BEATUS VIR

Studies in Early English and Norse Manuscripts

IN MEMORY OF PHILLIP PULSIANO

MEDIEVAL AND RENAISSANCE
TEXTS AND STUDIES
VOLUME 319

BEATUS VIR

Studies in Early English and Norse Manuscripts

IN MEMORY OF PHILLIP PULSIANO

edited by

A. N. Doane and Kirsten Wolf

ACMRS
(Arizona Center for Medieval and Renaissance Studies)
Tempe, Arizona
2006

Library of Congress Cataloging-in-Publication Data
Beatus vir : studies in early English and Norse manuscripts in memory of Phillip Pulsiano / edited by A.N. Doane and Kirsten Wolf.
    p. cm. -- (Medieval and Renaissance texts and studies ; v. 319)
Includes bibliographical references and index.
ISBN-13: 978-0-86698-364-8 (alk. paper)
ISBN-10: 0-86698-364-3 (alk. paper)
    1. Manuscripts, English (Old) 2. Manuscripts, Old Norse. 3. Manuscripts, Medieval--England--London. 4. English literature--Old English, ca. 450-1100--Criticism, Textual. 5. Old Norse literature--Criticism, Textual. 6. Transmission of texts. 7. Codicology. I. Doane, Alger Nicolaus, 1938- II. Wolf, Kirsten, 1959- III. Pulsiano, Phillip, 1955-

Z105.B43 2006
091--dc22
                                                                2006034012

∞
This book is made to last.
It is set in Adobe Minion Pro,
smyth-sewn and printed on acid-free paper
to library specifications.
Printed in the United States of America

TABLE OF CONTENTS

Acknowledgments

All the essays in this book are original and have been written with the standards and example of Phillip Pulsiano in mind. The editors wish to thank Tim Graham for his initial enthusiasm for this project, which he saw as a fitting memorial for Phill. We are grateful to Robert Bjork, director of the Arizona Center for Medieval and Renaissance Studies for agreeing to accept this book for publication in the MRTS series. Other folks at MRTS have been of invaluable assistance, especially Roy Rukkila, the managing editor, Todd Halvorsen, the production manager, Stephanie Volf, who did the troubleshooting and typesetting of a very difficult book, and Leslie MacCoull, who did the copy-editing. We had ongoing editorial help at all stages from the able project assistants, Matthew T. Hussey and Patrick J. Murphy. Patrick and Natalie Van Deusen compiled the index. We are grateful to all the contributors for their learning, help, enthusiasm, promptness, and patience during the long process from abstracts to print. Finally, we wish to thank, respectively, Marty and Anne for their ongoing support and love.

A. N. D. and K. W.

ABBREVIATIONS

AfdAdL	*Anzeiger für deutsches Altertum und deutsche Literatur*
ASE	*Anglo-Saxon England*
ASM	Anglo-Saxon Manuscripts in Microfiche Facsimile, ed. P. Pulsiano and A. N. Doane, Binghamton / Tempe, 1994– .
Archiv	*Archiv für das Studium der neueren Sprachen und Literaturen*
ASPR	The Anglo-Saxon Poetic Records, ed. G. P. Krapp and E. van K. Dobbie, 6 vols. New York, 1931–1953.
BaP	Bibliothek der angelsächsischen Prosa, ed. C. W. M. Grein and R. P. Wülcker. 13 vols. Cassel and Göttingen, 1872–1933.
BT	*An Anglo-Saxon dictionary, based on the manuscript collections of the late Joseph Bosworth*, ed. and supplemented by T. N. Toller. 2 vols. London, 1954, additions and corrigenda by A. Campbell (London, 1972).
BTS	"Bosworth-Toller Supplement," vol. 2 of the preceding item.
CCSL	Corpus Christianorum, Series Latina
CLA	*Codices Latini Antiquiores: A Palaeographical Guide to Latin Manuscripts Prior to the Ninth Century*, ed. E. A. Lowe, 13 vols. Oxford, 1934–1972.
CSASE	Cambridge Studies in Anglo-Saxon England
CSEL	Corpus scriptorum ecclesiasticorum latinorum
DOE	*Dictionary of Old English*, ed. A. diP. Healey et al. Toronto, 1986– [microform and CD-ROM]
EEMF	Early English Manuscripts in Microfiche Facsimile
EETS o.s., e.s., s.s.	Early English Text Society (original series, extra series, supplementary series)
Ker, *Cat.*	N. R. Ker, *Catalogue of Manuscripts containing Anglo-Saxon*. Oxford, 1957, rev. ed. 1990.
MGH AA	Monumenta Germaniae Historica : auctores antiquissimi

OED   *Oxford English Dictionary*, ed. J.A. H. Murray et al. 10 vols. in
             15. Oxford, 1888–1928; supplement, ed. R.W. Burchfield. 4 vols.
             Oxford, 1972–1986.

PG   Patrologia Graeca

PL   Patrologia Latina

TLL   *Thesaurus Linguae Latinae*. Leipzig, 1900–.

Wanley   Humphrey Wanley, *Librorum vett. septentrionalium, qui in
             Angliae Bibliothecis extant.... Catalogus Historico-Criticus*
             (Oxford, 1705).

ZfdA   *Zeitschrift für deutsches Altertum*

ZfdP   *Zeitschrift für deutsche Philologie*

List of Figures

PHILLIP PULSIANO 1955–2000

(photo by Kirsten Wolf)

BEATUS VIR:
STUDIES IN EARLY ENGLISH AND NORSE MANUSCRIPTS
IN MEMORY OF PHILLIP PULSIANO

Introduction

Eadig wer se ðe ne gewat on geþeahte arleas
7 on wege synfulra ne gestod 7 on heahsetle wolberendra ne siteð

Our dear friend and highly respected colleague Phillip Pulsiano died in Bryn Mawr, Pennsylvania, on 23 August 2000, just two weeks shy of his forty-fifth birthday, after a heroic four-year fight against cancer. He was laid to rest at Resurrection Cemetery in Madison, Wisconsin.

Phill was born in Astoria, New York, on 6 September 1955, and the state of New York remained his home for most of his life. He graduated from Saint Anthony's High School, Smithtown, in 1973, and then proceeded to Concordia University, Montreal, and The College of Saint Rose, Albany, where he received his B.A. (cum laude) in 1977, majoring in French and English. He studied briefly at the University of Kent and then turned to the State University of New York at Stony Brook for graduate study in English, completing his M.A. in 1980 and his Ph.D. (with distinction) in 1982 under the direction of Donald K. Fry. After two years of teaching at Stony Brook and Princeton University, Phill joined the faculty of Villanova University, Philadelphia, Pennsylvania, in 1984, where he taught a great variety of courses on topics ranging from Latin and paleography to *Beowulf* and Milton, moving swiftly through the ranks to full professor, and serving as chair of the Department of English for five years. With its strong foundations in the Augustinian tradition, Villanova University was in many ways for Phill an ideal place. He regarded it as a diamond in the rough, with much potential, and worked tirelessly on numerous committees. From 1983 to 1991 he also served as editor of the *Proceedings of the PMR Conference*, Villanova University's annual conference on Augustinian and related studies. Only three months before he died, Phill received Villanova's prestigious Outstanding Faculty Research Award. This award and an award twenty-three years earlier from The College of Saint Rose for excellence in scholarship frame a list of many institutional recognitions, including several grants from the National Endowment for the Humanities, a grant from the American Council of Learned Societies, and a Fulbright Collaborative Research Grant.

Phill's scholarship began with his doctoral dissertation on the Blickling Psalter. This six-hundred-page study set the course for his career interests in manuscript and psalter research, which culminated in his great combined critical edition of the Old English psalters. This was conceived as a four-volume work, including apparatus and commentary. By 1997, when the illness was diagnosed, Phill had brought the first volume on Psalms 1–50 (which was published by the University of Toronto Press in 2001) to completion. During the following three years, despite numerous surgeries and chemotherapy sessions, Phill managed to make the second volume (Psalms 51–100) almost ready for publication and made considerable progress on the third volume (Psalms 101–150). Phill's work on the psalters is being completed by his friend and former student Joseph McGowan.

Phill's work on the fourteen psalter manuscripts led to curiosity about a wide variety of manuscripts and resulted in a remarkable number of scholarly publications in a career compressed into a very few years. During those years, he edited or co-edited five books, completed some fifty scholarly articles and several other publications, and presented three dozen lectures or papers at various universities and scholarly conferences. His primary area of interest always remained Anglo-Saxon England, but his scholarship reached well beyond that, into Middle English and Chaucer, Old Norse-Icelandic literature, medieval Latin, bibliography, and hagiography, particularly female saints. In the last years of his life he planned and edited with A. N. Doane the major NEH-funded scholarly project "Anglo-Saxon Manuscripts in Microfiche Facsimile," which is making available on microfiche the images of about five-hundred complete manuscripts containing Old English along with original scholarly descriptions. He also did important service in the field of Anglo-Saxon; among other things he prepared the annual "Research in Progress" report for the *Old English Newsletter,* assumed the role of series editor for Ashgate Press, and served as an officer in the International Society of Anglo-Saxonists.

Although Phill lived with, and for, the vigor of the intellectual life, he found time for hobbies and family life. In 1988, he married Kirsten Wolf, who was then at the University of Manitoba, Canada, and throughout their marriage the two maintained a long-distance relationship, continuously traveling between Canada and the U.S. They worked closely together as colleagues; among other things, they co-edited *Medieval Scandinavia: An Encyclopedia* and collaborated on a couple of articles. Phill's daughter Anne, born about the time he became ill, was without question the love of his life and the force that sustained him in the many discomforts of cancer treatment, about which he rarely talked and never complained. Indeed, Anne's first words, first steps, potty-training, and bright intelligence were for Phill greater accomplishments than his scholarly publications; and watching fireflies, carouselling, building snowmen, or doing finger-painting with her were his happiest moments. An avid book collector, Phill spent much time in antiquarian bookstores and managed to build up an impressively large personal library. He was also renowned among friends for his culinary expertise, and he would often spend hours going through cookbooks and gourmet magazines looking for recipies pleasing to the most refined palates. Those who were well acquainted with him also know of his interest in and knowledge of art and art history. Phill himself did a great deal of painting, in oil and watercolor, and also experimented with charcoaling and silkscreening. Most of his art work is now housed in the Villanova University Art Collection. But what is known to very few is that Phill was a closet poet, who once would typically spend the wee hours on writings of a more personal nature. A little verse written in 1995 may justly prompt the hint of a smile among his colleagues:

> When I was twelve
> I used to paint graffiti
> on the columns
> underneath the Triboro bridge
> Now at 40
> I write papers
> for respected journals — graffiti
> in black and white

As his illness became increasingly serious, his writing darkened. The following undated note, the topic of which is obviously Phill himself, may well have been among his last endeavors within the field of creative writing:

> He was an unusually slender man, yet for all his ungainliness a graceful sort; I remember his hands most vividly, kind, gentle hands — the hands of an artist; the hands of a lover, long, thin fingers that spoke a language all their own. Yet his face was at first glance severe, long and thin like his fingers — a face marked by unknown sorrow. His eyes told a story much different. Oh, I've seen sternness in those eyes, eyes that often flashed arrogantly at some unsuspecting passer-by, eyes that could diminish a man at a glance — quick, severe, scolding. Still, lurking beneath that coldness, as though afraid to surface, were the gentlest blues and greens

and hazels. And I have seen those eyes sparkle, perhaps less often these days. But sometimes, as if for a moment unaware of their own too accustomed sternness, they would light up with the excitement and joy that in the past was ever present. I've never known him to be cruel, though I have heard stories of quick, impassioned anger-—rumors, perhaps; yet, certainly anger was not beyond him.

❖ ❖ ❖ ❖ ❖ ❖

Manuscripts are physical objects existing in time that must be preserved and described as unique material entities; they are text-bearing surfaces that allow us to abstract and idealize communications by processes of editorship and reading; they are practical objects of use and authority, taking their place in the lives of particular readers and communities; they are survivors of a deep past, eventually becoming objects of possession, study, and obsession for their own sake. As describer, editor, critic, and bibliophile, Phill contributed notably to all these angles of approach. This book pays tribute to him by presenting intersecting explorations of these aspects of the manuscript book.

The materiality of the book was a special interest of Phill's, his many studies in this area yielding many new insights and rewarding surprises. It is the topic, in the main or in part, of most of the studies included here. In "British Library Ms. Royal 15 A v: One Manuscript or Three," Gernot R. Wieland, defending his earlier assertion that the manuscript is a unity, scrutinizes in detail the three parts of a manuscript that consists of a "Norman" copy of Acts, an "Anglo-Caroline" copy of Arator's poem *Historica Apostolica*, and a "Norman" copy of a commentary on Arator in a hand very similar to that of the first part. As it happens, close codicological, paleographical, and orthographic analyses support the unity of the book almost too well, with the effect that the middle part, which was thought to be a late Anglo-Saxon production, is removed from the Gneuss canon altogether and joins the Norman ranks. What is a "text" is a very current question; Joyce Hill, in "Identifying 'Texts' in Cotton Julius E vii: Medieval and Modern Perspectives," tackles the theory by checking the material practice in a famous copy of Ælfric's *Lives of Saints* as that plays against scribal interventions and Walter Skeat's nineteenth-century textualist assumptions; in particular, she explores "the scribe's rationale in drawing up the contents list, since that gives a clue about his concept of 'the text'," which, she shows, is how a unit in the book functions liturgically, rather than how it derives from a specific historical act of writing.

The very existence of a text is in certain cases inextricably bound up with its physicality, not just in theory. In "The Werden Glossary: Structure and Sources," A. N. Doane untangles the complex history of the location and status of the few remaining dispersed leaves of a once impressive glossary collection originally written at Werden Abbey on the Ruhr about 820. As a preliminary to editing, the book as it was originally is reconstructed and its equally dispersed sources identified. Editorial recovery takes many forms, and, in contrast to the relatively traditional reconstruction of the large-scale Werden fragments, Kevin Kiernan, in "Odd Couples in Ælfric's *Julian and Basilissa* in British Library Cotton MS. Otho B. X," demonstrates methods of digital enhancement and manipulation now available for the editorial recovery of texts on what seemed hopelessly degraded burnt leaves; his practical explanation of new technologies is also an eloquent demonstration that these must, to mean anything, be combined with the most refined use of "old" technologies: philology, paleography, codicology, and historical analysis "to help editors deliver newly born Old English texts." Ólafur Halldórsson in "*Danakonungatal* in Copenhagen, Royal Library Barth. D III. Fol.: An Edition," must take yet another approach to the recovery of a text, since in this case the originals are represented not by fragments, but by late copies. The text is a brief genealogy of Danish kings from prehistoric times to the thirteenth century followed by a survey of the Danish monarchy in the late twelfth and early thirteenth centuries: it exists in a late seventeenth-century transcript on paper by Árni Magnússon and two other late paper copies. Halldórsson reconstructs the exact orthographic and paleographical forms that must have existed in the vellum copy that was Árni's exemplar and discusses the value of this text for the early history of Denmark. The text as a more abstract entity emerges in Marianne E. Kalinke's edition and translation "*Jóhannes saga gullmunns*: The Icelandic Legend of the Hairy Anchorite." The traces of the Low German source text showing through the Icelandic invite normalization of the text to highlight the German and Latin vocabulary and least distract from the sensational and entertaining material of the saga.

As Phill also showed in several of his studies, the materiality of the book leads sooner or later to the question of its handling, use, and reading. In "The Audience of Ælfric's *Lives of Saints* and the Face of Cotton Caligula A. xiv," Jonathan Wilcox progresses from a contemplation of a marginal drawing of a disembodied head to the uses that that manuscript and those texts might have had, whether for private or communal reading, among clerics or lay, men or women, and shows the many non-liturgical but specific occasions Ælfric may have had in mind when he composed and circulated his saints' lives. Kirsten Wolf, in "Female Scribes at Work? A Consideration of Kirkjubæjarbók (Codex AM 429 12mo)," considers the question of the involvement of Icelandic women, and nuns in particular, in scribal activites through an analysis of this late fifteenth-century collection of female saints' lives that was almost certainly written for the nuns at the Kirkjubær convent. While the book shows the patterns of veneration that were popular among women religious in Iceland, Wolf has to conclude that there is no evidence for, and much against, the possibility that the book was actually written by nuns at Kirkjubær, and, by extention, that Icelandic nuns did not concern themselves with writing.

An aspect of manuscript use is the *traditio* of texts copied from one generation of manuscripts to the next, which in the case of vernacular texts are, as Stephanie Würth emphasizes in "The Common Transmission of *Trójumanna saga* and *Breta sögur*," conditioned not just by scholarship and authority, but also by relevance, intelligibility, and entertainment value. *Breta sögur* is an Icelandic version of Geoffrey of Monmouth's *Historia regum Britannie*, which in the shorter version in *Hauksbók*, a huge early fourteenth-century historical compilation, favors the historicity of the events, while in the longer version of *Breta sögur* from the fourteenth-century *Ormsbók* (lost but represented by several later witnesses), a compilation of chivalric stories, the narrative elements of *Breta sögur* are selected, expanded, abridged, and reformed according to courtly literary fashion and popular entertainment.

The long "afterlife" of Old English literature was one of Phill's liveliest interests, that is, the interest in Anglo-Saxonica after its culture had expired; but when was that? In 1066, 1100, 1200, or later? Surveying a wide variety of twelfth-century manuscripts containing English texts and glosses, Elaine Treharne, in "Reading from the Margins: The Uses of Old English Homiletic Manuscripts in the Post-Conquest Period," argues for "Old English" as a necessary term distinct from "early Middle English" to denote the historical integrity of formal English language use for a long time after the Conquest; it is not "deviancy" that most importantly marks such English but rather a consciousness on the part of scribes that "late West Saxon was always a formal register of language" that signified "the most prestigious register of language for the composition of written texts." Thus, what to include in the canon of Old English literature should be decided not by inconsistency of forms or date but by the usefulness and intelligibility of such texts to actual audiences (which as far as can be told were confined to the great monastic cathedrals), whether undertaken to be privately read by monks, to instruct *conversi*, or to prepare for preaching to the laity. Joseph McGowen examines the peculiar configuration of "elliptical glosses," that is, glosses having the form "ax + bc" or "ab + cx" (as in Modern English phrases like "first- and secondhand source"); of the two terms used to gloss, either one or the other does not express the common second term. Glosses of this type were partially collected by Herbert Meritt, but many others remain to be noticed and McGowan gathers them together here for the convenience of present and future lexicographers.

An early modern aspect of the afterlife of Old English is explored by Peter J. Lucas's "Abraham Wheelock and the Presentation of Anglo-Saxon: From Manuscript to Print." Wheelock, the first lecturer in Anglo-Saxon at Cambridge University, was a prolific editor of Old English texts and he designed for them in the 1640s an extensive font showing thirty special sorts imitative of writing found in specific Anglo-Saxon manuscripts; he wished in his own editions "to recreate in print the authentic appearance of an archaic form of language." This was not the first or last of these special fonts, but perhaps the most impressive and historically meticulous; with matching meticulousness Lucas carries out "country-house murder" detective work to find which existing suspect manuscripts in Cambridge contributed to the idiosyncratic features of Wheelock's type-design. Even modern scholarship has an "afterlife" aspect to it: J. R. Hall, in "Three Studies on the Manuscript Text of *Beowulf*: Lines 47b, 747b, and 2232a," considers the respectable nineteenth- and twentieth-century legacy of piecemeal "restoration" of manuscript readings. What emerges is not just opinions on three minor textual cruces, but a meditation on the ontology and epistomology of the reading and emendation of manuscript texts as carried out by textual scholars. Hall's microscopic attention to details of flecks of ink in the *Beowulf* manuscript and misread or overlooked clues in the Thorkelin transcripts of *Beowulf* and what scholars see and missee, read and misread, do and misdo in successive editions and studies, is a fascinating lesson on the indeterminate nature of manuscript textuality as well as of the triumphs and foibles of various scholars from Thorkelin to Hall himself.

Whatever life a manuscript still lives, it must live it in its library home. The British Library is the greatest and largest collection of Anglo-Saxon manuscripts, a place where Phill and all the contributors to his memorial have spent many happy hours. From the mid-eighteenth century the British Museum (the British Library became a separate entity in 1972) has been acquiring, restoring, marking, and cataloging its manuscripts, and they carry the traces of that activity on them for ever, as palimpsests of a sort, stamps, accession and shelf-marks, foliations, rebindings. These traces are more often than not totally mysterious to their users, however learned, but as Andrew Prescott, in "What's in a Number? The Physical Organization of the Manuscript Collections of the British Library," is anxious to establish, they all once had their uses or still do. Writing from more than twenty years' experience as a curator in the Manuscripts Department, and with certainty that now that the collections have moved from Bloomsbury to their modern new home in St. Pancras, memory of the procedures and their relationships to marks will soon fade, he aims to preserve a record of the activities and physical layout of the old premises in which these marks were produced and to explain their meaning in terms of the way the manuscripts were stored, retrieved and conserved. It seems fitting to end this book of memory of a great book man with a memory of how the great books he loved were lovingly preserved and will continue to be preserved for many generations into the future.

A. N. D. and K. W.

PUBLICATIONS BY PHILLIP PULSIANO

2003

"The Passion of St Christopher: An Edition." In *Early Medieval Texts and Interpretations: Studies Presented to Donald G. Scragg*, ed. Elaine Treharne and Susan Rosser, 167–200. MRTS 252. Tempe, Arizona, 2003.

2002

"Jaunts, Jottings, and Jetsam in Anglo-Saxon Manuscripts." *Florilegium* 19 (2002): 189–216.

"The Old English Life of St. Pantaleon." In *Via Crucis: Essays on Early Medieval Sources and Ideas in Memory of J. E. Cross*, ed. Thomas N. Hall with assistance from Thomas D. Hill and Charles D. Wright, 61–103. Morgantown, WV, 2002.

2001

Ed. *Old English Glossed Psalters: Psalms 1–50*. Toronto: University of Toronto Press, 2001.

"Persius's *Satires* in Anglo-Saxon England." *Journal of Medieval Latin* 11 (2001): 142–55.

With Elaine Treharne, eds. *A Companion to Anglo-Saxon Literature*. Oxford: Blackwell, 2001.

With Elaine Treharne. "An Introduction to the Corpus of Anglo-Saxon Vernacular Literature." In *A Companion to Anglo-Saxon Literature* ed. Pulsiano and Treharne, 3–10.

"Prayers, Glosses and Glossaries." In *A Companion to Anglo-Saxon Literature* ed. Pulsiano and Treharne, 209–30.

2000

"The Old English gloss of the *Eadwine Psalter.*" In *Rewriting Old English in the Twelfth Century,* ed. Mary Swan and Elaine M. Treharne, 166–94. Cambridge Studies in Anglo-Saxon England 30. Cambridge: Cambridge University Press, 2000.

"William L'Isle and the Editing of Old English." In *The Recovery of Old English: Anglo-Saxon Studies in the Sixteenth and Seventeenth Centuries,* ed. Timothy Graham, 173–206. Publications of the Richard Rawlinson Center. Kalamazoo, MI, 2000.

Review of C. H. Talbot, ed. and trans., *The Life of Christina of Markyate: A Twelfth-Century Recluse. Arthuriana* 10 (2000): 124–25.

1999

"Blessed Bodies: The Vitae of Anglo-Saxon Female Saints." *Parergon* 16 (1999): 1–42.

"Psalter Glosses," "Benjamin Thorpe." In *The Blackwell Encyclopaedia of Anglo-Saxon England,* ed. Michael Lapidge, et al, 380–381, 447. Oxford, 1999.

Review, with Kirsten Wolf of Anne Clark Bartlett, and Thomas H. Bestul, eds., *Cultures of Piety: Medieval Devotional Literature in Translation* and Catherine M. Mooney, ed., *Gendered Voices: Medieval Saints and Their Interpreters. Envoy* 8.1 (1999): 17–29.

1998

With Elaine Treharne, eds. *Anglo-Saxon Manuscripts and Their Heritage.* Aldershot, 1998.

"The Prefatory Matter of London, British Libary, Cotton Vitellius E. xviii. In *Anglo-Saxon Manuscripts and Their Heritage,* ed. Pulsiano and Treharne, 85–116.

"Benjamin Thorpe." In *Medieval Scholarship: Biographical Studies on the Formation of a Discipline* 2: *Literature and Philology,* ed. Helen Damico, 75–92. Garland Reference Library of the Humanities 2071. New York and London, 1998.

"Abbot Ælfwine and the Date of the Vitellius Psalter." *American Notes and Queries* 11.2 (1998): 2–9.

"Glosses and Glossaries." In *Medieval England: An Encyclopedia* , ed. Paul E. Szarmach, *et al.*, 316–17. Garland Encyclopedias of the Middle Ages 3. New York and London, 1998.

1997

"'Danish Men's Words Are Worse than Murder': Viking Guile in *The Battle of Maldon.*" *Journal of English and Germanic Philology* 96 (1997): 13–25.

"The Originality of the Old English Gloss of the *Vespasian Psalter* and Its Relation to the Gloss of the *Junius Psalter.*" *Anglo-Saxon England* 25 (1997): 37–62.

"A Middle English Gloss in the Lambeth Psalter." *American Notes and Queries* 10.1 (1997): 2–9.

Review of Eric Gerald Stanley, *In the Foreground: Beowulf. Mediaevistik* 9 (1997): 321–22.

1996

Anglo-Saxon Manuscripts in Microfiche Facsimile 4: *Glossed Texts, Aldhelmiana, Psalms.* MRTS 169. Binghamton, 1996.

"Psalters." In *The Liturgical Books of Anglo-Saxon England, Old English Newsletter,* ed. Richard W. Pfaff, 61–85. Subsidia 23. Kalamazoo, 1996.

1995

"Language theory and Narrative Patterning in Augustine's *De Civitate Dei.*" In *The City of God: A Collection of Critical Essays,* ed. Dorothy F. Donnelly, 241–52. New York, 1995.

"The Twelve-Spoked Wheel of *The Summoner's Tale.*" *The Chaucer Review* 29 (1995): 382–89.

"Spiritual Despair in *Resignation B.*" *Neophilologus* 79 (1995): 155–62.

"Additional Evidence for an Old English 'Canterbury Vocabulary'." *Neuphilologische Mitteilungen* 95 (1995): 257–65.

Review of Stephanie Hollis and Michael Wright, *Old English Prose of Secular Learning. Parergon,* n.s. 12 (1995): 180–82.

Review of A. N. Doane, ed., *The Saxon Genesis: An Edition of the West Saxon Genesis B and the Old Saxon Vatican Genesis. Envoi* 3 (1995): 367–74.

1994

Anglo-Saxon Manuscripts in Microfiche Facsimile 2: Psalters I. MRTS 158. Binghamton, 1994.

"London, British Library, Cotton Otho E. i: A Neglected Latin-Old English Glossary." *American Notes and Queries* n.s. 7.4 (1994): 195–200.

"Old English *Nomina ventorum.*" *Studia Neophilologica* 66 (1994): 15–26.

With Joseph McGowan. "Four Unedited Prayers in London, British Library, Cotton Tiberius A.iii." *Mediaeval Studies* 56 (1994): 189–216.

"New Old English Glosses in the *Vitellius Psalter* (II)." *American Notes and Queries* n.s. 7.1 (1994): 3–6.

Review of Sarah Larratt Keefer, *Psalm-Poem and Psalter-Glosses: The Latin and Old English Psalter-Text Background to "Kentish Psalm 50."* Anglia 112 (1994): 177–79.

1993

With Kirsten Wolf (co-ed.), Donald K. Fry (assoc. ed.), and Paul Acker (assoc. ed.). *Medieval Scandinavia: An Encyclopedia.* Garland Encyclopedias of the Middle Ages 1. New York and London, 1993.

"*Bárðar saga Snæfellsáss,*" "*Bevis saga,*" "England: Norse in," "Old English Literature: Norse Influence on," "Stamford Bridge, Battle of." In *Medieval Scandinavia: An Encyclopedia,* ed. Pulsiano, Wolf et al., 35–36, 39, 166–170, 450–451, 608.

"New Old English Glosses in the *Vitellius Psalter.*" *American Notes and Queries,* n.s. 6.4 (1993): 180–82.

Review of Evert Wiesenekker, *Worde be Worde, Andgit of Andgite: Translation Performance in the Old English Interlinear Glosses of the Vespasian, Regius and Lambeth Psalters. Anglia* 111 (1993): 183–87.

Review of Orrin W. Robinson, *Old English and Its Closest Relatives: A Survey of the Earliest Germanic Languages. Germanic Notes* 24 (1993): 92.

1992

"A Proposal for a Collective Edition of the Old English Glossed Psalters." In *Anglo-Saxon Glossography: Papers Read at the International Conference Held in the Koninklijke Academie voor Wetenschappen, Letteren en Schone Kunsten van België, Brussels, 8 and 9 September 1986,* ed. R. Derolez, 167–88. Brussels, 1992.

1991

"Old English Glossed Psalters: Editions versus Manuscripts." *Manuscripta* 35 (1991): 75–95.

"The Old English Gloss to the *Lambeth Psalter* and Its Relations." *Neuphilologische Mitteilungen* 92 (1991): 195–210.

"Defining the A-type (*Vespasian*) and D-type (*Regius*) Psalter-gloss Traditions." *English Studies* 72 (1991): 308–27.

"The Old English Introductions to the *Vitellius Psalter*." *Studia Neophilologica* 63 (1991): 13–35.

"The Scribes and Old English Gloss of the *Eadwine's Canterbury Psalter*." In *Proceedings of the Patristic, Medieval, and Renaissance Conference* 14, 223–60. Villanova, PA, 1991.

With Joseph McGowan. "*Fyrd, Here,* and the Dating of *Beowulf*." *Studia Anglia Posnaniensia* 23 (1991): 3–13.

With Kirsten Wolf. "*Exeter Book* Riddle 57: Those Damned Souls, Again." *Germanic Notes* 22 (1991): 1–5.

With Kirsten Wolf. "The *hwelp* in *Wulf and Eadwacer*." *English Language Notes* 28 (1991): 1–9.

"Cotton Tiberius A.iii, fol. 59rv: An Unrecorded Charm in the form of an Address to the Cross." *American Notes and Queries* n.s. 4.1 (1991): 3–5.

1990

"Old English Names of Winds." *American Notes and Queries* n.s. 3.3 (1990): 103–104.

Review. With Kirsten Wolf of R. Simek and Hermann Pálsson, *Lexikon der altnordischen Literatur. Scandinvian Studies* 62 (1990): 356–358.

1989

"Redeemed Rhetoric and the Ending of *Troilus and Criseyde*." In *Sign, Silence, Discourse: Essays on the Theme of Language in Medieval Literature,* ed. Julian Wasserman, 153–74. New York, 1989.

"A *Gothic Grammar* with a Transcript of Anglo-Saxon Prayers (Columbia University)." *Old English Newsletter* 23 (1989): 40–41.

"The Blickling Psalter: *gladii: sweord*." *American Notes and Queries* n.s. 2.2 (1989): 43.

"*The Phoenix*: Lines 199b–207 and Psalm 101.7–8." *American Notes and Queries* n.s. 2.1 (1989): 3–7.

1988

An Annotated Bibliography of North American Doctoral Dissertations on Old English Language and Literature. Medieval Texts and Studies 3. Michigan, 1988.

"BL Cotton Tiberius A.iii: Fulgentius, Injunction." *American Notes and Queries* n.s. 1.2 (1988): 43–44.

1987

"Bees and Backbiters in the Old English *Homiletic Fragment I.*" *English Language Notes* 25 (1987): 1–6.

1986

"A Checklist of Books and Articles Containing Reproductions of Watermarks." In *Essays in Paper Analysis*, ed. Stephen Spector, 115–53. Washington and London, 1986.

1985

"The Latin and Old English Glosses in the 'Blickling' and 'Regius' Psalters." *Traditio* 41 (1985): 79–115.

"Hortatory Purpose in the OE *Visio Leofrici.*" *Medium Ævum* 44 (1985): 109–16.

"'Cames cynne': Confusion or Craft?" In *Proceedings of the Patristic, Medieval, and Renaissance Conference* 7, 33–38. Villanova, PA, 1985.

1984

With Jón Skaptason, ed. and trans., *Bárðar saga Snæfellsáss.* Medieval Texts in Translation Series A, No. 8. New York and London, 1984.

"The Blickling Psalter: *aqua uel is.*" *Notes and Queries* 31.3 (1984): 553–54.

"A New Anglo-Saxon Gloss in the *Liber Scintillarum.*" *Notes and Queries* 31.2 (1984): 151–53.

1983

"A New Look at the Anglo-Saxon Glosses in the *Blickling Psalter.*" *Manuscripta* 27 (1983): 32–37.

"The Sea of Life and the Ending of *Christ II.*" *In Geardagum* 5 (1983): 1–12.

1978

"'Things All Disjointed': Keats's *Epistle to Reynolds.*" *The Gypsy Scholar* 5.2 (1978): 96–101.

British Library, MS. Royal 15.A.v: One Manuscript or Three?[1]

Gernot R. Wieland

British Library Royal 15.A.v, written at an unknown scriptorium,[2] is a small book. With a folio size of 177 × 113 mm it is about the size of the Penguin edition of Bede's *Ecclesiastical History*. Royal 15.A.v contains the Evangelist

---

[1] When I gave an earlier version of this paper at the ISAS conference at Stanford in 1995, Phill confessed in the discussion afterwards that he was not convinced by my argument. He suggested that the paper needed a more theoretical framework with an examination of the co-operation of Anglo-Saxon with Norman scribes. I had fully intended to take Phill's criticism into account, to rewrite the paper and to present the results to him for further discussion. Unfortunately, his life was cut short before I was able to do so. Since the new version of this paper owes much to Phill, it is only fitting that it be dedicated to him. I only wish that in rewriting it I could have had the opportunity to draw on his considerable experience, to share some surprising finds which I made in re-examining the manuscript, and to discuss those areas where he still would not have been fully convinced. I would like to thank the University of British Columbia whose generous Humanities and Social Sciences grant enabled me to travel to London for a thorough examination of the manuscript under discussion.

[2] There is no internal evidence to place the book at a definite scriptorium. There are, however, two later additions, one on fol. 29v in a sixteenth-century hand, which speaks about "Thamesina iuuentus," the other on fol. 147v in a fifteenth-century hand, which mentions an owner by the name of "Wodson" or "Wodesson," who claims that "Winsor" is witness to his ownership of the book. Here is the full text:

> Possidet hunc librum vero sub nomine Wodson
> qui pro teste suo Winsor habere potest.
> Si quisquam dubitet cuius foret ista [sic] libellus,
> is dominum noscat Woddeson esse suum.

> "The owner of this book under his own true name is Wodson, and he can have Windsor as his witness. If anyone doubt whose book this is, let him know the owner is Woddeson."

Nothing can be found out about a "Wodson." The *Dictionary of National Biography* does not contain the name "Wodson," or any similar name such as "Woodson." If

Luke's Acts of the Apostles on folios 2v to 29r, Arator's poem *Historia apostolica*, which is a versified version of the Acts of the Apostles, on folios 30r to 81r, and a commentary on Arator's *Historia apostolica* on folios 86r to 147v.[3] The manuscript also contains a prose account of Arator's recitation of his poem at Rome on folio 81r (inc. *Beato domino petro adiuuante*), a six-line verse in praise of Arator on folios 81r to 81v (inc. *Versibus egregiis decursum clarus arator*), and, somewhat surprisingly, an unascribed poem with the incipit *Hec precepta legat deuotus et impleat actu*, which in many manuscripts is ascribed to one abbot Columbanus, but which appears in Dümmler's edition among the *carmina* of Alcuin.[4] The almost complete thematic unity of the manuscript would suggest that the three parts were from the very beginning destined to be bound together. In a 1985 article, I even suggested that Royal 15.A.v may have been used in the classroom, with the teacher using the commentary in order to explain the *Historia apostolica*.[5] The suggestion was somewhat premature, and Ray Page rightly rebuked me with these words: "I do not know of any evidence to show that the present arrangement represents that of the eleventh century, though of course early thread marks and sewing holes may have been recorded when the present rebinding was done. At any rate Wieland does not tell us, and he ought to."[6] Here, then, is a fuller account of the manuscript, including its codicology.

Aside from Page's comment, the manuscript has been mentioned by Helmut Gneuss and Michael Lapidge. Gneuss includes folios 30 to 85, the Arator section, but not folios 1 to 29 and 86 to 147, the Acts of the Apostles and the Commentary on Arator, in his "Handlist," thereby implicitly suggesting that the Arator section can be considered Anglo-Saxon, but the other two sections not. Lapidge is more explicit in his comments on the manuscript:

"Wodson" is an approximation of the name "Watson," it is still impossible to determine a Watson of the fifteenth century who lived along the Thames in or near Windsor. Though "Wodson" cannot be identified, he seems to have lived in the south of England, and thus a provenance from the south of England is a possibility. See Helmut Gneuss, *Handlist of Anglo-Saxon Manuscripts* (Tempe, AZ, 2001), no. 488.

[3] See A. P. Orbán, "Ein Aratorkommentar in HS. London, Royal MS. 15.A.v.," *Sacris Erudiri* 38 (1998–1999): 317–51, 40 (2000): 131–239.

[4] *Alcuini (Albini) Carmina*, ed. Ernst Dümmler, MGH Poetae Latini Aevi Carolini (Berlin, 1881; repr. 1964), 1: 275–81.

[5] G. Wieland, "The Glossed Manuscript: Classbook or Library Book?" *Anglo-Saxon England* 14 (1985): 153–73, at 156–57.

[6] R. Page, "On the Feasibility of a Corpus of Anglo-Saxon Glosses: The View from the Library," in *Anglo-Saxon Glossography: Papers Read at the International Conference held in the Koninklijke Academie voor Wetenschappen, Letteren en Schone Kunsten van België*, ed. R. Derolez (Brussels, 1992), 77–95, at 93.

Royal 15.A.V is a miscellaneous codex consisting in three parts which were apparently combined during the early twelfth century. The parts are as follows: Part I (fos. 1–29), the Vulgate Acts of the Apostles (Norman or International script, s.xii[1]); Part II (fos. 30–85), Arator (late Anglo-Caroline script, s.xi[ex]); Part III (fos. 86–147), a commentary on Arator (Norman or International script, s. xii[1]). It is difficult to say whether Parts I and III were written by the same scribe; they were quite possibly written in England. Part II (Arator) . . . was apparently in origin a separate book which was subsequently bound up with the other two parts by a librarian who was attempting to assemble in one codex all the material necessary for serious study of Arator.[7]

Lapidge's statement will serve as a starting point for the discussion of the manuscript. In particular, I would like to question the assumption that part II "was apparently in origin a separate book which was subsequently bound up with the other two parts," suggesting instead that the three parts belonged together from the very beginning. In order to support this suggestion, I will survey the extent to which Anglo-Caroline and Norman scribes cooperated in the post-Conquest era, compare Anglo-Saxon Arator manuscripts to BL Royal 15.A.v, examine the physical codex, discuss the relationship between the *Historia Apostolica* and the commentary on Arator, and end with a re-evaluation of the hands of the three sections.[8]

Cooperation of Anglo-Caroline and Norman Scribes

An argument for the scribe of part II (henceforth "scribe 2") writing at the same time as those of parts I and III must look at the larger context of cooperation between Norman and Anglo-Caroline hands. If it can be shown that no such cooperation existed, then an argument that Royal 15.A.v is an exception would be foolhardy. If, on the other hand, such cooperation occurred frequently, one necessary precondition for the scribes of Royal 15.A.v writing simultaneously would be fulfilled. By assigning scribe 2 to the late

---

[7] Michael Lapidge, "The Study of Latin Texts in Late Anglo-Saxon England: The Evidence of Latin Glosses," in *Latin and the Vernacular Languages in Early Medieval Britain*, ed. Nicholas Brooks (Leicester, 1982), 99–140, at 139, n. 106.

[8] On the concept of booklets, see P. R. Robinson, "Self-contained Units in Composite Manuscripts of the Anglo-Saxon Period," *Anglo-Saxon England* 7 (1978): 231–38. I do not wish to dispute that the three parts of Royal 15.A.v are three different booklets; rather, I would like to affirm that all three booklets were written at the same time and were bound together from the very beginning.

eleventh century and the other two scribes to the early twelfth century, Lapidge leaves open the possibility that Norman and Anglo-Caroline scribes cooperated, though he denies it in this particular instance. In his catalogue of manuscripts of early Norman England, Gameson gives a slightly later dating for scribe 2 of Royal 15.A.v, namely "xi/xii–xii^{in}," which would allow him to be contemporaneous with the other two.[9] N. R. Ker examines manuscripts containing patristic texts and therefore does not mention Royal 15.A.v, but he provides ample evidence that Anglo-Caroline scribes wrote side by side with Norman scribes.[10] Dumville does not discuss Royal 15.A.v individually, but claims that the Anglo-Caroline minuscule Style IV was written not only in the second half of the eleventh century, but even into the twelfth, thus also allowing writers of Anglo-Caroline minuscule to cooperate with Norman scribes.[11] Recent scholarship, moreover, has demonstrated that in Durham,[12] Salisbury,[13] and Canterbury[14] Anglo-Caroline and Norman hands were working next to each other. Such a cooperation is to be expected in a place such

---

[9] Richard Gameson, *The Manuscripts of Early Norman England (c. 1066–1130)* (Oxford, 1999), no. 557 (120). The date for the other two booklets is "xii^{in}."

[10] N. R. Ker, *English Manuscripts in the Century after the Norman Conquest* (Oxford, 1960), e.g. 22.

[11] David Dumville, *English Caroline Script and Monastic History: Studies in Benedictinism, A.D. 950–1030* (Woodbridge, 1993), 138.

[12] Michael Gullick, "The Scribes of the Durham Cantor's Book (Durham, Dean and Chapter Library, MS B.IV.24) and the Durham Martyrology Scribe," in *Anglo-Norman Durham 1093–1193*, ed. David Rollason, Margaret Harvey, and Michael Prestwich (Woodbridge, 1994), 93–109, at 93: "The Calendar was written by an English scribe who also worked in the Durham *Liber Vitae* and he appears to have been active from about the 1080s to the 1100s. . . . The two versions of the Rule had a different English scribe for each version." These English scribes clearly were active in the post-Conquest period, and their work appears side by side with that of Norman scribes.

[13] Teresa Webber, *Scribes and Scholars at Salisbury Cathedral c. 1075–c. 1125* (Oxford, 1992), 14–15, identifies scribes vii, x, xiii, xvi, and xvii of the Salisbury scriptorium as writing English Caroline minuscule, and shows their cooperation with Norman scribes in detail.

[14] Richard Gameson, "English Manuscript Art in the Late Eleventh Century: Canterbury and its Context," in *Canterbury and the Norman Conquest: Churches, Saints and Scholars, 1066–1109*, ed. Richard Eales and Richard Sharpe (London, 1995), 95–144, at 101: "We should not be surprised that old-style Anglo-Saxon scribes and decorators appear in post-Conquest books: the situation demanded all hands to the pump and the Anglo-Saxon hands were primarily what were available, at least at first;" 102: "The pronounced Anglo-Saxon hands, like this one, which occur in St Augustine's books. . . . , as also in books from Bury St Edmunds, of late eleventh- or even early twelfth-century date could well belong to scribes who were trained around the time of the Conquest if not before."

as Canterbury, where there was a continuity from Anglo-Saxon to Norman times, but it is surprising for Durham and Salisbury, since both were founded or refounded after the Conquest and could have excluded any scribes writing in the old style. The evidence of several monastic scriptoria thus suggests that a scribe trained in the Anglo-Caroline minuscule could easily cooperate with Norman scribes at the end of the eleventh or the beginning of the twelfth century. I am fully aware that the fact that Norman and Anglo-Caroline scribes were working together at various centers in itself is no proof that the three scribes of Royal 15.A.v were contemporaries, but at least it allows the possibility of their cooperation.

Comparison of Royal 15.A.v to Anglo-Saxon Arator Manuscripts

Once it has been established that scribe 2 could have cooperated with the two Norman scribes, the question needs to be asked whether the Arator of Royal 15.A.v exhibits the same features as other Anglo-Saxon Arator manuscripts. Did the text of the *Historia apostolica*, for instance, ever constitute a complete manuscript in Anglo-Saxon times, or was it always bound together with other texts? And how does the text of Royal 15.A.v compare to that of the Anglo-Saxon manuscripts? To the first question: if the *Historia apostolica* never occurs on its own in Anglo-Saxon manuscripts, then Lapidge's suggestion that Royal 15.A.v was "in origin a separate book" would *a priori* seem weakened; if, on the other hand, it does occur on its own, then his suggestion is strengthened. Anglo-Saxon copies of the *Historia apostolica* can be found in Cambridge, University Library, Gg.5.35 (s. xi med., St. Augustine's, Canterbury), in Paris, Bibliothèque National, lat. 8092 (s. xi), in Oxford, Bodleian Library, Rawlinson C 570 (s. x/xi, St. Augustine's, Canterbury), in British Library, Additional 11034 (s. ix), and in Cambridge, Trinity College, B.14.3 (s. x/xi, Christ Church, Canterbury). In CUL Gg.5.35, the *Historia apostolica* is one among a multitude of texts; in BN, lat. 8092 it is bound together with Sedulius' *Carmen Paschale*; in Bodleian, Rawl. C 570 and in CTC B.14.3 it is the only text; in BL Additional 11034 it takes up thirty-five of the forty folios — as in Royal 15.A.v the remaining five folios are filled with a Carolingian poem.[15] The evidence of the other Anglo-Saxon Arator manuscripts is therefore ambivalent: two have the *Historia apostolica* bound with other (long)

---

[15] Columbanus/Alcuin's poem in Royal 15.A.v; in BL Additional 11034, a poem with the incipit "Cęsareis carulus sapiens hec auribus hauri," ascribed in the manuscript to Naso, i.e. Moduin, takes up fols. 37r to 40v; for an edition see *Nasonis (Muaduuini) Ecloga*, MGH Poetae Latini Aevi Carolini 1: 384–91.

texts, three do not. Royal 15.A.v could therefore originally have been bound together with the other two texts, but it may also have existed separately.

While there is ambivalence on the first point, there is no ambivalence on the second: textually, Royal 15.A.v differs from the other Anglo-Saxon manuscripts. A collation of the Anglo-Saxon manuscripts[16] with Royal 15.A.v shows substantial differences, with Royal 15.A.v exhibiting some rather eccentric readings. It reads, for instance, *solebat* in line AI, 76, where all other manuscripts read *ardebat*;[17] *mitibus* in AI, 147 vs. *mentibus*; *vetus* in AI, 149 vs. *verus*; *intus* in AI, 157 vs. *unus*; *reduceret* in AI, 172 vs. *concederet*; *fenestra* in AI, 188 vs. *funesta*; *uitam solo* in AI, 354 vs. *solo uitam*; more differences of the first 500 lines of AI are given in the Appendix below. Partly these different readings characterize scribe 2 as careless (we shall return to this point below); partly they show that he is working from a tradition that differs from those of the Anglo-Saxons. This in itself is no proof that scribe 2 was working simultaneously with the other two scribes, but isolating him from the Anglo-Saxon tradition is a necessary prerequisite for my claim.

The Codicology of Royal 15.A.v

As Page has suggested, the codicology of the manuscript needs to be taken into account as well. He specifically asks for the thread marks and sewing holes, but the quiring, the opening and closing pages of the three booklets, the present and original page sizes, as well as the size of the writing grids must also be examined. Let us consider the sewing holes first: if it could be shown that all three booklets had identical late eleventh- or early twelfth-century stitch holes at, let's say, 12, 51, 90, 132, and 164 mm from the top of a folio, then we would have a very good argument that the three portions were all bound together at the same time. All three booklets do indeed have five stitch holes per sheet, and the distances between the stitch holes are roughly the same in all portions (and roughly those given above). This evidence,

---

[16] I have been unable to consult Paris, Bibliothèque Nationale, lat. 8092 and Cambridge, Trinity College B.14.3; since, however, Arthur Patch McKinlay, *Aratoris subdiaconi de actibus apostolorum*, CSEL 72 (Vienna, 1951) includes BN, lat. 8092 among "Classis I, Codices deteriores" and CTC B.14.3 among "Classis I, Codices meliores" their readings are taken into account in his edition, and I am confident that neither provides the eccentric readings of Royal 15.A.v.

[17] The abbreviations "AI" and "AII" refer to Arator, *Historia apostolica*, books I and II respectively.

however, does not help us at all. The manuscript was restored in 1969, and at that time all old stitching was removed, damaged sheets were repaired, and the quires were restitched. The even distances between the stitch holes are therefore new and do not allow any conclusions as to the original binding of the three booklets.[18]

Nor does the quiring help us. All three parts consist of quires of eight; the only exception is quire 4, the last of part I, which consists of four folios plus one singleton. Quires of eight, however, are so common for both late Anglo-Saxon and Norman manuscripts that the identical number of folios in the quires of the various parts means little.[19]

The evidence of the opening and closing pages of the three booklets is somewhat more helpful. If part II had for a time existed as a separate booklet, then one might expect that its first page had been exposed to light and would have yellowed more than the other pages or would show other signs of wear and tear. This, however, is not the case. Folio 30r differs little from other hair sides, and its ink does not seem to be rubbed to any discernible extent. This lack of yellowing and of wear and tear suggests, though not conclusively, that the initial page of part II had not been an opening page.

Final pages of independent booklets are frequently filled with contemporary *probationes pennae* or other scribbles. If, therefore, part II had been a separate booklet, one would expect such scribbles on folio 85v, the last page of part II. Part II, to be sure, does end with the poem *Hec precepta legat deuotus et impleat actu*, but that poem is written by hand 2 with the same calligraphic care as the *Historia apostolica*, and definitely does not constitute a *probatio pennae* or a scribble.[20] Folio 85v, the very last page of part II, is blank, except for a few scratched in letters (b u u e b[?]). The end of part I shows a similar absence of contemporary scribbles. Folio 29r has text in the first four lines but

---

[18] The British Library staff gave a negative answer to my question whether any records had been kept of the distances between the original stitch holes.

[19] Since in my opinion the three different scribes were at work at the same time, the last quire of part I does not contain the beginning of part II, nor does the last quire of part II contain the beginning of part III.

[20] According to Dümmler, there are no verbal overlaps between the *Historia apostolica* and *Hec precepta legat*. The inclusion of *Hec precepta legat* therefore remains a bit of a puzzle, unless one wishes to argue that the scribe did not wish to leave the remaining folios of his last quire empty and filled them with a poem of appropriate length. Since the poem *Hec precepta legat* has strong verbal overlaps with the *Disticha Catonis* which are well known as a school text, it is not so surprising to see *Hec precepta legat* included in a book that might have been used by a teacher.

no contemporary scribbles on the rest of the page nor on folio 29v.[21] The end of part III, on the other hand, has exactly the type of scribbles one would expect at the end of a manuscript. In a text totally unrelated to the commentary, an early twelfth-century scribe asks: "Dic m*i*hi qua etate erat ie*su*s quando baptizatus est baptismo iudeorum po*st* natiuitate*m*," and another scribe repeats the first words ("Dic mihi qua etate"). The lack of scribbles at the ends of parts I and II, but their presence at the end of part III, suggests that part III had always been the final portion of the manuscript, and that parts I and II had never been independent.

The idea that all three booklets had from the very beginning been designed to be bound together receives additional support from the size of the pages and of the writing grid. With minor fluctuations all pages measure about 177 × 113 mm. Since the small size of the manuscript is not typical for Anglo-Saxon Arator manuscripts,[22] one can argue that this particular size was conceived for all three booklets at the same time. Such an assumption seems more convincing than the counter-assumption that part II existed first and "was subsequently bound up with the other two parts." I find it difficult to believe that the "librarian who was attempting to assemble in one codex all the material necessary for serious study of Arator" would find one booklet of a size untypical for Anglo-Saxons already written and then request two additional booklets of the same size to be copied.

But were the three booklets originally all the same size, or were they trimmed to fit together? The Arator portion clearly shows signs of trimming: part of the gloss on fol. 30v (fig. 1.1) is cut off, with between two to three letters missing. Similar trimming of leaves, however, also appears in part I (e.g., fol. 14v [fig. 1.2]) and in part III (e.g., fol. 145v [fig. 1.3]), so that we can conclude

---

[21] Folio 29v does contain the sixteenth-century poem *Accede ad musas vatum Thamesina iuuentus,* which clearly was added much later. The full text of the poem is as follows:

> Accede ad musas vatum, Thamesina iuuentus,
>   perdocte ut valeas verba Latina loqui.
> Cedite, barbariem colitis quicumque, nec ullus
>   hac tanta vobis pareat urbe locus.

> "Oh, you young people living along the Thames, throng to the Muses of the poets so that you may learn to speak Latin like scholars. But you who cherish barbarian ways, be gone, and may no place in this great city be subject unto you."

[22] CTC B.14.3 measures 245 × 175 mm.; Oxford, Rawl. C 570 205 × 161 mm.; BL Additional 11034 230 × 144 mm.; CUL Gg.5.35 213 × 145 mm., and BN lat. 8092 measures 280/290 × 205/215 mm., i.e., the Anglo-Saxon manuscripts containing the *Historia apostolica* are all larger.

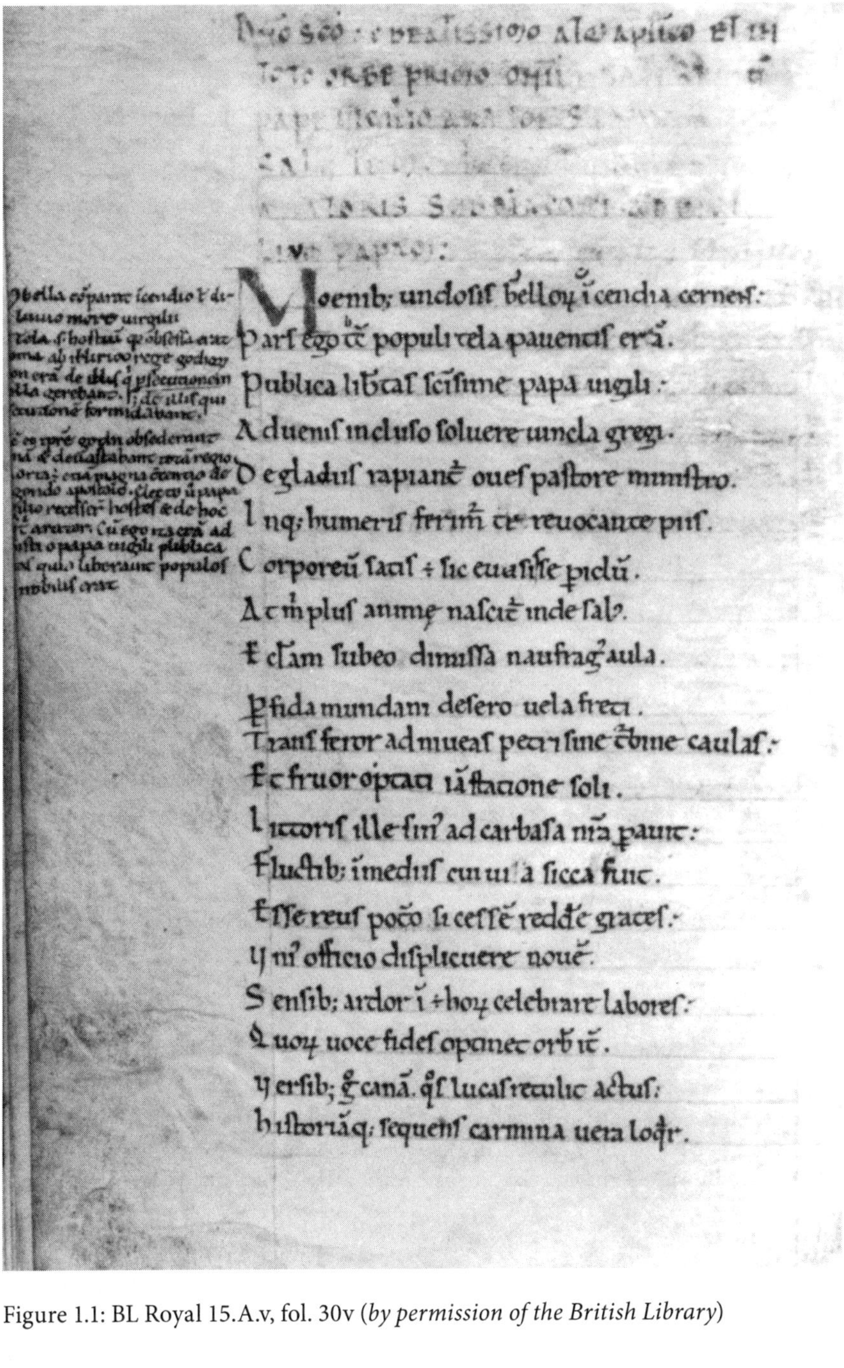

Figure 1.1: BL Royal 15.A.v, fol. 30v (*by permission of the British Library*)

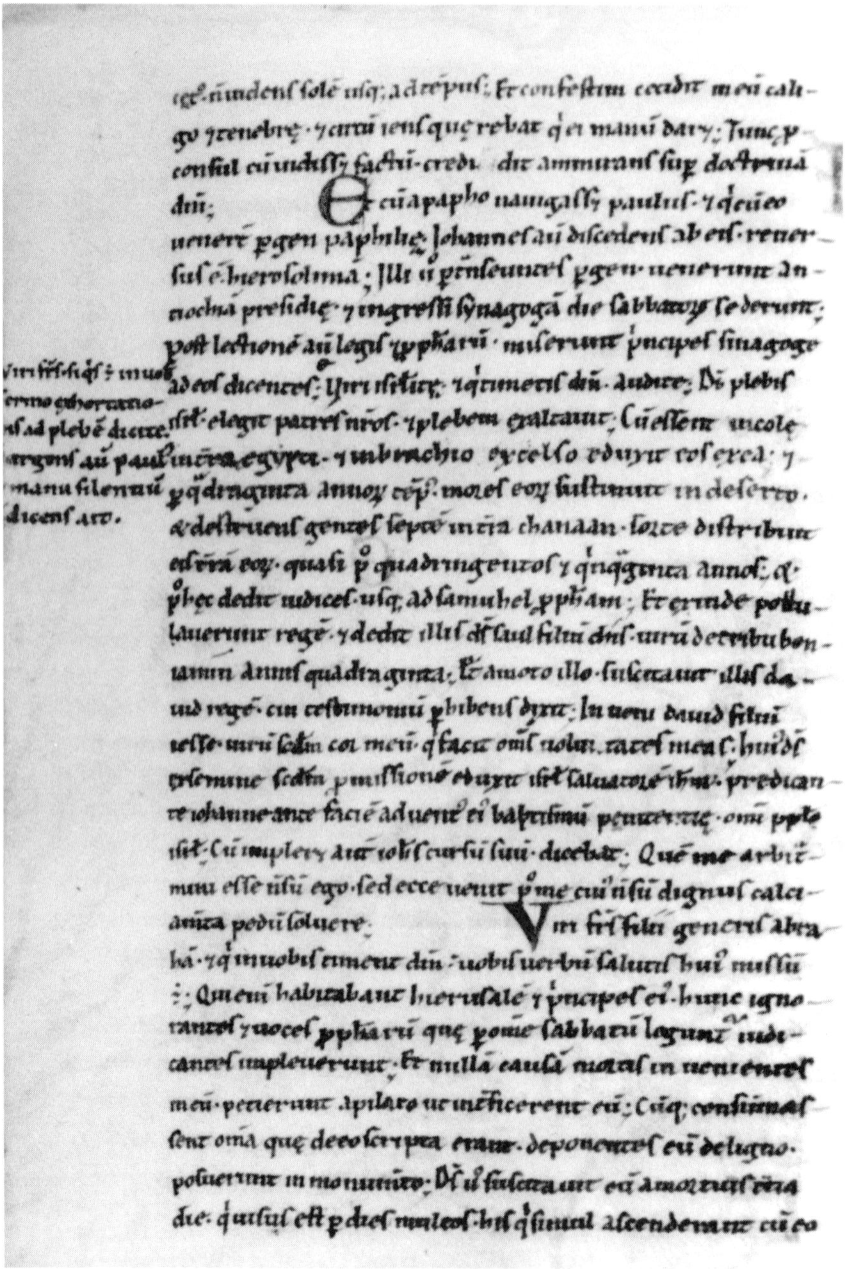

Figure 1.2: BL Royal 15.A.v, fol. 14v (*by permission of the British Library*)

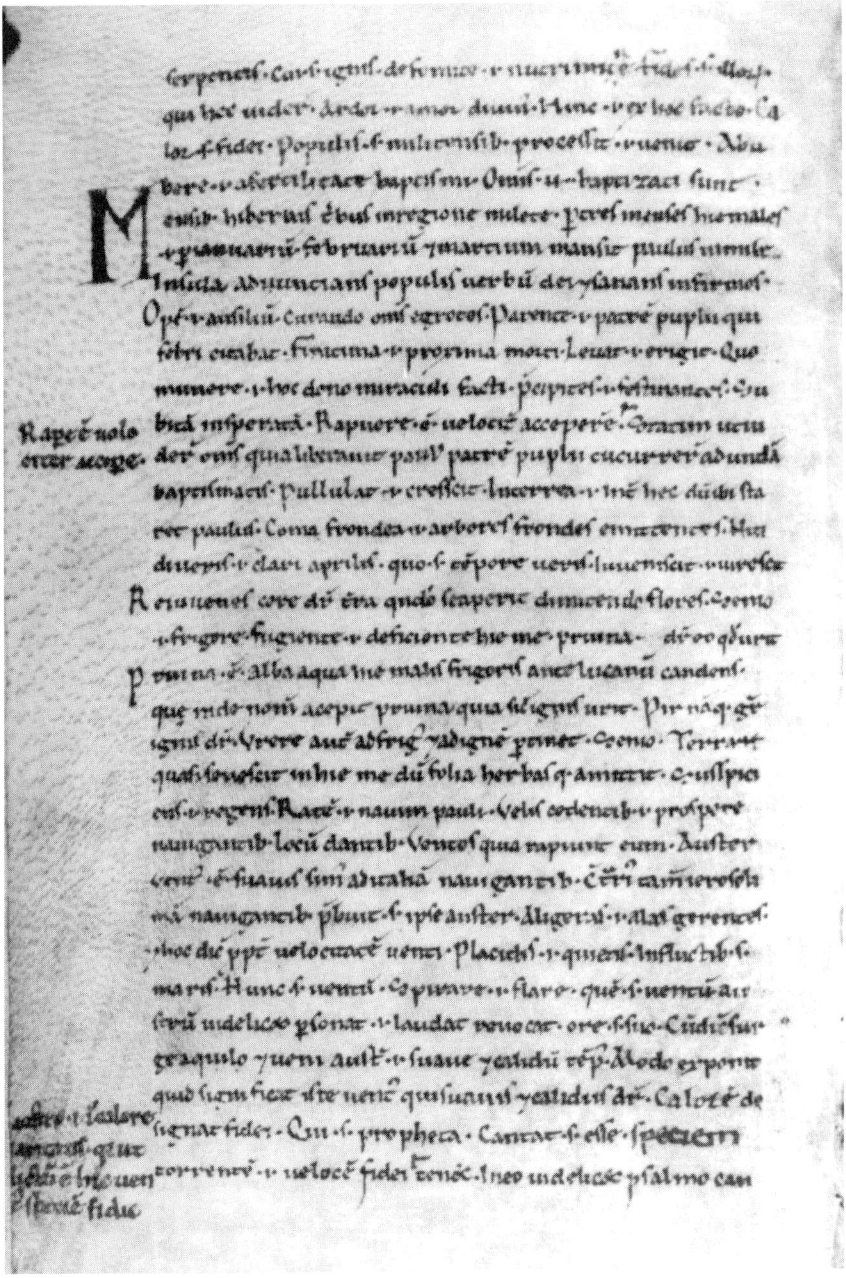

Figure 1.3: BL Royal 15.A.v, fol. 145v (*by permission of the British Library*)

that the trimming took place not when the three booklets were first bound together, but at a later date. This raises the question: what was the size of the booklets when they were first bound together?

Here, I think, the ruling of the individual folios can provide an answer. First, the ruling confirms what Lapidge has argued on palaeographic grounds, namely that parts I and III belong together. Both parts I and III are ruled at thirty-two lines per page, and the writing grid covers an area of about 133 × 77 mm. in part I, and of 133 × 77 mm. in part III (the ruling shows minor fluctuations of +/- 2 mm. from quire to quire). Part II has only twenty-six lines per page, and the writing grid is somewhat smaller at 133 × 66 mm. The smaller lateral dimension (66 mm instead of 77) need not surprise us since the *Historia apostolica* is poetry, and therefore does not need to fill the entire space between the left and the right margin, whereas the prose of parts I and III does. What is significant, in my opinion, is the fact that the distance between the top and bottom lines of part II is identical to that of parts I and III: 133 mm. This in turn suggests that the size of the original pages of all three parts was identical also. And because all three parts have identical vertical ruling and apparently originally the same page size, they all seem to have been prepared at the same time and in the same scriptorium.[23]

Relationship of the Commentary to the Glosses of the *Historia apostolica*

One further area has to be examined to determine whether this theory of an Anglo-Caroline hand collaborating with Norman ones is correct, and that is the relation of the glosses in part II (Arator) to those in part III (Arator commentary). Are they identical? Do they differ? If they differ, what conclusions can be drawn from the differences? If they are the same, what conclusion can we draw from that?

The glosses of part II are not numerous. Scribe 2 does not add any glosses whatsoever. Lack of space is probably the major reason for his not doing so, but a possible second reason may be his knowledge that a commentary was simultaneously being prepared, and that therefore there was no need for glosses. The glosses that are added are in Norman hands. I can discern two

---

[23] On this point Phill cautioned me that we might be dealing with what he called a "house style." This is indeed what I am arguing. House styles, however, change over time. In Royal 15.A.v we seem to have a house style of one specific time, namely the late eleventh or early twelfth century.

similar hands; both can be seen on e.g. fol. 40v where the glosses in the first twenty-one lines are by one hand, written in black ink, and the gloss in line 24 by the other, written in brown ink; this second glossator adds only a handful of glosses in the entire poem. Although both hands are Norman, neither is identical with the one which writes the commentary: the main glossator in part II uses a rounded abbreviation stroke for nasals, the "qr" combination for *quia*, an open-looped "g," and he tends to use double ligature in "er," i.e. both the top and lower loop of "e" connect with the "r" whereas the scribe of the commentary uses an angular abbreviation stroke for nasals, abbreviates q*uia* with a superscript "i," has a closed loop for "g," and uses only single ligature for "er," namely at the top. Nonetheless, as their scripts show, the two scribes are contemporaries or near-contemporaries, and the same can be said for the second glossing hand.

Now to the glosses themselves. The gloss on folio 30v7 (=letter to Vigilius 1) reads:

bella co*m*parat i*n*cendio *u*el di

luuio more uirgilii.

tela (30v8 = Vig. 2): s. hostiu*m* q*uia* obsessa erat

[r]oma ab illirico[24] (originally irlirico, but first r corrected to l) rege gothor*um*.

[n]on era*m* de illis q*ui* persecutionem

(*persecutionem* is underlined to indicate that it needs to be deleted)

[b]ella gerebant s*et* de illis qui

[per]secutione*m* formidabant.

These glosses form a group next to lines 7–10 and are cued with *signes de renvoi*. Also on the same page we find the marginal gloss:

---

[24] It is not entirely clear why the commentator mentions King "illiricus" (possibly "alaricus"?). Vigilius was pope from 537 to 555 A.D. In 536, i.e., one year before Vigilius became pope, Belisarius had defeated the Ostrogoths and taken Rome. Belisarius was recalled to Byzantium in 541, and the Ostrogoths rebelled under the leadership of King Totila. Belisarius returned in 547 and reconquered Rome. Since Arator speaks of the Goths as receding "electo uero papa uigilio," he seems to be referring to the Ostrogoths' defeat at the hands of Belisarius in 536, when Witigis was their king (he ruled from 536 to 540). "Illiricus" or "Alaricus" may have been inserted here since he was the best-known and most hated Gothic king conquering Rome. See Ilona Opelt, "Das Bild König Alarichs I. in der zeitgenössischen Dichtung," in eadem, *Paradeigmata Poetica Christiana: Untersuchungen zur christlichen lateinischen Dichtung* (Düsseldorf, 1988), 41–48.

[Tun]c eo tempore gothi obsederant

[ro]mam (first part of the first m is cut off) & deuastabant totam regio

[nem]. orta est etiam magna contentio de

[eli]gendo apostolo. Electo uero papa

[uig]ilio recesserunt hostes & de hoc

[loqu]itur arator. Cum ego ita eram ad

[uen]isti o papa uigili publica

[liber]tas quia liberauit populos

[uel quia] nobilis erat.

The corresponding texts in the commentary read:

> Bella comparat incendio uel diluuio more uirgilii./ Cernens. i. Intuens.
> Pars. i. un[i]us populi. Pauentis. i. intuen/tis. Tela. s. hostium quia ob-
> cessa [sic] erat roma ab ilirico rege gothorum./ Non eram de illis qui
> bella gerebant. set de his qui persecutionem for/midabant. Tunc. s. eo
> tempore quo gothi obsederant romam. &/ deuastabant totam regionem.
> Orta. est &iam magna contentio/ de eligendo (corr. from deligendo)
> apostolico. Electo uero papa uigilio. recesserunt hostes./ 7 de hoc loqui-
> tur arator. Cum ego ita eram aduenisti o papa uigili pu/blica libertas.
> quia liberauit populos. uel quia nobilis erat (fol. 86v, 15–23)

i.e., they are virtually identical (differences are *his, quo, apostolico* in the commentary vs. *illis*, [omitted], and *apostolo* in the marginal gloss. This would
suggest that the marginal gloss was taken from the commentary in the back.
Other identical readings seem to confirm this: (Glosses, both interlinear and
marginal, are shown in italics. If there are several glosses to a line, the lemmata will be repeated, and separated from the lemma line by a dash. Abbreviations in the glosses will be shown by underlined italics):

> Gloss 35v1 (AI, 195) Naturae percussit cui serior ortus: *.i. generationis per
> quod debebat nasci*
>
> Commentary 90v23–4 naturae. i. generationis per quod debebat nasci
>
> Gloss 35v16 (AI, 210) Mistica uis numeri gregis. pia forma nouelli: *.i. secreta
> quia trinitatem prefigurat. rectus numerus.*
>
> Commentary 91r5–6: Mistica uis. i. secr&a quia trinitatem prefigurat. pia
> forma.i. rectus numerus
>
> Gloss 62v21 (AII, 390) Nudus amore timor. paulus miseratus ab atro – nu-
> dus: *uacuus*; amore: *dei*; timor: *diaboli*
>
> Commentary 123r18 Nudus timor .s. diaboli. amore. s. dei.

However, differences exist, e.g.:

> Gloss 63r25 (AII, 420) Pena fugit. geminoque metu discrimina crescunt.–
> Pena: *apostolorum* (interl.)
>
> *Fugit poena. i. omnia uincula pauli et silę dissoluta sunt. discrimina. i. peri-
> cula gemino metu quia duplex timor custodi inhesit. terrę motus & hoc quod
> existimauit eos fugisse. & ob hoc interficere se uoluit* (marg.)
>
> Commentary 123v27 Poena s. apostolorum. Tormenta. s. carceris. Locum s.
> torquendi. Gemino. duplicato pauore. Gemino dicit. i. propter terrę motum
> 7 propter hoc quod in carcere erant paulus 7 silas.
>
> Gloss 35r26 (AI, 194) Festinas proferre reos: *quia antequam* sint creati sunt rei
>
> Commentary 90v22 quia antequam sint nati iam sunt rei

These differences indicate that the glossator did not copy from the commentary, but from another source. The identical glosses, on the other hand, rule
out the possibility that the glossator inserted into the text only those glosses
which differed from those in the commentary. The only conclusion can be
that the glossator of part II did not use the commentary as his source, but
drew either on the exemplar from which scribe 2 had copied the text, or on
another commentary.[25] I consider the glosses added later, possibly when the
system of flipping back and forth between commentary and text became too
cumbersome.

One further point deserves to be mentioned: the commentary does not
take the *Historia apostolica* of Royal 15.A.v as its lemma text. A few differences will quickly demonstrate this:

> 34v18 (AI, 160 primus at ille–90r30 primus ad ille
>
> 35r5 (AI, 173) fusus genetricis ab aluo–90v11 fusae
>
> 35r20 (AI, 188) fenestra piacula–90v18 funesta piacula
>
> 35v1 (AI, 195) cui serior ortus–90v25 cui tardior ortus

These differences in the text of the *Historia apostolica* as found in parts II and
III indicate that the commentary is independent of the Arator version in Royal
15.A.v. If the Arator text had been written before the commentary, and if the
commentary had been written for the Arator text, then one could expect the
scribe of the commentary to consult the text and correct either his commentary

---

[25] The error of *illirico* in the gloss, and of *ilirico* in the commentary for *alarico*, as in
Additional 11034, suggests that despite the differences between the commentary and the
gloss, both come from the same school.

or the text. Since neither was done, two possibilities open up: one, that scribes 2 and 3 wrote at the same time and could therefore not consult each other, or two, that scribes 2 and 3 wrote in different places and/or at different times, and that their independent booklets were later bound together. Taking into account that the opening page of part II is not yellowed, that only the end of part III has *probationes pennae*, and that the original size of the pages of parts II and III seems to have been identical, the first of the two possibilities seems more likely.

The Scribes of Royal 15.A.v

Now finally to the scribes of Royal 15.A.v. According to Lapidge, two or three hands are at work here: the easiest to identify is the one Lapidge calls the late Anglo-Caroline hand of folios 30r to 81r, writing late in the eleventh century or early in the twelfth century. Lapidge finds it "difficult to say whether parts I and III were written by the same hand." Several differences between the hands writing parts I and III suggest that the hands of these two sections are not identical. One difference between them is the abbreviation stroke, for which scribe 1 (=the scribe of part I) prefers a straight line, tapering to the right and slightly rising (e.g., in 8r1 [fig. 1.4]), while scribe 3 uses a line which begins with a marked downstroke, and often even ends with a downstroke (e.g., 119r2 [fig. 1.5]). Hand 1 writes a closed "ct" ligature, i.e. with the "c" continuing to form the cross bar of the "t" (e.g. 8r14 *octauo*), while scribe 3 leaves his open (i.e. with the "c" not forming the crossbar of the "t," e.g., 119r25 *facta*); scribe 1 writes an "a" with a headstroke (e.g., 8r1 *audite*), while the "a" of scribe 3 has no headstroke (e.g., 119r1 *quia lapideis*); scribe 1 tends to close the loop of his "g" (e.g., 8r3 *cognatione*), while scribe 3 tends to keep his open (e.g., 119r17 *dirigit*). Despite the general closeness of the hands, these four differences leave little doubt that two different scribes wrote parts I and III.

What about scribe 2 to whom I have so far referred as "Anglo-Caroline," following the lead of previous scholarship? Without doubt his hand is "Caroline." One of the major characteristics of late Anglo-Caroline, however, is its "roundedness."[26] A comparison of scribe 2 of Royal 15.A.v with some of the

---

[26] E.g. Teresa Webber, "Script and Manuscript Production at Christ Church, Canterbury, after the Norman Conquest," in *Canterbury and the Norman Conquest*, ed. Eales and Sharpe, 145–59, at 145: "The books display not only a number of Norman hands but also a new style of script based on Norman hands such as these. This distinctive, angular script, *so different from the rounded forms of the handwriting of the pre-Conquest scribes*, has long been associated with the arrival in 1070 of Lanfranc and monks from Norman monasteries such as Bec" (emphasis mine). Or Ker, *English Manuscripts*, 33: "one of the hands is old-fashioned *round* and upright in the stately English style" (emphasis mine).

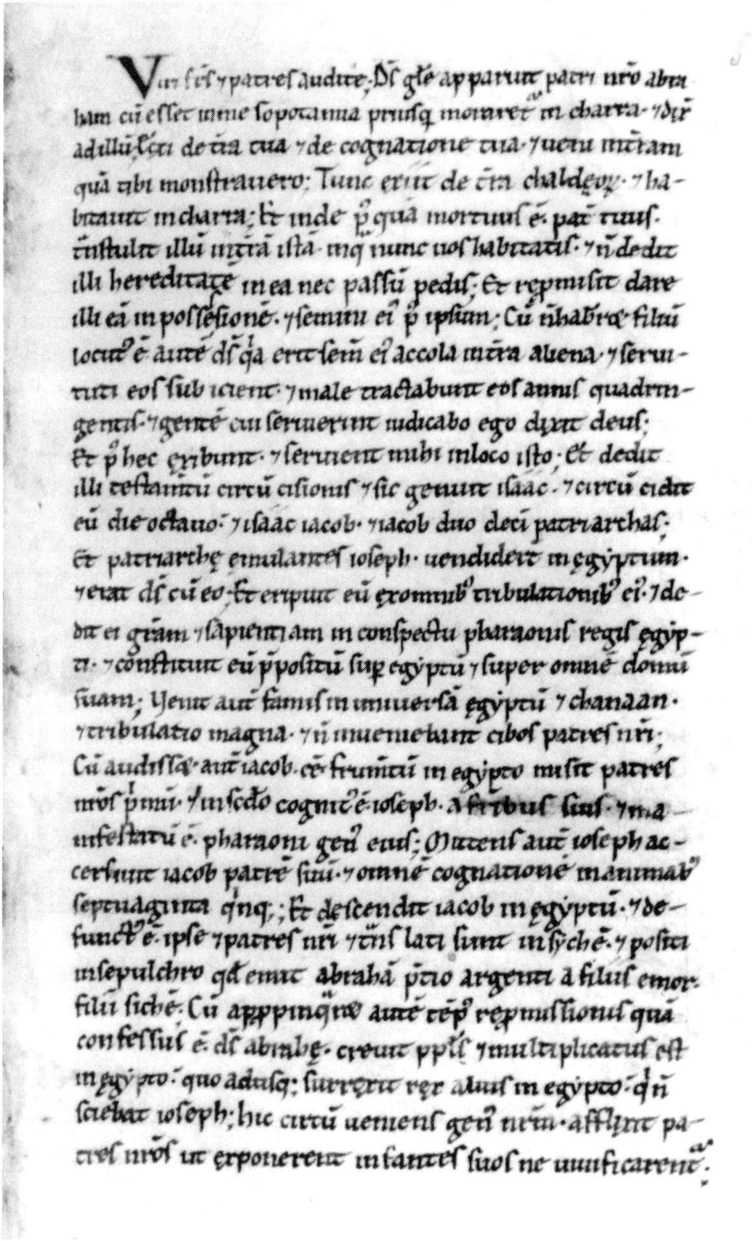

Figure 1.4: BL Royal 15.A.v, fol. 8r (*by permission of the British Library*)

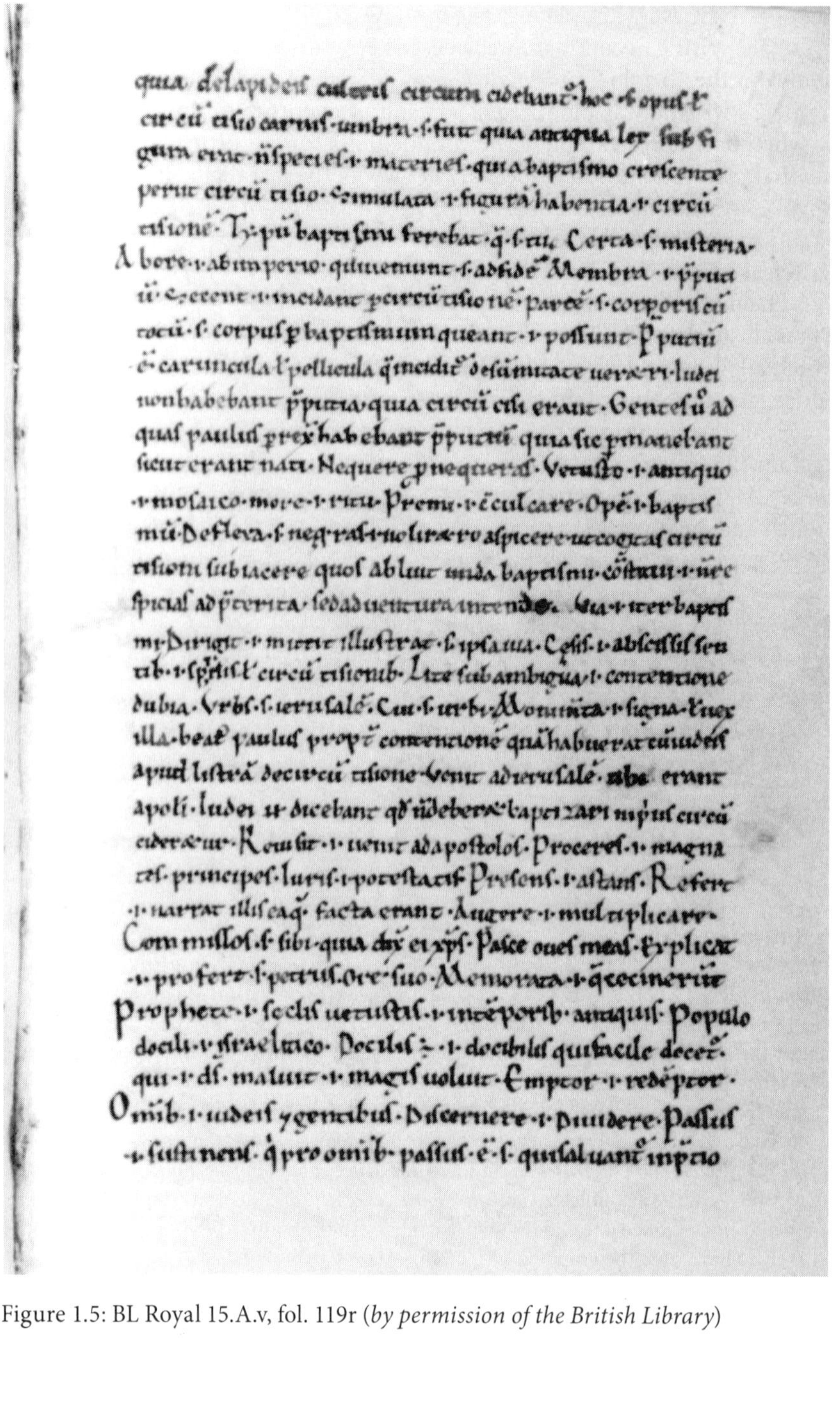

Figure 1.5: BL Royal 15.A.v, fol. 119r (*by permission of the British Library*)

plates given in Ker (e.g., plates 1 and 3) shows that scribe 2 lacks this rounded-ness. His writing in contrast can be described as angular, casting at least some doubt on the "Anglo-" of "Anglo-Caroline." It is impossible to say whether scribe 2's writing was modified as a result of exposure to the Norman style, or whether it never exhibited the roundedness typical of Anglo-Caroline in the first place. At any rate, especially in view of the fact that neither the size of Royal 15.A.v nor its text of the *Historia apostolica* conforms to those of Anglo-Saxon manuscripts, one must be very cautious about assuming that this writer of a Caroline hand was an Anglo-Saxon.

The manuscript even contains some evidence suggesting that scribe 2 was a French speaker. The *Historia apostolica* abounds with scribal errors, some of which allow a tentative conclusion as to the scribe's native language. The most noticeable one is this: of the sixteen times the word *baptisma* (or forms thereof) occurs in the *Historia apostolica*,[27] the scribe writes *baptima* (or forms thereof) four times: *baptima* 33v15 (AI, 117), *baptimatis* 35v10 (AI, 204), *baptimatis* 45r22 (AI, 646), *baptimate* 49v19 (AI, 849). The form without the "-s-" is Old French and anticipates the modern French *baptême*.[28] Other errors that might have been caused by the fact that the scribe was a French speaker are these:

1. *ignocui* 42r22 (AI, 513), *ignocuę* (for *innocuae*) 45v21 (AI, 671), and *in-signuans* (g erased) 67r14 (AII, 602) where a "-gn-" reproduces a Latin "-nn-" or "-n-" (*innocuus* and *insinuans*).[29]

2. *subcombit* 45v3 (AI, 653) and *circondata* 54v4 (AI, 1071) for *subcumbit* and *circumdata*, where the grapheme of an "o" for a "u" represents French scribal practice.[30]

---

[27] The word *baptisma* or forms thereof appear in lines 117, 204, 626, 646, 663, 744, 849, 864, and 956 of book I, and in lines 84, 280, 585, 586, 598, 604, and 807 in book II of the *Historia apostolica*.

[28] See M.K. Pope, *From Latin to Modern French with Especial Consideration of Anglo-Norman*, rev. ed. (London, 1952), 151: "The English pronunciation of words such as *aim* (<*ezmer*), *blame* . . . on the one hand, and of *beast, feast, host* . . . on the other, indicates that at the time of the Norman Conquest the voiced sound z was already modified or mute when prae-consonantal while the breathed sound s was still intact."

[29] On the shift of Latin "-gn-" to Old French nasalized "n," see Pope, *From Latin*, 133. In classical and medieval Latin, a "-gn-" was at times replaced by a "-nn-" or "-n-." See Peter Stotz, *Handbuch zur Lateinischen Sprache des Mittelalters*, vol. 3: *Lautlehre* (Munich, 1996), 306–7. In the examples given, we see the reverse process: an /n/ sound is given the grapheme "-gn-." Since late Old English speakers still pronounced /gn/ for "gn," they are unlikely to have used the grapheme "-gn-" for /n/.

[30] See Pope, *From Latin*, 166: "The sound u was represented by o or u, more rarely ou."

3. *iestare* (for *gestare*) 37r26 (AI, 286) and *magestatis* (for *maiestatis*) 41r4 (AI, 448), which suggests a confusion of "g" and "i" typical of Romance languages.[31]

4. *Illiriquos* (for *Illyricos*) 61r19 (AII, 315), where the apparent pronunciation of "qu" as /k/ suggests a French speaker.[32]

5. *oscure* (later corrected to *obscure*) 49v5 (AI, 841), where the assimilation of "-bs-" to "-s-" suggests Old French *oscure*.[33]

6. Addition of an h-sound where it is not needed, and omission of the sound where it is needed appears in many different language areas, but as French is among them, this point should not be neglected as a further indication that scribe 2 was a French speaker.[34] Examples of the first are *habraham* 60v9 (AII, 283), *habraham* 60v18 (AII, 292), *heliso* (for *eliso*) 63r8 (AII, 403), and of the second *ora* (for *hora*) 49v26 (AI, 856), *ebreus* 46r10 (AI, 681), *oṛẹ* 50v4, (AI, 881), *onestas* (later corrected to *honestas*) 55r4 (AII, 15), and *imnum* (later corrected to *himnum*) 63r22 (AII, 417). An example where scribe 2 both omits and adds an "h" occurs in the word *ebrehus* 44v14 (AI, 618).

These features strongly suggest that scribe 2 is a French speaker. Once, however, it is acknowledged that scribe 2 was not an Anglo-Saxon, then the largest obstacle against the theory that scribe 2 wrote at the same time as scribes 1 and 3 is removed.

The manuscript offers one further piece of evidence, though somewhat more tentative than the preceding one. Scribe 2 cannot be described as a careful worker. At times he omits entire lines, e.g. on folio 49r19, where a corrector supplies "Quẹ uitam de morte uides ut munera petrus" (AI, 828), on folio 60v27, where the corrector has to supply "Mater inest natusque dei de uirginis aluo" (AII, 300), and on folio 79r27, where he supplies "Quam dedit ipsa prius que culpe protulit ignem" (AII, 1174). Especially in the earlier sections scribe 2 commits numerous errors on each page. For instance, using a darker ink than scribe 2, a corrector changed the following errors on folio 37r:

37r3 reliqueret > reliquerat (AI, 263)

37r7 *carne* written in over erasure; the original word seems to have been *corde* (AI, 267)

---

[31] On "g" for "i," see Stotz, *Handbuch*, 3:140, and on "i" for "g," see Stotz, *Handbuch*, 3:206.

[32] Pope, *From Latin*, 91: "**w** was effaced . . . [w]hen standing between **k** and either **o** or **u**," and gives as examples *cot* for *quot* and *condam* for *quondam*.

[33] See Pope, *From Latin*, 149 on the word *oscure*.

[34] On the omission of "h" in Late Latin, see Pope, *From Latin*, 91. See also Stotz, *Handbuch*, 3:156–61.

37r9 et idola > atque idola (AI, 269)

37r15 similes quicumque prophetę> similes qui ore prophetę (AI, 275)

37r16 oscuris > obscuris; in the same line the word *manifesta* is written with a 5mm. space between *mani* and *festa*; an erasure suggests that the scribe had originally written something else. It cannot be ascertained whether scribe 2 or the corrector erased the incorrect word (AI, 276)

37r24 noxia: the 'x' is written in over an erasure (AI, 284)

Folio 67r exhibits a similar number of errors :

67r3 corporæ–the corrector erases the lower loop of the 'æ' to make the word read *corpore* (AII, 591)

67r3 mando > mundo (AII, 591)

67r11 palum > paulum (AII, 599)

67r14 insignuans > insinuans (AII, 602)

67r19 &psa > & ipsa (AII, 607)

67r24 laco > lacu (AII, 612)

Towards the end of the *Historia apostolica*, however, approximately on the last ten folios, the number of mistakes decreases noticeably. On folio 74r9, for instance, I could find only the correction of *redem* to *rudem* (AII, 925), and on folio 78v a *q;* written in over an erasure in line 13 (AII, 1143–the word is *quoque*), and a change of *figurem* to *figuram* in line 22 (AII, 1152). What is the reason for this sudden decrease in errors per page? It seems likely that someone drew scribe 2's attention to his large number of errors at around the time when he was writing folio 70, and consequently the number of mistakes per page decreased. Though there is no proof, this "someone" may have been the corrector since his corrections of scribe 2's errors clearly demonstrate that he was aware of them. To judge by the ductus and the angular letter forms of the supplied sentences, the corrector was a Norman. He seems to have inserted his corrections before the glossators, themselves Normans, began their work,[35] and he seems to have begun his corrections before scribe 2 had completed the *Historia apostolica*. Scribe 2, in other words, appears to have followed

---

[35] See fol. 66r5, where the glossator inserts an "s" between the abbreviation marks over the original *concius*, to create "conscius"; the gloss "ipse david" is written in above both the abbreviation marks and the added "s," and is, in effect obscuring the "s." It seems unlikely that the corrector would squeeze his correction into a place where it can barely be seen, and more likely that the glossator would add a gloss over a correction and in effect obscure the correction.

the instructions of a Norman corrector, and appears to have written his Caroline hand at the same time as the corrector wrote his Norman hand.

If scribe 2 was a contemporary of the Norman scribes and if he wrote simultaneously with them, why then did he not write the Norman or International script as they did? The answer, I believe, lies in the fact that the *Historia apostolica* is the centerpiece of the manuscript. As far as the content of Royal 15.A.v is concerned, it is not the palaeographically related parts I and III that belong together, but either parts I and II, that is the Vulgate Acts of the Apostles and Arator's versification thereof, or parts II and III, i.e. Arator's poem and the commentary explicating it. Arator's *Historia apostolica*, though palaeographically the outsider in the trio, occupies the central place of the manuscript as far as the content is concerned. To indicate this central place graphically, scribe 2 chose, or was instructed, to write in a more calligraphic script than the Norman or International script and he chose, or was instructed to choose, the Caroline script.

Conclusion

To sum up: research into manuscripts of the late eleventh/early twelfth century provides numerous instances of Anglo-Caroline and Norman hands cooperating; the text of the *Historia apostolica* of Royal 15.A.v differs from that found in Anglo-Saxon manuscripts; Royal 15.A.v is smaller than Anglo-Saxon manuscripts containing the *Historia apostolica*; the opening page of part II does not show the wear and tear one can expect from the opening page of a booklet; the last pages of parts I and II do not show the *probationes pennae* common to last pages of manuscripts, but the last page of part III does; the vertical ruling in all three booklets is the same, and the original page size of all three booklets was in all likelihood identical; the glosses of part II are not identical with the glosses in the commentary, and the lemmata in the commentary are not always identical to the text of the *Historia apostolica*. There is nothing in these points that indicates that scribe 2 did not write at the same time as scribes 1 and 3. When, however, we add to these points the thematic unity of the manuscript, the scribal errors that suggest that scribe 2 was a French speaker, as well as his possible obedience to the instructions of a Norman corrector, then there is little reason to retain the assumption that scribe 2 was not a contemporary of scribes 1 and 3. I therefore conclude that Royal 15.A.v is now, and has been from the very beginning, since sometime in the late eleventh or early twelfth century, one integral manuscript with three different scribes. I see no reason to assume that the three parts ever existed as three independent manuscripts or booklets which were at a later date bound together. I reiterate therefore the claim which I had made in 1985, and now with somewhat more confidence, namely that "in all probability . . . the teacher used the commentary in conjunction with the text,"[36] though of course I can no longer claim any portion of Royal 15.A.v for the Anglo-Saxons but have to concede all of it to the Normans.[37]

Appendix

The Appendix compares significantly different readings of the first 500 lines of Arator's *Historia apostolica* in Royal 15.A.v to those of Additional 11034, CUL Gg.5.35, and Rawlinson C 570. Mere orthographic differences are not taken into account; corrections, however, are mentioned with ">" meaning "corrected from."

line	15 A. v.	Add 11034	Gg.5.35	Rawl C 570
054	praelata	prᶒlecta	praelecta	prelecta
076	solebat	ardebat	ardebat	ardebat
097	extremas	externas >extremas	externas >extremas	externas
101	ocula	oscula	oscula	oscula
141	nunc	tunc	tunc	tunc
147	mitibus	mentibus	mentibus >mitibus	mentibus
147	instet >instat	instat	instat	instat
147	aestuet >aestuat	estuat	estuat	aestuat

---

[36] Wieland, "The Glossed Manuscript," 171.

[37] Gameson, *The Manuscripts*, 27 mentions that in the post-Conquest era very few Christian Latin poets, Arator among them, were copied, partly because "interest in the genre had passed its peak," and partly because of "the very strength of pre-Conquest holdings" in this area. Taking these two points into account one could — with all due caution — suggest that Royal 15.A.v was more likely to have been written in the late eleventh century when there was still some interest in the genre, rather than the early twelfth century, and that it was put together for a newly-founded monastery in the South of England which had no prior holdings. Canterbury had copies of Arator (CTC B.14.3 from Christ Church, CUL Gg.5.35 and Rawlinson C 570 from St. Augustine's) and was therefore less likely to need additional copies.

line	15 A v	Add 11034	Gg.5.35	Rawl C 570
149	vetus	verus	verus	verus
157	intus	unus	unus	unus
172	reduceret	concederet	concederet	concederet
188	fenestra	funesta	funesta	funesta
240	potis es	potis es	potis es	poteris
		>potis est		uel potis es
292	doctore	ductore	ductore	ductore
305	uouet	fouet	fouet	fouet
314	cohors	cadis	uechors	cadis
		>cohors?		
316	sumno	somno	somno	somno
354	uitam solo	solo uitam	solo uitam	solo uitam
385	per mistica	per mistica	per mistica	misteria
395	ambitione	ambitiose	ambitiose	ambitiose
405	quia	quia	quid	quod
		>quod?		
407	quae . . . uetant	quod . . . uitant	quod . . . uitant	quod . . . uitant
413	amplexu	amplexu	amplexus	amplexus
428	sponsio	falsi	falsi	falsi
434	fellere	fallere	fallere	fallere
438	plana	plena	plana	plena
		a over e		
455	dona	signa	signa	signa
464	species	facies	facies	facies
489	ferat	gerat	gerat	ferat
491	figurę	uidete	uidete	uidete

Bibliography

Alcuini (Albini) Carmina, ed. Ernst Dümmler. MGH Poetae Latini Aevi
    Carolini. Berlin, 1881; repr. 1964.

Dumville, David. *English Caroline Script and Monastic History: Studies in
    Benedictinism, A.D. 950–1030.* Woodbridge, 1993.

Gameson, Richard. "English Manuscript Art in the Late Eleventh Century:
    Canterbury and its Context." In *Canterbury and the Norman Conquest:
    Churches, Saints and Scholars, 1066–1109*, ed. Richard Eales and Richard
    Sharpe, 95–144. London, 1995.

———. *The Manuscripts of Early Norman England (c. 1066–1130)*. Oxford, 1999.

Gneuss, Helmut. *Handlist of Anglo-Saxon Manuscripts*. Tempe, AZ, 2001.

Gullick, Michael. "The Scribes of the Durham Cantor's Book (Durham, Dean and Chapter Library, MS B.IV.24) and the Durham Martyrology Scribe." In *Anglo-Norman Durham 1093–1193*, ed. David Rollason, Margaret Harvey, and Michael Prestwich, 93–109. Woodbridge, 1994.

Ker, N. R. *English Manuscripts in the Century after the Norman Conquest*. Oxford, 1960.

Lapidge, Michael. "The Study of Latin Texts in Late Anglo-Saxon England: The Evidence of Latin Glosses." In *Latin and the Vernacular Languages in Early Medieval Britain*, ed. Nicholas Brooks, 99–140. Leicester, 1982.

McKinlay, Arthur Patch. *Aratoris subdiaconi de actibus apostolorum*. CSEL 72. Vienna, 1951.

Opelt, Ilona. *Paradeigmata Poetica Christiana: Untersuchungen zur christlichen lateinischen Dichtung.* : Kultur und Erkenntnis 3. Düsseldorf, 1988.

Orbán, A. P. "Ein anonymer Aratorkommentar in HS. London, Royal MS. 15.A.v." *Sacris Eruditi* 38 (1996–1999): 317–51, 40 (2000): 131–239.

Page, R. I. "On the Feasibility of a Corpus of Anglo-Saxon Glosses: The View from the Library." In *Anglo-Saxon Glossography: Papers Read at the International Conference held in the Koninklijke Academie voor Wetenschappen, Letteren en Schone Kunsten van België*, ed. R. Derolez, 77–95. Brussels, 1992.

Pope, M. K. *From Latin to Modern French with Especial Consideration of Anglo-Norman*. Rev. ed. London, 1952.

Robinson, P. R. "Self-contained Units in Composite Manuscripts of the Anglo-Saxon Period." *Anglo-Saxon England* 7 (1978): 231–38.

Stotz, Peter. *Handbuch zur Lateinischen Sprache des Mittelalters*, vol. 3: *Lautlehre*. Munich, 1996.

Webber, Teresa. *Scribes and Scholars at Salisbury Cathedral c. 1075–c. 1125*. Oxford, 1992.

———. "Script and Manuscript Production at Christ Church, Canterbury, after the Norman Conquest." In *Canterbury and the Norman Conquest: Churches, Saints and Scholars 1066–1109*, ed. Eales and Sharpe, 145–59.

Wieland, Gernot. "The Glossed Manuscript: Classbook or Library Book?" *Anglo-Saxon England* 14 (1985): 153–73.

Identifying "Texts" in Cotton Julius E vii: Medieval and Modern Perspectives[1]

Joyce Hill

The particular questions implied by my title "Identifying 'Texts' in Cotton Julius E vii: Medieval and Modern Perspectives" are very large ones: what is a "text" and how does the concept of the text (whatever that is) vary across time? In other contexts we might wish to approach these questions philosophically but, capable as we are of engaging directly with the manuscript, I want to take a more practical approach, focusing on the manuscript contents list and comparing the rationale that brought it into being with the textual identities implied within the body of the manuscript and by other Anglo-Saxons who exploited this material. The manuscript merits attention because it is the best manuscript we have of Ælfric's Old English *Lives of Saints* collection, one of his major works, written sometime between 992 and 1002 at the request of his secular patron Æþelweard, who had evidently asked for an English version of the *passiones* and *vitae* "þe mynster-menn mid heora þenungum betwux him wurðiað", "whom monks in their services honor amongst themselves."[2]

The only edition to date, however, is that by Skeat, published progressively between 1881 and 1900, and it is with Skeat's edition that we must begin, since it is Skeat's textual divisions, editorial numbering, titles, and running

---

[1] My contribution to this memorial volume raises questions about the nature of textual identification and the relationship of manuscript and edition which were at the heart of Phill's academic interests. I remember having a vigorous discussion with him on these very topics after he had heard me give an earlier version of this paper at a conference some time ago. In celebration, therefore — since we should not here dwell on the sadness — my memorial contribution recalls the focus of his own work on the evidence of the manuscripts themselves, and the recurrent pleasure of his generous friendship, which we all enjoyed, and from which we all benefited, at conferences and in email exchanges.

[2] *Ælfric's Lives of Saints*, ed. Walter W. Skeat, 2 vols in 4 parts, EETS o.s. 76, 82, 94, 114 (London, 1881–1900), repr. as 2 vols (London, 1966), 1:4. References to this edition are to the two-volume reprint. All translations from Old English are my own.

heads which we all know and use and which therefore determine how we go about reading and interpreting the *Lives of Saints*. We know that this is "only" an edition, something highly mediated by the editor, and not the thing itself, but for practical purposes this is the collection for us. However, when we get behind Skeat's edition, the manuscript we encounter and the texts within it (however we choose to define them) are themselves already mediated since British Library MS. Cotton Julius E vii, which has the distinction of being the only manuscript witness to the *Lives of Saints* as a whole, is at some remove from the author and shows signs of non-authorial interference.[3] Admittedly, it has the advantage of being not far removed in date, since it is from the early eleventh century, and it still preserves the author's prefatory material, which in the Ælfrician corpus as in others tends to be dropped fairly early in transmission sequences. But even if we focus on Ælfric's own work in Julius E vii, there are some homiletic pieces which may have been added, possibly by the author or by others, which do not harmonize with the intention set out in the preface, so that, although we have no direct evidence to support the hypothesis, it may well be that what was originally produced for Æþelweard was a purer hagiographical collection than what now survives in this manuscript.[4] In addition, there were three completely independent works by Ælfric at the end of the manuscript which are not part of the *Lives of Saints* collection: the *Interrogationes Sigewulfi*, *De Falsis Deis*, and *De Duodecim Abusivis*, although loss of leaves from the manuscript means that part of *De Falsis Deis* and the whole of *De Duodecim Abusivis* are now lacking. These are included in the manuscript's contents list, as will be seen below; their juxtaposition with the *Lives of Saints* may be traceable to Ælfric, who sometimes had copies of independent

---

[3] The manuscript, which has a Bury St. Edmunds provenance on the basis of a thirteenth-century inscription on folio 3r, is described by N. R. Ker, *Catalogue of Manuscripts Containing Anglo-Saxon* (Oxford, 1957), 206–10. For a more recent reconsideration of the date of manuscripts with a Bury St. Edmunds provenance, see David Dumville, *English Caroline Script and Monastic History: Studies in Benedictinism, A. D. 950–1030* (Woodbridge, 1993), 30–48, 78–79. In J. Hill, "The Dissemination of Ælfric's *Lives of Saints*: A Preliminary Survey," in *Holy Men and Holy Women: Old English Prose Saints' Lives and Their Contexts*, ed. Paul E. Szarmach (Albany, 1996), 235–59, I discuss in more detail the evidence referred to in this paper and I provide a tabulated analysis of the manuscript distribution of all the material in the *Lives of Saints* part of Cotton Julius E vii.

[4] For a detailed discussion of how the *Lives of Saints* collection may have developed prior to the manifestation in Cotton Julius E vii, see Peter Clemoes, "The Chronology of Ælfric's Works," in *The Anglo-Saxons: Studies in Some Aspects of their History and Culture Presented to Bruce Dickins*, ed. idem (London, 1959), 212–47, esp. 219–23; and additionally M. McC. Gatch, *Preaching and Theology in Anglo-Saxon England: Ælfric and Wulfstan* (Toronto and Buffalo, 1977), 189, n. 49.

pieces added to the end of major collections as "file copies".[5] Finally, there are some anonymous items in Julius E vii, which is contrary to what Ælfric wished. In the Old English Preface to the *Lives of Saints* he insists:

> Ic bidde nu on godes naman gif hwa þas boc awritan wille . þæt he hi wel gerihte be þære bysne . and þær namare betwux ne sette þonne we awendon:[6]

> I pray now in God's name, if anyone wishes to transcribe this book, that he correct it well according to the exemplar, and set down in it no more than we have translated.

Yet despite this, the collection as we have it in Cotton Julius E vii contains the following items not by him: the Seven Sleepers (Skeat XXIII), Mary of Egypt (Skeat XXIIIB), Eustace (Skeat XXX), and Eufrasia or Euphrosyne (Skeat XXXIII).[7]

For the sake of completeness, it should also be noted here that St. Vincent, which Skeat prints in an appendix but with the sequential homily number XXXVII, survives uniquely in CUL Ii. 1.33. Its composition and use has nothing to do with the *Lives of Saints*, despite the impression that some readers may take from Skeat.[8]

Cotton Julius E vii thus presents us with a collection in which there has been significant intervening scribal activity. What the authorial concept was has already been noted: it was to meet the demands of Ælfric's secular patrons for a version in English of the passions and lives of the saints honored by the monks (as opposed to the saints honored by the English nation generally, who

---

[5] This is, of course, a purely pragmatic association, which could nevertheless be reflected in transmission, as the Julius E vii manuscript shows. There is a possible further example provided by the twelfth-century manuscript Cambridge University Library Ii. 1. 33, which includes the *Interrogationes Sigewulfi*, *De Falsis Deis*, and *De Duodecim Abusivis* in a context where texts from the *Lives of Saints* collection predominate. This is not an ordered manuscript, however, unlike Cotton Julius E vii, and the three additional texts are variously positioned instead of being grouped at the end after the material for the Feast of St. Thomas on 21December.

[6] *Ælfric's Lives of Saints*, ed. Skeat, I: 6.

[7] The scholarship which established that these pieces are not by Ælfric is reviewed by Hugh Magennis, who also shows that each is by a different author: "Contrasting Features in the Non-Ælfrician Lives in the Old English *Lives of Saints*," *Anglia* 104 (1986): 316–48.

[8] This homily's compositional context is discussed by Susan Irvine, "Bones of Contention: The Context of Ælfric's Homily on St. Vincent," *Anglo-Saxon England* 19 (1990): 117–32.

had already been included in the *Catholic Homilies*). But what exactly Ælfric produced for them, and how the collection developed in his own hands before it was further adapted by others, in the absence of any better manuscript evidence than Cotton Julius E vii now depends on a series of hypotheses. The situation for the *Lives of Saints* is thus radically different from that for the *Catholic Homilies*, where British Library MS. Royal 7 c. xii shows Ælfric working directly alongside the professional scribe in the preparation of the First Series,[9] and where CUL Gg. 3. 28, which preserves both Series, is "either a product of Ælfric's own scriptorium or a remarkably faithful copy of such a manuscript."[10]

Skeat's edition of the *Lives of Saints* part of Cotton Julius E vii is, then, a further mediation of something already mediated, but it is highly influential in determining how "texts" are identified, analysed, and discussed. Ker's *Catalogue,* on which we all depend, provides a classic example of what I mean in its treatment of Skeat XIX. On the basis of Ker's index (530) it seems that "Alban. Skeat, no. XIX" is a relatively popular subject, since there are references to its occurrence in six manuscripts. But this is misleading because what Ker refers to as "Alban" is in fact two items: a self-contained account of Alban's martyrdom beginning on folio 91v (Skeat XIX, 1–154) drawn from Bede's *Historia Ecclesiastica*, and an *item alia* beginning on folio 93r (Skeat XIX, 155–258), which is an equally self-contained piece using the Old Testament story of Absalom and Ahitophel (2 Samuel 15–16) as an exemplum in a homily on thieves and traitors. The narrative of St. Alban's martyrdom occurs only in three of the manuscripts listed by Ker in his index under the heading of "Alban"; it is Absalom and Ahitophel which occurs in six manuscripts, three times with Alban, twice independently, and once in a composite text, no doubt because, as a moral tale with practical application, it was more open to general use than the principal item in what is now Skeat XIX.[11] Furthermore, according to Wanley, the title given to the Absalom and Ahitophel material in Cotton Vitellius D xvii shows a response to it as a moral piece, rather than a narrative one, since it is called "De Iniustis", even though it here still has what was presumably its

---

[9] *Ælfric's First Series of Catholic Homilies (British Museum Royal 7 c. xii, fols. 4–218),* ed. Peter Clemoes and Norman Eliason, EEMF 13 (Copenhagen, 1966).

[10] *Ælfric's Catholic Homilies: Second Series. Text,* ed. Malcolm Godden, EETS s.s. 6 (London, 1979), xliii.

[11] The two items occur in sequence in Cambridge University Library Ii. 1. 33 (Ker 18 arts. 27 and 28), London, British Library Cotton Julius E vii (Ker 162 arts. 24 and 25), and London, British Library Cotton Vitellius D xvii (Ker 222 arts. 52 and 53). The Absalom and Ahitophel item occurs independently in Cambridge, Corpus Christi College 303 (Ker 57 art. 70) and Oxford, Bodleian Library Hatton 115 (Ker 332 art. 6), and is exploited in a composite homily on the dedication of a church in London, Lambeth Palace 489 (Ker 283, art. 6).

original position relative to Alban.[12] In presenting the Absalom and Ahitophel story from the Julius manuscript, Skeat naturally lists the manuscript's "item alia" title from folio 93r in his modern table of contents, and he gives it its own heading at the point where the text begins (424), although he supplements the manuscript's non-specific "item alia" title with an editorial adaptation of the more informative title from page 340 of Cambridge, Corpus Christi College MS 303, where it occurs as a separate piece. Even so, in Skeat's edition the Absalom and Ahitophel material shares the Alban number and is printed under the continuing editorial running title of "Passio Sancti Albani, Martyris", rendering it half invisible, and causing confusions in references and analysis of manuscript contents, as in Ker.

The independent use of the Absalom and Ahitophel text in CCCC 303 with an explicit title "Quomodo Acitofel 7 multi alii lacqueo se suspenderunt" is symptomatic — as is the presentation of the same text in Cotton Vitellius D xvii with its title of "De Iniustis" — of the fact that textual distinctions were fully recognized by medieval users, even though they were partly disguised (or one might say differently defined) by the method of presentation in Julius E vii and by Skeat's edition, which reduces the distinctions even more and which itself molds our perception of the macrocosmic and microscosmic text — the macrocosmic *Lives of Saints* as an entity (though that is problematic enough, as I have explained), and the microcosmic textual units which make it up.

Yet Skeat's textual identities, misleading though they can be, owe a great deal to the manuscript's contents list on folio 4v, which in turn is itself something of a hindrance to our understanding of the nature of the material within the *sanctorale* and consequently to any attempt we make to trace how this material was exploited elsewhere. As we can see (fig. 2.1), the list does not include Mary of Egypt, which was therefore presumably added after the manuscript's scribe drew up the table of contents, but it does include all the non-hagiographical items by Ælfric, which may or may not have been part of Ælfric's original conception, and all of the other non-Ælfric lives (Eustace, Efrasia or Euphrosyne, and the Seven Sleepers, even though these are probably also additions).[13] I am not so much concerned with the problems presented by added

---

[12] For most items in this manuscript, which was very badly damaged in the Cotton fire, we are dependent on the description by Humfrey Wanley, *Librorum Veterum Septentrionalium*, in vol. II of George Hickes, *Linguarum Veterum Septentrionalium Thesaurus* (Oxford, 1705).

[13] There is a change of hand at quires 16–18, where the Seven Sleepers (fols. 107v–22v) and Mary of Egypt (fols. 122v–36r) occur in sequence, together with some compression of the writing. The preceding quires are in the main hand, as are those that follow. For a discussion of the manuscript at this point, see *The Anonymous Old English Legend of the Seven Sleepers*, ed. Hugh Magennis, Durham Medieval Texts 7 (Durham, 1994), 7–8.

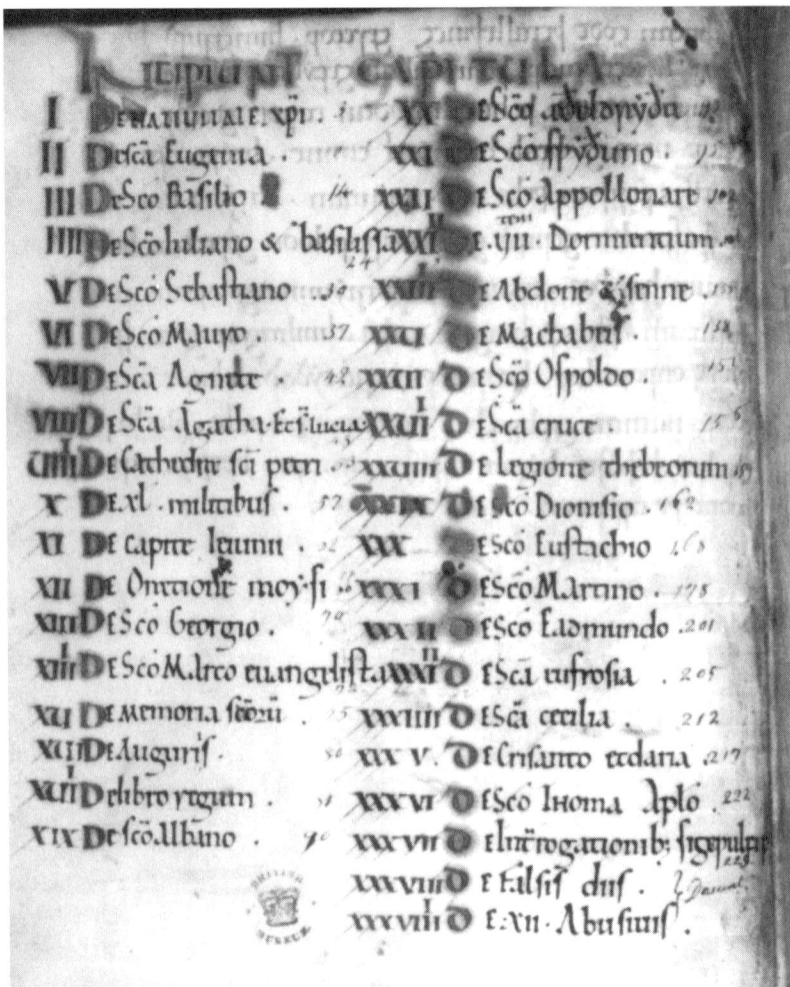

Figure 2.1: British Library MS. Cotton Julius E vii, fol. 4v (*by permission of the British Library*)

texts, however, as with understanding the scribe's rationale in drawing up the contents list, since this might give us a clue about his concept of "the text". As I hope to show, he was not motivated by a desire to identify texts in the sense of designating distinct textual identities, even though these were identities which other Anglo-Saxon scribes were quite willing to acknowledge, as we have seen with Absalom and Ahitophel, and as we can equally clearly see in the scribal treatment elsewhere of the "item alia" piece on fols. 152r–153r at the end of Maccabees (Skeat XXV, lines 812–862). This piece is a statement about the three orders of society and is mainly directed at monks. Skeat, however, supplements the manuscript's "item alia", which he prints in small type, with a longer Latin title, "Qui sunt oratores, laboratores, bellatores", which he prints in a larger font. This is not in Cotton Julius E vii, but is taken, with editorial emendation, from page 355 of Cambridge, Corpus Christi College MS 303, where it stands as a separate item headed "Qui sint Oratores. Laboratores. Bellatores."[14] In Cambridge, Corpus Christi College 178, where again it is independent of Maccabees, it has yet another title: "De tribus ordinibus saeculi", which Skeat could have borrowed just as well, once he had decided go beyond his base-manuscript.

If we now examine the contents list in detail, we see that the scribe does not acknowledge all the divisions in the manuscript: instead, he assigns one item number to each day and, with one exception, lists only one item per day (although he does not bring forward into his list the dates given in the manuscript's rubrics). For most days there is only one item in the manuscript and the scribe's method consequently causes no difficulties, but there are certain days when a saint's life (duly itemized and numbered in the scribal list) is followed in the body of the manuscript, as I have already indicated in two instances, by another item or items which may be significantly different. In these cases the scribe's omission of the additional pieces is, from a modern perspective, somewhat misleading, since it may disguise a marked change of subject. The omissions, however, are a logical consequence of the presentation of texts within the manuscript. What the scribe chooses to list are not textual units as such, but items that have a *specific* title; usually their rubrics also incorporate a date. What he ignores are companion pieces, which include no date in their rubric (since this is provided in the rubric to the immediately preceding item), and which, as companion pieces, have the non-specific title of "alia sententia", "item", or "item alia", whatever their subject may be. My

---

[14] This piece also occurs in Cambridge University Library Ii. 1. 33, following Maccabees proper, but without a separate title; and Oxford, Bodleian Library Hatton 115, independent of Maccabees but without a title.

analysis of the contents list (Table 1) gives Skeat's numbers and the scribe's numbers *as corrected* by him. I also show where these additional divisions occur.[15]

The extra material at Skeat VII (Agnes) is additional hagiographic material concerning Constance and Gallicanus, Terrentianus and John and Paul (rubric for the day, folio 32r; "alia sententia quam scripsit terrentianus", folio 48r). The first narrative for the day (21 January), the "De Sancta Agnete" narrative proper, describes how Agnes cured Constance of leprosy, which thus prepares naturally for the "alia sententia"; clearly the two pieces were written as a pair. The "item alia" at Skeat XV is information about the Four Evangelists (rubric for the day, folio 74r; "item alia", folio 75v); that at XIX is the Absalom and Ahitophel material, which I have commented on already. That at Skeat XXI (Swithun) describes how Macarius cures a maiden apparently transformed by a sorcerer into a mare.[16] Lines 496–98 of Skeat XXI are a formal homiletic conclusion. In the manuscript these words come at the end of the Swithun narrative (folio 103r), where they would be quite suitable, but an eleventh-century corrector marked them for transposition to the end of the Macarius narrative, and in this, as also in other instances, Skeat follows the corrector.[17] The "item alia" to Skeat XXIV is the letter of Christ to Abgarus (rubric for the day, folio 137r; "item alia", folio 138r) and that at the end of Maccabees (Skeat XXV 812–62) is the statement on the three orders of society, which I have referred to earlier. In addition, uniquely within the Maccabees narrative (folio 142v), "item" is used alone to mark a break which is also

---

[15] As will be seen from fig. 2.1, the list is arranged in the manuscript in two columns, with a Latinate form of capital D being used consistently in the first column, and the insular form in the second. Because the manuscript is too tightly bound to be opened fully for photography, only the first letter of *presbyteri* is visible at item XXXVII in fig. 2.1, but the rest of the word is present, abbreviated in the usual way. There is a scribal error in grammatical agreement at item XX, which is retained in the transcription.

[16] Rubric for the day, folio 96v; "item alia", folio 103r. The Macarius story, in a fuller form, is combined with *De Auguriis* and further material about Saul and the Witch of Endor in Cambridge, Corpus Christi College 178 and Oxford, Bodleian Library Hatton 116. This use of the Macarius material is discussed in *The Homilies of Ælfric: A Supplementary Collection*, ed. John C. Pope, EETS o.s. 259, 260 (London, 1967–1968), 2: 786–89, and by Audrey L. Meaney, "Ælfric's Use of his Sources in His Homily on Auguries," *English Studies* 66 (1985): 477–95.

[17] Geoffrey Needham, "Additions and Alterations in Cotton MS. Julius E VII," *Review of English Studies* n.s. 9 (1958): 160–64 (see 163, n. 3, for the Swithun/Macarius doxology). For Skeat's editorial responses to the Julius copy, see also Robert J. Alexander, "W. W. Skeat and Ælfric," *Annuale Medievale* 22 (1982): 36–53.

Table 1. Analysis of British Library MS. Cotton Julius E vii, fol. 4

Scribal Number	Skeat Number	Scribal Title: Contents List	Addition Divisions
		INCIPIUNT CAPITULA	
I	I	DE NATIUITATE *CHRIST*I	
II	II	De s*anct*a Eugenia	
III	III	De S*anct*o Basilio	
IIII	IV	DE S*anct*o Iuliano et bassilissa	
V	V	DE S*anct*o Sebastiano	
VI	VI	DE S*anct*o Mauro	
VII	VII	DE S*anct*a Agnete	(Agnes, Skeat VII, 1-295) Alia sententia quam scripsit terrentianus, Skeat VII, 296-429
VIII	VIII	DE S*anct*a Agatha	
	IX	Et s*anct*a lucia	
VIIII	X	DE Cathedra s*anct*i petri	
X	XI	DE xl. Militibus	
XI	XII	DE capite Ieiunii	
XII	XIII	DE Oratione moysi	
XIII	XIV	DE S*anct*o Gregorio	
XIIII	XV	DE S*anct*o Marco euangelista	(Mark, Skeat XV, 1-103) Item alia, Skeat XV, 104-226
XV	XVI	DE Memoria s*anct*orum	
XVI	XVII	DE Auguriis	
XVII	XVIII	De libro regum	
XIX	XIX	De s*anct*o Albano	(Alban, Skeat XIX, 1-154) Item alia, Skeat XIX, 155–258
XX	XX	DE S*anct*o æðeldryða	
XXI	XXI	DE S*anct*o swyðuno	(Swithun, Skeat XXI, 1-463, 496-98) Item alia, Skeat XXI, 464-95
XXII	XXII	DE S*anct*o Appollonare	
XXIII	XXIII	DE .VII.tem Dormientium	

Scribal Number	Skeat Number	Scribal Title: Contents List	Addition Divisions
	[XXIIIB	Mary of Egypt]	
XXIIII	XXIV	De Abdone *et* senne	(Abdon and Sennes, Skeat, XXIV, 1-80) Item alia, Skeat XXIV, 81–191
XXV	XXV	DE Machabeis	(Maccabees, Skeat XXV, 1–204) Item, Skeat XXV, 205-811 Item alia, Skeat XXV, 812-62
XXVI	XXVI	DE *Sancto* Oswoldo	
XXVII	XXVII	DE *Sancta* cruce	
XXVIII	XXVIII	DE Legione thebeorum	
XXIX	XXIX	DE *Sancto* Dionisio	
XXX	XXX	DE *Sancto* Eustachio	
XXXI	XXXI	DE *Sancto* Martino	
XXXII	XXXII	DE *Sancto* Eadmundo	
XXXIII	XXXIII	DE *Sancta* eufrosia	
XXXIIII	XXXIV	De *Sancta* cæcilia	
XXXV	XXXV	DE crisanto et daria	
XXXVI	XXXVI	DE *Sancto* THoma Ap*ostolo*	
XXXVII	XXXVII	De In*t*errogationbus Sigewulfi p*resbyter*[i]	
XXXVIII	XXXVIII	DE Falsis diis	
XXXVIIII	XXXIX	DE .xii. Abusiuis	

rhetorically signalled by Ælfric in the Old English text.[18] In all other extant copies of Maccabees, but not in Julius E vii, there are numbered sections in

[18] Ælfric begins this second part with the statement:

"We wyllað eac awritan hu þæt gewinn ge-endode .
and hu se ælmihtiga god þa arleasan afligde
mid mycelre sceama . swa swa us sægð seo racu ."
(*Lives of Saints*, ed. Skeat, 2:80, lines 205–207).

the longer, second part of Maccabees, so that a reader could easily subdivide further.[19] As divisions to assist a reader in coping with a long continuous narrative, however, these are not comparable to the textual division at the end on the three orders of society, or to the other examples I have just been commenting on — hence the different form of words: "item" alone, instead of "item alia" or "alia sententia".

My argument, then, is that the scribe's practice, when drawing up the contents list, was to recognize only the items which have a specific title and which usually also have a date in their rubrics. This is confirmed by his treatment of the companion narratives for Agatha and Lucy (Skeat VIII and IX). It is obvious from the opening of the Lucy narrative that Ælfric wrote these two lives as a consecutive pair, even though they do not have consecutive feast days, Agatha's being 5 February and Lucy's being 13 December. The Lucy narrative, following that of Agatha, begins without any further ado:

> Ða asprang Agathen hlisa ofer land . and sæ .
> swa þæt fram siracusa sohte mycel meniu
> ofer fiftig mila þæs mædenes byrgene .
> on catanensciscre byrig mid mycelre onbryrd-nysse .
> Þa com sum wydewe seo wæs geciged euthicia .
> betwux oðrum mannum. to þære mæran byrigene .
> and hire dohtor samod . seo gesælige lucia.[20]

> Then Agatha's fame spread over land and sea, so that a great crowd from Syracuse, fifty miles away, visited the virgin's tomb in the city of Catania with great devotion. Then, amongst others, a certain widow who was called Eutychia came to the tomb and her daughter as well, the blessed Lucy.

That these narratives were issued as a pair, and understood to be so subsequently, is further confirmed by their consecutive appearance in Cotton Vitellius D xvii, which is not an ordered collection. In the Julius manuscript, where they

---

"We will also write down how that contest ended, and how the almighty God put the impious men to flight with great shame, just as the story tells us."

[19] The other manuscripts are Cambridge University Library Ii. 1. 33 and Cambridge, Corpus Christi College MSS 198 and 303. It also occurred in London, British Library Cotton Vitellius D xvii, but this part of the manuscript was completely destroyed in the Cotton fire, so the detail of presentation is not known. There is also a fragmentary survival in Cambridge, Queens' College (Horne 75), but it is from the opening lines of the whole (Skeat XXV, 1–8).

[20] *Lives of Saints*, ed. Skeat, 1: 210, lines 1–7.

stand together as written, they are clearly intended for 5 February, since Agatha comes first, in the correct calendar position, and has a rubric specifying the date (folio 50r); Lucy follows without a date, as is normal for a companion piece in this manuscript, but the narrative is nevertheless provided with a specific title, "De sancta Lucia virgo", which, uncharacteristically for a companion piece, identifies the new subject (folio 53r). In the contents list the scribe at first followed his usual practice and listed Agatha only, which he numbered VIII. But in going through the manuscript he evidently noticed the distinctive title for Lucy and responded to it by carefully adding "Et sancta lucia" on the same line as Agatha, reducing the size of the lettering in order to squeeze it in. By its position and the use of "Et" it is clearly shown to be a companion-piece to Agatha and thus correctly shares the Agatha number. The scribe's numbering is supplied thereafter without a break, except that he omits Mary of Egypt altogether (presumably because it was not in the manuscript when the list was made), and he accidentally jumps from XVII (as corrected) to XIX in numbering the consecutive items "De libro regum" and "De sancto Albano".

Skeat, in his edition, dealt with Mary of Egypt by numbering it XXIIIB, even though it has no connection whatever with Skeat XXIII (Seven Sleepers). To Lucy he gave the number IX, treating it as an entirely separate piece from Agatha, with the result that for the next nine items his numbering differs from the scribe by one; the editorial and scribal sequences of numbers come together again at Alban, where the scribe jumped a number. Skeat was prepared to intervene editorially to "correct" the presentation of Lucy, when there was actually nothing to correct. As a result, he gives it a more independent textual identity than it has both in the contents list and in the body of the manuscript, where its relationship to Agatha is rhetorically apparent in Ælfric's wording and where this is respected in the rubrication and the manuscript's organization. The Agatha date, as I have already explained, is the governing factor, and Lucy, despite having a title, comes under that date, even though liturgically its date and thus its place in any legendary is more than ten months later.

In fact, in drawing up the contents list, the scribe had been perfectly consistent in his numbering method, though his rationale was liturgical and pragmatic, reflecting the organization of the manuscript; he was not primarily concerned with textual identity as a modern editor or reader might see it, or with itemizing what was present, in a kind of comprehensive index. It was not that his cultural context rendered him incapable of recognizing a greater number of discrete textual units than are listed on folio 4v because, as we have seen, contemporaries and near-contemporaries were well able to appreciate and make use of these independent identities in other manuscripts. It is, rather, an instance of where a scribal contents list, as we choose to call it, is not a contents list in the sense of systematically listing everything in the manuscript, but is a reflex of the manuscript's organization and textual presentation, which is not quite the same thing. For the scribe, at the moment when he was drawing up this list, the "text" was all the material for one day. This is a perfectly reasonable position for a mind dominated by the liturgy, but it is a definition of "the text" which does not come so readily to us.

Skeat, however, adopts a hybrid position, which confuses the picture for us, as I have shown earlier with Absalom and Ahitophel. On the one hand, Skeat gave Lucy a greater textual independence than the manuscript warrants, which then makes it look as if it is out of order. Yet he was otherwise not prepared to break free of the scribe's numbering in the contents list, which he imported into the body of the edition, where the numbers imply textual identity — for that is how we use them now — rather than liturgically-motivated manuscript organization — which is certainly not how we understand or use Skeat's numbers.

I said at the beginning that my title, "Identifying 'Texts' in Cotton Julius E vii: Medieval and Modern Perspectives", implied some very large questions. I have not provided any answers, but I did not intend to do so. What I hope I have done, however, is to identify the nature of the so-called contents list in Cotton Julius E vii, which certainly has important evidential value; to draw attention to the way in which, even in the Anglo-Saxon period, the apparent specification of texts can be understood only if we take account of immediate purpose; and to draw attention to Skeat's editorial practices in respect of the establishment of textual identities and the extent to which this imposes itself on modern scholarship. Facsimiles of medieval manuscripts, now in electronic form as well through more traditional media, allow us to study particular details and resolve some outstanding issues, but they also have the larger effect of releasing us from the tyranny of the standard edition, which sets particular kinds of limitations on the way we think about the material that has come down to us.

Bibliography

Ælfric. *The Homilies of Ælfric: A Supplementary Collection*, ed. John C. Pope. EETS o.s. 259, 260. London, 1967–1968.

Ælfric's Catholic Homilies: Second Series: Text, ed. Malcolm Godden. EETS s.s. 6. London, 1979.

Ælfric's First Series of Catholic Homilies (British Museum Royal 7 c. xii, fols. 4–218), ed. Peter Clemoes and Norman Eliason. EEMF 13. Copenhagen, 1966.

Ælfric's Lives of Saints, ed. Walter W. Skeat. 2 vols. in 4 parts. EETS o.s. 76, 82, 94, 114. London, 1881–1900; repr as 2 vols, London, 1966.

Alexander, Robert J. "W. W. Skeat and Ælfric." *Annuale Medievale* 22 (1982): 36–53.

Clemoes, Peter. "The Chronology of Ælfric's Works." In *The Anglo-Saxons: Studies in Some Aspects of their History and Culture Presented to Bruce Dickins*, ed. idem, 212–47. London, 1959.

Dumville, David. *English Caroline Script and Monastic History: Studies in Benedictinism, A.D. 950–1030.* Woodbridge, 1993.

Gatch, M. McC. *Preaching and Theology in Anglo-Saxon England: Ælfric and Wulfstan.* Toronto and Buffalo, 1977.

Hill, Joyce. "The Dissemination of Ælfric's Lives of Saints: A Preliminary Survey." In *Holy Men and Holy Women: Old English Prose Saints' Lives and Their Contexts*, ed. Paul E. Szarmach, 235–59. Albany, 1996.

Irvine, Susan. "Bones of Contention: The Context of Ælfric's Homily on St. Vincent." *Anglo-Saxon England* 19 (1990): 117–32.

Ker, N. R. *Catalogue of Manuscripts Containing Anglo-Saxon.* Oxford, 1957; rev. ed. 1990.

Magennis, Hugh. *The Anonymous Old English Legend of the Seven Sleepers.* Durham Medieval Texts 7. Durham, 1994.

———. "Contrasting Features in the Non-Ælfrician Lives in the Old English Lives of Saints." *Anglia* 104 (1986): 316–48.

Meaney, Audrey L. "Ælfric's Use of his Sources in His Homily on Auguries." *English Studies* 66 (1985): 477–95.

Needham, Geoffrey. "Additions and Alterations in Cotton MS. Julius E VII." *Review of English Studies* n.s. 9 (1958): 160–64.

Wanley, Humfrey. *Librorum Veterum Septentrionalium,* in vol. 2 of George Hickes, *Linguarum Septentrionalium Thesaurus.* Oxford, 1705.

THE WERDEN GLOSSARY:
STRUCTURE AND SOURCES[1]

A. N. DOANE

The Werden Fragments of the "Werden Glossary"

The "Werden Glossary" is one of the earliest and most important witnesses to the Anglo-Saxon glossary tradition. However, its parlous physical condition, the ongoing saga of its mysterious epistemologic status, and its checkered editorial history have hampered its proper study. In the 1980s the situation was improved somewhat by the publication of a good facsimile, along with its sister glossaries, the Épinal, Erfurt, and Corpus glossaries, but even this was fatally hampered by fragmentation and sudden appearances and disappearances.[2] Since the 1850s scholars at various times have reported the existence of a total of twenty-six leaves. N. R. Ker[3] described it as a fragmentary ninth-century volume of alphabetical glossaries, consisting of twenty-five leaves: six leaves in the Universitätsbibliothek, Münster, Paulinus 271; four leaves in the Bayrische Staatsbibliothek, Munich, Cgm. 187 III (e.4); seven leaves in the Pfarrhof, Werden; and eight leaves, formerly belonging to Ferdinand Deycks but "not found since his death in 1867." In other words, as far as Ker knew in 1957, there were seventeen located leaves and eight missing.

---

[1] For several years I have been working on the fragments called the Werden Glossary with an eye to editing the unique portion, known as "Werden A." Phill Pulsiano took a generous interest in this work and was most encouraging and helpful on the many occasions when we spoke of it. Unfortunately, I was not able to share a written version with him before he died. I dedicate this report to his memory.

[2] Bernhard Bischoff, Mildred Budny, Geoffrey Harlow, M.B. Parkes, and J.D. Pheifer, *The Épinal, Werden, and Corpus Glossaries*, Early English Manuscripts in Facsimile 22 (Copenhagen, 1988), henceforward referred to as EEMF 22.

[3] N. R. Ker, *Catalogue of Manuscripts Containing Anglo-Saxon* (Oxford, 1957), 483–84, item 39 of the appendix.

Turning to the authoritative facsimile edition of the Épinal, Erfurt, Werden, and Corpus glossaries (EEMF 22) already mentioned, one is surprised to learn that as of 1988 the eight Deycks leaves, "lost" to Ker, were in fact part of the Universitäts- und Landesbibliothek, Düsseldorf, MS. Fragment K19:Z9/1. But on the negative side, one learns that the six Münster leaves were destroyed in World War II (in 1945), a fact unbeknownst to Ker in 1957. As some compensation, there turned up in 1968 a previously unknown single leaf owned by the Füngling family of Rath, a suburb of Cologne, making a twenty-sixth leaf available for photography and hence for inclusion in EEMF 22; but in the same volume Geoffrey Harlow had to report that shortly before its publication the Cologne-Rath leaf had gone missing as well.

But, most surprising of all, Harlow, on behalf of the editors of EEMF 22, reported (9) that the seven Werden Pfarrhof leaves had simply vanished, were no longer in the secure place they were supposed to have been and not discoverable after prolonged search at the Werden Pfarrhof (now Probstei) and its environs. As I read this in 1995 I was astounded because sitting on the desk before me were photographs newly arrived of these same seven "lost" Werden leaves. Innocent of Harlow et al. and relying on Ker, I had ordered the photographs and they had duly arrived, courtesy of the authorities of the Werden Probstei. Were they old photographs? In 1894 J. H. Gallée had published two plates, a detail of folio 5r and a full shot of folio 7v, neither of very high quality, in his edition of Werden[4] and these were reproduced in EEMF 22. On the other hand, the black-and-white glossy prints I had received were a set of all seven leaves, of excellent quality and appearing to be recent. Moreover, pencil foliation had been added to folio 7 that does not appear in Gallée's photo. Unsure what to make of this, I wrote again to the Probst of Werden, Dr. Heinrich Engels, who kindly assured me that the fragments were indeed extant and available and invited me to come see them.[5] Which I did, in the summer of 1996.

Here is the history of these leaves, as far as I have been able to piece it together. Between November 1893, when J. H. Gallée of the University of Utrecht wrote the foreword to Altsaechsische Sprachdenkmaeler, and sometime in 1894, when it was published, he found out from Prof. F. Jostes of the existence of the leaves at Werden and made a hasty edition which he added as an appendix

---

[4] J. H. Gallée, ed., Altsaechsische Sprachdenkmaeler (Leiden, 1894), description and edition of the Werden leaves at 330–64. The photos appeared not in this book but in a supplement, Altsaechsische Sprachdenkmaeler, Facsimilesammlung (Leiden, 1895).

[5] The official designation is "Essen-Werden, Kath. Propsteigemeinde St. Ludgerus, Fragmente Nr. 2."

to his collection of Old Saxon texts.[6] Due to resistance by the Deycks family, which had them illegally in its possession at the time, Gallée was not able to see the Deycks (now Düsseldorf) leaves and took his readings from Deycks' edition.[7] He was able to compare the Münster and Werden fragments when they were lent to him at Utrecht. He did not know of the Munich fragments, which Steinmeyer announced in 1896 in a review of Gallée's work.[8] At the Werden Probstei is a letter of 24 June 1900 from Georg Goetz, the great glossographer, requesting that these fragments be sent to Jena for his research; apparently they weren't as he consulted them himself at Werden and for Münster depended on a transcript by his student, Paul Wessner.[9] It seems that at least from the turn of the century they were kept locked in a large safe in the attic on the fourth floor of the house in which the Pfarrhof or parish office was and is still located, and at some point were forgotten. In 1978 Dr. Engels, as the newly installed Probst, noticed this impressive antique safe but the key was lost until

---

[6] Gallée, *Sprachdenkmaeler*, 330, which will be referred to henceforth only as "Gallée." Gallée's transcriptions in general are error-prone, and particularly so in the case of the texts in the "Appendix," as has frequently been pointed out, no more so than in E. Steinmeyer's review, in *AfdAdL* 22 (1896): 266–80; see Harlow's extensive and helpful notes on the state of Werden scholarship, EEMF 22, 66 ff.

[7] Gallée, p. 333. The Deycks leaves were published as a pamphlet by Ferdinand Deycks, *Fragmenta Veteris Glossarii e Cod. Werthinensi S. XI, Index lectionum*, Academica Aschendorffiana (Münster, 1854/1855). With other medieval manuscripts at the abbey of Werden, after the secularization of the monastery in 1803 they found their way to the Landesbibliothek, Düsseldorf. These leaves were lent to Deycks for his use by the Düsseldorf archivist, T. J. Lacomblet, and after Deycks' death in 1867 the family refused to return them. W. Crecelius reports them still overdue in 1877 ("Ein Düsseldorfer Statiusfragment," *Rheinisches Museum für Philologie* n.f. 32 [1877]: 632–36, at 635–36). According to Harlow (EEMF 22, 9–10) they came to light in the Düsseldorf University Library even as the EEMF volume was at press (i.e., mid-1980s). The medieval holdings of the city archives were sent on permanent loan to the University Library in the mid-1970s. A history of the medieval acquisitions of the Düsseldorf University Library is given by Gerhard Karpp, "Mittelalterliche Handschriften und Inkunabeln in der Universitätsbibliothek Düsseldorf," *Codices Manuscripti* 7 (1981): 4–13, Werden manuscripts at 9.

[8] *AfdAdL* 22 (1896): 266–80, at 276.

[9] "Glossas, quarum in thesauro iam rationem habui" (he is referring here specifically to Werden Pfarrhof fol. 7). For Münster he relied on a transcript made by Wessner and Gallée's edition. See Georg Goetz, *De glossariorum Latinorum origine et fatis*, Corpus Glossariorum Latinorum 1 (Leipzig, 1923), vii, 161–65; henceforth CGL; cf. the introduction to the index, CGL 5, p. v. Wessner (1870–1933) was Goetz's student at Jena until 1896; see Conrad Bursian, *Jahresbericht über die Fortschritte der klassischen Altertumswissenschaft*, 4 Abt.: Nekrologe, 61 (1935) (I am indebted to Nancy McClements of the University of Wisconsin Memorial Library for this reference).

1985. Between 1978 and 1985 was precisely when unsuccessful attempts were being made to locate the fragments for the EEMF edition. When Dr. Engels and the present archivist, Johannes Fischer, located the key and opened the safe in 1985, they found about five hundred manuscript items, mostly late registry books of the parish and the like, but about a dozen fragments of items of pre-Carolingian and Carolingian date, including the missing glossary.[10]

The abbey of Werden on the Ruhr, about twenty-five miles northeast of Düsseldorf and now a suburb of Essen, was founded by Saint Liudger in the last years of the eighth century. Liudger had been trained by Anglo-Saxon masters at Utrecht, his native place, and studied for several years with Alcuin at York, bringing back to the continent many Anglo-Saxon books; the foundation of Werden took place as part of a concerted effort to Christianize the northwest low-German-speaking regions of the Carolingian realm. Liudger himself moved on to found the diocese of Münster, where he died as its first bishop in 809. Many early manuscripts, in both Insular and Carolingian script, now chiefly located in Berlin and Düsseldorf,[11] have been identified as

---

[10] The only published notice of the relocated glossary fragments at Werden that I know of is a brief mention by Eckhard Freise, "Von Mimigernaford zum *monasterium Liudgers*," in Thomas Küster and Franz-Josef Jakobi, eds., *Geschichte der Stadt Münster* (Münster, 1993), 1: 44. Unfortunately Freise confuses it with the "Corpus Glossary," an understandable mistake given the misleading presentation of the text by Gallée under that rubric, but standing for Corpus Gloss[ariorum Latinorum]. Dr. Gerhard Karpp, formerly of the manuscript department of the Universitätsbibliothek, Düsseldorf and now of Leipzig, arranged the photography for me. I want to thank Dr. Engel, Herr Fischer, and Dr. Karpp for their friendly information, help, and advice.

[11] The standard work is Wilhelm Stüwer, *Das Erzbistum Köln 3: Die Reichsabtei Werden an der Ruhr*, Germania Sacra n.f. 12, Die Bistümer der Kirchenprovinz Köln (Berlin, 1980). His description of the Werden Glossary, no. 20 (p. 65), gives the same data as Ker. Further information, particularly paleographical data, about the earliest history of Werden, compromised somewhat by the aim of proving the Werden origin of the *Heliand*, is found in Richard Drögereit, *Werden und der Heliand: Studien zur Kulturgeschichte der Abtei Werden und zur Herkunft des Heliand* (Essen, 1951). The manuscripts identified as from Werden, with their modern locations, are listed in a handy format by Sigrid Krämer, *Handschriftenerbe des deutschen Mittelalters, 2: Köln-Zyfflich*, Mittelalterliche Bibliothekskataloge: Deutschlands und der Schweiz, Ergänzungsband 1 (Munich, 1989), 826–28. None are listed as still being at Werden itself. She gives thirty-two Werden manuscripts as being at Düsseldorf. The Düsseldorf fragment of our glossary, Fgm. K 19: Z 9/1, is mentioned at the bottom of p. 827. Two lines up is mentioned as at the Düsseldorf UB "s.n. Glossar. (Fragm.), s. IX." Can this refer to the Werden leaves, for some reason temporarily at Düsseldorf after their being found, perhaps for photography? Stüwer, whose inventory differs somewhat from Krämer's, describes each of the former Werden manuscripts in detail (61–86).

ninth-century products of Werden; many are fragments released from bind-ings. No medieval work remains at Werden itself except for the recently found contents of the safe. It seems that in the later Middle Ages Werden was a very lax house, always in need of infusions of cash, and began at an early date to sell off its magnificent book collection, not least of which was the sixth-cen-tury "Codex Argenteus" of the Gothic Gospels now at Uppsala.[12] In the late fifteenth century the library was reorganized along "modern" lines: a systematic clearing out of older books began to take place, and an organized bindery operation was set up, for which many of the older books provided material.[13] It was in books rebound at the abbey that the known fragments of the Werden Glossary were preserved. The three ensembles known to exist (Munich, Düs-seldorf, and Werden) show a treatment consistent with other known Werden binding-materials that have been identified.[14] In 1803, under the pressure of the Napoleonic threat and Prussian reforms, the ancient monastery was dis-solved and the abbey church was converted to the Parish of St. Liudger of Essen-Werden. A few years later, the approximately 11,000 volumes still re-maining, both printed and manuscript, were dispersed.

In its original form, the "Werden Glossary" contained at least three glos-saries, all containing vernacular interpretations derived from Old English: one of these glossaries is more fully preserved in Erfurt, Wissenschaftliche Bibliothek, MS. Amplonianus 2° 42 and is known as the "Second Amplonian Glossary," or Erfurt 2; the Werden copy was named by Gallée "Werden B." The remains of "Werden B" comprise the four Munich leaves, plus folios "3" and "4" from the destroyed Münster ensemble, plus six of our Werden leaves (folios 1–6). Another of the glossaries in the Werden ensemble is the so-called "Glossae Nominum" or Erfurt 3 (Gallée's "Werden C"), batches of nouns and other nominals derived from a Latin-Greek glossary,[15] preserved elsewhere

---

[12] Stüwer gives the late medieval history of the Abbey's decline: *Reichsabtei Werden*, 97–107.

[13] "Archival evidence confirms that the abbey maintained its own active bindery (*of-ficina librorum*) from its acceptance of the Bursfeld reform in 1474 until around 1550; the accounts incorporate payments for leather, boards, chains, clasps and binders' tools": B. C. Barker-Benfield, "The Werden 'Heptateuch'," *Anglo-Saxon England* 20 (1991): 43–64, at 46; this article sums up what is known about the Werden Abbey library.

[14] Cf. Barker-Benfield, "Werden 'Heptateuch'," 48.

[15] See the descriptive analysis in W. M. Lindsay, *The Corpus, Épinal, Erfurt and Leyden Glossaries*, Publications of the Philological Society 7 (Oxford, 1921), 80–83, as reprinted in idem, *Studies in Early Mediaeval Latin Glossaries*, ed. Michael Lapidge (Aldershot, 1996); Gustav Loewe demonstrated its connections with the other English glossaries in *Prodromus Corporis Glossariorum Latinorum* (Leipzig, 1876), 126–37.

very imperfectly in Erfurt and more completely (though considerably altered and mixed in with other glossary material) in Cambridge, Peterhouse MS. 2.4.6 (s. xiii), ff. 1–144v.[16] "Werden C" comprises the six Düsseldorf leaves plus folios "2" and "5" from the destroyed Münster ensemble. A third, which Gallée called "Werden A," is found only in the Werden fragments. "Werden A" comprises remains of a single mutilated leaf among those recently recovered at Werden (folio 7)[17] and folios "1" and "6" of the lost Münster leaves, plus part of the Füngling leaf. The latter item also includes a fragment of a collection of "Differentiae" from several sources. The contents of the destroyed Münster leaves are now known only from Gallée's edition and Wessner's transcription as printed by Goetz.

That all the scattered Werden leaves stem from the same manuscript book and that its medieval provenance was Werden is without a doubt. It is well known that the oldest manuscripts in the city archives of Düsseldorf (whose medieval manuscripts were removed to the University Library in 1975) were from the secularized monastery;[18] Deycks knew of the Werden provenance of his leaves, doubtless informed by his friend Lacomblet, who had been Düsseldorf archivist since 1818.[19] The extant leaves are all in a single hand and of the same preparation throughout. The original manuscript was broken up probably at the end of the fifteenth century, when many of the older holdings were being reused and discarded.[20]

As a collection of glossaries, our manuscript is closely related to the collection in Erfurt: it contains two of the same glossaries, Second Amplonian (Erfurt 2/Werden B) and Glossae Nominum (Erfurt 3/Werden C). Moreover,

---

[16] The manuscript and glossary is described by Goetz, *CGL* 2, xliv–xlv. He dates it to the twelfth century. M. R. James says it is of the thirteenth: *A Descriptive Catalogue of the Manuscripts in the Library of Peterhouse* (Cambridge, 1899), 295–97.

[17] This is the numbering on the leaf itself and ought to be considered official. EEMF 22 identifies it on the page holding the facsimile, and elsewhere, as "Essen-Werden Pfarrhof, 'A', fol. 1v."

[18] Karpp, "Mittelalterliche Handschriften," 7. Why did some leaves leave Werden and some stay? Perhaps because the latter were used to bind parish record books?

[19] "Octo scilicet sunt folia eius formae quam quartanam solent nominare, quorum quidem quatuor ultima dimidia paginae parte sunt mutilata, quum librorum tegumento quondam inservierint. Fuerunt in bibliotheca olim celeberrima monasterii Werthinensis ad Ruram, quae inde a S. Ludgeri temporibus usque ad saeculi XVIII" (Deycks, *Fragmenta*, 5).

[20] The Munich leaves are from an incunable that had been in the possession of a student in the University of Cologne, and later in the library of the Palatine Elector of Wittelsbach, Karl Theodor, who died in 1777. (The Palatine bookplate is stuck to the verso of fol. 1 of Munich, Bayerische Staatsbibliothek, Cgm. 187 III (e.4), and may be seen in the reproduction in EEMF 22.)

these copies are closely related as to both text and paleographical features, as well as layout within the line. A comparison with the Erfurt Glossae Nominum suggests that Werden is a much more careful and accurate copy than Erfurt. Certainly it is more formal. For the Second Amplonian Glossary Werden and Erfurt are probably copies of the same Carolingian exemplar which was in turn probably written directly from an Anglo-Saxon exemplar in Insular handwriting (Erfurt can't be copied directly from Werden or vice-versa since both have entries not in the other).[21] The Erfurt manuscript is, according to Bischoff and Parkes (EEMF 22, 20–22), a product of Hildebald's scriptorium at Cologne and is thus before 819. Werden was within the archdiocese of Cologne and the two manuscripts are roughly contemporary, probably from the second decade of the ninth century. The page layout throughout Erfurt differs from Werden in having not a two- but a three-column format in 44–46 lines, a layout that is close to Épinal, Bibliothèque Municipale 72 (2) of the early eighth century, which like Erfurt has a copy of the "First Amplonian" or Épinal-Erfurt glossary containing hundreds of Old English interpretations. However, within the line the "accidentals" of most entries are practically identical in Werden and Erfurt.

Werden's leaves are pricked and ruled for two columns (two columns of lemmata and their glosses) in 31 lines (though not always are 31 written), in writing areas of a uniform size and with hair outside of most sheets where the arrangement can still be told. All three glossaries in Werden are in this format and all are written in a single distinctive early Carolingian hand showing pronounced Insular symptoms. The scribe had the habit of making a hooked vertical stroke with a brief horizontal stroke through it on the upper left of most pages, and these appear throughout all the dispersed parts, including the Füngling leaf. The script is rather eclectic in its letter forms, showing Insular, uncial, and rustic capitals introducing sections.[22] The general writing style is an elegant set minuscule of the Corbie type with headless closed *a* and closed *b* (distinct from the more current Insular minuscule hand of Erfurt),[23] with

---

[21] The retention of almost exactly the same Anglo-Saxon symptoms in both the Werden and Erfurt copies of the Second Amplonian (Erfurt 2) Glossary shows that their common exemplar was no longer in pure Insular handwriting, but was a copy in Carolingian script derived from an exemplar in Insular handwriting.

[22] B on Werden 1r, and insular capital B,C, D, and E in Düsseldorf, and uncial capital E in Münster, 1v (Gallée's facsimile, reprinted EEMF 22), as well as rustic-style capitals in Munich 1v and 4v.

[23] The script resembles that in two manuscripts from Werden, Berlin, Deutsche Staatsbibliothek Theol. Lat. Fol. 346 (s viii–ix) and Theol. Lat. Fol. 354 (s. viii²) (*CLA* 8:1066 and 1067a). Lowe places both of these at Corbie but the script has lost its Corbie peculiarities. The sample from fol. 2r of no. 1067a is particularly close to that of our manuscript.

long and thick ascenders and descenders in relation to the size of the bodies of the letters, and distinctive forms of *f* and *s* tending to descend below the line and bulge at the top of the vertical stroke, which Bischoff and Parkes associate with the "Maurdramnus" minuscule developed at Corbie in the last quarter of the eighth century.[24] The other striking peculiarity is the prevalence of Insular features, including the Insular form of *g* and *d* (uncial type, round-backed), though continental *g* and straight-backed *d* do sporadically occur. On Werden folio 7vb, line 4, occurs the form "sonð" (for OE *snōd*, "snood") which shows that the scribe was both comfortable writing exclusively Insular letters and unfamiliar with Anglo-Saxon. The predominantly Insular forms of these letters are not symptoms of the scribe's normal handwriting, since he occasionally slips into continental forms, but rather a conscious attempt to preserve the most characteristic features of a prestigious Anglo-Saxon exemplar in the background.[25] None of the vernacular interpretations in Werden A, usually marked "s" or "sax" by the scribe, have escaped being remodeled into Old Saxon, and the beginning of this process doubtless preceded our manuscript.

The Codicology of the Werden Glossary

This section describes the newly-recovered leaves and attempts to relate them codicologically to the other leaves of the original Werden glossary manuscript.[26] The fragments at Werden consist of seven leaves preserved as six physical items: two virtually complete bifolia (four leaves), two virtually complete single leaves, and two cut-down fragments from a single leaf. The first six leaves correspond to the Second Amplonian Glossary (Erfurt 2) and range through parts of the letters A, B, C, the tail end of D, and parts of E, S,

---

[24] EEMF 22, 21; Bischoff, review of Drögereit, *Werden und der Heliand*, *AfdAdL* 66 (1952): 9.

[25] Both Insular and Carolingian handwriting were being used at Werden in its earliest years. Several examples of manuscripts from Werden that were probably written in England are listed by Bischoff and Parkes (EEMF 22, 22, n. 118); the English connections of early Werden books are canvassed with much more detail and caution by Barker-Benfield ("Werden 'Heptateuch'," 52–60); the Werden Heptateuch, Düsseldorf Universitätsbibl. A. 19 + Tokyo, T. Takamiya collection, written in pointed insular minuscule 800 × 810 (*ibid.*, 61), is one of the insular-style manuscripts "on the cusp" between manuscripts written in England and in Germany. The Werden Glossary manuscript is of the next wave, manuscripts showing mixed Corbie and insular influences.

[26] The reconstruction offered in this section differs considerably from that given by Bischoff and Parkes, EEMF 22, 21. See the Appendix, 81–84, a diagram of the quiration.

and T.[27] The two cut-down fragments comprise part of a leaf from near the end of the unique glossary, "Werden A," the rest of which is now known only from Gallée's print of the destroyed Münster leaves. These have to be related to the other known fragments, namely the two bifolia at Munich, four bifolia at Düsseldorf, and three bifolia, now destroyed, formerly at Münster, plus the small cut-down Füngling leaf, whereabouts presently unknown.

Fragment 1 is a complete and intact bifolium (fols. 1 and 2), preserving the original size of the sheets, 404 × 277 mm. In the original volume, the bound page was about 200 × 277 mm. The leaf was reused in a volume having about the same page size: folio 1 served as the pastedown and folio 2 was the flyleaf, with the binder utilizing the original fold of the bifolium. This is consistent with the known method of reuse of old parchment in the Werden abbey bindery in the late fifteenth century.[28] The hair is outside. The pages are pricked on both margins and lightly ruled for 31 lines, with no scorings visible for columns on this leaf. Sewing holes in the center crease at 10, 69, 145, and 215 mm. from the top are original (comparing the Munich and Düsseldorf leaves),[29] while five other holes date from the later binding. Glue was smeared, not very evenly, over folio 1r, which was the side pasted down; the stiffness and darkness of this folio is from the glue, as folio 2 is supple and of a lighter tan. A faint pencil notation, '(IIa)' on the top left of folio 1r,[30] must date from the time when the fragments were released from the binding.

This sheet belongs directly outside the first Munich bifolium (which is slightly trimmed to 276 × 385 mm.). The binder subjected the two Munich bifolia to the same treatment as the Werden, as conjoint paste-down and fly, utilizing the original fold. Werden 1v ends "bilem" and Munich 1r begins

---

[27] A transcription of the "Second Amplonian," or Erfurt 2, fols. 14v–34v, has been printed by Goetz, *Placidus liber glossarum: Glossaria reliqua*, CGL 5 (Leipzig, 1894), 259–337; the 33 items having an Old English interpretation are edited by Henry Sweet, *The Oldest English Texts*, EETS o.s. 45 (London, 1885), 108–9. The best way to consult the glossary now, and the method used in the following discussion, is by way of the facsimile in EEMF 22, with references according to the index numbers printed there at the head and foot of each page-image.

[28] Barker-Benfield, "Werden 'Heptateuch'," 48.

[29] The four Düsseldorf bifolia have been trimmed more severely than Werden (and each separately); the three sewing holes on sheets 1,2,4 are (giving the extremes) 63 × 66, 134 × 138, 205 × 211 mm. from the top; on sheet 3, which has not been trimmed as deeply, the four original sewing holes are at 32, 115, 177, 221 mm. from the top. In Munich they are ambiguous because of wear, but are at about 210, 140, 62, 33 mm. from the top, with another perhaps at 17 mm. The variation would be because the sheets are from different quires, individually sewn, but they show a regular practice.

[30] Not visible in photo supplied to me, but clear on the leaf.

"bisum" (cf. Erfurt 2 "bilem, byssum" B71–72); Munich 2v ends "coryh" and Werden 2r begins "cornipes" (cf. Erfurt 2 "coryh, cornipes" C388–89), showing that Werden/Munich form the second and third sheets in the quire, respectively; Werden 2v ends with "conlegium" C508. Both sheets have the hair outside and are ruled for 31 lines. The missing inner bifolium would have accommodated 248 lines and there are 243 missing entries (comparing Erfurt 2: Munich 1v ends with "casabundus" C25 and Munich 2r begins with "cilex" C268). The first entry on Werden 1r is "auctimat" E661: 660 entries would occupy more than five folios in the Werden format, so this glossary began well into the preceding quire.

Werden Probstei Fragments 2 and 3 (fols. 3 and 4) are cut-down halves of a once-conjoint bifolium that has been released from a different volume than the previous fragment and are consistent with the bindery practices at Werden in the late fifteenth century for smaller volumes. The bifolium has been split to form two sheets of almost identical size (Fragment 2 is 260 × 190 mm., Fragment 3 a few millimeters smaller). They were turned sideways, roughly trimmed, and folded to form two leaves as pastedowns and flys in an octavo volume (presumably back and front pastedown and fly in the same volume; the old pencil markings 'Ia' on folio 4 and 'Ib' on folio 3 suggest that folio 4 was the front pastedown and folio 3 the back, the fragments being catalogued at the time the parchments were being released but before their true order was understood). Along the later central crease, running the same way as the writing, are at least six sewing holes to secure the leaves to the new binding. The sides once pasted down show the offset of the woodgrain of the board and the impressions of the leather cover folded in around the board under the pastedown. The pasted-down sides formed the outside and the flesh side of the original bifolium. On both glue-free sides are visible the offsets of the opposite side of the sheet from the time when the sheets were folded in on themselves. The prickings are visible on the (original) outer edges of the sheets, for 31 lines, while the scoring is faintly visible.

The last entry on Fragment 2, folio 3v is "eneruum" and the first on the top of Fragment 3, folio 4r (partly cut-off) is "enisus eluctatus" (= Erfurt 2 E108–109), showing that these two made up the inside sheet. The last entry on Werden 2r (Fragment 1) is "conlegium" C508 and the first on folio 3r (Fragment 2) is "duxit nutrix" D293. In Erfurt 2, between "conlegium" (C 508) and "duxit nutrix" (D293) there are 530 lines of writing, but 467 entries. Four Werden leaves (leaf *8 of the preceding quire and *1–3 of the present) allow for 496 lines, which is about right for 467 entries in the slightly more roomy columns of "Werden" compared to "Erfurt." The other side of the leaf ends at "excusit" E225.

Two of the lost Münster leaves (Gallée's Münster fols. 3 and 4) belonged next. According to Gallée's collation (pp. 350–52) these leaves ran from "inpubis"

I131 to "lapicidine" L55, and since there is no break between folio 3v and 4r ("incentiua" "intercipit" I 247–248), this was the innermost bifolium. If this was a quire in eight, we can expect that about 372 entries were on the three leaves at either side of this bifolium. The on-side would accommodate mate-rial to about the beginning of G ("Garrit"), actually 357 entries, and the last three leaves of the preceding quire would accommodate from "excusit" E225 through almost exactly all of F to "funus" F287 (374 entries, 372 lines), with a little wiggle-room between the quires. On the other side of the Münster quire, 372 lines takes us approximately to "naus" N5.

Werden Fragment 4 (fols. 5 and 6) is an almost intact bifolium that once formed the pastedown and fly in a configuration similar to that of fragment 1, though more severely trimmed in its broad dimension (380 × 280 mm.; a vertical strip on the outer edge, just inside the prickings, about 10 mm. wide, has been cut off); doubtless it formed the back pastedown in the same volume as Fragment 1, as shown by the old pencil marking '(IIb)'. The surface on the glue-free side is very clear and bright. On the glue side the impressions of the leather cover wrapped around the boards is visible, as well as some offset of the woodgrain and obvious marks of the glue brush. Some letters were pulled off with the glue when the parchment was released from the binding. Traces of original sewing holes, now obscured by glue, are detectable at 72, 145, and 217 mm. from the top. Hair is outside; the bifolium was scored from the out-side and the heaviness of the scores, especially on folio 5, suggest rescoring, since it cannot have been the outside sheet (see below).

As to text, Werden Probstei folio 5r begins "saba pappa" S38 and the verso ends with "seueritas" S151 and folio 6r begins "testudo densit[as][31] romanum" and ends at "trophetum" (T142). Fitting inside this bifolium as the inner sheet is the Munich bifolium (Munich fols. 3–4; 274 × 400 mm.), which begins "se-rio" S152 and runs to "tefore" T31. At just this place the text of Erfurt 2 is im-perfect, interrupted by loss of a leaf between folios 33 and 34, at "spartum" S259, resuming again at "tropeum signum uictoriae" T143, but by fortunate chance, Munich fols. 3v–4rv and Werden fol. 6 supply this portion of the text, and, luck-ily for the collation, Werden fol. 6v overlaps with Erfurt by two items, assuring that between the witnesses no text has been lost from S–T.[32] If this were a quire of 8, the two lost off-leaves, with 248 lines, would just accommodate, with some

---

[31] There is a wormhole where the missing letters are indicated. The items on Werden fol. 6 are T32–144. The resumption of Erfurt is at T143.

[32] The point of overlap is, given here as in Werden:

    Werden 110 (fol. 6v/27b) tropeum p⟨re⟩da de hostib⟨us⟩ facta
    Werden 111 (Erfurt T143) tropheum signu⟨m⟩ uictorię
    Werden 112 (Erfurt T144) troph⟨et⟩u⟨m⟩ d⟨icitu⟩r quoties deuicto hoste barbares
putate armis hostium occisorum ipsa sunt trophea [end of folio in Werden].

slight overruns, the 255 actual entries from T142 to "zozum" Z6, but probably
this is a quire of 10. On the on-side of the quire, two more leaves would push
the text back about only another 248 entries, approximately to "rudes" R133.
Between this place and "naus" N5 in Erfurt 2, the approximate place where
the lost remainder of the Münster leaves is calculated to have ended, are 3843
lines by calculation. Allowing 992 lines per quire of 8 in the Werden format (31
lines × 4 columns per leaf × 8 leaves), four quires of 8 yields only 3720 lines. But
if the Werden/Munich quire (that is, the quire containing Werden fols. 5–6)
was of 10, then another leaf may be added to the on-side so that 3720 + 124 =
3844. By the math it would seem that the Münster quire was of 8 and the following Werden-Munich quire was of 10. On the off-side, 5½ columns remain
to the end of the text of the Erfurt 2 Glossary, 245 lines, implying that our reconstructed Werden B glossary would have fit exactly onto the next two leaves,
perhaps running in a bit onto the last leaf of a quire of 10, with almost the whole
of this tenth leaf remaining blank or holding some other text.

The next quire must be the Düsseldorf ensemble, a single complete quire
of 8, consisting of four now split and trimmed bifolia containing the first part
of the Glossae Nominum (A–G), a glossary also partially preserved in Erfurt (fols. 34v/28c–36v). It is arranged hair outside on sheets 1, 3, 4 and flesh
outside on sheet 2 (HFHH). Of special interest here is that the bottom of the
last verso bears the heretofore unnoticed signature 'x', which helps establish
the correctness of the conjectural collation of the original volume as already
given (see p. 55 and Appendix).

Erfurt 2 ends at folio 34v/27c, the writing continuing without a break but
with a rubric, **Nunc aliae xiii**[33] **exiguae secuntur**; this heads the Glossae
Nominum (Erfurt 3). Such is the configuration in Werden too, the next quire,
consisting of the eight Düsseldorf (Deycks) leaves, containing the Glossae
Nominum, though perhaps with a leaf of other material intervening (if the
quire of 10 reconstruction is right). Goetz's edition in CGL[34] was based on the
late manuscript, Cambridge, Peterhouse MS. 2.4.6, running from A to U/V,
collated with Erfurt and Werden (that is Deycks plus Münster/Werden leaves
2 and 5 as reported by Wessner). The Düsseldorf quire holds about half the

---

[33] Or **xui**. The number is taken by Loewe and Lindsay (see n. 15 above) to refer to the
number of batches of glosses that were assembled to make up the complete Glossae Nominum, each batch grouping words by their ending.

[34] Georg Goetz and Gotthold Gundermann, ed., *Glossae Latinograecae et Graecola-
tinae*, Corpus Glossariorum Latinorum 2 (Leipzig, 1888), xlii–vi, 563–97. Sweet, *Oldest
English Texts*, 109–10, gives an edition of just the fifty-one items holding a vernacular interpretation. As with Erfurt 2, the best source is now the photographic facsimile in EEMF
22, though the image of fol. 37v is very faint in places.

text, from almost the beginning (the top of the sheet being trimmed) "abnegator negator" to "giler genus ligni" (= CGL 2.563.49–581.34).

The next quire, continuing Glossae Nominum, held leaves 2 and 5 of the destroyed Münster leaves, which Steinmeyer, the only person to give a detailed first-hand description of them, says were a bifolium.[35] What remains to fill this quire is only 17 pages in Goetz's edition and would not by itself quite fill another quire of 8; however a comparison of Erfurt and these Münster leaves with Peterhouse shows that the latter adds and subtracts items as compared to the earlier copies. Unfortunately, because leaf 2 corresponded more or less to Erfurt 3, Gallée and Steinmeyer only collated it for differences, leaving too much of the evidence for this leaf implicit. In any case the contents of Erfurt corresponding to Münster fol. 2 are consistent with the capacity of the lost pages. The available evidence requires a quire of 6 at this point:

fol. 1 "giler" (Goetz 2.581.2) to "intentus" (583.5) 80 items, a shortfall; Werden here must have had a longer list).

Münster 2 recto "inuuisus" – "interribilis" (= Goetz 2.583.6–584.15, 62 items)

verso "iuuenalis"[36] – "laberna" (= Goetz 2.584. 16–585.15, 60 items).

fol. 3
fol. 4 } approximately from "lappa" to "pistriensis". (Goetz 2.585.15–589.48, 289 items).[37]

Münster 5 "picens" – "puluinus" (pr. Gallée pp.361–64;[38] 125 items).

fol. 6 590.45 "pugilis," etc.

---

[35] Elias Steinmeyer, "Lateinische und altenglische Glossen," *ZfdA* n.f. 21 (1888): 242–51, at 243–44. The folio numbers assigned to the lost Münster leaves and used by Gallée and Steinmeyer are as they were arranged in their late-nineteenth-century library setting and are totally arbitrary as to contents and original disposition. They consisted of three bifolia which were arranged: bifolium 1–6, parts of Werden A; bifolium 2–5, parts of Glossae Nominum (Werden C, Erfurt 3); bifolium 3–4 (Werden B, Erfurt 2).

[36] CGL 2.584.16; both Gallée and Steinmeyer report Münster having 'iuuenalis'; Erfurt I113 has 'inuenalis' which is obviously correct both by its alphabetical position and gloss: 'q⟨uo⟩d uenale non ⟨est⟩'.

[37] It is not certain where Peterhouse and Münster splice at this point. Gallée gives as the first Münster item "picens peccator", which is not in Peterhouse; the second item, "pinguamen pinguido rien renes", corresponds to Peterhouse "Pignamen. pinguedo" (2.589.49).

[38] Also Steinmeyer in *ZfdA* n.f. 32 (1888): 245–47.

In Goetz's edition the rest of the text from "pugilis" has 472 entries or about three Werden folios plus 100 items. We must assume that one of these folios was folio 6 of this quire and the rest ran into the next quire.

In Erfurt the glossary lacks part of C, all of D–G, and almost all of H because of the loss of two leaves after folio 36 and the glossary (and the manuscript) ends abruptly in the midst of L, "lignarum ligneum et ÷ fin," indicating that that was as far as the exemplar went. The Werden scribe had an exemplar containing a more complete version of Glossae Nominum, probably to the end of the alphabet. There are no material remains of the next quire, which however must have contained Glossae Nominum P–U/V (Peterhouse ends with "Vsualis") on its first three leaves and the beginning of the unique glossary named by Gallée "Werden A."

Werden A must have extended from this quire and into the two following. Unfortunately, it has been very meagerly preserved, now represented only by Gallée's and Goetz's (ex Wessner) prints of one of the lost Münster bifolia (fols. "1" and "6"),[39] plus Werden Probstei fol. 7 (a single cut-down leaf), plus a few lines in the Füngling fragment. The Münster bifolium has, according to Gallée and Goetz, a mark "XIII" at the bottom of the last verso, doubtless the quire signature. This is valuable information that shows that this bifolium was the outside sheet of its quire and allows an accurate count back through the preceding collation.

Münster folio 1 holds 108 items as printed by Gallée (pp. 336–40), containing entries in C–D–E from "cratera" to "ex commode". The preceding quire (on the five-plus folios available) thus must have held A–B and most of C. Münster folio 6 has 113 items as printed, from "panigericis" to "purum". There are likely six missing intervening leaves between "ex commode" and "panigericis," space for 744 lines of writing. The Werden leaf, folio 7, which I shall discuss in some detail in a moment, contains entries covering T and U and was almost certainly on the offside of the quire, implying six leaves between "purum" and "telis", the first entry on folio 7.

Werden Fragments 5 and 6 together make up folio 7; it is a cut-down and split leaf that was turned into two pastedowns for a small volume, doubtless released from its front and back. Fragment 5 is 142 × 96 mm., the smaller dimension being the remaining width of the original leaf. Fragment 6 is 141 × 103 mm. The width of the two split sides combined, 199 mm., is consistent with the 200-mm. width of the other more complete leaves. About 9 mm. in from the split on either piece is a vertical crease where they were fastened into the (later) binding. There are about five deteriorated unoriginal sewing holes

[39] Supplemented by Steinmeyer's report, pre-Gallée and not systematic, of Münster fols. 1–6 and Werden fol. 7 (besides random remarks, he records only items containing vernacular interpretations) in *ZfdA* n.f. 21 (1889): 248–51.

along this crease. The writing size and preparation are identical to the other leaves. Eighteen lines and part of the nineteenth from the top remain, rectos and versos. The outer prickings are visible on both sides. The verso of the original sheet, the glueless side, seems to be the hair side and hence this leaf was most likely on the offside of the quire. The outside of the sheet shows the signs of the wrapped-around leather and some traces of the woodgrain of the boards. Because of the effects of the glue, but more because of the wear and tear at the crease, many letters are obscured or lost. The damage is particularly bad to the lemmata on the second column of the original recto.

The Füngling leaf is drastically cut down, containing twelve complete lines, from the top of the leaf, and part of a thirteenth. It is also split vertically, so that the partial leaf consists of two fragments and glue marks are visible. In other words, as rebinding material it received almost exactly the same treatment as Werden folio 7, though incorporated into a volume only two-thirds the height. It appears to be both the next leaf after the Werden leaf, continuing U–UU, and the last leaf containing this glossary, since the "differentiae" material occupies what remains of the second column and all of the reverse. It is known only from the photograph reproduced in EEMF 22, with virtually no codicological information given by the editors. It is likely that the differentiae on Füngling were added as filler to the last quire of the manuscript.

The structure of the book, according to the analysis above is:[40]

[I⁸], II⁸ lacks 1–2 and 7–8, III⁸ lacks 1–3 and 6–8, IV⁸ lacks 1–3 and 6–8, [V–VIII⁸], IX¹⁰ lacks 1–3 and 8–10, X⁸ (sig. `x'), XI⁶ lacks 1, 3–4, 6, [XII], XIII[⁸] three? inner bifolia gone (sig. `xiii'), XIV[⁸?] lacks all on-leaves and two? off-leaves.

To sum up, as it originally existed, the "Werden Glossary" was a large-format, carefully-executed volume of at least 112 leaves containing three interrelated but separate Anglo-Saxon glossaries. Werden B (Erfurt 2, "Second Amplonian") would have occupied about seventy-four leaves, Werden C (Glossae Nominum) about sixteen, and Werden A about twenty-two.

Approaching the Text: Sources and Problems

This article is intended to set the stage for my larger project of editing the "Werden A" glossary: it is a project that attracts because of the diversity of the sources, often reworked in original ways while still being in the mainstream

---

[40] For the sake of the argument, the recorded Münster leaves, although destroyed, are not counted as "lost" or "wanting."

of glossaries deriving from the early Anglo-Saxon tradition. There is something "fresh" about this glossary: despite its many old elements and manifest corruptions, one sense that new work and some thought has gone into it. Its miserable physical condition presents a challenge and also an opportunity, since its accidental brevity, some 280 items, allows one to contemplate doing a complete, in-depth investigation of each item, according to the source-stream and history of each.

An ancient glossary in manuscript is only the tip of a dangerous and forbidding iceberg: beneath the cold water lies a treacherous mass of precedent texts that have shifted and changed over the course of copying; chance and fate and deliberate choice have molded each successive ensemble according to particular needs and opportunities, since glossaries always had to be useful, one presumes, or at least appear to be so. Many of these problems are endemic to manuscript research, but with glossaries the situation is more exposed. The student sees the unique authority of each copy in its particularity and yet must search the massive tradition to make sense of the particular: the maintenance of the tradition was on one hand the basis and *raison d'être* of this class of text but it was constantly shaped to the needs and experiences of users. Any editing approach must be a flexible and systematic combination of "conservative" and "eclectic" methods of editing that respects the manuscript facts and also grapples with it as a distorted reflection not just of an "original" but of a trail of intermediaries that have the same "original" but "corrupt" status of the representative in hand. The usual calculus of the Werden glossaries has the additional complicating factor that much of it comes through the intermediary of unreliable modern editions.[41]

With the exception of the single detail of Münster folio 1v published by Gallée, showing items 55–68 and 82–84, and the recovered leaf 7 containing 220–80, and the items on the Füngling leaf,[42] our information depends on Gallée and Goetz under the influence of Gallée.[43] So, much depends on the

---

[41] In the discussions which follow, words taken as vernacular derivations of OE are in bold print; words that are preserved in manuscript or photos are marked ⊛.

[42] The Füngling leaf is not noticed further in the subsequent discussion, but contains as follows [; separates items, | indicates line breaks within items]: "uolumen a uoluendo; uoluntas animi uoluntas corpi[.] . . .; uorunculas moherth [for ?**mannherd** "miles," "mercenarius"?]; urbanus sapiens ⟨ue⟩l⟨ uir iucund[.] . . . ; urbane sapī electę sapientię; urbanę elegant̄ ⟨ue⟩l iucundę; uua assa uua sicca & cocca ante inl . . . | uasse ex in sole iterum siccata | adpendendum aut[em?] uasculo c[.] . . . | gentia seruatum; uua passa ꝗpatit̄ abscidi anter . . . | uulgo ubiq⟨ue⟩' At the bottom edge there is visible the top of a cut-off line, including remains of a vernacular word ". . . **lama**" (followed by "sax⟨onice⟩."

[43] Steinmeyer's partial collations (see notes 6 and 33, above) have some independent value. Werden A is printed in CGL 1.161–165. Goetz's own transcription of the Werden

reliability of Gallée. But the results, when we can check against manuscript and photo, are not encouraging. Such direct evidence as remains so often contradicts the testimony of Gallée/Wessner/Goetz that it seems best to look at them not as editions in the modern sense but as continuations of the tradition, like Hicke's editions of lost Anglo-Saxon texts, rife with mistranscriptions, inconsistencies, and omissions, not to mention Gallée's happy-go-lucky approach to resolutions and abbreviations and Goetz's tendency to introduce *Verbesserungen*. Nevertheless both these editions have at least the virtue that they are *intended* to present exactly what is on the manuscript page, even if the execution is far from perfect.[44]

Beyond getting the manuscript facts right, to understand an item's form and meaning requires extensive investigation of not only the history of the item itself, but the overall pattern of sources in the glossary as a whole. Werden A stems from a number, but a limited number, of sources, whose identity and form have often been obscured by revision and corruption through successive copyings; the trail is confused by the shuffling of items from distinct sources into a single alphabetized list. Werden A is part of an English tradition which had long since absorbed standard collections going back to second- and third-century word-lists glossing obsolete and rare words from Republican times; many others came from the so-called "Hermeneumata," Latin-Greek word lists that were originally intended for the use of Greek-speaking functionaries who had to contend with Latin as the official language of the Empire: these were later reversed into Greek-Latin glossaries for Latin-speakers seeking to learn Greek.[45] Seventh-century Spain produced two seminal glossaries, the "Abolita" and "Abstrusa," the former drawing on Virgil, Terence, Festus, and other early Latin sources, the latter on the Bible and Virgil; both these had long careers as

---

leaf often depends on Gallée, following him into error. The same dependence on Gallée is evident in Goetz's print of the Münster leaves, but one can't say for sure whether this is because Wessner's transcripts were influenced by Gallée or because Goetz trusted Gallée more than Wessner and emended the transcripts accordingly. Nevertheless, there is enough deviation between Goetz and Gallée, spiced with an occasional critical remark by the former, to establish Goetz as an independent, if unreliable, witness.

[44] Problems with Gallée's and Goetz's prints will be noted as they arise in the following discussion. On the shortcomings of Lindsay's brilliant but conjectural methods as compared to Gallée's more literal reporting, see Lapidge's introduction to *Studies in Early Mediaeval Latin Glossaries*, xiv–xv.

[45] See A. C. Dionisotti, "Greek Grammars and Dictionaries in Carolingian Europe," in *The Sacred Nectar of the Greeks: The Study of Greek in the West in the Early Middle Ages*, ed. Michael W. Herren and Shirley Ann Brown (London, 1988), 1–56; Johannes Kramer, ed., *Glossaria Bilinguia Altera (C. Gloss. Biling. II)*, Archiv für Papyrusforschung und verwandte Gebiete, Beiheft 8 (Munich/Leipzig, 2001), 15–18.

infiltrators of medieval glossaries.[46] Furthermore, the texts of Isidore of Seville were ransacked for clarification of obscure words that turned up in such lists.

These sources and others converged in the late seventh century in the circle around Theodore, Archbishop of Canterbury. Recent work has shown that bits of the teachings of Theodore and his students survived in glosses and glossaries showing influence of the Anglo-Saxon tradition.[47] Offshoots of this teaching became unalphabetized "glossae collectae" compiled from named texts and listed in the order of the discourse; these are most completely exemplified by the "Leiden Glossary," Leiden University Library, Vossianus Lat. 4° 69 (s. viii, St. Gall?) and other related glossaries copied on the continent between the ninth and twelfth centuries.[48] The earliest alphabetical glossaries draw from these collected glossaries: Épinal, Erfurt, Werden, and Corpus.[49] These manuscripts show their interrelatedness by their possession of so many common lemmata and glosses and their English origin by their ample residue of interpretations in Anglo-Saxon (or Old Saxon or Old High German revisions thereof). They are testimony not only of the Theodoran teachings in England in the 690s but to the Anglo-Saxon missions to Germany beginning in the early eighth century. As the following detailed discussion of its sources shows, Werden A vividly encapsulates the ontology of these early glossaries.

---

[46] Abolita and Abstrusa are most straightforwardly preserved together in an eighth-century Italian manuscript, Vatican, lat. 3321 (ed., CGL 4, 2–198), but much information can be gleaned about them from other glossaries they influenced, particularly those of the Corpus/Erfurt/Werden tradition. See L. M. Lindsay, "The 'Abolita' Glossary (Vat. Lat. 3321)," *Journal of Philology* 34 (1916): 267–82, and "The Abstrusa Glossary and the Liber Glossarum," *Classical Quarterly* 11 (1917): 119–31, at 120–21 (both reprinted in *Studies in Early Mediaeval Latin Glossaries*, see n. 15 above).

[47] Bernhard Bischoff and Michael Lapidge, eds., *Biblical Commentaries from the Canterbury School of Theodore and Hadrian* (Cambridge, 1994), 177 *et passim*.

[48] Glossaries derived from late seventh-century England, with the exception of Cambridge, Corpus Christi College 144 ("The Corpus Glossary") and a few other fragments and intrusions, preserved only in manuscripts from the continent (MSS listed by Ker, *Catalogue* 475–83), presumably because of the great destruction of manuscripts in England during the ninth century. There are surprising isolated survivals such as Aelfric's "praeruptum hengeclif" (WW. 1.180.4), an Abstrusa Virgil gloss (*Georgics* 2.156), corresponding exactly to Werden A, 186 "preruptum **haengi clif**"; see n. 90, below.

[49] Épinal, Bibliothèque Municipale 72 (2) (s. vii/viii, Mercia); Erfurt, Wissenschaftliche Bibliothek Amplonianus 2° 42 (810 × 820, Cologne); Cambridge, Corpus Christi College 144 (s. viii/ix, Canterbury); Werden (810 × 820, Werden) = Essen-Werden, Kath. Propsteigemeinde St. Ludgerus, Frag. Nr. 2 + Düsseldorf Universitäts- und Landesbibliothek MS Frag. K19:Z9/1 + Munich Bayerische Staatsbibliothek, Cgm. 187 III (e.4). These manuscripts are reproduced in EEMF 22, see n. 2, above.

"Leiden," that is, the general Anglo-Saxon-derived tradition of batch glossaries turning into alphabetical glossaries just discussed, is one of the main sources of Werden A.[50] Another main source, one that is special to Werden A, comprises the already discussed "Hermeneumata"-type glosses, most marked in the manuscript ".g." (g⟨rece⟩). Also strongly in evidence is the "Abstrusa" tradition, in ways that seem separate from the "Leiden/Corpus" tradition, but also many items not seen in "Leiden" are shared with "Erfurt/Corpus." There are other incidental sources as well, including a number which cannot be identified and show recent and independent extraction and glossing, including much fresh consultation of Isidore, even when the headword may come from an established glossary source. The following sets out as briefly as possible the structure of the sources for Werden A; editorial and interpretational problems will be illustrated as need arises. Werden items marked ⊛ exist in manuscript and/or photographs.

From the unalphabetized collected glosses as in "Leiden"[51]

Batch 1 (Glosae uerborum de canonibus) 13 curator et procurator (1.101), 94 ⊛epistua (1.49 epistilia), 185 presul (1.87), 206 procurator (1.101), 211 and 212 primicerius (1.103); **Batch 2 (Interpretatio sermonum de regulis [Benedicti])** 85 ⊛emina (2.86), 151 pedules **strapulas** (2.140 *sine interp.*); **Batch 3 (Uerba de S. Martini storia)** 90 ⊛ependiten

---

[50] In the discussions that follow the references to the items in Werden A are to Gallée's numbers, with some items subdivided as necessary.

[51] All Werden A items follow the numbering of Gallée. "Leiden" is a shorthand to indicate the tradition of Anglo-Saxon batch glosses as chiefly exhibited in Leiden University MS Voss. Qº Lat. 69, as edited by J. H. Hessels, *A Late Eighth Century Latin-Anglo-Saxon Glossary* (Cambridge, 1906), citations as in Hessels. CCCC 144 ("Corpus") is cited from Lindsay, *The Corpus Glossary*, supplemented by reference to the facsimile in EEMF 22. Épinal / Erfurt 1 (EE) is cited by reference to the facsimile index lines, supplemented by CGL 5.337–401 and for vernacular items by J. D. Pheifer, *Old English Glosses in the Épinal-Erfurt Glossary* (Oxford, 1974). Erfurt 2 is cited by reference to the facsimile index lines, supplemented by CGL 5.259–337. Michael Lapidge has noted briefly the connections of Werden A to Leiden and the occasional better readings in the former which show that it is not directly dependent on the Leiden manuscript itself, but on related batch glossaries: "Old English Glossography: The Latin Context," in *Anglo-Saxon Glossography*, ed. R. Derolez (Brussels, 1992), 45–47, at 52–53, repr. in idem, *Anglo-Latin Literature 600–899* (London, 1996), 169–81, at 174–80. For a detailed attempt to sort out the complex manuscript relations of the "Leiden" tradition, as far as the biblical glosses go, see J. D. Pheifer, "The Canterbury Bible Glosses: Facts and Problems," in *Archbishop Theodore: Commemorative Studies on his Life and Influence*, ed. M. Lapdige, CSASE 11 (Cambridge, 1995), 281–333.

(3.56),[52] 100 erapsa dapulas (3.54),[53] 139 pessuli (3.19), 149 per agerem (3.14–16),[54] 200 promontorium **hooh** (3.35), 238/239 ⊛toronicam /

---

[52] Though in the "Regula Benedicti" batch, this item, along with the others towards
the end of the batch, comes from Evagrius's version of Athanasius' "Vita S. Antonii":
Werden A has "ependiten tonica uel cocula"; Leiden 3.56 has "ependiten, tonica (→ tu-
nica) uel cocula (→ cuculla), uel omnis uestis desuper aliis uestibus pendens." The source
text has "Antonius . . . lauit ependytem suum" (PL 73.147).

[53] Probably a corruption of "[sata] erasa : stipulas." Ld. 3. 54 has "enrusa : dapulas." Hessels detected the source of the error. This item is derived from Athanasius' *Life of St. Antony*
as translated by Evagrius (chap. 24, PG 26.879–80), where Job 41:18 is being quoted; "reputa-
bit enim quasi paleas ferrum, et quasi lignum putridum aes" ("iron is judged as chaff, brass
as rotten wood"), and to this he adds, following Athanasius, words derived from verse 23,
"reputat quasi uas unguentarium" ("the sea accounted as a box of ointment"). Evagrius adds
the unbiblical phrase ". . . maria ut erasa . . ." ("the seas as if wiped out"). This insertion is not
confined to Evagrius's version: in the Latin version of Athanasius's text anciently and incorrectly ascribed to Jerome (ed. G. J. M. Bartelink, *Vita di Antonio* [Milan, 1974], 56) occurs the
phrase "mare quasi deletum" (MSS: *delictum*). Hessels (104) noted that some printed texts of
Evagrius's version have "maria ut sata erasa" ("the seas as if mown corn"); if this was what the
original gloss extractor saw, he naturally took the gloss from Job 41:20, "quasi stipulam aestim-
abit" ("counted as mown corn"). If this explanation is correct, the gloss was originally to "sata
erasa," the first word being lost at an early stage of transmission, before alphabetization. The
relation between Werden and Leiden suggests that for the Antony batch, there are at least
three degrees of separation between them: 1) "[sata] erasa : stipulas"; 2) "erasa : dapulas"; 3) a)
"erapsa" and b) "enrusa". My thanks to Leslie MacCoull for helping me clarify this note.

[54] According to Gallée, Werden A has "per agerem pro exercitu apuli inuitabor"
(Goetz differs slightly); it is a combination of several confused entries in the Leiden tradition: (3.14–16 + 30) "per aggerem : [*sine interp.*]; [*sine lemma*] : Pro exercitu; appulli :
huuitabar; reda : nomen uehiculi" ("along the road . . . ; . . . for the army; applied, was
called; 'reda', the name of a vehicle"; 30 "Appulli : inuitabant" "I applied, they invited").
The sources are Sulpicius Severus' *Dialogues*, 2.3.2: "interim *per aggerem* publicum plena
militantibus uiris fiscalis *raeda* ueniebat" ("meanwhile along the public roadway came a
government (treasury) wagon filled with servicemen") + Sulp. Sev. *Vita s. Martini* Epist.
Ded. 1.5: "Ego enim cum primum animum ad scribendum *appuli*" ("I, even when I first
applied myself to writing . . ."). Thus, in editing Werden A, it is necessary both to preserve
the errors faithfully transmitted from the Leiden tradition and to sort them out, that is, to
give the manuscript and reconstruct what should have been the original gloss sequence of
three items (even though it never probably existed correctly, or not for long), thus:
    per agerem : **** (gloss missing)
    [fiscalis] reda : pro exercitu
    apuli : inuitabor (→ inuitabar, *from* inuitabant).
Corpus F201 has "fiscalis reda : gebellicum **wægnfearu**" ("": fiscal, going by wagon"),
Lindsay explaining "gebellicum" as an adj. related to OF *gabelle* ("tax") and OE *gafol*
("payment").

⊛toracia (3.6, 3.38), 266 ⊛turno i⟨dest⟩ nodo (3.9 turnodo),[55] 276 ⊛uitalia (3.36), 278 ⊛uiridarum (3.62). **Batch 4 (Incipit in librum Ecclesiasticę Istorię)**[56] 4 curia (4.7), 9 cuniculum (4.94, lemma only), 33 de triuio (4.79),[57] 35 defectior (4.109), 38 defecatum (4.110–11), 39 dependisset (4.32), 50 dispicati (4.30), 71 edituum (4.6),[58] 80 elogis (4.68), 89 ⊛encratine (4.56), 109 panigericis (4.1), 110 parethris (4.45), 131 peripsima . . . **gisupop** (→ **gisuop**) (4.71),[59] 140 peculum (→ petulum) (4.34), 146 pessimus darent (4.41), 167 plexus (4.15), 179 pompa (4.63), 189 prestatio (4.31), 208 propositura → pre-) (4.105),[60] 219 pungius (4.20), 220 puncio (→ puncto[61]) (4.59), 221 purulont[a][62] (4.88), 222 purum extursum

---

[55] The correct form of lemma, ultimately from Abolita/Abstrusa, is preserved as Werden A 7 "cuturno **crincę**" and means the boot worn by the tragic actor, hence, "the high style," "eloquence," and "pride." The derivation and meaning of the OE gloss is obscure.

[56] That is, Rufinus's translation of Eusebius's *Ecclesiastical History*. This is one of several batches from this work in Leiden. Batch 4 is the one most heavily drawn upon by Werden A. Citations are from E. Schwartz and T. Mommsen, *Eusebius Werke*, 3 vols. (Leipzig, 1903–1909), by book, chapter, and paragraph.

[57] Also Leiden 35.238, another Eusebius/Rufinus batch, but Werden A never uses Batch 35 entries that are not also in Batch 4; 35 occasionally influences an interpretation, cf. nn. 59, 61, 64, 66 below.

[58] Werden has "edituum templum edituus". This is a confusion of Leiden 4.6 "Editus : ostiarius; Editum : templum" (→ aedituus : ostiarius; adytum : templum), "temple servant: doorkeeper; inner sanctum : temple."

[59] Werden A: "peripsima superhabundans purgamenta uel **gisupop**." Leiden 4.71 has "peripsima : **gaesuopę**" ("waste, leavings"). Leiden 35.195 has influenced Werden: "peripsima : purgamentum uel quisquilea." This entry illustrates how supplemental Latin interpretations gradually supplant the vernacular ones.

[60] Werden A has "propositura (→ prepositura) propositus (→ prepositus) id est uestis regiae" ("office of supervisor : overseer, that is, of the king's garments"). Leiden has reversed the lemma and gloss ("Propositus uestis regie : propositura"). The source text (*Eccl. Hist.* 7.32.3) has "et honorem ei contulerat purpurae praepositoram" ("and conferred on him the stewardship of the royal garments").

[61] Leiden has the correct form, "puncto." Gallée gives "puncio"; Goetz's "puncto" must be an emendation. The Leiden/Werden interpretation is wrong ("pede," a measurement); the context in *Eccl. Hist.* 5.1.27 is of torture, "puncto in nervo *pedes*", which shows the source of the error. It is correctly interpreted in Leiden batch 35: "puncto : foramine in quo pedes uinctorum in ligno tenentur cubitali spatio interiecto inter uinctos" ("a point : a hole in which the feet of the bound ones are held by bindings, spaced out yard by yard between the bindings")

[62] Gallée reports "purulontæ (*ntæ* undeutlich)", Goetz "purulenta (!)"; it is not clear if the ! is marking a mistake on Gallée's part or marking an emendation. Leiden has "purulenta."

(4.111),[63] 224 ⊛terebrantes **borendę**[64] (4.66), 228 ⊛thestéas (4.57),[65] 240 ⊛torices (4.97),[66] 250 ⊛trocleis **hlędrę** (4.74), 254 ⊛trallis (4.37). **Batch 5**[67] **(Item de Ecclesiastica Storia)** 34 de ogduade (5.6), 61 ⊛dorium (5.7), 112/114 paret' perstrigium; parcheris prestrigus (5.17–18),[68] 181 podagra (5.16), 209 proriginem **bloot** (→ pruriginem **blooc** [= blǣce, "itch"]), (5.15), 279 ⊛uirfibrarum i⟨dest⟩⟩ **dar** (5.22, Fibrarum ; **darmana** for OE *þearma*, "guts, entrails"). **Batch 7 (De Paralipomenon)** 111 panarethos (lemma) (7.1). **Batch 8 (De Salamone)** 153 pin (→ ptisones) g⟨rece⟩ **bere** (8.18).[69]

---

[63] The gloss is wrong in Leiden and Werden, drawing on a Hermeneumata-type (e.g., Herm. Mont. καταρον purum, *CGL* 3.315.27 "clean : pure") because the lemma is from Eusebius / Rufinus, *Eccl. Hist.*, "purum" having the sense "only," "merely" (three occurrences), e.g. 5.28.2, "haec haeresis purum hominem ... fuisse salvatorem confirmat," "this heresy holds that the Savior was only man" (i.e., had only one nature).

[64] Werden "terebrantes **borendę**" ("borings, perforations") is correct against Leiden 4.66 "borgenti"; cf. Leiden 35.187 "terebrantes : perforantes."

[65] Werden: "thestéas cęnas uel cęnas scelere"; Leiden 4.57 "thesteas : indiscretas concubitas." Werden better reflects the source, *Eccl. Hist.* 5.1.14, "Thyesteas cenas et incesta Oedipia perpetrantes." Gallée reports "thestéas (*e* oder *i*)" but the first "e" is perfectly clear in the photograph.

[66] Werden: "torices (→ thoraces) sa[r]apes" (the *i* is clear in "torices"; the *r* in the next word is written above a partially erased letter, probably *p*; Leiden 4.97 is "Thoraces : capud et pectus." The lemma is "thorax," a statue, bust. Werden better reflects the source (Rufinus' addition to *Eccl. Hist.* 11.29): "quod etiam thoraces Serapis ... abscisi sunt omnes et abrasi." The context is the destruction of the Serapion in Alexandria. Leiden 35.32 has "Thoraces : imagines."

[67] Another batch from Eusebius/Rufinus, *Ecclesiastical History*.

[68] Werden 112: "paret' (→ paredum) : perstrigium (→ prestigium) ("illusion"); Werden 114 "parcheris : prestrigus (prestigiis)" ("of illusions"). This separates by an item the inventory in the confused Leiden item 5.17–18: "paredum : prestigium; parchredis : prestrigiis." The source is *Eccl. Hist.* 2.14.5 "... et adhaerentis daemonicae virtutis, quam πάρεδρον vocant ..." "and adhering to demonic powers, which they call 'paredron' [a familiar spirit]."

[69] Werden 153 has "pin g⟨rece⟩ bere" ("prepared barley") and seems to be a curtailed version of the gloss as found in Corpus P841 (also Erfurt 2) "Ptysones **berecorn beorende**" ("bearing down on barleycorn"). The source is Proverbs 27:22, "si contuderis stultum in pila quasi *[p]tisanas feriente* desuper pilo ("if you should grind a fool as a pestle crushes down on hulled barley"). The note "grece" may indicate that the Werden item was not taken from a "Leiden" type gloss but directly from a Corpus-type list. In Leiden the gloss is more elaborated and loses the exactness of the match between source and gloss: "Ptis`a´nas : de ordeo fiunt grana. que decorticantur in pilo (→ pila) uel uase lapideo" ("grains made from barley, which are crushed in a mortar or stone vessel").

Batch 12 (De Ecclesiastico) 214 psalterium[70] (12.40). Batch 13 (In libro Isaiae prophete) 64a ⊛drómedarię (*sine interp.*) (13.60), 157 pilosi (13.24). Batch 14 (Incipit in Hieremia) 169 placentas (lemma, gloss from Isidore) (14.5), ⊛237a torte panis in modum coronę[71] (14.21). Batch 15 (Incipit in Hiezechiel) 164 pigmeus (15.13). Batch 18 (De Ose) 274 ⊛uinacia uuarum (18.3).[72] Batch 25 (De Marco et Luca et Iohanne) 36 decorio (→ decurio) (25.9).[73] Batch 30 (De calogo hieronimi in prol.) 49 dialogus (30.45), 101 etomologia[74] (30.56). Batch 34 (De Cassiano) 156 pinsit (24.25).[75] Batch 38 (De Clemente) 1 cratera (38.17), 228 ⊛thema figura (38.32–33).[76] Batch 39 (De Dialogorum [Gregorii]) 99 erucę (lemma) 39.7, 133 per fragmaticum (→ pragmaticum) per negationem (→ negotionem) (39.63). Batch 43 (Item de diuersis nominibus) 142

---

[70] Werden A 214 "psalterium triangulum est" seems to be a relic of Ld. 12.40, "Cyneris : nablis, idest citharis longiores quam psalterium . nam psalterium triangulum fit; theodorus dixit" ("Harps, that is cithers longer than the psaltery, because the psaltery is a triangle; Theodore said it."). This is one of the entries which led Bischoff and Lapidge to see Theodore (his school) as the moving force behind many of the Leiden batches (*Biblical Commentaries*, 177).

[71] Not "pauis" as Gallée. The *te* of "torte" are caught in the crease but legible in the photo.

[72] Werden A 274 "uinacia folciculi (→ folliculi) uuarum" ("husks, hard skin of grapes"); Ld. 18.3 "Uinacia : que remansit in uuis quando premuntur", also Leiden 15.33 (Incip. in Hiez.). Or is it from the Bible directly, Osee (3:1) "diligunt uinacia uuarum"? "uuarum" illustrates an occasional hazard: is it actually the remains of a vernacular interpretant (OE *wearr* "hard skin") or Latin "of grapes"? Probably the latter since it is not marked "sax".

[73] Werden: "decorio Nomen gradus ut centorio"; Leiden 25.9 (= Mark 15.43, Luke 23.50) "Decurio : princeps super × homines." But the interpretant may be from Hermeneuata: δηκάρχης decurio | ταξίαρχος centurio (Herm. Einsid. G.3.276.12–13)

[74] Goetz: "ecomologia".

[75] Both Werden and Leiden are corrupt, having "pinsit : densitudo." The source may be Cassian *Inst.*, 2.13, or *Collat.* 12.8, with a lemma *pinguedinem*. Or it may be two defective unrelated entries: *pinsit* : [***] : [***] : *densitudo*. Or the actual source may be Servius, *Comm. in Verg. Georg.* I. 267 (ed. Thilo [1887]) 3.192–93: "'nunc frangite saxo,' nam quod ait 'saxo frangite' potest accipi et pinsere, quod significat pilo tundere, quia et uulgo cauatum saxum pilam dicimus." The English tradition seems to reflect this Servian passage: EE (G.5.379.5) "pindere (→ pinsere) : pilo tundere" ("strike, crush with a pestle"), Corpus P395 "pinso: tundo." The correct reading for Leiden and Werden A may then be "pinsit pinso : tundit tundo."

[76] Werden collapses two entries: "Thema : doctrina; Schema : figura."

perendie die tertia (43.41–42).[77] **Batch 45 (Verba de multis)** 137 pedis-
equa (*sine interp.*) (45.22). **Batch 47 (Item alia)** 48 dispredulus : **acuaerna** uel sciron (47.88),[78] 172 platesa genus piscis **floc** (47.9), 267 ⊛turdus
staer (?for sturnus st<u>e</u>r 47.53). **Batch 48 (Item de Cassiano)** 180 posterula
(48.37).[79]

The sharing of the error at Werden 266 "turno i⟨d est⟩ node," Leiden 3.9
"turnodo," shows that Werden was being drawn from a copy that was in a line
that led also to Leiden Voss., but the many better readings also show that the
transmission was different and not directly from Leiden.[80] One also notices
that the glossator of Werden A was especially interested in the Eusebius/Ru-
finus batches and perhaps had access to only one or two of the several batches
available to the Leiden manuscript compiler. But the Werden compiler may
also have had access to some *glossae collectae* that were fuller than those in
Leiden, or at least made different selections, as the following rare or unique
items suggest:

> 107 expendere : tollerare ("pay out" : "endure") is probably from the Leiden
> tradition, since it is a Eusebius/Rufinus item reflected in Corpus (E542
> "expendere **to aseodenne**" "to pay out") and EE 40 "expendisse **throua-
> dae**" ("suffered"); *Eccl. Hist.* 9.10: "quod in ultimis vitae positus iustam
> esse vindictam dei et scelerum se poenas merentem profitetur expendere"
> ("so that in the last hours of his life he acknowledged that God's judgment
> was just and that he deserved to pay the penalty for his crimes").

---

[77] Leiden 43.41–42 is confused: "perende; **ofer tua nest** (→ **neht**); Posttriedie : post
III dies." But if the second lemma is merely misplaced in a late copy then Leiden can be
considered the source of Werden. Hermeneumata have the following type: *eis triten* : per-
endiae (Herm. Mont., G.3.296.14).

[78] "**acuaerna**" is "squirrel." The word "dispredulus" is unaccounted for. Goetz prints
"dispridulus" and implies in his index (7.691) "disperdulus," perhaps thinking of *disper-
do*, "destroy utterly." Leiden Batch 47 contains a large number of animal and bird names.
47.88 is "Perdulum : **hragra**" (heron), cf. Erf.1 (5.340.10) "ardea et dieperdulum **hragra**"
(heron). If the Erfurt form shows an intermediate corruption that could have entered a
predecessor of our glossary under DI-, then we may posit some unalphabetized glossary
showing "*dis*perdulum **hragra**, scira **acurna**," from which the middle two words dropped
out, perhaps in the process of excerpting for alphabetization. Perhaps the addition "uel
sciron" ("squirrel") was later by way of correction.

[79] Werden "posterula : ianua" ("postern gate"). The lemma is different from Leiden
48.37 "Postere : porte". The source is Cassian, *Inst.* 5.11.2 "posterae unius quamuis paruissimae" ("one postern however small"). Werden may be reflecting a reading such as in
Gazaeus's edition (printed PL 49.226–37) "posterulae unius, quamuis paruissimae."

[80] Lapidge notices this point: see n. 51, above.

The following items not in Leiden appear to be drawn from Cassian:

69 ⊛econemica disputatoria (→ dispensatoria). Cassian, *Collationes* 13.11 (PL 49.924), "quod etiam beatus David oeconomice tunc factum in psalmo centesimo quarto similiter declaravit dicens . . ." ("The blessed David likewise declared in Psalm 104 that this was done providentially then, saying . . .").[81]

86 ⊛embrimiis plumaci (→ plumaciis) "reed bundle : pillow". This certainly derives from Cassian, *Collationes* 1.23.4 (PL 49.522) "iisdem ipsis quibus insidebamus psiathiis admonens incubare, embrimiis pariter capiti nostro ceruicalium uice suppositis, grossioribus papyris in longos gracilesque fasciculos coaptatis. Quae pedali interuallo pariter colligata . . ." ("advising us to lie down on the same mats [*psiathiis*] that we were sitting on, and instead of a pillow [*ceruicalium*] to put under our heads little bundles [*embrimiis*] which are gathered into long slender bundles. These are tied together with heavier papyrus cords at intervals of a foot . . .").

118 paxmatium : demedia libra II pax⟨matia⟩ lib⟨ra⟩ una "*paxmatium* is half a pound, two *paxmatia* is a pound". This is the daily bread ration, two *paxmatia*, as given in Cassian, *Collationes*, e.g., 12.15 (PL 49.896): "et mortificatus ab omni ira ac sollicitudine, curaque mundana, duobus tantum paximaciis fuerit quotidiana refectione contentus" ("who has mortified himself from all anger and care of the world will be content with a daily ration of two *paxmatii*)". Cf. also 2.21, 2.24, 2.26, 19.4, *De Coenobiorum Institutis* 4.14 (PL 4.169); this source is also reflected in Erfurt 2 P100 "paxmatis quadr⟨ang⟩ulatus" ("bread cut in quarters").

171 plectrans (→ plectas) fundes de palmulis ("cords [made of] of palmleaves"). Cassian, *Collationes* 18.15 (PL 49.1116): "absconditum codicem inter plectas palmarum" "the hidden book among the palm-fibre cords." Apparently related is Corpus P465 "plectra (→ plecta) : **auunden**" ("woven").

The following appear to be from Jerome:

22 degustatos depastos ("tasted : consumed"). This seems to be drawn from Ep. 52.5 (PL 11.532): "Crebra munuscula et sudariola et fasciolas

---

[81] For the revision of the interpretant, cf. Corpus E10 "economia : dispensatio." "Economice" means "by God's grace" (A. Souter, *A Glossary of Later Latin to 600 A.D.* [Oxford, 1959], s.v.).

et uestes ori applicitas et oblatos ac degustatos cibos blandasque et dul-
ces litterulas sanctus amor non habet." ("Frequent presents and hankies
and ribbons and cloths applied to your lips and already-tasted pleasant
dishes and sweet little notes have nothing to do with holy love.")

115 parafrasten non translatorem ("a paraphraser, not a translator"). Jerome, "Praef. in libros Samuel et Malachim" (PL 28.557): "et cum intel-
lexeris quod antea nesciebas, uel interpretem me aestimato, si gratus es,
uel παραφραστήν, si ingratus, quamquam mihi omnino conscius non
sim mutasse me quippiam de hebraica ueritate." ("and when you understand what before you were ignorant of, if you are pleased, call me a
translator, of, if not pleased, a paraphraser, though I am not at all aware
of having deviated from the Hebrew truth.")

117 pancratiasten [graece[82]] luctator ("wrestler"). This may be from Jerome's *Comm. in ep. ad Titum* (PL 26.567C): "pugilem et pancratiasten"
but it could just as well be from Hermeneumata, e.g. Herm. Mont. (CGL
3.172.67–68): "paleste luctatores | pancratiaste pancratiaste" [*sic*].

There are two related items from Priscian: 52 dionimus qui duo nomina
habet. 256 ⊛trionimus g⟨rece⟩ qui tria nomina habet. Priscian, *Inst. Gramm.*
2.29 (Keil 2.60–61): "in propriis quoque hanc vim habent dionyma uel tri-
onyma vel tetraonyma. . . ."
The following are apparently Bible glosses, not in Leiden and slenderly
represented in other glossaries:

5 curiosi dicuntur qui uocant (→ uacant) sibi otio et detraunt (→ detra-
hunt) ("they are called 'the curious' who are themselves empty because
of idleness and disparage others"), from 1 Tim. 5:13: "curiosae loquentes
quae non oportet");

73 egregi[us] salta israel egregi[us] cantator ("favorite psalmist of Israel
: favorite singer") from 2 Sam. 23:1 "egregius psalta Israhel";

97 ⊛epistolia (→ peribolia) g⟨rece⟩ q⟨uo⟩d ⟨est⟩ la⟨tine⟩ op⟨er⟩torium
("garment"). Psalm 101:27: the lemma is from the LXX, περιβόλαιον, the
gloss from the Gallican, "et sicut opertorium mutabis eos."

125 paneos (→ panemos) g⟨rece⟩ similitudo dicitur. This appears to be
the confusion of two entries with "grece" after the lemma causing haplo-
graphy. The first part is the name of the Greek month and must represent
something like *paneos grece : september* [or *iulius*] *mensis* (cf. Lib. Gl.

---

[82] Reported by Goetz, not Gallée.

CGL 5.230.24–25 and Bede);[83] the second part requires a lemma to "similitudo" and this is supplied for the English tradition by Corpus P685, "problesma : similitudo" ("riddle") and the source for that is probably Judges 14:15: "blandire viro tuo et suade ei ut indicet ubi quid significet problema" ("soothe thy husband and persuade him to tell you what the riddle means").

136 pellicentes maculantes ("deceiving, defiling") A gloss in Cod. Vat. 1468 (CGL 5.509.48) corresponds to this: "pellaicientes : meretricantes," and both this and Werden probably go back to 2 Peter 2:14, "pellicentes animas instabiles" ("deceiving unstable souls").

199 proaulum (→ proaulium) proatrium ("προαύλιον : area in front of the *aula*," "forecourt"), from Mark 14:68 "καὶ ἐξῆλθεν ἔξω εἰς τὸ προαύλιον καὶ ἀλέκτωρ ἐφώνησεν," "Et exiit foras ante atrium et gallus cantavit" ("and he went out in front of the court and the cock crew").[84]

203 prop[h]etatio prophetia ("prophecy"), 1 Cor. 12:10 "alii prophetatio," the gloss based on the "Hispanic" reading of Augustine, MSS C G* H T and Theodulf, while the gloss "prophetia" is the reading of the Amiatinus and Fuldensis and the Alcuinian recension.[85]

Besides the items listed above in "Leiden" and many of those below in "Hermeneumata," the following are identical to or closely related to Corpus, Épinal, Erfurt 2, and are not in "Leiden," showing various sources: 12a cumba (→ tumba) (lemma, Corpus T 350 tumba, Abolita, attracted to Abstrusa "cumba : navis," cf. Corpus C 9732),[86] 26 denotare (→ deuotare) (Corpus D84 defotabat, ?Aldhelm 38.19), 28 defexum decliuium ęsdyni (→ ęfdyni) (Corpus D140, Abolita), 41 disparuit (Corpus D273),[87] 43 discolatis (→ disco-

---

[83] *De rat. temp.* 14 (CCSL 123B.1, 328) "Iulius, Panemos."

[84] *"Proatrium"* seems to be a nonce calque. See TLL 10.2.10, 1441, 1223, s.v. *proaulium, proatrium*. The same corrupt form, "proaulum", is found in Vat. 1469 (CGL 5.525.10) but apparently applying to the Jerusalem temple: "porta prima est ab oriente" (cf. e.g. Ezech. 40:6–19).

[85] J. Wordsworth et al., *Nouum Testamentum D.N.I.C. Latine*, 2d ed., S. Hieronymi, Pars 2. Epp. Paulinae (Oxford, 1913–1941), 242.

[86] The confusion is deep in the English tradition, cf. Corpus T350 "tumba : nauis uel sepulchrum." The Werden interpretation has been expanded from some Roman topography.

[87] Werden 41 disparuit : exoleuit ("separated : disappeared"); Corpus D273 Disparuit : **ungesene wearð**; EE D59 Disparuit : **ungiseem uard**. The interpretants in Latin and OE correspond in meaning: perhaps the lemma is from Vulg. Lat. *disparere* > OF *disparoir*, "disappear, cease to be visible." See Pheifer, *Épinal-Erfurt Glossary*, 82, n. 333.

lis) . . . quasi **sterolesum** (→ **steorleasum**) (Corpus D281, Abolita/Abstrusa),
55 ⊛dolatoriu⟨m⟩ grece ascia latine **aetsa** (→ **aesca**) saxonice (EE D28 "dala-
turae **braedlaestu aesc**", Abolita, from Jerome Ep. 106), 63 ⊛dracontopedes
(Ps-Clement/Rufinus, *Recogn.* 1.29),[88] 65 ⊛duellum (lemma, Corpus D375,
Abolita/Abstrusa), 66 ⊛dudum **ungeora** (Corpus D382, Abstrusa), 77 eludit
saigdę (Corpus E111 eluderet **awwaegde** "outmaneuver," Abolita, Oros. 3.1.6),
78 elegans (Corpus E 105, 141, Abstrusa), 106c ex asse : ex uno siue ex omni-
bus (Erf2 E86,)[89] 117 pauxillum (Corpus P173, Abstrusa), 120 patricius pater
patrię (Erf2 P105), 127 perduellio (Erf2 P182, Corpus P205, Abolita/Abstru-
sa), 141 peles (→ **pelex**) (Corpus P372, P 355, Abolita), 144 p⟨et⟩ulcum (Corpus P219 petulci, Abolita peculcum, CGL 4.142.45), 170 plagearii (Corpus P
475, Abstrusa), 182 posteritas (lemma Corpus P491, Abolita; gloss Isidore),
186 preruptum **haengi clif**,[90] 198a prosapia[91] (Corpus P 667, Abstrusa), 198b
presagia (lemma, Corpus P 586, Abstrusa), 215 pug[io][92] (Corpus P873, Abolita), 218 puu⟨et⟩enus (→ **pube tenus**) **oð middil** (Corpus P 854, Abstrusa),
225 ⊛terga (Corpus T 62), 226 ⊛termas p⟨ro⟩ cal[or]e (Épinal T6, perhaps
Hermeneuta), 230 ⊛thia[93] (Épinal T5, Abstrusa), 247 ⊛tr[i]dentes creagras

---

[88] ". . . non δρακοντόποδες, ut Graecorum fabulae ferunt, sed immensis corporibus
editi" (PG 1.1223: "not 'dragonfooted' as Greek fables report, but born with huge bodies").

[89] Erfurt has "exasreresto : exintegro exomnipatrimoni", reconstructed by Goetz
(CGL 6.401) "ex asse : heres esto ex integro, ex omni patrimonio" ("you will be sole heir
of the whole patrimony").

[90] Probably an Abstrusa Virgil gloss ("praeruptis : excisse rupis extreme," *Georgics*
2.156, "praeruptis oppida saxis"); though the form of the lemma differs from those in
Corpus (P610) "praeruptus" and Épinal-Erfurt (P 747) "praerupta"; the gloss reappears
in the form "praeruptum **hengeclif**" in a surprising context, a "Supplement" to Aelfric's
glossary, by T. Wright and R. P. Wülcker, *Anglo-Saxon and Old English Vocabularies*, 2nd
ed. (London, 1884, repr. Darmstadt, 1968), 1.180.4.

[91] Gallée reports "prosapia presagia futurorum uel genus," which is a conflation of
two Abstrusa glosses:
    prosapia : genus (4.149.38)
    presagia : [indicia] futurorum (4.156.2–3)

[92] Goetz "Pugio (incohaverat Pugill)"; Gallée "pug*ulum* (*ulum* undeutlich)."

[93] Gallée prints "thia .g. amita latine siñ pat he dicuntur extranea." Goetz is slightly
different: "Thia g. amita latine sēn paī he dicuntur extranea." The item, which is on the pre-
served leaf 7, clearly reads: 'thia g amita latina soř paī he dñr | extranea[.]'. The letters 'or' of
'sor' are partly flaked off: one could make the case perhaps for the "n", but not "i". Goetz expands in his index to "senex patris." But the characteristic mid-stroke of an *e* is not present
and the letter is probably "o". There seems to be an "r" like the *r* in 'figura' four lines above
this place, with a blunt hook to the left and short descender, not like the *r* in 'scelere' two lines
up, with a longer descender and a wider left hook. The basis of the entry is the widespread
Abstrusa gloss "amita: soror patris" as it shows up in, for example, Épinal-Erfurt (EE)

(EE C149 creagras tridentes, Abstrusa), 252 ⊛tribulibus tribubus (? = tribuli, Corpus T 305, Abolita), 253 ⊛tropheum pretia **herihyd** (Corpus T 271, Abolita), 255 ⊛traducem (Corpus T269), 257 ⊛tribunal **dom sedil** (Corpus T245, Werden B 103 [= Erf2] tribunalia cathedrẹ, Abstrusa), 261 ⊛triphinas (*recte* sciniphes) **micg**[94] (Corpus S175, Abolita, Isidore), 269 ⊛uectigal (Erf2 U66, Abstrusa), 271 ⊛uitta **sonð** (→ **snod**, "snood," "headgear") (Corpus U224, Abolita). The English Glossae Nominum (in our manuscript as Werden C), drawn from Hermeneumata items, seems to have little independent influence on Werden A, only perhaps 273: "uicarii custodes locorum uicar. enim custus est locibus," which matches G.N. "uicarius : custos loci" (CGL 2.597.21).[95]

There are few if any Abolita glosses in Werden A that are not mediated by "Leiden" or by the Corpus/Épinal/Erfurt tradition, or at least found there. However there are a few independent uses of Abstrusa, suggesting the influence of an Abstrusa list unmixed with Abolita: 37 derogat (CGL 4.48.30, Festus), 59 ⊛dorcus **girec** (→ doricus **grec**) (4.58.28, Isidore), 72 egis .g. habes (Abstrusa 4.61.3: "egent : indigent, necessae habent," cf. Mark 2:17), 166 phalances turbe (4.73.44),[96] 204 prologus (4.148.42), 210 prunus lignum, prunum fructus i⟨dest⟩ **plum[e]** (two contiguous Abstrusa items [4.152.19–20]: "prunus : arbor / prunum et pruna : poma,")[97] 281 ⊛uilicus (4.192.12).

The following are items whose glosses appear to be taken directly from Isidore.[98] Items whose lemmata are paralleled in the Anglo-Saxon tradition are starred. Unless otherwise noted, the Isidore material (and the reference) is from the *Etymologies*:

T5 "thia vel amita soror patris"; "latina" rather than "latine" seems definite. The correct reading must be: "thia g⟨rece⟩ amita latina sor⟨or⟩ pat⟨ris⟩ he d⟨icu⟩n⟨tur⟩ extranea[e]."

[94] Gallée: "triplunas .g. nuge"; Goetz: "triphinas g. nugc." Neither *triplunas* nor *triphinas* would appear to be genuine Greek words. The photo clearly shows **migc**, "midge"; the lemma must be a corruption of *sciniphes, scinifes* (as in Abavus and Isidore), perhaps *sci-* in pointed Insular minuscule being misread as "tsi-" and subsequently realphabetized. The correct form of the interpretant was pointed out by Steinmeyer in his review of Gallée (*AfdAdL* 22 [1896]: 271).

[95] There occur many incidental matches of lemmata between Werden A and Glossae Nominum, all better attributed to other sources and connections; on fol. 7 alone are: torques, triclinium, tribunus, tribunal, tutela, turdela, tubus, uulturus.

[96] The form of the lemma suggests the item is directly from Abstrusa: "falangas : multudines," not through Corpus, etc.: Erf2 F11 "falanx : multitudo militum."

[97] Making it likely an Abstrusa-list was the direct source, perhaps mediated in some way by the English tradition, since Corpus has P456 plumum (→ prunum) **plumae**, P449 plunas (→ prunus): **plum treu**. But it should be borne in mind that Insular precursors of the extant Werden manuscript probably had vernacular interpretations as a matter of course.

[98] All citations of the *Etymologies* are from W. M. Lindsay, ed., *Isidori Hispalensis episcopi Etymologiarum sive Originum libri XX*, 2 vols. (Oxford, 1911).

2b *cirographa (5.24.23),[99] 4 curia conuentus (interp., 15.2.28),[100] 8
*curricula (5.35.9), 12b [curatores] a curando (9.4.34), 16 curiales et
decuriones (9.4.24), 19a/b dactulus (17.7.1),[101] 20 defensores (epitome
of 9.4.18), 21 dilator (10.77), 44 differenda (1.31), 47 *dilicatis (10.70),
64b [dromones] (19.1.14),[102] 68 ⊛eculium (5.27.21) 82 ⊛elifantiac⟨us⟩

---

[99] The entry is defective: "cirographa" could be lemma or gloss. If the former, the
entry should be "cirographa : [cautiones]" as *Etym.* 5.24.23, "Chirographum : Cautio";
if the latter, we see a Hermeneumata-type as represented by Glossae Nominum (CGL
2.571.41) "Cautio cirographum."

[100] This is part of a confusing complex. Gallée as his nos. 2–4 gives:
    crates gaerdes. cirographa
    cur[ia senatus culfus sinus maris [enatus de cunctis
    curia conuentus et contio idem est i. curas
Gallée's presentation seems to indicate that the manuscript appeared thus:

                    ia senatus culfus sinus maris
    crates gaerdes. cirographa cur\
                            enatus de cunctis
    curia conuentus et contio idem est i. curas\

This would give five entries:
    crates **gaerdes**
    cirographa [*sine interp.*]
    curia senatus
    culfus sinus maris
    curia conuentus et contio idem est i. cura senatus de cunctis
Things are further complicated by Goetz, who (not employing line-by-line division of
items) reports: "crates gaerdas (*et supra scr. .s.*) cirographa, Culfus sinus maris [enatus
decuntis ([*signum distinctionis est.* Gallée praemittit Curia [senatus), Curia conuentus et
contio idem est .i. curas." In other words Goetz implies that Gallée's third item "curia senatus" is not there and indicates, I guess, an entry "Culfus sinus maris enatus decunctis" (?
"A gulf is a bay of the sea pushed back from everything"), cf. Leiden 36.3 (De Orosio) "Sinus ubi mare intrat in terram." But Gallée's report is more plausible, the last item "curia
conventus et contio idem est i<dest> cura s|enatus de cunctis" being directly from *Etym.*
15.2.29, "Curia dicitur eo quod ibi cura per senatum de cunctis administretur." "Contio"
is an Abstrusa lemma. "Curia conuentus" is Leiden 4.7.
[101] Gallée/Goetz 19: "dactulus fructus digito similis. dactulus grece digitus." This is
two entries, the first from Isidore, the second Hermeneumata.
[102] MS (i.e., Gallée's photo): 'dromedarię naues dñr .xxx. in qō semi|gant gubernant
& trahunt draconem | capiunt. l. Ɨ lx. homines.' Gallée and Goetz both read "remigant,"
a silent emendation. The lemma is from Leiden 13.60 "Dromedarię; castrati cameli", the
interpretant lost. The second part appears to be from *Etym.* 19.1.14, "longae naves sunt
quas dromones vocamus. . . ."

(4.18.12),[103] 88 ⊕*enigma (1.37.26), 92 ⊕*epentiditen et *colophium (19.22.24),[104] 102 *etomologia (1.29.1), 103 equa lance (18.7.5), 123 *pa-pauer (17.9.31),[105] 132 *peryzoma (19.22.5), 138 pecodes (12.1.6), 145 petulcus (10.231, ex Servius), 152 *pelues (20.6.8), 158 piscarius (*Diff.* 2.467), ?168 plageatur (→ -tor) (10.220), 169 *placentas (20.2.17), 176 poma (17.6.24),[106] 182 posteritas (lemma from Abolita, 9.5.26), 187 pre-lum (20.14.12), 190 precentor (7.12.27), 191 *pretores ex (→ et) prefecti (9.3.27, 9.4.16), 192 presides (9.3.38), 193 proceres (9.4.17), 202 proximus (9.6.2), 205 proelium (18.1.8),[107] 213 *princeps (9.3.21), 225 ⊕*terga[108] (11.1.91), 229 ⊕th[e]atrum (15.2.34, 18.42.1), 233 ⊕toga dicta (19.24.3), 234 ⊕*tor[q]u[e]s **halsberigolth** (19.31.11),[109] 235 ⊕*toga palmata (19.24.5), 249 ⊕*tr[ag]elapus (?12.1.20), 258 ⊕traducere (17.5.33), 260 ⊕tribuni (9.4.18), 263 ⊕*triclinium (15.3.8), 269 ⊕uectigal (16.18.8).

A feature of this glossary often noted is its interest in Greek words. There are more Hermeneumata-types than any other class (even leaving out those Hermeneumata derivations that come by way of "Leiden"). Many of these are

---

[103] Theodore, EvII 13 (*Biblical Commentaries*, 398), "Morbus regius ['leprosy'] et elefans unum sunt. Elefanciosus dicitur qui perdit aliquid membrum et fit paene totum corpus emortuum," etc. may be the occasion for the word's entry into the gloss tradition. The interpretant is from Isidore.

[104] "epentiditen" is Leiden 3.56; "colophium" is paralleled in Anglo-Saxon tradition, Corpus C514 "Colobium : **hom**" ("cloak"), sim. EE C13.

[105] This is a Hermeneumata-type; Corpus P166 papver : **popei**, P542 popaver : **popaeg**, Épinal popauer **popaeg**. Werden brings in Isidore to replace the vernacular gloss.

[106] The interpretant is defective: "poma generaliter dicuntur" but probably is for *Etym.* 17.6.24 "poma dicta ab optimo."

[107] Gallée: "proelium pars pugne pugnaumus `diei´," a minim error?; Goetz's "proeli-um pars pugne pugna unius diei" must represent a silent emendation, cf. Isidore's "pugna unius diei, proelium pars pugnae est."

[108] The manuscript reads 'terga hominu⟨m⟩ s⟨unt⟩ ter[..] animaliu⟨m⟩'. Gallée gives "terga *dorsa* hominum sunt terga animalium," silently emending from Corpus T62, or the probable source, Abstrusa (CGL 4.183.20) or Isidore. Goetz follows Gallée verbatim rather than the manuscript.

[109] sax<onice> "tor[.]u[.]s **halsberigolth** circula aurei sunt"; Lapidge noted "torques halsberigold" in an Isidore epitome in Paris, Bibliothèque Nationale 1750, fols. 140–152 (s. viii/ix) copied by a continental scribe from an Anglo-Saxon insular minuscule exemplar written, Lapidge supposes on linguistic grounds, about 700 (M. Lapidge, "An Isidorian Epitome from Early Anglo-Saxon England," *Romanobarbarica* 10 [1988–1989]: 445–83, at 452). In a later article he concludes that the Werden gloss is drawn from the same glossed Isidore manuscript that Paris used, not Paris itself ("Old English Glossography," 52).

within the English tradition but not appearing in the Leiden batches. Hermeneumata-types with Isidore glosses mentioned in the preceding paragraph
are 19a, 123, 168, 176, 260, 263. Those marked "g⟨rece⟩" in the manuscript are
followed by ".g." with a reference to a representative source-type as given in
CGL. Many of these retain a vernacular interpretant and it must be assumed
that many if not most or all once had them (any item corresponding to the
"Corpus" group or with a vernacular interpretant is marked *).

2a *crates **gaerdes** (2.262.60), 2b *cirographa (see Isidore section), 3b
culfus (2.352.37), 10 cupellulus **bula** (3.197.69), 14 *curcilio (2.433.46),
19b *dactulus .g. (5.513.55), 23 *deuote .g. (2.268.54), 24? delibras delibras,[110] 25 dexe .g. **tene**, 40 *desinteria **utsynht** (→ utsyht) (3.599.41), 42
disiria (→ disuria) (3.599.31), ?45 diocisus .g., 51 dipondio (2.44.8), 54
*dos id est **uuidome** (2.55.27),[111] 60 ⊕docheatas (3.136.30), 67 ⊕ebratio
(2.366.33), 74/75 egero .g., egiro .g. (2.283.35), 79 elein .g. (2.318.12–15),
84 ⊕*epistola (*Gl. Steph.*, 3.447.12), 86 ⊕emorphor (→ eumorphos) .g.
(2.318.35–36), ?91 ⊕*epilentici (3.510.5, or Abolita/Abstrusa?), 93 ⊕epi-
dicta (2.307.45), 96 ⊕epicaustoriu⟨m⟩ (→ [h]ypocaustorium) (2.466.31–
32), 101 erchese (→ erchesai) .g. (2.314.62), 119 *pala **scoful** (3.195.62),
123 *papauer (lemma, 2.141.51), 135 *pegulium (→ pulegium) (3.16.45),
143 pensor qui penderator (→ ponderator) (2.153.19),[112] 150 petra .g. ly-
targicus (cf. 2.406.32, 2.360.49),[113] 154 pius (→ opoios) .g. (2.385.33), 155
pison (→ poieson) .g. (2.411.18), 160 *pinguido (→ pinguitudo 3.176.59),
161 *pistillus (2.224.51), 163 pipones (→ pepones) .g. (5.510.4), 174 polit-
ica (→ politicus) (2.412.12), 184 *prȩsto est (2.157.46, etc., but cf. Leiden
1.52), 188 *prassus (→ prassinus) **groeni** (3.174.8), 195 programma
(2.416.51), 207 proton (2.159.15), 217 *pugillum **handful** (2.164.30), 223
⊕telis .g. (2.327.18), 232 ⊕titulatio (2.342.40), 237b ⊕torton (→ ton ar-
ton) .g. pane (2.246.10), 246 ⊕*t[rifo]lia **claefrȩ** (3.360.1), 259 ⊕trien .g.

---

[110] Maybe eyeskip deriving from such Greek-Latin glosses as *dialerō* : deliro ("to
rave"), *dialepizōdendron* : delibro ("to strip") (*CGL* 2.272.18–19).

[111] Gallée gives "dos mui dome sāx" (Goetz: "dosmui"). But this is not a grammatical
gloss: "give to me," but a Hermeneumata Latin-Greek type: "dos *phērne prōix*," "dowry."
Werden is like Corpus D347 "dos: **wituma** uel **wetma**," with the seven minims of the editors' *mui* representing "i⟨d est⟩ uui" i.e, "dos id est **uuidome**." The OE interpretant has
been turned into its OHG counterpart.

[112] Lemma and gloss have exchanged places.

[113] Probably the residue of two separate Hermeneumata items.

(2.459.48–52), 264 ⊛*tubuli [.]emnę **theuta**[114] (2.338.42), 267 ⊛*turdus **staer**[115] (3.18.1), 268 ⊛tu (→ tou) .g. illa, 280 ⊛*uicus **uuic** (2.257.41).

There are elements unparalleled in the English gloss tradition, including items reflecting a topography of Rome and other original (non-gloss tradition) observations (12a, 17, 96, 129, 159, 173/177, 216, 227, 272, 275, 277, 282) referring to the shrines of saints in various cemeteries, church furniture, and architectural highlights. There is a stray Aldhelm item: 122 pastinare uineas plantare;[116] an item from (a glossed?) version of Ps.-Apuleius' *Herbarium*: 128 personacia **clifę** i⟨d⟩ est **clata. clatacrop** ("burdock"?);[117] several Bede items, 61 ⊛domuncula domus d[omicilium][118], 106 exarcus patricus (*De temp. rat.* 66, "patricium et exarchum"), 125a paneos (the Greek month of September, *ibid.* 14). These exiguous items, together with more than a dozen others that are not presently identifiable or are merely incoherent, will form the basis for another study.

The analysis of sources shows that the Werden A glossary is, like most alphabetical glossaries, a catchment of various sources, with a strong base in the Anglo-Saxon tradition stemming from the school of Canterbury, as exemplified by "Leiden" and by the alphabetized glossaries deriving from this tradition that was strong throughout the eighth century in areas subject to Anglo-Saxon missions and teaching. Men setting out for the formidable wildernesses of

---

[114] Gallée reads "tubuli *stemn* etheuta," a bit ingenuous since he indicates an emendation but does not indicate that letters are gone because of a hole. The photo shows '. . . emnę'. Goetz reads as Gallée without indicating any loss or emendation. Steinmeyer in his review of Gallée (*AfdAdL* 22 [1896]: 271) indicates the most probable reading, "laemnę theuta" ("clay pipes"), the second word being a Germanized version of OE *þeote*, "pipe."

[115] Turdus ("thrush") : **staer** ("starling"), is unique to Werden. The lemma may be a corruption or confusion of "sturnus," which would relate this item to Leiden 47.53 "sturnus **stęr**," Corpus 526 "stuirnus **stær**," which Lindsay sources to Hermeneumata. The English tradition is dominated by variants of "turdus **scric**" (Corpus T324), "shrike."

[116] This might be related to Corpus P13 "pastinare : **settan**," but Werden seems to reflect Aldhelm's wording directly: "et eruitis passionum radicibus fructiferos uirtutem surculos pastinare Christo plantante possimus" (*De uirg.*, Ehwald MGH AA 1.5.245.28).

[117] "Personacia" is burdock. In the Anglo-Saxon versions of the *Herbarium* **clate**, **geclyfia**, **clefia** gloss "Philantropos," goose-grass, clivers; "personacia" is glossed "**bete**" ("beet") probably wrongly (cf. de Vriend, EETS 286.84–85, 218–19).

[118] The last word is *diṁi* and so Goetz (his index has "diminutiue"); Gallée silently reads "dimidium," going over to the latter in his "Collation," 378. But it must stand for "domicilium," as in Bede, *De Orth.* (CCSL 123A.1 20.331) "domuncula : conclauium, domus domicilium; nidus auis." It is presented as two items in Vat. 1469: "Domuncula conclauium domus / Domiciliam nidus auis" (CGL 5.521.32–33).

Germany must have clutched their glossaries as talismans of Latinate culture. A forebear of Werden has incorporated many items from one or more Hermeneumata lists not part of the Leiden/Épinal-Erfurt/Corpus tradition, but from some Anglo-Saxon tradition, since so many still retain their vernacular glosses. These sources had doubtless settled into a pattern similar to the one in Werden A decades before it was copied.

However, it is interesting to note at least two glosses that seem to be clearly continental in origin which have nevertheless acquired Anglo-Saxon vernacular interpretations, suggesting activity of Anglo-Saxon scholars on the continent, perhaps close to the date of our manuscript and perhaps indicating nodes of compilation activity.[119] They probably originate much closer to the time of our manuscript, when the continuous compiling activities that gave birth to Werden A had moved to the continent.

There is a clearly Frankish-influenced gloss, with an English interpretant, vividly illustrating the intertextual and intercultural play of many glossary items: 53 "dilaturas **lybisnę** sax⟨onice⟩" ("delayers : bundles, amulets"). The lemma "dilaturas," (→ dilatores) "delayers," does not in any remote way match the gloss and neither does a similar word, *delatores*, "denouncers," although the confusion between *delator* and *dilator* "delayer" was sufficiently common that Isidore includes them in his "Differentiis" (PL 83.27). The Old English gloss "lybisnae" means "amulets" (charms made with magic potions). It is related to OE *lybb*, "poison," OLG *lubbe*, OHG *luppi*. It is found in Gothic, in the translation of Galatians 5:20, "lubjaleisei" for Greek *pharmakeía*. Steinmeyer[120] guessed that the lemma ought to be *ligaturas* "bound-up things, amulets," but it remained a guess, though the correct one, as it turns out. The OE gloss word occurs in English glosses with different lemmata: Corpus S569 "strenas **lybesne**," "signs, prognostics, omens" from an unknown source, and the EE O54 Corpus O43 items "obligamentum : *lyb*, *lybsn*" ("band, bond"). Lindsay thought this gloss derived from Orosius.

The source, however, is some Frankish penitential, as will be seen, and as continental penitentials do not begin to appear until the early eighth century, the gloss has to be from a post-Theodoran layer, perhaps though the mediation of the Bonifatian mission.[121] Our gloss is from a penitential in which the

---

[119] Background in W. Levison, *England and the Continent in the Eighth Century* (Oxford, 1946): see chap. 6 (132–73).

[120] *ZfdA* 33 (1889): 250.

[121] Boniface, *Sermo* VIII (PL. 89.859C): "Auguria et incantationes et ligaturas nolite exercere, nec illis credere, quia diabolica haec sunt" ("you must not use augury or charms or amulets, nor believe in them, because they are diabolical"; idem, *Epist.* 49 (PL 89.747A): "Dicunt quoque se uidisse ibi mulieres pagano ritu phylacteria, et ligaturas et in brachiis et cruribus ligatas habere et publice" ([referring to contemporary Roman customs] "They

phrase "ligaturas fecerit" was glossed correctly as "lybisnae": then in a sub-sequent copy or use the item containing the phrase was replaced by a differ-ent item occupying the same relative position in the text and containing the phrase "delaturas fecerit"; the latter ultimately goes back to the 73rd Canon of the Council of Elvira (305) which sanctions those who denounce Christians to the authorities.[122] Later, the gloss was mechanically copied over the new word in the same relative position: "delaturas fecit : lybisnae." The situation is exactly illustrated by two texts:

Burgundian Penitential (ca. 700–725), items 37–38:[123]

Si quis uirginem uel uiduam raptus fuerit, III ann. pen[e] cum pane et aqua ("if anyone rapes a virgin or a widow, three years penance on bread and water")

Si quis *delaturas fecerit* quod detestabile est superioris uersus sentenci-am accipiat. ("If anyone gives information [i.e. against Christians to the pagan authorities], which is abominable, he shall receive the sentence of the preceding item")

Merseburg Penitential (ca. 800), items 35–36:[124]

Si quis uiduam uel uirginem raptus fuerit, etc.

---

say . . . that they have seen there women with amulets and bracelets of heathen fashion on their arms and legs, offering them for sale to willing buyers" (tr. Ephraim Emerton, *The Letters of St. Boniface* [New York, 1973], 82).

[122] Concilium Eliberitanum, LXXIII: "Delator si quis extiterit fidelis, & per dela-tionem ejus aliquis fuerit proscriptus, vel interfectus, placuit, eum nec in fine accipere communionem": Mansi, *Sacrorum Conciliorum Collectio* (Florence, 1759, repr. Leipzig: H. Welter, 1901), 2:17. This scenario, in an entirely different connection, is suggested by John T. McNeill and Helena M. Gamer, *Medieval Handbooks of Penance* (New York, 1938), 277, n. 13.

[123] Brussels, Bibl. reg. Cod. Burgund. 8780–873 fol. 6r, ed. H. J. Schmitz, *Die Buss-bücher und das kanonische Bussverfahren nach handschriftlichen Quellen* (Düsseldorf, 1898), 322. Cf. items 33–34 in Bobbio Penitential (s. vii/viii), items 29–30 in Paris Peni-tential, Paris BN Lat. 7193, fol. 41r (s. vii), ed. Schmitz, Bussbücher, 325, 329. On the Frankish penitentials in general, see Rosamond Pierce (McKitterick), "The 'Frankish' Penitentials," in *The Materials, Sources and Methods of Ecclesiastical History*, ed. D. Baker, Studies in Church History 11 (Oxford, 1975), 31–39.

[124] Ed. Schmitz, *Bussbücher*, 1.362; cf. also the Vienna Penitential, Wiener Univ.-Bibl. 2225 (s. ix²), fol. 1, arts. 38–39, ed. *ibid.*, 353. The 36th Merseburg canon also appears as canon 40 in Haltigar's *Penitential* (ca. 830) (PL 105.722C) and with slightly different wording in Hrabanus's *Poenitentium Liber ad Otgarium* (PL 112.1417C), cap. 59.

Si quis *legatura fecerit* in erbas uel qualibet ingenio malo incantaberit et super Christianum ligaberit, scias eum fidem Dei amisse, III ann. pen. I ex his in pane et aqua. ("If anyone makes herbal amulets or casts spells with evil intent and ties them on a Christian know he has lost the Christian faith, three years penance, one on bread and water").

What apparently happened is that an excerptor taking glosses from an intermediate version which contained both the *Burgundian Penitential* item 38 and the *Merseburg* item 36 skipped from *ligaturas* to *delaturas* in writing the lemma, having the gloss "amulet" already firmly in mind. This is probably, in a surprisingly "writerly" context, an instance of the oral mindset of early medieval scribes, who wrote what they said as much as what they saw.[125]

In editing an entry such as this one has to account for the floating nature of the text. Although it would be easy to emend to "ligaturas : *lybesnae*," given the history of the entry this would be a misrepresentation. I believe the manuscript reading should be left, with the history of the gloss being featured on the page; we are sure what the source of the lemma was (since the "erroneous" form *dilatores/dilaturas* must have been taken directly from a form in a manuscript of a penitential and thus constitutes the "original" of this item), yet we also know that this "original" is itself a deviation from the original that produced the interpretation: thus I would choose to present the edited entry in this style:

> dilaturas (→ delatores; *aliter* ligaturas) : *lybesnae* sax⟨onice⟩

Item 46 is unparalleled, but revealing: "discarruta (→ discarica) solue carrum idest **ondhlelth**" (OE **onhlideð** "unload"), "unload a wagon". This appears to be from the prose *Life of St. Médard* written ca. 600;[126] St. Médard's cult was restricted to northwest Francia and suggests someone in that area. Nevertheless it was someone who glossed in Anglo-Saxon; moreover, the OE gloss is accurate ("unload"), whereas the Latin is not ("unhitch"), suggesting that the Latin gloss has been added later and that this item was added at a time when probably all the items still had their English *interpretamenta*. Perhaps,

---

[125] A case I have made elsewhere and which is newly argued with great particularity by Roy M. Liuzza, "Scribal Habit: The Evidence of the Old English Gospels," in *Rewriting Old English in the Twelfth Century*, ed. Mary Swan and Elaine M. Treharne (Cambridge, 2000), 143–65, at 145–47.

[126] "et data oratione discarecantes quae tulerant laxati pergunt itinera" (ed. B. Kursch, MGH AA 4.2.70); "and [Médard] having prayed for the unloading, those (carts) they brought were lightened and they resumed their journey."

given the source, at this point the compilation was in the care of an English person, perhaps at Corbie itself not very long before our copy was made.[127]

The Leiden scribe concluded his work, "Sicut inueni scripsi ne reputes scriptori," "as I found it I wrote it, don't blame the scribe." Scribes were well aware of the pitfalls of their work, which could not be checked against better exemplars; moreover, their work was further conditioned by space and material limitations, the state of a copyist's understanding of words and things, and sheer competence or lack thereof. Beyond all this, the glossary traditions belong to great interrelated families, with various nodes of relatively original activity discernable and unevenly acted out in dozens of individual copies. What an edition of a glossary has to find is a way of indicating and presenting its contingent and floating nature without at the same time relegating everything on the page to the category of "error" or "corruption." The problem is to discern the use-value of glosses in their specific historical situations, to explain what produced the forms that we see. Errors and miswritings must be taken account of, without effacing the glossators' and scribes' activities, sources, knowledges, desires, ignorance, and mistakes — for that is the whole calculus of an early medieval glossary. Editorial controversies in recent times have revolved around "conservative" versus "constructive," that is, between those who would save the manuscript readings at all cost and those who would emend according to stemmatic evidence and/or contextually-derived conjecture. The editing of glosses demands that both approaches be adopted, a conservative presentation keeping the evidence and problems on display, while comparative, stemmatic, and conjectural work attempts to elucidate the scribal performance and show the cultural and cognitive processes which have fed into it.

Bibliography

Barker-Benfield, B. C. "The Werden 'Heptateuch'." *Anglo-Saxon England* 20 (1991): 42–64.

Barwick, Karl. "Paul Wessner." *Jahresbericht über die Fortschritte der klassischen Altertumwissenschaft*, 4 Abt.: Nekrologe, 62 (1935): 18–34.

---

[127] See David Ganz, *Corbie in the Carolingian Renaissance* (Sigmaringen, 1990), 41 ff. on the presence of Insular script there and the consequent developments. Ganz thinks Abbot Grimo (before 744) had close ties to Boniface (20) and there is evidence of English influence from earliest times (19); Alcuin donated books, and Corbie books went to Liudger and hence to Werden (24). In the first years of Louis the Pious the Saxon daughter house, Corvey, was founded.

Bischoff, Bernhard, Mildred Budny, Geoffrey Harlow, M.B. Parkes, and J.D. Pheifer. *The Épinal, Werden, and Corpus Glossaries.* EEMF 22. Copenhagen, 1988.

——, and Michael Lapidge, eds. *Biblical Commentaries from the Canterbury School of Theodore and Hadrian.* CSASE 10. Cambridge, 1994.

Crecelius, W. "Ein Düsseldorfer Statiusfragment." *Rheinisches Museum für Philologie* n.f. 32 (1877): 632–36.

de Vriend, Hubert Jan, ed. *The Old English Herbarium and Medicina de Quadrupedibus.* EETS, o.s. 286. London, 1984.

Deycks, Ferdinand. *Fragmenta Veteris Glossarii e Cod. Werthinensi S. XI, Index lectionum.* Academica Aschendorffiana. Münster, [1854/1855].

Dionisotti, A. C. "Greek Grammars and Dictionaries in Carolingian Europe." In *The Sacred Nectar of the Greeks: The Study of Greek in the West in the Early Middle Ages*, ed. Michael W. Herren and Shirley Ann Brown, 1–56. London, 1988.

Drögereit, Richard. *Werden und der Heliand: Studien zur Kulturgeschichte der Abtei Werden und zur Herkunft des Heliand.* Essen, 1951.

Emerton, Ephraim, tr. *The Letters of St. Boniface.* New York, 1973.

Eusebius. *Eusebius Werke*, ed. E. Schwartz and T. Mommsen. 3 vols. Leipzig, 1903–1909.

Freise, Eckhard. "Von Mimigernaford zum *monasterium* Liudgers." In Thomas Küster and Franz-Josef Jakobi, eds., *Geschichte der Stadt Münster.* 1:1–51. Münster, 1993.

Gallée, J. H., ed. *Altsaechsische Sprachdenkmaeler.* Leiden, 1894.

——, ed. *Altsaechsische Sprachdenkmaeler, Facsimilesammlung.* Leiden, 1895.

Goetz, Georg, ed. *De glossariorum Latinorum origine et fatis.* Corpus Glossariorum Latinorum 1. Leipzig, 1923.

——, ed. *Placidus liber glossarum: Glossaria reliqua.* Corpus Glossariorum Latinorum 5. Leipzig, 1894.

——, and Gotthold Gundermann, eds. *Glossae Latinograecae et Graeco-latinae.* Corpus glossariorum Latinorum 2. Leipzig, 1888.

Hessels, J. H. *A Late Eighth Century Latin-Anglo-Saxon Glossary.* Cambridge, 1906.

Isidore of Seville. *Isidori Hispalensis episcopi Etymologiarum sive Originum libri XX*, ed. W. M. Lindsay. 2 vols. Oxford, 1911.

James, M. R. *A Descriptive Catalogue of the Manuscripts in the Library of Peterhouse.* Cambridge, 1899.

Karpp, Gerhard. "Mittelalterliche Handschriften und Inkunabeln in der Universitätsbibliothek Düsseldorf." *Codices Manuscripti* 7 (1981): 4–13.

Ker, N. R. *Catalogue of Manuscripts Containing Anglo-Saxon.* Oxford, 1957.

Kramer, Johannes, ed. *Glossaria Bilinguia Altera (C. Gloss. Biling. II).* Archiv für Papyrusforschung und verwandte Gebiete Beiheft 8. Munich/Leipzig, 2001.

Krämer, Sigrid. *Handschriftenerbe des deutschen Mittelalters, 2: Köln-Zyfflich.* Mittelalterliche Bibliothekskataloge: Deutschlands und der Schweiz, Ergänzungsband 1. Munich, 1989.

Lapidge, Michael. "An Isidorian Epitome from Early Anglo-Saxon England." *Romanobarbarica* 10 (1988–1989): 445–83.

———. "Old English Glossography: The Latin Context." In *Anglo-Saxon Glossography*, ed. R. Derolez, 45–47. Brussels, 1992; repr. in idem, *Anglo-Latin Literature 600–899*, 169–81. London, 1986.

Levison, Wilhelm. *England and the Continent in the Eighth Century.* Oxford, 1946.

Lindsay, W. M. "The 'Abolita' Glossary (Vat. Lat. 3321)." *Journal of Philology* 34 (1916): 267–82, repr. in idem, *Studies in Early Mediaeval Latin Glossaries*, ed. Michael Lapidge. Aldershot, 1996.

———. "The Abstrusa Glossary and the Liber Glossarum," *Classical Quarterly* 11 (1917): 119–131, repr. in idem. *Studies in Early Mediaeval Latin Glossaries*, ed. Lapidge.

———. *The Corpus Glossary.* Cambridge, 1921.

———. *The Corpus, Épinal, Erfurt and Leyden Glossaries.* Publications of the Philological Society 7. Oxford, 1921; repr. in idem. *Studies in Early Mediaeval Latin Glossaries,* ed. Lapidge.

Loewe, Gustav. *Prodromus Corporis Glossariorum Latinorum.* Leipzig, 1876.

Luizza, Roy M. "Scribal Habit: The Evidence of the Old English Gospels." In *Rewriting Old English in the Twelfth Century,* ed. Mary Swan and Elaine M. Treharne, 143–65. Cambridge, 2000.

Mansi, G. D., ed. *Sacrorum Conciliorum Collectio.* Vol. 2. Florence, 1759; repr. Leipzig, 1901.

McKitterick, Rosamond (see Pierce)

McNeill, John T. and Helena M. Gamer. *Medieval Handbooks of Penance.* Records of Civilization 29. New York, 1938.

Pheifer, J. D. "The Canterbury Bible Glosses: Facts and Problems." In *Archbishop Theodore: Commemorative Studies on his Life and Influence,* ed. M. Lapidge, 281–333. CSASE 11. Cambridge, 1995.

———. *Old English Glosses in the Épinal-Erfurt Glossary.* Oxford, 1974.

Pierce, Rosamond (McKitterick). "The 'Frankish' Penitentials." In *The Materials, Sources, and Methods of Ecclesiastical History*, ed. D. Baker, 31–39. Studies in Church History 11. Oxford, 1975.

[Pseudo-Jerome], *Vita di Antonio*, ed. G. J. M. Bartelink. Milan, 1974.

Schmitz, H. J., ed. *Die Bussbücher und das kanonische Bussverfahren nach handschriftlichen Quellen.* 2 vols. Düsseldorf, 1883–1898.

Souter, A. *A Glossary of Later Latin to 600 A.D.* Oxford, 1959.

Steinmeyer, Elias. "Lateinische und altenglische Glossen." *ZfdA* n.f. 21 (1888): 242–51.

———. Review of Gallée, *Altsaechsische Sprachdenkmaeler. Anzeiger für deutsches Altertum und deutsche Litteratur* 22 (1896): 266–80.

Stüwer, Wilhelm. *Das Erzbistum Köln 3: Die Reichsabtei Werden an der Ruhr.* Germania Sacra n.f. 12, Die Bistümer der Kirchenprovinz Köln. Berlin, 1980.

Sweet, Henry. *The Oldest English Texts.* EETS o.s. 45. London, 1885.

Wordsworth, J., and H. J. White. *Nouum Testamentum D.N.I.C. Latine.* 2nd ed. Oxford, 1913–1941.

Wright, Thomas, and R. P. Wülcker. *Anglo-Saxon and Old English Vocabularies.* 2nd ed. London, 1884; repr. Darmstadt, 1968.

Appendix: Quiration Diagram

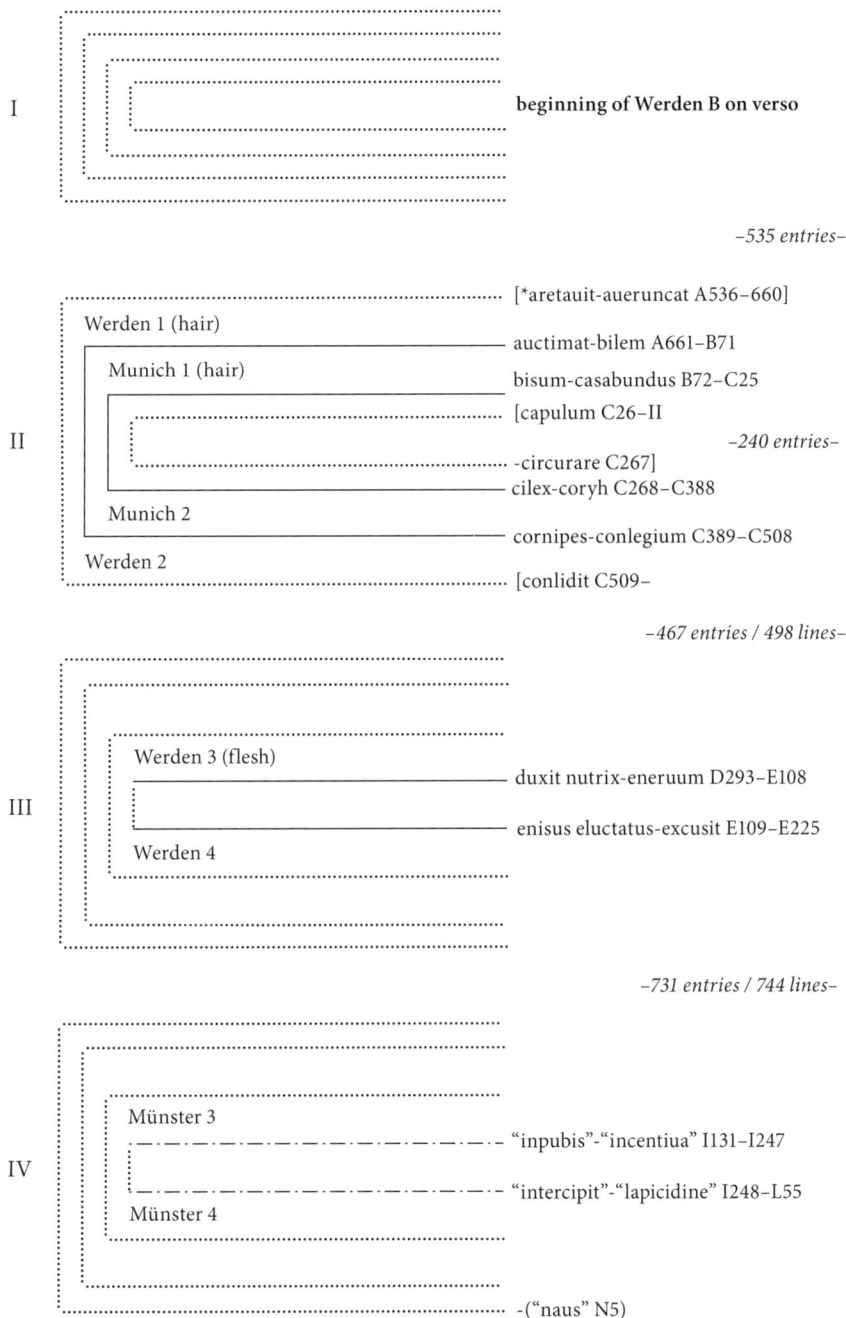

I

beginning of Werden B on verso

–535 entries–

[*aretauit-aueruncat A536–660]

Werden 1 (hair)

auctimat-bilem A661–B71

Munich 1 (hair)

bisum-casabundus B72–C25

[capulum C26–II

II

–240 entries–

-circurare C267]

cilex-coryh C268–C388

Munich 2

cornipes-conlegium C389–C508

Werden 2

[conlidit C509–

–467 entries / 498 lines–

Werden 3 (flesh)

duxit nutrix-eneruum D293–E108

III

enisus eluctatus-excusit E109–E225

Werden 4

–731 entries / 744 lines–

Münster 3

"inpubis"-"incentiua" I131–I247

IV

"intercipit"-"lapicidine" I248–L55

Münster 4

-("naus" N5)

V

VI

VII

VIII

Erfurt 3843 lines / Werden IV 6–7, V–VIII, IX 1–3 = 3844 lines

IX

Werden 5 (hair)

Munich 3 (hair)

— saba pappa-seueritas S38–S151

— serio-stuprum S152–S274

— stragulat-tefore S275–T31

Munich 4

— testudo-trophetum T32–T144

Werden 6

[tropus- T144–

255 entries -zozum Z6] *(end of Werden B on verso)*

[leaf blank or with filler text]

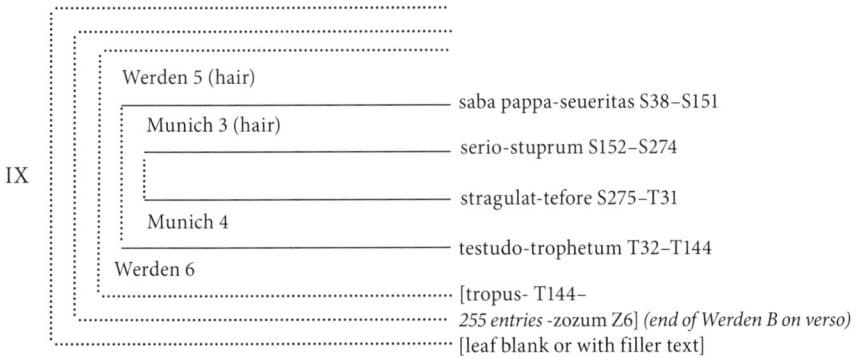

Düsseldorf Quire of 8

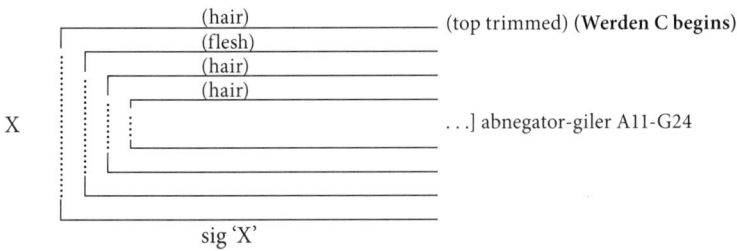

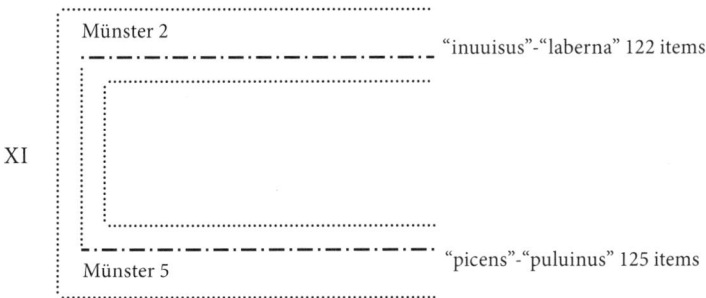

X

(hair)   — (top trimmed) **(Werden C begins)**
(flesh)
(hair)
(hair)

...] abnegator-giler A11–G24

sig 'X'

XI

Münster 2

"inuuisus"-"laberna" 122 items

"picens"-"puluinus" 125 items

Münster 5

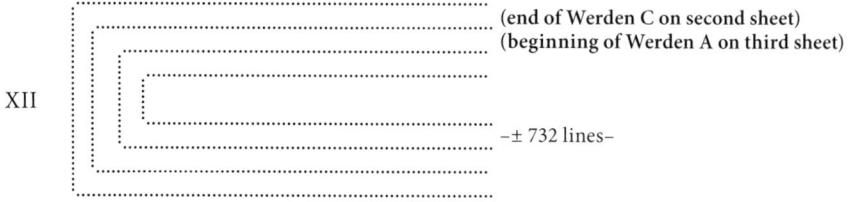

XII

(end of Werden C on second sheet)
(beginning of Werden A on third sheet)

−± 732 lines−

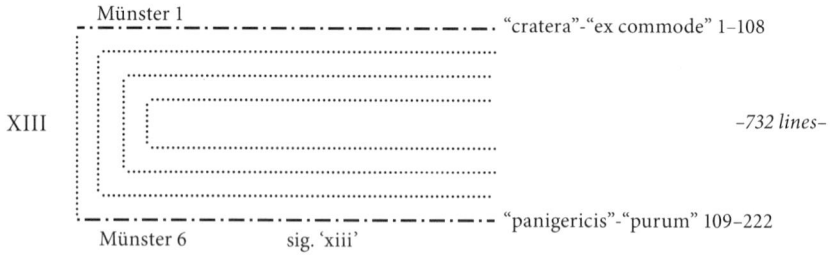

XIII

Münster 1

"cratera"-"ex commode" 1–108

−732 lines−

Münster 6   sig. 'xiii'

"panigericis"-"purum" 109–222

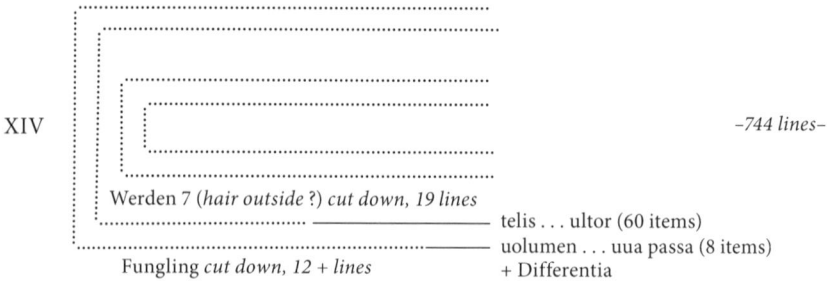

XIV

−744 lines−

Werden 7 (hair outside ?) cut down, 19 lines

telis . . . ultor (60 items)

Fungling cut down, 12 + lines

uolumen . . . uua passa (8 items)
+ Differentia

Odd Couples in Ælfric's *Julian and Basilissa* in British Library Cotton, MS. Otho B. x[1]

Kevin Kiernan

The unusual marriage of Julian and Basilissa features two saints-to-be who vow on their wedding night in their wedding bed not to consummate their marriage.[2] Their connubial plans extol chastity, Old English *clænnysse*, ensuring immediate female sanctity for Basilissa[3] and a more perfect union for the couple in heaven by the end of the story. Julian superfluously earns his sainthood through more active, manly virtues, including a violent martyrdom by beheading. Notwithstanding its chaste setting, the fragmentary, appropriately headless, version of this story semi-saved in British Library Cotton MS. Otho B. x has led to a productive and even reproductive marriage of text and technology. I use the term "technology" in a broad sense, alluding to Anglo-Saxon writing or copying, modern printing, medieval and modern textual encoding, early-modern and modern bookbinding and rebinding of burnt manuscript fragments in individual paper frames, as well as the more obvious modern technology of computers and digital cameras with all their coupled hardware and software. My goal, to illustrate how medieval and

---

[1] My continuing work on this badly damaged codex is part of an interdisciplinary project, "The Digital Atheneum: New Techniques for Restoring, Searching, and Editing Humanities Collections," supported by the National Science Foundation, IBM's Shared University Research grant, the British Library, and the University of Kentucky's Center for Computational Sciences. The principal investigators are Kevin Kiernan for the humanities (with the invaluable assistance of Linda Cantara) and Brent Seales and James Griffioen in Computer Science.

[2] The "Passion of St. Julian and His Wife Basilissa" is edited by Walter W. Skeat, *Ælfric's Lives of Saints . . . edited from British Museum Cott. MS. Julius E. vii with variants from other manuscripts*, EETS o.s. 76, 82 (London, 1881–1900),1: 90–115.

[3] As Clare Lees observes, "the transformation of sexuality into the gift of chastity is the prime component of the female saint's life" in "Chastity and Charity: Ælfric, Women, and the Female Saints," in eadem, *Tradition and Belief: Religious Writing in Late Anglo-Saxon England*, Medieval Cultures 19 (Minneapolis, 1999), 133–53, at 147.

modern technology can unite to help editors deliver newly born Old English texts, may seem remote from the lives of saints. Yet in the end these burnt fragments of manuscripts can rejoice with the martyrs and say, *We ferdon þurh fyr 7 wæter, 7 þu us læddest on celincge.*[4]

Cotton Otho B. x was grievously injured in the disastrous fire in 1731 that destroyed or seriously damaged nearly one-quarter of the magnificent collection of over a thousand manuscripts amassed by Sir Robert Cotton following the dissolution of monasteries in the sixteenth century.[5] Very little of the *Passion of St. Julian and His Wife Basilissa* survived. Walter Skeat, its modern editor, wrongly thought that only one folio had made it through the fire. His edition is based on the complete manuscript of Ælfric's *Lives of Saints* preserved in British Library MS. Cotton Julius E. vii, but he collated this fragment with his edition (lines 27–91) and recorded nine variant readings from "Otho B. x. fol. 7 (*as now numbered*)" (his italics, p. 92). To help scholars find their way among the extremely disordered fragments of Cotton Otho B. x,[6] I have devised a "virtual" foliation, which keeps track of the correct order of the surviving bits of leaves, but also gives the official British Library foliation number in parentheses. In this case, fol. 10(7) means that the leaf is numbered 7 in the British Library foliation of the disordered manuscript, but that it should come tenth in the correct order of the surviving leaves. The line references provide both folio lines and Skeat's verse lines. Thus fol. 10(7)r3:29 identifies a reading on line 3 of the recto, which corresponds to Skeat's verse line 29.[7] As we shall see, without a special foliation and dual lineation, it would be extremely difficult for anyone to keep track of the other surviving portions of this text.

Figure 4.1 provides a greatly reduced overview of fol. 10(7), recto and verso, as it is now framed in its nineteenth-century paper binding. Far superior to the limitations of print facsimiles, an electronic facsimile allows one

---

[4] "We have passed through fire and water, and thou hast led us into a cool place," line 340.

[5] Andrew Prescott, "'Their Present Miserable State of Cremation': The Restoration of the Cotton Library," in *Sir Robert Cotton as Collector: Essays on an Early Stuart Courtier and His Legacy*, ed. C. J. Wright (London, 1997), 391–454.

[6] To read the surviving leaves in the correct order using the official British Library foliation, one must begin with fol. 60v, then 36v, then 49, 1, 3, 5, 4, 50, and 6, before getting to the misplaced folios of *Julian and Basilissa*. There is another misplaced leaf following BL fol. 4 at the Bodleian Library, Oxford.

[7] For a discussion of this virtual foliation and the disorder of the manuscript that makes it essential, see Kevin Kiernan, W. Brent Seales, and James Griffioen, "The Reappearances of St. Basil the Great in British Library MS Cotton Otho B. x," *Computers and the Humanities* 36 (2002): 7–26.

Figure 4.1: fol. 10(7), recto and verso

to study a dynamic image of the folio in detail at high resolution, in full color, enhanced by ultraviolet, and much enlarged.[8] At its normal size one is able to see where Sir Frederic Madden identified the text in pencil as "SS Julianus and Basilissa" in the upper-left frame, recto. As the shape of the burnt leaf indicates, the greatest losses of text are concentrated in the beginning of the first nine lines on the recto, and the ends of the first nine lines on the verso.

A substantial part of the folio survives and most of what survives is relatively easy to read, except for sections obscured by gauze and tape, which were somewhat recklessly used, after Skeat's time, to forestall further deterioration. These obscure sections are made more legible with ultraviolet fluorescence (fig. 4.2).

In the following transcription the surviving text is in **bold**, with Skeat's restorations bracketed in *italics*. The folio boundaries for lines 1–9 are conjectural.

> *7 him þa begeaten.*] **Þa wurd**[*on gegearcode þa*
> *gyftu æfter gewunan*] **7 hi butu beco**[*man on anum*
> *bedde tosomne.*] **Hwæt þa iulianus** [*hine georne*
> *gebæd to ðam hælende*] **criste þæt he** [*hi*]**ne gehælde** [*wið*

---

[8] All images from Otho B. x were digitized by David French and Kevin Kiernan for the Digital Atheneum project and are used with permission of The British Library Board.

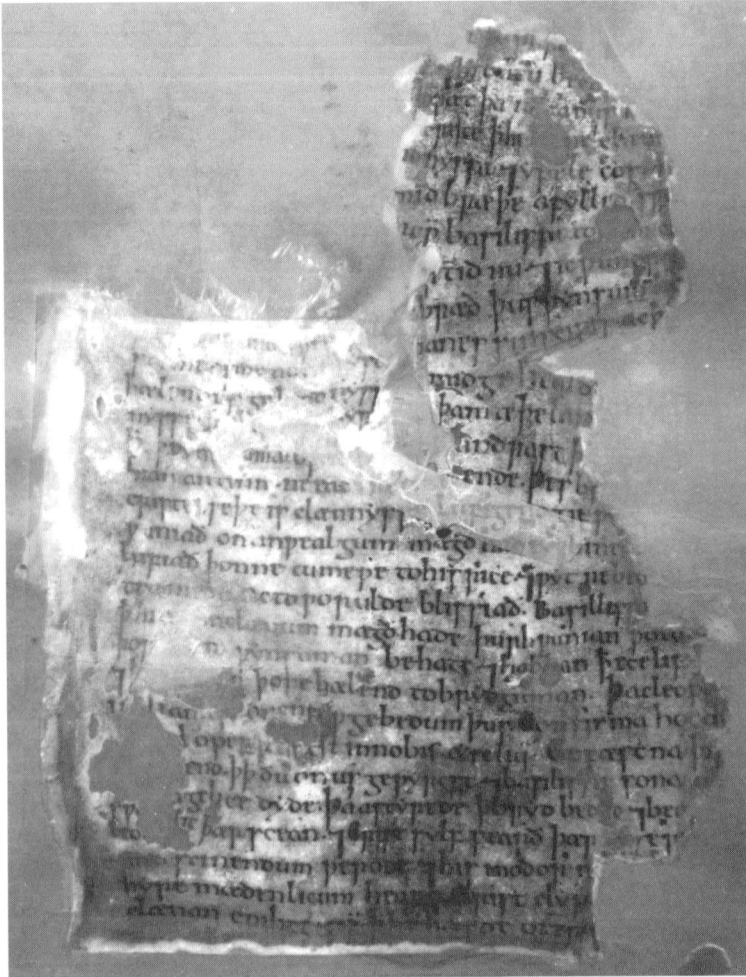

Figure 4.2: fol. 10(7) recto, enhanced by ultraviolet

5   *ealla onten*]dnyssa 7 yfele costn[*unga. Ða wearð*
      þæt brydbed] mid bræþe afylled swy[*lce þær lægon*
      lilie 7 rose. Ð]a cwæð basilissa to [*þa*]m c[*lænan*
      brydguman, Hit is winte]rtid nu 7 ic wundrie
      þearle hwanon] þes [*wyrt*]bræð þus wynsumlic[*e*
10   steme 7 me nu ne lyst nanes sinscipes. ac þ[*æs*
      hælendes geþeodnyss[*e*] mid geheald[*enre clen-*

nysse. Iul[*ianus and*]wyr[*de*] þam æðelan [*mædene*
Þes wynsuma bræð þ[*e ðu w*]undrast þ[*earle næfð*
nan anginn . ne eac n[*ænne*] ende. Þes br[*æð is of*
15 criste seþe is clænnysse lufigend gif wy[*t þurh-*
wuniað on anwealgum mægðhade. 7 hine [*clænlice*
lufiað þonne cume we to his rice. 7 wyt ne beo[*ð to-*
twæmede ac a to worulde blyssiað. Basilissa [*cwæð*
þæt heo on clænum mægðhade þurhwunian wolde
20 for [*ða*]m wynsuman behate 7 habban þæt éce lif
7 þone hælend to brydguman. Þa cleopo[*de*
Iulianus on cneowgebedum þus. Confirma hoc d[*eus*
quo]d operatus est in nobis et reliqua. Gefæstna þis
hæl]end. þæt þæt ðu on ús gewyrcst. 7 basilissa sona
25 swa gelice dyde. Þa astyrede þæt brydbedd 7 beor[*ht*
leoht þær scéan. 7 Crist sylf wearð þær gesew[*en*
mid scinendum werode. 7 his modor m[*aria mid*
hyre mædenlicum heape. Crist clyp[*ode þa to ðam*
clænan cnihte 7 cwæð þæt he hæfde ofers[*wiðod*

For the recto Skeat in his collation records only five variants, none of which are scribal blunders, and two are arguably superior to the readings in Cotton Julius E. vii. The five variant readings Skeat notes are *anwealgum* for *ansundum* r16:43; *we* for *wit* r17:44; *wyt* for *wit* r17:45; the omission of *a* r17:45; and the expansion of the phrase, *crist wearð*, to *crist sylf wearð þær* r26:54.

Although *ansund*, "sound, entire, unhurt," appears often in his writings, it is plausible that Ælfric, in keeping with the alliterative style of this text, here used *anwealg* (i.e., *onwealg*), "sound, uninjured, uncorrupted": *gif wyt þurh-wuniað on anwealgum mægðhade.*[9] The use of *we*, "we," for *wit*, "we two" is unremarkable (Ælfric often uses both), as is the spelling variation, characteristic of both manuscripts, of *y* for *i* in *wit*. The omitted *a*, "ever," is almost certainly a mistake, because Ælfric frequently uses *a to worulde*, but *a* is actually redundant in the phrase *to worulde*, "for ever." The most significant variant reading is *crist sylf wearð þær* [*gesewen*], which explicitly states that "Christ himself was [seen] there," rather than the more ambiguous *crist wearð* [*gesewen*], which Skeat translates, "Christ was [visible]." Skeat fails to note 15 additional variant readings on 10(7) recto: *beco*[*mon*? (*beco-*, not *co-*, follows *butu*) for *coman*

---

[9] For *anwealg* in reference to chastity, see Bosworth-Toller under *onwealh* ii. The Toronto *Dictionary of Old English* cites the Julius E. vii reading from *Julian & Basilissa* for *ansund, onsund*, "whole, sound, having integrity," in its figurative sense, b.ii, "of virginity, chastity: uncorrupted, unblemished, immaculate."

r2:28; *ontendnyssa* (partitive genitive plural) for *ontendnysse* r5:31; *bræþe* for *bræðe* r6:32; *sinscipes* for *synscipes* r10:37; *clen]nysse* for *clennisse* r11–12:38; *wynsuma* (weak masculine nominative singular) for *wynsuman* r13:40; *anginn* for *angin* r14:41; *ende* for *ænde* r14:41; *seþe* for *seðe* r15:42; *wyt* for *wit* (again) r15:43; *þone* for *ðone* r21:48; *cleopode* for *clypode* r21:49; *þus* for *ðus* r22:49; *brydbedd* for *brydbed* r25:53; and *modor* for *modur* r27:55.

As is usually true of the fire-damaged Cotton manuscripts that Henry Gough inlaid, the paper frames cover bits of the text along the damaged edges of the fol. 10(7) verso (fig. 4.3), and the use of fiber-optic backlighting will reveal additional covered readings.

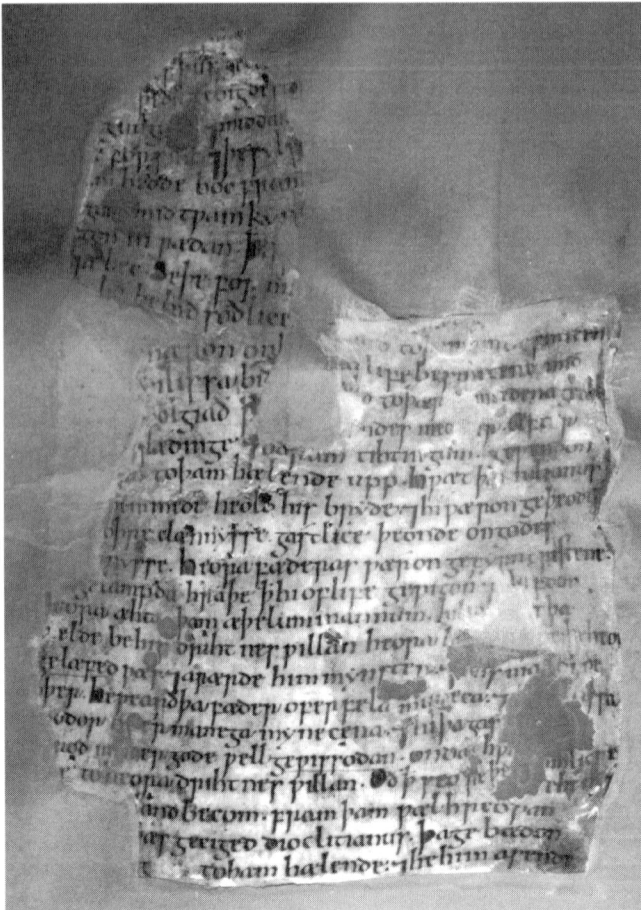

Figure 4.3: fol. 10(7) verso, enhanced by ultraviolet

In the following transcription of fol. 10(7) verso the surviving text is in **bold**, with Skeat's restorations bracketed in *italics*. The folio boundaries for lines 1–9 are still of course conjectural.

    woruldlice gælsan 7 þone g]**ram**[*lican feond. Of Marian*
    werode wæ]**s þus gec**[*lypod, Eadig eart þu Basilissa*
    forþan] **þe ðu gebigdest** [*þin mod to halwendum*
    myne]**gungu**[*m*] **7 middan**[*eardlice swæsnysse*
5   *mid eall*]**e forsihst 7 þe sylf**[*e gearcost to wuldre. Þa*
    com to ða]**m bedde boc fram** [*þam Hælende. 7 twegen*
    his hal]**gan mid twam kyn**[*ehelmum arærdan hi þa*
    upp 7 he]**ton hi rædan. Þa r**[*ædde Iulianus þas*
    word on þæ]**re bec. Se þe for mi**[*nre lufe middan*]**ear**[*d*
10 *fors*]**yhð he bið soðlice** [*ge*]**teald to þam unbesmiten**[*um*
    halgum, þe] **næran on h**[*eo*]**ra life besmitene mid**
    wifum. Ba]**silissa bið** [*get*]**eald to þær**[*a*] **mædena getæ**[*le*
    þe Marian] **folgiað þ**[*æs hæl*]**endes meder. Æfter**
    þissere] **rædinge 7 oðrum tihtingum. gewendon**
15 *þa hal*]**gan to þam hælende upp. Hwæt þa iulianus**
    unge]**wæmmede heold his bryde. 7 hi wæron geðeodd**[*e*
    mid s]**oþre clænnysse gástlice þeonde on godes**
    gewyt]**nysse . Heora fæderas wǽron gefyrn cristene .**
    hit] **gelamp ða hraþe þæt hi of life gewitan 7 læfdon**
20 *h*]**eora æhta þam æþelum mannum . Iulia**[*nu*]**s þa**
    dælde be his drihtnes willan heora l[*and a*]**re . þe heo**[*m*
    gelæfed wæs . 7 arærde him mynster . 7 his mædene
    o]**þer . He wearð þa fæder ofer fela muneca . 7** [*Basi*]**lissa**
    m]**odor ofer manega mynecena . 7 hi þa gas**[*tlican*
25 *we*]**rod under gode well gewissodan . on dæ**[*g*]**hwamlicre**
    lar]**e to heora drihtnes willan . Oð þæt seo reþe ehtnys**[*se*
    on Egypta] **lande becom . fram þam wælhreowan**
    casere þe w]**æs geciged dioclytianus . Þa gebædon**
    þa hal]**gan hi to þam hælende . 7 he him asende**

For the text on the verso Skeat notes only four variants, *hraþe* for *raðe* v19:79, *willan* for *wyssunga* v21:81, *fela* for *fæla* v23:84, and *well* v25:86, which the Julius scribe omits. Skeat overlooks nineteen additional variant readings on 10(7) verso: *ðu* for *þu* v3:60; *gebigdest* for *gebygdest* v3:60; *Þa* for *Ða* v8:67; *fors*]*yhð* for *forsihð* v10:68; *s*]*oþre* for *soðre* v17:76; *ða* for *þa* v19:79; *gewitan* for *gewytan* v19:79; *æþelum* for *æðelum* v20:80; *heo*[*m* for *him* v21:82; *gelæfed* for *læfed* v22:82; *oþer* for *oðer* v23:83; *gewissodan* for *gewyssodon* v25:86; *drihtnes* for *dryhtnes* v26:87; *willan* for *wyllan* v26:87; *Oð* for *oþ* v26:88; *seo* for *se* (*ehtnys* is feminine nominative singular, not masculine) v26:88; *reþe* for *reðe* v26:88; *ehtnys[se* for *æhtnysse* v26:88; *wælhreowan* for *welhreowan* v27:89. In short, Skeat lists only nine of the forty-three variant readings on folio 10(7).

To make the results of any and all collations accessible for later investigation and analysis, an editor of an electronic edition must encode or tag everything (variant readings, pointing or punctuation, abbreviations, erasures, corrections, ultraviolet enhancements, descriptions of damage and misplacements, and any other physical features of the manuscript record). Comprehensive tagging or encoding in conformance with what is called a Document Type Declaration (or DTD)[10] paves the way for later interactive searching and analysis by scholars who may hold diametrically opposite views of the evidence. Basically, in order to help, a computer must have some encoded way to locate the things we want it to find. A traditional scholarly edition collects textual data and normally displays it in textual notes, as Skeat does here. But Skeat's notes do not make it possible to discover, for example, how often the Otho scribe used *y* where the Julius scribe used *i* in any or all words, or where the scribal pointing in both manuscripts coincides. It is customary in Old English editions to pass over many minor spelling variants, such as *y* for *i* or *þ* for *ð*, from collations with other manuscripts, as Skeat may have done deliberately here, and to ignore such manuscript features as scribal pointing in another manuscript, as Skeat does, and even scribal abbreviations, which Skeat however records in his text by means of italics.

Exhaustive textual details, however, are prohibitively expensive and drastically clutter traditional print editions. In an electronic edition, on the other hand, it is advantageous to tag or encode exhaustively, because textual details cost nothing but the editor's time and trouble, and there is no need to display the results unless someone is actually looking for them. For example, it is a simple matter to encode scribal pointing as metrical or syntactic or both, which would allow scholars to weigh the manuscript evidence for each kind of pointing. Then, with the aid of electronic search facilities, users of the edition will be able to fashion their own individual investigations, looking in a moment, for example, for differences in scribal practice in the use of *thorn* and *eth* or *i* and *y*, for the use or non-use of abbreviations, for different spellings of the same words in the same or different manuscripts, for Old English synonyms like *ansund* and *anwealg* meaning "sound" and "uncorrupted," or for adjectives modifying *mægðhad*, "virginity, maidenhood."

---

[10] I will refrain in this essay from discussing in detail or resorting to the terminology of the XML technologies we are using. As Ælfric says at one point in *Julian and Basilissa, Þeos race is swiðe langsum fullice to gereccenne, / ac we hit sæcgað eow on þa scortostan wisan*, "This story is very tedious, to tell it all, but we tell it you in the briefest way" (lines 139–140).

An edition of the fragmentary text of *Julian and Basilissa*, consisting of only parts of three folios of an original seven,[11] is part of a larger project to provide an electronic edition of what survives from Otho B. x as a collection. The use of fragments, usually reduced by collation to a few footnotes as in Skeat's edition, as a primary text has the effect of reversing the goals of a traditional standard edition like Skeat's. The fragment becomes the main text, using Skeat's text to restore lost sections, but relegating his text to variant readings wherever text survives in the fragment. In order to understand the fragments in their original context, it is necessary to create a full glossary of the new composite of Skeat's text with the fragments embedded to replace it wherever readings survive. To create a readable and ultimately searchable electronic edition of sometimes almost completely illegible manuscript fragments, I first collated the readable bits of text with Skeat's online edition available through the *Complete Corpus of Old English in Electronic Form*.[12] Using specialized mark-up or tags conforming to a "DTD" designed for damaged manuscripts from the Cotton Library, I next make transcripts of the fragments as the primary texts, and encode Skeat's text as variant readings. The first stage of tagging, then, separates the text into folios and folio lines, while tagging as well Skeat's verse lines. Using style sheets designed for the purpose, I can then transform the encoded files into Hypertext Markup Language (HTML), and use a web browser to display both transcripts and modern editions from the same tagged document. Graphical interfaces we are developing will allow users to integrate images, transcripts, modern editions, comprehensive glossaries, editorial annotations, ancillary materials, and search facilities to provide unprecedented access to these previously unedited texts.

After the first stage of tagging has identified the folios and folio-lines, tagged the verse lines of Skeat's edition, integrated any readings that differ from Skeat's text, tagged the latter as variants, and added the Cotton Library DTD, I use this "lightly tagged" document to generate an exhaustive word

---

[11] Approximately a page (26 lines of verse) is missing before fol. 10(7). As Wanley indicated, *Julian and Basilissa* began with its rubric on a verso, following the *Passio Sancti Mauri Abbatis*, a text totally destroyed in the fire of 1731. Two folios are missing between 10(7) and 11(67r), and one and a half following 12(67Lv)r. With 101 verse lines missing at the end, *Julian and Basilissa* probably ended a few lines into the verso, followed by the *Passio Sancti Sebastiani Martyris*, which as Wanley says began on 39 verso of the old foliation before the fire. For Wanley's foliation before the fire, see Ker, *Catalogue*, 225.

[12] Antonette di Paolo Healey, with Richard Venezky and Peter Mielke, eds., Dictionary of Old English Project, Centre for Medieval Studies, University of Toronto, January 2000.

list in preparation for making a glossary. We have developed a very useful
Electronic Editing tool for the purpose.[13] The tool processes the encoded file
and presents a working environment, with wordlist and corresponding text
on one side and templates for all parts of speech on the other, as shown in
Figure 4.4:

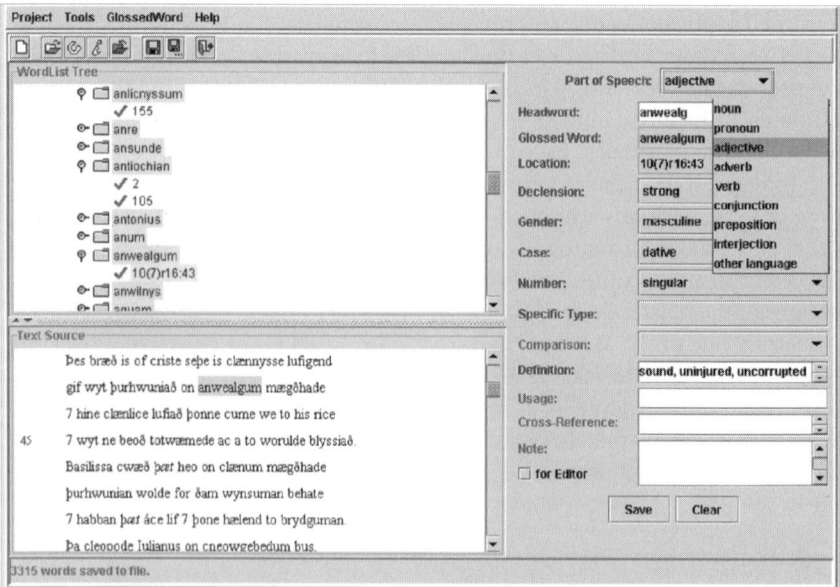

Figure 4.4: Glossary Tool

When the editor chooses a word from the text to gloss (in this case *anwealgum*), the word is simultaneously highlighted in the text in the lower left to
provide its context, in the wordlist in the upper left, and as default entries
in the "glossed word" and "location" fields on the right side of the Glossary
Tool. Since *anwealg* is an adjective, the editor then selects "adjective" from the
templates, and fills in the required information to define the word and describe its grammatical properties. All of these fields are automatically tagged

---

[13] The tool was programmed by my research assistant, Ionut Emil Iacob, and extensively used by my students, Kenneth Hawley, Demorah Hayes, and Jocelyn Taylor, as well
as by students in my Spring 2002 seminar on Electronic Editing.

in XML for use in the database, making it possible to search and otherwise access all features and any combination of them throughout the glossary.

Standard editorial work proceeds on the text, as well, and everything is likewise encoded for use in the database (these collations serve to encode variant readings, emendations, conjectural restorations, ultraviolet readings vs. daylight readings, etc.). The glossary production tool ensures that any editorial changes to the text must be updated in the glossary. A browser interface with programmed applications displays image and text together, allows for precise linking between them, and accesses the database for apparatus, glossary, translation, and user-defined searches. The browser interface used while editing the text will ultimately be included in the user's version of the edition to allow users to emend or develop the glossaries. By compiling a single comprehensively encoded file with multiple style sheets, users may display text as a diplomatic transcript, or as prose or verse with or without editorial brackets and italics, and without losing access to textual information of any kind. Using a collection of customized style sheets and a transforming processor, users can also develop their own transformations of the master document and display the results in a browser.

Surely one of the strangest looking folios in all Old English manuscripts is folio 67 (fig. 4.5), the last "leaf" of Cotton Otho B. x, as its charred remnants were mistakenly ordered in a mid-nineteenth-century restoration. It looks like a surreal jigsaw puzzle of a domestic disturbance involving a raised frying pan (or perhaps a pie).

Figure 4.5: fol. 67, recto and verso

It is so difficult to read that Skeat understandably failed to realize that "folio 67" belonged to *Julian and Basilissa* when he collated readings from Otho B. x with Cotton Julius E. vii. N. R. Ker in his *Catalogue of Manuscripts containing Anglo-Saxon* was apparently the first scholar after Frederic Madden to recognize not only that "folio 67" comes from *Julian and Basilissa*, but that it is actually the remnants of two different folios.[14] In his *Catalogue* entry, Ker tersely observes:

> 5. [f. '32ᵛ' **Idus Ianuarii. Passio Sancti Iuliani Et Sponse Eius Bas-ilissa.** 'Iulianus wæs gehaten . . .'.] As Skeat, i. 90. 'þa . . . asende' and 'þystru[m] . . . ðam' (Sk., ll. 29–91, 219–333) remains in part (ff. 7: 67 fragm. 2, 67 fragm. 1).

He notes elsewhere without further comment, "67 fragm. 1 . . . reversed" (225). Given Ker's extremely taciturn style, it will be helpful here to explain and illustrate what he means. His catalogue entry records that the *Passio Sancti Iuliani Et Sponse Eius Basilissa*, celebrated on the Ides of January (13 January),[15] was the fifth item in Otho B. x, and that it began on the verso of folio 32 in the foliation recorded by Humfrey Wanley. The reference to Skeat is to volume 1 of his edition, beginning on page 90. The remaining fragments correspond to lines 29–91 for fol. 10(7) and to lines 219–333 for the two folios combined on "BL fol. 67" of Skeat's edition (fig. 4.6). It will be easier to visualize the correct order of the fragments by graying out sections that are out of sequence.

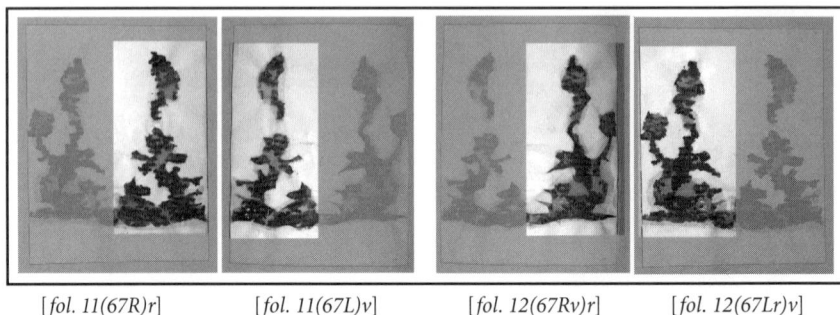

   [*fol. 11(67R)r*]   [*fol. 11(67L)v*]   [*fol. 12(67Rv)r*]   [*fol. 12(67Lr)v*]

Fig. 4.6: fols. 11(67R) recto and 12(67Rv) recto in order

---

[14]Ker §177–178. Madden must have known that the fragments were two folios, not one, in order to reconstruct the text even to the point that he did, but it remains a mystery why he allowed his talented restorer, Henry Gough, to frame them as if they were parts of the same folio.

[15]As Skeat notes (91 note 1), the actual feast day is 9 January.

Figure 4.6 illustrates that the part of so-called "folio 67" that should be next after fol. 10(7) verso is the right (R) side, instead of the left, as Gough mistakenly thought when he framed the two fragments. Its virtual foliation number is therefore 11(67R) recto. But when the page is turned, the verso of this fragmentary leaf is now on the left (L) side, hence properly called fol. 11(67L) verso. As Ker indicates, the next fragmentary leaf was "reversed," that is, pasted in back to front. Thus the real recto is on the right side of the verso (Rv). I therefore call it fol. 12(67Rv) recto. The last page is the one erroneously framed first in the sequence, here called fol. 12(67Lr) verso.

As Figure 4.7 illustrates, a diplomatic transcription alone is relatively useless:

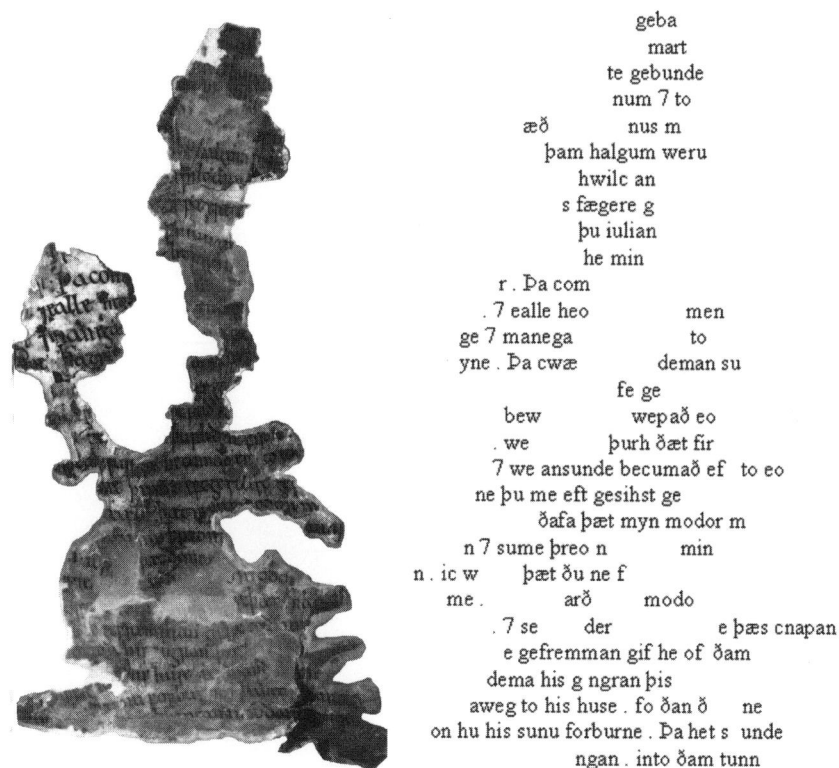

```
                                    geba
                                    mart
                               te gebunde
                               num 7 to
                     æð          nus m
                    þam halgum weru
                         hwilc an
                        s fægere g
                        þu iulian
                         he min
                   r . Þa com
                   . 7 ealle heo          men
                 ge 7 manega               to
                 yne . Þa cwæ          deman su
                             fe ge
                   bew          wepað eo
                   . we         þurh ðæt fir
                7 we ansunde becumað ef  to eo
              ne þu me eft gesihst ge
                        ðafa þæt myn modor m
            n 7 sume þreo n           min
         n . ic w      þæt ðu ne f
           me .            arð     modo
               . 7 se     der        e þæs cnapan
                 e gefremman gif he of ðam
                 dema his g ngran þis
               aweg to his huse . fo ðan ð   ne
           on hu his sunu forburne . Þa het s unde
                 ngan . into ðam tunn
```

Figure 4.7: transcript of fol. 12(67Lr) verso, enhanced by ultraviolet.

When filled in by collation with Skeat, lines 304–333, the transcript of the folio assumes what must have been close to its form before the fire:

binnan þam cwearterne 7] **geba**[*d mid þam Cristenum,*
oð þæt Martianus hi to þam] **mart**[*yrdome gefette.*
*Hi wurdon þa gebroh]*te **gebunde**[*ne on racen-*
*teagum ealle to þam tun]*num 7 to [*þære ontend-*
5   *nysse.* Þa cw]æð [*martia]*nus m[*id mycelre*
angsumnysse to] þam halgum weru[*m 7 to his*
agenum suna, eala] hwilc an[*wilnys 7 geortruwad*
*wylla, þurh ða þeo]*s **fægere** g[*eogað nu for-*
wurðan sceall. Eala] þu iulian[*e, þe awendest*
10   *minne sunu swa þæt]* he min [*ne ræcð ne eac*
*þære mede]*r . Þa com [*seo modor mid*
*mycelre sarnyss]*e . 7 ealle heo[*re hyredmen to*
*þære heofun]*ge 7 manega [*oðre menn]* to [*þære mycclan*
*wæfers]*yne . Þa cwæ[*ð þæs]* deman su[*nu to his*
15   *dreorigan fæder, Ne þur]*fe ge [*us bemænan*
*ne urne si]*þ . bew[*epan be]*wepað eo[*w sylfe, we siðiaþ to*
heofonum] . we [*farað]* þurh ðæt fir [*unforhte*
þurh God] 7 we ansunde becumað ef[*t]* to eo[*wrum*
*gesihþum. Þon]*ne þu me eft gesihst ge[*sundne*
20   *of þam fyre, ge]*ðafa þæt myn modor m[*e ge-*
*spræca]*n 7 sume þreo n[*iht on]* min[*um ræde*
*beo]*n . ic w[*ene]* þæt ðu ne f[*orleosa naðor ne*
hi ne] me . [*Þa we]*arð [*seo]* modo[*r on mode*
geblissod,] . 7 se [*fæ]*der [*cwæð þæt h]*e þæs cnapan
25   *willan wold]*e **gefremman** gif he of ðam [*fyre come.*
Þa het se] dema his g[*i]*ngran þis [*don, 7 eode mid*
his wife] aweg to his huse . fo[*r]*ðan ð[*e he]* ne [*mihte*
*gese]*on hu his sunu forburne . Þa het s[*e]* unde[*r-*
*gerefa hi ealle gebri]*ngan into ðam tunn[*um 7*

A thorough encoding of the damage to and restoration of this folio would include tagging for cause of damage (fire, hole, tear, water, other), its description, extent, and source of transcription (high-intensity light, microfilm, or ultraviolet image), in addition to sources of restoration (here Skeat's edition along with ultraviolet fluorescence and image processing [fig. 4.8]).

The restoration of fol. 11(67R) (fig. 4.9), corresponding to lines 219–245 in Skeat, presents many interesting textual and technical problems. Ker indicates that the first surviving recognizable word on the fragment is *þystru*[*m*] r4, but there are other bits of text preceding it that image processing discloses.

Figure 4.8: fol. 12(67Lr) verso, ultraviolet, detail

At the tip of the fragment an *e* and most of *m* from [*c*]*em*[*pan*] survive; be-low that in line 2 is -*um þær*- from [*weardmann*]*um þær*[*a*], and in line 3 -*ft gecirr*- from [*æ*]*ft gecirr*[*on*] is still visible. And the final –*um* from [*blind*]*um* remains before *þystru*[*m*] in line 4:

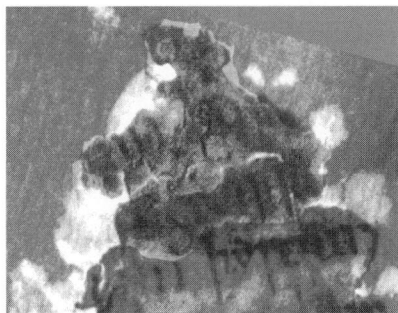

Figure 4.9: fol. 11(67R)r1–4, ultraviolet processed

A painstaking collation with Skeat's text continues to recover, line by line, expected bits of the succeeding text until line 8, when for five consecutive lines on a postage-stamp-sized bit of vellum, completely unexpected and uncollatable letters appear: *min* 11(67R)r8:223, *iste 7 ða* r9:224, *eofodo* r10:225, *or he* r11:226, and *ser* r12:227.

Figure 4.10: fol. 11(67R)r8–11

In view of the obvious mismatch of the text on this fragment, it seemed most probable that Henry Gough had pasted the fragment on the wrong folio. A futile search for combinations of these letters in close proximity anywhere in *Julian and Basilissa* seemed to prove, moreover, that they came from another text entirely. The mystery was temporarily compounded when the expected and collatable letters, *hte* 11(67L)v8:223, *urdon* v9:224, *oðra* v10:225, and *æs* v11:226, were found on the other side of this fragment (less text is visible on the verso, because of the retaining edges of the paper frames) (fig. 4.11).

> *nysse his dri*]**hte**[*n þæt he foresceawode hu*
> *hi gefullode w*]**urdon** [*Þær wæron binnan þære*
> *byrig seofan gebr*]**oðra** [*Cristena, þæs caseres cynnes*
> *7 heora fæder w*]**æs** [*Cristen, þam alyfde se casere*
> [fol. 11(67R)r8–11 restored with misplaced 11(67L)v8–11]

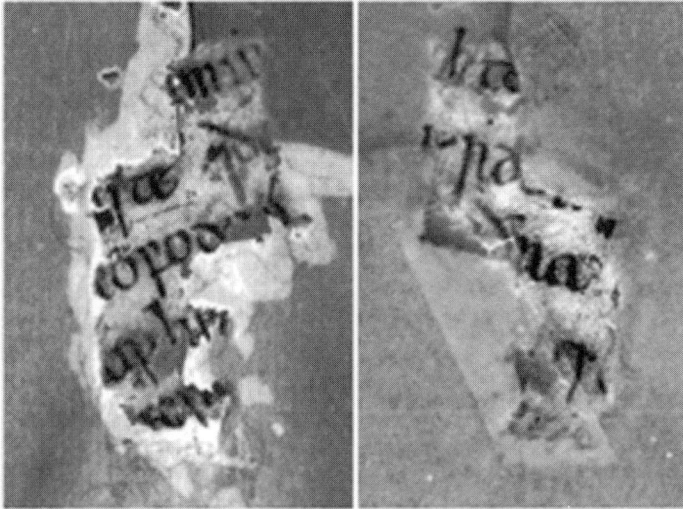

Figure 4.11: fols. 11(67R)r8–11 and 11(67L)v8–11 are reversed

With the assurance that the fragment was in its correct place on the recto, it became apparent that the unrecognized text from the recto that could not be collated with anything must contain spelling variants. Moreover, the fragment reading *iste 7 ða* was now easy to find in line 9 of the verso:

> *me to his Cr*]iste 7 ða *[seofan cnihtas þe be*

With this line as a guide, *min* became easy to place with *minne* in line 8, and *ser* likewise fell in with *casere* in line 12. Knowing from the collation of folio 10(7) with Skeat's edition that the Otho scribe used the spelling variant *cleopode* for *clypode* and *heom* for *him*, I then realized that the Otho scribe had spelled *lyfedan* as *leofodon* at line 10, and *hyra* as *heora* at line 11:

> *ealle tobrytte, 7]* min[*ne sunu gebygde fram*
> *me to his Cr*]iste 7 ða[*seofan cnihtas þe be*
> *þinre leafa l*]eofodo[*n buton ehtnysse on*
> *þyssere byrig f*]or heo[*ra mycclum gebyrde.*
> *Þa asende se ca*]ser[*e þisne cwide ongean, gif*
> [fol. 11(67L)v8–12 restored with misplaced 11(67R)r8–12]

There was yet another unsolved (or rather, unnoticed) mystery on this folio, attesting to its practically unreadable condition without special lighting, image processing, and magnification. At lines 18 and 19 the bit of vellum containing what appears to be a couple of words in the same ink but in some unknown language with a peculiar script.

Figure 4.12: fol. 11(67R)r18–19

What happened is that Gough pasted the fragment in the right place but upside down:

Figure 4.13: fol. 11(67R)r18–19 right side up

Once set aright, the text fits in where it belongs:

> ge[*fullode*] . **Hi eodon ða** [*on niht 7 Godes ængel*
> **hi** [*lædde*] 7 ð[*æt*] **cwearter**[*n geopenade mid his handa*

The same problem occurs, of course, on the verso, where the words *þa godes* and *hi* are upside down at lines 18 and 19:

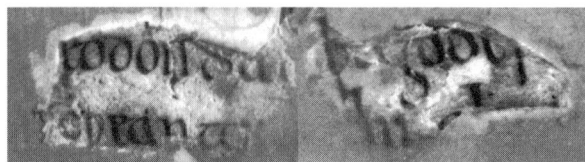

Figure 4.14: fol. 11(67L)v18–19 upside down and right side up]

When set right side up, the appropriate text emerges, although the top of insular *s* is gone in *godes*, and only the tops of *ah* in *aht* survive:

> *Martianus*] **þa gode**[*s me*]**n gef**[*eccan 7 axode*
> *Iulianum hweðer*] **hi** [*aht sme*]**adon** [*ymbe hyre.*

At the bottom of the same folio a collation of fol. 11(67R)r26–29 with Skeat's edition (lines 241–245) reveals that the Otho scribe has omitted exactly two lines of verse. To my knowledge, no one has noticed this omission. The missing text comes from the last two lines, a section of the damaged leaf that is tolerably well preserved and legible, although the left side of the fragment is confusingly misaligned with the right side:

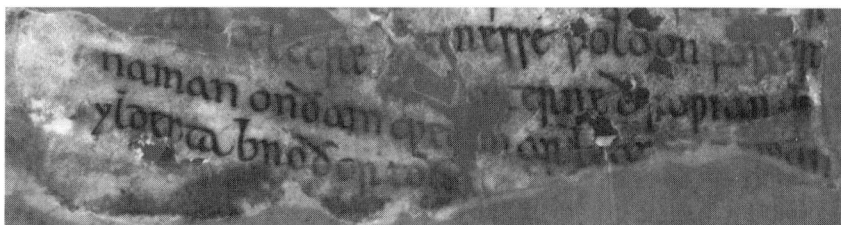

Figure 4.15: fol. 11(67R)r27–29, enhanced by UV

Skeat's text reads,

> woldon for cristes naman on þam cwearterne þrowian .
> Þa het se cwellere hi . of þam cwearterne gelædan .
> and axode hwi hi woldan butan ehtnysse þrowian .
> Þa cwæð se yldesta broðor to ðam arleasan deman[16]

The version in Otho B. x (here digitally realigned) appears to be a deliberate revision, removing the potentially merciful action of the judge: "They were willing for Christ's name to suffer in the prison. Then said the eldest brother to the impious judge . . .":

---

[16] "They were willing for Christ's name to suffer in the prison. / Then the tormentor bade them be led from the prison / and asked why they wished, without persecution, to suffer. / Then said the eldest brother to the impious judge . . ." (lines 242–245). The Otho version omits verses 243–244.

Figure 4.16: fol. 11(67R)r27–29, with left side realigned

. . . woldon for cr[*istes*
naman on ðam cwearterne ðrowian. Þ[*a cwæð se*
yldesta broðor to ðam arleas[*an de*]man. . . .
    [11(67R)r27–29]

Restored by collation with Skeat and with the misplaced bits in their proper
places, the remaining text on the fragment of fol. 11(67R) recto is:

   Þa cwædon þa c]em[*pan þe se cwellere gesette þam halgum*
   to weardmann]um Þær[*a wæron twentig, Unrihtlic*
   us bið, þæt we æ]ft gecirro[*n fram þysum*
   beorhtan leohte to blind]um þystru[*m fram*
5 *life to deaðe, fram soðe to l*]easu[*n*]ge . Hi f[*eollon*
   þa ealle to Iulianes fotum] mid gelea[*fan herigende*
   þæs Hælendes nam]an . Iulianu[*s þa bæd mid onbryrd-*
   nysse his dri]hte[*n þæt he foresceawode hu*
   hi gefullode w]urdon [*Þær wæron binnan þære*
10 *byrig seofan gebr*]oðra [*Cristena, þæs caseres cynnes*
   7 heora fæder w]æs [*Cristen, þam alyfde se casere*
   heora cristendom to healdenne butan ælcere
   ehtnysse for ðam arwurðan cynne. Hi hæfdon
   ænne mæssepreost swiðe mæres lifes, Antonius
15 *gehaten, þ*]e him mæ[*ssan gesang. Þas geneosode*
   se Hæ]lend 7 het hi [*gan to þam cwearterne mid*
   heora] mæssepreoste [*þæt þa men wurdon*
   ge[*fullode*] . Hi eodon ða [*on niht 7 Godes ængel*
   hi [*lædde*] 7 ð[*æt*] cwearter[*n geopenade mid his handa*
20 *hrepunge. Þ*]a sædo[*n þa*] geb[*roðra þæt se*
   hæ]lend hi asænde mid [*heora mæssepreostæ*
   þa men to fu]lligenne. Iulianus þa son[*a þæs*
   ða[*ncode God*]e 7 wearð þa gefu[*llod se fore-*

sæda cna[*pa 7 his f*]æder cempan on [*Cristes*
25 naman en[*demes.*] Þis wearð þa ge[*cyd þam*
cwellere m[*arti*]ane þæt ða seofon ge[*b*]r[*oðra*
bu]ton ælcere [*eh*]tnesse woldon for cr[*istes*
naman on ðam cwearterne ðrowian . Þ[*a cwæð se*
yldesta broðor to ðam arleas[*an de*]man

The restored text on fol. 11(67L) verso is:

Andsæte bið þæt treow þe æfre grewð on leafum 7 næfre
nænne wæstm his scyppende ne bringð swa synd we
Cristene gi]f ure c[*ristendom ne bið acunnod.*
Þa het se c]wellere [*hi to þam cwearterne ge-*
5 *lædan, 7 sen*]de his gewr[*it to þam wælhreowan*
casere, Ge]help uru[*m godum 7 hat to þe gefeccan*
þisne dry] Iulianum [*þe ure goda anlicnysse mid*
ealle tobrytte, 7] min[*ne sunu gebygde fram*
me to his Cr]iste 7 ða [*seofan cnihtas þe be*
10 *þinre leafa l*]eofodo[*n*] [*buton ehtnysse on*
þyssere byrig f]or heo[*ra mycclum gebyrde.*
Þa asende se ca]ser[*e þisne cwide ongean, gif*
Iulianus þurhwunað mid his geferum on þysum
nim fela tunnan 7 do hi þær on innan, onæl hi
15 *siððan e*]alle oðr[*um mannum to bysne. 7 gif he*
þurh his] dr[*y*]cræft [*þæt fyr adwescan mæg*
gewitna h]i ealle loc[*a hu þu wylle. Þa het*
Martianus] þa godes [*me*]n gef[*eccan 7 axode*
Iulianum hweðer] hi aht [*sme*]adon [*ymbe hyre*
20 *agene þearfe o*]n [*þæ*]re h[*wile oðþæt. Iulianus*
sæde, ure] geþanc is s[*wa s*]wa h[*it wæs*
gif þu æn]ig wite beþohtest we [*synd gearwe to þam.*
Þa mi]d þissere spræ[*ce bæron menn*] on
ðære stræt] anes hæð[*enes mannes*] lic 7 se
25 *heardhe*]orta dema [*het beran þo*]ne deadan
to his dom]setle . cwæð þa [*to Iuliane*] eower
Crist] arærde þa deadan [*to*] life læt nu [*ge*
swu]telian gif he soð g[*od*] sy 7 ge þisne aræron .
Þa andwyrde iulianus þam] arleasan deman

The strange case of British Library "folio 67" and its companion in *Ju-*
lian and Basilissa teaches a valuable lesson about odd couples and the difficult nature of collaboration. We know that Sir Frederic Madden had correctly

identified the bits and pieces of two distinct folios from *Julian and Basilissa*. It is unlikely in the extreme that he instructed Henry Gough to frame them together as if they were one folio, much less to put 12(67Lr)v back to front and frame it before 11(67R)r, or to place one small piece of 11(67R) back to front and another small piece upside down. While Gough achieved a restoration that has kept all of these pieces intact for a century and a half, "folio 67" also represents the breakdown of an otherwise fruitful collaboration of an odd couple, Madden and Gough, keeper and conservator, scholar and technical expert. Just as Madden did not have the technical expertise to rebind these fragments, so Gough did not have the expertise to read Old English. They stopped working together too early on this puzzle. A patient and sustained collaboration is likewise essential between another truly odd couple, humanities and computer science, for digital libraries to achieve their full potential for restoring, searching, and editing currently inaccessible humanities collections.[17]

Bibliography

Kiernan, Kevin, W. Brent Seales, and James Griffioen. "The Reappearances of St. Basil the Great in British Library MS Cotton Otho B. x." *Computers and the Humanities* 36 (2002): 7–26.

Lees, Clare. "Chastity and Charity: Ælfric, Women, and the Female Saints." In eadem, *Tradition and Belief: Religious Writing in Late Anglo-Saxon England*, 133–53. Medieval Cultures 19. Minneapolis, 1999.

Prescott, Andrew. "'Their Present Miserable State of Cremation': The Restoration of the Cotton Library." In *Sir Robert Cotton as Collector: Essays on an Early Stuart Courtier and his Legacy*, ed. C. J. Wright, 391–454. London, 1997.

Skeat, Walter W. *Ælfric's Lives of Saints*. EETS o.s. 76, 82. London, 1881.

---

[17] I presented an early version of this paper as "Electronic Editions of Damaged Manuscripts" for a special session on "Whose Standards? MLA Committee on Scholarly Editions" for the Modern Language Association in December 2000. My student, Jocelyn Taylor, made a related presentation on "Creating a Glossary for a Damaged Old English Manuscript" for the National Conference for Undergraduate Research in Lexington, Kentucky, in March 2001. This essay was completed in June 2000.

DANAKONUNGATAL IN COPENHAGEN, ROYAL LIBRARY BARTH. D III. FOL.: AN EDITION

ÓLAFUR HALLDÓRSSON

The text edited and discussed in this article is preserved in the extensive col-lection of historical documents collected and copied mainly from Icelandic and Norwegian diplomata and manuscripts by the Icelandic philologist Árni Magnússon (1663–1730) for the benefit of the Danish historiographer Thom-as Bartholin (1659–1690). The text is in two sections: the first is a brief gene-alogy of Danish kings from prehistoric times to the late thirteenth century; the second, and the primary one, is a concise survey of the Danish monarchy from Sigurðr hringr to Valdemar II (1170–1241).

Introduction

In 1683, at the age of twenty, Árni Magnússon landed in Copenhagen. The city was the home of Thomas Bartholin, a young scholar, born in 1659, who had already studied at several universities elsewhere in Europe. In 1682, at the tender age of twenty-three, he had been appointed to a chair, and in 1684, a year after Árni's arrival, he was promoted to one of the most prestigious official posts in Denmark, that of Royal Antiquary. In this same year, Árni was recruited as his amanuensis and began to collect materials relating to the pre-Reformation church history of Denmark, Norway, and Iceland. His main task was to find and copy relevant texts in Icelandic and Norwegian historical and documentary sources, including old poetry, and to make Latin versions of them for Bartholin's benefit. Bartholin died before his time in 1690, and by then he and his collaborators had collected a massive archive of extracts, thousands of pages in large format, now preserved in some twenty-five vol-umes in the Royal Library in Copenhagen, catalogued under the general title,

"E donatione variorum Bartholiniana". Nine of these volumes were written in whole or in part by Árni Magnússon.

On pages 819–27 in one of these volumes, Don. var. 1, fol., Barth. D (III) fol., there is a text in Árni's hand which begins with a brief account of Haraldr hárfagri's lineage followed by a genealogy of Danish kings from Ívarr víð-faðmi to Queen Ingeborg, wife of King Magnús lagabœtir (d. 1287) and her kinsman, King Eiríkr klipping (r. 1259–1286), son of Kristófórus I.[1] After this genealogical section comes a concise survey of the Danish monarchy, which I shall refer to here as *Danakonungatal.* At the head of this Árni cites his source: "Ex Ms. membraneo Bibliothecæ publicæ Acad. Hafn. in 4to post Sverris sögu in capsa rubra minori." Árni also refers to this piece in Copen-hagen, Arnamagnaean Institute 1045 4to, a list he compiled of the contents of volumes A–K in the Bartholin collection, where on folio 19r we read: "Genea-logia Regum Daniæ, usqvæ ad Valdemarum II. Islandicè. Manu Arnæ Mag-næi, ad calcem Historiæ Sverri Regis." On a slip with Copenhagen, Arnamag-naean Institute 79 fol. there is a list made by Árni of manuscripts of *Sverris saga.* He first notes "1. Codex meus in 4to, optimus [. . .]" (that is, Copenha-gen, Arnamagnaean Institute 327 4to), and then: "2. Codex Academiæ Haf-niensis in 4to mutilus qvidem passim, at egregius. 3. Codex alter Academiæ Hafniensis in 4to. et ille qvidem satis bonus."[2] *Danakonungatal* was either at the end of no. 2 or no. 3 of these. Gustav Storm thought no. 2 was the more likely source but there is no evidence to prove that it was.[3]

After the genealogical section, Árni drew a line across the page and wrote below it in an ink just a little paler than that used in the text itself: "Ex eodem Codice." This is followed by a space answering to three lines of writing, and then *Danakonungatal* begins. At the end of *Danakonungatal,* Árni first noted "aliqva forte desunt," but he subsequently crossed this out and wrote "duo," only to cancel this and insert "tria" above the line, continuing with "enim ul-tima folia abscissa sunt, in qvibus an aliquid exaratum fuerit incertum est." Later again he bracketed this and wrote "nihil deesse puto."

It would seem distinctly odd if three leaves were left empty at the end of the manuscript. It seems to have been customary for a scribe to allow

---

[1] In view of the nature of the texts considered in this paper, I use conventional Old Icelandic forms for Danish names throughout.

[2] Kr. Kålund, *Katalog over Den arnamagnæanske håndskriftsamling,* 2 vols. (Copen-hagen, 1888–1894), 1: 59–60.

[3] Gustav Storm, ed., *En oldnorsk Saga om Danekongerne* (Christiania [Oslo], 1879), 11.

the extent of the matter to decide the size of the last gathering in a volume, leaving at most a single blank folio at the end. If three leaves had been left unwritten, it is, of course, highly probable that before long they would have been cut out for other use. Árni's doubts as to whether something was missing at the end must have been prompted by the fact that the text concludes with a complete sentence at the bottom of the page. Since this was a text which in the time of Árni and Bartholin existed only in this one vellum copy, we shall never know for sure whether it was longer at some stage than it is at present. That makes it more difficult to decide when *Danakonungatal* was first put together.

The genealogical section and *Danakonungatal* were first printed by Jacob Langebek.[4] Langebek speaks of two texts — the genealogical section and *Danakonungatal* — and attributes them to different authors, whom he assumed to be Icelanders. He thought *Danakonungatal* could be dated to between 1221 and 1223, while pointing out that the genealogies come down to 1260. He says that his edition is based on a copy which he had taken many years before from a Bartholin manuscript, and as far as he could recall this text had been in Árni Magnússon's hand. He adds that he had also used another copy, made by Hannes Finnsson from a paper manuscript, no. 76 fol. in "Archivi Antiqvitatum Regii" in Stockholm, written, it was thought, by Páll Hallsson (d. 1663).[5] The identification of the source as Stockholm, Royal Library Papp. fol. no. 76 is correct, but not the identification of the scribe. Langebek's print is in two columns, with the Icelandic text on the left, a Latin version of it on the right; the Latin was the work of Jón Ólafsson of Svefneyjar. Langebek's footnotes include comments on the text and references to sources: Adam of Bremen, *Knýtlinga saga*, *Maríu saga* (on Julian the Apostate), Matthew of Westminster, William of Malmesbury (on the monastery founded by King Knútr at Bury St Edmunds), *Heimskringla*, Sven Aggesøn, and others.

The texts were next edited by Storm and published by him with a brief introduction and postscript.[6] Storm gave a diplomatic transcript of Árni's text but with some modifications. Thus he gives proper names an initial capital, silently expands abbreviations, prints *gg, nn, rr* where Árni has small capital

---

[4] Jacob Langebek, ed., *Scriptores rerum Danicarum medii ævi* (Copenhagen, 1773), 2: 422–33.

[5] Páll Eggert Ólason, *Íslenzkar æviskrár frá landnámstímum til ársloka 1940*, 5 vols. (Reykjavík, 1948–1952), 4: 120.

[6] Storm, ed., *En oldnorsk Saga*, 1–15.

G, N, R, roman *f* and *v* for Árni's Insular þ and ρ,[7] *hann* for *han*, and, as he says, "borttager de nyislandske Udtaleformer, som han [Árni] undertiden har indblandet" (takes away the modern Icelandic pronunciations which he has sometimes included).

Storm maintains that the genealogical section and *Danakonungatal* belong together, to be taken as a single work by a single Norwegian author. This conclusion of his is based on the argument that, since the same dialectal features and the same orthography are found in both texts, they must have been in one hand in the vellum exemplar from which they were copied, and that, since the texts are free from scribal errors or other misunderstandings, that source must have been the author's original. He thought that the genealogies served as an introduction to *Danakonungatal* and, if they were compiled after 1263, then *Danakonungatal* could not have been composed at an earlier date. In consequence he believed that something was certainly missing at the end of *Danakonungatal*, material which would have brought it down to the dates concluding the genealogical section. The whole work should then be assigned to the period between 1263 and 1286 and it was probably composed on behalf of Queen Ingeborg; after saying this Storm then inserts 1280 in parenthesis.[8]

These texts have been again and most recently edited by Bjarni Guðnason.[9] Bjarni finds Storm's conjecture that they were compiled for the benefit of Queen Ingeborg a convincing one; he notes that she received her royal title in 1261 and doubtless retained it till her death in 1287. Bjarni countenances the possibility that this epitome of the history of the royal house of Denmark was the work of Sturla Þórðarson.[10]

---

[7] The term "Insular" is here used for letters and forms of letters adopted from Anglo-Saxon.

[8] "Arne Magnusson har skilt de to Stykker, som fulgte efter hinanden i Codex; men det er aabenbart, at de høre sammen. Forfatteren har først skrevet de danske Kongers Slægttavle og paavist deres Slægtskab med den norske Kongeæt efter den islandske Fremstilling; derpaa leverer han en kort dansk Historie, hvori han fornemmelig dvæler ved de danske Kongers Forhold til Norge og fremstiller dette efter islandske Kilder (Snorre); Slægttavlen har de samme dialektiske Egenheder, de samme Bogstavformer (ρ for v) som Krøniken, — kort, alt taler for, at begge Stykker hører sammen, at Slægttavlen er en Indledning til Krøniken" (Storm, ed., *En oldnorsk Saga*, 11; see also 12).

[9] Bjarni Guðnason, ed., *Danakonunga sǫgur*, Íslenzk fornrit 35 (Reykjavík, 1982), 323–36.

Storm was convinced that these texts at the end of the *Sverris saga* codex were written by a Norwegian, because Árni's copy evidenced all the linguistic features

> som røber den norske Dialekt af det norrøne Maal (r for hr, l for hl, øy for ey, Mangel paa u-Omlyd, gjennemgaaende Vokalharmoni o. s. v.) [. . .] Den norske Skrivemaade er i det hele saa gjennemført i denne Saga, at man ikke kan tvivle om, at den er forfattet i Norge; alle Navne findes i norsk Form som Ragnilldr, Astrið, Eirikr; der bruges norske Udtryk som herra om Prinser [. . .], som hertugi for isl. hertogi, som Franz for isl. Frakkland el. Frakkariki; der benyttes Ord, som i 13de Aarhundrede var brugelige i Norge, men paa Island enten aldeles ikke kjendtes eller endnu ikke var optagne, f. Ex. rikti, rettari (Dommer), fullkomliga, strið (Kamp,) stríða (kjæmpe), landsherra.'[11]

Storm is right in saying that there are many Norwegian features in the language of these pieces — more indeed than he mentions. On the other hand, there are also mistakes in the Norwegian for which it seems that Árni cannot be held responsible. I return to these later.

---

[10] Bjarni Guðnason, ed., *Danakonunga sǫgur*, clxxxviii–cxci.

[11] "which reveal the Norwegian dialect of the Norse language (r for *hr*, l for *hl*, øy for *ey*, lack of u-mutation, consistent vowel harmony, etc.) [. . .] The Norwegian orthography is so consistent in this saga that there is no doubt that it is composed in Norway; all names appear in their Norwegian forms, such as Ragnilldr, Astrið, Eirikr; Norwegian expressions are used, such as *herra* for *prinser* [. . .] *hertugi* for Icelandic *hertogi*, *Franz* for Icelandic *Frakkland* or *Frakkariki*; words are used, which in the thirteenth century were usable in Norway but which in Icelandic were totally unknown or had not been adopted, such as *rikti*, *rettari* (judge), *fullkomliga*, *strið* (fight), *stríða* (to fight), *landsherra*" (Storm, ed., *En oldnorsk Saga*, 12–13).

The Text[12]

1.1   1.1Haralldr harfagri þar ſon haldanar sparta, Guðroðar ſonar hins | 2gavfuglata. haldanar s. hins millda oc hins matarilla, Æÿstæins ſ. | 3haldanar ſ: hþitbeins, Olafsſ: tretelgio, Ingiallz ſ. hins illraða, Onþndar ſ: | 4Ingialldur hinn illraði atti gꜹtilldi dottur algꜹta .ſ. gꜹtz er gꜹtland er | 5þið kennt.   moðir haralldz harfagra þar ragnilldur dotter Sigurþar hiartar, | 6moðir hans þar Aflꜹg dotter Sigurþar orms i ꜹga. | 7Raðbarðr kongr i holmgarði þeck þnnar dottur Iþars `hins´ þiðfaðma, | 8þeirra ſon þar Randþerr broðir haralldz hillditannar. hans ſon þar | 9Sigurþr Ringr. hans .ſ. Ragnar loðbrok. hans .s. þar Sigurþr ormur i | 10auga. hans .s. hꜹrða knþtr. hans .ſ. þar Gormr. hans .ſ. haralldur. hans | 11.s. var Sþeinn tíþgu ſkeɢ. hans .s. knþtr hinn riki. hans syner þoro þeir | 12hꜹrða knþtr, haralldr, oc Sþein.   Spæinn kongur tiþgufſkeg atte | 13dottor er Astrið het, hana atte Ulfr Iarl spraka legs ſon, þeirra ſon þar | 14Sþeiɴ er magnus het ꜹðru nafne, hans ſon þar hinn helgi Knþtr kongr oc | 15Eirikr ᶒgoðe. ſon Eiriks þar hertuge knþtr hinn helgi, hans ſon þar | 16Ualldemar. ſon Walldemars het oc Walldimarr, hans ſon þar hinn helgi | 17Eirikr kongr faðir Ingi borgar drottningar i Noregi. kristofor þar broðir | 18Eiriks kongs. hans ſon Eirikr.

Ex eodem Codice

| 19I þenna tima er Carll kongr |:er kallaðr er Magnus, oc þm ſiðir þarð | 20keifari|: ſtyrði rumþeria riki. hÿggio þær riki oc kongdom haft hafa a | 21norðrlꜹndum. Sigurþ Ring faður Ragnars loðbrokar. þann Sigurþ ſegia | 22meɴ þerit haþa broðor ſon, haralldz hillditannar. Carll keifari andaðiz a | 23þþi are er liðit þar fra burð þars herra Iesu Kristi .vííj. hundrat oc .xv. | 24ár.   Loþis ſon karls keifara tok keifaradom æftir foður ſiɴ. han let | 25skira ut i meiðinz borg haralld kong af Jwtt landi. Epter haralld kong | 26þar Eirikr kongr er kirkiþ let gera gera i Sleiþik, Epter han þar annaʀ | 27Eirikr er kirkiu let gera i Ripum. Eptir daga þefsa Eiriks kongs lagði ſa | 28kongur þnder ſek Danmork alla er Gormr (<Gormur) het, harðr ok | 29heiðinn. hans drotning þar Thÿri Danmarkar bot. I þenna tima þar uppi i | 30Noregi haralldr harfagri er þnder ſik lagði Noreg allan. hann þekk þa | 31kono af Danmork er Ragnilldr het, oc hÿggio þer hana þerit hafa dottor |

---

12 In the following a diplomatic transcript of Árni Magnússon's copy is provided. Expansion of abbreviations is indicated by italic; what is written superscript is marked by ` ´, what is deleted by {}, what is written in the margin by ´´, correction to-from by <. Where Árni leaves larger gaps between sentences and paragraphs, these are retained in the print. Superscript numerals in text indicate lineation in the copy.

The Text

Haraldr hárfagri (the Fairhaired) was the son of Halfdan svarti (the Black), son of Guðrøðr inn gǫfugláti (the Venerable), son of Halfdan inn mildi og inn matarilli (the Gentle but the Bad Entertainer), son of Eysteinn, son of Halfdan hvítbein (Whiteleg), son of Óláfr trételgja (the Tree-feller), son of Ingjaldr illráði (the Evil-worker), son of Önundr. Ingjaldr the Evil-worker was married to Gauthildr, daughter of Algauti, son of Gautr, from whom Gautland receives its name. The mother of Haraldr hárfagri (the Fairhaired) was Ragnhildr, daughter of Sigurðr hjǫrtr (Hjort); his mother was Áslaug, daughter of Sigurðr ormr í auga (the Snake-eyed). King Raðbarðr in Hólmgarðr[13] was married to Unnr, daughter of Ívarr viðfaðmi (Vidfavne); their son was Randvér, the brother of Haraldr hilditǫnn (Wartooth). His son was Sigurðr hringr (Ring). His son was Ragnarr loðbrók (Lodbrok). His son was Sigurðr ormr í auga (the Snake-eyed). His son was Harda-Knútr. His son was Gormr. His son was Haraldr. His son was Sveinn tjúguskegg (Forkbeard). His son was Knútr inn ríki (the Great). His sons were Harda-Knútr, Haraldr, and Sveinn. King Sveinn tjúguskegg (Forkbeard) had a daughter by the name of Ástríðr. She was married to Earl Úlfr, son of Sprakalegg. Their son was Sveinn, who was also called Magnús. His sons were King Knútr the saint and Eiríkr eygóði (the Good). Eiríkr's son was Duke Knútr the saint. His son was Valdimarr. The son of Valdimarr was also called Valdimarr. His son was the King Eiríkr the saint, the father of Queen Ingeborg of Norway. Kristófór was the brother of King Eiríkr. His son was Eiríkr.

From the same codex

At this time when King Karl, who is called Magnús and who eventually became emperor, ruled over the Roman empire, we believe that the realms and kingdoms in the northern countries were held by Sigurðr hringr (Ring), the father of Ragnarr loðbrók (Lodbrok). Men say that this Sigurðr was the nephew of Haraldr hilditǫnn (Wartooth). Emperor Karl died eight hundred and fifteen years after the birth of our Lord Jesus Christ. Lovís, the son of Emperor Karl, ruled the empire after his father. He had King Haraldr of Jutland baptized in Mainz. After King Haraldr Eiríkr became king, who had a church built in Sleivík. After him there was another Eiríkr, who had a church built in Ribe. After the days of this King Eiríkr, the king who is named Gormr, stern and heathen, conquered all of Denmark. His queen was Thyri Danmarkarbót (Dannebod). At this time Haraldr hárfagri (the Fairhaired) lived in Norway, who conquered all of Norway. He married a woman from Denmark named Ragnhildr, and we believe that she was the

---

[13] The country of Russia bordering on the lakes Ladoga, etc.

³²Eiriks kongs hins sidaʀa af Iutlandi er fẏʀ ꝑar nefndr. þeirra ſon var |
³³Æirikr bloðæẏx.   Haralldr kongur blatann tok riki ï Danmork æfter |
³⁴Gorm kong fɑdur sinn, a hans dogum heriaði a Danmork Otte keiſare |
³⁵hinn fẏrſti með þꝑi nafne er kallaðr er Magnus oc ſigraðe han oc ʽhanʼ |
³⁶let ſkira haralld kong oc Sꝑein ſon hans. oc ꝑeitti honom ſialfr | ³⁷guðſifiar,
oc kalladi han Svein Otto. þenna Svein kalla daner oc | ³⁸Nordmenn tiꝑgu
ſkegg. þa tok oll danmork ꝑið kriſtni. A þꝑi are ꝑar | ³⁹lidit fra burð ꝑars
herra Ieſu Kristi ix hundrut oc fim tiger ara. haralldr | ⁴⁰kongr blatann hellt
2.1   ꝑel ſiðan kriſtni. A ſiðarſtum dogum hans ſtriddi til || ²·¹landz i mote honom
Sveinn ſon hans, oc i þeim bardaga er þeir atto ꝑarð | ²haralldr kongr ſaʀ, oc
flẏði til Joms borgar i ꝑindland oc andaðiz þar | ³allra heilagra meſso oc ꝑar
fluttr til Rooſkelldo oc jarðaðr þar. þa hafði | ⁴han ꝑerit fim tigi ꝑetra kongr
æfter foður ſinn, han hafði gort mẏkit | ⁵herꝑirki i Noregi. |
     ⁶Sꝑeinn tiuguſkegg tok riki i Danmork æfter foður ſinn, han hellt illa |
⁷kriſtni. a hans riki heriaði æirikr ſigr ſæli Sꝑia kongr oc rak han Svein | ⁸kong
af riki oc hellt ſiþan Dana riki til dɑða dags. Æfter dɑða Eiriks | ⁹kongs feck
Sꝑeiɴ kongr riki ſitt i Danmork.   I þenna tima heriaðo | ¹⁰Iomsꝑikingar
i Noregi at a æggian Sꝑeins kongs. Morgum ꝑetrꝑm ſiðaʀ | ¹¹borduz þeir
Sveinn kongr oc Olafr Sꝑia kongr, oc Æirikr Iarl ſon | ¹²hakonar Iarls rika
af Noregi, ꝑið Olaf trẏgua ſon Noregs kong er þar | ¹³hellt fẏrſt kriſtni, oc
fengo ꝑnnit ꝑm ſiðir. þa kallaði Sꝑeiɴ kongr ſer | ¹⁴þriðiꝑng af Noregi, Æfter
þat heriaði han i ængland oc lagdi ꝑnder ſek. | ¹⁵han andadiz þar ſkiotlega
i hꝑilu ſinni oc birtiz ſꝑa nockorum monnom, | ¹⁶ſem hinn helgi Edmundr
hefði drepit han med þꝑi moti ſem Mercurius | ¹⁷riddari drap Julianꝑm
apostatam þa hafðe Sveiɴ kongr ꝑerit kongr eꝑter | ¹⁸foður ſin . . . . . . Knꝑtr
er Landbertus het skirnar nafne oc kalladr er a | ¹⁹danſka tꝑngu oc norrena
Knꝑtr ʀiki, tok kongdom i Dan mork æfter | ²⁰Sꝑein kong faður ſinn .x. ꝑetra
gamall. En þrim ꝑetrꝑm ſiðaʀ heriaði | ²¹han til ænglandz oc æfter margar
oroſtur ꝑann han ꝑnder ſek, a þꝑi are. | ²²Uar han ſiðan kongr ẏfer þeſsum
tꝑeim þioðlondom þar til er han for | ²³med .xij. hundrut ſkipa I Noreg oc
lagði unðer ſec allt kongriki en hinn | ²⁴helgi Olafr kongr atte oc han hafði
fullkomlega til kriſtni ſnꝑit. ꝑarð þa | ²⁵hinn helgi Olafr kongr at rẏma landit
firer knꝑti kongi, oc for han fẏrſt | ²⁶i Sꝑia riki, oc ſiðan auſtr i holmgarð, oc
þa er han hafðe ꝑerit þar einn | ²⁷ꝑetr ꝑende han aptr i Noreg oc fell þa i
þrondeime a ſticla ſtoðum ꝑirer | ²⁸landzher. knꝑtr kongr gaf konga nofn

daughter of King Eiríkr II of Jutland, who was mentioned earlier. Their son was Eiríkr blóðøx (Bloody-axe). King Haraldr blátǫnn (Bluetooth) became king after his father, King Gormr. In his days Emperor Otto, the first with that name, who was called Magnús, waged war on Denmark and he was victorious and had King Haraldr and his son Sveinn baptized and he himself offered him sponsorship and called him Sveinn Otto. The Danes and Norwegians call this Sveinn tjúguskegg (Forkbeard). Then all Denmark accepted Christianity. In that year nine hundred and fifty years had passed from the birth of our Lord Jesus Christ. Since then King Haraldr blátǫnn (Bluetooth) observed Christianity well. Towards the end of his life his son Sveinn engaged in battle against him in order to conquer the land, and in their battle King Haraldr was wounded and fled to Jómsborg[14] in Wendland and died there on All Saints' Day and was brought to Roskilde and buried there. He had then been king after his father for fifty years, and he had done much ravaging in Norway.

Sveinn tjúguskegg (Forkbeard) ruled in Denmark after his father. He observed Christianity badly. Eiríkr sigrsæli (the Victorious), king of the Swedes, waged war on his kingdom and he drove King Sveinn from the kingdom and held sway over Denmark until his death. After the death of King Eiríkr King Sveinn regained his kingdom in Denmark. At this time the Jómsvíkingar[15] harried in Norway at the instigation of King Sveinn. Many years later King Sveinn and Óláfr, king of the Swedes, and Earl Eiríkr, son of Earl Hákon ríki (the Mighty) of Norway, fought against King Óláfr Tryggvason of Norway, who was the first to become Christian there, and eventually conquered him. Then King Sveinn claimed for himself a third of Norway. After that he harried in England and conquered it. He died suddenly there in his sleep, and some men had the vision that St. Edmund had killed him in the manner in which the knight Mercurius killed Julian Apostata. Then King Sveinn had been king after his father ...... Knútr, whose baptismal name was Landbertus and who is called Knútr inn ríki (the Great) in Danish and Norse tongue, became king of Denmark after King Sveinn, his father, when he was ten years old. But three years later he waged war on England, and after many battles he conquered it in that year. He was then king over these two countries until he went with twelve hundred ships to Norway and conquered the entire kingdom which King Óláfr the saint ruled and had made completely Christian. Then King Óláfr the saint had to give up the country to King Knútr, and he first went to Sweden and then east to Hólmgarðr, and when he had been there one winter, he returned to Norway and fell in Þrándheimr[16] at Stiklastaðir in fight against insurgents among his

---

[14] The city of Jóm. Jóm is a county in Pomerania, where the Danish had an ancient colony and stronghold.

[15] The Vikings of Jóm.

[16] Modern Trondheim.

.íij. fonþm finþm, haralldi i ænglande. Hꜹrða knþte i danmorko. Speine konge i Noregi. hans moðir | ³⁰þar Alfiþa. Dottor knþtz kongs Gunnilldi atte herra Heinrekr er fiðan | ³¹þarð keifare. Spa fegia Danfkir menn at knþtr kongr þann þnder fek | ³²æiftland. han for til Roms oc han let fetia Clauftr i Edmundarborg. han | ³³andadiz i Englandi Idus Novembris. þa þar liðit fra burð þars herra Iesu | ³⁴Kristi .m. oc .xxx. oc .íííj. uetr. þa hafðe knþtr þerit kongr ẏfer | ³⁵Danmork .víj. uetr oc .xx. En ẏfer ænglandi .íííj. þetr (<uetr) oc .xx. En | ³⁶ẏfer Noregi .vj. uetr.

| ³⁷Hꜹrða knþtr fon knþtz kongs rika þar kongr i Dan morko æfter | ³⁸faður fiɴ .víij. uetr. han þar oc kongr ẏfer ænglandi .íííj. uetr. han gerdi | ³⁹fett oc kȯrleik þið ᴍagnus kong goða af noregi fon hins helga Olafs | ⁴⁰kongs með þeim skildaga at fa þeirra fem lengr lifði fkilldi taka riki | ⁴¹æfter þann er fẏʀí andaðiz ef sa ætte engan fon æfter. han andaðiz af | ⁴²fott.¹⁷ |

⁴³Magnus kongr goði (i<e) af Noregi tok riki efter hꜹrða knþt i Danmork, | ⁴⁴Sumer landz herrar i Danmorko þoro honom otrygger oc ftriddo i moti || ³·¹honom oc hofðo iafnan legra lut, þa heriaðo þinðr i danmork. oc || ²Magnus kongr barðiz þið þa, oc gaf þeim fþa mikit flag a lẏrskogs heiði | ³at þar fello af þinðum .xv. þufundrað manna. han andaðiz i danmorko | ⁴attanda kalendas dag Novembris, Norðmenn fluttu lic Magnus kongs til | ⁵Noregs, oc hþilir han i criftz 'corrige clementz` kirkio i Niðarofi. þa | ⁶hafdi han þerit fim þetr kongr ẏfer Danmork. |

⁷Sveinn er Magnus het oðru nafne son þlfs Iarls tok kongdom i | ⁸Danmorko æfter Magnus kong goða. Moðir Speins kongs þar Aftrið | ⁹dottir Sueins Tẏugufkegs, fẏfter knutz kongs rika. han hafði lengi ofrið | ¹⁰oc ftrið þið haralld kong harðraða af Noregi broðor hins helga Olafs | ¹¹kongs. Speinn kongr atte .xíííj. fẏne þa fem or bernfko komo, oc þurðu | ¹²af þeim .v. æinþalldz kongar i Danmorko, han gifti Ingiriði dottor fina | ¹³olafi kongi kẏʀa af Noregi fẏní haralldz kongs harðraða. han þard | ¹⁴fottdꜹdr ⊦ oc ⊣ þa hafdi han þerit kongr .ix. uetr oc .xx. |

¹⁵Haralldr er kallaðr þar hein tok kongdom æpter Svein kong | ¹⁶faður fiɴn oc rikte íííj þetr, han þarð fott dꜹðr.¹⁸ |

¹⁷Knþtr hinn helgi annaʀ fon Sueins kongs tok riki æpter haralld kong | ¹⁸brodor finn. han þar .víj. þetr kongr. han þar goðr rettare oc reffte miok | ¹⁹ran oc o fiðu. firer þat gerðu Daner famnað at honom oc drapo han oc | ²⁰Benedict broðor hans i hæilagri (<hæilagre) kirkio i oðins æẏ i Fione: | ²¹hans meffo dagr er vj⁰ Idus Julii. |

---

¹⁷ af sott *written after* Noregi *at the end of the next line.*
¹⁸ sott dꜹðr *written in the next line after* Su (*where there is line-division in* Sueins).

own people. King Knútr bestowed the title of king on his three sons, Haraldr in England, Harda-Knútr in Denmark, King Sveinn in Norway. His mother was Alfífa. King Knútr's daughter Gunnhildr was married to Lord Heinrekr, who later became emperor. The Danish say that King Knútr conquered Estonia. He went to Rome and he established a monastery in Edmundsbury. He died in England on 13 November. Then one thousand and thirty-four years had passed from the birth of our Lord Jesus Christ. Knútr had then been king of Denmark twenty-seven years and of England twenty-four years and of Norway six years.

Harda-Knútr, the son of King Knútr inn ríki (the Great), was king of Denmark after his father for eight years. He was also king of England for four years. He made peace and an agreement with King Magnús góði (the Good) of Norway, the son of King Óláfr the saint, on the condition that the one who lived longer should rule after the one who died first if he was survived by no son. He died from illness.

King Magnús góði (the Good) of Norway took over the kingdom after Harda-Knútr in Denmark. Some landlords in Denmark were unfaithful to him and fought against him and always got the worst of it. Then the Wends harried in Denmark, and King Magnús fought against them and at Lyrskov Heath he defeated them to such an extent that fifteen thousand Wends fell there. He died in Denmark on 25 October. The Norwegians brought King Magnús's body to Norway, and he has been laid to rest in Christ Church in Niðaróss.[19] He had then been King of Denmark for five years.

Sveinn, with the other name Magnús, the son of Earl Úlfr, became king of Denmark after Magnús góði (the Good). King Sveinn's mother was Ástríðr, daughter of Sveinn tjúguskegg (Forkbeard) and sister of King Knútr inn ríki (the Great). For a long time he was at war with King Haraldr harðráði (the Stern) of Norway, the brother of King Óláfr the saint. King Sveinn had fourteen sons who lived to become adults, and five of them became absolute kings in Denmark. He married his daughter Ingiríðr to King Óláfr kyrri (the Quiet) of Norway, the son of King Haraldr harðráði (the Stern). He died from illness when he had been king for twenty-nine years.

Haraldr, who was called Hein (Whetstone), became king after King Sveinn, his father, and ruled for four years. He died from illness.

St Knútr, King Sveinn's second son, became king after King Haraldr, his brother. He was king for seven years. He was a good protector of law and order and greatly punished plunder and abuses. For that reason the Danes gathered together against him and killed him and his brother Benedikt in Holy Church in Odense on Funen. His feast day is 10 July.

---

[19] Modern Trondheim.

²²Olafr þriði ſon Sueins kongs tok kongdom efter hinn helga knþt |
²³broðor finn, hans drotning þar Ingigerðr dotter haralldz kongs harðraða |
²⁴af Noregi. han þar .víіj. þetr kongr oc þarð ſottdaðr. |
²⁵Eirikur er kallaðr þar egoðe fiorðe ſon Sueins kongs tok kongdom |
²⁶æfter Olaf kong broðor finn. A hans dogum þar ſettr erkibiscops ſtoll i |
²⁷Lþnd i Danmorko. Auzſur ærkibiscop þar þar fŷrſtr. han andaðiz ut i |
²⁸Cipr þa er han for ut til Iorsala, þa hafði han kongr þerit .víіj. þetr. |
²⁹Nicholas hinn .v. son Sueins kongs tok kongdom efter Eirik kong |
³⁰broðor finn. han atte Margretto dottor Inga Steinkels ſonar Spía kongs. |
³¹þeirra ſon þar herra Magnus ſterke, Margretto atte fŷʀ Magnus ber fęttr |
³²Noregs kongr ſon Olafs kŷʀa. Siðarliga á dogum Nicholas kongs drapo |
³³þeir Magnþſs ſon hans oc Heinrekr ſkotulær með spikum hinn helga | ³⁴knþt
hertuga i Siolande ſon Eiriks ægoða. þat var .víj. Idus dag Ianuarii. | ³⁵Efter
þetta hofz i moti Nicholasi kongi Eirikur er kallaðr er Emuni ſon | ³⁶Eiriks
kongs egoða broðer hins helga knþtz hertuga, oc atto þeir mikla | ³⁷orroſto i
ſkane. þar fello .vj. biscopar oc þar fell Magnus sterki ſon | ³⁸Nicholas kongs
oc Heinrekr ſkaʋtulær ſon Speins Speins ſonar kongs. | ³⁹Nicholas kongr flŷði
or bardaganþm til Iutlandz oc þar ſiþan drepin i | ⁴⁰heiðabŷ. þa hafðe han
þerit kongr .xxx. þetra. |

⁴¹Eirikr Emuni tok riki oc kongdom efter Niccholas kong, han atte |
⁴²Malmfridi drottning er fŷʀ hafði att Sigurþr kongr `i Noregi´ Jorſala |
⁴³fare, han for med her i Noreg oc med honum Magnus kongr blindi ſon
⁴⁴Sigurþar kongs Jorsalafara, þeir brændo ſtaðinn i Oflu oc ſþa hallþarðz ‖

4.1   ⁴·¹kirkio oc þunnþ ecki til fregðar i þeirri ferð. Ingi oc Sigurþr ſŷner | ²harallz
kongs Gilla þoro þa kongar i Noregi born at alldri, Eirikur let | ³drepa
haralld keſio broðor finn oc .íj. fŷni hans. Eirikr kongr þar | ⁴drepinn a þingi
j Jþtlandi, Sa het Plogr Sparte er þa konginn, þa hafði han kongr þerit íííj
þetr. |

⁶Eirikr Spaki er ſumer menn kalla Lamb fŷſturſon Eiriks kongs |⁷ empna
tok kongdom æfter han. I faður ętt þar han kominn af Magnþſi | ⁸kongi
goða. I mote honom striddi til rikis Olafr ſon Harallz keſiu, oc | ⁹þeir atto
.víіj. bardaga a æino are oc einn tima borðuz þeir þrŷſþar a | ¹⁰æinþm degi. A
aðru are ʀikis Eiriks kongs fell Olafr firer honom. Eirikr þar | ¹¹kongr .víіj.
þetr. hann gaf sek i clauftr oc andaðiz han mþnkr i oðins | ¹²æŷ. |

¹³Epter þat þoro kongar .íj. i ſenn ŷfer Danmorko. Toko Skanþngar | ¹⁴ser
til kongs Sþein er kallaðr þar ſuiðandi ſon Eiriks kongs Emþna. En | ¹⁵Jutar
toko ſer til kongs knut ſon herra Magnus ſterka, þeſſir kongar | ¹⁶ſtriddu

Óláfr, the third son of King Sveinn, became king after St Knútr, his brother. His queen was Ingigerðr, the daughter of King Haraldr harðráði (the Stern) of Norway. He was king for eight years and died from illness.

Eiríkr, who was called Eigóði (the Good), the fourth son of King Sveinn, became king after King Óláfr, his brother. In his days the archiepiscopal see was established in Lund in Denmark. Assur was the first archbishop there. Eiríkr died in Cyprus on his way to Jerusalem. He had been been king for eight years.

Nikulás, the fifth son of King Sveinn, became king after King Eiríkr, his brother. He was married to Margreta, the daughter of Ingi Steinkelsson, king of the Swedes. Their son was Lord Magnús sterki (the Strong). Margrét had previously been married to King Magnús berfættr (Bareleg) of Norway, the son of Óláfr kyrri (the Quiet). Late in the life of King Nikulás his son Magnús and Heinrekr skǫtulær (Magpie-thigh) treacherously killed Duke Knútr the saint in Zealand, the son of Eiríkr eigóði (the Good). That was on 7 January. After this Eiríkr, who is called Emuni (the Unforgettable), the son of King Eiríkr eigóði (the Good) and the brother of Duke Knútr the saint, rose up against King Nikulás, and they fought a great battle in Scania. Six bishops fell there, and Magnús sterki (the Strong), the son of King Nikulás, and Heinrekr skǫtulær (Magpie-thigh), the son of King Sveinn Sveinsson, fell there. King Nikulás fled from the battle to Jutland and was subsequently killed in Hedeby. He had then been king for thirty years.

Eiríkr Eimuni (the Unforgettable) came to power and took over the kingdom after King Nikulás. He was married to Queen Málmfríðr, who had previously been married to King Sigurðr Jórsalafari (the Crusader) of Norway. He went with an army to Norway and with him King Magnús blindi (the Blind), son of King Sigurðr Jórsalafari (the Crusader). They burned down Oslo township and Hallvard's church and did not earn themselves any fame in this journey. Ingi and Sigurðr, the sons of King Haraldr Gilli, children of age, were then kings in Norway. Eiríkr had his brother Haraldr kesja (halberd) and his two sons killed. King Eiríkr was killed at an assembly in Jutland. The one who slew the king was called Plógr svarti (the Black). He had then been king for four years.

Eiríkr spaki (the Meek), whom some men call Lamb, son of the sister of King Eiríkr Eimuni (the Unforgettable), became king after him. On his father's side he was descended from King Magnús góði (the Good). Óláfr, the son of Haraldr Kesja, fought against him over the kingdom, and they had eight battles in one year, and once they fought three times in one day. In the second year of King Eiríkr's reign Óláfr fell at his hands. Eiríkr was king for eight years. He entered a monastery and died as a monk in Odense.

After that there were two kings over Denmark at the same time. The Scanians took as their king Sveinn, who was called Svíðandi (the Scorcher), the son of King Eiríkr Eimuni (the Unforgettable). But the Jutes took as their king Knútr, the son of Lord Magnús sterki (the Strong). These kings

lengi þm rikit oc þeitti knþti kongi jafnan þẏngra, þar til er | [17]Walldimar ſon hins helga knþtz hertuga kom til liðſemðar þið knþt | [18]kong. þar þa gefit Walldimar kongs nafn. En Speinn kongr þarð at | [19]flẏía i þẏðiſkt land. han þar harðr maðr oc ſþikall. Litlu ſiðarr ſættuz | [20]þefsir .ííj. kongar, oc ſkiptu þeir þa Danmork millim ſin i þriðiþnga, oc | [21]þegar æfter þat ſþeik Speinn kongr baða þa, knþt kong oc Walldimar | [22]kong. þar þa knþtr kongr þeginn. En Walldimar kongr þarð farr oc | [23]komz þið þat þndan. þetta þar i Roskelldo a Lᴀrenz meſso aptan. knþt | [24]kong ſegia menn helgan. knutr þar vííj. þetr kongr. Nockoro ſiðarr | [25]borðuz þeir Walldimar kongr oc Speinn kongr a þeirri heiði er Grathe heiter. | [26]þar fell Speinn kongr. þa hafdi han þerit kongr .ix. þetr. |

[27]Epter þetta æignaðiz Walldimar kongr alla Danmork, oc þar agætr | [28]kongr, han atte Suffiþ dottor Walaðar kongs af Polenia, þeirra fẏner | [29]þoro þeir knþtr kongr oc Walldemar kongr. Cristofor hertogi þar oc ſon | [30]Walldimars kongs. Toþa het moðir hans. herra Wilialmur af Brþnsþik | [31]broðir Otta keiſara þeck dottor Walldimars kongs, oc aðra feck | [32]Philippus kongur af Franz. hina þriðio atte Eirikr Spiakongr, hon het | [33]Rikiza. Walldimar kongr kristnaði mikinn lþt af þind landi. han ſtẏrkti | [34]Magnus kong Erlings ſon frænda ſinn til Noregs, oc for fialfr med her | [35]ſinn i Noreg til Tþnsbergs (<Tunsbergs) þa er honom þotte Erlingr | [36]Skacke þaðir Magnus kongs. haþa brotit æinka mal þeirra. Litlo ſiðaʀ for | [37]Erlingr til Danmarkar oc geck a þalld Walldimars kongs, oc gaf | [38]kongurinn honum þa Iarls nafn, Walldimar kongr let upp taka helgan | [39]dom hins helga knþtz hertoga faður ſins. han þar kongr .vi. þetur oc .xx. | [40]oc andaðiz In feſto johannis ante portam Latinam. |

[41]Knþtr tok kongdom æfter Walldimar kong faður ſinn. En | [42]Walldimar broðir hans þar hertogi firer ſþnan a i Jþtlandi, þerſer bræðr | [43]kriſtnaðu þindland til fullz. knþtr þar rikr kongr oc goðr. han andadiz a | [44]þvi ſama are ſem Sverrir kongr i Noregi. þa hafði han þerit kongr .xx. | [45]þetr. Walldimar hertogi toc kongdom æfter knþt kong broþor ſinn. han | [46]feck dottor kongſens af Bȯm Margrætto er ſþmer kalla Dagmȯẏ. þeirra ||

5.1 [5.1]ſon þar Walldimar er kongr þar með feðr ſinum nockora uetr. Siðarr | [2]atte Walldimar kongr Berengario dottor kongſens af Portugal. þeirra | [3]fẏner þoro þeir Eirikr oc Abel oc Cristofor. Walldimar kongr atte oc .íj. | [4]frillu fẏne (e<i). hertuga knþt oc Græifa Nicholas. Walldimar kongr | [5]þaɴ þnder ſek mikin lþt af æiſt lande (e<i) oc criſtnaði. oc let gera ſterka | [6]borg j reþalum, han þann oc mikit af þẏðerſko. han for oc i Noreg til | [7]tþnsbergs oc `let´ gæfa kongs nafn Erlingi er hans menn kallaðu | [8]ſtæinþegg oc ſon Magnus kongs Erlings ſonar. Valldimar er kallaðr | [9]agætaztr Danakonga.

fought over the kingdom for a long time, and King Knútr always got the worst of it until Valdimarr, the son of Duke Knútr the saint, came to the assistance of King Knútr. Valdimarr was then given the title of king. But King Sveinn had to flee to Germany. He was a stern and treacherous man. A little later these three kings came to terms, and they then divided Denmark in three parts amongst themselves, but immediately after that King Sveinn betrayed both of them, King Knútr and King Valdimarr. King Knútr was then slain. But King Valdimarr escaped having been wounded. This took place in Roskilde on the eve of the feast day of St. Laurence. King Knútr is said to be a saint. Knútr was king for eight years. Sometime later King Valdimarr and King Sveinn fought on the heath that is called Grath. There King Sveinn fell. He had then been king for nine years.

After that King Valdimarr obtained all of Denmark and was an excellent king. He was married to Suffía, the daughter of King Valaðar of Poland. Their sons were King Knútr and King Valdimarr. Duke Kristófór was also the son of King Valdimarr. His mother's name was Tófa. Lord Viljálmr of Brúnsvík, the brother of Emperor Ótti, got the daughter of King Valdimarr in marriage, and King Philippus of France got another. Eiríkr, king of the Swedes, was married to a third; her name was Ríkiza. King Valdimarr Christianized a large part of Wendland. He supported King Magnús Erlingsson, his nephew, to obtain Norway, and himself went with an army to Tunsberg in Norway, when he thought that Erlingr skakki (the Skew), King Magnús's father, had broken their personal agreement. A little later Erlingr went to Denmark and submitted to King Valdimarr, and then the king bestowed upon him the title of earl. King Valdimarr saw to the translation of the relics of Duke Knútr the saint, his father. He was king for twenty-six years and died on 6 May on the feast of St. John before the Latin Gate.

Knútr became king after King Valdimarr, his father. But Valdimarr, his brother, was duke south of the river in Jutland. These brothers completely Christianized Wendland. Knútr was a mighty and good king. He died in the same year as King Sverrir of Norway. He had then been king for twenty years. Duke Valdimarr became king after King Knútr, his brother. He married Margareta, whom some call Dagmey, daughter of the king of Bohemia. Their son was Valdimarr, who was king together with his father for some years. Later King Valdimarr married Berengaria, daughter of the king of Portugal. Their sons were Eiríkr and Abel and Kristófór. King Valdimarr also had two sons by a concubine, Duke Knútr and Count Nikulás. King Valdimarr conquered a great part of Estonia and Christianized it, and he made a strong castle in Reval. He also conquered much of Germany. He also went to Tunsberg in Norway and had the title of king given to Erlingr, whom his men called Steinveggr (Stonewall), and the son of King Magnús Erlingsson the title of king. Valdimarr is considered the most excellent king of the Danes.

Translated by Kirsten Wolf

The manuscripts and their orthography

Árni Magnússon copied a vast number of texts for Bartholin.[20] I have flicked through these volumes, chiefly looking for texts from *Óláfs saga Tryggvasonar en mesta*, but stopping to look at others that seemed interesting. This comparatively casual inspection has led me to believe that Árni made it a matter of principle to provide diplomatic transcripts of documents and extracts from old books and, when particularly engaged by some source, even to imitate the script as well. On the other hand, when copying from late paper manuscripts, he used the orthography that came naturally to him. He copied the genealogical section and *Danakonungatal* letter by letter from the original, though not without a good many mistakes. In nominatives, especially of personal names, he often writes "ur" for *r*, for example. That usage was doubtless inadvertent, for there is otherwise nothing in the orthography to suggest that his source was written after the time when the svarabhakti came to be realised with any frequency in either Norwegian or Icelandic script.

Árni seems to have retained abbreviated forms only in very small measure. It is true that in the genealogical section he most often writes just ".f." for the word *son*, which was doubtless the practice of his source, but in *Danakonungatal* he writes "son" in full. The *er/ir* sign occurs once in his transcript at the end of a line; a macron is sometimes written over *n* and a dot to indicate gemination over *g* and *t*. He abbreviates Jesus Christ in the same way as in his source, and his abbreviation for the preposition *við* is doubtless also copied from the exemplar (I come back to this abbreviated form below). Árni always has the form "kongr" for *konungr*: probably the word was regularly abbreviated in his source but not as *kr*, *kg*, *ks* in the usual Icelandic fashion but as *kñgr*, *kñg*, *kñgs*, which Árni may have taken to represent the contracted form. It is further likely that the scribe of the vellum abbreviated the plural of *bróðir* in the conventional way as "℔", which Árni reproduces as "bræðr". He consistently writes the copulative as "oc", and that was undoubtedly the way it was spelt in the vellum exemplar in accordance with the common practice in thirteenth-century Norwegian script and in Icelandic manuscripts written at Þingeyrar in the latter part of the thirteenth century.[21] It is probably of no account whether Árni has "er" or "ir" in the words *bróðir, dóttir, faðir, móðir, synir*, since it may well be that these were all abbreviated in the source. He writes "biskup" with *i*, not *y*, and it is tolerably certain that that was the spelling of

---

[20] Már Jónsson, *Árni Magnússon. Ævisaga* (Reykjavík, 1998), 31–40.

[21] Stefán Karlsson, "Elsta brot Karlamagnús sögu og Rekaþáttur Þingeyrabókar," in *Stafkrókar: Ritgerðir eftir Stefán Karlsson gefnar út í tilefni af sjötugsafmæli hans 2. desember 1998*, ed. Guðvarður Már Gunnlaugsson,(Reykjavík, 2000), 206–24, esp. 214 (§ 4.20).

his source, though it too might have been abbreviated. And we may expect that still more abbreviated forms were in the text he copied, *Danmörk* for instance, the dative of which Árni always writes as "danmorko". In attempting to get at the orthography of the vellum exemplar through the medium of Árni's copy we must thus cautiously discount any words that we suspect were not written out in full in the source. On the other hand, where Árni uses old letter-forms, he probably derives most of them from his exemplar. He wrote tall ∫ and ordinary round *s* where these letters were there to copy, and he often writes court-hand *s* in a form most like the *h* of cursive black letter. (In the text above this letter is reproduced as ordinary *s*.) Árni may be expected to have followed the vellum in his use of *d*, *ð* and *þ*, of small capitals ɢ, ᴍ, ɴ and ʀ, and of dotted *g* and *t* to indicate gemination. The exemplar most probably also dictated his use of Insular ꝼ, made by Árni like *y* but with *y* itself distinguished by a superior dot, again following the practice of his source. On the other hand, it is difficult to believe that his rare use of Insular ꝥ (7 examples) truly reflects the incidence of this form in the vellum. We may instead be virtually certain that the Insular form was used throughout that text: it was hardly so antique a piece of writing that Roman *f* was extensively employed in it, not if the scribe was Norwegian or, as it might be, Icelandic.

Two other manuscripts containing these texts need to be introduced at this point. The genealogical section and *Danakonungatal* are in Stockholm, Royal Library Papp. fol. no. 76, folios 1–5r14. They are followed by lists of kings, evidently derived from texts that Árni had himself copied from Codex Resenianus: their source may have been the pages in Árni's hand now preserved in Copenhagen, Arnamagnaean Institute 1 eβ II fol., folios 85v–91r, or some other close copy. Some lines in Stock. Papp. fol. no. 76, folios 8v6–29, are taken up by three stanzas of a *hrynhent* poem, in fact all that remains of a memorial *drápa* on King Magnús lagabætir. These were first published by Jón Þorkelsson,[22] who rightly concluded that they were ultimately derived from Codex Resenianus. It is, however, evident that, like the preceding matter in Stock. Papp. fol. no. 76, their immediate source was to be found in copies made by Árni Magnússon.[23] The same hand is then found on what follows in Stock. Papp. fol. no. 76: "Um syni Nóa og skiptingu heimsins" (9r–9v9); "Um stórþing" (9v10–10v2); "Keisaratal" (10v3–11r); "Ártíðaskrá" (11v–13v11). Quite a different script, large and straggly, doubtless that of another writer, is then seen on folios 13v12–18v, "Langfedga Tal till nockurra Danmerkur og Norges kónga." Folios 19r–297 are then taken up by a copy of Copenhagen,

---

[22] Jón Þorkelsson, ed., *Småstykker 1–16*, Samfund til udgivelse af gammel nordisk litteratur 13 (Copenhagen, 1884–1891), 289–92.

[23] Stefán Karlsson, "Alfræði Sturlu Þórðarsonar," in *Stafkrókar*, 279–302, esp. 287.

Royal Library 1157 fol., the Codex Regius version of *Grágás*. Árni Magnússon began to check the copy but his marginal and interlinear corrections are
found only on the first three pages.[24]
Vilhelm Gödel thought that Stock. Papp. fol. no. 76 was all the work of
one writer: "Volymen är skrifven af Jón Eggertsson, utan tvifvel under hans
vistelse i Köbenhavn 1683–88."[25] It is likely enough that folios 13v12–18v and
the *Grágás* copy were written by Jón Eggertsson, though the latter is in a
changed hand-style, but the script of the opening part, folios 1–13v11, is quite
different.

The orthography of the genealogical section and *Danakonungatal* in
Stock. Papp. fol. no. 76 is largely the same as in Árni's copy, but letter-forms
differ. Long gaps left in a line or marking paragraph division are the same in
both manuscripts with these exceptions in Stock. Papp. fol. no. 76: 1.5 "moðir"
and 1.12 "Spæinn" start the line with no indication of a gap or new paragraph;
before "Lopis" in 1.24 there is an ordinary word-space; after "bloðæ̈yx" 1.33
is a paragraph division where Árni leaves a long gap; after 4.45 "petr" Stock.
Papp. fol. no. 76 begins a new paragraph where Árni has an ordinary word-
space. We have no means of knowing whether the vellum original showed
precisely the same spacing as that in Árni's copy and Stock. Papp. fol. no. 76. It
seems very likely, however, that the *Danakonungatal* text in the exemplar was
divided into sections with a new paragraph for each new reign; and it is possible that in the first part Árni left a long gap in the line where the exemplar had
a paragraph division. The agreement between Árni's copy and Stock. Papp. fol.
no. 76 in this particular does, however, suggest that Stock. Papp. fol. no. 76 was
derived from Árni's copy, though not from the one now in Barth. D III fol.

The genealogical section also exists in a copy by Jón Eggertsson in Stockholm, Royal Library Papp. fol. no. 64, folio 264r–v. Some forms in this copy
agree with those in Stock. Papp. fol. no. 76; both, for example, always write "au"
where Árni has "av" or "ɑ" (except once "havrda" in 64), and "son", "sonar", in
full where Árni has ".f."; both write "u" or "v" as appropriate where Árni has
Insular "ρ", and "gg", "nn" and "rr" where Árni has small capital G, N, R. Further
examples of agreement between Stock. Papp. fol. no. 64 and Stock. Papp. fol. no.
76 are (Árni's copy] Stock. Papp. fol. no. 76, Stock. Papp. fol. no. 64):

> 1.4 illraði] illrade. 5 haralldz] Harallz. 6 Sigurþar] Sigurdar. 9 Sigurþr]
> Sigurdr. 12 Spein] Sveinn. 16 Walldimarr] Valldemar.

[24] A. I. Arwidsson, *Förteckning öfver Kongl. bibliothekets i Stockholm isländska handskrifter* (Stockholm, 1848), 98.
[25] Vilhelm Gödel, *Katalog öfver Kongl. bibliotekets fornisländska och fornnorska
handskrifter* (Stockholm, 1897–1900), 208.

In Árni's copy there is a gap larger than an ordinary word-space before 1.4 "Ingialldur", 5 "мoðir", 7 "Raðbarðr" and 12 "Spæinn". Stock. Papp. fol. no. 64 has the gap before "Ingialldur" but not before the others. A particular point in favor of not counting Stock. Papp. fol. no. 64 a copy of Árni's copy is that, while in 1.7 Árni has "þeirra" written in full, Stock. Papp. fol. no. 64 has the abbreviation "þra". On the other hand, in l.18 both Stock. Papp. fol. no. 64 and Árni's copy have "þeirra" written out in this way. There is probably no need to take account of Jón Eggertsson's er/ir spellings in the words *bróðir, dóttir, faðir, móðir, synir.* In the genealogical section Stock. Papp. fol. no. 76 has these words in exactly the same form as in Árni's copy, but in Stock. Papp. fol. no. 64 Jón Eggertsson once has "i" where Árni's copy has "e" (5 "dotter") and six instances of "e" where Árni's copy has "i" (5 "мoðir", 6 "moðir", 8 "broðir", 17 "faðir" and "broðir"). In 1.7 Árni's copy has "holmgarði", Stock. Papp. fol. no. 76 "holmgardi", but Stock. Papp. fol. no. 64 "Holm garde"; in 1.15 Árni's copy and Stock. Papp. fol. no. 76 have "hertuge", Stock. Papp. fol. no. 64 "hertugi". We can hardly be confident that these endings were lifted by Jón Eggertsson from his exemplar, since in other texts in Stock. Papp. fol. no. 64 his use of "i" (and more often "e") in endings appears to be indiscriminate. A final point to note is that Árni and Stock. Papp. fol. no. 76 write "oc" throughout, while Stock. Papp. fol. no. 64 writes "og" and once "ok".

Beside the start of the text in Stock. Papp. fol. no. 64 there is a marginal note: "aþ gamallri skript og gamallri Membr:"; and another beside 1.4–5: "huadan Gatland haþe sitt naþn." After the genealogies comes the Our Father with the title: "Oratío Domíníca Ex Eadem Membr:" The spelling here is quite different from that of the genealogical section, and Jón was evidently making a close copy of his original.[26] If he was right in saying that the Lord's Prayer was in the same codex as *Sverris saga* and the genealogies, then it is clear that these texts were not all the work of one scribe. His imitation of the exemplar's script appears to be close, and this suggests that he was copying from the vellum itself. His remarks indicate that he was aware that the genealogical section existed in the same codex, whether in fact he made his copy directly from that source or from some other transcript of it. If he copied the genealogies from the codex, one might reasonably expect him to have attempted to follow its orthography, but in general we have to be wary of taking Jón Eggertsson's allusions to "ancient vellums" at their face value.[27]

---

[26] Stefán Karlsson, "Drottinleg bæn á móðurmáli," in *Biblíuþýðingar í sögu og samtíð*, Studia theologica islandica 4 (Reykjavík, 1990), 145–74, esp. 150–51.

[27] Már Jónsson, *Árni Magnússon*, 62–63.

In Árni's copy proper names are written variously with and without an initial capital. The same is true of Stock. Papp. fol. no. 76 and Stock. Papp. fol. no. 64, but there are numerous discrepancies, itemized as follows:

1.1 haldanar *ÁM*, Halfdanar *76*, Haldanar *64*. Guðroðar *ÁM*, Gudrodar *76*, guðroðar *64*. 2 and 3 haldanar[1,2] *ÁM*, *64*, Haldanar *76*. 2 Æýstæins *ÁM*, *76*, æýstæins *64*. 4 gɑtilldi *ÁM*, gautilldi *64*, Gautilldi *76*. algɑta *ÁM*, Algauta *76*, *64*. gɑtz *ÁM*, gautz *64*, Gautz *76*. gɑtland *ÁM*, gautland *64*, Gautland *76*. 5 haralldz *ÁM*, Harallz *76*, *64*. ragnilldur *ÁM*, Ragnilldr *76*, Ragnilldur *64*. Sigurþar *ÁM*, *76*, sigurdar *64*. 6 Sigurþar *ÁM*, Sigurdar *76*, sigurdar *64*. 7 holmgarði *ÁM*, holmgardi *76*, Holm garde *64*. þnnar *ÁM*, Vnnar *76*, Wnnar *64*. 8 haralldz *ÁM*, *64*, Haralldz *76*. 9 Sigurþr[1] *ÁM*, *76*, sigurdur *64*. Ringr *ÁM*, Ringur *64*, ringr *76*. Sigurþr[2] *ÁM*, Sigurdr *76*, sigurdur *64*. 10 hɑrða knþtr *ÁM*, haurda knutur *64*, Haurda knutr *76*. haralldur *ÁM*, *64*, *76*. 11 Sþeinn *ÁM*, Sveinn *76*, sveinn *64*. 12 hɑrða knþtr *ÁM*, havrda knutur *64*, Haurda knutr *76*. haralldr *ÁM*, Haralldr *76*, Haralldur *64*. Sþein *ÁM*, Sveinn *76*, sueinn *64*. 13 Ulfr *ÁM*, *76*, ulfur *64*. 14 Sþeiɴ *ÁM*, Sveinn *76*, sueinn *64*. ᴍagnus *ÁM*, magnus *76*, *64*. 16 Walldemars *ÁM*, *76*, walldimars *64*. 17 Noregi *ÁM*, *76*, noregi *64*. kristofor *ÁM*, Kristofor *76*, Kristophor *64*.

The names Sigurður and Sveinn are written in Stock. Papp. fol. no. 64 with a small round *s* in no way distinguishable from the form it has in other words. Nor can any clear distinction be seen between initial *k* in Knútr and the same letter at the beginning of ordinary words. Most proper names in Stock. Papp. fol. no. 76 are written with a capital, certainly more than had such an initial in the source, and probably Árni is similarly over-generous in the insertion of capital letters. Stock. Papp. fol. no. 76 agrees with Árni's orthography rather more often than Stock. Papp. fol. no. 64 does, though on occasion Stock. Papp. fol. no. 64 is closer: thus, for example, Jón Eggertsson, like Árni, always has the contracted form *kóngr* while Stock. Papp. fol. no. 76 has "konongr". Jón also regularly uses insular *f* (ꝼ) but it would not be safe to conclude that this was the letter-form he found in his exemplar. These points, along with the use of capitals in proper names, show that Stock. Papp. fol. no. 64 was not copied from Stock. Papp. fol. no. 76, and it is hardly conceivable that either of these was copied from Árni's copy in Barth. III D.

Bjarni Guðnason inserts "landit" after 2.21 "han"[2] and "landi" after 5.6 "þyðerſko".[28] With these words supplied the text becomes a good deal more

---

[28] Bjarni Guðnason, ed., *Danakonunga sǫgur*, 329.13, 335.19.

natural, and the conclusion that they were lacking in the vellum exemplar can hardly be avoided. It is unlikely that Árni Magnússon would have omitted them if they had been in the manuscript in front of him, but he did not see fit to correct the text. Storm printed 1.26 "Sleivik" as "Slesvik",[29] Bjarni Guðnason as "Slésvík",[30] both doubtless assuming that "ei" was an error for "es" or possibly a spelling that represented *é*. If the vellum had "slefʃik", we should have to believe that the tall *ʃ* had been worn or reduced in some way when Árni made his transcript so that he could only read it as *i* — though in that case one would have expected him to offer some comment. As far as I know, the place-name form "Sleivík" is not found in any other Norse-Icelandic source, but possibly Árni regarded it as permissible (cf. German Schlei). These three putative errors in Árni's copy all remain in Stock. Papp. fol. no. 76, which clearly demonstrates that Stock. Papp. fol. no. 76 was derived from the same original as Árni's copy, but of course does not tell us whether it was copied directly from that original or from some intermediate transcript.

In two places Stock. Papp. fol. no. 76 omits words found in Árni's copy (and doubtless in his source), and in one instance it has a word not in Árni's copy: 2.20 Sʃein] ÷ Stock. Papp. fol. no. 76; 2.25 kongr] ÷ Stock. Papp. fol. no. 76; 2.2 flyði] + hann Stock. Papp. fol. no. 76. Otherwise Stock. Papp. fol. no. 76 is word for word the same as Árni's copy, although there is naturally no repeat of the double "gera gera" in 1.26, and in 1.35–36 "'han' let" appears as "let hann". The third singular masculine pronoun is always "han" in Árni's copy (except twice "hann" 1.30 and 4.11), while Stock. Papp. fol. no. 76 has the Icelandic form "hann". Other variants in Stock. Papp. fol. no. 76, either alterations made willy-nilly by the writer or forms which may suggest the spelling of the original, are chiefly these (Árni's copy] Stock. Papp. fol. no. 76):

1.4 Ingialldur] Jngialldr. 1.5 haralldz] Harallz. ragnilldur] Ragnilldr. 1.7 'hins'] hins. 1.9 ormur] Ormr. 1.10 haralldur] Haralldr. 1.12 kongur] konongr. 1.16 Walldimarr] Valldemar. 1.19 Carll] Karll, *but* 1.23 Carll. 1.23, 39 og 2.33–34 I*esu Kristi*] Jhesu Christi. 1.26 Eirikr] Eirikur. Epter] Efter *and elsewhere*. 1.29 drotning] drottning. 1.30 sik] sig. 1.39 hundrut] hundrud. 1.40 fiðarʃtum] Siþarʃtu. 2.7 Svein] Svæinn (!). 2.12 trỹgua] Tryggva-. 2.18 fin] finn. 2.20 En] Enn. 2.21 orostur] orrostur. 2.23 en] er. 2.24 kriʃtni] Christni. 2.25 fỹrʃt] firʃt. 2.31 fegia] feigia. 3.12 æinʃalldz] ænvalldz. 3.20 hæilagri] heilagri. 3.23 drotning] drottning. 3.25 Eirikur] Eirikr. 3.26 erkibiʃcops] erkipiskups (*probably abbreviated*. "erch. bpc"

[29] Storm, ed., *En oldnorsk Saga*, 2.19.
[30] Bjarni Guðnason, ed., *Danakonunga sǫgur*, 327.2.

in the vellum). 3.27 ærkibifcop] ærkibifcup. 3.29 .v.] þ. 3.33 Magnpfs]
Magnus. 3.34 hertuga] hertoga. Ianuarii] Januarij. 3.35 Eirikur] Eirikr.
3.36 knptz] Knuts. 3.44 brændo] brendu. 4.2 Eirikur] Eirikr. 4.7 ętt] ætt.
4.11 mpnkr] mukr. 4.14 Spein] Sveinn. 4.16 jafnan] iafnan. 4.21 þat] þad.
4.29 knýtr] Knutr. Walldemar] Valldimar. 4.30 Wilialmur] Vilialmr.
4.32 kongur] konongr. 4.33 ftýrkti] stirkti. 4.35 Tpnsbergs] Tungsbergs.
4.38 kongurinn] konongrinn. 4.40 In] i. 4.42 þerfer] þerfser. 4.46 Mar-
grætto] Margrættu. kalla] calla. 5.3 Cristofor] Christofor. 5.4 Græifa]
Græfa. 5.7 `let´] let.

Among the Norwegian characteristics noted by Storm in Árni's copy was consistent vowel harmony. As observed above, it is safest to disregard the vowels
in any endings which may be thought to have been abbreviated in the vellum
source. The existence of the vowel harmony rule is not fully substantiated by
the occurrence of *e/i* and *ö/u* in final syllables in Árni's copy and Stock. Papp.
fol. no. 76, and these two copies do not always show the same ending vowel.[31]
Examples of such variation are as follows (the first group from the text also
known in Stock. Papp. fol. no. 64):

> 1.13 dottor Árni's copy, dottur Stock. Papp. fol. no. 76, dotter Stock.
> Papp. fol. no. 64. 1.14 nafne Árni's copy, Stock. Papp. fol. no. 76, napni
> Stock. Papp. fol. no. 64. helgi Árni's copy, Stock. Papp. fol. no. 64, helge
> Stock. Papp. fol. no. 76. l.15 hertuge Árni's copy, Stock. Papp. fol. no. 76,
> hertugi Stock. Papp. fol. no. 64.

In *Danakonungatal* we find these variants in Stock. Papp. fol. no. 76 [Árni's
copy] Stock. Papp. fol. no. 76):

> 1.23, 4.9 *and* 4.44 are] ari. 1.33 riki] rike. 2.1, 3.1 *and* 4.35 honom] honum.
> 2.3 and 3.21 mefso] mefsu. 2.13 kriftni] kriftne. 2.15 monnom] monnum.
> 2.22 þioðlondom] þiodlondum. 3.3 þinðum] vindom. 3.3 *and* 3.37 fello]
> fellu. 3.12, 4.28, 31 *and* 46 dottor] dottur. 3.13 sýní] sýne. 3.19 drapo]
> drapu. 3.31 fterke] Sterki. 3.36 atto] attu. 3.44 brændo] brendu. 4.1 *and*
> 4.25 þeirri] þeirre. 4.3 broðor] brodr. 4.4 Sparte] Svarti. 4.8 mote] moti.

And there are these variants in Árni's copy (Árni's copy] Stock. Papp. fol. no.
76):

---

[31] Bjarni Guðnason, ed., *Danakonunga sǫgur*, cxc, n. 5.

1.27 kirkiu] kirkio. 2.7 sæli] sæle. 2.16 moti] mote. 2.29 knᵽte] knuti. 2.44 ſtriddo] ſtriddu. 3.9 dottir] dotter. 3.16 rikte] rikti. 3.19 firer] firir.

I include here the accusative of *dóttir* and the dative of *hann, sonr, menn*, but it may be safely assumed that these forms were not written out in full in the vellum exemplar. I have, on the other hand, not included words ending in *de/ di* and *ðe/ði*. This is because we know that when *d* came to be generally written with a curved ascender (Ð) scribes tended to write *e* after *d* and *ð* without regard to the quality of the preceding vowel and to ligature the *e* with the bowl of the *d* or *ð*.[32] It is thus reasonable to believe that *di* and *ði* endings in Árni's copy, Stock. Papp. fol. no. 76 and Stock. Papp. fol. no. 64 might be deviations from the spelling of their ultimate source. Árni's copy shows these examples of *di/ði* spellings where Stock. Papp. fol. no. 76 and Stock. Papp. fol. no. 64, one or both, have *de/ðe*:

1.4 illraði Árni's copy, illrade Stock. Papp. fol. no. 76, Stock. Papp. fol. no. 64. 1.7 holmgarði Árni's copy, Stock. Papp. fol. no. 76, Holm garde Stock. Papp. fol. no. 64. 1.19 fiðir] fider. 1.25 Jwtt landi] Jutlande. 1.27, 30 *and* 2.23 lagði] lagde. 1.34 *and* 2.20 heriaði] heriade. 3.39 flýði] flÿde. 4.42 broðir] broder.

Examples of *di* in Stock. Papp. fol. no. 76 where Árni's copy has *de/ðe*:

2.29 ænglande] Ænglandi. 3.25 fiorðe] fiordi. 3.34 Siolande] Siolandi. 5.5 æist lande] æist landi.

But there are numerous examples of *di/ði* in both Stock. Papp. fol. no. 76 and Árni's copy:

1.22, 3.3, 4.11, 40 *and* 43 andaðiz. 1.32 Iutlandi. 1.37 kallaði. 2.33, 35 *and* 38 Englandi. 4.4 jᵽtlandi. 4.14 fuiðandi. 4.27 æignaðiz. 4.33 ᵽind landi. 5.5 criſtnaði.

It may further be noted that the third person preterite singular of *hafa* is always "hafdi" in Stock. Papp. fol. no. 76; Árni's copy shows eight instances of "hafði", four of "hafðe" (2.17, 26, 34 and 3.40).

The vowel harmony rule is broken in one instance shared by all three manuscripts, Árni's copy, Stock. Papp. fol. no. 76 and Stock. Papp. fol. no. 64, viz. 1.4 "atti". Árni's copy and Stock. Papp. fol. no. 76 have a few more similar

---

[32] Stefán Karlsson, "Elsta brot Karlamagnús sögu," 209–10 (§ 4.4).

instances in common. I start with words whose endings may be reliably assumed not to have been abbreviated in the source:

2.43 goði. 2.44 moti. 3.5 Niðarofi. 3.11 bernſko. 3.18 reffte. 3.20 hæilagri.
3.35 moti. 3.44 Oslu. 4.6 Spaki. 4.9 æino. 4.29, 42 *and* 45 hertogi. 4.32
þriðio. 4.36 Litlo. 4.43 kristnaðu.

In both manuscripts the kinship nouns, *bróðir, faðir, móðir*, are more often
with "ir" than "er"; *dóttir* and the nominative plural of *sonr* more often with
"er". Oblique cases of *bróðir* in the singular are written in both with the ending "or" (nine examples, with 4.3 "brodr" an exception in Stock. Papp. fol. no.
76), but *faðir* in similar cases with "ur" (11 examples: 'faður] "fauður" once,
"faður "six times, "foður" four times). An exception is 5.1 "feðr" (dative). It
is noteworthy that the unmutated instances are the same in Stock. Papp. fol.
no. 76 and Árni's copy. The spelling variety in these forms indicate that they
were written out in the vellum and not reduced to "f.".

The word *eftir* occurs 16 times with the ending "er", twice with "ir"; *fyrir*
(always spelt with "i" in the first syllable) occurs once with "ir", four times
with "er"; *undir* six times with "er", never with "ir"; *yfir* seven times with "er",
never with "ir".

Insular *f* occurs seven times in Árni's copy: 1.7 ꝧeck, 1.30 ꝧekk, 2.17 eꝧter,
2.27 ꝧirer, 3.17 æꝧter, 4.31 ꝧeck, 4.36 ꝧaðir. A type of Insular *f* is used throughout Stock. Papp. fol. no. 64; it does not occur at all in Stock. Papp. fol. no. 76.

An accent mark over a long vowel is seen only thrice in Árni's copy, twice
over *a*, in the word *ár* 1.24 and the preposition *á* 3.32, and once over Insular
ꝧ in the name Knútr 4.29. No distinction is otherwise made between short
and long vowels except in the place-name Hróarskelda, Roskilde, which is
spelt with double *o* in 2.3 "Rooskelldo", and *w* in 1.25 "Jwtt landi" probably
indicates *ú*.

Unmutated short *a* is found in the eke-name "blatann", twice written so
(1.33 and 40); and in "faður" 1.21, 2.20, 2.38, 3.16, 4.39, 4.41 (six examples);
"heriaðo" 2.9 and 3.1; "hundrat" 1.23 but "hundrut" 1.39, 2.23; "kallaðu" 5.7;
"kristnaðu" 4.43; "siðarſtum" 1.40; "þufundrað" 3.3.

Mutated forms are: "gavfuglata" 1.2; "borduz" 2.11, "borðuz" 4.9 and
4.25; dative plural of *dagr*, "dogum" 1.34, 1.40, 3.26, 3.32 (four examples);
oblique cases of *faðir*, "foður" 1.24, 2.4, 2.6, 2.18, "faður" 4.7 (five examples);
"Morgum" 2.10; dative plural of *land*, "norðrlɏndum" 1.21, "þioðlondom"
2.22; "skotulær" 3.33, "skɏtulær" 3.38; *öðru*, written "ɏðru" 1.14, 4.10, "oðru"
3.7; "Onꝧndar" 1.3. The dative singular of the pronoun *hann* always has *o* in
the first syllable: "honum" 3.43, 4.38, "honom" 1.36, 2.1, 2.44, 3.1, 3.19, 4.8,
4.10, 4.35 (ten examples). It may well be however that in the vellum this word
was abbreviated in the conventional way ("hm").

"æ" is often written for *e* at the beginning of a word but according to no observable rule: for instance, *eftir* is spelt 19 times with "æ" and only three times with "e"; *England* four times with "æ" and not at all with "e". In medial positions "æ" is rare but does occur: "brændo" 3.44, "gæfa" 5.7, "Margrætto" 4.46. The diphthong in the name Sveinn is spelt "æi" and "ei" in a ratio of 8 to 1. Other words have "ei" rather more often but "æi" is well represented (eight examples in all). "ey" does not appear but there are three instances of "æẏ": "Æẏstæins" 1.2, "oðins æẏ" 3.20 and 4.11–12, and once "òẏ": "Dagmòẏ" 4.46. There is one instance of "æẏ" for "ø": "bloðæẏx" 1.33.

This use of "æ" for "e" is an early Norwegian scribal custom which became relatively common in Icelandic manuscripts after about 1250.[33] In the transcripts the vowel in (-)eng(-) is most often written "e", occasionally "æ", never "ei".

The relative particle *er* appears once as "en" 2.23 in Árni's copy; it is "er" in Stock. Papp. fol. no. 76.

The preposition *í* is written "i" but it is difficult to know whether Árni meant "I" or "j" in initial positions, particularly in proper names.

The word *son* is always written with "o", not with "u" as was commonly done in Norwegian. The geographical name *Jótland* is written with some form of "u" in the first syllable, "u" or Insular "v" (ꝩ) and once "w", which probably stands for "ú": "Iutlandi" 1.32, "Iutlandz" 3.39, "Jꝩtlandi" 4.4, "Jꝩtlandi" 4.42, "Jwttlandi" 1.25; similarly "Jutar" 4.15.

The feminine name Þyri is written with "Th": "Thẏri" 1.29; and the Jutish moorland named Graðarheiðr in *Knýtlinga saga* is called "Grathe" 4.25.

"u" is normally written for *u* and *ú* especially in medial positions, but "v" or "ꝩ" occasionally occur, and in one instance "ꝩ" with an accent appears for *ú*: "knꝩtr" 4.29. Both "v" and "ꝩ" are written for *v*. An isolated form with "ẏ" for *i* is found in 3.9 "Tẏgufkegs" (also spelt that way in Stock. Papp. fol. no. 76), probably lifted straight from a Danish source.[34]

The neuter of the adjective *mikill* is spelt with "y" in "mẏkit herꝩirki" 2.4–5, but elsewhere all genders appear with "i": "mikit" 3.2., "mikla" 3.36, "mikinn" 4.33, "mikin" 5.5, "mikit" 5.6. The word *fyrir* is always written "firer" or "firir", and the preterite of *skulu* appears as "skilldi" 2.40, but it is doubtful whether these words were spelt out in the vellum.

"æ", "e" or "ę" are written for *æ* (i-mutation of *á*): "ætte" 2.41, "fættuz" 4.19; "e" in, for example, fett 2.39, "legra" 3.1, "fregðar" 4.1; and "ę" in "ętt" 4.7. The cognomen of King Eiríkr eygóði is once written "ęgoðe" 1.15 (the same in Stock. Papp. fol. no. 76 and Stock. Papp. fol. no. 64), once "egoðe"

---

[33] Stefán Karlsson, "Elsta brot Karlamagnús sögu," 217–19 (§§ 5.3 and 7.1).

[34] Gunnar Knudsen and Marius Kristensen, eds., *Danmarks gamle Personnavne*. 1: *Fornavne*, 2: *Tilnavne* (Copenhagen, 1954–1964), 2: 1137–38.

3.25, and once "ægoða" 3.34. The cognomen of King Eiríkr eymuni similarly appears as "Emuni" 3.35, 3.41, "empna" 4.7 and "Empna" 4.14. There is
no reason to think that in writing "ęgoðe" Árni was doing anything except
faithfully copying his source, but in that case it is most likely that the scribe
of the vellum followed an exemplar in which the name was spelt "ægoðe". In
Danish sources both these eke-names, "eymuni" and "eygóði," are most often
spelt with initial e, but æ and æi also occur.[35]

A particular letter-form for æ (i-mutation of ó) is found only once, and
then inappropriately, in the accusative of kærleikr: "kòrleik" 2.39. In the whole
text, however, there are only three words in which æ would be proper: substan-
tive "bræðr" 4.42, written with "æ" but possibly abbreviated "ƀ" in the vellum;
the adjective norrænn, dative "norrena" 2.19; and the eke-name of King Magnús berfœttr, spelt in the nominative "ber fęttr" 3.31 (in Stock. Papp. fol. no. 76
all these words are spelt in the same way as in Árni's copy). The whole text thus
contains no word in which correct distinction is made between æ and œ.

ǫ is variously rendered by "o" and "a", never by "au"; for diphthong au either "a" or "au" is written.

ø is spelt "o" in "Guðroðar" 1.1 and "æẏ" in "bloðæẏx" 1.33.

vá appears as "pa": "spa" 2.15, 3.2, 3.44, "Spa" 2.31, "pa" 4.4, "pars" 1.23,
1.39, 2.33; for older vǫ́ in the third plural preterite of vera we find "po": "poro"
1.11, 2.44, 4.2, 4.13, 4.29, 5.3.

The first person plural pronoun is "per" 1.31, "pær" 1.20.

The reflexive pronoun sik is spelt seven times with "e" in the Norwegian
fashion: "fek" 1.28, 2.21, 2.31, 5.5, "sek" 2.14, 4.11, "fec" 2.23, once "sik" 1.30.

The chief consonantal features to be noted are the following:

The third singular masculine pronoun in the nominative is twice written "hann" 1.30 and 4.11, but 58 times "han". Single "g" is written in "spraka
legs" 1.13, "tivgufkeg" 1.12, "Tyugufkegs" 3.9. Small capital letters that stand
for geminated consonants are ɢ, ɴ, and ʀ.

The voiced dental spirant is generally written "ð" except in the personal
name Sigurður which is always written with "þ"; "þ" also occurs in "broþor"
4.45 and "fiþan" 2.8, 3.39. There are also some 20 instances of "d" written for ð,
and since these most often occur in a single line or within a few lines of text it is
conceivable that the vellum was worn in these places and the loop of ð no longer visible. We find "pinðr" 3.1 and "pinðum" 3.3, but "pindland" 2.2, 4.43, and
"pind landi" 4.33. One back spelling exists in "unðer" 2.23. t for older ð is found
in "hundrat" and "hundrut", and in the preterite of styrkja, "ftyrkti" 4.33.

[35] See Knudsen and Kristensen, eds., Personnavne, 2: 243–44, 248–49.

The definite article is with initial "h". Initial *hl* and *hr* are spelt "l" and "r": "lut" 3.1, "lþt" 4.33, 5.5; "lyrskogs heiði" 3.2; "Ringr" 1.9, "Ring" 1.21.

As observed earlier, the copulative is always "oc". Elsewhere "c" is rare: the Emperor Charlemagne's name is spelt "Carll" 1.19 and 22, "karls" 1.24; other instances are "claustr" 4.11, "cristnaði" 5.5, "Criftofor" 4.29, 5.3, "lic" 3.4, "toc" 4.45.

At 3.19 the form is "samnað", not the later form with *-fn-*.

The word *eftir* is spelt with both "ft" and "pt".

There is a solitary example of the Norwegian practice of writing "rs" for long *s*, "þerfer" 4.42.

The middle voice ending is *z*.

The nominative of Ástríðr is "Aftrið" 1.13, 3.8. Initial *h* is lost in *hildr* when it occurs as the second element in a personal name, for example. "rag-nilldur" 1.5, "Ragnilldr" 1.31, "gꝩtilldi" 1.4, "Gunnilldi" 2.30. Such forms are common in Norwegian sources, less so in Icelandic.[36] The genitive of the name of the first wife of King Valdemarr II appears as "Margrætto" 4.46, which presupposes nominative Margretta or Margreta, a name-form common in Denmark and Norway.[37] We read that Valdemarr I "atte Suffiþ dottor Walaðar kongs af Polenia." This lady has the same name in *Fagrskinna*,[38] and another Suffía is referred to in *Hákonar saga gamla* in Fríssbók.[39]

Some place-names are not written according to Icelandic custom: "Franz" 4.32, "heiðabý" 3.40, "Sleiþik" 1.26, "þrondeime" 2.27. Johan Fritzner cites the form Franz only from *Karlamagnús saga* and *Elís saga ok Rósamundu*.[40] The East Norse *býr* for *bœr* occurs in Norwegian and Icelandic sources of the thirteenth and fourteenth century.[41] Sleivik is probably an adaption of a German form of this place-name (Schlei; see above). Þrándheimr spelt with *o* or *ó* is a Norwegian form but crops up in Icelandic manuscripts, e.g. in Copenhagen,

---

[36] See E. H. Lind, ed., *Norsk-isländska dopnamn ock fingerade namn från medeltiden* (Uppsala, 1905–1915), 303–4, 409–11, 842–44, 1051–53, 1178.

[37] Knudsen and Kristensen, eds., *Personnavne*, 1: 899–909; Lind, ed., *Norsk-isländska dopnamn*, 760–64.

[38] Finnur Jónsson, ed., *Fagrskinna. Nórges konunga tal*, Samfund til udgivelse af gammel nordisk litteratur 30 (Copenhagen, 1902–1903), 300.23.

[39] C. R. Unger, ed., *Codex Frisianus. En Samling af norske Konge-Sagaer* (Christiania [Oslo], 1871), 568.

[40] Johan Fritzner, *Ordbog over Det gamle norske Sprog*, 3 vols. (Kristiania [Oslo], 1886–1896).

[41] The form is quite common in *Kringla*: see, for example, Den arnamagnæanske Kommission, ed., *Ordbog over det norrøne prosasprog: A Dictionary of Old Norse Prose* 1– (Copenhagen, 1995–), 2: 1032–33.

Arnamagnaean Institute 325 4to VI from the latter part of the fourteenth century.[42] The adjective *þýskur* appears in the forms "þyðiſkt" 4.19 and "þyðerſko"
5.6; both are common in other sources.[43]

Word-forms not attested in early sources and unusual in Icelandic are:[44]
"fullkomlega" 2.24, "herra" 2.30, 3.31, 4.15, 4.30, used as a title, "landz herrar" 2.44, "rettare" 3.18, "rikte" 3.16, and the verb *stríða*: "ſtriddi" 1.40, 4.8,
"ſtriddo" 2.44, "ſtriddu" 4.16. According to Fritzner, *réttari* first occurs in
Skáldskaparmál in *Snorra Edda*[45] and the so-called articles entered by Magnús
Þórhallsson in *Flateyjarbók* from Styrmir's *Óláfs saga helga* are probably the
oldest Icelandic source in which *stríða* is found in the sense of "fight";[46] otherwise it is attested in the same sense in Icelandic sources from the second half
of the thirteenth century.

All the Norwegian features in spelling and word-forms that are apparent
in these texts would lead one to conclude with little doubt that the writer was
Norwegian — if only the confusion between "æ" and "œ" did not exist, see p.
132 above.

On three occasions Árni writes the preposition *við* as Insular þ followed by
the 3-like abbreviation for *eð*: "þ3" 1.5, 1.38, 4.23. The preposition *með* written
m with this abbreviation sign is very common, but I know of no example of *við*
written in this way in Norwegian manuscripts. Bjarni Einarsson pointed the
same form out to me in the *Heiðarvíga saga* text in Stockholm, Royal Library
Perg. 4to no. 18. It occurs there at folio 2r11, "*ok mælti við hann*," and in the introduction to his facsimile edition of this manuscript he remarks that this use
of the abbreviation sign in the word *við* "appears quite unparalleled."[47] This instance is in the oldest part of the codex, written scarcely later than soon after
about 1250. Nothing is certainly known about the ultimate provenance of the
manuscript but it must be thought most likely that it was written at Þingeyrar.

It has been borne in on me when considering the orthography of these
texts that they have many features reminiscent of the scribal habits apparent
in Copenhagen, Arnamagnaean Institute 310 4to, a manuscript of *Óláfs saga*

---

[42] Oscar Albert Johnson and Jón Helgason, eds., *Saga Óláfs konungs hins helga. Den
store saga om Olav den hellige* (Oslo, 1941), 6.18.

[43] Ólafur Halldórsson, "Þýskan í Grænlendinga sögu," *Gripla* 8 (1993), 282–84.

[44] Storm, ed., *En oldnorsk Saga*, 13.

[45] Finnur Jónsson, ed., *Edda Snorra Sturlusonar* (Copenhagen, 1931), 161.19.

[46] Guðbrandr Vigfússon and C.R Unger, eds., *Flateyjarbók. En Samling af norske
Konge-Sagaer*, 3 vols. (Christiania [Oslo], 1860–1868), 3: 239.2.

[47] Bjarni Einarsson, ed., *The Saga of Gunnlaug Serpent-Tongue and Three Other Sagas. Perg. 4:o nr 18 in the Royal Library Stockholm*, Early Icelandic Manuscripts in Facsimile 16 (Copenhagen, 1986), 21.

Tryggvasonar by Oddr munkr Snorrason. Other manuscripts in the same hand are Copenhagen, Arnamagnaean Institute 655 4to XII–XIII and XIV, the *Grágás Rekaþáttr* in Copenhagen, Arnamagnaean Institute 279a 4to and a fragment of *Karlamagnús saga* in Oslo, Norsk Riksarkiv 61. Stefán Karlsson attributes all these to the Þingeyrar scriptorium.[48]

There is nothing problematic about assigning to the same hand the genealogical section and *Danakonungatal* in the vellum manuscript copied by Árni Magnússon. The genealogies were apparently put together about 1261 or soon afterwards (see p. 137 below). Before that date they and *Danakonungatal* could not have been written at the end of the *Sverris saga* manuscript followed by Árni. To judge by letter-forms and spelling they could not have been written many years later either. That does not mean that the genealogical section and *Danakonungatal* always existed in combination and are necessarily equally old in origin.

The Genealogies. Commentary

The genealogies start with the lineage of Haraldr hárfagri but are mostly devoted to the descent of the kings of Denmark. Haraldr hárfagri's ancestry is traced back to Sigurðr ormr í auga. The generations agree in the main with those enumerated in *Ynglinga saga* and *Hálfdanar saga svarta* in *Heimskringla*. Guðrøðr, father of Hálfdan svarti, is called "hinn gǫfugláti," as in *Jöfraskinna*, while in *Kringla* and *Flateyjarbók* he is referred to as "inn mikilláti, en sumir kǫlluðu hann veiðikonung."[49] Gauthildr, wife of Ingjaldr hinn illráði, is described as the daughter "Algauta s(onar) Gauts er Gautland er við kennt." This corresponds to *Heimskringla*:[50]

Ok er Ingjaldr var roskinn, þá bað ǫnundr konu til handa honum, Gauthildar, dóttur Algauta konungs, hann var sonr Gautreks konungs ins milda, sonar Gauts er Gautland er við kent.

---

[48] Stefán Karlsson, "Om norvagismer i islandske håndskrifter," in *Stafkrókar*, 173–87, esp. 181–82.

[49] Finnur Jónsson, ed., *Heimskringla. Nóregs konunga sǫgur af Snorri Sturluson*, 4 vols., Samfund til udgivelse af gammel nordisk litteratur 23 (Copenhagen, 1893–1901), 1: 81.3–4; Stefán Karlsson, "Gǫfuglátur veiðikonungur," in *Pétursskip búið Peter Foote sextugum 26. maí 1984* (Reykjavík, 1984), 51–54.

[50] Finnur Jónsson, ed., *Heimskringla*, 1: 62.16–63.2. "And when Ingjaldr was full-grown, Ǫnundr asked for a women for him, Gauthildr, the daughter of King Algauti; he was the son of King Gautrekr the Mild, the son of Gautr, from whom Gautland is named."

Bjarni Guðnason takes the view that the genealogy depended on *Heimskringla* and that a generation had been skipped in the maternal line of Ingjaldr ill-ráði.[51] If such an omission is to be credited to the author or a later copyist, it is probable that the original source read: "Gauthildi dóttur Algauta konungs, sonar Gautreks konungs, sonar Gauts [. . .]," and he jumped from the first "konungs" to the second (*saut du même au même*). In that case we have to reckon with a source that contained royal pedigrees but not with *Heimskringla* itself. Of course, it could well be that the author of that text (if it existed) made use of *Heimskringla*, unless it and *Heimskringla* were both following the same older source — which seems, in fact, to be the most likely explanation.

The Danish kings are traced from Ráðbarðr in Hólmgarðr to Eiríkr Kristófórusson (r. 1259–1286). From King Ráðbarðr to the sons of Knútr ríki (Cnut the Great, king of England and Denmark) the regnal list agrees with other such catalogues that are thought to be derived from *Skjöldunga saga*.[52] The only known source to trace connections between Ívarr víðfaðmi, his daughter Unnr, Ráðbarðr and Randvér, father of Sigurðr hringr is *Sögubrot af fornkonungum*.[53] Ráðbarðr is there said to be king in Garðaríki while in the genealogy here he is referred to as king in Hólmgarðr. This may point to the use of a text different from that preserved in *Sögubrot*, and the statement that Randvér was the brother of Haraldr hilditǫnn suggests the same: according to *Sögubrot*, they were half-brothers. There are passages in *Óláfs saga Tryggvasonar en mesta* that bear witness to this same source.[54]

In the later part of the genealogy the line is traced from Sveinn tjúguskegg to Eiríkr klipping, son of Kristófórus I. Sveinn Úlfsson is mentioned in the same way in both the genealogy and *Danakonungatal*: "Sveinn er Magnús hét ǫðru nafni." A comparable expression is in *Knýtlinga saga*: "[. . .] Sveinn, sá er sagt er Magnús héti ǫðru nafni."[55] The cognomen Magnús is derived from Danish sources: "Sveno. Magnus" in *Series regum Danie ex necrologio Lundensis* and *Series ac brevior historia regum Danie a Dan ad Waldemarum*;[56] but the direct source of the Icelandic texts probably had the same phrasing as *Wilhelmi abbatis genealogia regum Danorum*: "Iste Sveno, cognomento Magnus."[57]

---

[51] Bjarni Guðnason, ed., *Danakonunga sǫgur*, 325, n.1.

[52] Bjarni Guðnason, *Um Skjöldungasögu* (Reykjavík, 1963), 116–17.

[53] Bjarni Guðnason, ed., *Danakonunga sǫgur*, 46–71.

[54] Ólafur Halldórsson, *Danish Kings and the Jomsvikings in the Greatest Saga of Óláfr Tryggvason* (London, 2000), 7–8, 47, 86–87.

[55] Bjarni Guðnason, ed., *Danakonunga sǫgur*, 128.18.

[56] M. Cl. Gertz, ed., *Scriptores minores historiæ Danicæ medii ævi. Ex codicibus denuo recensuit*, 2 vols. (Copenhagen, 1970), 1: 157.13, 165.3.

[57] Gertz, ed., *Scriptores*, 178.28.

Ingeborg, daughter of Eiríkr IV, is given the title of queen in the genealogy. She married Magnús lagabætir in 1261 and was crowned queen that same year. Her father had been killed in 1250, and the genealogy calls him "hinn helgi Eiríkr." Eiríkr, son of Kristófórus I, is named last in the line and is given no title; he became king at the age of ten in 1259 and in the first years of his reign played no part at all in affairs of state. It is clear that the genealogy was compiled after Ingeborg became queen in 1261. If the compiler was tracing the dynasty soon after her coronation, it might be understandable that he did not bother to give young Eiríkr his kingly title. On the other hand, he is not punctilious in giving a title to every monarch in his list, and he may have thought that as a contemporary Eiríkr was too well known to need one. Soon after 1261 is a likely date for the origin of the genealogy but it cannot be counted certain.

Danakonungatal: An Epitome of the Reigns of the Danish Kings. Commentary

The observations made in the opening clauses of *Danakonunungatal* are those of the writer himself, speaking in the first person plural, "hyggjo vér." His conclusion that Sigurðr hringr ruled in the Northern realms when Charlemagne was emperor is not a fantasy but very likely a calculation based on the sequence he gives: Haraldr blátönn ← Gormr hinn gamli ← Hörða-Knútr ← Sigurðr ormr í auga ← Ragnarr loðbrók ← Sigurðr hringr. Five generations from Sigurðr hringr at 30 years apiece make 150 years. Charlemagne died on 28 January 814, having been king and emperor for 46 years. In 964, 150 years after his death, the king of the Danes was Haraldr blátönn. It was reasonable to conclude that the great-grandfather of his grandfather had been a contemporary of Charlemagne.

The first words of *Danakonungatal*, "Í þenna tíma," would appear to refer to some preceding narration as it does in other contemporary Norse texts and also hereafter in this text. As the opening of an independent text *Í þann tíma* would be a more natural expression, and it may be that "þenna" in *Danakonungatal* is a misreading of "þann" in the exemplar. The vague reference to the source of the comment on Sigurðr hringr's kin, "þann Sigurð segja menn verit hafa bróðurson Haralds hilditannar," could equally imply an oral or a written account, but if the author of the genealogies and *Danakonungatal* were the same man, he would hardly have expressed himself in this way.[58] It

---

[58] Storm, ed., *En oldnorsk Saga*, 11: "Slægttavlen har de samme dialektiske Egenheder, de samme Bogstavsformer (þ for v) som Krøniken — kort, alt taler for, at begge Stykker hører sammen, at Slægttavlen er en indledning til Krøniken."

is noteworthy that Charlemagne is twice named Karl, written "Carll," and on
the first occasion introduced as "Carll kongr" followed in parenthesis by "er
kallaðr er Magnús ok um síðir varð keisari." His obit is given as 815, a date
found also in Icelandic annals, other than *Konungs annáll* and *Flateyjar annáll*,
which both have the correct date, 814.

Louis the Pious, son of Charlemagne, is given the French form of his name,
Lovís ("Lopis"). In *Veraldar saga* he is called "Lvdovicvs" ("lodovicus"), in *Óláfs
saga Tryggvasonar en mesta* "Hlöðver," in *Konungs annáll* and *Lögmanns
annáll* "Lodovicus," in *Skálholts annálar* "Lòðvér," in *Gottskálks annáll* "Hloduer,"
in *Flateyjar annáll* "hloduer lodouicus," and in *Oddverja annáll* "Loduijk."[59] On
the other hand, Icelandic annalists refer to Ludwig/Louis VI, VII, VIII, and IX
as Lovís, so they at least must have been familiar with the French form.

The next four sentences go back to Adam of Bremen: (1) "han —Jwtt
landi"; (2) "Epter — Sleipik"; (3) "Epter — Ripum"; (4) "Eptir —heiðinn."[60]

(1) *Annales regni Francorum* and Adam of Bremen say that Haraldr
was baptized in Mogontia, *Óláfs saga Tryggvasonar en mesta* says in
Meginzuborg, both names referring to Mainz. *Danakonungatal*'s "meið-
inz borg" belongs with "Meitheburg" in a Danish work on the Øm monastery (*Exordium monasterii quod dicitur Cara Insula*), referring to
Magdeburg.[61] In *Danakonungatal* Haraldr is king in Jutland, and *Óláfs
saga Tryggvasonar en mesta* also names him among Jutland kings, but in
Annales regni Francorum and Adam of Bremen he is always called king
of the Danes ("Rex Danorum").

(2) and (3) Both the kings named here as Eiríkr are called Horic by
Adam and in other Latin sources, for example, the *Annales Fuldenses*, but Hárekr in *Óláfs saga Tryggvasonar en mesta* and *Resens annáll*
(which drew on the same source as *Óláfs saga Tryggvasonar en mesta*).
All the relevant Danish sources are in Latin, and they variously give his
name as Eric, Ericus, or Hericus.[62]

[59] Jakob Benediktsson, ed., *Veraldar saga*, Samfund til udgivelse af gammel nordisk
litteratur 61 (Copenhagen, 1944), 71.6 and v.l.; Ólafur Halldórsson, ed., *Óláfs saga Tryggvasonar en mesta*, 3 vols., Editiones Arnamagnæanæ, Ser. A, 1–3 (Copenhagen, 1958–
2000), index; Gustav Storm, ed., *Islandske Annaler indtil 1578* (Christiania [Oslo], 1888),
index; Peter Foote, *The Pseudo-Turpin Chronicle in Iceland: A Contribution to the Study
of the Karlamagnús saga* (London, 1959), 27–28.

[60] Rudolf Buchner, ed., *Ausgewählte Quellen zur deutschen Geschichte des Mittelalters: Quellen des 9. und 11. Jahrhunderts zur Geschichte der Hamburgischen Kirche und
des Reiches* (Darmstadt, 1976), 186.26–32, 198.12–15, 202.5–16, 226.32–228.4.

[61] Gertz, ed., *Scriptores*, 2: 252.23.

[62] See the index in Gertz, ed., *Scriptores* 2, 1:468–69.

(4) No king is mentioned between the second Eiríkr and Gormr. In the next sentence Gormr's wife is called "Thyri Danmarkar bot," so this Gormr is evidently "hinn gamli" (the Old). Danish regnal lists[63] include numerous kings between the second Eiríkr and Gormr gamli, but their absence in *Danakonungatal* does not justify the conclusion that no such Danish list was known to the *Danakonungatal* author. These strings of names are not of a kind to warrant the attention of anyone of reasonable intelligence.

The beginning of the next paragraph, "I þenna — bloðæÿx," refers to the reign of Gormr gamli and ends with an intervention by the author, again speaking in the first person plural: "hyggio vér." That Haraldr hárfagri subdued all Norway was common knowledge and not to be traced to any particular source. The *Heimskringla* account of the origin of his wife, Ragnhildr, bears partial resemblance to that in *Danakonungatal*: "Haraldr [. . .] fekk þeirar konu, er Ragnhildr hét, dóttir Eiríks konungs af Jótlandi [. . .] þeira sonr var Eiríkr blóðøx."[64] Ragnhildr is also mentioned in the separate *Óláfs saga helga* but the phrasing there is different: "[. . .] Ragnildr dóttir Eiríks konungs ór Danmǫrku."[65] In fact, the way this is expressed in *Danakonungatal* looks closer to some original text than the *Heimskringla* and *Óláfs saga helga* versions. *Danakonungatal* speaks of "kono af Danmǫrk," cf. *Óláfs saga helga* "ór Danmǫrku"; *Heimskringla* says "dóttir Eiríks konungs af Jótlandi," but *Danakonungatal* "ok hyggjo vér hana verit hafa dóttor Eiríks konungs hins síðara af Jútlandi."

The phrasing at the beginning of the section on Haraldr Gormsson is related to *Knýtlinga saga*:

Danakonungatal	*Knýtlinga saga*
Haraldr kóngr blátann tók ríki í Danmǫrk eptir Gorm kóng fǫður sinn. Á hans dǫgum [. . .]	Haraldr Gormsson var tekinn til konungs í Danmǫrk eptir fǫður sinn [. . .] Á dǫgum Haralds konungs Gormssonar [. . .].[66]

In *Danakonungatal* Haraldr is called blátǫnn. He has the same cognomen in *Færeyinga saga* ("[. . .] Haraldr konungr Gormsson er kallaðr var blátǫnn,"[67] *Ágrip*,[68] *Annales vetustissimi*, *Skálholts annálar* (s.a. 907), *Flateyjar annáll*

---

[63] Gertz, ed., *Scriptores*, 1: 145–94.

[64] Finnur Jónsson, ed., *Heimskringla*, 1: 126.12–15.

[65] Johnsen and Jón Helgason, eds., *Den store saga*, 6.12.

[66] Bjarni Guðnason, ed., *Danakonunga sǫgur*, 93.2–5 and 21.

[67] Ólafur Halldórsson, ed., *Færeyinga saga* (Reykjavík, 1987), 2.23–24.

[68] Bjarni Einarsson, ed., *Ágrip af Nórgeskonunga sǫgum; Fagrskinna — Nórges konunga tal*, Íslenzk fornrit 29 (Reykjavík, 1984), 14.5.

(s.a. 904), and in a fragment of a translation of Adam of Bremen.[69] No other Icelandic sources give him this addition. The earliest Danish source for it is apparently *Chronicon Roskildense*.[70]

Danakonungatal and *Knýtlinga saga* go on to tell of Emperor Otto's warfare against Denmark, though with the difference that *Danakonungatal* describes him as "Otte keisari hinn fyrsti með því nafni, er kallaðr er Magnús [. . ."], that is, Otto I, but *Knýtlinga saga* as "keisari í Saxlandi Ottó inn rauði,"[71] that is, Otto II. Adam of Bremen gives Otto I the appellation Magnus.[72] In Copenhagen, Arnamagnaean Institute 415 4to we read: "Otti keisari hinn ra[v]ði er fyrstr var með þvi namni."[73] Here "ravði" shows an unclear correction to "riki" and "riki" is also written in the margin. *Danakonungatal* evidently derived this from Adam, presumably in Icelandic translation, cf. *Danakonungatal* "Otte keisari hinn fyrsti með því nafni" and "Otti keisari [. . .] er fyrstr var með því namni."[74] What follows in *Danakonungatal* also makes it clear that it was based on a translation of Adam's history:

Danakonungatal	*Alfrœði III*
Ok hann lét skíra Harald kóng ok Svein, son hans, ok veitti honum siálfr guðsifjar ok kallaði hann Svein Ottó.	[. . .] hét Haraldr at láta skírask ok kristna alla Danmǫrk. Var þá Haraldr konungr skírðr ok kona hans, Gunnhildr drottning, ok sun hennar ungr, er keisarinn veitti guðsifjar ok lét kalla Svein Ottó.
[. . .] Haraldr kóngr blátann helt vel síðan kristni.	Haraldr konungr blátǫnn helt vel trú meðan hann lifði.[75]

    [69] Kr. Kålund, ed., *Alfrœði íslenzk. Islandsk encyklopædisk litteratur* 3, Samfund til udgivelse af gammel nordisk litteratur 45 (Copenhagen, 1917–1918), 60.11–12 and 33; Guðbrandr Vigfússon and Unger, eds., *Flateyjarbók*, 1: 17.21–22, 18.3–4.
    [70] Eric Christiansen, trans., *The Works of Sven Aggesen, Twelfth-Century Danish Historian* (London, 1992), 121, n. 88; see also Knudsen and Kristensen, eds., *Personnavne*, 2: 85.
    [71] Bjarni Guðnason, ed., *Danakonunga sǫgur*, 93–94.
    [72] Buchner, ed., *Quellen*, 232.16.
    [73] Kålund, ed., *Alfrœði íslenzk*, 59.17–18.
    [74] Kålund, ed., *Alfrœði íslenzk*, 59.17–18.
    [75] Cf. Finnur Jónsson, ed., *Heimskringla*, 1: 305.8–9: "Haraldr Dana-konungr helt vel kristni alt til dauðadags."

Danakonungatal

Á síðarstum dǫgum hans stríddi til lands í móti honum Sveinn son hans, ok í þeim bardaga er þeir átto varð Haraldr kóngr sárr ok flýði til Jómsborgar í Vindland ok andaðisk þar allra heilagra messo ok var fluttr til Róskeldo ok jarðaðr þar. Þá hafði hann verit fimm tigi vetra kóngr eptir fǫður sinn [. . .].

Sveinn tjúguskegg tók ríki í Danmǫrk eptir fǫður sinn. Hann helt illa kristni.

Á hans ríki — Danmǫrk (1.40–2.9).

Alfræði III

En þá er Haraldr tók at eldask vildi Sveinn s(on) hans taka ríki af feðr sínum.[. . .] þeir lǫgðu bardaga við Harald *konung. [. . .] Ór þessi orrostu flýði Haraldr konungr sárr til Vindlands ok andaðisk við Jómsborg allra heilagra messudag. Lík hans var flutt til Róiskeldu ok jarðat at Kristskirkjo þeiri er hann sjalfr lét gjǫra. Hann var konungr fimm tigi ára.

Eptir Harald konung blátǫnn tók ríki Sveinn son hans ok helt illa kristni.

Cf. Hann — konungs.[76]

Danakonungatal inserts a passage which is independent of Adam:

Þenna Svein kalla Danir ok Norðmenn tjúguskegg. Þá tók ǫll Danmǫrk við kristni. Á því ári var liðit frá burð várs herra Jesú Kristí níu hundruð ok fimm tigir ára (1.37–39).

The closest parallel to the sentence "Þá tók ǫll Danmǫrk við kristni" (1.38) is in *Jómsvíkinga saga* in Stockholm, Royal Library Perg. 4to no. 7: "Var þá kristnuð ǫll Danmǫrk."[77] The dating to A.D. 950 probably came by some roundabout route from Adam. He says that these events took place in the twelfth year of the archiepiscopate of Adaldag: "Anno archiepiscopi factum est hoc XII."[78] Adaldag was consecrated in 937; his twelfth year was thus 949, and some Icelandic annals actually give that date (*Konungs annáll, Skálholts annálar, Gottskálks annáll*, with 950 in *Flateyjar annáll*). Previously Adam reports that Unni, Adaldag's predecessor, died 936 years after the Incarnation, in the first

---

[76] Kålund, ed., *Alfræði íslensk*, 61.1–12.

[77] F. N. Blake, ed. and trans., *Jómsvíkinga saga—The Saga of the Jomsvikings*, Nelson's Icelandic Texts 3 (London, 1962), 8.13.

[78] Buchner, ed., *Quellen*, 238.3.

year of the reign of Otto Magnus.[79] In *Alfræði íslenzk*, it is said that Emperor Otto "fór hann með her sinn upp á Dani á tólfta ári ríkis síns";[80] that would be in 948, according to Adam's dating. Whoever translated this passage from Adam probably took his date from a collection of annals. *Konungs annáll* puts Otto's succession under 938.

The passage on Haraldr blátönn in *Danakonungatal* ends with a sentence not drawn from Adam: "Hann hafði gǫrt mikit hervirki í Nóregi." *Jómsvíkinga saga*, *Fagrskinna*, and *Heimskringla* tell of an attack on Norway by Haraldr after Hákon Hlaðajarl withheld the tribute he was supposed to pay.[81] The writer of *Danakonungatal* clearly knew some such report, but his source is not identifiable.

Adam of Bremen does not give the year of Haraldr blátönn's death but says that he reigned fifty years and died on All Saints' Day, 1 November. In this he is followed by *Danakonungatal*. By inference from Adam's account editors have put Haraldr's death in 986,[82] but historians are now disposed to think 987 was the true date.[83]

It is noteworthy that the translator of this matter from Adam interposed a comment of his own: "Í þessum ófriði hyggjum vér verit hafa Hákon jarl ok barisk við Ottó keisara, sem segir í Vellleklu" [spelt "vell hęklo"] ok veitt lið Eiríki konungi vin sínum eða mági."[84] The reference is to Eiríkr sigrsæli, king of the Swedes. Adam says that he had heard, but not from Sveinn Úlfsson, that when Eiríkr ruled Denmark, he fought against Otto III and was defeated by him.[85]

In this passage the translator speaks in the first person plural in exactly the same way as the author of *Danakonungatal* (see pp. 137 and 139). His comment shows that he had some inkling that Hákon jarl had fought on the Danish king's side against the Saxon emperor and recognized that this warfare was referred to in *Vellekla* (st. 26–29), but there is nothing to indicate that he knew other sources telling of these events: *Jómsvíkinga saga*, *Fagrskinna*, *Heimskringla*, or *Knýtlinga saga*. In his *Óláfs saga Tryggvasonar* Oddr Snorrason

[79] Buchner, ed., *Quellen*, 232.6–16.

[80] Kålund, ed., *Alfræði íslenzk*, 59.17–22.

[81] Carl af Petersens, ed., *Jómsvíkinga saga efter Arnamagnæanska handskriften N:o 291 4:to* (Copenhagen, 1882), 35.13–25; Finnur Jónsson, ed., *Fagrskinna*, 79–80; Finnur Jónsson, ed., *Heimskringla*, 1: 315.

[82] Buchner, ed., *Quellen*, 262, n. 120.

[83] Niels Lund, "Cnut's Danish Kingdom," in *The Reign of Cnut*, ed. Alexander R. Ruble (London and New York, 1994, repr. 1999), 27–42, esp. 27 and n. 2. See also Ólafur Halldórsson, ed., *Jómsvíkinga saga* (Reykjavík, 1969), 40–41.

[84] Kålund, ed., *Alfræði íslenzk*, 61.34–62.1. "We believe that Earl Hákon was in this battle and fought against Emperor Ótto, as is told in *Velleklu*, and offered King Eiríkr, his friend or brother-in-law, support."

[85] Buchner, ed., *Quellen*, 274.9–15; Kålund, ed., *Alfræði íslenzk*, 61.15–19.

says that Eiríkr sigrsæli was married to Unnr, daughter of Hákon Hlaðajarl.[86] That could have been the source of the translator's knowledge of the marriage ties between Hákon jarl and Eiríkr sigrsæli.

The latter part of the *Danakonungatal* passage on Sveinn tjúguskegg is not based on Adam of Bremen's account. The chronology is obscure. "Í þenna tíma" at the outset refers to the years after Sveinn regained power in Denmark. It is told that the Jomsvikings attacked Norway "at áeggjan Sveins kóngs" — *Jómsvíkinga saga* or some source derivative from it was evidently known to the writer. The part played by King Sveinn in fomenting the attack is not mentioned in Oddr's *Óláfs saga Tryggvasonar*. *Danakonungatal* says that the battle fought against Óláfr Tryggvason by Sveinn tjúguskegg, Óláfr Svíakonungr, and Eiríkr jarl occurred many years after the foray of the Jómsvíkingar but it tells neither when nor where that battle took place. On the other hand, the words "ok fengo unnit um síðir" (2.13) suggest that the writer had some particular knowledge of the battle's progress. The matter in the rest of this section is related to *Knýtlinga saga*,[87] but the wording points to no close affinity.

Danakonungatal has the same account of the death of Sveinn tjúguskegg as is found in *Óláfs saga helga*, *Heimskringla*, *Óláfs saga Tryggvasonar en mesta*, and *Knýtlinga saga* but not the same phrasing:

Danakonungatal	*Óláfs saga helga, Heimskringla*	*Knýtlinga saga*
Eptir þat herjaði hann í England ok lagði undir sek. Hann andaðisk þar skjótlega í hvílu sinni, ok birtisk svá nǫkkorum mǫnnum sem hinn helgi Edmundr hefði drepit hann með því móti sem Mercurius riddari drap Julianum apostatam (2.14–17).	Þat sama haust er Óláfr konungr kom til Englands urðu þau tíðendi þar, at Sveinn konungr Haraldsson varð bráðdauðr um nótt í rekkju sinni, ok er þat sǫgn enskra manna at Játmundr enn helgi hafi drepit hann með þeim hætti sem enn helgi Merkíríús drap Júliánúm níðing[88]	[. . .] Sveinn konungr varð bráðdauðr um nótt í rekkju sinni, ok segja þat enskir menn at Játmundr konungr inn helgi hafi drepit hann með þeim hætti sem inn helgi Merkúríús drap Júliánúm níðing[89]

---

[86] Finnur Jónsson, ed., *Saga Óláfs Tryggvasonar af Oddr Snorrason munk* (Copenhagen, 1932), 14–15.

[87] Bjarni Guðnason, ed., *Danakonunga sǫgur*, 98.

[88] Johnsen and Jón Helgason, eds., *Den store saga*, 42.1–5; Finnur Jónsson, ed., *Heimskringla*, 2: 15.9–14.

[89] Bjarni Guðnason, ed., *Danakonunga sǫgur*, 98.17–21.

The text in *Óláfs saga Tryggvasonar en mesta* was derived from a manuscript of *Óláfs saga helga*.[90]

In *Óláfs saga helga, Heimskringla*, and *Knýtlinga saga*, Mercurius is called "hinn helgi" and Julian "níðingr"; in *Danakonungatal*, Mercurius is called "riddari" and Julian given his Latin cognomen, "apostata." *Maríu saga* has two accounts of Julian's death at the hands of Mercurius. In *Maríu saga*, Mercurius is called "hinn helgi" (in one manuscript, Copenhagen, Arnamagnaean Institute 234 fol.) and Julian is called "níðingr";[91] elsewhere in this work Julian is "guðníðingr," while Mercurius is called "þessi helgi riddari,"[92] and it is as a knight that he appears when he kills Julian;[93] otherwise he is called "hinn helgi."[94] With reference to Sveinn's sudden death *Danakonungatal* says: "[. . .] ok birtisk svá nǫkkorum mǫnnum [. . .]," while *Óláfs saga helga, Heimskringla*, and *Knýtlinga saga* credit the story to Englishmen. The oldest source to tell of this supernatural assassination of King Sveinn is *De Miraculis Sancti Edmundi* by Hermannus archidiaconus, composed a little before 1100.[95] Hermannus relates that St Edmund appeared to Egelwin, monk of Beodricsworth (Bury St Edmunds), where Edmund's shrine was, and later that Edmund killed King Sveinn:

> Ecce! martyr EADMUNDUS, potentia signorum mirificus, æquiparatur Mercurio martyri ulciscenti injuriarum blasfemias apostatæ Juliani, in genitricem Dei Basiliumque virum Domini. Uterque [. . .] confringunt reges in die suæ vindictæ, ad levamen et auxilium suorum, conquassando capita fortium in terra multorum Quia de torrente, id est, morte pro Christo biberunt, propterea eorum exaltatur caput.[96]

Thus, saints had shattered the heads of many mighty men who had opposed Christ, and William of Malmesbury explains Svein's death in the same way:

> Dicitur quod terram sancti Edmundi depopulanti martyr idem per visum apparuerit, leniterque de miseria conventum suorum, insolentiusque

[90] Óláfur Halldórsson, *Text by Snorri Sturluson in Óláfs saga Tryggvasonar en mesta* (London, 2001), 8 and xvii.

[91] C. R. Unger, ed., *Maríu saga. Legender om Jomfru Maria og hendes Jertegn* (Christiania [Oslo], 1868–1871), 73.13–14.

[92] Unger, ed., *Maríu saga*, 700.30–31.

[93] Unger, ed., *Maríu saga*, 701.25, 27.

[94] Unger, ed., *Maríu saga*, 701.5, 16.

[95] Thomas Arnold, ed., *Memorials of St. Edmund's Abbey* (London, 1890), 1: xxv–xxix.

[96] Arnold, ed., *Memorials*, 1:36. The quotations are from Psalm 109:5–7.

respondentem, in capite perculerit; quo dolore tactum, in proximo, ut prædictum est, obiisse.[97]

These accounts do not, however, say that Sveinn died "skiótliga í hvílu sinni" (*Danakonungatal*; "varð bráðdauðr um nótt í rekkju sinni," *Óláfs saga helga, Heimskringla, Knýtlinga saga*). That information must stem from a more reliable source.

The author of *Danakonungatal* had no source to tell him how long Sveinn tjúguskegg ruled after the death of his father and left a space to be filled in. Sveinn died on 3 February 1014, but our chief guide to the date of Haraldr blátönn's death is Adam of Bremen, who says that it occurred in Archbishop Adaldag's last days — Adaldag died 29 April 988.[98]

Danakonungatal's remark, "Knútr er Landbertus hét skírnarnafni," probably goes back to Adam of Bremen: "Chnut filius Suein regis abiecto nomine gentilitatis in baptismo Lambertus nomen accepit."[99] Further points in *Danakonungatal*'s account of Knútr agree with other sources, as follows:

It is said in the *Þingamanna þáttr* (in *Flateyjarbók*) and *Knýtlinga saga* that Knútr was ten years old when his father died and that he went to England three winters later.[100] In the *Legendary Saga of St Óláfr* Knútr's age when his father died is not given, but it is said that he went to England three winters later.[101]

Danakonungatal says that Knútr "fór með tólf hundruð skipa í Nóreg"; cf. Theodoricus monachus: "[. . .] nam mille ducentarum navium fertur classis ejus fuisse";[102] *Óláfs saga helga*: "Siglir sunnan af Jótlandi yfir Limafjǫrð með tólf hundruð skipa";[103] *Fagrskinna*: "[. . .] ok kom í Limafjǫrð ok sigldi

---

[97] William Stubbs, ed., *Willelmi Malmesbiriensis monachi De Gestis Regum Anglorum*, Rerum Britannicarum medii ævi scriptores, Rolls Series 90 (London, 1887), 212.18–22.

[98] Buchner, ed., *Quellen*, 262–64; cf. p. 142 above.

[99] Buchner, ed., *Quellen*, 290; cf. E Schol. no. 37. On the form Landbertus, see Knudsen and Kristensen, eds., *Personnavne*, 1: 822–24.

[100] Ólafur Halldórsson, "Þingamanna þáttr," in *Sagnaþing helgað Jónasi Kristjánssyni sjötugum 10. apríl 1994*, ed. Gísli Sigurðsson, Guðrún Kvaran, and Sigurgeir Steimgrímsson, 2 vols. (Reykjavík, 1994), 2: 617–40, esp. 620, 622, 627–28; Bjarni Guðnason, ed., *Danakonunga sǫgur*, 100–1.

[101] Oscar Albert Johnsen, ed., *Óláfs saga hins helga. Efter pergamenthandskrift i Uppsala Universitetsbibliotek, Delagardieske samling nr. 8ᴵᴵ*, Det norske historiske kildeskriftfonds skrifter 47 (Kristiania [Oslo], 1922), 9.17–21.

[102] Gustav Storm, ed., "Theodorici monachi Historia de antiquitate regum Norwagiensium," in *Monumenta historica Norvegiæ* (Kristiania [Oslo], 1880), 30.10–11.

[103] Johnsen, ed., *Óláfs saga hins helga*, 64.2–3.

þaðan til Nóregs með tólf hundruð skipa [. . .]";[104] *Óláfs saga Tryggvasonar en mesta*: "Hann hafði eigi færa en tólf hundruð skipa."[105]

All sources which tell that St Óláfr fled Norway on the arrival of King Knútr say that he first went to Sweden and from there east to Garðaríki. The only difference in *Danakonungatal* is that the name Garðaríki is not mentioned and we read instead that he went "fyrst í Svíaríki ok síðan austr í Hólmgarð"; cf. *Óláfs saga helga*: "Þaðan fór hann austr í Garðaríki ok var annan vetr í Hólmgarði [. . .]."[106]

What is told of the children of Knútr in *Danakonungatal* agrees in the main with Adam of Bremen and was probably derived from his history but through the medium of Danish annals.[107] For comparison Gustav Storm prints a passage from *Annales Lundenses* in a note in his edition.[108] Most of this[109] was evidently lifted from Adam.[110] *Danakonungatal* does not name Emma, Knút's queen, and there is no identification of the mother (or mothers) of his children, Haraldr, Hörða-Knútr, and Gunnhildr,[111] but Sveinn is said to have been son of Álfífa. According to Adam, Hörða-Knútr and Gunnhildr were children of Knútr and Emma, and Haraldr and Sveinn sons of concubines.[112]

"Svá segja danskir menn at Knútr kóngr vann undir sek Eistland." This is a report found otherwise only in a Danish annal and a Danish regnal list. Storm refers to *Annales Ryenses*:[113] "Estonicam etiam gentem subdidit."[114]

"Hann fór til Róms" (2.32) — recorded in many sources; see the comprehensive survey by Bjarni Guðnason.[115]

"[. . .] hann lét setja klaustr í Edmundarborg." Langebek refers to Matthew of Westminster on this monastery founded by Knútr:[116]

---

[104] Bjarni Einarsson, ed., *Ágrip-Fagrskinna*, 191.13–14.
[105] Ólafur Halldórsson, ed., *Óláfs saga Tryggvasonar en mesta*, 2: 327.14.
[106] Johnsen, ed., *Óláfs saga hins helga*, 71.19–20.
[107] Cf. *Annales Ryenses* (Ellen Jørgensen, ed., *Annales Danici Medii Ævi* [Copenhagen, 1920], 69).
[108] Storm, ed., *En oldnorsk Saga*, 5.
[109] Jørgensen, ed, *Annales Danici*, 59–60.
[110] Cf. Buchner, ed., *Quellen*, 316.13–16.
[111] These are counted the children of Knútr and Emma in *Óláfs saga helga*, *Heimskringla*, *Knýtlinga saga*, and *Óláfs saga helga* in *Flateyjarbók*.
[112] Ólafur Halldórsson, "Þingamanna þáttr," 631–32.
[113] Storm, ed., *En oldnorsk Saga*, 5, n. b.
[114] Jørgensen, ed., *Annales Danici*, 69a. 22–23; cf. also Gertz, ed., *Scriptores*, 1: 171.11, *Series et genealogiæ regum Danorum*.
[115] Bjarni Guðnason, ed., *Danakonunga sǫgur*, civ–cv.
[116] Langebek, ed., *Scriptores*, 2: 427, n.x.

An. 1020. Rex Anglorum & Danorum CNUTO, *constructo Regali Monasterio*, cum competentibus officinis, in loco, qvi *Bederichesvurthe* nuncupatur, ubi beatissimus Rex & Martyr EADMUNDUS, incorrupto corpore, diem beatæ resurrectionis expectat, consilio EMMÆ Reginæ & Episcoporum simul & Baronum Angliæ, Monachos in eo constituit [. . .]

Langebek also refers to William of Malmesbury (who does not give the place-name).[117] The author of *Danakonungatal* used a source which had Edmundsbury or Edmundiburgum instead of the earlier Bedrichesworde. (Langebek refers to Bromton and other authors.)

Danakonungatal records the death of King Knútr and the length of his reign in virtually the same way as *Óláfs saga helga*, *Heimskringla*, and *Knýtlinga saga*:

Danakonungatal	*Óláfs saga helga*	*Heimskringla*	*Knýtlinga saga*
Hann andaðisk í Englandi Ídús Nóvembris. Þá var liðit frá burð várs herra Jesú Kristí eitt þúsund ok þrír tigir ok fjórir vetr. Þá hafði Knútr verit kóngr yfir Danmǫrk sjau vetr ok tuttugu, en yfir Englandi fjóra vetr ok tuttugu, en yfir Nóregi sex vetr (2,32–36).	En Knútr enn ríki andaðisk þann vetr[118] á Englandi Ídús Nóvembris. Þá hafði hann konungr verit yfir þremur þjóðlǫndum, Englandi, Danmǫrk, Nóregi, vetr sjau, en yfir Englandi ok Danmǫrk tuttugu ok fjóra. En fyrst yfir Danmǫrku einni þrjá. Þá var hann at aldri þriá tigi ok sjau vetra.[119]	Þat sama haust andaðisk Knútr inn ríki í Englandi Ídús Nóvembris. Hann var jarðaðr í Vincestr. Þá hafði hann verit konungr yfir Danmǫrk sjau vetr ok tuttugu, en bæði ok yfir Englandi fjóra vetr ok tuttugu, en þar með yfir Nóregi sjau vetr.[120]	[. . .] ok um haustit andaðisk hann Ídús Nóvembris [. . .] Þá hafði hann at aldri sautján vetr ok tuttugu. Þá hafði hann verit konungr yfir Danmǫrku sjau vetr ok tuttugu, en ráðit fyrir Englandi fjóra vetr ok tuttugu, en fyrir Nóregi sjau vetr.[121]

---

[117] See Stubbs, ed., *Willelmi Malmesbiriensis monachi*, 220.6–12.

[118]That is, in the same winter as Sveinn Álfífuson died.

[119] Johnsen and Jón Helgason, eds., *Saga Óláfs konungs hins helga*, 619.10–14.

[120] Bjarni Aðalbjarnarson, ed., *Snorri Sturluson: Heimskringla*, 3 vols., Íslenzk fornrit 26–28 (Reykjavík, 1941–1951), 3: 11.12–16.

[121] Bjarni Guðnason, ed., *Danakonunga sǫgur*, 123–24.

No other early Norwegian or Icelandic sources give the day of Knútr's death. The date in the above texts, 13 November (the Ides), was undoubtedly derived from English sources. The *Anglo-Saxon Chronicle* (C and D) record his death on ".ii. ID. Nove*mbris*,"[122] Florence of Worcester on "secundo Idus Novembris,"[123] that is, 12 November.[124] We may assume that ".ii." or "secundo" had been omitted in the original or archetype of the texts quoted above. *Óláfs saga helga* and *Knýtlinga saga* note that Knútr was thirty-seven when he died, but the year of his death is not given in *Óláfs saga helga*, *Heimskringla*, and *Knýtlinga saga*. *Danakonungatal*, *Knýtlinga saga*,[125] and *Þingamanna þáttr* in *Flateyjarbók* say he was ten when his father, Sveinn, died and he was acknowledged as king; his age when he died was probably calculated in relation to this: he became king when he was ten and ruled the Danes for twenty-seven years. The *Anglo-Saxon Chronicle* C (D) records his death in 1035, E (F) in 1036.[126] The year 1034 in *Danakonungatal* is matched in no other known source.

Danakonungatal, *Óláfs saga helga*, *Heimskringla*, *Knýtlinga saga*, and *Þingamanna þáttr* agree in allotting Knútr twenty-four years as king of England.[127] The information offered by these texts on the length of his reign in Denmark and in England was not drawn from English sources. It depended rather on a calculation from 1008 (or 1007, see above), the date of Sveinn tjúguskegg's death given in most of the Icelandic annals — Knútr became king that same year and died twenty-seven years later, in 1035. If the arithmetic was based on 1034 as the year of his death (see above), it might be thought that twenty-seven years were calculated from a source which used the Gerlandus chronology and gave 1007 as the date of Sveinn tjúguskegg's death instead of 1014. But in the common original of the sources (Icelandic annals) which give 1008 as the year of Sveinn tjúguskegg's death and relate Knútr's age and death to it, it is more likely however that the Roman numeral ".viij." existed as a misreading of ".xiu.";[128] for comparable errors in reading "v" and "x" in Roman numerals see the examples quoted on pp. 159 and 161 below.

What is told of King Knútr in *Danakonungatal* was probably not dependent on a single source; there is no reference to any except Danes as authority

[122] Ch. Plummer, ed., *Two of the Saxon Chronicles Parallel*, 2 vols. (Oxford, 1892–1899), chap. 1 (158) and chap. 2 (208).
[123] Benjamin Thorpe, ed., *Florentii Wigorniensis monachi Chronicon ex chronicis* (London, 1848), 1: 190.
[124] Bjarni Guðnason, ed., *Danakonunga sǫgur*, 124, n. 1.
[125] Bjarni Guðnason, ed., *Danakonunga sǫgur*, 100.6–7.
[126] Dorothy Whitelock, trans., *The Anglo-Saxon Chronicle* (London, 1965), 102.
[127] Ólafur Halldórsson, "Þingamanna þáttr," 622.
[128] Ólafur Halldórsson, "Þingamanna þáttr," 628.4–7.

for the claim that Knútr subdued Eistland (see above). Possibly some matter in this part was derived from a lost *Knúts saga ríka*.[129]

On the reign of Hörða-Knútr in England and in Denmark Storm refers respectively to comparative material in *Annales Lundenses* and *Annales Ryenses*.[130] The first of these says: "[. . .] et successit Harthaknut et regnavit 8 annis"; the second: "Harald uero 4 tantum annis regnauit et mortuus est, cuius regnum Harthæknut rex suscepit."[131]

Icelandic sources, *Morkinskinna*, *Fagrskinna*, *Óláfs saga helga*, *Heimskringla*, *Knýtlinga saga*, and annals, mostly agree that Haraldr, who called himself the son of Knútr ríki, ruled England for five years and that Hörða-Knútr ruled Denmark and England for two years. This reckoning must depend on English sources (*Anglo-Saxon Chronicle* and Roger of Howden).[132] But as Storm indicated, *Danakonungatal* depends on Danish annals.

The treaty between Hörða-Knútr and King Magnús góði Óláfsson is referred to in numerous sources: Theodoricus monachus, *Ágrip*, *Fagrskinna*, *Óláfs saga helga*, and *Heimskringla*[133] and it finds mention in Danish sources too, *Chronicon Roskildense* and *Annales Ryenses*.[134] On the other hand, *Knýtlinga saga* is totally silent on the pact between the kings. The wording of these texts varies and *Danakonungatal* produces yet another version, though possibly one that echoes Theodoricus (perhaps both were derived from the same source): "[. . .] mutant in melius consilium [. . .] non solum concordes, verum etiam amicissimi,"[135] cf. *Danakonungatal*: "Hann gerði sætt ok kærleik [. . .]" (2.38–39) .The clause "ef sá ætti engan son eptir" is reminiscent of *Óláfs saga helga*: "[. . .] ef misdauði þeira yrði svá at sá andaðisk sonlauss."[136]

In the passage on King Magnús góði, Sveinn Úlfsson is not named among the rulers of Denmark who waged war against him, although it is clear that the author of *Danakonungatal* had heard of many battles between Magnús and the Danes, since he observes that these always came off worse, "hǫfðu jafnan lægra hlut" (3.1). Magnús's victory over the Wends is recorded in kings'

---

[129] See Bjarni Guðnason, ed., *Danakonunga sǫgur*, xci–cix, esp. xcii and cvii–cviii.

[130] Storm, ed., *En oldnorsk Saga*, 5, nn. c and d.

[131] Jørgensen, ed., *Annales Danici*, 59, 69.

[132] Whitelock, trans., *The Anglo-Saxon Chronicle*, D, 104–6; William Stubbs, ed., *Chronica magistri Rogeri de Houedene*, 2 vols. (London, 1868–1871), 2: 235.27–32.

[133] Storm, ed., "Theodorici monachi Historia," 45.24–46.12; Bjarni Einarsson, ed., *Ágrip-Fagrskinna*, 211–12; Johnsen and Jón Helgason, eds., *Saga Óláfs konungs hins helga*, 627.11–16; Bjarni Aðalbjarnarson, ed., *Snorri Sturluson: Heimskringla*, 3: 12–13.

[134] Gertz, ed., *Scriptores*, 1: 22.8–12; Jørgensen, ed., *Annales Danici*, 69b.2–6.

[135] Storm, ed., "Theodorici monachi Historia," 46.7, 11–12.

[136] Cf. also Storm, ed., "Theodorici monachi Historia," 46.8–11.

sagas and Danish annals. The source followed by *Danakonungatal* contained
the name Hlýrskógsheiðr and the figure of 15,000 Wendish dead. Theodoricus gives the place-name; *Morkinskinna, Fagrskinna, Óláfs saga helga,
Heimskringla*, and *Knýtlinga saga* give both place-name and date, on the eve
of (*Knýtlinga saga*: the day before) Michaelmas, that is, 28 September. Storm
refers to *Annales Lundenses*, which report that the battle was fought outside
Hedeby and that 15,000 men fell there.[137] This notice comes from Adam.[138]
The date of Magnús's death, "áttanda kalendas dag Novembris," that is, 25
October, was presumably derived from a calendar.[139] The same date is given
in *Tómasskinna* ("átta kalendas Novembris") and *Morkinskinna* ("þrem nótt-
um fyrir messudag Símonis ok Jude").[140]

That Magnús was brought home for burial is told in *Ágrip, Morkinskinna, Fagrskinna, Heimskringla*, and *Knýtlinga saga. Ágrip, Morkinskinna*,
and *Fagrskinna* say that he was buried in Christ Church in Niðarós (*Ágrip*:
Þrándheimr), "þar sem faðir hans hvílir"; "fyrir útan kór, en nú er þat innan kórs fyrir rúmi erkibyskups"; "fyrir útan kórinn."[141] According to *Heimskringla* he was buried "at Clemenskirkju. Þar var þá skrín ins helga Óláfs
konungs";[142] *Tómasskinna* also has "at Clemenskirkju."[143] *Knýtlinga saga* does
not record his burial-place. When Árni Magnússon made this transcript of
Danakonungatal, he undoubtedly remembered that in *Heimskringla* Magnús
is said to have been buried "at Clemenskirkju," and this led him to underline
"criſtz" and write "corrige clementz" in the margin.[144] The sources which refer
to Christ Church are older than *Heimskringla*.

Danakonungatal says that Magnús was "fimm vetr kóngr yfir Danmǫrk"
(3.6). This corresponds to Theodoricus: "Hic Magnus regnavit annis undec-
im, ex quibus quinque utrique regno [sc. Denmark and Norway] præfuit."[145]

[137] Storm, ed., *En oldnorsk Saga*, 5, n. h.
[138] See Buchner, ed., *Quellen XI*, 320.12–18.
[139] See Jón Þorkelsson, ed., *Íslenzkar ártíðaskrár eða Obituaria Islandica með athugasemdum, xxv ættarskrám og einni rímskrá* (Copenhagen, 1893–1896), *Ártíðaskrá Oddaverja*, 31; *Helgafells ártíðaskrá*, 87, 91; *Ártíðaskrá Vestfirðinga*, 118.
[140] Johnsen and Jón Helgason, eds., *Saga Óláfs konungs hins helga*, 836.7–8; Finnur
Jónsson, ed., *Morkinskinna*, Samfund til udgivelse af gammel nordisk litteratur 53 (Copenhagen, 1932), 143.37–38.
[141] Bjarni Einarsson, ed., *Ágrip-Fagrskinna*, 37.11–12; Finnur Jónsson, ed., *Morkinskinna*, 147.28–29; Bjarni Einarsson, ed., *Ágrip-Fagrskinna*, 249.13.
[142] Bjarni Aðalbjarnarson, ed., *Snorri Sturluson: Heimskringla*, 3: 107.21–22.
[143] Johnsen and Jón Helgason, eds., *Saga Óláfs konungs hins helga*, 836.9.
[144] Cf. Storm, ed., *En oldnorsk Saga*, 12.
[145] Storm, ed., "Theodorici monachi Historia," 55.21–22.

The passage on Sveinn Úlfsson in *Danakonungatal* is closely related to *Knýtlinga saga* (Ólafur Halldórsson, "Um Danakonunga sögur," 93):

Danakonungatal	*Knýtlinga saga*
Sveinn er Magnús hét ǫðru nafni, son Úlfss jarls, tók kóngdóm í Danmǫrko eftir Magnús kóng góða. Móðir Sveins kóngs var Astrið, dóttir Sveins tjúguskeggs, systir Knúts kóngs ríka. [. . .] Sveinn kóngr átti fjórtán syni þá sem ór bernsku kómu [. . .] (3.7–11).	[. . .] Sveinn, sá er sagt er Magnús héti ǫðru nafni. Hann var son Úlfss jarls Þorgilssonar sprakaleggs. Móðir Sveins var Ástríðr, dóttir Sveins konungs tjúguskeggs. Var hon systir Knúts konungs gamla [. . .]. Hann átti fjórtán sonu, þá er ór barnœsku kómusk.[146]

Sveinn is called "Sveno Magnus" in *Chronicon Roskildense*, the Lund necrologium, *Series ac brevior historia regum Danie*; "Sveno, cognomento Magnus" in *Wilhelmi abbatis genealogia regum Danorum*.[147]

William of Malmesbury reports that Sveinn had fourteen sons and names those who were kings after him: Haraldr, three years, Knútr, Óláfr, eight years, "Henricus" (that is, Eiríkr eygóði) who died at sea on pilgrimage to Jerusalem when he was twenty-nine years old, and Nikulás the fifth who, William says, is reigning at the present time:

[. . .] Henricus [. . .] Is, viginti et novem annis modeste vivens, Jerosolimam abiit, medioque mari spiritum evomuit. Quintus nunc Nicolaus in regno subsistit.[148]

In the *Anglo-Saxon Chronicle* (D and E) Sveinn Úlfsson's death is recorded s.a. 1076,[149] and it seems pretty clear that the author of *Danakonungatal* had that date in mind[150] and that the dating in *Knýtlinga saga* and Icelandic annals also depend on it. Danish annals assign his death to 1074.[151]

---

[146] Bjarni Guðnason, ed., *Danakonunga sǫgur*, 128.18–129.1, 135.4–5.

[147] Gertz, ed., *Scriptores*, 1: 23.17, 157.13, 165.3, 178.28, 179.21.

[148] Stubbs, ed., *Willelmi Malmesbiriensis monachi*, 319–20.

[149] Whitelock, trans., *The Anglo-Saxon Chronicle*, 158.

[150] Calculated from 1034 as the year of Knútr ríki's death plus 8 years for the reign of Hörða-Knútr, 5 for the reign of Magnús góði, and 29 for the reign of Sveinn Úlfsson = 1076.

[151] Jørgensen, ed., *Annales Danici*, 61a, 69b, 71b, 150a, 163a, 192a.

Except to some degree in *Chronicon Roskildense*, Danish sources pay only brief attention to Haraldr hein. There and in other Danish regnal lists he is said to have succeeded his father and reigned for seven years: "Post cuius mortem filius eius Haroldus in regnum successit et regnauit annos .VII."[152] Sven Aggesøn and other regnal lists give him the cognomen "Hen." Rather more is told of him in *Knýtlinga saga*, where similar phrasing to that in *Danakonungatal* is found: "Danir kǫlluðu hann Harald hein. En er hann hafði konungr verit fjóra vetr, þá varð hann sóttdauðr."[153] *Danakonungatal*, *Knýtlinga saga*, and most of the Icelandic annals agree on four years as the length of his reign (1076–1080, so *Konungs annáll* and others), but the list in the *Lund Necrologium* records that he ruled from 1074 to 1080.[154]

Danakonungatal says that St. Knútr was king for seven years and that he died "vj° Idus Julii," 10 July. *Knýtlinga saga* says the same but adds that the king was killed on a Saturday: in 1087 10 July fell on a Saturday.[155] This is the year under which his death is entered in Icelandic annals, and the same year is implied when *Heimskringla* says that he reigned for seven years.[156] The earliest Danish sources give the year 1086, but though they share the same day date, 10 July, as *Danakonungatal* and Icelandic writings, they identify it as a Friday: ".VI. Idus Julii et .VI. feria."[157]

Gustav Albeck preferred Saturday 10 July 1087 to Friday 10 July 1086 as Knútr's death-day. He argued that the Odense monks wanted the description of the martyrdom to parallel as closely as possible the death of Christ and consequently rejected 1087 in order to let Knútr die on a Friday; the calendar dating, 10 July, on the other hand, was a point they could not alter.[158] His argument has not won general acceptance.

---

[152] Gertz, ed., *Scriptores*, 1: 23.20–21.

[153] Bjarni Guðnason, ed., *Danakonunga sǫgur*, 145.6–8.

[154] Aksel E. Christensen, "Tiden 1042–1241," in *Danmarks historie* (Copenhagen, 1977), 1:211–399, esp. 236–37.

[155] Bjarni Guðnason, ed., *Danakonunga sǫgur*, 200.

[156] Bjarni Aðalbjarnarson, ed., *Snorri Sturluson: Heimskringla*, 3: 207. Four sons of Sveinn Úlfsson are named in chap. 5 of *Óláfs saga kyrra* in *Heimskringla* with a note of the length of their reigns. The starting-point of the chronology is "fall Haraldanna", that is the death of Haraldr harðráði and Harold Godwineson in 1066: Haraldr hein became king ten years after that date and ruled for four years (1076–1080), Knútr ruled seven years (1080–1087), Óláfr for eight (1087–1095), and Eiríkr góði (eygóði) for eight (1095–1103).

[157] M. Cl. Gertz, *Knud den Helliges Martyrhistorie. Særlig efter de tre ældste Kilder* (Copenhagen, 1907), 2–5, 70–71.

[158] Gustav Albeck, *Knýtlinga: Sagaerne om Danmarks Konger* (Copenhagen, 1946), 127–29.

Danakonungatal says of Knútr that he was "góðr réttari ok refsti mjǫk rán ok ósiðu" (3.18–19). There is similar phrasing in *Knýtlinga saga*: "Knútr konungr var ríkr maðr ok refsingasamr ok hegndi mjǫk ósiðu."[159] *Danakonungatal*'s clause "ok refsti mjǫk rán" might suggest that the writer knew *Blóð-Egils þáttr*.[160] Acquaintance with the same text could also explain the sequel in *Danakonungatal*, "fyrir þat gerðu Danir samnað at honum ok drápu hann" (3.19); cf. the end of the *þáttr* in *Knýtlinga saga*:

Eptir þetta viku hǫfðingjar til sundrþykkis við konunginn ok tóku mjǫk at stirðna við hann, ok þar eptir gerði alþýðan. Þótti þeim hann ríkr ok refsingasamr, en þeir áðr vanir sjálfræði.[161]

Danish sources refer to the church in which Knútr was killed as St. Alban's.[162] The patron saint is not named in *Danakonungatal* or *Knýtlinga saga*.

In the last part of what *Knýtlinga saga* tells of Óláfr Sveinsson, these sentences are mostly in accord with the entry in *Danakonungatal*:

Óláfr konungr Sveinsson átti Ingiríði,[163] dóttur Haralds konungs Sigurðarsonar Nóregskonungs [...] Óláfr var konungr átta vetr í Danmǫrku. Hann varð sóttdauðr [...].[164]

Neither *Knýtlinga saga* nor *Danakonungatal* give dates, but Icelandic annals (*Konungs annáll* and others) record that Óláfr succeeded in 1087 and died in 1095, which agrees with the *Lund Necrologium*.[165]

That Eiríkr eygóði was king for eight years, as told in *Danakonungatal* and *Knýtlinga saga*, is in accord with the *Lund Necrologium* and Icelandic annals. *Knýtlinga saga* calls him "inn góði,"[166] *Danakonungatal* "egóði"; in *Nomina regum Danorum* he appears as "hin egothæ," but in other Danish sources generally as "bonus."[167]

---

[159] Bjarni Guðnason, ed., *Danakonunga sǫgur*, 147.

[160] Bjarni Guðnason, ed., *Danakonunga sǫgur*, 152–63.

[161] Bjarni Guðnason, ed., *Danakonunga sǫgur*, 162–63: "After this, the chieftains turned against the king and became rough towards him, and after that the common people did. They considered him mighty and a severe punisher, and they were used to independence."

[162] Gertz, *Knud den Helliges Martyrhistorie*, 2 and 18.

[163] "Ingiríði" is an error in *Knýtlinga saga* for "Ingigerði" in *Danakonungatal* and *Heimskringla*.

[164] Bjarni Guðnason, ed., *Danakonunga sǫgur*, 211.6–7, 16–17.

[165] Gertz, ed., *Scriptores*, 1: 157.17.

[166] Bjarni Guðnason, ed., *Danakonunga sǫgur*, 214.11–12.

[167] Gertz, ed., *Scriptores*, 1:176; Knudsen and Kristensen, eds., *Personnavne*, 2: 243–44.

154 ÓLAFUR HALLDÓRSSON

Danakonungatal has more to tell of Nikulás than of the other sons of Sveinn Úlfsson, but he was the last of them and his reign longer than theirs. Comparable matter in *Knýtlinga saga* with the same or similar wording as in *Danakonungatal* is as follows:

> Nikulás Sveinsson tók nú konungdóm í Danmǫrk eptir Eirík konung, bróður sinn. [...] Hann fekk Margrétar Ingadóttur. Hana hafði fyrr átta Magnús berbeinn af Nóregi. [...] Síðan tóksk þar mikil orrosta [...] Þar fellu sex biskupar af liði Nikuláss konungs. [...] Nikulás konungr flýði ór bardaganum [...] ok fór suðr til Jótlands. Síðan fór hann til Heiðabjár [...]. Síðan var hann af lífi tekinn. Þá hafði hann verit konungr þrjá tigu vetra.[168]

Danakonungatal tells that "hinn helgi Knútr hertugi" was killed by Magnús sterki, son of King Nikulás, and Heinrekr skǫtulær ".víj. Idus dag Ianuarii," that is 7 January. The date accords with Danish annals and with *Knýtlinga saga*: "einni nótt eptir inn þrettánda dag jóla."[169] Heinrekr skǫtulær is identified as the son of Sveinn, son of Sveinn Úlfsson, in *Danakonungatal, Fagrskinna, Heimskringla*, and *Knýtlinga saga*.[170] Danish annals give him the same "skǫtulær" cognomen as in *Danakonungatal* and *Fagrskinna*,[171] while *Heimskringla* and *Knýtlinga saga* call him "halti."[172]

As in most Danish records, *Danakonungatal* gives "emuni" as the ekename of Eiríkr, son of Eiríkr eygóði. In Icelandic sources the name is variously spelt "eimuni" and "eymuni."[173]

The battle fought in Skåne between King Nikulás Sveinsson and Eiríkr eymuni is mentioned in numerous sources. *Knýtlinga saga* and Icelandic annals locate the battle at "Fótvík" in Skåne, information that probably came

---

[168] Bjarni Guðnason, ed., *Danakonunga sǫgur*, 240.16–17, 241.3–5, 261.5–7, 262.6–8, 263.7–9.

[169] Jørgensen, ed., *Annales Danici*, 42 and 138; Bjarni Guðnason, ed., *Danakonunga sǫgur*, 255.18–19.

[170] Bjarni Einarsson, ed., *Ágrip-Fagrskinna*, 326.11–12; Bjarni Aðalbjarnarson, ed., *Snorri Sturluson: Heimskringla*, 3: 369.5–6; Bjarni Guðnason, ed., *Danakonunga sǫgur*, 254.8.

[171] Gertz, ed., *Scriptores*, 1: 130.26, 131.19, 2: 32.6.

[172] Knudsen and Kristensen, eds., *Personnavne*, 2: 968. "Skötulær" means "magpie-thigh" (Old Danish "skata," modern "skade"). Presumably Heinrekr got the name, and alternative "halti," because he had some deformity which made his gait reminiscent of a magpie's hop.

[173] Knudsen and Kristensen, eds., *Personnavne*, 2: 248–49.

from Danish sources (Sven Aggesøn, *Series ac brevior historia regum Danie,
Vetus chronica Sialandie*, and others),[174] while *Danakonungatal* refers to
Skåne but does not mention Fótvík. *Danakonungatal* and *Knýtlinga saga*[175]
say that six bishops were killed in the battle, and the same number is reported
in Icelandic annals s.a. 1134 (*Gottskálks annáll, Flateyjar annáll*, and *Oddverja
annáll*). The number varies from four to seven in Danish annals, but some
of them also say six.[176] Apart from *Danakonungatal, Knýtlinga saga* is the
only source that records the death of Heinrekr skǫtulær in this battle.[177] *Danakonungatal* also agrees with *Knýtlinga saga* on King Nikulás's flight from the
battlefield and his violent end in Hedeby, as well as on thirty years as the
length of his reign. All this must depend on Danish sources.

The beginning of the section on Eiríkr eymuni in *Danakonungatal* is in
better accord with the *Konungs annáll* entry s.a. 1134 than with *Knýtlinga
saga*:

Danakonungatal	*Konungs annáll*	*Knýtlinga saga*
Eiríkr emuni tók ríki ok kóngdóm eftir Nicholas kóng (3.41).	Eiríkr eimuni tók ríki í Danmǫrku.[178]	Eptir fall Nikuláss konungs var Eiríkr Eiríksson til konungs tekinn í Danmǫrk um allt land.[179]

Later there are closer parallels between *Knýtlinga saga* and *Danakonungatal*:

> Hann átti Málmfríði dróttningu, dóttur Haralds konungs Valdimars-
> sonar, Jarizleifssonar, austan ór Hólmgarði, systur Engilborgar, er átti
> Knútr lávarðr, bróðir hans. Málmfríði hafði fyrr átta Sigurðr Jórsalafari
> Nóregskonungr. [. . .] Hann lét drepa Harald kesju, bróður sinn, ok sonu
> hans tvá [. . .]. En konungr brenndi bœinn í Ósló ok svá Hallvarðskirkju
> [. . .].[180]

---

[174] See the indices in Gertz, ed., *Scriptores* and Jørgensen, ed., *Annales Danici*.

[175] Bjarni Guðnason, ed., *Danakonunga sǫgur*, 261.7.

[176] See Jørgensen, ed., *Annales Danici*, 75 (*Annales Ryenses*), 144, 163, and further *Vetus chronica Sialandie* and *Chronica archiepiscoporum Lundensium* (Gertz, ed., *Scriptores*, 2: 34.20–23, 107.3–5).

[177] Bjarni Guðnason, ed., *Danakonunga sǫgur*, 262.2.

[178] Gustav Storm, ed., *Islandske Annaler indtil 1578* (Christiania [Oslo], 1888), 113.

[179] Bjarni Guðnason, ed., *Danakonunga sǫgur*, 263.11–12.

[180] Bjarni Guðnason, ed., *Danakonunga sǫgur*, 263.19–264.4 and n. 1, 265.17–18, 267.14–15.

Danakonungatal and *Knýtlinga saga* say only that Eiríkr eymuni had two sons of Haraldr kesja killed; they do not name the victims. *Chronicon Roskildense*, Sven Aggesøn, and Saxo name Bjǫrn járnsíða and Eiríkr djákn as the two sons of Haraldr whom Eiríkr eymuni drowned beside the castle in Hedeby harbor a year before he had Haraldr kesja and his eight other sons put to death.[181] It could well be that the author of *Danakonungatal* followed a Danish source which had an entry on the death of Bjǫrn járnsíða and Eiríkr djákn but separated by some intervening text from a report of the death of the eight other brothers. But it could also be that two in *Danakonungatal* ("ij.") was a misreading of an original ten ("x.").

Gustav Albeck and Bjarni Guðnason have reckoned that the *Knýtlinga saga* account of the attack on Norway by Eiríkr eymuni and Magnús blindi was derived from *Heimskringla*.[182] In fact, the end of the passage is closer to *Morkinskinna* than to *Heimskringla*:

Knýtlinga saga	*Morkinskinna*	*Heimskringla*
Þótti Eiríki konungi eigi sér svá reynask sem Magnús konungr hafði sagt honum, at laust mundi liggja ríkit fyrir í Nóregi ok engi maðr mundi skapti skjóta í móti honum, ok lézk aldregi skyldu vera hans vin jafnmikill sem áðr.[183]	En Eiríki þótti Magnús ok lið hans hafa logit at sér at Nóregr mondi auðr fyrir liggja ok eigi mondi spjóti skotit í móti þeim, ok lézk aldregi þeim skyldu slíkr vinr sem áðr.[184]	[. . .] ok líkaði Eiríki konungi illa við Magnús ok hans menn ok þóttu þeir hafa mjǫk spottat sik, er hann hafði komit í þessa ferð, lézk ekki síðan skyldu vera þeira vinr slíkr sem áðr.[185]

But in the passage on the burning of St. Hallvard's church and the Oslo township the phrasing in *Knýtlinga saga* accords better with *Danakonungatal* than with *Morkinskinna* and *Heimskringla*:

---

[181] Gertz, ed., *Scriptores*, 1: 31.5–7; Jørgen Olrik and H. Ræder, eds., *Saxonis Gesta Danorum* 1 (Copenhagen, 1931), 367–68; see Bjarni Guðnason, ed., *Danakonunga sǫgur*, 265, n. 2., and Christiansen, trans., *The Works of Sven Aggesen, Twelfth-Century Danish Historian*, 134.

[182] Albeck, *Knýtlinga*, 198–202, and Bjarni Guðnason, ed., *Danakonunga sǫgur*, cl.

[183] Bjarni Guðnason, ed., *Danakonunga sǫgur*, 267.22–26.

[184] Finnur Jónsson, ed., *Morkinskinna*, 419.2–5.

[185] Bjarni Aðalbjarnarson, ed., *Snorri Sturluson: Heimskringla*, 3: 308.23–26.

Danakonungatal	Knýtlinga saga	Morkinskinna	Heimskringla
Þeir brenndu stað-inn í Oslu ok svá Hallvarðskirkju (3.44–4.1).	En konungr brendi bœinn í Ósló ok svá Hall-varðskirkju.[186]	En þeir Eiríkr lǫgðu eld í Hall-varðskirkju ok allan bœinn ok brenndu upp með hringum.[187]	Eiríkr konungr lét leggja eld í Hallvarðskirkju ok víða um býinn ok brenndi allt upp með hringum.[188]

But none of the other sources has the comment of *Danakonungatal*: "ok unnu ekki til frægðar í þeiri ferð" (4.1).

The death of Eiríkr eymuni is told in this way in *Danakonungatal*: "Eiríkr kongr var drepinn á þingi í Jútlandi. Sá hét Plógr svarti er vá kónginn." This is doubtless translated straight from a Danish source, cf., for example, *Annales Essenbecenses* s.a. 1139: "Ericus Emun rex occisus est in Jutia a Plog nigro."[189] Other annals (*Annales Ryenses* and *Annales Slesuicenses*) report that he was killed at an assembly.[190] *Knýtlinga saga* gives a close description of Plógr svarti and the killing of the king, to some extent parallel to Saxo's account of the event.[191] As in *Danakonungatal*, *Knýtlinga saga* says that Eiríkr eymuni reigned for four years; this accords with Danish annals.

The next Eiríkr is called "spaki" in *Danakonungatal*, but the writer goes on "er sumir menn kalla lamb." He has "lamb" as his cognomen in *Morkinskinna*,[192] *Knýtlinga saga*,[193] and in Icelandic and Danish annals with the exception among the latter of *Annales 67–1287*,[194] where he appears in the accusative as "Ericum Spake regem." He has this same eke-name in the lections for the feast of the translation of St. Knútr,[195] in Helmold's Chronicle of the

---

[186] Bjarni Guðnason, ed., *Danakonunga sǫgur*, 267.14–15.
[187] Finnur Jónsson, ed., *Morkinskinna*, 418.23–25.
[188] Bjarni Aðalbjarnarson, ed., *Snorri Sturluson: Heimskringla*, 3: 308.11–13.
[189] Jørgensen, ed., *Annales Danici*, 144–45.
[190] Jørgensen, ed., *Annales Danici*, 77, 133.
[191] Bjarni Guðnason, ed., *Danakonunga sǫgur*, 268–69, 269–70, n. 3.
[192] Finnur Jónsson, ed., *Morkinskinna*, 234.17.
[193] Bjarni Guðnason, ed., *Danakonunga sǫgur*, 231.12, 270.20 and 22.
[194] Jørgensen, ed., *Annales Danici*, 136, s.a. 1140.
[195] M. Cl. Gertz, ed., *Vitae sanctorum Danorum* (Copenhagen, 1908–1912), 202.10.
[196] Bernhardus Schmeidler, ed. *Helmolds Slavenchronik*, 3rd. ed (Hannover, 1937), 124.23.

Slavs,[196] and *Nomina regum Danorum*.[197] At the end of the passage describing the accession of Eiríkr *Knýtlinga saga* adds: "Hann var kallaðr Eiríkr inn spaki,"[198] and he is so called throughout the saga thereafter. He has the same addition in *Orkneyinga saga*.[199] The descent of Eiríkr is traced in both *Morkinskinna* and *Knýtlinga saga* but not in the same way. *Knýtlinga saga* has the sequence: Magnús góði, his daughter Ragnhildr married to Hákon jarl Ívarsson, their daughter Sunnifa, her son Hákon norrœni married to a daughter of Eiríkr eygóði, their son Eiríkr lamb.[200] *Morkinskinna* differs in making Eiríkr lamb the son of Hákon Sunnifuson by a daughter of Sveinn Úlfsson.[201] *Danakonungatal* counts Eiríkr spaki a sister's son of Eiríkr eymuni, a fact that also finds mention in Danish annals and is in accord with the pedigree traced in *Knýtlinga saga*.[202]

Danakonungatal's entry on the battles between King Eiríkr and Óláfr, son of Haraldr kesja, is most closely paralleled by *Annales Ryenses*, s.a. 1140, 1142, and 1143:

> 1140. Olauus, filius Haraldi, quem quedam pars fecerat regem, surrexit contra Ericum Lam [. . .]

> 1142. Bellum fuit Distling ter uno die et uno anno 13 uicibus inter Ericum et Olauum, et semper fugit Olauus ante Ericum [. . .]

> 1143. [. . .] Olauus Haraldi filius in bello occiditur.[203]

The account of this warfare in *Knýtlinga saga* mostly agrees with *Danakonungatal*:

> Óláfr, son Haralds kesju, hófsk til ríkis í móti Eiríki inum spaka á inu fyrsta ári ríkis Eiríks, ok á inu þriðja ári áttu þeir Eiríkr konungr ok Óláfr átta orrostur ok þrjár á einum vetri,[204] ok hafði Eiríkr sigr í ǫllum.

---

[197] Gertz, ed., *Scriptores*, 1: 176.79.

[198] Bjarni Guðnason, ed., *Danakonunga sǫgur*, 270.23.

[199] Finnbogi Guðmundsson, ed., *Orkneyinga saga*, Íslenzk fornrit 34 (Reykjavík, 1965), 89.12.

[200] Bjarni Guðnason, ed., *Danakonunga sǫgur*, 231.

[201] The text in *Morkinskinna* is corrupt; see Jón Helgason and Jakob Benediktsson, eds., *Hákonar saga Ívarssonar*, Samfund til udgivelse af gammel nordisk litteratur 62 (Copenhagen, 1952), xxv.

[202] Jørgensen, ed., *Annales Danici*, 77, 133, 145, 150, 163.

[203] Jørgensen, ed., *Annales Danici*, 77.

[204] The word "vetri" in *Knýtlinga saga* is an error for "degi".

Þeir váru þrjá vetr hǫfðingjar í Danmǫrk báðir. En á inu fjórða ári áttu
þeir enn orrostu, ok í þeiri orrostu fell Óláfr, son Haralds kesju.[205]

But it is most likely that the writer of the saga took this passage straight from
Danish annals and did not depend on *Danakonungatal*. Cf. the following:

Annales Ryenses	*Knýtlinga saga*	*Danakonungatal*
1) Olauus, filius Haraldi, [. . .] surrexit contra Ericum Lam [. . .]	Óláfr, son Haralds kesju, hófsk til ríkis í móti Eiríki [. . .]	Í móti honum stríddi til ríkis Óláfr son Haralds kesju,
2) Bellum fuit [. . .] ter uno die et uno anno 13 uicibus inter Ericum et Olauum,	[. . .] á inu þriðja ári áttu þeir [. . .] átta orrostur ok þrjár á einum vetri,	ok þeir áttu átta bardaga á einu ári, ok einn tíma bǫrðusk þeir þrysvar á einum degi (4.8–10).
3) et semper fugit Olauus ante Ericum.	ok hafði Eiríkr sigr í ǫllum.	

Nevertheless, *Danakonungatal* and *Knýtlinga saga* clearly go back to the same
source. It is equally clear that the 1143 entry in *Flateyjar annáll* depends on
Danakonungatal or some parallel text: "Eirekr lamb ok Ólafr son Haralds
kesju börðust þrysvar á einum degi."[206]

Most Danish annals agree in saying that Eiríkr and Óláfr fought thirteen
battles in a single year; *Danakonungatal* and *Knýtlinga saga* make the number eight. Some copyist must have confused X and V in the Roman numerals XIII and VIII; cf. p. 161 below. No matter whether XIII or VIII represents
the original, it is evident that either the number came into *Danakonungatal*
and *Knýtlinga saga* from a common source or that *Knýtlinga saga* here follows *Danakonungatal*, and this alternative conclusion is not supported by the
rest of the passage in *Knýtlinga saga*. *Danakonungatal* says that Óláfr fell in
battle in the second year of Eiríkr's reign where *Knýtlinga saga*, in agreement
with Danish annals, says it was in his fourth year, and Icelandic annals differ
(*Resens annáll* and *Høyers annáll* 1142, *Flateyjar annáll* 1145). In Árni Magnússon's copy the word *öðru* is written "ᴁðru", which is probably how it was
written in his exemplar. If this is a mistake of two for four in *Danakonungatal*
it would be easiest to attribute it to a copyist and would be one point among
others to show that the text in the *Sverris saga* manuscript was not in the hand
of the author of *Danakonungatal*. But the possibility that *ǫðru* was the original reading of *Danakonungatal* cannot be dismissed.

---

[205] Bjarni Guðnason, ed., *Danakonunga sǫgur*, 271.5–11.
[206] Guðbrandr Vigfússon and Unger, eds. *Flateyjarbók*, 3:513.

Most Danish annals give 1139 as the date of Eiríkr's accession following the assassination of Eiríkr eymuni and 1147 as the year of his death. Icelandic annals have the same. If we assume that he was a monk in Odense in the last year of his life, this gives his reign a span of eight years, which agrees with *Danakonungatal* and *Knýtlinga saga*. *Danakonungatal* and *Knýtlinga saga* have similar statements about his death:

Danakonungatal	*Knýtlinga saga*
Hann gaf sek í klaustr, ok andaðisk hann munkr í Óðinsey (4.11–12).	Hann skilði sik sjálfr frá ríkinu ok fór í klaustr ok andaðisk munkr í Óðinsey [. . .][207]

The information comes from Danish annals; cf. *Annales Lundenses*: "1147. Ericus Lamb monachus factus est; obiit Othensø"; *Annales Ryenses*: "1147. [. . .] Ericus Lam obiit, factus monachus in Odenseh."[208]

The matter in *Danakonungatal* on Sveinn svíðandi, Knútr Magnússon, and Valdemarr Knútsson is in general agreement with *Knýtlinga saga* and there is some similarity in wording:[209]

Danakonungatal	*Knýtlinga saga*
Eptir þat váru kóngar tveir í senn yfir Danmǫrko. Tóku Skánungar sér til kóngs Svein er kallaðr var svíðandi, son Eiríks kóngs emuna, en Jútar tóku sér til kóngs Knút, son herra Magnúss sterka (4.13–15).	Sveinn, son Eiríks konungs eymuna, var til konungs tekinn á Skáni eptir Eirík konung inn spaka, en Jótar tóku til konungs Knút, son Magnúss ins sterka Nikulássonar.
Hann (*Sveinn*) var harðr maðr ok svikall (4.19).	[. . .] því at hann var við allt fólk harðr ok grimmr.
Knút kóng segja menn helgan (4.23–24).	Segja Danir hann helgan.[210]

Sveinn's cognomen is mentioned later in *Knýtlinga saga*: "Hann kǫlluðu Danir Svein svíðanda";[211] cf. *Danakonungatal* "er kallaðr var." It is noteworthy that

---

[207] Bjarni Guðnason, ed., *Danakonunga sǫgur*, 272.1–2.
[208] Jørgensen, ed., *Annales Danici*, 79.
[209] Bjarni Guðnason, ed., *Danakonunga sǫgur*, 272–94.
[210] Bjarni Guðnason, ed., *Danakonunga sǫgur*, 272.5–8, 275.5–6, 288.29–30.
[211] Bjarni Guðnason, ed., *Danakonunga sǫgur*, 275.5.

the writer of the saga also refers to Danes when he speaks of the sanctity attributed to Knútr Magnússon, while *Danakonungatal* has "segja menn."

Danakonungatal says that Knútr was king for eight years, Sveinn svíðandi for nine. The same is implied in the statement in *Knýtlinga saga* that Valdemarr won "einvald yfir ǫllu Danaveldi [. . .] Þá váru níu vetr liðnir frá andláti Eiríks konungs ins spaka, en einn vetr frá drápi Knúts konungs Magnússonar."[212] Most Danish annals record the death of Eiríkr spaki s.a. 1147, but show much variation in the dates, from 1156 to 1158, under which the deaths of Knútr Magnússon and Sveinn svíðandi are entered; some of them assign their obits to the same year. None of them corresponds precisely with *Danakonungatal* and *Knýtlinga saga*. The dates given by the Danish annals also disagree with other Danish accounts which say that Knútr and Sveinn spent twelve years at war (*Annales Lundenses* and *Annales Ryenses*): "[. . .] et facta est pugna inter eos 12 annis";[213] and cf. *Chronicon Roskildense*.[214] Bearing in mind that in the last year of his life Knútr fought no battle against Sveinn, we can assume that a source which reckoned that Knútr was king for eight years gave seven years as the span of his warfare with Sveinn, using a Roman numeral VII, which then became XII in the archetype of the Danish texts. It is an open question whether the same sort of error was not introduced when it is told in Danish sources that Eiríkr spaki and Óláfr, son of Haraldr kesja, fought thirteen battles in one year, with VIII there read as XIII (see p. 159 above). *Danakonungatal* reports that Knútr was killed on the eve of St. Laurence's day, that is on 9 August, a date presumably obtained from Danish annals.[215] The date is not given in *Knýtlinga saga*.

The *Danakonungatal* text appears to be closer to Danish sources than to *Knýtlinga saga;* see, for example, *Chronicon Roskildense* and *Series et genealogiæ regum Danorum*.[216] It is, however, clear that no extant Danish source can have provided the matter of *Danakonungatal*. The statement that Knútr reigned for eight years and Sveinn for nine, for instance, finds no correspondence in any of the Danish writings, but it is in agreement with other Icelandic texts, *Knýtlinga saga* and annals.[217] It is also worth noting that Sveinn's cognomen, *svíðandi*, is found only in Icelandic sources, *Danakonungatal*, *Knýtlinga saga*, Copenhagen, Arnamagnaean Institute 415 4to, and annals.[218] But the remark in *Knýtlinga saga*, "Hann kǫlluðu Danir Svein svíðanda," indicates reference to a Danish source, most likely a written one.

---

[212] Bjarni Guðnason, ed., *Danakonunga sǫgur*, 294.4–8 and n. 3.
[213] Jørgensen, ed., *Annales Danici*, 79.
[214] Gertz, ed., *Scriptores*, 1: 32.22–23.
[215] Jørgensen, ed., *Annales Danici*, 80–81.
[216] Gertz, ed., *Scriptores*, 1: 32.18–33.19, 173.10–23.
[217] Bjarni Guðnason, ed., *Danakonunga sǫgur*, 294.6–8.
[218] See Knudsen and Kristensen, eds., *Personnavne*, 2: 1109.

The matter in the *Danakonungatal* passage on Valdemarr Knútsson is largely comparable to *Knýtlinga saga* but it is differently presented:

Danakonungatal	*Knýtlinga saga*
Eptir þetta eignaðisk Valdimarr kóngr alla Danmǫrk [...]²¹⁹	Eptir orrostu þessa þá fekk Valdimarr konungr einvald yfir ǫllu Danaveldi.²²⁰
Hann átti Suffíu dóttur Valaðar kóngs af Pólenía.	Eptir þetta gipti Knútr konungr Valdimar Suffíu, systur sína sammœdda. Hón var dóttir Valaðars konungs af Pólínalandi.
Þeira synir váru þeir Knútr kóngr ok Valdemarr kóngr.	Bǫrn Valdimars konungs ok Suffíu dróttningar váru þau Knútr konungr ok Valdimarr gamli, er síðan var konungr í Danmǫrk [...]
Cristofor hertogi var ok son Valdimars kóngs. Tófa hét móðir hans.	Kristófórús hét son Valdimars. Hann var frilluson. Tófa hét móðir hans.
	Kristófórús hertogi var ok son Valdimars konungs ok Tófu [...]
Herra Viljálmr af Brúnsvík, bróðir Otta keisara, fekk dóttur Valdimars kóngs, ok aðra fekk Philippús, kóngr af Franz. Hina þriðju átti Eiríkr Svíakóngr. Hon hét Ríkiza (4.27–33).	Engilborg var ok dóttir Valdimars konungs Knútssonar, er átti Philippús Frakkakonungr [...] ǫnnur dóttir Valdimars konungs var Ríkiz, er átti Eiríkr Svíakonungr Knútsson. [...] Þriðju dóttur Valdimars konungs átti Vilhjálmr digri, son Heinreks hertoga af Brúnsvík, bróðir Ottó keisara.²²¹

---

²¹⁹ Cf *Annales Lundenses*: "[...] et Waldemarus totum regnum obtinuit [...]" (Jørgensen, ed., *Annales Danici*, 83).

²²⁰ Cf *Annales Ryenses*: "[...] atque Waldemarus obtinuit monarchiam totius Dacie" (Jørgensen, ed., *Annales Danici*, 83).

²²¹ Bjarni Guðnason, ed., *Danakonunga sǫgur*, 294.4–5, 280.1–3, 315.11–13, 280.4–5, 315.25–26, 315.16–25.

There is a chapter in *Fagrskinna* A with the title: "Ættartala Danakonunga hefr hér." Valdemarr Knútsson and his wife and children are entered there in terms similar to those found in *Danakonungatal* and *Knýtlinga saga*:[222]

> Valdimarr Danakonungr fekk Suffíu, dóttur Valaðs konungs á Púlína-landi ok Ríkizu dróttningar. Bǫrn þeira Valdimars konungs ok Suffíu var Knútr konungr ok Valdimarr konungr ok Ríkiza dróttning. [...] Ríkizu dróttningu átti Eiríkr konungr í Svíþjóð Knútsson.[223]

Knýtlinga saga has a long account of Valdemar's attacks on Wendland but *Danakonungatal* only a single sentence: "Valdemarr kóngr kristnaði mikinn lut af Vindlandi." What *Danakonungatal* tells of Valdemar's dealings with Erlingr skakki and Magnús, his son, is not dependent on *Knýtlinga saga*. Bjarni Guðnason referred to *Heimskringla*,[224] and it is true that everything here in *Danakonungatal* could have been drawn from *Heimskringla* if only it was demonstrable that *Danakonungatal* was composed later than *Heimskringla*. In fact, *Fagrskinna* might equally well be envisaged as the source, unless we choose to entertain the notion of some still older work.

Knýtlinga saga does not mention that Valdemarr saw to the translation of the relics of Knútr lávarðr, but his initiative comes out clearly in Danish sources.[225] *Danakonungatal* was probably following some Danish account.

Danakonungatal and *Knýtlinga saga* agree in saying that Valdemarr was king for twenty-six years and died on 6 May, but they do not word it in the same way:

Danakonungatal	*Knýtlinga saga*
Hann var kóngr sex vetr ok tuttugu ok andaðisk in festo Johannis ante Portam latinam (4.39–40).	Valdimarr konungr andaðisk af sótt þessi annan Nónas Maii. [...] Þá hafði hann verit einvaldskonungr at allri Danmǫrk sex vetr ok tuttugu.[226]

The date in *Danakonungatal* was probably derived from a calendar with obits.

---

[222] Bjarni Guðnason, ed., *Danakonunga sǫgur*, clxix–clxx.
[223] Finnur Jónsson, ed., *Fagrskinna*, 300.22–26, 301.8–9.
[224] Bjarni Guðnason, ed., *Danakonunga sǫgur*, 334, n. 39.
[225] Cf., for example, Gertz, ed., *Vitae sanctorum Danorum*, 202–4, 219.
[226] Bjarni Guðnason, ed., *Danakonunga sǫgur*, 315.4–8.

King Knútr Valdemarsson is the subject of the last three chapters of
Knýtlinga saga, where most attention is paid to the battles he and Archbishop Absalon fought against the Wends. This account covers only the first five
years of Knútr's reign and is chiefly derived from Saxo.[227] The little that *Dana-*
konungatal tells of Knútr Valdemarsson does not depend on a text like that in
Knýtlinga saga. I have found no direct source for the statement that Valdemarr,
Knútr's brother, "var hertogi fyrir sunnan á í Jútlandi." Most Danish annals
call Valdemarr Valdemarsson *dux*, but *Annales Nestvedienses 821–1300* style
him "dux Jutiæ" and *Annales Sorani 1202–1347* "dux Iucie et Holsacie."[228] After his coronation in Lund cathedral he adopted the title of "Danorum Sclauo-
rumque rex, dux Jucie, dominus Nordalbingie."[229] I know of no other Icelandic
source which refers to the territory "fyrir sunnan á" in Jutland. We meet it,
however, in Danish sources, both in Latin and the vernacular. In the document
(ca. 1175) recording the donation of Valdemarr I to the church of St. Peter in
Hedeby (Slesvig) we find: "Preterea dimidiam capitalem porcionem patrimo-
nii nostri sed et aliarum acquisicionum nostrarum sunnen. a. [. . .]."[230] Since
the seventeenth century the river in question has been called Kongeåen, but its
old name was Skodborg Å (cf. Skotborgará in *Ágrip, Morkinskinna*, and *Heims-*
kringla). It divided the kingdom of Denmark and the duchy of Slesvig.[231]

According to Danish sources, Knútr came to the throne in 1182 and died
in 1202 (on 12 November). *Danakonungatal* gives no date but says that he
"andaðisk á því sama ári sem Sverrir kóngr í Nóregi."

What *Danakonungatal* has on Valdemarr Valdemarsson and his wives
and children agrees with Danish sources. His wife Margareta is called Dag-
mar in several Danish annals[232] and the reason is given in these terms in *An-*
nales Ryenses: "1212. Obiit Margareta regina que propter precipuam forme
pulchritudinem dicta fuit Daghmar."[233] Old Danish sources say that she was a

---

[227] Bjarni Guðnason, ed., *Danakonunga sǫgur*, clv–clvii.

[228] Jørgensen, ed., *Annales Danici*, 90–91, 94, 142.

[229] Christensen, "Tiden 1042–1241," 373.

[230] *Diplomatarium Danicum* ser. 1, vol. 3 (Copenhagen, 1976–1977), 72.24–25. See
further *Den danske Rigslovgivning indtil 1400*, 59.20, 144, variant to l. 76, 160.97; John
Kousgård Sørensen, *Danske sø- og ånavne* (Copenhagen, 1968), 8, 357; *Ordbog over det*
danske Sprog (1919), 1b. 38–43.

[231] Britta Olrik Frederiksen has supplied me with all this material on "fyrir sunnan
á", and she has my warmest thanks for it.

[232] See Jørgensen, ed., *Annales Danici*, 214, index.

[233] Jørgensen, ed., *Annales Danici*, 99; Storm, ed., *En oldnorsk Saga om Danekongerne*,
10, n. d. Cf. *Annales Ripenses*: "1212. Obiit regina Margareta, que dicta est Dagmar pre-
cipue propter pulchritudinem" (Jørgensen, ed., *Annales Danici*, 151).

daughter of the king of Bohemia.[234] They do not give the name of her father, but Hal Koch identifies her as daughter of King Ottokar I of Bohemia.[235] Gunnar Knudsen and Marius Kristensen interpret the name as follows: "(*Dag-mar* ɔ: '*Dag-mø*') [...] dannet ud fra Dronningens slaviske Navn *Dragomir*),"[236] while Aksel E. Christensen writes: "I 1205 ægtede han [sc. King Valdemarr] Dragomir [Dagmar] af Przemyslidernes gamle bøhmiske slægt."[237] *Konungs annáll* s.a. 1205 refers to her in much the same way as *Danakonungatal*: "Valdemarr Danakonungr fekk Margretar, er Danir kǫlluðu Dagmey. Hon var dóttir konungs af Bœheim." And under the same year *Flateyjar annáll* has: "Valdimarr Danakonungr fekk Margretar dóttur konungs af Barheimi. Hana kǫlluðu Danir Dagmey."[238] The Czech encyclopedia, *Ottův slovník naučný*, 6. *díl* (1893), gives the name of this princess as Markéta, daughter of King Přemysl I and Adléta from Meissen. In an article on Drahomíř, wife of the Czech prince Vratislav I, the same work notes that the name Drahomíř was spelt Dragomir in all sources down to the beginning of the fourteenth century, with Drahomíra its more modern form.[239]

The name "Bóm" in *Danakonungatal* is presumably an adaptation of the Latin form, Boemia or Bohemia, found in Danish sources; the closest parallel I have noticed is "Boem" in *Høyers annáll*, s.a. 1271.[240] *Danakonungatal* does not say precisely how long the joint reign of Valdemarr III and his father lasted. Danish annals record that Valdemarr III was acknowledged as king in 1215, crowned in 1218, and died in 1231,[241] but in *Incerti auctoris genealogia*

---

[234] Jørgensen, ed., *Annales Danici*, 96–97.

[235] Hal Koch, *Danmarks historie* 3: *Kongemagt og Kirke 1060–1241* (Copenhagen, 1969), 417. Ottokar I was king in Bohemia 1197–1230.

[236] "(*Dag-mar* ɔ: *Dag-mø*) [...] formed from the queen's Slavic name Dragomir" (Knudsen and Kristensen, eds., *Danmarks gamle Personnavne*, 1: 183).

[237] "In 1205 he [sc. King Valdemarr] married Dragomir [Dagmar] of the Przemyslids' old Bohemian family" (Christensen, "Tiden 1042–1241," 379).

[238] Storm, *Islandske Annaler*, 122; Guðbrandr Vigfússon and Unger, *Flateyjarbók*, 3:522.

[239] I owe this information to Professor Helgi Haraldsson, Oslo. I also owe to him the translation of following passages from an article on Dagmar in the encyclopedia: "**Dagmar**, Danish queen, wife of Valdemarr II (*1186–⁺1213); her native name was Markéta, daughter of the Czech king Přemysl I and Adléta from Meissen. [...] A Danish embassy came to Adléta in 1204: Strange Ebbesen, Limberg the Young, Oluf Lykke, Petr the Bishop (*probably Peder Sunesøn Bishop of Roskilde*) and Albert of Eskidsön, to ask for the hand of Markéta for Valdemarr II: her reputation for beauty and kindness of heart had reached even to Denmark [...] Their wedding was celebrated in Lübeck in 1205."

[240] See the index in Jørgensen, ed., *Annales Danici*, 222, and Gertz, ed., *Scriptores*, index 3, 2: 102; Storm, *Islandske Annaler*, 68.

[241] Jørgensen, ed., *Annales Danici*, 100, 101, 104, 105, 108, 109.

regum Danie it is said that his father allowed him to rule jointly with him after the kingly title was conferred on him, and that he did not live long: "[. . .] quem in regem electum fecit sibi conregnare. Qui paruo viuens tempore a seculo nimis mature subtractus est."[242] The author of *Danakonungatal* probably followed a source like this both at this point and again when he records Valdemar's second marriage and his sons by his second wife: "Síðar átti Valdimarr kóngr Berengarió dóttur kóngsins af Portúgal. Þeira synir váru þeir Eiríkr ok Abel ok Cristofor." (Cf.: "Post cuius matrem defunctam aliam duxit uxorem, nomine Berengariam, filiam regis Portugallie, de qua tres genuit filios his nominibus: primus nominatus Ericus, medius Abel, ultimus Christoferus.")[243] This piece gives neither the names nor the number of the illegitimate sons of Valdemarr. *Danakonungatal* gives the names of two of them, "hertuga Knút ok greifa Nicholás," both of whom find mention in Danish annals.

Valdemar's expedition against Eistland (Estonia) in 1219 is mentioned in Danish annals, for example in *Annales Ryenses*:

> Rex Waldemarus congregato exercitu permaximo cum mille quingentis longis nauibus Estoniam intrauit atque post multa bella totam terram illam ad fidem Christi conuertit et Danis subdidit usque in presens.[244]

His expedition to Norway is similarly recorded:

> 1204. Expeditio facta est in Norwegiam per regem Waldemarum, qui Ærlingum constituit ibi regem et Philippum ducem, qui ambo facti sunt homines regis apud Tunsbyærgh.[245]

Some Danish annals call this Erlingr the son of King Magnús.[246] Icelandic sources report that he claimed to be the son of Magnús Erlingsson;[247] *Danakonungatal* says that his men called him "steinvegg ok son Magnúss kóngs Erlingssonar." His eke-name does not appear in Danish sources but it was regularly used by Icelandic writers, in *Böglunga sögur, Hákonar saga gamla,* and annals.

---

[242] Gertz, ed., *Scriptores,* 1: 188.24–26.

[243] Gertz, ed., *Scriptores,* 1: 188.26–29.

[244] Jørgensen, ed., *Annales Danici,* 105; see also Gertz, ed., *Scriptores,* 1: 459.1–6.

[245] *Annales Ryenses,* Jørgensen, ed., *Annales Danici,* 95; see also Gertz, ed., *Scriptores,* 1: 441.2–4.

[246] See the index in Jørgensen, ed., *Annales Danici.*

[247] Hallvard Magerøy, ed., *Soga om Birkebeinar og Baglar. Bǫglunga sǫgur,* Norsk Historisk Kjeldeskrift-Institutt, norrøne tekster 5 (Oslo, 1988), 11–12.

Danakonungatal ends with this sentence: "Valdimarr er kallaðr ágætastr Danakónga." Bjarni Guðnason cites in comparison the sentence in *Knýtlinga saga* where Valdemarr is first introduced: "[. . .] Valdimarr gamli [. . .] er einhverr hefir verit ágætastr konungr hingat á Norðrlǫnd,"[248] and another sentence in *Hákonar saga gamla*, where the *Eirspennill* text comes closest to *Danakonungatal*: "[. . .] Valdimarr konungr í Danmǫrk [. . .] er þann tíma var ágæztr konungr á Norðrlǫndum."[249] Here there is a difference between *Danakonungatal* and *Knýtlinga saga* in that the former uses the present tense, "er kallaðr," and the latter the perfect, "hefir verit." But it would be hasty to conclude from this that Valdemarr was alive when *Danakonungatal* was composed and dead when the saga was written.

The origins of *Danakonungatal*

There are various references to sources in *Danakonungatal* but there is nothing in the wording to indicate whether they were oral or written:

Þann Sigurð segja menn [. . .] (1.21–22). — þenna Svein kalla Danir ok Norðmenn tjúguskegg (1.37–38). — Svá segja danskir menn [. . .] (2.31). — Eiríkr spaki er sumir menn kalla lamb [. . .] (4.6). — Knút kóng segja menn helgan (4.23–24). — [. . .] Margrettu er sumir kalla Dagmey (4.46).

A precise dating to a year occurs twice, in each case counted from the birth of Christ, not from the Incarnation. When Denmark became Christian "var liðit frá burð várs herra Jesú Kristí níu hundruð ok fimm tigir ára" (see p. 141–42 above), and when Knútr ríki died "var liðit frá burð várs herra Jesú Kristí .M. ok .xxx. ok .íííj. uetr" (2.33–34). Knútr Valdemarsson is said to have died in the same year as King Sverrir in Norway, but the year is not given. Otherwise we are told only the length of each king's reign: Hörða-Knútr Knútsson 8 winters, Magnús góði Óláfsson 5 winters, Sveinn Úlfsson 29 winters, Haraldr hein Sveinsson 4 winters, Knútr hinn helgi Sveinsson 7 winters, Óláfr Sveinsson 8 winters, Eiríkr eygóði Sveinsson 8 winters, Nikulás Sveinsson 30 winters, Eiríkr eymuni Eiríksson 4 winters, Eiríkr spaki Hákonarson norrœna 8 winters, Sveinn svíðandi Eiríksson eymuna 9 winters, Valdemarr Knútsson hertoga 26 winters, Knútr Valdimarsson 20 winters —he died in the same year as King Sverrir, that is in 1202. This sequence makes 166 years between

[248] Bjarni Guðnason, ed., *Danakonunga sǫgur*, 336, n. 42, 315.12–14.
[249] Finnur Jónsson, ed., *Eirspennill* (Kristiania [Oslo], 1913–1916), 614.4–6.

Knútr ríki and Valdemarr gamli, two years less than the correct span from
the death of Knútr ríki to the death of Knútr Valdemarsson. The discrepancy must represent the two years missing in the time allotted to the reign
of Haraldr hein in *Danakonungatal* and other Icelandic sources (see p. 152
above).

The periods of rule ascribed to the Danish kings in *Danakonungatal* are
not in accord with any extant Danish source but they agree for the most part
with the record in Icelandic annals, *Konungs annáll, Lögmanns annáll, Gottskálks annáll,* and *Flateyjar annáll.* The author of *Knýtlinga saga* gives no date
for the death of Knútr ríki; he appears to assume that Hörða-Knútr ruled
Denmark for seven years; and he does not tell us how long Magnús góði's
reign there lasted. But the figures he gives for the reigns from Magnús góði to
Knútr Valdimarsson are the same as in *Danakonungatal.*

Icelandic annals occasionally have sentences which are in better accord
with *Danakonungatal* than with other sources:

Danakonungatal	*Icelandic annals*
Haraldr kóngr blátǫnn tók ríki í Danmǫrk [. . .] (1.33).	Haraldr blátǫnn Gormsson tók ríki í Danmǫrku (*Skálholts annáll* 907 and *Flateyjar annáll*).
Á síðustum dǫgum hans stríddi til lands í móti honum Sveinn son hans. [. . .] Sveinn tjúguskegg tók ríki í Danmǫrk eptir fǫður sinn. [. . .] (1.40–2.1 og 2.6).	Sveinn tjúguskegg tók konung-dóm (ríki *Annales vetustissimi, Flateyjar annáll*) ok stríddi við fǫður sinn (*Resens annáll, Annales vetustissimi,* and *Flateyjar annáll*). Sveinn tjúguskegg stríddi til ríkis við fǫður sinn (*Skálholts annáll* 958).
[. . .] ok einn tíma bǫrðusk þeir (*Eiríkr lamb and Óláfr, son of Haraldr kesja*) þrysvar á einum degi (4.9–10).	Eirekr lamb ok Óláfr son Haralds kesju bǫrðusk þrysvar á einum degi (*Flateyjar annáll* 1143).[250]

Danakonungatal cannot, however, be seen to be dependent on any of the annals cited above, but a few instances of similar phrasing and the almost exact
correspondence in the regnal years of the Danish kings given in these sources indicate close relationship between them. The likeliest explanation is that

[250] Storm, ed., *Islandske Annaler.*

Icelandic annal-writers and the author of *Knýtlinga saga* knew and used *Danakonungatal*. If that was the case, it is obvious that the text existed in more manuscripts than the Codex Resenianus containing *Sverris saga*.

From the comparison between *Danakonungatal* and related texts undertaken above, it seems evident that the author of *Danakonungatal* drew on a Danish set of annals, now lost. It is also clear that he made some use of English records. He had a translation of matter from Adam of Bremen, but I can see no evidence to suggest that he knew either *Heimskringla* or *Knýtlinga saga* — both these were doubtless written later than *Danakonungatal*. There is every likelihood that he knew Icelandic writings on the Danish kings, work that was related to *Sögubrot af fornkonungum*, and learnt about Haraldr Gormsson's forebears from them; and he also had some knowledge of sagas of the kings of Norway, from Haraldr hárfagri to Ingi Bárðarson. The author's use of sources in *Danakonungatal* does not suggest that he also wrote the genealogical section which precedes it in Árni Magnússon's transcript; and it is obvious that the text copied by Árni was not in the author's own hand.

I have not so far considered the date of composition of *Danakonungatal*, though in an earlier article I attempted to establish its age by looking at the way Valdemarr II and his sons are referred to in the text.[251] There is no note of the death of Valdemarr II — Valdemarr gamli as he is usually called — or of the death of Valdemarr, his son: Valdemarr II died in 1241, his son before him in 1231. Two of his illegitimate sons are given titles: hertogi Knútr (rank bestowed in 1219) and greifi Nikulás (rank bestowed in 1216; d. 1218); but his sons by his second wife, Berengaria, are named without titles: Eiríkr, given the title of king in 1231; Abel, hertogi in 1232, king in 1250; Kristófórus, king in 1252. On this basis we might conclude that *Danakonungatal* was composed after 1219 and before 1231.

As remarked earlier (p. 110), Gustav Storm and Bjarni Guðnason conjectured that *Danakonungatal* was composed on behalf of Ingeborg, Magnús lagabætir's queen. If that were the case it must be counted extraordinary, indeed incomprehensible, that in *Danakonungatal* her father, Eiríkr, is referred to neither as king nor as saint.

The nationality of the scribe of the genealogies and *Danakonungatal* in the Codex Resenianus of *Sverris saga* is in reality a problem that defies solution. Linguistic features and scribal practice are so decidedly Norwegian that it is unlikely that it was written by an Icelander, but then again a Norwegian could hardly be expected to muddle *œ* and *æ* as comprehensively as the text reveals (see p. 132). It is still less likely that we shall ever know for sure the

---

[251] Ólafur Halldórsson, "Um Danakonunga sögur," *Gripla* 7 (1990): 73–102.

nationality of the author of *Danakonungatal* itself. When he refers to Norwegian rulers he most often says specifically that they were kings in or of or from Norway, which I take to indicate that he was not himself in that country when he wrote *Danakonungatal*:

"Í þenna tíma var uppi í Nóregi Haraldr hárfagri" (1.29–30); "[...] ok Eiríkr jarl, son Hákonar jarls ríka af Nóregi, við Óláf Tryggvason Nóregskóng, er þar helt fyrst kristni" (2.11–13); "Hann gerði sætt ok kærleik við Magnús kóng góða af Nóregi" (2.38–39); "Magnús kóngr góði af Nóregi" (2.43); "Hann hafði lengi ófrið ok stríð við Harald kóng harðráða af Nóregi" (3.9–10); "Hans dróttning var Ingigerðr, dóttir Haralds kóngs harðráða af Nóregi" (3.23–24); "Hann átti Málmfríði dróttning er fyrr hafði átt Sigurðr kóngr í Nóregi Jórsalafari" (3.41–43).

He had access to Danish sources, took matter from English records, and knew Icelandic kings' sagas older than *Heimskringla*. What he tells of Haraldr blátǫnn, Sveinn tjúguskegg, and Knútr the Great is in part derived from Adam of Bremen — and it is an open question whether the bits from Adam (see p. 140) were not translated by the writer of *Danakonungatal* himself. He was a learned man, literate in Latin and the vernacular. I have here only considered the possibility of an Icelandic or a Norwegian author, but learned and literate men certainly also existed in Orkney and the Faroes, and Greenland too for that matter, especially at the cathedral churches of those communities. Not that I intend to point to any of them as the likely home of the writer of *Danakonungatal*, mindful as I am of the old adage, "Eigi veit hvar óskytja ör geigar" (one never knows where a bad marksman's arrow will stray). I leave it to others to solve the riddle of his origin and environment.

English translation by Peter Foote

Bibliography

Albeck, Gustav. *Knýtlinga: Sagaerne om Danmarks Konger.* Copenhagen, 1946.

Arnold, Thomas, ed. *Memorials of St. Edmund's Abbey* 1. London, 1890.

Arwidsson, A. I. *Förteckning öfver kongl. bibliothekets i Stockholm isländska handskrifter.* Stockholm, 1848.

Bjarni Aðalbjarnarson, ed. *Snorri Sturluson: Heimskringla.* 3 vols. Íslenzk fornrit 26–28. Reykjavík, 1941–1951.

Bjarni Einarsson, ed. *Ágrip af Nóregskonunga sǫgum; Fagrskinna — Nóregs konunga tal.* Íslenzk fornrit 29. Reykjavík, 1984.

————. *The Saga of Gunnlaug Serpent-Tongue and Three Other Sagas. Perg. 4:0 NR 18 Royal Library Stockholm.* Early Icelandic Manuscripts in Facsimile 16. Copenhagen, 1986.

Bjarni Guðnason, ed. *Danakonunga sǫgur.* Íslenzk fornrit 35. Reykjavík, 1982.

Blake, F. N., ed. and trans. *Jómsvíkinga saga — The Saga of the Jomsvikings.* Nelson's Icelandic Texts 3. London, 1962.

Buchner, Rudolf, ed. *Ausgewählte Quellen zur deutschen Geschichte des Mittelalters. Quellen des 9. und 11. Jahrhunderts zur Geschichte der Hamburgischen Kirche und des Reiches.* Darmstadt, 1976.

Christensen, Aksel E. "Tiden 1042–1241." In *Danmarks historie* 1:211–399. Copenhagen, 1977.

Christiansen, Eric, trans. *The Works of Sven Aggesen, Twelfth-Century Danish Historian.* London, 1992.

Diplomatarium Danicum. Ser. 1, vol. 3. Copenhagen, 1976–1977.

Finnbogi Guðmundsson, ed. *Orkneyinga saga.* Íslenzk fornrit 34. Reykjavík, 1965.

Finnur Jónsson, ed. *Heimskringla. Nórges konunga sǫgur af Snorri Sturluson.* 4 vols. Samfund til udgivelse af gammel nordisk litteratur 23. Copenhagen, 1893–1901.

————, ed. *Fagrskinna. Nórges konunga tal.* Samfund til udgivelse af gammel nordisk litteratur 30. Copenhagen, 1902–1903.

————, ed. *Eirspennill.* Kristiania [Oslo], 1913–1916.

————, ed. *Edda Snorra Sturlusonar.* Copenhagen, 1931.

————, ed. *Morkinskinna.* Samfund til udgivelse af gammel nordisk litteratur 53. Copenhagen, 1932.

————, ed. *Saga Óláfs Tryggvasonar af Oddr Snorrason munk.* Copenhagen, 1932.

Foote, Peter. *The Pseudo-Turpin Chronicle in Iceland: A Contribution to the Study of the Karlamagnús saga.* London, 1959.

Gertz, M. Cl., ed. *Knud den Helliges Martyrhistorie. Særlig efter de tre ældste Kilder.* Copenhagen, 1907.

————, ed. *Vitae sanctorum Danorum.* Copenhagen, 1908–1912.

————, ed. *Scriptores minores historiæ Danicæ medii ævi.* 2 vols. Copenhagen, 1970.

Guðbrandur Vigfússon and C. R. Unger, eds. *Flateyjarbók. En Samling af norske Konge-Sagaer.* 3 vols. Christiania [Oslo], 1860–1868.

Gödel, Vilhelm. *Katalog öfver Kongl. bibliotekets fornisländska och fornnorska handskrifter*. Kongl. bibliotekets handlingar 19–22. Stockholm, 1897–1900.

Jakob Benediktsson, ed. *Veraldar saga*. Samfund til udgivelse af gammel nordisk litteratur 61. Copenhagen, 1944.

Johnson, Oscar Albert, ed. *Ólafs saga hins helga*. *Efter pergamenthandskrift i Uppsala Universitetsbibliotek, Delagardieske samling nr. 8*. Det norske historiske kildeskriftfonds skrifter 47. Kristiania [Oslo], 1922.

———, and Jón Helgason, eds. *Saga Óláfs konungs hins helga*. *Den store saga om Olav den hellige*. Oslo, 1941.

Jón Helgason and Jakob Benediktsson, eds. *Hákonar saga Ívarssonar*. Samfund til udgivelse af gammel nordisk litteratur 62. Copenhagen, 1952.

Jón Þorkelsson, ed. *Småstykker 1–16*. Samfund til udgivelse af gammel nordisk litteratur 13. Copenhagen, 1884–1891.

———, ed. *Íslenzkar ártíðaskrár eða Obituaria Islandica með athugasemdum, xxv ættarskrám og einni rímskrá*. Copenhagen, 1893–1896.

Jørgensen, Ellen, ed. *Annales Danici medii ævi*. Copenhagen, 1920.

Knudsen, Gunnar, and Marius Kristensen, eds. *Danmarks gamle Personnavne*. 1: *Fornavne*, 2: *Tilnavne*. Copenhagen, 1954–1964.

Koch, Hal. *Danmarks historie 3: Kongemagt og Kirke 1060–1241*. Copenhagen, 1969.

Kousgård Sørensen, John. *Danske sø- og ånavne*. Copenhagen, 1968.

Kålund, Kr. *Katalog over Den arnamagnæanske Håndskriftsamling*. 2 vols. Copenhagen, 1888–1894.

———, ed. *Alfræði íslenzk. Islandsk encyklopædisk litteratur 3*. Samfund til udgivelse af gammel nordisk litteratur 45. Copenhagen, 1917–1918.

Langebek, Jacob, ed. *Scriptores rerum Danicarum medii ævi 2*. Copenhagen, 1773.

Lind, E. H., ed. *Norsk-isländska dopnamn ock fingerade namn från medeltiden*. Uppsala, 1905–1915.

Lund, Niels. "Cnut's Danish Kingdom." In *The Reign of Cnut*, ed. Alexander R. Ruble, 27–42. London and New York, 1994; repr. 1999.

Magerøy, Hallvard, ed. *Soga om Birkibeinar og Baglar. Bǫglunga sǫgur*. Norsk Historisk Kjeldeskrift-Institutt, norrøne tekster 5. Oslo, 1988.

Már Jónsson. *Árni Magnússon. Ævisaga*. Reykjavík, 1998.

Ólafur Halldórsson, ed. *Óláfs saga Tryggvasonar en mesta*. 3 vols. Editiones Arnamagnæanæ, Ser. A:1–3. Copenhagen, 1958–2000.

———, ed. *Færeyinga saga.* Reykjavík, 1987.

———. "Um Danakonunga sögur." *Gripla* 7 (1990): 73–102.

———. "Þýskan í Grænlendinga sögu." *Gripla* 8 (1993): 282–84.

———. "Þingamanna þáttr." In *Sagnaþing helgað Jónasi Kristjánssyni sjötugum 10. apríl 1994,* ed. Gísli Sigurðsson, Guðrún Kvaran, and Sigurgeir Steingrímsson, 1: 617–40. 2 vols. Reykjavík, 1994.

———. *Danish Kings and the Jomsvikings in the Greatest Saga of Óláfr Tryggvason.* London, 2000.

Olrik, Jørgen, and H. Ræder, eds. *Saxonis Gesta Danorum.* Copenhagen, 1931.

Páll Eggert Ólason. *Íslenzkar æviskrár frá landnámstímum til ársloka 1940.* 5 vols. Reykjavík, 1948–1952.

Pertz, Georgius Heinricus, ed. *Gisleberti Chronicon.* MGH 21. Hannover, 1869.

Plummer, Ch., ed. *Two of the Saxon Chronicles Parallel.* 2 vols. Oxford, 1892–1899.

Schmeidler, Bernhard, ed. *Magistri Adami Bremensis Gesta Hammaburgensis Ecclesiae Pontificum.* MGH. Scriptores rerum Germanicarum in usum scholarum 2. Hannover and Leipzig, 1917.

Stefán Karlsson. "Gǫfuglátur veiðikonungur." In *Pétursskip búið Peter Foote sextugum 26. maí 1984,* 51–54. Reykjavík, 1984.

———. "Drottinleg bæn á móðurmáli." In *Biblíuþýðingar í sögu og samtíð,* 145–74. Studia theologica islandica 4. Reykjavík, 1990.

———. "Om norvagismer i islandske håndskrifter." In *Stafkrókar: Ritgerðir eftir Stefán Karlsson gefnar út í tilefni af sjötugsafmæli hans 2. desember 1998.* ed. Guðvarður Már Gunnlaugsson, 173–87. Reykjavík, 2000.

———. "Elsta brot Karlamagnús sögu og Rekaþáttur Þingeyrabókar." In *Stafkrókar,* 206–24.

———. "Alfræði Sturlu Þórðarsonar." In *Stafkrókar,* 279–302.

Storm, Gustav, ed. *En oldnorsk Saga om Danekongerne.* Christiania [Oslo], 1879.

———, ed. "Theodrici monachi Historia de antiquitate regum Norwagiensium." In *Monumenta historica Norvegiæ* 1:1–68. Oslo, 1880.

———, ed. *Islandske Annaler indtil 1578.* Christiania [Oslo], 1888.

Stubbs, William, ed. *Chronica magistri Rogeri de Houedene.* 2 vols. London, 1868–1871.

———, ed. *Willelmi Malmesbiriensis monachi De gestis regum Anglorum.* Rerum Britannicarum medii ævi scriptores. Rolls Series 90. London, 1887.

Thorpe, Benjamin, ed. *Florentii Wigorniensis monachi Chronicon ex chronicis*. London, 1848.

Unger, C. R., ed. *Mariu saga. Legender om Jomfru Maria og hendes Jertegn*. Christiania [Oslo], 1868–1871.

———, ed. *Codex Frisianus. En Samling af norske Konge-Sagaer*. Christiania [Oslo], 1871.

Whitelock, Dorothy, trans. *The Anglo-Saxon Chronicle*. London, 1965.

JÓHANNES SAGA GULLMUNNS: THE ICELANDIC LEGEND OF THE HAIRY ANCHORITE

MARIANNE E. KALINKE

I. Introduction

The apocryphal legend of St. John Chrysostom, known as the legend of the hairy anchorite, was immortalized by Albrecht Dürer in 1497, when he produced a copper engraving depicting a voluptuous nude reclining against a tree while nursing a baby. In the background one sees a small male figure crawling on all fours.[1] The tale that inspired this work of art became the object of Martin Luther's scorn and derisive commentary, when he published it in 1537 under the title *Die Lügend von S. Johanne Chrysostomo*.[2] In choosing to designate this apocryphal story as a *Lügend* (lying story), Luther was playing on the German loan *Legende* (from Latin *legenda*, "to be read"), the generic designation for saints' lives. With the neologism, Luther proclaimed as fiction a type of narrative that was accepted by many believers as transmitting historical reality. Although his publication was addressed to the pope, the cardinals, and other members of the ecclesiastical hierarchy assembled at Whitsun at the Council of Mantua, as the dedication in the title indicates,[3]

---

[1] For a reproduction of this engraving, as well as a similar one by Lucas Cranach the Elder from 1500, see Paul Schubring, "Die Chrysostomus-Legende," *Zeitschrift für Bildende Kunst* n.F. 24 (1913): 110. For the text that presumably inspired both Dürer and Cranach and for a discussion of the legend in general, see Charles Allyn Williams, *The German Legends of the Hairy Anchorite*, Illinois Studies in Language and Literature 18 (Urbana, 1935).

[2] "Die Lügend von S. Johanne Chrysostomo. 1537," in *D. Martin Luthers Werke*, Kritische Gesamtausgabe, vol. 50 (Weimar, 1914), 48–64. The legend was published in Wittenberg, Augsburg, and Strassburg.

[3] Luther, "Die Lügend," 52.

the very fact of its publication made widely available a type of text denounced by Luther as "verzweivelte lugen und abgoettery," "rechte luegenden, erstunckene, Teuffelische luegen" (53).[4]

The redaction of the legend of St. John Chrysostom published by Luther was taken from one of the many editions of *Der Heiligen Leben* then circulating in the German-language area. To judge by its dissemination and impact, *Der Heiligen Leben* was the most important vernacular collection of saints' lives in the Middle Ages. The work, which originally included 251 texts, is extant in 197 manuscripts and thirty-three High German and eight Low German imprints.[5] The oldest extant imprint was published by Günther Zainer in 1471/1472, while the last edition appeared in Strassburg in 1521.[6] The legendary was most likely compiled in the years between 1396 and 1410 in the context of a reform of the Dominican women's monastery in Nürnberg, its legends most probably intended for reading in the refectory.[7] These legends, drastically reduced versions of older texts,[8] transmit merely the bare facts. Authorial commentary is eliminated while behavior and events are unmotivated; dialogue is avoided in favor of third-person narrative; and the legends' paratactic style mimics the flat, undifferentiated presentation of narrative detail.[9] Werner Williams-Krapp aptly characterized the legends in *Der Heiligen Leben* as "abbreviierte, unkommentierte, zumeist auch völlig enthistorisierte und entrhetorisierte Legendenfassungen."[10] Not all the sources of the texts in the legendary have been identified.[11] This is the case with the apocryphal legend of St. John Chrysostom.

---

[4] Luther, "Die Lügend," 53.

[5] Werner Williams-Krapp, *Die deutschen und niederländischen Legendare des Mittelalters: Studien zu ihrer Überlieferungs-, Text- und Wirkungsgeschichte* (Tübingen, 1986), 188.

[6] Williams-Krapp, *Legendare*, 237–38.

[7] Williams-Krapp, *Legendare*, 300.

[8] Williams-Krapp, *Legendare*, 272.

[9] On the basis of the legends of Henry and Cunegund, George, and Gregorius peccator, Volker Mertens summarized the character of the texts as follows: "Kürzung auf die Summa facti, Abbau von individualisierenden Darstellungsmomenten, Ausklammerung einer differenzierten Problematik und im Stilistischen eine vergleichbare Tendenz zur syntaktischen Reihung mit Nivellierung komplexer Abhängigkeitsverhältnisse" ("Verslegende und Prosalegendar. Zur Prosafassung von Legendenromanen in 'Der Heiligen Leben'," in *Poesie und Gebrauchsliteratur im deutschen Mittelalter*, Würzburger Colloquium 1978, ed. Volker Honemann et al. [Tübingen, 1979], 265–89, at 287).

[10] Williams-Krapp, *Legendare*, 367.

[11] Williams-Krapp, Legendare, 279–92.

St. John Chrysostom (345/349/354–407), who was born in Antioch, ordained a priest in 386, and consecrated bishop of Constantinople in 398, "was the most gifted Christian preacher of his age."[12] His eloquence earned him the cognomen "Chrysostomos," that is, Goldmouth. His large œuvre includes exegetical and occasional homilies as well as writings in defense of the ascetic and monastic life and in celebration of virginity. Before he was ordained, he lived for an extended period as a hermit, from c. 373 to c. 381.[13]

The apocryphal legend that came to be associated with John Chrysostom tells of a fantastic episode that supposedly occurred during St. John's sojourn in the wilderness. The story is a frame narrative, in which the tale constituting the frame demonstrates the efficacy of prayer for the deceased and provides the motivation for the saint's ordination as a priest at the — historically inaccurate — tender age of sixteen.

> An unidentified pope, while engaged in prayer one day, hears a sorrowful voice calling out to him. A suffering soul informs him that it will not be released from its torments until the soon-to-be born son of a couple named Seidmer and Anthusa becomes a priest and has celebrated his sixteenth Mass.

The frame story resurfaces near the end of the legend when fifteen years later St. John learns of the prenatal incident and immediately says the necessary number of Masses, at the end of which the soul is freed from its suffering. This miracle tale, illustrating the intercessory power of prayer, encloses a narrative that combines the fantastic with the miraculous in what may be considered a sacred romance.

> On the day of his ordination St. John renounces the world to devote himself to penance. He withdraws to an isolated spot and embarks on a life of penance. The fantastic intrudes when a princess is carried off by a whirlwind and deposited near his cave. St. John reluctantly takes her in, but his attempt to live a life of penance with the maiden comes to naught. He seduces her, is contrite, but fears that he will again succumb to passion.

---

[12] Peter Brown, *The Body and Society: Men, Women, and Sexual Renunciation in Early Christianity* (New York, 1988), 306.

[13] K. S. Frank, "J. Chrysostomos," in *Lexikon des Mittelalters* (Munich, 1990), 5:563–64; "Chrysostom, St. John," in *Oxford Dictionary of the Christian Church*, 3rd ed. F. L. Cross and E. A. Livingstone (Oxford, 1997), 342–43; Otto Wimmer and Hartmann Melzer, *Lexikon der Namen und Heiligen* (Innsbruck, 1984), 430. See Brown, *The Body and Society*, chap. 15, "Sexuality and the City: John Chrysostom," 305–22.

He solves his dilemma by throwing the maiden off a cliff. Remorseful, he travels to Rome to seek absolution from the pope, and when the latter refuses to grant this, John returns to the wilderness and vows to crawl on all fours until he is given a sign that his sins have been forgiven. For fifteen years he undergoes this penance. Then the parents of the princess have another child, and it refuses to be baptized by anyone other than the holy man John. No one knows who this might be, but one day the emperor's hunters bag a marvelous creature, which the baby addresses as his spiritual father John and whom the baby informs that his sins have been forgiven. The saint is restored to full beauty. A final miracle rounds off the tale. The emperor wishes to bury his daughter, but when St. John leads him to the place of his misdeed, the princess is found safe and sound.

This apocryphal tale, widely disseminated through inclusion in *Der Heiligen Leben*, presumably derives from a fourteenth-century Italian text, "Istoria di San Giovanni Boccadoro."[14] A fifteenth-century Italian painting on a hope chest, depicting three scenes of the fantastic tale, attests the currency of the legend that came to be transmitted to the German-language area.[15]

The apocryphal tale of St. John Chrysostom that is edited here, *Jóhannes saga gullmunns*, "Saga of John Goldmouth," is one of twenty-five legends in *Reykjahólabók*, the Book of Reykjahólar, a monumental legendary produced in Iceland during the second quarter of the sixteenth century, as the Reformation began to gain a foothold in that country.[16] With the exception of three texts that are copies of already existing Icelandic translations from the Latin — *Ambrosius saga*, *Laurencius saga*, and *Stefanus saga*[17] — the legends in *Reykjahólabók* are translations from Low German.

Reykjahólabók contains three legends relating to the life of Christ (the legends of St. Anne and the Virgin Mary, the Three Wise Men, and Lazarus); seven legends devoted to martyrs, several of them the so-called Holy Helpers (Christopher, Erasmus, George, Lawrence, Oswald, Sebastian, and Stephen);

---

[14] Dietz-Rüdiger Moser, "Chrysostomus," in *Die deutsche Literatur des Mittelalters. Verfasserlexikon*, 2nd rev. ed., ed. Kurt Ruh (Berlin, 1978), 1:1269.

[15] See Wolfgang Braunfels, ed., *Lexikon der christlichen Ikonographie* (Rome, 1968–1976), 7:101; Federico Patetta, *Di una tavola della R. Galleria Estense con rappresentazioni tolte dalla leggenda di S. Giovanni Boccadoro*, Memorie della R. Accademia di Scienze, Lettere ed Arti in Modena, ser. 3, 7 (Sezione Arti) (Modena, 1907), esp. 6–7.

[16] Agnete Loth edited the text under the title "Johannes Gullmunnr" in *Reykjahólabók. Islandske helgenlegender*, Editiones Arnamagnæanæ, A, 16 (Copenhagen, 1969), 2:167–91 (hereafter *Rhb*).

[17] See Marianne E. Kalinke, *The Book of Reykjahólar: The Last of the Great Medieval Legendaries* (Toronto, 1996), 80–95.

five Doctors of the Eastern and Western Church (Ambrose, Augustine, Gregory the Great, Jerome, John Chrysostom); two popes (the aforementioned Gregory and Silvester); one bishop (Servatius); two friars (the Augustinian Nicholas of Tolentino and the eponymous founder of the Dominican Order); one desert father (Anthony) and one hermit (Roch); one martyr king (the aforenamed Oswald); one emperor (the above Henry II) and one empress (Cunegund); and, finally, the apocryphal Barlaam and Josaphat, Gregorius peccator, and the Seven Sleepers.

Reykjahólabók, named after the place of its origin in the Westfjords of Iceland, has singular value for our understanding of hagiography in the late Middle Ages, inasmuch as the sources of the twenty-two legends translated from Low German are no longer extant. *Reykjahólabók* was written by Björn Þorleifsson († ca. 1554), probably the wealthiest Icelander of his time, and circumstantial evidence suggests that he was not only the scribe but also the translator.[18] He belonged to a family well known for its literary interests, the members of which produced nineteen books in the period 1420 to 1560.[19] In addition to the legends in *Reykjahólabók*, fragments of four other saints' lives are extant in Björn's hand, suggesting that he had also produced another legendary, one devoted to the apostles and evangelists.[20] Furthermore, we possess his fragmentary translation of the Book of Revelation, a translation from German.[21] We do not know how Björn Þorleifsson came to be in possession of the Low German texts that he made available in translation to his countrymen.

Until recently the source of the translated legends in *Reykjahólabók* was thought to be *Dat Passionael*, the Low German translation of *Der Heiligen Leben*. In the 1960s, Ole Widding and Hans Bekker-Nielsen published two articles on *Reykjahólabók*, in which they posited the *Passionael* as the chief source of all but one of the translated legends.[22] They interpreted discrepancies between the Low German and Icelandic texts as the work of the translator. A detailed study of the legends in *Reykjahólabók* and a comparison

---

[18] See *Rhb*, 1:xxix; xxxix–xl; Kalinke, *The Book of Reykjahólar*, 29–30.

[19] Stefán Karlsson, "Ritun Reykjafjarðarbókar. Excursus: Bókagerð bænda," in *Opuscula*, 4, Bibliotheca Arnamagnæana 30 (Copenhagen, 1970), 137–40; Kalinke, *The Book of Reykjahólar*, 30–31.

[20] See Mariane Overgaard, ed., *The History of the Cross-Tree Down to Christ's Passion*, Editiones Arnamagnæanæ, B: 26 (Copenhagen, 1968), xcix–ciii.

[21] Agnete Loth, "Et islandsk fragment fra reformationstiden. AM 667, x, 4to," in *Opuscula* 4, 25–30.

[22] Ole Widding and Hans Bekker-Nielsen, "En senmiddelalderlig legendesamling," *Maal og Minne* (1960): 105–28; eidem, "Low German Influence on Late Icelandic Hagiography," *Germanic Review* 37 (1962): 237–62.

with German antecedents other than *Dat Passionael/Der Heiligen Leben* has shown, however, that the Icelandic versions, all of which are much longer accounts than those in the *Passionael*, are translations not of the short texts in the prose legendary but most likely of some of the very sources of those texts.[23] In other words, some legends on which the compiler of *Der Heiligen Leben* drew and which he condensed were in all probability the High German texts that Björn Þorleifsson knew in Low German translation. This is in all likelihood the case with *Jóhannes saga gullmunns*.

The Icelandic legend of St. John Chrysostom extends to nearly twenty-five pages in the large printed edition, averaging 36 lines per page.[24] It consists of two discrete, albeit conjoined legends, the apocryphal tale of the hairy anchorite[25] and the saint's biography.[26] The apocryphal legend about St. John Chrysostom takes up more than two-thirds of the text. The transition from the apocryphal story to the saint's vita is somewhat confusing. The narrative proper of the apocryphal tale ends with the following, apparently authorial statement, and a reference to a Venetian church dedicated to the saint:

> Og endist þessi historía hér fyrst að sinni um þetta efni af því að sumlegir meistarar vilja segja að hún sé ekki sönn fyrir því að þeir þykkjast ekki so skýrt finna hana í latínu skrifaða sem aðrar historíur. En þó greinir so að í <Italíu>[27] liggur einn mektugur staður er Fenedien heitir og í þessum greindum stað sé honum helguð ein kirkja með eins og historían segir til og hér fyrir greinir. En hvað sannast sem hér um er þá veit það guð best.[28]

> (And for the present the legend ends here about this matter, concerning which some teachers claim that it is not true because they do not think that it is manifestly written in Latin like other legends. But it reports that a mighty city is found in Italy which is called Venice and in this city there is a church dedicated to him, just as the legend says and here records. But what the truth in the matter is, God knows best.)

---

[23] See Kalinke, *The Book of Reykjahólar*, 51–64; 95–105.

[24] *Rhb.* 2: 167–91.

[25] *Rhb.* 2: 167–84:33.

[26] *Rhb.* 2: 185:3–191:24.

[27] The manuscript has a space of six letters here (*Rhb.* 2: 184.34); presumably Björn's source did not name the country and the space was left to be filled in subsequently, once the country had been identified.

[28] *Rhb.* 2: 184.30–185.3.

The statement above seems to suggest that the church in Venice attests to the truth of the story that has just been told, but this cannot be the case. The corresponding passage in the *Passionael* sheds some light on what the author of the German source had actually written:

> Etlike wyllen dat dysse hystorie nycht waer sy. wente me vindt se nicht in dem latine beschreuen. men de hystorie de hijr tohant nauolget is de rechte hystorie van sunte Johanne Crisostimo. wo deme nu sy is gode bekant. men to Uenedie vind me ene kerke in sunte Johannes crisostimus eere ghebuwet. daer steyt de hystorie so ghemalt alze se hijr vortellet is.[29]

> (Some insist that this legend is not true, since it is not found in Latin. But the legend that now follows is the real story of St. John Chrysostom. Whatever the case may be, God knows. But in Venice there is a church built in honor of St. John Chrysostom. There the story is painted just as it is told here.)

The church in Venice is that of San Giovanni Crisostomo, and the reference to the story being depicted there must be to the vita that follows, that is, the actual biography. Unlike Albrecht Dürer and Lucas Cranach the Elder, who depict St. John as a small creature crawling on all fours, Sebastiano da Piombo's altarpiece portrays St. John as archbishop of Constantinople, engaged in writing and surrounded by a group of saints.[30]

Björn Þorleifsson was aware of the discrepancies between the two accounts he was transmitting, for at the beginning of St. John's vita he notes that the saint was born in Antioch "en ekki í Róm sem fyrr greinir" ("but not in Rome as was reported before"),[31] but he goes on to say that his mother and father nevertheless had been the same "sem fyrr segir" ("as was told before").[32]

While *Jóhannes saga gullmunns* is not a translation of the legend in *Der Heiligen Leben*, or, to be more exact, of the Low German version "Van sunte Johannes Crisostimo" in *Dat Passionael*,"[33] it most likely represents the longer German version that is the source of the abbreviated text in *Der Heiligen*

---

[29] The Low German text is cited from *Dat Passionael* (Lübeck: Steffan Arndes, 1492), CCCxlix.b. Abbreviations in the text, indicated by a nasal stroke, have been silently expanded.

[30] See "Johannes, Chrysostomus," in Braunfels, ed., *Lexikon der christlichen Ikonographie*, 7:99–100.

[31] *Rhb.* 2: 185.10

[32] *Rhb.* 2: 185.10–11.

[33] *Dat Passionael*, CCC.xlv ii.a–CCC.xlix.b.

Leben/Dat Passionael. Despite the drastic condensation in the German legend, the affinity between the Icelandic translation and the extant Low German version is quite evident, extending at times to word-for-word correspondence.[34] This is sporadic, however, since the Low German text is so drastically abbreviated. The following example, the scene in which the princess is carried off by a tornado, will serve to show both the affinity between the Low German and Icelandic texts and the discrepancies between them. The scene is depicted in the *Passionael* as follows:

> Eynes daghes in deme somer ginck des keysers dochter mit velen yuncfrouwen in den wolt vmme tijdvordrijff. vnde wolden de blomen vnde de lustycheyt beseen. do quam daer eyn so groet wynd dat he des keysers dochter vp vorde hoch in de lucht vnde de yuncfrouwen wusten nicht woer dat se bleeff.[35]

> (One day during the summer the emperor's daughter went with many maidens into the woods for amusement. And they wanted to look at the flowers and the pleasant views. Then there came such a great wind that it lifted the emperor's daughter high into the air and the maidens did not know what became of her.)

Although the Icelandic version exhibits a more expansive and leisurely narrative style vis-à-vis the Low German redaction, it nonetheless reveals its Low German origins and relationship to the text in the *Passionael*:

> Þá einn dag um sumar tíma vildi keisarans dóttur ganga með sínum meyjum og spacera út í mörkina til forlystingar og að safna sér til gamans blóma af grösum og sætleg aldin eður ávöxtu af trjám og so til annarra lystigheitar er hún girntist og meyjar hennar að forvitnast um. En í þessu bili kom yfir keisaradóttur so sem einn vindbylur eða hvirfilvindur og tók hana í loft upp so hátt at þær meyjar er með henni voru vissu ekki hvað af henni varð og eigi sáu þær til hennar að því sinni meira. En hinar er með henni voru sakaði ekki neitt.[36]

---

[34] See Marianne Kalinke, "The Icelandic Legend of the Hairy Anchorite," in *Sagnaþing helgað Jónasi Kristjánssyni sjötugum 10. apríl 1994* (Reykjavík, 1994), 2: 485–96.
[35] *Dat Passionael*, CCC.xlvii.d.
[36] *Rhb.* 2: 174.24–32.

(One day during the summer the emperor's daughter wanted to go walking with her maidens in the forest for amusement, and to collect for their delight flowers from the meadows and sweet fruits and other produce from the trees, and for other pleasures that she and her maidens desired to experience. But at this moment something like a strong wind blast or whirlwind descended on the princess and took her so high up into the air that the maidens who were with her did not know what became of her and did not see her any longer. But those who were with her were not harmed.)

The passage contains three loans from Low German — *spacera, forlysting, lystigheit* — only one of which is also found in the *Passionael*, that is, *lustycheyt*. Their occurrence in the amplified text of the saga suggests, however, that they were present in Björn Þorleifsson's Low German source and were simply transferred into the Icelandic version.

Like the other translated texts in *Reykjahólabók, Jóhannes saga gullmunns* represents a German version of the legend that was narratively superior to and much longer than the text in *Der Heiligen Leben* and *Dat Passionael*. The Icelandic legend attests that prior to the end of the fourteenth century, when German legends were abridged for inclusion in *Der Heiligen Leben*, an apocryphal frame-narrative about St. John Chrysostom circulated in the German-language area at the heart of which was a story of seduction, murder, penance, and forgiveness. That the great Doctor of the Church should have become associated with such a titillating story is difficult to fathom unless one reads the tale in the context of St. John's writings on virginity and a questionable practice of his day, that is, syneisaktism, the chaste cohabitation of members of the clergy with women.[37] The great saint who argued that such couples "would not enjoy such a despicable reputation nor would there be so many scandals, if a violent and tyrannical pleasure were not found in their cohabitation,"[38] himself became the subject of a narrative in which he was to experience the pleasures of cohabitation and which he thought to be able to escape only by resorting to violence. While Martin Luther chose to focus on the absurdity of the tale, the apocryphon nevertheless effectively transmits a profound lesson on the efficacy of penance and the unfathomable mercy of God.

---

[37] On syneisaktism and John Chrysostom's position in the matter, see Dyan Elliott, *Spiritual Marriage: Sexual Abstinence in Medieval Wedlock* (Princeton, 1993), 32–38.

[38] Cited in Elliott, *Spiritual Marriage*, 35.

II. On the Edition and Translation

The language of *Reykjahólabók* is a strange amalgam of early Modern Icelandic and late Middle Low German, in respect to both lexicon and syntax. The text is here presented in normalized modern Icelandic orthography, but where Low German, and also Latin, loans occur, their origin is left transparent. The text is based on Agnete Loth's edition, though photocopies of the manuscript have been consulted.[39] Loth's emendations or suggested readings have been silently accepted, unless otherwise noted, and incorrect readings or typographical errors in the edition have been emended, with a note to that effect.

Whereas orthography is normalized, variant forms are not. The edition thus retains such variants as *aldrei* and *aldregi, eða* and *eður*. The ending of the first person singular, present tense, of both strong and weak verbs with but two exceptions occurs as *-r*, e.g., *ég biður, býður, bindir, getur, segir, sér, treystir, verður, þórir*, and this deviation from modern Icelandic is retained in the edition. The saint's name is alternately given in Icelandic and Latin as *sankti Jóhannes* and *sanctus Johannes*, and in the latter case, it is even declined as in Latin. This distinction is preserved. Throughout, Middle Low German loans — words, translations, syntax — occur. Björn Þorleifsson sometimes incorporates the loan word without explanation, such as *heimuglegt mak* ("private chambers") or *celle* ("cell"); at other times a Low German loan becomes part of a synonymous pairing, one member of which is Icelandic, for example, *ávexti* and *frukt*, or *jagari* and *veiðimaður*, or, on occasion, the loan is given as an alternative to the common Icelandic word, such as "hundarnir . . . er sumir menn kalla þá styfara."[40]

The translation into English of German loan words in *Jóhannes saga gullmunns* is somewhat problematic, commencing with the word *historía*.[41] The word occurs in sixteenth-century Icelandic imprints where its meaning vacillates, just as it does in the German of this time. While in German the fable

---

[39] I am grateful to Ragnheiður Mósesdóttir, Det Arnamagnæanske Institut, Copenhagen, for having sent me photocopies of the text in the manuscript.

[40] I am grateful to Kirsten Wolf, who made available to me proofs of her edition of *Saga heilagrar Önnu* (Reykjavík, 2001), to which I refer in notes concerning MLG loans, cited as KW with page number.

[41] I am greatly indebted to Sverrir Tómasson, Stofnun Árna Magnússonar á Íslandi, for answering my many questions concerning linguistic problems in difficult passages in the text.

(*Fabel*) is considered fictional and history (*Histori*) factual,[42] in Icelandic the word *historía* seems to have been used to refer both to factual and fictional accounts.[43] The word occurs in several other texts in *Reykjahólabók* and is used both for apocryphal narratives[44] and for attested vitae.[45] In the two instances that the word occurs in *Jóhannes saga gullmunns*, I translate it with "legend". A number of German words unattested in Icelandic at the time *Reykjahólabók* was written have subsequently entered the Icelandic language but taken on a somewhat different meaning from that in German. Since Björn Þorleifsson most likely simply transferred the loans from his Low German source, I translate, where contextually appropriate, the respective words according to their Low German meaning. A striking example of the need to consider the original meaning of a word is the preposition *in*, found in both MLG and Icelandic. St. John's question, why the princess, thought to be dead, is sitting "alone on the rock" ("allene in deme stene") is rendered in Icelandic by "einsömul í steini þessum" ("alone in this rock"), which is obviously incorrect. The translator did not realize that the MLG preposition *in* meant not only "in" but also "on" (see n. 141 of the ed.).

---

[42] See Jacob and Wilhelm Grimm, *Deutsches Wörterbuch* (Leipzig, 1877; repr. Munich, 1984): "Ich will dir etwas erzählen, und es gilt gleichviel, ob du es für eine Histori oder für eine Fabel annehmest"; the word was used "in dem Sinne einer wahrhaften begebenheit der fabel entgegengesetzt"(10:1580).

[43] Christian Westergård-Nielsen, *Låneordene i det 16. århundredes trykte islandske litteratur*, Bibliotheca Arnamagnæana 6 (Copenhagen, 1946), 157–58.

[44] *Rhb*, "Barlaham og Josaphat," 1: 97.2; "Gregorius peccator," 2: 35.15.

[45] *Rhb*, "St. Gregory the Great," 2: 56.21.

III. Edition

Jóhannes Saga Gullmunns

1. Historía[46] þessi[47] byrjar so og víkur á er hún[48] segir so að í Róm var einn páfi sem margur annar, þó að hans eiginlegt nafn sé og ekki hér inn sett eður greint. En þá hafi þetta eftir skrifaða efni þó í fyrstu so til borið sem hér mun greint verða og upp hefur[49] sitt mál með þessum hætti og segir að páfinn þessi hafi haft eitthvert nauðsynja erinda er hann vildi ríða í burtu af Rómaborg, sem hann og gerði. Og hafði mikinn fjölda fólks með sér. Nú hafði og þessi páfinn eina venju hvað nær sem hann vildi góðfúslega sínar bænar fram flytja í augliti guðs, þá gekk hann burtu frá öllum mönnum til þess að hann mætti því betur og ástuðlegar þjóna so guði og síður yrði hann ómakaður af sínum góðum vilja og verkum. So bar og nú til að þá sem hann var farinn úr staðnum Róma sem fyrr segir og var kominn nokkurn langan veg frá staðnum þar sem hann vildi þá hvíla sig, þá gjörði hann eftir sinni venju er hann vildi biðjast fyrir að hann tók sig í burtu einsamall frá öllu sínu föruneyti fram í eina þykkva mörk eður skóg og ætlaði að spacera[50] þar á meðan[51] að hann flutti fram sínar bænar. Og þá sem hann hafði nokkura stund gengið í mörkinni og var að lesa, þá fékk hann að heyra eina rödd mjög syrgilega og hryggilega kallandi. Þá staldraði hann við og vildi so vita hvort honum hafði ekki misheyrist. En þá var samt kallað.

---

[46] *Historía* derives ultimately from Latin but is here borrowed from Low German. There is no corresponding passage in *Dat Passionael* (1492) (henceforth abbreviated *Pass.*) but when *historía* recurs at the end of the legend, the word also occurs in the *Pass.* See Westergård-Nielsen, *Låneordene*, 157–58; Oskar Bandle, *Die Sprache der Guðbrandsbiblía: Orthographie und Laute Formen*, Bibliotheca Arnamagnæana 17 (Copenhagen, 1956), 273 (henceforth cited as Bandle with page number); KW, cxxii.

[47] Corrected from the manuscript, which writes *þessa*. Bandle (353) notes sporadic occurrences of *þessa* in *Guðbrandsbiblía* for the nom.sg.fem., but considers them typographic errors.

[48] Corrected from the manuscript, which writes *hann*.

[49] The construction with the preposed prefix derives from MLG *upheven* "to begin." This is not idiomatic Icelandic.

[50] The word *spacera* is ultimately a loan from Italian, but here it entered Icelandic from MLG. Westergård-Nielsen, *Låneordene*, 315, and Bandle, 429, normalize the word to *spásséra*, but the form in *Rhb* is the same as in MLG and hence that spelling is retained here. Cf. KW, cxxx; Jón Helgason, *Málið á Nýja Testamenti Odds Gottskálkssonar*, Safn Fræðafjelagsins 7 (Copenhagen, 1929), 361 (henceforth *NT* with page number), which has *spaztseru veg*.

[51] See Bandle, 455 for the occurrence of the conjunction *á meðan* in the *Guðbrandsbiblía*.

IV. Translation

THE LEGEND OF JOHN GOLDMOUTH

1. This legend[52] begins thus and turns to where it tells that there was a pope in Rome like many another, though his real name is not put down here or recorded. And according to the written record this is what happened at the beginning, as will be told here, and the story begins in this way and tells that this pope had some pressing business so that he wanted to ride from Rome, which is what he did. And he had a large entourage with him. Now this pope also had a habit that whenever he wanted to say his prayers devoutly in the presence of God, he went off by himself from everyone so that he might all the better and more lovingly thus serve God, lest he become unworthy through his own good will and works. And so it now also happened that when he had left the city of Rome, as was said before, and had come quite a long distance from the city to a place where he wanted to rest, he did as was his wont when he wanted to pray that he went off by himself from his entire retinue and into a thick forest or woods, and he intended to walk about there while he was reciting his prayers. And when he had been walking in the forest for some time and was reading his prayers,[53] he heard a voice crying out very sadly and sorrowfully. He stopped then and wanted to find out whether he had not heard wrong. But it kept crying out.

---

[52] The word used in Icelandic, *historía*, is a loan from Latin via Low German, where it could mean either "story"or "history." I have decided to translate the word as "legend," since it also occurs in other texts in *Rhb* where it refers to both saints' vitae, such as the legend of St. Gregory the Great, and apocryphal tales, such as the legend of Gregorius peccator. See the Introduction and n. 46.

[53] The Icelandic text merely says that he was reading, but I interpret this to mean that he was reading the prayers or psalms from his breviary.

Þá mælti hann sem við sig sjálfan, so segjandi: "O herra guð, hvað klög-
unlega⁵⁴ og aumlega kallar þessa rödd og fýsir mig í guðs trausti að vita þetta
gjör," og gekk þá enn lengra fram í skóginn eftir hljóðinu, en honum heyrðist
hljóðið þá vera hryggilegra en fyrr og gekk þá enn lengra.

En samt var altíð honum fyrir eyrum hljóðið, nema honum þótti röddin
vera æ því aumlegri sem hann þóttist koma henni nærri og mælti þá enn og
fyrir munni sér: "Hversu lengi sem þetta hljóð fer og undan mér, þá verður
ég nú með guðs fulltingi að fá vita hvað það hefur að þýða. En þó undrar mig
mest um það að ég þykist heyra þetta hljóð allt nærri⁵⁵ mér, en ég sé þó ekki
neitt nýlegt, og má þetta ekki so lengi fara," sagði hann og gekk þá enn nokkura
stund. En þetta var eins að hann heyrði kallið en sá þó öngvan heldur en fyrri.

Þá stöðvaði sig páfinn og mælti: "Nú frá því að ég heyri til þín en ég sér
þig ekki, þá býð ég þér í nafni Jesu Christi⁵⁶ að þú segir þá mér hver að þú ert."

Þá var honum svarað: "Ég er ein örm fátæk sál. Ó vé, minn kæri faðir,
þvíað ég má ekki so langa hvíld eða stund hafa án pínu að ég megi svar gefa
eða augna blik upp og aftur."⁵⁷

Þá grét páfinn er hann heyrði þetta og mælti: "Seg mér þá," sagði hann,
"hvort að ég má ekki hjálpa þér."

Hún svaraði og sagði: "Nei."

Páfinn svarar: "Það er mér af hjarta leitt⁵⁸ að ég má þér ekki hjálp veita, og
guð hefur mér mikið vald þó gefið að ég megi syndir manna uppgefa, og það
ég bindir á jörðu það skyldi vera bundið á himni og það sem ég leysti á jörðu
það væri og leyst á himni og jafnvel í helviti."

---

⁵⁴ The word *klögunlega* derives from *klaga*, a loan from MLG; see Westergård-
Nielsen, *Låneordene*, 180; *NT*, 297; Bandle, 429; Veturliði Óskarsson, *Middelnedertyske
låneord i islandsk diplomsprog frem til år 1500* (Uppsala, 2001), 199–200 (henceforth VÓ
with page number). *Pass* writes here: "O we wat ys de klegelike stemme" (CCC.xlvii.a).

⁵⁵ The use of the comparative form *nærri* but in a positive sense occurs both in the
1540 New Testament translation and in the *Guðbrandsbiblía*: see *NT*, 175; Bandle, 439.
Instances of this use of *nærri* are also found in chaps. 6, 7, 8, and 9.

⁵⁶ The manuscript consistently uses the Latin — rather than the Icelandic — form
(and declensional endings) of the name.

⁵⁷ augna blik — aftur] The phrase, which is elliptical, is more easily comprehensible if one reads it against the text in *Pass*: "yk mach nicht so lange ane pyne wezen als
eyn oghe vp vnde to geyt" (CCC.xlvii.b). See Westergård-Nielsen, *Låneordene*, 17–18,
on *augnablik* for parallel passages where the compound is clearly construed to mean the
"blinking of the eyes."

⁵⁸ This is not idiomatic Icelandic but replicates a Low German expression which occurs in the corresponding passage in the *Pass*: "Dat is my van herten leed" (CCC.xlvii.b).
The same expression occurs on several subsequent occasions in the text.

He then spoke as if to himself, saying: "O Lord God, how woefully and wretchedly this voice is crying and, confident in God, I would like to investigate this," and he went even deeper into the woods, following the sound, and he heard that the sound was even more sorrowful than before and he then went still farther.

And the sound was in his ears the whole time, except that he thought the voice was all the more wretched the closer he thought he came to it, and he spoke once more to himself: "No matter how long this sound escapes me, I am now going to find out with God's help what that means. But what surprises me most is that I think I hear this sound quite close to me, yet I don't see anything different, and this can't go on for long," he said and walked on a while longer. But it was all the same that he heard the crying but saw no one just as before.

The pope then stopped and spoke: "Now since I hear you but don't see you, I order you in the name of Jesus Christ to tell me then who you are."

Then came the answer: "I am a wretched poor soul. O woe, my dear father, for I am not allowed to have rest or relief long enough from the pain, not even for the blink of an eye,[59] as to be able to give an answer."

The pope then wept, when he heard this, and spoke: "Tell me then," he said, "whether I cannot help you."

The soul answered and said: "No."

The pope answers: "I am sorry with all my heart that I cannot give you help, and yet God has given me great power to be able to forgive men's sins, and what I bind on earth shall be bound in heaven, and what I loose on earth will also be loosed in heaven as well as in hell [cf. Matthew 16:19]."

---

[59] The passage is not clear in Icelandic but the reading in the *Passionael* — "yk mach nicht so lange ane pyne wezen als eyn oghe vp vnde to geyt" ("I am not long enough without pain for an eye to open and shut" [CCC.xlvii.b]) — suggests that *augna blik* is to be taken literally here, in the same sense as MLG *ogenblick* "blinking" or "glance" of the eye.

Sálin svarar: "Með öngu móti megið þér sjálfir rétta hjálp veita mér, en
það má vel ske að ég megi njótandi verða yðvarra ráða og so verka að ég verður
frelstur. En þó sker það ekki nema með einu móti."
Páfinn glaðist þá og bað hann[60] segja sér ef það væri nokkur sá hlutur er
hann mætti leysast fyrir og hann mátti ráða.
Sálin svarar: "Nú í dag áður en þér fundið mig þá var mér kunngjört[61]
sem ég hefur nú traust á að ég muni leysast, þó mér þykir seint vera. Og er so
háttað að í Róm býr einn ærlegur[62] mann er Seidmir heitir. Hann á og eina
göfuga kvinna og er nafn hennar Anthusa.[63] Þessi hin ágæta kvinna hefur nú
nýlega tekið við ávexti og mun sú frukt[64] blessuð verða og mjög kær guði er
hún gengur með. Og er sonur og á nafn hans vera Jóhannes, og so mun hann
verða eiga einn góður kennimaður. Og nær hann hefur sungið þá sína sext-
anda messu, þá verður ég og fátæk sál fra öllum mínum pínum."
Hér með greindi sálin og fyrir páfanum á hverju strætinu þar í Róm að
þessi fyrirsögð hjón bjuggu í. En eftir þetta skildist páfinn þar við sálina og
reið heim aftur í Róm. En so lengi sem hann mátti hljóðið heyra, þá heyrði
hann að sálin kveinaði sér og kallaði allt jafnt.

2. Nú sem páfinn kom aftur til föruneytis síns og valdramanna og var mjög
hryggur á líta. Þá þorði engin frétta hann eftir hvað honum væri eða hvað hann
hafði dvalið er hann hafði so lengi í burtu verið. Nema þá sem hann fann sína
góða menn er með honum voru, þá benti hann þeim til að þeir skyldu snúa
heim aftur til Róm. Og á öllum veginum er hann fór þá var hann hryggur en
stundum grét hann. En so snart sem hann kom í Rómaborg aftur, þá sendi
hann bæði eftir manninum og so kvinnunni að þau skyldu koma til fundar við
hann. Og sem þau voru komin, þá tók hann við þeim með miklum kærleika.

[60] The manuscript is inconsistent in its use of the pronoun for *sál*, which is feminine.
Here the translator slips and uses the masculine pronoun.
[61] The word is a loan from MLG. The *Pass* writes: "My is huden wes kundich gedaen"
(CCC.xlvii.b). See *NT*, 300, for usage in the 1540 translation of the New Testament. Cf.
VÓ, 204–5.
[62] *ærlegur* derives from MLG *êrlik*; see Westergård-Nielsen, *Låneordene*, 403–4; Bandle,
317; *NT*, 411; KW, cxxxiv.
[63] The manuscript writes *Avthvsa*. The name of John Chrysostom's mother was Anthusa. The corresponding passage in the *Pass* is abridged and the mother is not named.
[64] *frukt* is borrowed from MLG *vrucht*. There is no corresponding passage in the
Pass, but the phrase has its origin in the New Testament's "benedictus fructus ventris tui,"
which is translated into Icelandic as: "Blessaður er ávöxtur kviðar þíns." It is noteworthy
that the loan *frukt* is used in *Rhb* together with the Icelandic *ávöxtur*. This is common
practice in *Rhb* and recurs several times in this text, e.g., in the collocation *jagara eður
veiðimenn* (cf. n. 126).

The soul answers: "There is no way that you yourself can give me proper help, yet it may happen that I can profit from your counsel and also deeds and be freed. But that will happen in only one way."

Then the pope rejoiced and asked the soul to tell him if there were some thing he could resolve and carry out.

The soul answers: "Today, before you met me, something was revealed to me which now gives me confidence that I will be freed, though it seems to me slow in coming. The case is thus that there lives in Rome an honorable man named Seidmir. He has a noble wife and her name is Anthusa. This excellent woman has recently become pregnant and the fruit of her womb[65] that she is carrying will become blessed and very dear to God. And it is a son and his name is to be John, and he is going to become a good priest. And when he has said his sixteenth Mass, then I, poor soul, will be released from all my suffering."

The soul also explained to the pope on which street in Rome the afore-mentioned couple lived. And after this the pope parted there from the soul and rode back home to Rome. And as long as he could hear a sound, he heard the soul wailing and crying out the whole time.

2. Now when the pope came back to his retinue and mighty men, he appeared very sorrowful. No one dared then to ask him what was the matter with him or what had delayed him that he was gone for such a long time. But when he met up with the good men who were with him, he directed them to turn back home to Rome. And everywhere he went, he was sorrowful and at times he wept. And as soon as he came back to Rome, he sent a message to both the man and the woman that they should come to meet with him. And when they arrived, he received them with great affection.

---

[65] The discourse is biblical and is indebted to Luke 1:42, where Elizabeth greets Mary with the words: "Benedicta tu inter mulieres, et benedictus fructus ventris tui." The Ice-landic text literally reads: "This excellent woman has recently received a fruit and that fruit will become blessed" (cf. also Luke 1:13–17 on the prophecy of the birth of John the Baptist).

Síðan mælti hann til kvinnunnar Anthusa: "Dóttir," sagði hann, "ekki má annars vera um þinn hag en þú munt sæl vera, fyrir því að nú fyrir lítlu hefur mér að vilja guðs so verið tilkynnt að þú munt hafa tekið göfuglegum ávexti af þínum manni Seidmir og til marks um þetta þá er það sveinbarn og á heita Jóhannes og verður góður maður í augliti guðs."

Þá svarar kvinnan: "Minn herra," sagði <hún>, "til þessa hluta veit ég ekki eða varla kunna[66] yður svar hér til gefa, nema vilji guðs verði á mér fullkomlega eftir hans vild og fyrirætlun."

Þá sagði páfinn: "Þá býður ég ykkur bæði saman að þið látið mig fá það vita nær sem það kemur til, þvíað ég skal skyldbinda mig sjálfan til að skíra það og allt kristilegt embætti því veita, so að ég vil þaðan í frá vera hans andlegur faðir."

En greind hjón þökkuðu honum sín orð og lofun og tóku síðan orlof heim aftur. En hann veitti þeim það góðfúslega og gaf þeim sína blessun og skildist so við hann.

Nú þá sem sveinninn var til kominn sem páfinn sagði þeim fyrir, þá gjörðu þau honum boð til þess, en hann varð þeim boðskap glaður og fór til þeirra og skírði barnið og lét það heita Jóhannes. Síðan fór páfinn heim aftur, en Jóhannes ólst upp hjá föður sínum og móður þar til að hann var sjö vetra. En eftir það var hann settur til skóla og fór það vel með það fyrsta á meðan að hann lærði stafrofið og þó nokkuð meira. En þaðan í frá[67] að hann átti hafa les og kynna sér ritninginu, þá gjörðust hann stórlega tornæmur, so að hann fékk oftsinnis af sínum skóla bræðrum og líka af sínum meistara miklar og margar ávitanar sakir, en sumlegir hæddu hann og spéuðu[68] með mörgum ónytju orðum og aðhlátri. En Jóhannes lét ekki á sér finna, þó hann væri kallsaður og hélt sömu fram um sitt að hvað sem óvinir hans röbbuðu, útan sakir ungleika hans að hann fór sem hjá sér fyrir þeirra orðtak og skammaðist.

---

[66] See Bandle, 383–84, for a similar use of the ending -a in the 1st pers. sg. pret. subj. in the Guðbrandsbiblía.

[67] On the occurrence of þaðan í frá in Oddr Gottskálksson's translation of the New Testament, see NT, 175.

[68] The verb spéa is borrowed from MLG spien, spigen. Westergård-Nielsen, Låneordene, 316–17, notes that the MLG word occurs only with the meaning of "spuere, vomere," and this is confirmed in Karl Schiller and August Lübben, Mittelniederdeutsches Wörterbuch, 5 vols. (Bremen, 1875–1880; repr. Vaduz, 1986), 4: 324 (henceforth MNW with volume and page). Nonetheless, the related noun spe, spei, "mockery," "scorn," "derision" and such compound forms as spewort and spen rede (MNW, 4: 306–7) suggest how the Icelandic loan came about. See Bandle, 428; NT, 362 (spjea).

He then spoke to the woman Anthusa: "Daughter," he said, "as far as you are concerned, you will be blessed, for just a short time ago it was revealed to me through the will of God that you have become fruitful[69] by your husband Seidmir, and as a sign of this, it is a boy and is to be called John, and he will become a holy man in the sight of God."

The woman then answers: "My lord," she said, "I know nothing about these things and I can hardly give you an answer about this other than that the will of God be fully done in me according to his will and design."

Then the pope said: "Then I ask both of you to let me know when that comes about, because I will pledge to baptize the child myself and perform all Christian rites, so that I shall from then on be his spiritual father."

And the couple in question thanked him for his words and pledge and then took leave to go back home. And he willingly granted this to them and gave them his blessing, and thus they parted from him.

Now when the boy was born, as the pope had predicted, they sent him a message about this, and he was happy at the news and went to them and baptized the child and had it called John. The pope then went back home, and John was brought up by his father and mother until he was seven years old. And after this he was put in school, and at first things went well as he learned the alphabet and some other things. But from then on, when he was to learn to read and write, he was very slow to learn, and for this reason he was frequently rebuked a great deal by his fellow pupils and similarly by his teacher, and some scoffed at him and ridiculed him with many disparaging words and derisive laughter. But John did not let it show, even though he was taunted, and kept right on no matter what nonsense his enemies spouted, except that because of his youth he was nearly beside himself on account of their talk and was ashamed.

---

[69] The text reads literally: "you have received a noble fruit."

En þó gekk hann samt og áður í skólann ef honum mætti nokkuð lærast og vildi ekki forlíta[70] sig með öllu fyrir þetta og setti sitt traust til almáttugs guðs og jungfrú Maríu að þau mundu sjá nokkuð gott ráð með sér so að sér dugði, og setti í sitt hjarta með stöðugri trú og fullri þau orð sem drottinn sjálfur kenndi sínum lærisveinum er hann so mælti: "Biðjið þér og mun yður veitast, leitið þér og munuð þér finna, klappið þér og mun verða fyrir yður upp látið." Þessi dæmi tók Jóhannes fyrir sig fyrir því að hann sá það fyrir að hann mundi ekki sér einhlítur vera um fyrir sagt efni að kynna sér heilaga ritningu eftir því sem hans hjarta girntist að vita og skilja hennar grundvöll. Og tók það í venju fyrir sig að <hann> gekk í eina kirkju og lagði sig þar niður fyrir altari því er helgað var jungfrú Maríu til að leita þar eftir nokkuri líkn og hjástöðu af þeirri er þar væri helguð.[71] Hér með flutti hann fram sitt erindi með mjúkum bænum hjartans og tára úthellingu sinna augna til að hnýja og so að berja á hurð miskunnarinnar hver að[72] María var, sem full er af náð og miskunn og öngum synjar sinnar hjálpar er á hana kalla. Og bað hana að þiggja fyrir sig af spektar brunninum sjálfum, syni sínum Jesum Christum,[73] so að hann mætti læra betur en áður gjörði hann. Þetta bað <hann> oftlega jungfrú Maríu um og hann mætti að heldur so forðast mega annarra manna ávítanar orðum og bakmælgi.

3. Þá einu sinni er hann lá á bæn sinni sem hann var vanur og um sama efni og aðra hluti sem hann vildi og nauðsynlegir voru, þá birtist honum jungfrú María og mælti til hans:

"Jóhannes, þú góði sonur, ég hefur lítið á þitt vankvæði sem þú hefur mesta sorg fyrir og þó eigi aðeins á sjálfs þíns vegna nema á annarra ranglátra manna sem ekki vilja líta á sannleikinn, hvað[74] því veldur að þú getur ekki lært so vel sem þeir, hvað þér er ekki sjálfráð um það og öngum öðrum sem so er háttað, fyrir því að þá ástgjöf hefur enginn af sjálfum sér til og af öngum öðrum nema af guði einum og þrennum. Og hefur nú sonur guðs og minn séð vilja þinn og hjarta hvað þér til þessa gengur og hefur hann heyrt bæn mína er ég hefur frammi látið á þína vegna í hans augliti, so að <ég> megi

---

[70] *forlíta* is formed with the prefix *for-*, borrowed from MLG, rather than with the customary Icelandic prefix *fyrir-*, as in *fyrirlíta* "to consider worthless," "to despise." Cf. Westergård-Nielsen, *Låneordene*, 72–74, 103; KW, cxx; *NT*, 251, where the word translates German *verachten*.

[71] Corrected from the manuscript, which writes *helgað* (*helgat*).

[72] See *NT*, 133–34, for examples of the use of *hver að*.

[73] One would expect here the dative rather than accusative endings for the name, in keeping with the Icelandic syntax.

[74] On the use of *hvað* as a relative pronoun, see Bandle, 365.

Nonetheless he went to school as before in order to learn whatever he could, and he did not wish to despise himself at all for this and placed his trust in almighty God and the Virgin Mary that they would come to his aid in some useful way, and he set in his heart with steadfast and full confidence the words that the Lord Himself taught His disciples when He spoke: "Ask and you shall receive, seek and you shall find, knock and it shall be opened to you" [Matthew 7:7]. John took this example to heart, since he foresaw that he would not be relying on himself alone in this matter, in studying the sacred scriptures, as his heart desired to know them and understand their basis. And he made it a habit to go into a church and lie down before the altar dedicated to the Virgin Mary and to seek there some help and assistance from her who was there venerated. And he expressed his concern with meek prayers from the heart and with tears streaming from his eyes as he knelt and knocked on the door of mercy that is Mary, who is full of grace and mercy and refuses no one her help who calls upon her. And he asked her to obtain for him from the font of wisdom Himself, her son Jesus Christ, the ability to learn better than he had done so far. He asked this often of the Virgin Mary and also that he might be able to escape the rebukes of others and their backbiting.

3. Then one time as he was prostrate in prayer, as was his wont, concerning the same matter and other things that he wanted and that were necessary, the Virgin Mary appeared to him and spoke to him:

"John, you good son, I have considered the troubles that most worry you and not only on your own account but also that of other unrighteous men who do not want to look at the truth, at the reason that you are not able to learn as well as they, which is not something you yourself can determine or anyone else to whom it happens, for no one has the gift of love on his own or from anyone else but from God, one in three. And the Son of God and mine has now seen your desire and heart in this respect and He has heard my prayer which I offered up before Him on your behalf so that I might grant you

veita þér það þú hefur beðið. Og gakk hingað til mín og minnast við mig. Muntu þá eigi síður kunna að læra og so að skilja það sem þú les<t> en hinir er þig dáruðu og fundu að við þig með hæðni og spotti."

En þá hann heyrði þessi hennar orð, þá slóg[75] sem nokkurn ótta yfir hann, og mælti: "O þú miskunnsamlegasta brúður guðs og móðir, slíkt þórir ég ekki að gjöra, þvíað ég er þessa hlutar óverðugur."

Þá svarar jungfrú María honum: "Jóhannes, gjör sem ég býð þér og gakk til mín án hræðslu eður nokkurs ótta í mínu leyfi ok kyss mig, so fær þú að læra það þú vilt og nytsamlegt er."

Síðan gekk hann til hennar og minntist við hana af mikilli auðmjúkt og fékk þar þá að læra himneskan konst[76] og lærdóm hver að frágengur[77] yfir allan veraldlegan lærdóm og skilning, sem raun bar honum þegar eftir á satt vitni um, að frá þeirri stundu voru[78] honum nálega allar ritningar ljósar og kunnigar so að honum þraut aldregi nokkurs hlutar andsvara til útskýringa heilagra ritninga framar en nokkurir meistarar aðrir. Eftir það hvarf jungfrú María frá honum en Jóhannes gekk í skóla sem hann var vanur.

Annan daginn eftir var Jóhannes kominn í skóla að læra sem aðrir hans félagar, og sem hann leit í bókina þá var honum allt kunnigt, eigi aðeins hans eiginar bækur útan jafnvel annarra bækur þeirra sem langt fyrir honum þóttust áður vera og mest straffaði[79] hann með háði. En þá er þeir sáu þetta og skildu að slíkt væri ekki jarteiknalaust, þá horfðu þeir ýmist til hans eða hver þeirra til annars og tóku að undrast hvað títt var. Þá hlógu sumlegir að honum og fréttu hann eftir hvernin að þá væri um hans hag að hann væri nú so vel lærður og næmur orðinn hjá því er hann væri vanur að vera, so að með höggum og öðrum lamningum gátu menn hann ekki lært og væri því oftlega dáraður, en nú á lítilli stundu væri hann so mikill meistari orðinn að hann kynni langt um betur en nokkur þeirra þar og þó að víðara væri leitað. En hann þagði við þeim og var að sinni iðju sem áður að lesa.

Þá gengu nokkurir fram að honum og horfðu so á hann rétt í asjónuna á honum. En eftir það leit hver þessara til annars og "sé hér hvern undarlegan hlut að hér má líta á þessum manni Jóhannes, þar sem oss sýnist öllum sem

---

[75] On the addition of -g after ó- in the 3rd pers. sg. pret., see Bandle, 135.

[76] konst is a loan of MLG kunst "knowledge"; cf. Westergård-Nielsen, Låneordene, 187. The Pass reads: "vnde soch dar vth alle hemmelsche kunst"(CCC.xlvii.c).

[77] The word fráganga with the meaning here does not exist in Icelandic; it derives from MLG vorgân "to exceed," "to be superior to."

[78] Corrected from the manuscript, which writes var.

[79] The word straffa is borrowed from MLG straffen. See Westergård-Nielsen, Låneordene, 328–29; Bandle, 429; NT, 365; KW, cxxxi.

what you have asked. And come here to me and kiss me. You will then be no less able to learn and understand what you read than those who made fun of you and criticized you with mockery and ridicule."

And when he heard her words he was struck with fear and he spoke: "O you most merciful bride and mother of God, I do not dare do this, for I am unworthy of these things."

The Virgin Mary then answers him: "John, do as I tell you and with my permission come to me without fear or any fright and kiss me, and you will learn whatever you want and what is useful to you."

He then went to her and kissed her with great meekness and he then acquired there the heavenly knowledge and learning that surpasses all worldly learning and understanding, as was demonstrated afterwards according to true testimony, that from this hour on nearly all texts were clear and understandable to him so that he never lacked for any kind of answer in interpreting the sacred scriptures better than some other teachers. After this the Virgin Mary disappeared and John went to school as he was wont.

The next day John came to school to learn like his other schoolmates, and when he looked into the book he understood everything, not only his own books but also the other books that before were thought to be far above him and for which he was most rebuked. And when they saw this and realized that this could not be without a miracle, they looked now at him and now at each other and they began to wonder what was going on. Some then laughed at him and asked him how it could be that he had now become so very learned and erudite compared to what he used to be, when even with beatings and blows people could not teach him, and he was thus often made fun of, but now in a short time he had become such a great scholar that he knew far more than any of them there and even others far afield. But he was silent and kept to his task of reading as before.

Some then went up to him and looked him straight in the face. And then each looked at the other and "see here, what a wondrous thing we can see on this fellow John, who seems to all of us to have a golden ring around his entire

hann hafi einn gullegan hring kring um munninn allan. Og er það ekki undur þó hann kunni meir[80] og betur en aðrir," og sögðu allir sem með einum munni: "Fyrir víst," sögðu þeir, "hver sem[81] honum hefur gefið þennan hringinn, sá hefur gefið honum fleira en vér vitum eða megum skilning á bera," og báðu hann mjúkum orðum að undirvísa[82] þeim hvernin að hann hefði fengið þenna hringinn. En hann greindi þeim þá allt hvernin farið hafði með jungfrú Maríu og sér. En þeir allir fögnuðu þá er áður dáruðu[83] hann, og gjörðu hann að sínum yfirmeistara, hvað vel og mátti þvíað engin fannst hans líki sem hans konst[84] vissi allan og kölluðu hann síðan Jóhannes gullmunn og sögðu so: "Sannlega er þér með réttu það nafn gefið þvíað öll þín orð virðist oss vera gulli lík sem fram fara af þínum munni." Og með því sama nafni var hann bæði nefndur og kenndur upp frá því meðan hann lifði.

4. Þá ekki langt eftir það sem nú fyrir lítlu var um glósað vegna Jóhannes gullmunn<s>, hvað jungfrú María hafði veit honum kom til eyrna páfanum, so og hversu mikill meistari að hann var orðinn þaðan í frá. Af þeirri fregn varð páfinn glaður þvíað hann hafði Jóhannes sér kæran. Og þegar að páfinn frétti að nokkuð lén[85] var laust orðið sem ærlegar personur andlegar höfðu áður haldið, þá veitti hann það þegar Jóhannes og af því varð hann innan lítils tíma eður fárra so að reikna[86] mjög ríkur að veraldlegum auðæfum en lifði þó guðrækilega og heilaglega. Og sem páfinn fregnar af Jóhannes hversu hreinlegt og gott dagferði er hann framdi, þá vildi hann gjarnan flýta forlögunum og hjálpa þeirri fátækri sálu er hann hafði fundið fyrir nokkurum árum sem fyrr segir. Og lét senda eftir Jóhannes og vígði hann til prest<s> er hann var sextán vetra, til þess að hún yrði frelst sem fyrst. En þó að heilagur faðir páfinn[87] vildi

---

[80] On the lack of an ending in the comparative of the adverb, see Bandle, 445.

[81] On the use of *hver sem* with the meaning of *quicumque*, see *NT*, 132.

[82] The word is a loan from MLG *underwisen* "to teach," "to explain;" cf. Westergård-Nielsen, *Låneordene*, 359–60, *undirvísa*; *NT*, 385; KW, cxxxii.

[83] The verb *dára* is a loan from MLG *doren* "to be a fool," "to be foolish." See VÓ, 169–70.

[84] The *Pass* reads: "wente nemand konde sine kunst" (CCC.xlvii.c). Cf. n. 76.

[85] The word is a loan from MLG *lên* "benefice." See Westergård-Nielsen, *Låneordene*, 200; VÓ, 208. While the corresponding passage in *Pass* uses the word *prouene*, which is synonymous with *lên*, the text continues: "de vorlenede he em" (CCC.xlvii.c).

[86] The word is a loan from MLG *rekenen, reken* "to calculate," "to count," but also "to consider," "to esteem," "to reckon" (*MNW*, 3: 456–57). Here the word is used in the second sense. Cf. VÓ, 230; *NT*, 336. The same loan occurs in *Önnu saga*, where we read: "Hún reiknast og hins mikla og ins blessaða kóngs Davíðs móðir og dóttir" ("She is also considered the mother and daughter of the great and blessed King David" [*Rhb*, 2:345.9–10]).

[87] Corrected from the manuscript, which has the metathesis *fapen*.

mouth. And no wonder that he knows more and better than others," and all said as with one voice: "For sure," they said, "whoever has given him this ring has given him more than we know or can give an explanation for," and in humble words they asked him to explain to them how he had gotten this ring. And he then told them all that had happened with the Virgin Mary and him. And then all rejoiced who before had poked fun at him, and they made him their master teacher, which was only right since there was no one like him who had all his knowledge, and from then on they called him John Gold-mouth, and said: "This name is given to you by right, for all your words seem to us like gold, those which come from your mouth." And by this very name he was both called and known henceforth as long as he lived.

4. Now not long after what has just now been explained about John Gold-mouth, what the Virgin Mary had granted him came to the ears of the pope, and also what a great teacher he had become from then on. The pope rejoiced at this news because he was fond of John. And when the pope found out that a certain benefice had become available which honorable ecclesiastics had held before, he granted it to John at once, and on account of this he was within a short time or less reckoned very rich in worldly goods, yet he lived in a pi-ous and holy manner. And when the pope hears in what a pure and good way John conducted himself, he wanted very much to speed up destiny and to help the poor soul that he had encountered some years earlier, as was told above. And he had John sent for and ordained him a priest when he was sixteen years old, so that the soul would be released as soon as possible. And even though the holy father, the pope, wanted to have happen what has been reported,

að so yrði sem nú var greint, þá verður þó engin hlutur fyrr en guð vill að sé
og sannast orðskviðurinn í þessu er so víkur að: "Veit hvað vill, en eigi hvað
verða kann, þvíað leyndir eru dómar⁸⁸ guðs," og so var nú um þetta efni sem
brátt má heyra.

Nú sem Jóhannes hafði tekið við prestvígslunni og hann var að syngja
sína fyrsta messu, þá í messunni var hann hugsandi í sínu hjarta þau orð sem
hér segir: "O herra guð," sagði hann, "hvað mjög ungur er ég og óverðugur til
þess, drottinn minn, að höndla þinn blessaða líkam og það að ég er kominn
í þá stétt að heita prestur. Hvað mér er leitt af öllu hjarta⁸⁹ að ég so ungur er
til slíks embættis, það og annað að veraldleg auðæfi gjöra minni sálu mikinn
skaða. Þar fyrir vil ég gjarnan armur og fátækur vera fyrir guðs skyld heldur
en eiga nokkurn þann hlut er mín sál megi týnast fyrir frá mínum skapara
og hans boðorði er þvert á móti. Og fyrir víst skal ég nokkuð hér til gjöra
það snarasta er ég má," og leit upp fyrir sig til himins með þeirri hugsan⁹⁰ að
messan yrði úti sem fyrst. En er messan var úti þá gengu allir til borðs með
mikilli verðugheit,⁹¹ og gjörði Jóhannes sig vel glaðan undir borðinu í manna
augliti að því síður skyldi nokkurir gruna um hans hag og fyrirætlan.

En þá sem máltíðinn var úti og hver var kominn í sitt heimuglegt mak,⁹²
þá vildi Jóhannes fylla það með verkinu sem hann hafði áður sett sér með
hugunum, og lét sinn smásvein fá sér fátæks manns klæðabúning og so var
gjört, en hann klæddist sig⁹³ so engin vissi nema sveinninn. Og gekk síðan
burt úr staðnum og út í eyðimörkina og var þar í margan dag með lítilli hvíld,
sem seinna mun sagt verða, hversu lengi að hann var þar.

---

⁸⁸ Corrected from *domat* in the manuscript.

⁸⁹ Hvað — leitt] as above (cf. n. 58). The corresponding passage in *Pass* reads: "dat is
my leed"(CCC.xlvii.c).

⁹⁰ On the occurrence of *-an* and *-un* in the singular of feminine i-stems, see Bandle, 231.

⁹¹ *verðugheit* is a loan from MLG *werdicheit*, here meaning "pomp," "ceremony," "fes-
tivity." The corresponding passage in the *Pass* does not use this word: "do gingen se mit
groten vrouden to der tafelen" (CCC.xlvii.d). While *verðugur* and *verðuglega* occur elsewhere (see Bandle, 304, 433; *NT*, 397), the nominal form seems to be limited to *Rhb*,
where it is used both with the meaning above, e.g., in the legend of St. Anthony (*Rhb* 2:
275.25) and with the meaning of "inner worthiness" (*Rhb* 2: 256.5) as well as "high sta-
tion," "honor" in the legend of Henry and Cunegund (*Rhb* 1: 65.5).

⁹² Both *heimuglegt* and *mak* are Low German loans, *heimuglegt* deriving from MLG
heimelik, hemelik "private," "secret" (*MNW*, 2: 237), and *mak* from *mak* "private chambers," "a comfortable room" (*MNW*, 3: 7). Here the noun *mak* has a meaning different
from the one attested in other sixteenth-century Icelandic texts, where the word has the
sense of "peace," "quiet." See Westergård-Nielsen, *Låneordene*, 212; Bandle, 273; *VÓ*, 210.
The phrase *heimuglegt mak* also occurs in *Ósvalds saga* (*Rhb* 1: 79.14).

⁹³ Corrected from the manuscript which writes *honum* (*honvm*).

yet nothing happens before God wills it, and the proverb proves true, which goes: "No matter what one knows, one doesn't know what will happen, for the judgments of God are hidden" [Romans 11:33], and thus it was in this case, as you will shortly hear.

Now when John had been ordained a priest and he was to say[94] his first Mass, he started thinking in his heart during the Mass with the words that here follow: "O Lord God," he said, "how very young I am and unworthy, my Lord, to touch Your blessed body and to have attained a position to be called a priest. What I am sorry about with all my heart is that I am so young for such an office, and also that worldly riches cause great harm to my soul. Therefore I gladly want to be poor and destitute for the sake of God rather than own anything on account of which my soul might be lost for my creator and which is contrary to His commandments. And I certainly am going to do something about this as soon as I can," and he looked up to heaven with the hope that the Mass would be over as soon as possible. And when the Mass was over, all went to table with great ceremony, and John behaved at table as though he was very happy for all to see lest anyone suspect anything about his state and intention.

And when the meal was over and everyone had gone to his private quarters, John wanted to carry out in deed what he had earlier determined in his mind, and he had his page fetch for himself a poor man's garb and this was done, and he got dressed so that no one knew this but the page. And he then left the city and went into the wilderness and he was there for many a day with little repose, as will be told later, for as long as he was there.

---

[94] Although the Icelandic uses the word *syngja* "to sing," it is unlikely and indeed there is nothing to indicate that this was a sung Mass. The corresponding passage in the *Pass* reads: "Do lasz sunte Johannes de misse mit groter andacht" (CCC.xlvii.c).

En þá sem páfinn og aðrir herrar í staðnum Róma urðu varir við hans burthvarf, þá varð hann og margir með honum hryggir um hans burtför og þóttu mikið um það, og létu leita eftir honum í alla staði er þar voru í nándir og fannst hann ekki að heldur.

En í annan stað er það að segja að Jóhannes linnti sinni ferð ekki fyrr en hann kom sér út í eyðimörk og gekk þar langan tíma áður en hann þóttist finna þann stað er honum virðist bíkvæmur⁹⁵ vera til að þjóna guði í. Og fann hann þann stað ekki fyrr en hann bað til guðs að hann vísaði sér þann stað er hann blessaður vildi sína þjónustu þiggja. Þegar lítlu seinna fann hann einn uppsprettu brunn og varð þá glaður. Þar fann hann og einn steinn mikinn og var holur innan ofan til, en niður undir steininum þá rann vatnið.

Þá mælti hann: "Lofaður sé guð og fyrir víst skal þessi steinn vera mitt heimili."

Og reiddi sér efterá gras og þakti með steininn. En síðan gjörði hann fyrir hurð og gætti so að síður mætti dýr sem grimm væri gjöra honum mein. Og fæddi sig með grösum og rótum. Oftlega leit hann upp til himinin<s> til <að> biðja sér miskunnar af almáttugum guði. Og þjónaði þar síðan sínum herra og skapara með föstum og vökum, með bænum og öðrum harðindum er hann lagði á sig.

5. So finnst og skrifað að í þann tíma var einn keisari sem vel elskaði guð og hans heilagt lögmál. Hann hafði eina borg sem lá nær mörkinni þessari sem sanctus⁹⁶ Johannes var í, og þá sem það bar til tíðinda þar hafði keisarinn sína drottningu og með sér þar og dóttur með öðrum mörgum hans vildarmönnum, er þetta skeði sem brátt má heyra. Þá einn dag um sumar tíma vildi keisarans dóttur⁹⁷ ganga með sínum meyjum og spacera út í mörkina til forlystingar⁹⁸ og að safna sér til gamans blóma af grösum og sætleg aldin eður

---

⁹⁵ *bíkvæmur* is a loan from MLG *bequeme* "suitable," "fitting," "appropriate." The corresponding passage in the *Pass*, though phrased somewhat differently, has the cognate: "mit ener bequemen stede" (CCC.xlvii.d). See Westergård-Nielsen, *Låneordene*, 26–27, who lists only the adjectival and adverbial forms *bíkvæmiligur* and *bíkvæmiliga*, but not *bíkvæmur*.

⁹⁶ The manuscript alternates between the Latin and Icelandic forms, that is, *sanctus* and *sankti* (written *sancte*); I follow suit and distinguish in spelling the name as in Latin, *Johannes*, or Icelandic, *Jóhannes*. Cf. KW, cxxix.

⁹⁷ Thus the manuscript. On the vacillating declension of *dóttir* (*faðir, móðir*) in the singular in the sixteenth century, see Bandle, 263–67, who writes: "Einerseits endet der Nom oft auf -*ur*, andererseits ist -*ir* aus dem Nom in den GenDatAkk eingedrungen" (265).

⁹⁸ *forlysting* is a loan from MLG *vorlusten* "to amuse," "to find pleasure" (*MNW*, 5: 400).

And when the pope and the other lords in the city of Rome became aware of his disappearance, the pope and many with him were distressed at his departure and were worried, and they had him looked for everywhere in the vicinity and he was not found anywhere.

On the other hand it can be told that John did not end his journey before he had come into the wilderness, and he walked there for a long time before he thought he had found the place that seemed suitable to him for serving God. And he did not find that place until he had asked God to show him the place where He, the Blessed One, wanted to accept his service. A little while later he found a spring and he was then happy. There he also found a large rock and on the upper part there was a hollow in it, but below the rock there ran water.

Then he spoke: "Praised be God, for this rock will certainly become my dwelling" [cf. Psalm 27:5; Job 30:6, 39:28].

And he collected grasses afterwards and covered the rock with them.[99] And then he put a door in front and arranged it so that ferocious animals would be less likely to do him any harm. And he nourished himself with plants and roots. Often he looked up to heaven and asked for mercy from almighty God. And there he then served his Lord and Creator with fasts and vigils, with prayers and other ascetic practices that he imposed upon himself.

5. It is also written that at this time there was an emperor who dearly loved God and His holy commandments. He had a castle in the vicinity of the forest in which St. John was, and at the time this took place the emperor had his queen there with him and his daughter and many other friends of his, when there happened what you will soon hear. One day during the summer the emperor's daughter wanted to go and take a walk with her maidens in the forest for amusement and to collect for their pleasure flowers from the meadows and sweet fruits

---

[99] St. John is actually covering the hollow in the rock. In the *Pass* we read: "vnde nam grasz vnde bedekkede sine celle. vnde makede dar ene dore voer" (CCC.xlvii.d). The text here anticipates that the hollow in the rock will function as St. John's cell.

ávöxtu af trjám og so til annarra lystigheitar[100] er hún girntist og meyjar hennar
að forvitnast um. En í þessu bili kom yfir keisaradóttur so sem einn vind-
bylur eða hvirfilvindur og tók hana í loft upp so hátt at þær meyjar er með
henni voru vissu ekki hvað af henni varð og eigi sáu þær til hennar að því
sinni meira. En hinar er með henni voru sakaði ekki neitt.

Þetta undraði þær og vissu nú ekki hvað þær vildu til gjöra og óttuðust
reiði keisarans og urðu stórlega mjög um hennar burthvarf hryggar og mæltu
sín á milli: "Góðar systur, hvað svar eigum vér að gefa vorum kærustum herra
um dóttur hans og so líka móður hennar?" En allar svöruðu sem með einu
hljóði og orðtaki að þær so segja mundu sem skeði, en það kynni þær ekki
honum segja hvert að hún væri niður komin.

En so[101] vill skriftin víkja á að sjá vindur hafi hana ekki fyrri niður látið að
forlagi og fullum vilja almáttugs guðs en fyrir jarðholinu, fyrir hreysi sankti
Jóhannes, án nokkurs mótlætis eður sárenda so henni mátti skaða. Og þá sem
hún var niður komin, þá vissi hún ekki hvert í frá[102] að hun átti snúast sér til
bjargar og leit á báðar síður. Og þá sem hún hafði snúist nokkura hríð, þá fékk
hún að líta beint niður hjá steininum þeim er hún stóð á hvar ein jarðhola var
og um hana var so búið sem hurð mætti vera fyrir ef það vildi gjöra.[103] Þá sté
hún ofan af steininum og leit inn í holuna og sá að þar lá einn maður á bæn
sinni á grúfu niður á hnjánum og lá so höfuðið á honum á jörðunni. Þá varð
hún hrædd og skoðaði á báðar hlíðar hvort að nokkur maður annar mundi
vera í nándir að sjá sig, so að hún mætti hlaupa þangað sér til hjálpar. En er
hún skildi það með íblæstri ins helga anda að hún mundi vera horfin frá öllum
mönnum, þá veik hún sér aftur að jarðholunni er hún sá fyrri og kallaði með
hárri röddu á þann sem inni fyrir var, so segjandi:

"Heyr mig, góði herra, veit mér fátækri leyfi að ég megi ganga inn til
þín."

En þegar að sanctus Johannes heyrði kallið stóð hann upp og sá hvar þessi
jungfrúin var með skrautlegum búningi og eina gyllega kórónu á höfðinu
á sér og var hugsandi hvað þetta mundi. Þá kallaði hún annað sinni og bað
hann góðmótlega að lofa sér inn til sín, en hann þagði við henni. Þá kallaði

---

[100] *lystigheit* is a loan from MLG *lusticheit* "attraction," "delight" (*MNW*, 2: 753).
Pass writes that the emperor's daughter and her companions "wolden de blomen vnde de
lustycheyt beseen" (CCC.xlvii.d). Westergård-Nielsen, *Låneordene*, lists only *lystiliga* and
lystiligur (210). Cf. Bandle, 71, 305.

[101] On *so* (*svo*) to introduce clauses, see *NT*, 145.

[102] See Bandle, 450–51, on the pleonastic use of *í* before the preposition *frá*.

[103] ef — gjöra] corrected from the manuscript, which writes *þótt það vildi*. This
makes no sense. There is no corresponding text in the *Pass* that might provide an explanation as to how this phrase, undoubtedly in error, was generated.

or other produce from the trees and for other delights that she and her maidens desired to experience. But at this moment something like a strong wind blast or whirlwind descended on the princess and lifted her so high up into the air that the maidens who were with her did not know what became of her and did not see her any longer. But those who were with her were not harmed.

They wondered at this and did not know now what they should do and they feared the emperor's anger and became very sorrowful at her disappearance, and they spoke among themselves: "Good sisters, what answer are we to give our dearest lord about his daughter, and also her mother?" And all answered as with one voice and in the same words that they should just say what happened, and that they could not tell him where she had been set down.

And the story turns to where that wind did not set her down any sooner, in keeping with the providence and perfect will of almighty God, than in front of the hollow, before St. John's den, without any mishap or harm having come to her. And when she had been set down, she did not know where to turn for protection, and she searched on both sides. And when she had turned back and forth for a while, she saw that straight down by the rock on which she was standing there was a hollow and it was of such a kind that one might have a door in front of it if one wanted to make one. She then stepped down from the rock and looked into the hollow and saw that a man was prostrate in prayer on his knees and his head was touching the ground. She then became frightened and looked on both sides to see whether there might be someone else near who might see her, so that she could run there for help. But when she realized through the inspiration of the Holy Spirit that she was far from all people, she turned back to the hollow that she had seen before and called out with a loud voice to the person who was inside, saying thus:

"Hear me, good sir, permit me, wretched woman, to come inside to you."

And as soon as St. John heard the cry, he stood up and saw this maiden standing there in splendid garments and with a golden crown on her head, and he wondered what this might mean. Then she called out once more and asked him kindly to permit her to come in, but he remained silent. She then

hún í þriðja sinni og bað hann fyrir guðs skyld að leyfa sér inn til hans[104] so að
dýr eður aðrar meinvættir gjörði sér ekki mein og mælti:

"Þú góði herra," sagði hún, "ekki þurfi þér að þegja við mér eður undur
slá í hug yðvarn um mig, hver ég er eða hvernin að ég er hér komin. En ég veit
fyrir víst að þú ert einn kristinn maður líka sem[105] ég er. Þar fyrir byrjar þér
að hjálpa mér so ég deyji ekki af reiðuleysi hér fyrir þínum dýrum. So veistu
það vel sjálfur ef þú mátt hjálpa mér en vilt ekki og dey ég af hungri eður
grimmleik dýra, þá gjörir þú í því mikla synd og muntu þá eiga að gjalda guði
skyn fyrir mig á dómsdegi."

En þá sem sanctus Johannes heyrði þessi hennar áklögunar orð, þá gekk
hann að dyrunum og lét hana inn, og frétti hana eftir hver hún væri og so
hvernin að hún væri þar komin.

Hún svarar: "Góði herra," sagði hún, "af því kann ég yður ekki annað að
segja en það hafi guðs vilji verið."

Þá stóð hann og hugsaði með sér: "Ef hún er kristin sem hún segist vera
og deyr hún úti af mínum völdum, þá er það víst sem hún sagði, að ég mun
eiga svara þar fyrir[106] á dómsdegi. Sé það og einn blekkingar andi, þá mun ég
og í guðs trausti vilja reyna hverja freistni að hún muni gjöra mér," og leyfði
henni að vera þar hjá sér.

Þá gladdist hún og féll til jarðar fyrir honum og lofaði guð. Þá vildi hún
sakir huggunar er hann veitti henni minnast við fætur hans, en hann vildi
það með öngu móti og bað hana upp standa.

6. Þá nú eftir þetta þeirra tal, sem nú var greint, þá tók hann staf sinn og reist
með honum einn reit um þvert gólfið og mælti síðan til hennar: "Nú vil ég
að þú haldir það boð sem ég býð þér, en það er fyrst að þú skalt vera í öðrum
arminum burtu fra þeim reitnum er þú sér hér á gólfinu. En ég skal vera í
öðrum arminum og skal hvorki ganga til annars yfir takmarkið. Þar með[107]
skaltu afleggja þann glyslega búninginn sem þú ber á þér. Og guði góðfúslega
skaltu þjóna með harðlífi, með föstum og vökum og guðlegum bænum."

Hún kvaðst þetta gjarnan gjöra vilja og hans góðum ráðum fylgja. Og
sofnaði síðan út af og hafði lítla ró[108] eður hvild fyrr en þá sem dagurinn kom.

---

[104] The use of the personal pronoun here rather than the possessive *til sín* as above, may
have been generated by a German *to em*. There is no corresponding passage in the *Pass.*

[105] On the use of *líka sem*, see *NT*, 149.

[106] On the combination of a locative adverb with a preposition, see Bandle, 442.

[107] Cf. the preceding note; see Bandle, 443.

[108] lítla ró] thus the manuscript; Loth reverses the words in her edition (*Rhb* 2:
176.24), but this seems unnecessary.

called a third time and asked him for God's sake to ler her come in so that wild animals or other monsters would not harm her, and she spoke:

"You, good sir," she said, "you need not remain silent or wonder in your heart about me, who I am or from where I have come. And I know for sure that you are a Christian just as I am. For that reason it behooves you to help me so that I won't die from neglect here in front of your door. And you yourself know that if you can help me but won't and I die from hunger or the ferocity of animals, you will commit a great sin by this and you will have to give an accounting to God for me on Judgment Day."

And when St. John heard her words of accusation, he went to the door and let her in, and he asked her who she was and how she had come there.

She answers: "Good sir," she said, "I cannot tell you anything other than that it has been God's will."

Then he stood and thought to himself: "If she is a Christian as she says she is and she dies outside on my account, then it will surely be as she said, that I shall have to answer for that on Judgment Day. But should this be an evil spirit, then with trust in God I want to see what temptation she will pose for me," and he let her stay with him.

Then she became happy and fell to the ground before him and praised God. Then, because of the comfort he granted her, she wanted to kiss his feet, but he did not at all want that and told her to stand up.

6. Now after this conversation of theirs, which was reported above, he took his staff and drew a line with it across the ground and then he spoke to her: "Now I want you to do what I tell you, and that is first of all that you shall stay in the other corner, away from the line that you see here on the ground. And I will stay in this corner, and neither shall go to the other over the line. Moreover, you shall take off the splendid garments that you are wearing. And you shall serve God piously with ascetic practices, with fasts and vigils and devout prayers."

She said that she would gladly do this and follow his good counsels. And she then went to sleep but had little rest or repose before day came. After she

Eftir það að hún var uppstaðin, þá var hún hugsandi um það sem hún átti að neyta og sagði við sjálfa sig: "Nú þó að ég er komin hjá mennskum manni, þá hefur hann ekki það neitt að ég getur etið og mun ég því verða að þola harðindi á sjálfri mér."

En í öðrum stað var sanctus Johannes að biðjast fyrir og sá hann hennar hug og ástundan. Lítlu seinna stóð hann upp af bæn sinni og sagði til hennar: "Heyr, dóttir," sagði hann, "guð sér altíð best fyrir öllum og so hvað hver þarf."

Síðan kenndi hann henni hvernin hún skyldi biðjast fyrir, en eftir það mælti hann: "Förum nú," sagði hann, "og leitum okkur að fæðslu," og sýndi henni þá þau grös og rætur og aldin er hún átti að taka til fæðslu sér, þvíað þeirra fæða var engin önnur en krydd og aldin. Og neyttu þess margan dag með allri auðmjúkt fyrir hungurs sakir, og þjónuðu þar með guði nætur sem daga með vökum og bænum.

Þessi dygðarverk þoldi andskotinn ekki so að hann gjörði ekki eitthvað til og bjó sín bölvuðu skeyti til ef hann mætti spilla þessum sauðum guðs og koma þeim af réttum veg og á rangan stíg með saurlegu hugskoti til losta-girndar þeirra á milli. Og laust sanctus Johannes með einni þessari eiturfullri ör í hans hjarta til að girnast að stíga yfir það markið er hann sjálfur hafði sett þeim báðum til lögvarnar. Og jók blíðlæti við hana, so hann tók hana í faðm sér ljúflega með annarri þeirri blíðu er hann veitti henni af sér til, so að hún féll af hans völdum í stóra synd. Eftir þeirra misræði og syndlega verk er þau höfðu framið á móti guði, þá tóku þau að iðrast sína synd og þótti báðum mikið að þau sinn skapara so illa reitað höfðu[109] á sig og grétu sárlega.

Þá mælti sankti Jóhannes við sjálfan sig og sagði: "O herra guð, hvað illa hefur ég nú gjört, að það lítla sem ég hefur áður hingað til gott gjört, þá er nú það allt farið og týnt."

En hún og líka í annan stað klagaði sig í augliti guðs með þessum orðum fyrir sitt misfelli er hún hafði í fallið, so segjandi: "O sæti herra Jesus Christ-us, hvað mikið er mér það að ég hefur reitað þig í mínum glæp á móti mér. Hvað mér er nú það leitt að so sé af öllu hjarta[110] og biður ég þig líknar og miskunnar og hér ofan spillt og svívirðlega týnt mínum heiðri þeim er ég hefði hugað þér að offra. Þessa hluti fyrirgef þú mér drottinn Jesus."

---

[109] að — höfðu] see *NT*, 168, on the placement of the verb in final position in depen-dent clauses, which also occurs in Oddr Gottskálksson's translation of the New Testa-ment.

[110] Hvað — hjarta] concerning this idiom, see n. 58. The *Pass* has a corresponding passage: "dat is my van gantzeme herten leed" (CCC.xlviii.b).

had gotten up, she began to think about what she was to eat and said to herself: "Now even though I have found a human being, he does not have anything for me to eat, and I am thus going to have to suffer hardship."

For his part, St. John was praying and he saw her worry and concern. A little later he got up from his prayer and said to her: "Listen, daughter," he said, "God provides best for everyone and what everyone needs."

He then taught her how she should pray, and after that he spoke: "Let us now go," he said, "to look for food for us," and he showed her the plants and roots and fruit that she was to collect for food, for their food was nothing but herbs and fruit. And they ate this for many a day with great humility on account of their hunger, and they also served God night and day with vigils and prayers.

The devil could not stand this virtuous life without doing something about it, and he prepared his accursed arrows to see if he could not corrupt these lambs of God and lead them off the right road and onto the wrong path with filthy minds bent on lust for each other. And he struck St. John in the heart with one of these poisonous arrows so that he yearned to cross the line that he himself had drawn for both their protection. And his affection for her increased, and he took her lovingly into his arms and along with his other caressing she fell into great sin on account of him. After the misdeed and sinful act that they had committed against God, they began to regret their sin and they both thought it terrible that they had grievously angered their Creator, and they wept sorely.

Then St. John spoke to himself and said: "O Lord God, what evil have I now done, for the little that I previously did that was good is now completely gone and has been lost."

And similarly, on her part, she lamented before God with these words on account of the sin into which she had fallen, saying thus: "O sweet Lord Jesus Christ, how sorry I am that I have angered you through my offense against you. How sorry I am now with all my heart that this is so, and I ask for your forgiveness and mercy that I have, moreover, besmirched and disgracefully lost my honor which I had intended to offer up to you. Forgive me for these things, Lord Jesus."

Nú sem andskotinn sá og skildi þeirra uppsáttur[111] að þau vildu iðrast þeirra synd og bæta að miskunnar dómi guðs almáttugs, þá vildi hann og ekki láta dvína sína illsku þeim í gegn og herjaði enn á hug og hjarta Jóhannes með þeim íblæstri, ef so væri að þessi kvensvift væri þar lengur nærri honum að þá mundi hann oftar enn syndgast með henni og sér væri það betur að koma henni með einhverjum hætti í burtu frá sér. Og því verr að þessu óráði fylgði hann er hinn vondi[112] andi skaut í huginn á honum.

Og kallaði síðan á hana að hún skyldi ganga út úr jarðhúsinu er þau voru í og so gjörði hún. En þegar að hún var komin út á steininn er húsið þeirra var á, þá hratt hann henni út af steininum. Og gekk inn aftur í celle[113] sín jafnt og ekki neitt hafði í gjörst. En þá sem hann var inn í cellann kominn og hann vildi gjöra eftir sínum iðulegum vana að biðjast fyrir og þjóna guði og sínum skapara, þá snerist hans <hjarta>[114] á annan veg og kom honum þá í hug hvað verk er hann hafði þá enn fyrir stystu gjört og tók að gráta og að iðrast síns ins ljóta verks, og mæltist við sig sjálfan á þessa lund:

"Ó drottinn, hvað ósálugur maður er ég[115] í þínu augliti. Nú hefur ég sannlega gjört morð og rænt lífi þessarar góðrar kvinnu sem ég hýsta og gaf henni sök ranga fyrir sjálfs míns synd og vilja skyld, þar sem hún hafði öngva synd gjört eða hugsað, hefði ég ekki komið henni þar til[116] og blekkt, og líf léteg hana nú þar ofan saklausa. Og þessa synd og ótrúleika er ég gjörða mun guð hefna á mér æfinlega."

Og með þessari umræðu gengur hann í burtu ur kofanum er hann var í og setti það óráðvendi í hug sér að hann vildi guð ekki lengur þjóna og sín þjónusta mundi vera farin hvort sem væri, og sagði að guð mundi hafa gleymt sér.

---

[111] The word, written *vppsathvr* in the manuscript, does not exist in Icelandic; it is a loan of MLG *upsat*, *upsatte* "decision," "intention" (*MNW*, 5: 126).

[112] The manuscript has *ondi*.

[113] The word is taken directly from MLG; *Pass* reads here: "vnde gink wedder in de celle" (CCC.xlviii.b). When the word recurs in the next sentence, it is Icelandicized, however, and construed as a weak masculine; the manuscript writes *cellan* and this is normalized in the edition to *cellann*.

[114] The word is missing in the manuscript. Loth suggests *hugur* here, but given the *kom honum þá í hug* in the following clause, *hjarta* seems more appropriate.

[115] hvað — ég] this corresponds to *Pass*: "Ach ik vnsalige man" (CCC.xlviii.b). The adjective *ósálugur* is borrowed from MLG *unsalich*.

[116] See Bandle, 443, on the combination of the locative adverb *þar* with the preposition *til*. In this case the MLG origin is obvious. *Pass* writes: "hadde yk se dar to nicht ghebrocht" (CCC.xlviii.a).

Now when the devil saw and realized that their intention was to repent of their sin and to amend their lives relying on the merciful judgment of Almighty God, he did not want to cease his machinations against them, and he again harried the mind and heart of John with the thought that if this woman were to stay there any longer with him, he would again often sin with her, and that it would be better for him if he could get rid of her in some way. Even worse, he followed the evil advice that the evil spirit shot into his mind.

And he then called to her and told her to leave the hollow in which they were, and she did so. And as soon as she had come out on the rock in which their dwelling was, he pushed her off the rock. And he went back into his cell as though nothing had happened. And when he had come into his cell and wanted to do as he was wont, to pray and serve God and his Creator, his heart was moved, and he reflected on what deed he had again committed only a moment ago, and he began to cry and regret his evil deed, and he spoke to himself in this manner:

"O Lord, what a wretched person I am in your sight. I have now truly committed murder and taken the life of this good woman whom I sheltered and whom I blamed for my own sin and willful deed, even though she would not have committed any sin or intended to do so had I not brought this on her and seduced her, and I have now in addition taken the life of her who is innocent. And this sin and infidelity that I have committed God will avenge on me eternally."

And with this argument he leaves the cell in which he was and came to the wicked decision not to serve God any longer and that his service would be over no matter what happened, and he said that God must have forgotten him.

7. Nú í annarri grein skal enn þar að víkja að sanctus Johannes var kominn í stóra hugsan og áhyggju um sinn hag og breytni, sem fyrr segir, so nálega var allt hans ráð á reikun komið. Þá var enn fyrir honum sem fyrir ótölulegum mörgum sker að miskunn guðs er nærri til hjálpar en menn ætla eður forþénan[117] er til, sakir þess að hann öngum týna vil úr sínu tali er til náðar vil leita. Og af íblæstri ins helga anda setur hann fyrir sig stöðugt ráð og hjálpsamlegt að hann vil fara á fund páfans og fá lausn og líkn á sínum málum, sem hann og gjörir. Og gekk aftur til Róm og fann páfann, sem hans skírifaðir var, og féll til fóta honum og bað á guðs vegna at hlýða sér og sinni játningu, en[118] páfinn játaði honum því. Hann sagðist vera einn bersyndugur og inn glæpafullasti maður, en ekki þekkti páfinn hann. Nú sem hann hafði játað allar sínar syndir, þá á milli annarra artikula[119] sem páfinn gaf honum svar uppá, þá sagði páfinn að hann hefði illa gjört við þá fátæka er nærri honum hafði verið og straffaði hann stórlega fyrir það, so að nokkuð af þeirri sök er hann sjálfan snerti vildi páfinn ekki gefa honum lausn fyrir.

Það angraði hann stórlega og varð mjög hryggur og mælti við hug sinn sér til styrktar: "Nú þó að heilagur faðir páfinn vilji mér ekki fulla lausn gefa sakir minna illgjörða, þá skal ég þó ekki mistreysta um miskunn guðs af því að ég sannlega veit að hún er meiri og máttugri en allar mínar syndir eru."

Og með þennan hug gekk hann út aftur í eyðimörkina og inn í cella sinn er hann var áður í og bað guð nætur sem daga að veita sér fyrirgefning sinna synda og þiggja af sér bót og betran so hann mætti hjálpast, og mælti: "Drottinn," sagði hann, "þigg þú þessa bót mína er ég vil viljuglega sjálfur setja og undir ganga mér til hjálpar og lausnar af mínum syndum og þú drottinn minn veist að ég hefur fyrir þínum umboðsmanni í ljósi látið. Og er það fyrst að frá þessum degi meðan ég lifi skal ég aldregi mínu höfði réttu upp halda til himins nema heldur[120] ganga á höndum og fótum sem önnur ferfætt skepna, þangað til að ég fæ nokkura sanna vitneskju af þinni blessaðri og eiginlegri náð og miskunn að mínar syndir sé bættar og fyrirgefnar í þínu augliti," hvað hann og fullkomlega héllt í mörg ár að hann kraup á höndum og fótum so

---

[117] forþénan is borrowed from MLG vordênst; see Westergård-Nielsen, Låneordene, 130; KW, cxxi.

[118] The edition has a typographical error and writes ne (Rhb 2: 178.32).

[119] The word derives from Latin via MLG; see Westergård-Nielsen, Låneordene, 17; Bandle, 281. Here the word refers most likely to the articles of faith, as in the Nicene Creed.

[120] aldregi — nema heldur] this is not idiomatic Icelandic. Variations of this construction occur elsewhere in Rhb, e.g., in Ósvalds saga (Rhb, 1: 71.13). The phrase may be analogous to at heldur, translating German sondern, in the 1540 translation of the New Testament. See NT, 218.

7. Now we must once more return to where St. John was engaged in deep thought and anxiety about his state and condition, as was said before, that all his plans had well-nigh come to naught. But then once again it happened to him as to innumerable others that the mercy of God is closer with help than men think or they deserve, because God does not want to lose anyone from His number who is willing to seek grace. And through the inspiration of the Holy Spirit he made the firm and helpful decision to go see the pope and obtain forgiveness and mercy for his misdeeds, which is what he did. And he went back to Rome and met the pope, who had baptized him, and he fell at his feet and asked him for God's sake to listen to him and his confession, and the pope agreed to do so. He said that he was a sinner and a most wicked man, but the pope did not recognize him. Now when he had confessed all his sins, including matters of faith[121] about which the pope gave him an answer, the pope said that he had behaved badly toward the poor woman who had been with him, and he rebuked him greatly for that, so that for some of the misconduct he mentioned the pope did not want to grant him absolution.[122]

He was very upset about this and he was very sorrowful, and he spoke to himself in order to get courage: "Now even though the Holy Father, the Pope, does not want to grant me complete absolution for my misdeeds, I shall nonetheless not despair of the mercy of God, since I truly know that it is greater and more powerful than all my sins are."

And with this thought he went back into the wilderness and into his cell, where he had been before, and he asked God night and day to grant him forgiveness for his sins and to accept his penance and atonement so that he might be helped, and he spoke: "Lord," he said, "accept my penance, which I freely want to take upon myself and undergo for my salvation and the release from my sins, which you, my Lord, know I have revealed to your representative. First of all, from this day on and as long as I live, I will never hold my head upright toward heaven again, but rather crawl on my hands and feet just like the four-footed animals, until I receive some clear sign of your blessed and real grace and mercy that my sins have been atoned for and forgiven in your sight," which is what he fully carried out for many years, so that he crept on his hands and feet so long that even if he had wanted to stand up straight,

---

[121] I am translating the Icelandic *artikula* with "matters of faith." The Latin loan word presumably refers to the articles of faith in the Creed.

[122] It is not quite clear what is meant here. The *Pass* writes: "vnde vmme andere dinge de em vp de hant quemen absolueerde he ene nicht" (CCC.xlviii.b "and on account of some other things that surprised him, he did not grant him absolution").

lengi að þó hann hafði viljað upprétta sig, þá gat hann ekki það gjört. Og þau
lítlu fötin er hann hafði haft á sér þá voru af honum öll og var allur loðin, so
að engin mátti þekkja hann fyrir mennskan mann, sem raun gafst að því og
brátt má heyra.

8. Þá nú að þessi guðs vinur hafði verið í eyðimörkinni nærri fimtán ár með
mikilli vosbúð af hungri og kulda og öðru mótlæti á sínum líkama og nú
mátti heyra, þá bar enn so til að drottning keisarans þess ins sama af Róm ól
enn eitt barn og var það borið til páfans og beðið hann að skíra það. Nú þá
sem páfinn vildi þetta embætti fullgjöra við barnið, þá tók hann það upp í
hönd sér og leit á barnið. En í því kallaði það og sagðist ekki vilja skírast láta
af honum.

Þetta orð óttaðist páfinn mjög og sagði: "Sé," sagði hann, "heyrið hér allir
góðir herrar andlegir og veraldlegir, hvað þetta barn segir eða hvað þenkjið[123]
þér að þetta mun þýða?" Og sagði þá en við barnið: "Seg þú í guðs nafni enn
hvort að þú vilt þiggja skírn af mér eða eigi."

En barnið svaraði sömu að það vildi ekki skírn af honum þiggja og af
öngum öðrum en af sankti Jóhannes, þeim heilögum manni sem nú er í
eyðimörkinni, "þvíað guð mun snarlega[124] senda hann hingað til vor."

En þá sem páfinn heyrði það, þá fékk hann fósturmóður barnsins aftur
barnið og gekk síðan til drottningarinnar og sagði hann henni hvað títt væri,
og frétti hann hana eftir ef hún kynni gjöra sér nokkura grein á því hver
Jóhannes að[125] það mundi vera er barnið ætti að skíra. En hún kunni honum
öngva grein á því gjöra og engin heldur annar að því sinni.

Þá í þenna sama tíma er þetta var, þá hafði keisarinn sent út í mörkina
sína jagara[126] eður veiðimenn[127] til að fá sér dýr og fugla til barns ölsins. Og

---

[123] þenkja is a loan of MLG denken; see Westergård-Nielsen, Låneordene, 399; Bandle,
430; NT, 406–7; KW, cxxxiv.

[124] snarlega is borrowed from MLG snarliken "quickly." See NT, 360. The Pass uses
a different adverb, however, and writes: "God wert ene tohant vth deme elende heer sen-
den" (CCC.xlviii.c).

[125] hver — að] On the use of hver + að in the 1540 translation of the New Testament,
see NT, 133–34.

[126] The word is a loan from MLG jeger "hunter"; see Westergård-Nielsen, Låneordene, 170; cf. KW, cxxiii. While the Pass has a corresponding passage, the episode features only one hunter: "do hadde de keyser sinen yeger in den wolt heten ryden" (CCC.
xlviii.c, "Then the emperor had told his hunter to ride into the woods"). The same collocation also occurs in the legend of St. Anthony, where we read: "So bar til eitt sinni að
einn jagari eða veiðimaður . . . kom til sankti Antoníus" (Rhb, 2: 259.21–23).

[127] The manuscript incorrectly writes veiðamenn (veida menn).

he nevertheless could not do so. And the few clothes he had on his back fell off him and he was completely matted with hair, so that no one was able to recognize him as a human being [cf. Daniel 4:33], as proved to be the case and will soon be heard.

8. Now when this friend of God had been in the wilderness for close to fifteen years in great misery from hunger and cold and other bodily affliction, as could now be heard, it happened yet again that the queen of the same emperor of Rome gave birth to another child, and it was taken to the pope and he was asked to baptize it. Now when the pope wanted to perform this rite on the child, he took it into his arms and looked at the child. But at this it called out and said that it did not want to be baptized by him.

The pope was quite afraid at these words and said: "See," he said, "listen here, all you good lords, both ecclesiastical and secular, what this child is saying, and what do you think this means?" And he then said to the child: "Tell me, in God's name, once more whether you want to be baptized by me or not."

But the child answered just as before that it did not want to be baptized by him but by no other than St. John, the holy man who is now in the wilderness, "for God will quickly send him here to us."

And when the pope heard that, he handed the baby back to its foster-mother[128] and then went to the queen and told her what had happened, and asked her if she had some idea who this John might be who was supposed to baptize the child. But she could not give him any explanation for this and neither could anyone else at this time.

At the same time that this was happening, the emperor had sent out into the woods his hunters or huntsmen to catch some animals and birds for the

---

[128] The *Pass* identifies the woman as the baby's *amme* "nursemaid" (CCC.xlviii.c). The translation vacillates; here she is identified as the *fósturmóðir* (*Rhb* 2:180.9) but subsequently as *barnfóstra* "nursemaid" (*Rhb* 2:131.16).

sem þeir voru komnir inn í þykkva mörkina nær eini mílu vegs, þá heyrðu
veiðimenn keisarans að hundarnir sem þeir höfðu sleppt, er sumir menn kalla
þá styfara,[129] geyðu með miklum ákafa, en þeir eru þó so vandir að þeir geyja
aldrei fyrr en þeir líta eitthvað til nýlynda hversu lengi sem þeir hlaupa og
renna um skóginn. En þegar að veiðimaðurinn heyrir ljóð hundsins þá veit
hann víst hvert að hann á <að> leita að dýr eru. So er og líka að soddan[130]
hundar þagna og aldrei af þeirra hljóðum frá því að hann sér dýrið og til þess
að veiðimaðurinn kemur til hans. So verður og nú að þegar veiðimenn heyrðu
hljóð hundanna, þá höfðu þeir sig eftir hljóðinu. Og þegar að þeir komu í nánd
hundunum, þá fengu þeir að líta þar eitt mikið dýr og þó undarlegt að sjá og
stóð fyrir hundunum. En þeir verða hræddir við og þykkjast nú ekki vita hvað
þeir vildu gjöra. Og ræddu sín á milli hvort að þeir skyldi skjóta það eða eigi.

Og sögðu so: "Ef vær[131] skjótum það og tekur ekki til dauða, þá má vera að
vær ýfum það þá upp og drepur það oss eftirá alla, því það er ógurlegt að líta, og
<vær> viljum heldur fara heim aftur og sem vær höfum ekki neitt fundið."

Þá svarar annar að keisarinn mundi þá vera þeim reiður ef þeir kæmi so
heim og færðu honum ekki neitt.

Þá mælti enn einn þeirra: "Hvað má vita, bræður," sagði hann, "hversu
grimmt að þetta dýr er fyrr en reynt <er>, þvíað mér virðist það vera kyrt og
spakt," og gjörði krossmark fyrir sig og kvaðst vildu[132] reyna hvort það mundi
sækja að sér ef hann gengi nærri því. Og með þessu gekk hann að þessu
dýrinu er honum sýndist. En það stóð kyrt fyrir honum og lagði sig niður.
Síðan fór hann úr kápu sinni og breiddi yfir það. En eftir það batt hann á því
bæði hendur og so fætur,[133] og þótti nú vel að fara að hann mátti sínum herra
soddant undarlegt dýr færa. En þó undraði hann það allra mest að það var so
tamið og auðmjúkt þó það væri og stórt og hræðilegt að líta. Og þreif belti sitt
og batt það síðan við söðulinn á hesti sínum og færði hann so þetta dýr heim
sínum herra keisaranum uppá borgina[134] er hann var og drottning hans.

---

[129] The word is a loan from MLG stover "hunting dog" (*MNW*, 4: 424).

[130] The adjective soddan, borrowed from MLG sodân, is indeclinable, but occasionally the form soddant occurs in the nom. and accus. sg. neuter, as happens below. See
Bandle, 376–77; *NT*, 360, 369.

[131] This form of the 1st pers. pl. pronoun occurs not only in this text, but throughout
Rhb. On similar usage in the *Guðbrandsbiblía*, see Bandle, 345–46, where, however, *vær*
occurs alongside *vér*.

[132] *vildu* appears to be a past infinitive, presumably formed by analogy to *mundu*, as
in "en hann sagðist mundu vel finna það (chap. 9).

[133] The manuscript repeats *á því* after *fætur*.

[134] The phrase "uppá borgina" corresponds to *Pass* "vp de borch" (CCC.xlviii.c). See
Bandle, 451–52; *NT*, 173.

child's baptismal feast. And when they had gone about a mile deep into the woods, the emperor's huntsmen heard that the hounds which they had let loose, which some people call spoor dogs, were barking vehemently, but these dogs are trained never to bark until they see something strange, no matter how long they leap and run about in the woods. And as soon as the huntsman hears the sound of the hound he knows for sure where he is to look for the game. Similarly, such hounds do not stop barking from the time it sees the animal until the huntsman reaches it. And that is what happened now, for as soon as the huntsmen heard the sound of the hounds, they took off after the sound. And as soon as they came near the hounds, they caught sight there of a large animal, quite strange in appearance, and it stood still before the hounds. And they became afraid and did not know what they ought to do. And they discussed among themselves whether they should shoot it or not.

And this is what they said: "If we shoot it but don't kill it, it may happen that we then rile it up and it ends up killing all of us, for it is frightful to look at, and we would rather go back home and pretend we have not found anything."

Then someone else answers that the emperor would then be angry with them, if they came home and did not bring anything back for him.

Yet another one of them then spoke: "How can we know, brothers," he said, "how fierce this animal is before we test it, for to me it seems calm and gentle," and he made the sign of the cross over himself and said that he wanted to test whether it would attack him if he went near it. And with this he went up to the animal as he thought fit. But it stood still before him and then lay down. He then took off his cloak and spread it over the animal. And after that he tied both its hands and also its feet, and he thought it turned out fine that he could bring his lord such a wondrous animal. Yet he wondered most of all that it was so tame and gentle, even though it was both large and frightful to look at. And he pulled off his belt and then tied the animal onto the saddle of his horse, and that is how he took the animal home to his lord the emperor up in the castle where he was with his queen.

Þá komu þangað mikill fjöldi fólks, menn og kvinnur, og vildu líta þessa undarlega skepnu. En það skammaðist sín og kraup þangað er það sá skuggann og undir bekkina og vildi so fela sig. Þá á milli margra annarra er þangað komu að sjá þetta dýrið, þá kom þar og barnfóstra keisarans og hafði barnið með sér í fanginu og bað fólkið að sýna sér dýrið sem öllum öðrum. Þá vildu það margir veita henni en það vildi ekki fara út undan bekknum og skugganum er það faldi sig í. Þá kom einn maður að með langa stöng og steytti það út úr bekknum, en það hafði sig þegar jafn snart upp aftur í myrkurið. Þá steytti hann það þaðan í annað sinni, en það hafði sig þegar í burtu aftur og í myrkurið. Þá gjörir maðurinn þetta enn í þriðja sinni og lemur það undan bekknum, en þá það kom fram þá stóð það kyrt í allan máta.

Þá mælti barnið so að allir heyrðu: "Sé hér, Jóhannes, minn kæri herra, ég á að taka skírn af þér en öngum öðrum."

Þá svaraði hann sem dýrið átti að vera og sagði: "Er það vilji guðs að so sé og eigi að vera, þá seg þú það enn eitt sinni."

Þá svarar barnið og sagði so: "Minn kæri andlegur faðir Jóhannes, af þér á ég fyrir víst að fá skírn og hennar beiðumst ég af þér."

Þetta undruðust allir er þetta heyrðu og mæltu hver við annan, so segjandi: "Mikill er guð og undarlegur í sinni dýrð og so í sínum verkum undarlegum."

En í annan stað kallaði sankti Jóhannes til drottins vors Jesu Christi með hug og ástsamlegu hjarta á þessa lund að hann[135] bað drottin um að barnið skyldi birta þar fyrir öllum hvort að hans syndir væri honum uppgefnar eða eigi, og sagði so: "Heyr þú drottinn, láttu birtast út af þessa barns munni hér fyrir öllum hvort að ég hefur bætt mínar syndir með þinni miskunn."

Þá svarar barnið: "Jóhannes, vertu glaður, þvíað guð hefur allar þínar syndir þér fyrirgefið, og til marks um það þá verður þú heill og vel til reika af öllum saurlegum hlutum sem á þér eru. Og þar fyrir stattu upp og skír mig í nafni heilagrar þrenningar."

Sýndi þá drottinn fagurt tákn sínum ástvin eftir því sem barnið sagði fyrir, að so snart sem hann stóð upp, þá féll niður af honum hár er hann var allur vaxinn með og önnur óhreinsan er á honum var, so að allur hans líkamur og hold var so fagurt og hvítt sem á það hefði hár eður duft ekki komið. Síðan var honum fengin ágæt klæði á sig og sýndist hann þá vera enn allra tigulegasti herra. Lofuðu þá allir guð er þetta tákn sáu. En eftir það tók páfinn barnið og margir herrar með honum er því áttu undir að halda, en sanctus Johannes skírði það með góðfýsi.

---

[135] Corrected from the manuscript, which writes *had.*

A large crowd of people then came there, men and women, and they wanted to look at this wondrous creature. But it was shy and it crept to where it saw cover and got down under the bench and wanted to hide itself this way. And among many others who came there to see this animal, there also came the emperor's nursemaid[136] and she had the child in her arms and asked the people to show her, like the others, the animal. Many wanted to grant her that, but the animal did not want to come out from under the bench and the cover where it was hiding. Then there came a man with a long pole and he flushed it out from under the bench, but just as quickly it took itself back into the dark. Then he flushed it out from there once more, but it took itself at once back into the dark. Then the man did this a third time and flushed it out from under the bench, and when it came out, it stood there completely calm.[137]

Then the child spoke so that all heard: "See here, John, my dear lord, I am to be baptized by you and no other."

Then he who was supposed to be an animal answered and said: "If it is the will of God that this is so and is to be, then say this once more."

Then the child answers and said this: "My dear spiritual father John, I am most certainly to be baptized by you and I am asking this of you."

All who heard this wondered at this and they spoke to each other, saying: "God is great and wondrous in His glory and also in His wondrous works" [Psalms 26:7, 105:2, 145:5].

On his part, St. John called upon Our Lord Jesus Christ with his mind and loving heart in such fashion that he asked the Lord to have the child reveal there before everyone whether his sins had been taken away or not, and he said: "Hear, o Lord, let it be revealed by the mouth of this child, here before all, whether I have atoned for my sins in keeping with your mercy."

Then the child answers: "John, rejoice, for God has forgiven you all your sins, and as a sign of this you will become whole and cleansed of all the filth that is on you. And, therefore, stand up and baptize me in the name of the Holy Trinity."

The Lord then granted a beautiful sign to his beloved friend in keeping with what the child had foretold, for as soon as he stood up, the hair that had grown all over him fell off him as well as the other filth that was on him, so that his entire body and skin were so fair and white as though no hair or dirt had ever been on it. He was then clothed with splendid garments and he then appeared to be once more the most noble among men. Then all who saw this sign praised God. And after this the pope took the child, along with many lords who were to hold it at baptism, and St. John baptized it with devotion.

---

[136] See n. 128.

[137] This entire episode bears a striking resemblance to one in the French lai *Bisclavret*, which was translated into Old Norse, where it is entitled *Bisclaretz ljóð*. In the lai it is a man-turned-werewolf who is ashamed of being seen in his hairy state.

9. Þá eftir þetta sem nú var í frá sagt bað páfinn sankti Jóhannes að ganga með sér til keisarans og sitja nærri honum um daginn til máltíðar og það gjörði hann. Og sem þeir höfðu setið undir borðum nokkura hríð þá, þá mælti sankti Jóhannes til páfans so segjandi: "Kæri faðir, þekkið þér mig nú ekki?"

Páfinn svarar og sagðist ekki neitt þekkja til hans.

Jóhannes sagði þá: "Ég er þín andlegur sonur er þú skírðir og settir mig til skóla og veittir mér mikið lén og so vígðuð þér mig til prests þá ég var sextán vetra. Og kom mér þá í hug að ég mundi vera nógu ungur þar til slíks embættis. Og þá ég hafði sungið mína fyrsta messu, þá fór ég í burtu með leynd og út í eyðimörkina, og sagði ég við sjálfan mig að það væri ekki vel tilheyrilegt og sameiginlegt að ég jafn ungur og gálauss skyldi höndla líkam drottins míns með mínum bernsklegum höndum." Og sagði honum síðan í frá öllu því sem honum hafði til handa borið, frá því fyrsta að hann kom þar og til þess að jagarinn eður veiðimaður keisarans hafði sig þaðan. Og jafn vel greindi hann honum í frá[138] hversu að jungfrúin hafði komið þangað til og so hvernin að hann skildist við hana. Hér ofan á greindi hann og honum í frá að hann hafði farið til fundar við hann og hafði skriftast fyrir honum, sem fyrr segir. Þetta varð keisarinn áheyrsla og féll hans hjarta nærri því hann hugsaði þá þegar um dóttur sína er hann missti og setti það fast í sinn hug að hún mundi fyrir verið hafa og stillti sig þó vel og sagði til sankti Jóhannes: "Munið þér ekki kunna segja nokkurum manni til hvar sá staður væri er sú píkan[139] missti líf sitt er þið talið um so að bein hennar mætti grafast hjá öðrum kristnum mönnum."

Sankti Jóhannes svaraði: "Fyrir víst, herra," sagði hann, "má það vel verða ske með því móti, ef yðvar jagari treystir sér til að finna þann sama stað sem hann fann mig, þá treystir ég <mér> að finna hinn staðinn <sem> hún fórst."

Þá varð jagarinn um þetta fundinn, en hann sagðist mundu vel finna það. Síðan reið sanctus Johannes í mörkina og jagarinn með honum og sem <þeir> komu að steininum er hún var hrundin út fyrir og ætluð fyrir löngu dauða, sem hér fyrir má heyra, þá sat hún nú heil og lífs og ósködd í allan máta. En er Jóhannes sá þetta, þá veit það einn guð hvað glaður hann varð í sínu hjarta og hélt upp sínum höndum til himna lofandi og þakkandi guð<i>

---

[138] On the use of the "pleonastic" *í* before the preposition *frá*, see Bandle, 450–51.

[139] *píka* came into Icelandic from the other Scandinavian languages, but the word derives ultimately from Finnish *piika*. See Westergård-Nielsen, *Låneordene*, 256; Bandle, 273; KW, cxxviii.

9. Then, after what has now been reported, the pope asked St. John to go with him to the emperor and to sit by him during the day at meals, and he did that. And when they had been sitting at table for a while, St. John spoke to the pope and said: "Dear father, don't you recognize me now?"

The pope answers and said that he did not know him.

John then said: "I am your spiritual son whom you baptized and placed in school, and you granted me a large benefice and then ordained me a priest when I was sixteen years old. And it occurred to me then that I was somewhat young for such an office. And when I had said my first Mass, I left secretly and went into the wilderness, and I told myself that it was not appropriate and fitting that, young and careless as I was, I should touch the body of my Lord with my childish hands." And he told him then about everything that had happened to him, from the beginning when he came there up to the time when the emperor's hunter or huntsman took him away from there. And just as thoroughly he told him how the maiden had come there and how he had gotten rid of her. In addition he also told him about how he had gone to see him and had confessed to him, as was told before. The emperor overheard this and his heart was touched, for he thought at once about the daughter whom he had lost and he was convinced that she must have been there,[140] but he remained calm and said to St. John: "Would you not be able to tell someone where that place might be where that young girl you talked about lost her life, so that her body might be buried alongside other Christians?"

St. John answered: "Certainly, lord," he said, "that may very well be; if your hunter trusts himself to find the same place he found me, then I trust that I can find the place she died."

Then the hunter was located, and he said that he could easily find the place. Then St. John rode into the forest and the hunter with him, and when they came to the rock off which she had been pushed and long thought dead, as was heard before, she sat there now safe and sound and completely unhurt. And when John saw this, only God knows how happy his heart became, and he raised his hands to heaven, praising and thanking God for His mercy.

---

[140] The text is somewhat puzzling. The corresponding passage in the *Pass* reads: "do wart em sin herte swaer. vnde dachte. dat ys vorwar myn dochter gewezen" (CCC.xlviii.d, "His heart became heavy and he thought: 'That was surely my daughter'").

sína miskunn. Síðan mælti hann so til hennar: "Hvar fyrir situr <þú> hér," sagði hann, "einsömul í steini þessum?"[141]
Hún svarar og spurði hann eftir hvort hann þekkti sig ekki. En hann sagði nei fyrir. Hún sagði þá: "Minn herra," sagði hún, "ég er sú in sama jungfrúin sem kom til yðvars cella og þér hrunduð burtu frá yður af steininum."
Hann segir: "Hver hefur þá holpið þér það þú hefur lifað so lengi."
Hún svarar: "Guð hefur mig geymt með sinni miskunn og guðlegum almætti so að mig hefur ekki sakað."
Og so væn var hún þá að lít ok líka hennar klæði sem hún væri þar ný komin. Þetta undraði stórlega hann og bauð henni að fara með sér til föður hennar og það gjörði hún. En faðir hennar og móðir fögnuðu þeim þá vel og lofuðu guð fyrir að þau höfðu dóttur fundið aftur. Síðan frétti keisarinn faðir hennar hana eftir hvernin hún hafði farið meðan að hún hefði í burtu verið.
Hún svarar: "Guði er engin hlutur ómögulegur það sem hann vil veita og so vera láta, og er það í fljótu máli yður að segja að mig hefur ekki grandað eður mein gjört, regn eður snjór, eigi frost eður kuldi, eigi heldur hungur eður þorsti, so og eigi heldur ofurhíti eður nokkuð meinlæti af dýrum, fiskum eður fuglum, ormum eður pöddum og öngu öðru. Og þar með læt ég so standa að ég segir yður ekki fleira."
Þessa fagra jarteikn lofuðu margir almáttugan guð fyrir, sem vel verðugt var.

10. Eftir þetta fór páfinn heim aftur í Róm og hafði sanctus Johannes með sér og gjörir síðan boð eftir föður hans og móður og lætur segja þeim að Jóhannes sonur þeirra væri heim <kominn>. En þau urðu full af fagnaði er þau frétta það og fóru til fundar við páfann og sankti Johannem[142] og varð þar mikill fagnaður með þeim. Síðan frétti páfinn Johannem að hversu margar messur er hann hafði sungið. Hann svarar og sagðist ekki sungið hafa fleiri en eina áður en <hann> gekk í eyðimörkina. Páfinn svarar og sagði: "O vei, þú fátæka sál, hvað langa pínu hefur þú og að þola, þar sem ekki er enn lengra komið."
Þá frétti sankti Jóhannes hvað hann meinti með þessu orði. Þá sagði páfinn honum í frá hversu hann heyrði eitt sinni eina sál hrópa og kveina sér og greindi honum að hún hafði sagt sér að hún vissi eina kvinnu hafa nýlega

---

[141] The sentence replicates the *Pass* text: "worumme sittestu hijr allene in deme stene" (CCC.xlix.a, "why are you sitting here alone on this rock?"). When the prepositional phrase was rendered "í steini þessum" the meaning was changed, since Icelandic *in* can here mean only "in," which context shows is incorrect. The MLG preposition *in* had additional meanings, however, including "on" (*MNW*, 2: 352–53), which is how the word is used here.
[142] In this instance, the Icelandic *sankti* occurs with the Latin form of the name.

Then he spoke to her thus: "Why are you sitting here," he said, "all alone on this rock?"[143]

She answers and asked him whether he did not know her. And he said that he did not. She said then: "My lord," she said, "I am the same maiden who came to your cell and whom you pushed off the rock."

He says: "Who has helped you then that you should have stayed alive so long?"

She answers: "God has protected me in His mercy and with His divine power so that nothing has hurt me."

And she was so beautiful in appearance as were her clothes that it seemed as though she had just arrived there. He wondered greatly at this and he asked her to go with him to her father, and she did so. And her father and mother welcomed them and praised God that they had found their daughter again. Then the emperor, her father, asked her how things had gone for her while she was away.

She answers: "Nothing is impossible for God [Luke 1:37], whatever he wants to grant and have happen and, to answer in few words, nothing has harmed or hurt me, neither rain nor snow, neither frost nor cold, neither hunger nor thirst, and not even great heat or trouble from animals, fish or birds, snakes or insects or anything else. And I'll let this suffice and not tell you any more."

Many praised God for this beautiful miracle, as was indeed appropriate.

10. After this the pope went back home to Rome and took St. John along, and he then sends for his father and mother and has them told that their son John had come home. And they became filled with joy when they learned this, and they went to see the pope and St. John and there was much rejoicing among them. Then the pope asked John how many Masses he had said. He answers and says that he had not said more than one before he went into the wilderness. The pope answers and says: "O woe, you poor soul, what long suffering you have had to endure, since there has not been any further progress."

Then St. John asked him what he meant by this statement. The pope then told him about how he had heard a soul crying one time and wailing, and he told him that it had told him that it knew that a woman had recently become

---

[143] Considering the fact that St. John went to the very spot where he had thrown the princess off the rock and that he praised and thanked God when he saw her, his question and subsequent denial that he knows her strike one as odd, to say the least. The same happens in the *Pass* (CCC.xlix.a).

tekið göfugri frukt af sínum manni "og nefndi fyrir mér þessa tvo menn er hér nú standa, og það barn er hún gengi þá með skyldi Jóhannes heita. Og þetta ið sama sagða ég þeim þegar eftirá. En þau játuðu því að so hefði verið. Og fyrir því vígða ég þig so ungan til prests stéttar að nær sem[144] þér hefðuð sungið yðra sextánda messu þá væri hún frelst af öllum pínum, og frá því að guð vildi láta sér sóma að kynna mér til þessa að þér munið þá veita henni hjálp að hún leysist af sínum nauðum."

Hann svarar: "Heilagur faðir," sagði hann, "hvað sem þér viljið mér bjóða þá vil <ég> það fúslega gjöra."

Og söng messu hvern dag eftir annan þar til að sextán voru, en sálin varð frelst eftir því sem páfinn sagði honum áður fyrir.

Og endist þessi historía hér fyrst að sinni um þetta efni af því að sumlegir meistarar vilja segja að hún sé ekki sönn fyrir því að þeir þykkjast ekki so skýrt finna hana í latínu skrifaða sem aðrar historíur.[145] En þó greinir so að í <Italíu>[146] liggur einn mektugur staður er Fenedien heitir og í þessum greindum stað sé honum helguð ein kirkja með eins og historían segir til og hér fyrir greinir. En hvað sannast sem hér um er þá veit það guð best.

---

[144] See Bandle, 457, on the use of *nær sem* as a conjunction.

[145] Corrected from the edition which has *historiar*. The *Pass* has a corresponding passage: "Etlike wyllen dat dysse hystorie nycht waer sy. wente me vindt se nicht in dem latine beschreuen" (CCC.xlix.b "Some say that this story is not true since one does not find it written in Latin").

[146] The manuscript has a space of six letters here (*Rhb* 2:184.34); presumably Björn's source did not name the country and the space was left to be filled in subsequently, once the country had been identified.

pregnant by her husband, "and it named these two people for me who are now standing here, and said that the child she was carrying was to be named John. And I told them the same afterwards. And they confirmed that this was so. And for this reason I ordained you as a priest when you were so young so that when you had said your sixteenth Mass the soul would be freed from all its torments, and also because God saw fit to reveal to me that you would help the soul so that it would be freed from its distress."

He answers: "Holy Father," he said, "whatever you want to command me I will gladly do."

And he said one Mass a day until there were sixteen in all, and the soul was freed in accordance with what the pope had foretold.

And for the present the legend ends here about this matter, concerning which some teachers claim that it is not true because they do not think that it is manifestly written in Latin like other legends. But it reports that a mighty city is found in Italy which is called Venice, and in this city there is a church dedicated to him, just as the legend says and here records. But what the truth in the matter is, God knows best.

Bibliography

Bandle, Oskar. *Die Sprache der Guðbrandsbiblía: Orthographie und Laute Formen.* Bibliotheca Arnamagnæana 17. Copenhagen, 1956.

Braunfels, Wolfgang, ed. *Lexikon der christlichen Ikonographie.* 8 vols. Rome, 1968–1976.

Brown, Peter. *The Body and Society: Men, Women, and Sexual Renunciation in Early Christianity.* New York, 1988.

Cross, F. L., and E. A. Livingstone, eds. *Oxford Dictionary of the Christian Church.* 3rd ed. Oxford, 1997.

Elliott, Dyan. *Spiritual Marriage: Sexual Abstinence in Medieval Wedlock.* Princeton, 1993.

Frank, K. S. "J. Chrysostomos." In *Lexikon des Mittelalters* 5: 63–64. Munich, 1990.

Grimm, Jacob, and Wilhelm Grimm. *Deutsches Wörterbuch.* Leipzig, 1877; reprt. Munich, 1984.

Jón Helgason. *Málið á Nýja Testamenti Odds Gottskálkssonar.* Safn Fræða-fjelagsins 7. Copenhagen, 1929.

Kalinke, Marianne E. *The Book of Reykjahólar: The Last of the Great Medieval Legendaries.* Toronto, 1996.

Karlsson, Stefán. "Ritun Reykjafjarðarbókar. Excursus: Bókagerð bænda." In *Opuscula* 4, 137–40. Bibliotheca Arnamagnæana 30. Copenhagen, 1970.

Loth, Agnete, ed. *Reykjahólabók. Islandske helgenlegender.* 2 vols. Editiones Arnamagnæanæ A:15–16. Copenhagen, 1969.

———. "Et islandsk fragment fra reformationstiden. AM 667, x, 4to." In *Opuscula* 4: 25–30. Bibliotheca Arnamagnæanæ 30. Copenhagen, 1970.

Luther, Martin. "Die Lügend von S. Johanne Chrysostomo. 1537." In *D. Martin Luthers Werke,* Kritische Gesamtausgabe. 50: 48–64. Weimar, 1914.

Mertens, Volker. "Verslegende und Prosalegendar. Zur Prosafassung von Legendenromanen in 'Der Heiligen Leben'." In *Poesie und Gebrauchsliteratur im deutschen Mittelalter,* ed. Volker Honemann et al. 265–89. Wurzburger Colloquium 1978. Tübingen, 1979.

Moser, Dietz-Rüdiger. "Chrysostomus." In *Die deutsche Literatur des Mittelalters: Verfasserlexikon* 1, ed. Kurt Ruh, 1269. 2nd rev. ed. Berlin, 1978.

Overgaard, Mariane, ed. *The History of the Cross-Tree Down to Christ's Passion.* Editiones Arnamagnæanæ B:26. Copenhagen, 1968.

Patetta, Federico. *Di una tavola della R. Galleria Estense con rappresentazioni tolte dalla leggenda di S. Giovanni Boccadoro.* Memorie della R. Accademia di Scienze, Lettere ed Arti in Moderna, ser. 3, 7 (Sezione Arti). Modena, 1907.

Schiller, Karl, and August Lübben. *Mittelniederdeutsches Wörterbuch.* 5 vols. Bremen, 1875–1880; repr. Vaduz, 1986.

Schubring, Paul. "Die Chrysostomus-Legende." *Zeitschrift für Bildende Kunst* n.F. 24 (1913): 109–12.

Veturlíði Óskarsson. *Middelnedertyske låneord i islandsk diplomsprog frem til år 1500.* Uppsala, 2001.

Westergård-Nielsen, Christian. *Låneordene i det 16. århundredes trykte islandske litteratur.* Bibliotheca Arnamagnæana 6. Copenhagen, 1946.

Widding, Ole, and Hans Bekker-Nielsen. "En senmiddelalderlig legendesamling." *Maal og minne* (1960): 105–28.

———. "Low German Influence on Late Icelandic Hagiography." *Germanic Review* 37 (1962): 237–62.

Williams, Charles Allyn. *The German Legends of the Hairy Anchorite.* Illinois Studies in Language and Literature 18. Urbana, 1935.

Williams-Krapp, Werner. *Die deutschen und niederländischen Legendare des Mittelalters: Studien zu ihrer Überlieferungs-, Text- und Wirkungsgeschichte.* Tübingen, 1986.

Wimmer, Otto, and Hartmann Melzer. *Lexikon der Namen und Heiligen.* Innsbruck, 1984.

Wolf, Kirsten, ed. *Saga heilagrar Önnu.* Stofnun Árna Magnússonar á Íslandi, Rit 52. Reykjavík, 2001.

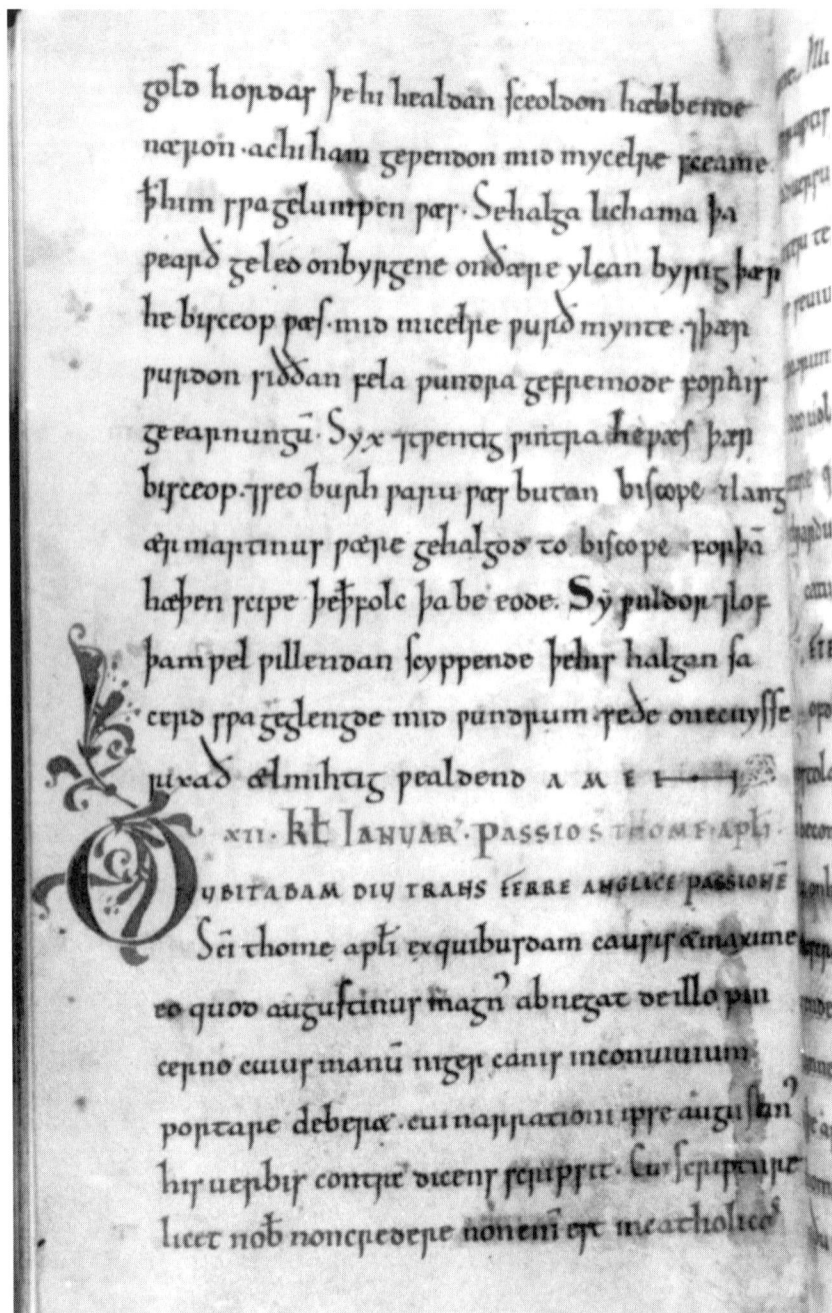

Figure 6.1: BL Cotton Caligula A. xiv, fol. 111v (*by permission of the British Library*)

THE AUDIENCE OF ÆLFRIC'S *LIVES OF SAINTS* AND THE FACE OF COTTON CALIGULA A. XIV, FOLS. 93–130

JONATHAN WILCOX

Part way down folio 111v of British Library, MS. Cotton Caligula A. xiv, resting against the final flourish of a closing *amen* at line 13, lies a small ink drawing of a head. Bearded, and calmly smiling, the head looks out at the manuscript's reader. Fitting neatly into the writing block, only slightly larger than a regular character, and in the same color ink, the head discreetly occupies a small space on the right of the page [see figure 7.1]. This modest drawing does not immediately catch the eye, which is drawn instead to the effusive initial in the left margin. That display capital, considerably enlarged and ornamented with foliate patterns of a type common in late Anglo-Saxon manuscripts, serves a familiar function in the layout of the page: the assertion of the opening of a new item. It enters into the hierarchy of beginnings and endings signaled through other visual elements at this point: the extended fancy capitals of the *AMEN*, the red display script of the following rubric, the subsequent line in capitals, and the enlarged initial at the start of the next line. To all this characteristic paratextual work, the head is a supplement, not necessary to the function of the texts and easily overlooked.[1] Yet it surely has some significance for those who would return its gaze.

Phillip Pulsiano was not one to overlook such an intriguing detail. One hallmark of Phill's work was a meticulous eye for the minutiae of manuscripts, as well as an appreciation for the unlikely and the offbeat. My essay in honor of Phill will accordingly begin by contemplating the significance

---

[1] It is not mentioned in the published descriptions of the manuscript, namely Humphrey Wanley, *Librorum vett. septentrionalium, qui in Angliae Bibliothecis extant . . . Catalogus Historico-Criticus* (Oxford, 1705), 190; *A Catalogue of the Manuscripts in the Cottonian Library Deposited in the British Museum* (London, 1802); N. R. Ker, *Catalogue of Manuscripts Containing Anglo-Saxon* (Oxford, 1957), no. 138 (172–73).

of this offbeat and minor manuscript detail. In doing so, I will place it in the context of other incongruous faces and heads that peer out of Anglo-Saxon manuscripts more often than one might expect. The head in Cotton Caligula A. xiv lies between two of Ælfric's *Lives of Saints*. Gazing back at the head provides one tiny clue for tackling the vexed question of the use made of *Lives of Saints*. There is something puzzling about the dissemination of *Lives of Saints* — a puzzle that I will tackle head-on in this essay, grounding my discussion in a consideration of the materiality of manuscripts and their circulation, a materiality that was at the center of Phill's work. Pondering this puzzle will allow me to construct the reading communities of Anglo-Saxon England likely to have engaged with this vernacular pious reading matter.[2]

Cotton Caligula A.XIV, fols. 93–130

British Library, MS. Cotton Caligula A. xiv, fols. 93–130, is a fragmentary manuscript written at an unknown place of origin in the middle of the eleventh century. It was bound together with an unrelated neumed Latin hymnal, the Illustrated Cotton Troper, presumably in early modern times. Its five surviving quires contain two of Ælfric's *Lives of Saints*: the Life of St. Martin (Skeat xxxi) for 11 November, lacking both the opening and a single folio within the text and now bound partly out of order (the fragment begins on fols. 125r–130v, after which one folio is missing, and continues on fols. 93r–111v) and the Life of St. Thomas (Skeat xxxvi) for 21 December (on fols. 111v–121v).[3] These are followed by the fragmentary opening of an anonymous Life of St. Mildred for 13 July (fols. 121v–124v).[4] While this particular vernacular version is unique, it is part of an extended legend concerning Mildred and other Kentish royal saints that circulated widely in Latin and the vernacular in late Anglo-Saxon England.[5] The fragment thus seems to preserve part of

---

[2] My thanks to Nick Doane, Denise Filios, Malcolm Godden, and Stacy Klein for suggestions about versions of this essay.

[3] Ed. W. W. Skeat, *Ælfric's Lives of Saints*, EETS, o.s. 76, 82, 94, 114 (London, 1881–1900; repr. as 2 vols., 1966).

[4] Ed. Oswald Cockayne, *Leechdoms, Wortcunning, and Starcraft of Early England*, vol. 3 (London, 1866), 422–29, and by M. J. Swanton, "A Fragmentary Life of St. Mildred and Other Kentish Royal Saints," *Archæologia Cantiana* 91 (1976 [for 1975]): 15–27.

[5] See D. W. Rollason, *The Mildrith Legend: A Study in Early Medieval Hagiography in England* (Leicester, 1982). Rollason suggests the script of the Caligula fragment is "similar to that which N. R. Ker assigns to Exeter" although Ker refrains from making such an identification (*Mildrith*, 30).

an unordered collection of vernacular saints' lives drawn from Ælfric's *Lives of Saints*. This type of book survives a few times from Anglo-Saxon England, as will be seen below, but its form presents a number of puzzles that will be addressed in this essay.

The head comes between Ælfric's Lives of Martin and Thomas. This version of Martin survives in two other manuscripts, BL MS. Cotton Julius E. vii, and, in modified form, Oxford, Bodleian Library, MS. Bodley 343 (the manuscripts are described in more detail below), but in neither other case is a head drawn at the end. The Life of Thomas survived in three other manuscripts. It is preceded by a Latin note, as here, in Julius E. vii and in BL, MS. Cotton Vitellius D. xvii, while it also circulated without the note in Cambridge, University Library, MS. Ii. 1. 33. In none of these cases is a head drawn at its head.

Heads and Faces in Anglo-Saxon Manuscripts

The head in BL Cotton Caligula A. xiv, fol. 111v, is not the same as the fantastic marginal drolleries — the babewyns and grotesques — that are such a characteristic part of Gothic manuscript illumination. From the late twelfth century onwards, carnivalesque elements riot in the margins of illuminated manuscripts in ironic and complex interplay with the text of the pages they occupy. These later forms have been the subject of significant scholarly attention.[6] The head under consideration here predates such developed and profuse marginal manuscript play and is far more restrained.[7]

Even before the Gothic proliferation of marginalia, Anglo-Saxon England certainly produced a fair share of richly decorated manuscripts. Cotton Caligula A. xiv belongs to a different tradition, however. It is a plain, workaday Anglo-Saxon manuscript in which the text is presented without the aid of a program of illustrations. Accordingly, the head is apparently less fundamental than such a decorative element in an illuminated manuscript. Yet it is far from unparalleled in other unilluminated manuscripts. Indeed, there is a surprising profusion of such figures in workaday Anglo-Saxon manuscripts.

---

[6] Most notably Michael Camille, *Image on the Edge: The Margins of Medieval Art* (London, 1992), and Lilian M.C. Randall, *Images in the Margins of Gothic Manuscripts* (Berkeley, 1966).

[7] For a reading of faces in a fourteenth-century literary manuscript, see Paul F. Reichardt, "Paginal Eyes: Faces Among the Ornamented Capitals of MS Cotton Nero A.x, Art. 3," *Manuscripta* 36 (1992): 22–36, who reads the faces as more literal pointers to particular passages.

Occasionally such drawings provide straightforward illustration. Two figures in CCCC 9, a copy of the Cotton-Corpus legendary from the second quarter of the eleventh century, are squeezed into the right of the text block on a single line at fol. 13r, column a, for example. These ink drawings have been added by a correcting and glossing hand of the second half of the eleventh century to an originally blank line end. The figures, one of whom is lacking an eye, are identified in a caption as Hysimbardus and Wyngardus, two characters described in the following text within the *De miraculis Sancti Saluii*.[8] A scribe who made interlinear entries in this text chose to provide a miniature illustration of this scene in a blank line end.

More often, though, the figures are puzzling and apparently unrelated to the surrounding text. The Corpus Sedulius, CCCC 173, part II, written in the second half of the eighth century, has a series of heads, faces, and body parts drawn in ink and in drypoint in the margin, probably in the ninth or tenth century.[9] The manuscript was used as a classbook, with many glosses in both Latin and Old English, and in the course of such use apparently acquired sketches unrelated to the text of Sedulius's *Paschale Carmen*. In another example, a copy of Archbishop Wulfstan's Commonplace Book, CCCC 265, part I, written in the middle and second half of the eleventh century, probably at Worcester, has three marginal sketches of human heads added in the second half of the eleventh century or in the twelfth century.[10] One (on p. 197) is a bichrome ink drawing, partly painted; two further (on pp. 303 and 325) are ink drawings resembling in size and detail the drawing in Caligula A. xiv, although more clearly separated from the text block in the margin [figure 7.1].

Such figures as these have received little attention in the scholarly literature. Examples from manuscripts at Corpus Christi College Cambridge are admirably inventoried and described in Mildred Budny's catalogue, if with little discussion of their significance, but many more surely exist in other manuscript collections, unremarked in the scholarly literature. In one such case, a face has been drawn into an initial *O* of MS Copenhagen, Kongelige Bibliotek, Gamle Kongelige Sammlung 1595, another copy of Wulfstan's commonplace book from the eleventh century, at fol. 15r. The codicology and palaeography of this manuscript are described at length by its recent editors,

[8] See Mildred Budny, *Insular, Anglo-Saxon, and Early Anglo-Norman Manuscript Art at Corpus Christi College, Cambridge: An Illustrated Catalogue*, 2 vols. (Kalamazoo, 1997), description at 1: 619–20; illustrated at 2: 567.
[9] Described by Budny, *Illustrated Catalogue*, at 1: 84–87; illus. at 2: 10–21.
[10] Described by Budny, *Illustrated Catalogue*, at 1: 607–8; illus. at 2: 552, 558, 559.

& diacon̄ secutur̄. & sic pcedat sacerdos inchorū
ducentib; eū duob; presbiteris. Apud quosdā alius
subdiacomb; pcedentib; ille qui lectione lecturus̄ē
cū euangło. retro diacon̄ epm pcedit. Coram q̄ duo
acoliti cū candelabris uns q: cū tribulo ante cedunt.
Quib; utiq: inhoc consentiendū eē uolunt. acoliti
ut inchorū uenerint cū candelabris se diuidant.
quatuor indextrā. tres insinistra. sic diacon̄ facian̄.
Subdiacom̄ aut̄ ut inchorū uenerint. quasi quadā
linea porrecti. inclinent se cora altari. et quatuor
indextro corum. in insinistro consistant. Pontifex
aut̄ post quā in medietat̄ chori pducitur. prbisq̄ eū
ducebant & diaconis mari et osculantib; ppria q: repe-
tentib; loca. inclinans se. dm ppeccatis suis depcetur.
Tunc erectus. pmū duob; prbis deinde diaconis pacis
oscula dabit. Inquibus dā locis usus̄ē & consuetudo.
ut his finitis. minister cū tribulo subdiaconū eugłm
postant̄ē ante cedat ad altare. In aliis inueniun̄
non incensum poni ante q oblationes altari sup po-
nantur. his pactis. cū gloria cantatur. eps ducendus̄ē
ad supiore gradū. non ad altare. Inquo loco gressus̄ē
figendus. quousq: oms osculentur. Post quā in altiora
ascendent. glā patri canentib; & subdiaconis in
chorū reuestentib; . quatuor indextro choro trib;
insinistro standū erit. Quib; finitis uersus cantat̄.
&pontifex usq: ad medietat̄ē altaris ducendus est.

but they make no mention of this face — an omission all the more striking as it is reproduced in color as the frontispiece to the facsimile.[11]

Similar examples occur in vernacular as well as Latin manuscripts. The Old English translation of Bede in CCCC 41, written in the first half of the eleventh century, has a disembodied head drawn in ink to the left of the writing block at p. 410. This head, like that in Caligula A. xiv, is one line high and drawn at an angle, although here facing downwards rather than up and without a beard. It was drawn in the first half of the eleventh century before the marginal homiletic text was added, as Budny shows [figure 7.2].[12] It bears no obvious specific relation to the text, which recounts the return from death of Dryhthelm (*Ecclesiastical History* V.13). The margins of CCCC 162, a collection of homilies of the end of the tenth or beginning of the eleventh century from southeastern England, have been used, probably in the eleventh century, to sketch a series of part-length and full-length figures, male and female, ecclesiastical and secular, in plummet, ink, or drypoint throughout the later part of the manuscript.[13] The sketches, including a small head on p. 301, seem unrelated to the homilies they share the page with. In all these examples, the drawings are unaccounted for and seem external to the use of the manuscripts' texts. An angelic head in the Exeter Book is drawn in drypoint in the margin beside *The Wanderer*; although the angel might be thematically related to the end of that poem, the fact that it is in drypoint means that it is not easily visible and therefore not a major signifying part of the visual program of the manuscript.[14]

An example which has received more scholarly attention illustrates well the conundrums such drawings present. CCCC 57 is a Latin copy of the Rule of St. Benedict and associated monastic texts written in insular minuscule at the end of the tenth or beginning of the eleventh century, perhaps at Canterbury, and subsequently used at Abingdon. In a careful description, Timothy Graham has concluded: "Through the character of its contents and the evidence for its use, the manuscript can justly claim to be the outstanding surviving

---

[11] *The Copenhagen Wulfstan Collection: Copenhagen Kongelige Bibliotek, Gl. Kgl. Sam. 1595*, ed. James E. Cross and Jennifer Morrish Tunberg, Early English Manuscripts in Facsimile 25 (Copenhagen, 1993).

[12] Described by Budny, *Illustrated Catalogue*, at 1: 522; illus. at 2: 438.

[13] Described by Budny, *Illustrated Catalogue*, at 1: 470–73 (and see 465–66); illus. at 2: 344–81.

[14] Exeter Cathedral Library, MS. 3501, fol. 78r, illustrated in a drawing by A. Morris in Patrick W. Conner, *Anglo-Saxon Exeter: A Tenth-Century Cultural History* (Cambridge, 1993), plate XVII.

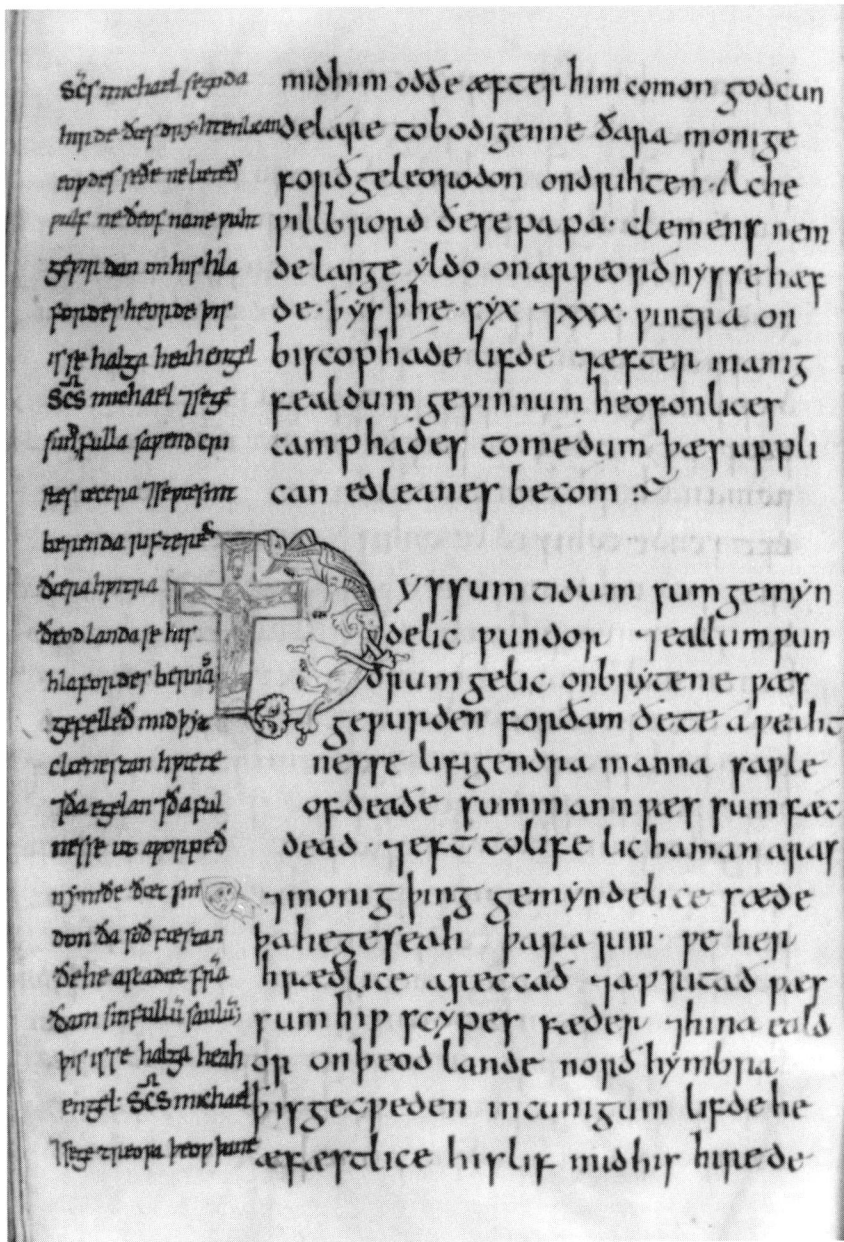

Figure 7.2: CCCC 41, p. 410 (*by permission of the Master and Fellows of Corpus Christi College, Cambridge*)

example of an Anglo-Saxon chapter-house book."[15] Yet this sober and serious book includes a series of faces drawn in ink into the bow of numerous enlarged capital letters throughout the manuscript [figure 7.3].[16] Some of these heads are clearly tonsured, presenting the monk who read this copy of the monastic rule with the returning gaze of a representation of himself comically peeking out from the hortatory text. This manuscript also contains a number of subsequent drypoint sketches of figures, including a scene on fol. 152r characterized by Budny as "Comic group of human or demonic figures."[17] Such drypoint work is by its very nature not central to the impact of the manuscript since it is not easily visible. The faces, on the other hand, are far more integral to the text's appearance and, apparently, to its production. In a more conventional feature of eleventh-century manuscript production, the initial letters are often highlighted through an infilling of coloration, here in yellow pigment. By examining one such case through a microscope, Graham is able to establish that the drawing of the face preceded the infilling, suggesting that the faces were an early part of the conception of the look of the manuscript, not the addition of some mischief-maker.[18] Indeed, they are so fundamental to the conception of the manuscript that a replacement leaf, carefully supplied in the middle of the eleventh century, adds a head to the curve of the the initial S written in red as the beginning of a chapter heading at fol. 22r.[19]

Graham concludes of this manuscript that it was used for reading aloud in the meeting of monks in the chapter-house and probably also for private contemplation in the course of a monk's study. In neither case does a smiling face peering from the capital letters seem particularly appropriate, yet in pondering the use of an Anglo-Saxon manuscript, we need to consider its impact, heads and all. What did the reciting monk make of the heads looking up at him from within the text? It is hard to believe that they were intended to serve the same function as the smiling face that accompanies the imprecation to SMILE! SMILE! SMILE! on a local supermarket check-out as the clerk makes a customer's change. What did the monk engaged in private study reflect from

---

[15] Timothy Graham, "Cambridge Corpus Christi College 57 and its Anglo-Saxon Users," in *Anglo-Saxon Manuscripts and their Heritage*, ed. Phillip Pulsiano and Elaine M. Treharne (Aldershot, 1998), 21–69, here 54.

[16] Graham, "Cambridge Corpus Christi College 57," describes such faces as occurring on fols. 11v, 12r, 12v, 108v, 124v, 144v, 146v, 147r, and 160r. They are described also by Budny, *Illustrated Catalogue*, at 1: 449–53; illust. at 2: 297–320.

[17] Budny, *Illustrated Catalogue*, 1: 453.

[18] Graham, "Cambridge Corpus Christi College 57," 29.

[19] See Graham, "Cambridge Corpus Christi College 57," 30 and Budny, *Illustrated Catalogue*, at 1: 449; illus. at 2: 300.

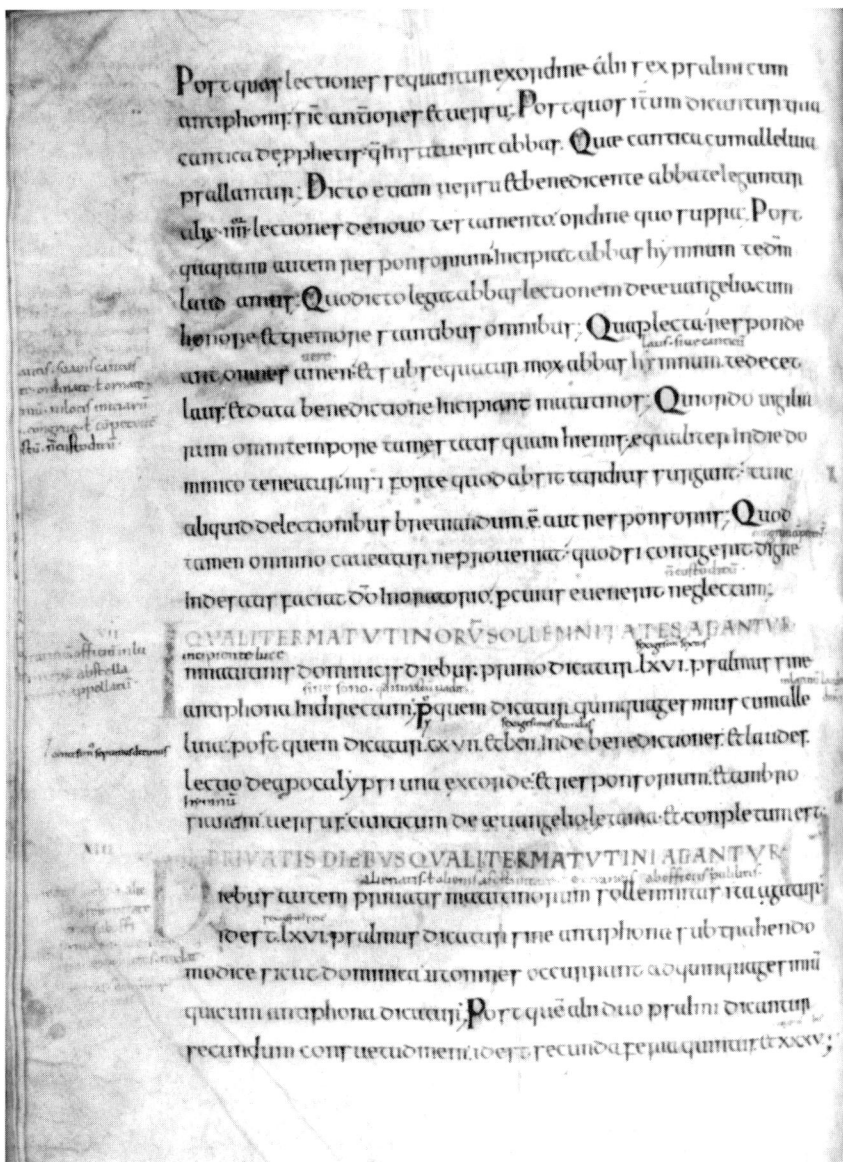

Figure 7.3: CCCC 57, fol. 12v (*by permission of the Master and Fellows of Corpus Christi College, Cambridge*)

such playful faces? Such a private reader seems a slightly more likely audience for these figures than the public reciter since, at the least, he could pause to gaze and reflect, while the reciter needed to just keep reading.

One final example is worth considering because it occurs in another manuscript of *Lives of Saints*. Cambridge, University Library, MS. Ii. 1. 33 includes two heads at the foot of fol. 153v, drawn in a light-washed ink similar to that of scribbles and circles in the opposite margin. These are very different in style from the head in Caligula A. xiv and it is hard to say when they were added. These heads will be worth revisiting because they occur in a manuscript of *Lives of Saints*.

The head in Caligula A. xiv is not, then, an especially unusual feature, even if its purpose, like that of many of its parallels, is enigmatic. It may offer a hint regarding the use of the manuscript. To pursue that hint, it is necessary to consider the use of the texts it lies among, a book of vernacular saints' lives based upon Ælfric's *Lives of Saints*. The uses of such a collection should be recoverable since there are multiple surviving copies, written mostly by a known author, who expressed his intentions in prefaces to his works. I will next consider the circulation and use of Ælfric's *Lives of Saints* before returning to specific consideration of the use of Caligula A. xiv and the meaning of its head.

Circulation of Ælfric's *Lives of Saints*

Ælfric's *Lives of Saints* survive in far fewer manuscripts than do his two series of *Catholic Homilies*. Thirty-four manuscripts or fragments survive of the first series of *Catholic Homilies*, for example, two of which come from Ælfric's own scriptorium, while that collection's editor infers the existence of a further fifty lost manuscripts.[20] Twenty-seven manuscripts and fragments of the second series of *Catholic Homilies* survive. Saints' lives from *Lives of Saints*, on the other hand, survive (or once survived) in only eleven manuscripts, four of which contain very few saints' lives in a predominately homiletic context, while seven may have been predominately hagiographic. No manuscript survives from Ælfric's own scriptorium and, as a consequence, it is not possible fully to recreate Ælfric's intentions for the series. The best text is that in BL Cotton Julius E. vii, which preserves the prefaces and some twenty-nine works by Ælfric for the sanctorale, but demonstrably fails to reproduce

---

[20] Peter Clemoes, ed., *Ælfric's Catholic Homilies: the First Series*, EETS, s.s. 17 (Oxford, 1997), 134–68.

his intentions since it includes four non-Ælfrician items, despite his request in the preface that any copiest "þær na mare betwux ne sette þonne we awendon."[21] It also includes non-hagiographic pieces by Ælfric that may or may not have been part of the original conception, in addition to three further works saved at the end.[22]

The circulation of Ælfric's *Lives of Saints* has been catalogued in a pair of articles by Joyce Hill.[23] As she shows, the seven manuscripts containing any extensive range of material from the *Lives of Saints* collection, in approximate chronological order, are:

- BL Cotton Julius E. vii, written at the beginning of the eleventh century at an unknown center and later at Bury St. Edmunds;

- Cambridge, Queens' College (Horne) 75 and Bloomington, Lilly Library, Poole 10: binding fragments from the beginning of the eleventh century, place of origin and provenance unknown;

- BL Royal 8 c. vii, fols. 1 and 2: binding fragments from the beginning of the eleventh century, place of origin and provenance unknown;

- BL Cotton Otho B. x, written in the first half of the eleventh century, place of origin and provenance unknown;

- BL Cotton Vitellius D. xvii, fols. 4–92, written in the middle of the eleventh century, place of origin and provenance unknown;

---

[21] The preface is ed. Jonathan Wilcox, *Ælfric's Prefaces*, Durham Medieval Texts (Durham, 1994), as Preface 5b; quoted from lines 33–34: "may not place any more among them than we have translated." All citations of Ælfric's prefaces are from this edition.

[22] See Ker, *Catalogue*, no. 162; Peter Clemoes, "The Chronology of Ælfric's Works," in *The Anglo-Saxons: Studies in Some Aspects of their History and Culture Presented to Bruce Dickins*, ed. idem (London, 1959), 212–47; and Roland Torkar, "Zu den Vorlagen der altenglischen Handschrift Cotton Julius E. vii," *Neuphilologische Mitteilungen* 72 (1971): 711–15.

[23] Joyce Hill, "The Dissemination of Ælfric's Lives of Saints: A Preliminary Survey," in *Holy Men and Holy Women: Old English Prose Saints' Lives and Their Contexts*, ed. Paul E. Szarmach (Albany, NY, 1996), 235–59, and eadem, "The Preservation and Transmission of Ælfric's Saints' Lives: Reader-Response in the Early Middle Ages," in *The Preservation and Transmission of Anglo-Saxon Culture*, ed. Paul E. Szarmach and Joel T. Rosenthal (Kalamazoo, 1997), 405–30. See also Hill's article in this volume, 27–40.

- BL Cotton Caligula A. xiv, fols. 93–130, from the middle of the eleventh century, place of origin and provenance unknown;

- Cambridge, University Library, Ii. 1. 33, written in the second half of the twelfth century, place of origin possibly Canterbury, provenance perhaps Ely.[24]

Three of these manuscripts are fragments, and the two sets of binding fragments, in particular, provide only the tiniest glimpses of circulation. Two others fared badly in modern times: Otho B. x and Vitellius D. xvii were both largely destroyed by the fire at the Cotton library in 1731. Enough survives to indicate that they were fairly full collections, although Vitellius D. xvii, in particular, combined *Lives of Saints* material with homilies on saints drawn from *Catholic Homilies*. Neither manuscript seems particularly close to Ælfric's intentions for the series, since both lack the prefaces. Ii. 1. 33 is a radically reorganized late collection, also mixing *Lives of Saints* items with homilies from the two series of *Catholic Homilies*. Slight use is made of hagiographic items from *Lives of Saints* in four further homiletic manuscripts, while the non-hagiographic items circulated somewhat more widely in further homiletic collections.[25]

It is striking that Ælfric's *Lives of Saints* are preserved for the most part in manuscripts that are puzzling in their circulation: most are of unknown origin or provenance. Little work has been done on the textual relations of these manuscripts, a project vitiated by the parlous state of most of the texts and by the lack of a fully collated edition. Both Skeat and Ker point to the particular closeness of the text in Caligula A. xiv to that in Julius E. vii,[26] and the two manuscripts do, indeed, share a number of errors not shared by CUL Ii.

---

[24] William Schipper, "A Composite Old English Homiliary from Ely: Cambr. Univ. MS Ii.1.33," *Transactions of the Cambridge Bibliographical Society* 8 (1983): 285–98, argues for Ely origin and provenance, but such an origin is convincingly refuted by Elaine M. Treharne, "The Dates and Origins of Three Twelfth-Century Old English Manuscripts," in *Anglo-Saxon Manuscripts and Their Heritage*, ed. Pulsiano and eadem, 227–53, here 240–44, who establishes instead a south-eastern origin. More recently, Oliver Martin Traxel, "Language, Writing and Textual Interference in Post-Conquest Old English Manuscripts: The Scribal Evidence of Cambridge, University Library, Ii. 1. 33" (unpublished Ph.D. dissertation, Cambridge University, 2000), argues for an East Midlands origin of one booklet, a probable St. Augustine's, Canterbury, origin for the bulk of the manuscript, and a possible later Ely provenance.

[25] As Hill shows, "Dissemination," particularly at 243–47.

[26] *Lives of Saints*, 2: xv, and *Catalogue*, 173.

1. 33,[27] but Caligula A. xiv is unlikely to be a direct copy of Julius E. vii since it does not reproduce an error in the arrangement of chapters within the Life of Martin.[28] The manuscript evidence suggests that *Lives of Saints* circulated in a more restricted manner than *Catholic Homilies*, and apparently in less well-known centers.

Ælfric's *Lives of Saints*: The Question of Use

While the place of origin and provenance of most *Lives of Saints* manuscripts presents a puzzle, a yet more fundamental puzzle is presented by the question of the use of the series. Even though the two series of *Catholic Homilies* include a number of saints' lives,[29] the intended use of *Catholic Homilies* is strikingly different from that of *Lives of Saints*. It will be handy to briefly review the case of *Catholic Homilies* before returning to consider the use of *Lives of Saints*.

Ælfric's *Catholic Homilies* provide pieces for preaching in church on a Sunday or a saint's festival, in two series. Ælfric's intentions are made explicit in the prefaces. Here he initiates their circulation by sending them to Sigeric, the archbishop of Canterbury, expecting them to be recited by the ministers of God to the faithful in church over the course of a year.[30] Such intentions are evident stylistically in the homiletic voice and the exhortation that runs throughout the homilies, in the frequent allusions within them to the preaching context, and in the consistent short length of the pieces. Occasional other uses are suggested by a few other clues. A note preserved at the end of the preface to the first series in CUL, Gg. 3. 28 records a direction for Ealdorman Æthelweard to receive a special copy with 44 rather than 40 pieces.[31] Perhaps Æthelweard used his copy for private reading — and hence his desire for an advance publication copy of four additional pieces — although he might

---

[27] These include two inappropriate semantic substitutions, namely *scipa* for *scira* at line 30 and *wundrigende* for *wuldrigende* at line 233, and a grammatical error, namely *adræfde* for *adræfdon* at line 260; see Skeat, *Lives of Saints*, 2: 401, 414, 415.

[28] Julius E. vii misnumbers chapter xiv as a second xiii.

[29] There are 19 items for the sanctorale in *Catholic Homilies* I and 15 or 16 in *Catholic Homilies* II, as is shown by Michael Lapidge, "Ælfric's Sanctorale," in *Holy Men and Holy Women*, ed. Szarmach, 115–29.

[30] Ed. Wilcox, Preface 1a, lines 18–20. On the rhetorical form of the prefaces, see Mark Griffith, "Ælfric's Preface to Genesis: Genre, Rhetoric and the Origins of the *Ars dictaminis*," *Anglo-Saxon England* 29 (2000): 215–34.

[31] Ed. Wilcox, Preface 1b, 92–94.

also have had the homilies read out to his household in a pseudo-liturgical manner. A few notes in Latin preserved in manuscripts close to Ælfric show that he anticipated some readers literate in Latin for whom further explanation was appropriate. At places Ælfric anticipated a mixed audience including monks, nuns, and secular priests, in addition to the laity, and Malcolm Godden detects increasing concern for the clergy in the second series.[32] Nevertheless, the principal use for the homilies is clear. Ælfric explicitly spelled out the obligation of priests to preach in the vernacular in his pastoral letters written for Bishop Wulfsige and Archbishop Wulfstan.[33] That such a performance in church was in fact the primary use of the homiletic series is seen in their distribution: massive dissemination from Canterbury saw copies of the homilies going to centers throughout England.[34] The audience for them was implicitly a range of social classes, both men and women, gathered in a church on a Sunday or a saint's festival. The performance of these homilies in churches across the country must have contributed to a novel sense of national unity.[35]

Such is precisely not the performance context for *Lives of Saints*. Ælfric is explicit in his preface to this series that these works are for those saints not celebrated with secular church festivals, in contradistinction to the lives provided in the two series of *Catholic Homilies*:

> Nam memini me in duobus anterioribus libris posuisse passiones vel vitas sanctorum ipsorum quos gens ista caelebre colit cum veneratione festi diei, et placuit nobis in isto codicello ordinare passiones etiam vel vitas sanctorum illorum quos non vulgus sed coenobite officiis venerantur. (Preface 5a, 5–9)

> For I remember having set forth in two previous books the passions and lives of those saints which this people commonly honor with the veneration of a feast day, and it has pleased us in this little book to arrange the passions and lives of those saints which the monks and not the laity honor with offices.

---

[32] Malcolm Godden, "The Development of Ælfric's Second Series of *Catholic Homilies*," *English Studies* 54 (1973): 209–16.

[33] "Se mæssepreost sceal secgan Sunnandagum and mæssedagum þæs godspelles angyt on englisc þam folce": Letter for Wulfsige, §61, ed. Dorothy Whitelock, *Councils and Synods I.i: 871–1066* (Oxford, 1961), 191–226, here 208; "Se mæssepreost sceal mannum bodian þone soþan geleafan 7 hym larspel secgan": First Old English Letter for Wulfstan, §175, ed. Whitelock, *Councils and Synods*, 294.

[34] See Clemoes, *The First Series*, 134–68.

[35] See further J. Wilcox, "Ælfric in Dorset and the Landscape of Pastoral Care," in *Pastoral Care in Late Anglo-Saxon England*, ed. Francesca Tinti (Woodbridge, 2005), 55–62.

He makes effectively the same statement in the Old English preface, stressing that these are passions and lives "þe mynstermenn mid heora þenungum betwux him wurðiað" (5b, 9–10, "which people in monasteries honor among their services").

Such monastic celebration of saints' days is abundantly attested. It is enjoined by the Benedictine Rule and by the *Regularis Concordia*.[36] Record of such observance is preserved in Ælfric's own consuetudinary, the so-called Letter to the Monks of Eynsham, including liturgical reading for those feasts not observed by the laity.[37] Passionals and legendaries containing Latin lives used in such a context survive from the eleventh century and later.[38] Especially important is the Cotton-Corpus legendary, which, augmented with English lives, provided the likely source for most of Ælfric's sanctorale.[39] Yet Ælfric's *Lives of Saints* do not fit in such a context: in a monastery, such reading should be in Latin. Ælfric's act of translation makes these lives available outside the realm of monastic *literati*, precisely where there is no obvious performance context for such lives.

The non-liturgical nature of the saints' lives within *Lives of Saints* is evident in the style of the pieces. They lack much of the exhortation that is such a marker of Ælfric's homiletic voice, often providing instead apparently unmediated narrative. Their unhomiletic nature is well illustrated by one of the lives that survives in Caligula A. xiv. Martin is the only saint with a life in both *Catholic Homilies* and *Lives of Saints*.[40] The version in *Catholic Homilies* (CH II.xxxiv) radically abbreviates the sources — Sulpicius Severus and

---

[36] *Rule of St. Benedict*, chap. 14; *Regularis Concordia: The Monastic Agreement*, ed. Thomas Symons (London, 1953), chap. 54.

[37] *Ælfric's Letter to the Monks of Eynsham*, ed. Christopher A. Jones, CSASE 24 (Cambridge, 1998), §55: "In aliis uero festiuitatibus quas populus non celebrat"; see also §73 for a requirement to read saints' lives, and Jones's notes to both provisions.

[38] Helmut Gneuss, "Liturgical Books in Anglo-Saxon England and their Old English Terminology," in *Learning and Literature in Anglo-Saxon England: Studies Presented to Peter Clemoes on the Occasion of his Sixty-Fifth Birthday* (Cambridge, 1985), 91–141 lists four surviving collections with discussion at 125–27.

[39] See Patrick H. Zettel, "Saints' Lives in Old English: Latin Manuscripts and Vernacular Accounts: Ælfric," *Peritia* 1 (1982): 17–37; and Peter Jackson and Michael Lapidge, "The Contents of the Cotton-Corpus Legendary," in *Holy Men and Holy Women*, ed. Szarmach, 131–46.

[40] Stephen the protomartyr receives two treatments, one in *Catholic Homilies* I and one in *Catholic Homilies* II, but no other saint receives more than one life, even though sanctorale items like Christmas are provided with multiple works. See, further, Lapidge, "Ælfric's Sanctorale."

Gregory of Tours largely mediated through Alcuin — so that the account of Martin's life and death "on ðisum dæge" (line 328) takes 332 lines of a modern edition. This version is well adapted for preaching in the context of the saint's festival. The account in *Lives of Saints* (LS xxxi), by contrast, translates the sources far more fully, taking 1495 lines of a modern edition, presented in fifty-five numbered chapters, which would be unwieldy for recitation within a service and more suited to either contemplative reading or recital in a relaxed and extended context, such as over a meal.[41]

Anglo-Saxon Reading

The most common assumption about *Lives of Saints* is that they are narrative reading pieces.[42] This is an interesting but complicated suggestion in the context of transitional literacy occurring in late Anglo-Saxon England. Recent theoretical work has convincingly challenged a model that sees literacy as a radical and abrupt shift and replaced it with a model of developing restricted literacies.[43] The very idea of narrative reading pieces begs the question of who was doing the reading and how.

One obvious possibility within Anglo-Saxon England is the monastery, and the reading practices of monasteries are well documented and have been the subject of much discussion.[44] Monastic practice based on the Benedictine Rule required monks to engage in private devotional reading, providing for extended reading time during the day, and such provisions are repeated in

[41] Ed. Godden, *Second Series*, 288–97, and Skeat, *Lives of Saints*, 2: 218–312, respectively, although it should be noted that Godden edits Ælfric's rhythmical prose as continuous prose whereas Skeat edits it in separated lines. For a careful reading of Ælfric's distinctive weighting of his sources in the two lives, see Frederick M. Biggs, "Ælfric as Historian: His Use of Alcuin's *Laudationes* and Sulpicius's *Dialogues* in his Two Lives of Martin," in *Holy Men and Holy Women*, ed. Szarmach, 289–315.

[42] As suggested by Clemoes, "Chronology."

[43] See, especially, Kathryn A. Lowe, "Lay Literacy in Anglo-Saxon England and the Development of the Chirograph," in *Anglo-Saxon Manuscripts and their Heritage*, ed. Pulsiano and Treharne, 161–204.

[44] On reading in Anglo-Saxon England, see Nicholas Howe, "The Cultural Construction of Reading in Anglo-Saxon England," in *The Ethnography of Reading*, ed. Jonathan Boyarin (Berkeley, 1993), 33–62, repr. in *Old English Literature: Critical Essays*, ed. R.M. Liuzza (New Haven, 2002), 1–22; and Hugh Magennis, "Audience(s), Reception, Literacy," in *A Companion to Anglo-Saxon Literature*, ed. Phillip Pulsiano and Elaine Treharne (Oxford, 2001), 84–101.

the tenth-century *Regularis Concordia* and in Ælfric's own consuetudinary.[45] Such reading may have involved articulation aloud or may have been silent but was certainly slow and meditative: the Benedictine Rule apparently envisages a monk receiving a new book every year at Lent.[46] The monastery also provided extensive contexts for reading aloud, primarily in the course of the liturgy, but also at the monastic meal during which the Rule of St. Benedict suggests edifying reading, possibly from lives of saints.[47] Monastic reading ought to be in Latin, although it is easy to imagine that the learned language might not be comprehensible to all members of the community and that vernacular reading might be a concession to practical circumstances, particularly in the less formal condition of reading over the meal.

Outside the monastery reading practices are harder to recover. Priests were clearly literate in view of their liturgical and pastoral obligations. In his Pastoral Letter for Bishop Wulfsige, Ælfric requires the mass-priest to have *boclare*, "book-learning," to teach the people.[48] Ælfric itemizes the books it is necessary for a priest to own.[49] Such expectations suggest full literacy in Latin, but the reality on the ground may have been different. Wulfstan's account of ordination practices makes provision for ordaining priests who are *samlæredne*, "half-educated," when necessary, provided they pledge to continue learning.[50] Byrhtferth directs his account of the computus to priests, since they need to be able to calculate the date of festivals, and, significantly, he writes his explanation in English as well as in Latin.[51] Local churches owned by the local landowner, which were becoming increasingly common in this period, probably relied upon a priest who was close to the surrounding community, which leads Karen Louise Jolly, in a study of the real-world pressures on rural priests, to speculate about their low level of education.[52] The educational situation may have been better in some of the larger minsters. The most

---

[45] *The Rule of St. Benedict*, chaps. 8, 48; *Regularis Concordia*, chaps. 19, 25, 29, 40, 54, 55, 56; Ælfric, *Letter to the Monks of Eynsham*, §§2, 14, 60.

[46] *Rule of St. Benedict*, chap. 48; see M.B. Parkes, "*Rædan, areccan, smeagan*: How the Anglo-Saxons Read," *Anglo-Saxon England* 26 (1997): 1–22, here 9–10.

[47] *Rule of St. Benedict*, chaps. 38, 42.

[48] Pastoral Letter for Bishop Wulfsige, §66, ed. Whitelock, *Councils and Synods*, 209.

[49] Pastoral Letter for Bishop Wulfsige, §§ 51–54, and First Old English Letter for Wulfstan, §§157–58, ed. Whitelock, *Councils and Synods*, 206–7, 291–92.

[50] Examination of Candidates for Ordination, §16, ed. Whitelock, *Councils and Synods*, 425.

[51] *Byrhtferth's Enchiridion*, ed. Peter S. Baker and Michael Lapidge, EETS, s.s. 15 (Oxford, 1995).

[52] Karen Louise Jolly, *Popular Religion in Late Saxon England: Elf Charms in Context* (Chapel Hill, 1996), 62–66.

elaborate examples were the unreformed communities in cathedrals where a daily round based, for example, on the Enlarged Rule of Chrodegang implies an organization parallel to that of the monasteries.[53] Both here and, especially, in small communities, the standard of Latinity was probably lower than in reformed monasteries. In both local churches and in minsters, priests would have constituted a literate class, but their literacy might have been more reliable in English than in Latin. It is notable that the various pastoral letters aimed at the clergy usually circulated in English and these groups likely constituted a demand for religious work in the vernacular.

Beyond the religious orders, secular literacy is best attested around the processes of government and the charters and wills that documented land-ownership and inheritance.[54] Some literacy in Latin is implied in the process of administration, alongside more widespread literacy in English, which was promulgated in King Alfred's famous educational program from the end of the ninth century. The very survival of vernacular literature implies some practice of secular reading, albeit one hard now to recreate. The model of private reading and public recital may well have operated in the secular world as well as the religious. While some reading could have occurred in private contexts — if Ælfric's secular patrons, Æthelweard and Æthelmær, were really recreating a monastic round in their secular households, this could have included private devotional study — the more common pattern was probably for recital across a broad and mixed audience, somewhat in the manner of monastic mealtimes, but incorporating a broader cross-section of society, including young and old, men and women, and people of high rank and low. Understanding such general patterns of literacy and performance is necessary for considering how the *Lives of Saints* were being read in late Anglo-Saxon England.

Reading *Lives of Saints*

The most straightforward answer as to who was reading the *Lives of Saints* is Ealdorman Æthelweard and his son Æthelmær. Ælfric says as much in the prefaces. He addresses the Old English preface to Æthelweard in epistolary form and makes clear that he has undertaken the translation:

---

[53] *The Old English Version of the Enlarged Rule of Chrodegang together with the Latin Original*, ed. Arthur S. Napier, EETS, o.s. 150 (London, 1916).

[54] See Susan Kelly, "Anglo-Saxon Lay Society and the Written Word," and Simon Keynes, "Royal Government and the Written Word in Late Anglo-Saxon England," in *The Uses of Literacy in Early Mediaeval Europe*, ed. Rosamond McKitterick (Cambridge, 1990), 36–62, 226–57 respectively; and Lowe, "Lay Literacy."

for þan þe ðu, leof swiðost, and Æðelmær swylcera gewrita me bædon, and of handum gelæhton, eowerne geleafan to getrymmenne mid þære gerecednysse, þe ge on eowrum gereorde næfdon ær.

(Preface 5b, 3–6)

because you, dearest sir, and Æthelmær asked for such writings from me, and received them from my hands, in order to strengthen your faith with that narrative, which you did not possess before in your language.

The two noblemen asked for the writings and are imagined in tangible proximity to the resulting book, receiving it "of handum." Ælfric is just as explicit about their responsibility in the Latin preface:

Non mihi inputetur quod divinam scripturam nostrae lingue infero, quia arguet me praecatus multorum fidelium, et maxime Æþelwerdi ducis et Æðelmeri nostri, qui ardentissime nostras interpretationes amplectuntur lectitando. (Preface 5a, 28–31)

Let it not be charged against me alone that I turn divine scripture into our language because the entreaty of many of the faithful charges me, and especially that of ealdorman Æthelweard and of our friend Æthelmær, who most ardently favour our translations by often reading them.

His patrons bear responsibility for his acts of translation and are envisaged as enthusiastic readers of those works. Ealdorman Æthelweard is named a third time as the instigator for the translation of the Life of Thomas in that work's Latin preface, further reinforcing his role as principal reader.[55]

Æthelweard and Æthelmær appear to have been voracious consumers of Ælfric's works. Æthelweard had a personal augmented copy of *Catholic Homilies* I, as indicated by the note in CUL Gg. 3. 28 (Preface 1b, 92–94), described above. Æthelweard is also explicitly evoked as the commissioner of Ælfric's translation of Genesis (see Preface 4, 1–5 and 111–14) and of his translation of Joshua (see Letter to Sigeweard, lines 405–409).[56] Æthelmær is explicitly and respectfully associated with Ælfric's transfer from Winchester to Cerne

---

[55] The note is edited as Wilcox, Preface 5d; see especially lines 10–11. See further the explication of Malcolm Godden, "Ælfric's Saints' Lives and the Problem of Miracles," *Leeds Studies in English* n.s. 16 (1985): 83–100, here 88–90.

[56] The Letter to Sigeweard is edited as "On the Old and New Testament" by S. J. Crawford, *The Old English Version of the Heptateuch*, EETS, o.s. 160 (London, 1922 for 1921; repr. with a suppl. by N. R. Ker, London, 1969), 15–75.

Abbas in the Old English preface to CH I (Preface 1b, 3–5) and mentioned as founder of Eynsham at the beginning of the Letter to the Monks of Eynsham (Preface 8b, 2). Æthelweard and Æthelmær, then, provide tangible and immediate readers for much of Ælfric's work.

In some ways this is surprising, both because of their high-profile political lives and because of Æthelweard's demonstrable literacy in Latin. Æthelweard, ealdorman of the western provinces 975–c. 998, would have been involved as ealdorman in both fighting and negotiating with the Vikings: in 994 the Anglo-Saxon Chronicle records that he escorted the Viking leader Anlaf to King Æthelred at Andover. Æthelmær was apparently displaced from his position in court by a palace revolution in 1005, whereupon he presumably retired to the monastery at Eynsham, but he had re-emerged by 1013, when, according to the Anglo-Saxon Chronicle, he led the thanes of the west in submission to the Viking leader Swein, who was briefly to displace Æthelred as king of England.[57] Both were in regular attendance at meetings of the Witan as their signatures on charters attest. Their sponsorship of Ælfric suggests that in the midst of all this political activity they led pious lives, as is also suggested by their joint founding of Cerne Abbas in 987 and Æthelmær's founding of Eynsham in 1005. Æthelweard's piety extended all the way to literacy in Latin, as is attested by his translation of the Anglo-Saxon Chronicle into hermeneutic Latin.[58] Æthelweard, therefore, and probably the son with whom he is closely associated, did not strictly need Ælfric to translate works from Latin for him, yet evidently appreciated those translations.

Of course, Ælfric's saints' lives, like his homilies, are more than just translations to the extent that he selected and combined sources, often abbreviating and rationalizing them and adding his own perspective, and so the noblemen might have appreciated them as original compositions. Ælfric's additions to some of the lives, such as the discussion of just warfare at the end of the translation of Maccabees, suggest that he was writing with powerful secular leaders like Æthelweard in mind.[59] Moreover, the implicit piety of these sponsors and their associations with reformed monasteries may hint at their intentions for *Lives of Saints*. Even amid their active political lives, they may

---

[57] See Simon Keynes, *The Diplomas of Æthelred "the Unready" 978–1016: A Study in their Use as Historical Evidence* (Cambridge, 1980), 209–14.

[58] *Chronicon Æthelweardi: The Chronicle of Æthelweard*, ed. A. Campbell (London, 1962). On the style of Æthelweard's Latin, see Michael Lapidge, "The Hermeneutic Style in Tenth-Century Anglo-Latin Literature," *Anglo-Saxon England* 4 (1975): 67–111, here 97–98.

[59] The idea is developed by Godden, "Problem of Miracles," 94–97.

have pursued some of the practices of a monastic house, including a pseudo-liturgical celebration of those saints honored in the monastery. If such celebration involved the reading aloud of the relevant saints' lives, the audience for the readings would have been the whole household maintained by a powerful ealdorman, presumably including an extended family, children and youths in the ealdorman's foster care, a group of professional fighting men, perhaps with wives and further family of these men, and numerous servants. In such a wide-ranging household, most of the audience would not have understood Latin. If the pious ealdorman expected these followers to attend to the readings, they would have to be in English.

The household of Æthelweard and Æthelmær, then, provides one context for both the reading and the recital of *Lives of Saints*, which were to be received "sive legendo seu audiendo" ("either by reading or listening") according to Preface 5a.4; but it is certainly not the only likely context. In the passage from the Latin preface cited above, Ælfric attributes his work to the "entreaty of many of the faithful" in addition to the two nobles. If this is more than a conventional appeal, these must include other secular and clerical people who knew the writings of the prolific monk in Cerne Abbas. We know of some such faithful from Ælfric's correspondence, albeit mostly dating from after his promotion to the abbacy of Eynsham in 1005. A brief letter dealing with Christian prohibitions and fashions is addressed to "Brother Edward," perhaps a biological brother.[60] From Eynsham, Ælfric wrote to the otherwise unknown Wulfgeat of Ylmandun in response to an enquiry now lost, providing a catechetical *narratio* followed by advice on how to live a moral life (Assmann i).[61] Ælfric wrote to the otherwise unknown Sigefyrth a homily on virginity stressing clerical celibacy (Assmann ii). He wrote to the otherwise unknown Sigeweard of Eastheolon, who specifically requested his writings, and provided him with a synopsis of Christian history interwoven with notices about his previous writings (Letter to Sigeweard).[62] Ecclesiastical correspondents included Wulfsige, bishop of Sherborne 993–1002, in which diocese Cerne Abbas lies, for whom Ælfric wrote a pastoral letter, and Wulfstan, bishop of Worcester 1002–1016 and archbishop of York 1002–1023, for whom Ælfric wrote a personal letter and a series of pastoral letters in Latin

---

[60] Edited and discussed by Mary Clayton, "An Edition of Ælfric's *Letter to Brother Edward*," in *Early Medieval English Texts and Interpretations: Studies Presented to Donald G. Scragg*, ed. Elaine Treharne and Susan Rosser, MRTS 252 (Tempe, 2002), 263–83.

[61] *Angelsächsische Homilien und Heiligenleben*, ed. Bruno Assmann, BaP 3 (Kassel, 1889; repr. with a suppl. intro. by Peter Clemoes, Darmstadt, 1964).

[62] See n. 56 above.

and English from about the time of his move to Eynsham. Any of these correspondents could have added their entreaties to those of Æthelweard and Æthelmær to commission the *Lives of Saints*.

Even where a specific dedicatee is named, in a predictable economy of effort, Ælfric intended his occasional works to be reused in other contexts. The Letter to Wulfgeat, for example, opens in its epistolary version (in Oxford, Bodleian Library, MS. Laud Misc. 509) with the observation "Nis þis gewrit be anum men awriten ac ys be eallum" (Assmann i.1: "this letter is not written for a single person but for all"), and the work duly survives in no less than three different homiletic adaptations.[63] The Letter to Sigeweard likewise circulated in its epistolary form in Laud Misc. 509, where it bears the generalized rubric "Incipit libellus de veteri testamento et novo" and opens "Ðis gewrit wæs to anum men gediht ac hit mæg swaðeah manegum fremian" (Preface 8c, 1–2: "this treatise was composed for one man but it may nevertheless help many"). In addition, it circulated in an adapted form as a generalized homily in Oxford, Bodleian Library, MS. Bodley 343.[64]

It is no surprise, then, that Ælfric envisages a wider audience for *Lives of Saints* than whoever commissioned the series. He explains in the Latin preface his desire to profit others (*aliis*), "quia estimo non esse ingratum fidelibus" ("for I do not reckon it to be disagreeable to the faithful": Preface 5a.4–5). In the Old English preface, Ælfric observes that these saints' lives serve a generally edifying purpose, "mannum to getrymminge" ("as an exhortation for people": Preface 5b.29). He posits the effect of saints' lives as the ability to revive those flagging in faith (Preface 5a.13–15). In other words, these lives will benefit a general Christian audience, even if Ælfric does not spell out how that audience will get to hear them.

Such were Ælfric's intentions for all his works. As that corpus built up, he apparently came to conceive of it as a coherent body of work, since he freely provided cross-references to earlier discussions rather than repeating points. This is particularly evident in the Letter to Sigeweard, which both provides a conspectus of Christian history and adverts to how much of the story Ælfric has already dealt with. Allusions here to *Lives of Saints* might provide a clue

---

[63] A version close to the letter but without its opening is in Hatton 115, fols. 95r–99v; a more truncated adaptation is in Junius 121, fols. 124r–130v; and a version in a different context, perhaps not assembled by Ælfric, is in Vitellius C. v, fols. 1r–v, 4r–5v, ed. as Pope xia. See Clemoes, "Suppl. Intro.," xi–xvi, and John C. Pope, *The Homilies of Ælfric: A Supplementary Collection*, EETS, o.s. 259–60 (London, 1967–1968), 1: 453–75.

[64] Short excerpts survive as freestanding items in Vitellius C. v, fols. 33r–35r, and in BL Harley 3271, fols. 125v–126r and 126r–128v.

to the expected audience, although the evidence proves equivocal. There are numerous allusions to the *Catholic Homilies*, but allusions to *Lives of Saints* are more limited. Ælfric does refer to his translations of Kings (LS xviii) and of Maccabees (LS xxv) — "ic awende hig on Englisc ⁊ rædon gif ge wyllað eow sylfum to ræde!" ("I translated them into English and read them yourselves if you want to for counsel," lines 836–838) — but, as biblical translations, these might have had an identity and a circulation beyond *Lives of Saints*.[65] He also alludes to writing lives of the apostles:

> Ealra þissera apostola geendunge ic hæbbe awriten buton Mathian anes, þe ic ofacsian mihte: ða ge mihton rædan ⁊ eow aræman on þam, gif ge holde wæron eowrum agenum sawlum. (Letter to Sigeweard, lines 1006–1009)[66]

> I have written the ending of all these apostles except Matthias alone, which I could learn of: those you could read and raise yourselves up through them, if you were loyal to your own souls.

With the exception of Thomas, though, all the other apostles are covered in the two series of *Catholic Homilies*. Ælfric does unambiguously refer back to one item in *Lives of Saints*, namely the epilogue to the Life of St. Agnes (LS vii) concerning Gallicanus, in the tract "Wyrdwriteras Us Secgað" (Pope xxii, 56–58), a late work which both Clemoes and Pope speculate may derive from an occasional letter.[67] Such an allusion suggests that Ælfric expected his *Lives of Saints* to be available to the audience of this late homily, which seems to be aimed at high-ranking secular nobles.[68]

These kind of allusions do not provide a definitive sense of the use of Ælfric's works, as the example of the homily on Judith nicely exemplifies. He says of the Judith piece in the Letter to Sigeweard that it serves as an example, "þæt ge eowerne eard mid wæmnum bewerian wið onwinnendne here" (lines

---

[65] The translation of Kings survives in a non-hagiographic context in Hatton 115, fols. 131v–139v; the translation of Maccabees is preserved in a non-hagiographic manuscript in CCCC 303, 341–55 and 355–56.

[66] Crawford, *Heptateuch*, 60, emends by adding a *ne* before *mihte*, thereby making the dependent clause refer negatively to the unavailable story of Matthias rather than positively to the stories of the other apostles. Sense and significance remains the same with or without the emendation.

[67] See Pope's introduction, *Homilies*, 2: 725–27 and also Godden, "Problem of Miracles," 94.

[68] See Pope, *Homilies*, 2: 726.

778–780, "that you defend your land against an invading army with weapons"), clearly signaling a secular male audience for the work. His conclusion to the homily itself (Assmann ix), however, addresses "min swustor" and requires maintaining the chastity promised to God (lines 434–437), clearly suggesting that the work was aimed at a female religious audience. The disparity is pointed to in an analysis by Mary Clayton, who shows that Ælfric is variously offering literal, typological, and tropological interpretations of the story aimed at different audiences.[69] Adaptation to varied audiences is visible in the version in Otho B. x, which closes with the address to a female religious audience but opens with a generalized address, almost certainly not by Ælfric, of "Leofan men" (Assmann ix.1). While it is unsurprising that a single work could serve more than one audience, the range in this example from martial secular men to pious women is striking. Such a range may relate also to the actual uses of *Lives of Saints*.

The example of Judith usefully demonstrates an audience of both sexes for Ælfric's work. Presumably women also constitute a likely audience for *Lives of Saints*.[70] It is striking that six of the lives are of women, which makes up a goodly proportion of all the surviving female saints' lives in the vernacular from Anglo-Saxon England.[71] Apart from these six lives by Ælfric, there are two further female lives associated with the series in Julius E. vii, and one other associated with it in Caligula A. xiv.[72] Excluding pieces on the Blessed Virgin Mary, only a handful of further female lives survive in Old English.[73] The relatively high number of exemplary stories of women in *Lives of Saints* might have particularly appealed to women — or might have been envisaged by Ælfric as particularly salutary for a female audience.

---

[69] Mary Clayton, "Ælfric's *Judith*: Manipulative or Manipulated?" *Anglo-Saxon England* 23 (1994): 215–27. Clayton shows that the epilogue to the homily is addressed to a community of religious laywomen.

[70] Susan Groag Bell, "Medieval Women Book Owners: Arbiters of Lay Piety and Ambassadors of Culture," *Signs* 7 (1982): 742–68, charts female book ownership and use throughout Europe in the 9th to 15th centuries.

[71] Eugenia (Skeat ii), Agnes (Skeat vii), Agatha (Skeat viii), Lucy (Skeat ix), Æthelthryth (Skeat xx), Cecilia (Skeat xxxiv).

[72] Mary of Egypt (Skeat xxiiib) and Euphrosyne (Skeat xxxiii) in Julius E. vii; the Life of Mildred in Caligula A. xiv.

[73] Namely three prose lives of Margaret, one of Veronica, another fragment of the Mildred legend, and the poetic lives of Elene and Juliana. For a catalogue of Old English prose saints' lives, see E. Gordon Whatley, "An Introduction to the Study of Old English Prose Hagiography: Sources and Resources," in *Holy Men and Holy Women*, ed. Szarmach, 3–32.

Lives of Saints, a monastic sequence written in the non-monastic language of English, presents a problem that needs explaining. A somewhat analogous case may help in speculating about a likely performance context. Ælfric translated into English a work of monastic admonition that he considered to be by Basil, the *Admonitio ad filium spiritualem*, which survives in a fragmentary state in a single manuscript, Oxford, Bodleian Library, Hatton MS. 76, of the first half of the eleventh century, of unknown place of origin and Worcester provenance.[74] In describing the point of his translation in a preface to this work, Ælfric emphasizes the significance of Basil's monastic rule as a precursor to and influence on Benedict. He offers the translation into English with a specifically monastic audience in mind: "Heo gebyrað to munecum and eac to mynecenum, þe regollice libbað for hyra Drihtnes lufe" ("It is fitting for monks and also for nuns, who live according to the rule on account of their love of the Lord").[75] Although the precise Latin manuscript of Ælfric's source has not been identified, Ker points to the similarity of chapter divisions with the twelfth-century Latin text in Oxford, Bodleian Library, MS. Bodley 800. Yet why did Ælfric translate monastic admonitions aimed specifically at monks and nuns into English when monastic literacy required those groups to have a facility in reading Latin and the work was circulating in Latin? A hint lies in Ælfric's specific addition of *mynecena*, "nuns," to his imagined audience of monks. This inclusiveness is not evident in the Latin version, which is so clearly targeted at a male *filius*. (The exhortation to sexual abstinence in chapter 7, for example, stresses male-centered abstinence from a woman's body.) Ælfric, then, takes a work that is rhetorically directed at a monk but of interest to all regular religious for its connection with Benedict's Rule and, in translating it, stresses its suitability for both monks and nuns. Ælfric's translation envisages a monastic community that is not as capable in Latin as the tradition of reformed monasticism would require, and it is conspicuous that in thinking of this audience his mind turns to nuns. It is possible that the female monastic communities of reformed monasticism had a lower level of Latin literacy than the male ones — or, at least, that Ælfric viewed English translations of monastic works as particularly useful for women's houses — and this would explain why he added explicit reference to nuns as the target of this translated work.

---

[74] Ed. Henry W. Norman, *The Anglo-Saxon Version of the Hexaemeron of St. Basil . . . and the Saxon Remains of St. Basil's Admonitio ad Filium Spiritualem* (London, 1848), 31–55; and Lawrence E. Mueller, "Ælfric's Translation of St. Basil's *Admonitio ad Filium Spiritualem*: An Edition" (unpublished Ph.D. dissertation, University of Washington, 1974). Modern scholarship considers the attribution to Basil as spurious.

[75] Ed. Wilcox, Preface 6, 12–13.

Ælfric apparently deemed the *Admonitio ad filium spiritualem* as appropriate for the same audience as *Lives of Saints* since, in contextualizing Basil in the opening of the preface, he alludes to an earlier account of the writer: "Basilius se eadiga, be ðam we ær awriton" ("Basil the blessed, about whom we have written before"), which probably alludes to his account of Basil in *Lives of Saints* (Skeat iii).[76] Ælfric apparently assumed that the kind of audience that would appreciate monastic precepts translated into the vernacular would also appreciate monastic lives in the vernacular. This might particularly have been houses of nuns. Other vernacular works aimed specifically at such female monastic audiences survive, namely the Old English Rule of St. Benedict in BL MS. Cotton Faustina A.x, fols. 102–151, in which many personal forms were originally feminine although they have been altered to masculine, and the translation of the *Regularis Concordia* that has been adapted for female use in CCCC 201.[77]

It might also have been communities of priests — the minsters peopled by clerks or secular priests who were not monks. Within such a community, if the standard of Latin was lower than in reformed monastic houses, it is possible that the reading for private study, the edifying reading over meals, and, just possibly, even some of the reading within the liturgy, might take place in English. This is particularly likely in the smaller minsters where both resources and education were likely to be more restricted than in the large institutions.[78] Monastic readings translated into English suggest the existence of communities who wanted to follow the monastic life and yet did not have access to the monastic language of Latin.

One final likely audience for the *Lives of Saints* is one that leaves the least material record and yet that is implicit in the model of reading described above: a secular audience, including the non-social elite. Servants and children, relatives and visitors were presumably present in the households of Æthelweard and Æthelmær, as also in other social settings where the lives were read, and they may not have shared the lord's desire to enact the religious life of monks in the vernacular. Other secular listeners may have been

---

[76] It might just refer to his translation of the *Hexaemeron*, which is drawn in part from Basil.

[77] See, on the Benedictine Rule, Ker, *Catalogue*, no. 154B and Mechthild Gretsch, *Die Regula Sancti Benedicti in England und ihre altenglische Übersetzung* (Munich, 1973); and, on the *Regularis Concordia*, Joyce Hill, "The 'Regularis Concordia' and Its Latin and Old English Reflexes," *Revue Bénédictine* 101 (1991): 299–315, here 309–11.

[78] See John Blair, ed., *Minsters and Parish Churches: The Local Church in Transition, 950–1200* (Oxford, 1988).

attached to some of the minster communities, where the presence of married priests implies some place for women and children. And the literate priest in a small community may have read from a book of *Lives of Saints* to entertain the full cross-section of village life with whom he came into contact. These secular readers may have been less disciplined readers and less focused on the edifying than their religious conterparts. They may well have listened for the sensational plot and the gripping storytelling, appreciating the pleasure of the text more than the utility of its message.

Ælfric anticipated such a response even in the very form of his work. The rhythmical prose that is the norm throughout the *Lives of Saints* exploits the pleasure that comes from the metrical form of poetry without fully being Old English poetry.[79] Ælfric adapted the traditional poetic form of the alliterative line, but in a way that is metrically looser than traditional Old English verse and that lacks the distinct diction that is peculiar to poetry. It is as if he wanted his works to seduce the reader with their rhetorical power, but not to seduce too far to the extent that pleasure in the rhetoric might distract from their edifying point. Yet, as modern interpretive theory rightly stresses, this is an impossible thing for the author to control. Just as Ælfric's intentions for the circulation of his works in splendid purity from those of other vernacular writers were more often ignored than honored, so too he would have lost control over their reception once the works circulated in reading communities. In some of the multiple places where these works would have been heard, pleasure in the narrative and in its telling may have reared its ugly head in Ælfric's audience, in addition to pious devotion to the edifying message and pseudo-monastic contemplation.

The Return of the Head

At this point it might be useful to reconsider the manuscript evidence for the circulation of *Lives of Saints*. The prevalence of manuscripts of unknown place of origin has already been remarked. It is tempting to associate that ignorance with our shadowy knowledge of manuscript production in female houses or in small minster communities in the late Anglo-Saxon period. Female houses were presumably copying manuscripts as well as their male counterparts, yet their output has been identified far less successfully than that of major male monastic or cathedral centers like Canterbury, Winchester, and

---

[79] The best introduction is John C. Pope, "Ælfric's Rhythmical Prose," chap. 5 of his introduction to *Homilies of Ælfric: A Supplementary Collection*, 1: 105–36.

Worcester.[80] Just as "anonymous" might always be a woman, "unknown place of origin" may be a female scriptorium.

The material format of the surviving books provides an ambiguous hint for the use of the series. While it is impossible to be certain of the original size of Anglo-Saxon books since they have been subject to cropping in the process of rebinding, the surviving copies of *Lives of Saints* are noticeably small books. Julius E. vii has demonstrably been cropped since the lower part of a decorative Æ has been lost at fol. 67v. The book now measures a portable 273 × 185 mm. Cotton Caligula A. xiv is a smaller 222 × 132 mm. and CUL Ii. 1. 33 is 220 × 158 mm. It is hard to know the original measure of the two burnt manuscripts: the best-preserved leaves of Cotton Otho B. x now measure ca. 195 × 140 mm., those of Cotton Vitellius D. xvii, which Wanley reported as in quarto, now measure ca. 135 × 90 mm. The strips of Cambridge, Queens' College (Horne) 75 and Bloomington, Lilly Library, Poole 10 suggest a somewhat larger book, now measuring at most 303 × 60 mm., while those of BL Royal 8 c. vii, fols. 1 and 2, have been cut down to ca. 230 × 160 mm., compatible with coming from a small volume. These dimensions contrast with the larger format of manuscripts of *Catholic Homilies*. BL Royal 7 C. xii measures 310 × 205 mm., and CUL Gg. 3. 28 measures ca. 275 × 218 mm., to cite the two manuscripts probably produced at Cerne Abbas. Bodley 343 is ca. 308 × 200 mm.; CCCC 162 is ca. 297 × 203 mm., although other volumes are smaller than this. While the distinction is not clear-cut and consistent, it is possible that manuscripts of *Catholic Homilies* incline to larger stature because they were placed upon a lectern for recital aloud, whereas manuscripts of *Lives of Saints* are smaller because they were intended to be portable as a reading book in the many contexts where such reading is likely.

One form of such reading is hinted at by the head on fol. 111v of Caligula A. xiv, with which this essay began. While the example of the Benedictine Rule in CCCC 57 cautions against any too-easy assumption, since faces there appear in a book that was certainly used for recital, if perhaps also for private reading, the head in Caligula A. xiv would only signify to a full extent if it was encountered in the practice of private contemplative reading. The monk or nun or secular noble using this volume for private devotional reading would

---

[80] See Michelle P. Brown, "Female Book-Ownership and Production in Anglo-Saxon England: The Evidence of the Ninth-Century Prayerbooks," in *Lexis and Texts in Early English: Studies Presented to Jane Roberts*, ed. Christian Kay and Louise Sylvester (Amsterdam, 2001), 45–67; and Jonathan Wilcox, "Transmission of Literature and Learning: Anglo-Saxon Scribal Culture," in *A Companion to Anglo-Saxon Literature*, ed. Pulsiano and Treharne, 50–70, here 54–55.

have the opportunity to pause between saints' lives and look at the head staring back at the reader and ponder what it means, whereas the head could not contribute to the more public performance practice of reading aloud.

And what would the head suggest for such a reader as he or she finished the Life of St Martin and paused before reading the Passion of St Thomas? A drawing of a head can always be simply part of a life drawing. Some of the heads inventoried above are drawn with shoulders or torsos more or less complete. The head in Caligula A. xiv, though, conspicuously lacks any association with a body. While the face may be smiling, the very completeness of the facial features and lack of any space or hint of attached body parts emphasizes that this is a disembodied head. And disembodied heads have a special resonance in *Lives of Saints*. Neither of the surrounding lives here features head removal — neither Martin, who dies lying on the earth surrounded by his followers, nor Thomas, who is slain with a sword after torture, is decapitated — and so such a head is not straightforwardly illustrative of the surrounding texts. Yet to lose one's head is not an unusual fate for a saint. Alban is beheaded (Skeat xix, 116). Oswald is conspicuously decapitated on the battlefield, his head displayed as a trophy on a stake until recovered by his brother and taken with reverence to Lindisfarne (Skeat xxvi, 162–68). Most memorably of all, Edmund's head is lopped off and hidden in the woods by the evil Viking attackers but is subsequently found, guarded by a wolf, after it calls attention to itself with the memorable line (for a trunkless head) of "her, her, her" ("here, here, here"), after which it is reverently buried with the body (Skeat xxxii, 122–67).[81] The severed head appears to carry particular interest for Anglo-Saxon culture: ritual beheading is central both to *Beowulf* and to *Judith*.[82] It bears particular resonance among saints' lives. The severed head emblematizes the grisly but memorable detail through which saints' narratives achieve their effect.

In addition to its general appropriateness to a series of saints' lives, the head in Caligula A. xiv may have a specific resonance. While it is impossible to be certain of the organization in such a brief fragment as Caligula A. xiv,

---

[81] See James W. Earl, "Violence and Non-Violence in Anglo-Saxon England: Ælfric's 'Passion of St. Edmund'," *Philological Quarterly* 78 (1999): 125–49, here 139–41 for a stimulating reading of this scene.

[82] On the ritual implications of beheading, see John Edward Damon, "*Desecto capite perfido*: Bodily Fragmentation and Reciprocal Violence in Anglo-Saxon England," *Exemplaria* 13 (2001): 399–432, and the earlier studies of Ann W. Astell, "Holofernes's Head: *Tacen* and Teaching in the Old English *Judith*," *Anglo-Saxon England* 18 (1989): 117–33, and Mary Flavia Godfrey, "*Beowulf* and *Judith*: Thematizing Decapitation in Old English Poetry," *Texas Studies in Literature and Language* 35 (1993): 1–43.

and while the following Life of Mildred suggests the manuscript was not ordered by the liturgical year, the jump from Martin, whose date is not speci-
fied in *Lives of Saints*, but who was celebrated on 11 November, to Thomas,
who was celebrated on 21 December, would raise for the liturgically savvy
reader a sequence of missing lives. As provided by Ælfric in *Lives of Saints*,
these are Saints Edmund (20 November), Cecilia (22 November), and Chry-
santhus and Daria (29 November). Edmund's story, in particular, revolves
around his bodyless head, as may be hinted, too, by the two heads sketched
into CUL Ii. 1. 33, described above, which appear in the lower margin of the
Life of Edmund. Whether part of the original design or added by a reader, the
head in Caligula A. xiv may, therefore, stand in for Edmund for the viewer
who gazes at it with the right expectations. Gazing now at that head may help
construct the reader who did such gazing.

Conclusion

By considering the material evidence of Ælfric's reception and probable
Anglo-Saxon reading communities that have left some record, it can be established that the *Lives of Saints* probably saw use, either through reading or
listening, in many or all of the following circumstances:

as private reading by the literate and pious nobles Æthelweard and
Æthelmær;

for public recital (in a pseudo-liturgical context or over meals) to the
extended household of Æthelweard and Æthelmær, incorporating
both men and women of different social ranks and different ages;

as private reading by other secular nobles, including those with
whom Ælfric corresponded;

for public recital to the households of those other secular nobles incorporating both men and women of different social ranks and different ages;

as private reading by the bishops with whom Ælfric corresponded;

for reading aloud to the episcopal household of the bishop's palace;

as pious private reading by a monastic audience not fully literate in
Latin, especially that in a female monastic house;

for edifying public reading, to be recited over meals, to a monastic audience not fully literate in Latin, especially that in a female monastic house;

as pious private reading by a non-monastic religious community not fully literate in Latin, especially that in a minster of secular priests;

for edifying public reading, to be recited over meals or elsewhere, to a non-monastic corporate audience not fully literate in Latin, especially that in a minster of secular priests;

for private devotional reading by an isolated priest in the community;

as potentially uplifting reading to a complete village community by the isolated priest out in the field.

These are some of the multiple reading communities implicit in the idea that the *Lives of Saints* are narrative reading pieces. The range of different audience members suggests that the lives were likely heard and interpreted in different ways by different folks and served multiple purposes. They were probably given the edifying and pious attention that Ælfric surely intended, serving as a vernacular simulacrum of the monastic round of pious readings in Latin. Equally edifying and pious, if not Ælfric's explicit intention, would have been the use of these vernacular lives to displace the Latin liturgical reading of the monastery. Once circulating among multiple reading communities, though, the *Lives of Saints* would have received some audiences less centered on the pious and the edifying, audiences who would have listened to the exploits and travails of these saints for the pleasure of the story, the excitement of the plot, and the beauty of the form. The disembodied head of Caligula A. xiv serves principally as a focus for pious reflection on the ultimate sacrifice of God's chosen ones, yet it could also provide a focus for an exciting story well told, as in other secular stories of Anglo-Saxon England that center on a beheading.

Pinpointing the uses of Ælfric's *Lives of Saints*, even to the extent done here, has required attentiveness not just to Ælfric's writings as recorded in printed editions but also to the material evidence of the manuscripts, exemplified in this essay by the face in Caligula A. xiv. Phillip Pulsiano worked tirelessly in his professional life to focus scholarly attention on Anglo-Saxon manuscripts. In his role as general editor of the series Anglo-Saxon Manuscripts in Microfiche Facsimile, in particular, Phill labored to make access to the manuscripts widely available to the community of scholars. As someone who benefited from his meticulous editing of my own contribution to that series, I dedicate this essay on the joy of Anglo-Saxon manuscripts to his memory.

Bibliography

Assmann, Bruno, ed. *Angelsächsische Homilien und Heiligenleben.* BaP 3. Kassel, 1889; repr. with a suppl. intro. by Peter Clemoes, Darmstadt, 1964.

Astell, Ann W. "Holofernes's Head: *Tacen* and Teaching in the Old English *Judith.*" *Anglo-Saxon England* 18 (1989): 117–33.

Baker, Peter S., and Michael Lapidge, eds. *Byrhtferth's Enchiridion.* EETS s.s. 15. Oxford, 1995.

Bell, Susan Groag. "Medieval Women Book Owners: Arbiters of Lay Piety and Ambassadors of Culture." *Signs* 7 (1982): 742–68.

Biggs, Frederick M. "Ælfric as Historian: His Use of Alcuin's *Laudationes* and Sulpicius's *Dialogues* in his Two Lives of Martin." In *Holy Men and Holy Women: Old English Prose Saints' Lives and Their Contexts,* ed. Paul E. Szarmach, 289–315. Albany, NY, 1996.

Blair, John, ed. *Minsters and Parish Churches: The Local Church in Transition, 950–1200.* Oxford, 1988.

Brown, Michelle P. "Female Book-Ownership and Production in Anglo-Saxon England: The Evidence of the Ninth-Century Prayerbooks." In *Lexis and Texts in Early English: Studies Presented to Jane Roberts,* ed. Christian Kay and Louise Sylvester, 45–67. Amsterdam, 2001.

Budny, Mildred. *Insular, Anglo-Saxon, and Early Anglo-Norman Manuscript Art at Corpus Christi College, Cambridge: An Illustrated Catalogue.* 2 vols. Kalamazoo, 1997.

Camille, Michael. *Image on the Edge: The Margins of Medieval Art.* London, 1992.

Campbell, A., ed. *Chronicon Æthelweardi: The Chronicle of Æthelweard.* London, 1962.

Clayton, Mary. "Ælfric's *Judith*: Manipulative or Manipulated?" *Anglo-Saxon England* 23 (1994): 215–27.

Clemoes, Peter, ed. *Ælfric's Catholic Homilies: The First Series.* EETS s.s.17. Oxford, 1997.

———. "The Chronology of Ælfric's Works." In *The Anglo-Saxons: Studies in Some Aspects of their History and Culture Presented to Bruce Dickins,* ed. idem, 212–47. London, 1959.

Cockayne, Oswald. *Leechdoms, Wortcunning, and Starcraft of Early England.* 3 vols. London, 1864–1866; repr. London, 1961.

Crawford, S. J. *The Old English Version of the Heptateuch.* EETS o.s.160. London, 1922 [1921]; repr. with a suppl. by N. R. Ker, London, 1969.

Cross, James E., and Jennifer Morrish Tunberg, eds. *The Copenhagen Wulfstan Collection: Copenhagen Konigelige Bibliotek, Gl. Kgl. Sam. 1595.* EEMF 2. Copenhagen, 1993.

Damon, John Edward. "*Desecto capite perfido*: Bodily Fragmentation and Reciprocal Violence in Anglo-Saxon England." *Exemplaria* 12 (2001): 399–432.

Earl, James W. "Violence and Non-Violence in Anglo-Saxon England: Ælfric's 'Passion of St. Edmund'." *Philological Quarterly* 78 (1999): 125–49.

Gneuss, Helmut. "Liturgical Books in Anglo-Saxon England and their Old English Terminology." In *Learning and Literature in Anglo-Saxon England: Studies Presented to Peter Clemoes on the Occasion of his Sixty-Fifth Birthday*, ed. idem and M. Lapidge, 91–141. Cambridge, 1985.

Godden, Malcolm. "Ælfric's Saints' Lives and the Problem of Miracles." *Leeds Studies in English* n.s. 16 (1985): 83–100.

———. "The Development of Ælfric's Second Series of *Catholic Homilies*." *English Studies* 54 (1973): 209–16.

Godfrey, Mary Flavia. "*Beowulf* and *Judith*: Thematizing Decapitation in Old English Poetry." *Texas Studies in Literature and Language* 35 (1993): 1–43.

Graham, Timothy. "Cambridge Corpus Christi College 57 and its Anglo-Saxon Users." In *Anglo-Saxon Manuscripts and their Heritage*, ed. Phillip Pulsiano and Elaine M. Treharne, 21–69. Aldershot, 1998.

Griffith, Mark. "Ælfric's Preface to Genesis: Genre, Rhetoric, and the Origins of the *Ars dictaminis*." *Anglo-Saxon England* 29 (2000): 215–34.

Hill, Joyce. "The Dissemination of Ælfric's Lives of Saints: A Preliminary Survey." In *Holy Men and Holy Women*, ed. Szarmach, 235–59.

———. "The Preservation and Transmission of Ælfric's Saints' Lives: Reader-Response in the Early Middle Ages." In *The Preservation and Transmission of Anglo-Saxon Culture*, ed. Paul E. Szarmach and Joel T. Rosenthal, 405–30. Kalamazoo, 1997.

Jackson, Peter, and Michael Lapidge. "The Contents of the Cotton-Corpus Legendary." In *Holy Men and Holy Women*, ed. Szarmach, 131–46.

Jolly, Karen Louise. *Popular Religion in Late Saxon England: Elf Charms in Context.* Chapel Hill, 1996.

Jones, Christopher A. *Ælfric's Letter to the Monks of Eynsham.* CSASE 24. Cambridge, 1998.

Kelly, Susan. "Anglo-Saxon Lay Society and the Written Word." In *The Uses of Literacy in Early Medieval Europe*, ed. Rosamond McKitterick: 36–62. Cambridge, 1990.

Keynes, Simon. *The Diplomas of Æthelred "the Unready" 978–1016: A Study in their Use as Historical Evidence.* Cambridge, 1980.

———. "Royal Government and the Written Word in Late Anglo-Saxon England." In *The Uses of Literacy in Early Medieval Europe*, ed. McKitterick, 226–57.

Lapidge, Michael. "Ælfric's Sanctorale." In *Holy Men and Holy Women*, ed. Szarmach, 115–29.

Lowe, Kathryn A. "Lay Literacy in Anglo-Saxon England and the Development of the Chirograph." In *Anglo-Saxon Manuscripts and Their Heritage*, ed. Pulsiano and Treharne, 161–204.

Magennis, Hugh. "Audience(s), Reception, Literacy." In *A Companion to Anglo-Saxon Literature*, ed. Phillip Pulsiano and Elaine M. Treharne, 84–101. Oxford, 2001.

Mueller, Lawrence E. "Ælfric's Translation of St. Basil's *Admonitio ad Filium Spiritualem*: An Edition." Ph.D. diss, University of Washingon, 1974.

Napier, Arthur S., ed. *The Old English Version of the Enlarged Rule of Chrodegang together with the Latin Original.* EETS o.s. 150. London, 1916.

Norman, Henry W. *The Anglo-Saxon Version of the Hexaemeron of St. Basil . . . and the Saxon Remains of St. Basil's Admonitio ad Filium Spiritualem.* London, 1848.

Parkes, M. B. "*Rædan, areccan, smeagan*: How the Anglo-Saxons Read." *Anglo-Saxon England* 26 (1997): 1–22.

Pope, John C. *The Homilies of Ælfric: A Supplementary Collection.* EETS o.s. 259–260. London, 1967–1968.

Randall, Lilian M. C. *Images in the Margins of Gothic Manuscripts.* Berkeley, 1966.

Rollason, D. W. *The Mildrith Legend: A Study in Early Medieval Hagiography in England.* Leicester, 1982.

Schipper, William. "A Composite Old English Homiliary from Ely: Cambr. Univ. MS Ii.1.33." *Transactions of the Cambridge Bibliographical Society* 8 (1983): 285–98.

Skeat, Walter W. *Ælfric's Lives of Saints.* EETS o.s. 76, 82, 94, 114. London, 1881–1900; repr. as 2 vols., London, 1966.

Swanton, Michael. "A Fragmentary Life of St. Mildred and Other Kentish Royal Saints." *Archæologia Cantiana* 91 (1976 [1975]): 15–27.

Symons, Thomas, ed. *Regularis Concordia: The Monastic Agreement.* London, 1953.

Torkar, Roland. "Zu den Vorlagen der altenglischen Handschrift Cotton Julius E. vii." *Neuphilologische Mitteilungen* 72 (1971): 711–15.

Traxel, Oliver Martin. "Language, Writing, and Textual Interference in Post-Conquest Old English Manuscripts: The Scribal Evidence of Cambridge, University Library, Ii. 1. 33." Ph.D. diss., Cambridge University, 2000.

Treharne, Elaine M. "The Dates and Origins of Three Twelfth-Century Old English Manuscripts." In *Anglo-Saxon Manuscripts and Their Heritage*, ed. Pulsiano and eadem, 227–53.

Whatley, E. Gordon. "An Introduction to the Study of Old English Prose Hagiography: Sources and Resources." In *Holy Men and Holy Women*, ed. Szarmach, 3–32.

Wilcox, Jonathan, ed. *Ælfric's Prefaces*. Durham Medieval Texts. Durham, 1994.

———. "Transmission of Literature and Learning: Anglo-Saxon Scribal Culture." In *A Companion to Anglo-Saxon Literature*, ed. Pulsiano and Treharne, 50–70.

———. "Ælfric in Dorset and the Landscape of Pastoral Care." In *Pastoral Care in Late Anglo-Saxon England*, ed. Francesca Tinti, 52–62. Woodbridge, 2005.

Whitelock, Dorothy, M. Brett, and C. N. L. Brooke, eds. *Councils and Synods, with Other Documents Relating to the English Church*, Vol. 1, *A.D. 871–1066*. Oxford, 1961.

Zettel, Patrick H. "Saints' Lives in Old English: Latin Manuscripts and Vernacular Accounts: Ælfric." *Peritia* 1 (1982): 17–37.

FEMALE SCRIBES AT WORK?
A CONSIDERATION OF KIRKJUBÆJARBÓK
(CODEX AM 429 12MO)

KIRSTEN WOLF

I

Undoubtedly as a result of the reenvisioning of women's history in the late 1970s and 1980s, a good deal of research within the field of Old Norse-Icelandic literature has in recent years centered on women in medieval Icelandic society. Historians have exploited the corpus for what it reveals about the social and political status of women, and literary critics have made forays into the agendas of its authors and examined the portrayal of women and their roles in the literary works.

Despite this recovery of the "hidden history" of medieval Icelandic women, the question of their contribution to the creation and especially the transmission of Old Norse-Icelandic literature remains largely unanswered.[1] To be

---

[1] Of the works that have named authors, almost all the authors are males. No prose work has been attributed to a woman, and of the approximately 250 poetic works that have been preserved by named authors, only a fraction has been attributed to women (Helga Kress, *Máttugar meyjar: Íslensk fornbókmenntasaga* [Reykjavík, 1993], 17; Sandra Ballif Straubhaar, "Ambiguously Gendered: The Skalds Jórunn, Auðr and Steinunn," in *Cold Counsel: Women in Old Norse Literature and Mythology*, ed. Sarah M. Anderson and Karen Swenson [New York and London, 2002], 261–71, esp. 269). Else Mundal, "Kvinner og dikting. Overgangen frå munnleg til skriftleg kultur — ei ulukke for kvinnene?" in *Förändringar i kvinnors vilkor under medeltiden. Uppsatser framlagda vid ett kvinnohistoriskt symposium i Skálholt, Island, 22.–25. juni 1981*, ed. Silja Aðalsteinsdóttir and Helgi Þorláksson, Ritsafn Sagnfræðistofnunar 9 (Reykjavík, 1983), 11–25, esp. 13–16, considers it likely that more poems by women than by men have been lost. Her view is shared by Shaun F. D. Hughes, "The Reemergence of Women's Voices in Icelandic Literature, 1500–1800," in *Cold Counsel*, 93–128, esp. 94–95. Guðrún P. Helgadóttir, *Skáldkonur fyrri alda*, 2 vols. (Akureyri, 1961–1963), 2: 16, notes that in lists of authors, it was not uncommon to omit women writers or to write their names in the margin, and she draws attention to the fact that Jón Ólafsson (Grunnavíkur-Jón; 1705–1779) apologizes for including women among poets.

sure, women have been accorded a significant role in the oral transmission of Old Norse-Icelandic poetry,[2] but their contribution to the written transmission of the literary works has not been the subject of analysis. While it has generally been acknowledged — usually with reference to the charming vignette in the monk Gunnlaugr Leifsson's (d. 1218/19) *Jóns saga helga* about a certain Ingunn who studied ("var . . . í fræðinæmi") at the cathedral school at Hólar, where Latin books were read to her while she sewed or played games[3] — that a few women were given the opportunity to study, their involvement in scribal activity has been a matter of speculation, for on this topic the source material is silent, and no Old Icelandic manuscript has presented evidence of having been written by women. Nonetheless, Anna Sigurðardóttir takes it for granted that the nuns in the two Icelandic convents, Kirkjubær at Síða (founded 1186) and Staður in Reynisnes (founded 1295 or 1296), both Benedictine houses, not only copied manuscripts, but also illuminated them, and points to monasteries abroad to substantiate her argument.[4] Helga Kress and Jón

---

[2] Cf. Helga Kress, *Máttugar meyjar*, 13: "Margt bendir til að það hafi einkum verið konur sem í upphafi stunduðu munnlega frásagnarlist og stóðu fyrir munnlegri hefð skáldskaparins. Þetta má greinilega sjá í mörgum eddukvæðum, einkum hetjukvæðunum, sem fjalla mjög um kvenlega reynslu og hafa oft kvenlegt sjónarhorn. Skáldskapnum tengdist spádómslistin seiður og einnig læknislistin, sem hvort tveggja heyrði kvennamenningunni til" (Many things suggest that it was especially women who originally occupied themselves with the art of oral narration and were responsible for the oral transmission of poetry. This is obvious from many eddic poems, especially the heroic poems, which deal with female experience in particular and often present a female point of view. Poetry was associated with the magic called *seiðr* and with leechcraft, which both belong to female culture).

[3] Jón Sigurðsson and Guðbrandur Vigfússon, ed., *Biskupa sögur*, 2 vols. (Copenhagen, 1858–1878), 1: 241.

[4] Anna Sigurðardóttir, *Allt hafði annan róm áður í páfadóm: Nunnuklaustrin tvö á Íslandi á miðöldum og brot úr kristnisögu*, Úr veröld kvenna 3 (Reykjavík, 1988), 41, 52–53, 155–56, 228. In discussing the 1397 inventory of the Kirkjubær convent, which mentions twenty books in Latin and Norse (see below), Anna Sigurðardóttir (52) says: "Þessar bækur hafa systurnar efalaust skrifað sjálfar eftir bókum sem þær hafa fengið að láni. Sumar systranna hafa verið listaskrifarar og aðrar eða þær sömu hafa jafnframt lýst bækurnar, eins og títt var erlendis í nunnuklaustrum" (The nuns without doubt copied these books themselves from books which they had borrowed. Some of the nuns were artists and others or the same ones also illuminated the books as was common in convents abroad). Cf., however, Gerda Lerner, *The Creation of Feminist Consciousness: From the Middle Ages to Eighteen-seventy* (Oxford, 1993), 29, who says: "The fame and notoriety of 'learned women' of the Middle Ages and the early Renaissance attest to their rarity — with a few exceptions, they were noted more for existing at all than for their accomplishments. Up to the 17th century, learned women are extremely rare. We can identify perhaps thirty learned nuns in the period up to 1400, and some of the most accomplished of these, such as Hildegard of Bingen and Mechthild of Magdeburg, were unable to write in Latin. In the period 1350–1530, which is regarded by historians as a time when

Viðar Sigurðsson also consider it highly likely that Icelandic nuns worked as copyists.[5] Inga Huld Hákonardóttir is more cautious and comments that the nuns may have engaged in literary activity.[6]

It is the purpose of this article to consider these conjectures about medieval Icelandic women's involvement in scribal activity in the light of an examination of Copenhagen, Arnamagnaean Institute 429 12mo, which, it is argued, offers compelling indications of having been written for use in the Kirkjubær convent and may well have its provenance there.

II

The codex AM 429 12mo is an all-female legendary similar to, for example, Osbern Bokenham's (ca. 1393–ca. 1463) *Legendys of Hooly Wummen*,[7] the German *Passienbüchlein von den vier Hauptjungfrauen* and *Das Buch von*

---

learned women are particularly numerous, a leading scholar on the subject, Margaret King, has identified no more than thirty-five such women in Italy. The medievalist Roland Bainton, in his three-volume work on women of the Reformation in Europe, adds no more than ten names of learned women to those mentioned by King. One can safely say that up to 1700 there are fewer than 300 learned women in Western Europe known to historians."

[5] Helga Kress, *Máttugar meyjar*, 17, says: "Mikið af ritstörfum miðalda hefur farið fram í klaustrunum. Á þessu tímabili voru tvö nunnuklaustur á Íslandi . . . og þar hefur að öllum líkindum verið unnið að ritstörfum eins og í munkaklaustrunum og nunnuklaustrum erlendis." Jón Viðar Sigurðsson, "Utenlandske kvinnehelgener på Island i høymiddelalderen," in *Samtíðarsögur: The Contemporary Sagas. The Ninth International Saga Conference, Akureyri 31.7–6.8. 1994*, 2 vols. (Reykjavík, 1994), 2: 423–34, esp. 426, emphasizes the fact that the named translators and redactors of saints' lives are all priests and monks and that the nuns probably were not involved in the choice and translation of the legends, but argues that it is nonetheless highly likely that the nuns were active as copyists ("det [er] likevel fullt mulig at nonnene har vært aktive som kopiister").

[6] Inga Huld Hákonardóttir, "Í nunnuklaustri — Kirkjubær og Reynistaður," in *Kristni á Íslandi*, ed. Hjalti Hugason, 4 vols. (Reykjavík, 2000), 2: 225–29, esp. 226.

[7] Bokenham's legendary is preserved in a single manuscript, London, British Library, MS. Arundel 327, written in Cambridge in 1447. Sheila Delany, trans., *A Legend of Holy Women: Osbern Bokenham*, Legends of Holy Women (Notre Dame and London, 1992), who is evidently not familiar with the German *Passienbüchlein* (see n. 8 below), claims that "Bokenham's *Legend* is unique in the history of hagiography, for it is the first all-female hagiography in any language" (xxvii). She notes, however, that there were partial models and antecedents, among them Aldhelm's (639–709) didactic tract *De laudibus virginitatis*, which is divided into male and female virgins; the Franciscan friar Nicole Bozon's (late thirteenth–early fourteenth centuries) lives of nine female saints, although it is not known if they were intended as a set; and Christine de Pizan's (ca. 1365–ca.1430) *Livre de la cité des dames*, in which stories of a group of women saints form a small portion.

den heiligen Mägden und Frauen,[8] and in some respects the Danish *De hellige kvinder,*[9] but in Old Norse-Icelandic hagiographical literature it is the only extant legendary devoted exclusively to legends of female saints.[10]

AM 429 12mo is a small, stout volume now consisting of 84 leaves, which are divided into 11 gatherings. Gathering 1 consists of 10 bifolia. Gatherings 2–5 are of the ordinary type, each containing 8 bifolia (folios 11–18, 19–26, 27–34, 35–42).[11] Gathering 6 also consists of 8 leaves (folios 43–50), but the two middle leaves, folios 46 and 47, have joints extending to folios 48r and 46v, respectively. Gathering 7 is a normal gathering of 8 bifolia (folios 51–58). Gathering 8 has 6 bifolia (folios 59–64). Gathering 9 consists of 8 leaves (folios

---

[8] Sibylle Jefferis and Konrad Kunze, "Passienbüchlein von den vier Hauptjung-frauen," in *Die deutsche Literatur des Mittelalters: Verfasserlexikon,* ed. Kurt Ruh, 2nd rev. ed. (Berlin and New York, 1989), 325–28, esp. 326, date the *Passienbüchlein* to the first half of the fourteenth century, although the manuscripts and imprints preserving the work are considerably younger; the oldest manuscript is Uppsala, University Library, MS. C 497 from ca. 1400. Werner Williams-Krapp, *Die deutschen und niederländischen Legendare des Mittelalters: Studien zu ihrer Überlieferungs-, Text- und Wirkungsgeschichte* (Tübingen, 1986), 30, dates *Das Buch von den heiligen Mägden und Frauen,* extant in Karlsruhe, Badische Landesbibliothek, cod. Licht. 69, to around 1460.

[9] *De hellige kvinder* is extant in Stockholm, Royal Library, MS. K 4 from the mid-fif-teenth century. It is comprised of fourteen items, representing various genres of legends. The first two items, "om joachim oc anna oc maria" and "om vorherræ fødelssæ," make up the *Evangelium Pseudo-Matthaei;* the third item, "Aff vorherræ pyne," gives the story of the passion based primarily on Matthew; the fourth item is *Transitus Mariae;* and the fifth is *Visio Pauli.* These New Testament (apocryphal and canonical) narratives are fol-lowed by legends of seven female virgin saints (Margaret of Antioch, Christina, Cecilia, Catherine of Alexandria, Lucy, Agnes, and Sophia and her daughters). The thirteenth item is the legend of St Marina. The legendary concludes fragmentarily with miracles at-tributed to the Virgin Mary.

[10] Copenhagen, Arnamagnaean Institute 238 fol. I (ca. 1300) and fol. II (ca. 1300–1350) may be remnants of legendaries of female saints. The former manuscript now con-sists of only two leaves containing fragments of the legends of St Mary of Egypt and St Agnes. The latter manuscript consists of six leaves. The first four contain fragments of the legends of St Andrew the apostle and St Basil; the last two, fragments of the legends of St Catherine of Alexandria, St Agnes, and St Agatha. Because of the different size of the last two leaves, Gustav Morgenstern, "Notizen," *Arkiv för nordisk filologi* 11 (1895): 95–97, esp. 97, suggested that originally they did not belong with the first four, and it may be that they are the remaining part of a legendary devoted to female saints.

[11] Between the second and third gathering, it appears that a gathering consisting of 10 leaves is missing (see below).

65–72), but only folios 67 and 70 are bifolia; the others are loose leaves with joints (the joint of folio 65 extends to 72r, that of folio 66 to 71v, that of folio 68 to 69r, that of folio 69 to 68r, that of folio 71 to 67v, and that of folio 72 to 65r; the sewing is in the joint of folio 68). Gathering 10 has 5 leaves (folios 73–77), but only folios 73 and 77 are bifolia. Folios 74, 75, and 76 have joints; the sewing is in the joint of folio 74 to which the joint of folio 76 is extended and that of folio 75 glued. Gathering 11 consists of 7 leaves (folios 78–84); folio 80 has a joint extending to folio 83r. There is no pattern regarding hair and flesh sides of the vellum; vellum was expensive in Iceland, and no doubt efforts were made to utilize as much of the skin as possible.

The vellum is undoubtedly calfskin. The pages, which measure 11.5 × 8.8 cm., are regular in size, though the outer margin of folios 60, 82, and 84 have been trimmed. Some minor trimming may also have taken place on folios 67, 70, and 72. The vellum is of good quality, though on folios 68 and 72 there are folds, and on folios 8, 20, 28, 47, 49, 66, 69, 75, and 83 there are small holes. Moreover, the bottom corner of folio 27 has been ripped off, and folio 50 is torn almost right across.

The spine shows evidence of altogether eight cord sewings, from which it may be concluded that the codex was once bound. Presumably, the original cover was a leather cover. The codex has been rebound, probably during Árni Magnússon's (1663–1730) time. The present cover consists of soft, grey cardboard plates. Folio 1, which is part of the first gathering, is a pastedown and appears to be contemporaneous with the present binding.

There are 16–18 (occasionally 14, 15, and 19) lines of writing to the single-columned pages (except where a gap is left at the end of a section). At least four hands may be distinguished in AM 429 12mo. Hand I is responsible for folios 2r–13r, 15r–39v12, 40r6–44v5, and 44v9–84v. Hand II appears only twice and writing only a few lines, that is, folios 39v12–40r5 and 44v6–8. It distinguishes itself from hand I primarily by its use of *æ* and *a*. Hand III, which is found on folio 13v (a Latin prayer to St Catherine of Alexandria), is altogether different from hands I and II. Its main characteristics as opposed to hands I and II are its single-storey *a* and triangular-shaped descender of *g*. Hand IV appears on folio 59v (a Latin verse about and prayer to St Dorothy). It is quite similar to hand I, except that its long *s* does not descend below the line. Hand I changes somewhat in the course of the manuscript. Among other things, the scribe begins on folio 61r to make use of small capital *n* (*N*) to denote the geminate and starts on folio 61v to regularly furnish *j* with a crossbar, while the occasional use of small capital *s* (*S*) with a superior dot is abandoned after folio 59r. The differences suggest that the manuscript was written over an extended period of time, during which the scribe's habits changed, but the possibility that more scribes were involved cannot be excluded.

Kr. Kålund, Jón Þorkelsson, and Didrik Arup Seip date the manuscript to around 1500.[12] C. R. Unger dates it to about half a century earlier.[13] His view is shared by Konráð Gíslason, who maintains that it is from approximately the same time as Copenhagen, Arnamagnaean Institute 621 4to, which he dates to the mid-fifteenth century.[14] Jón Helgason, however, comments, that Konráð Gíslason's dating is "hardly correct."[15]

The manuscript contains a prose legend of St Margaret of Antioch (folios 2r–13r), a Latin verse in praise of Sts Catherine of Alexandria and Celia (folio 13v), a prose legend of St Catherine of Alexandria (folios 15r–27r),[16] a prose and a poetic legend of St Cecilia (folios 29r–45v; 46r–47v),[17] a prose and a poetic legend of St Dorothy (folios 49r–57r; 57r–59r),[18] a Latin verse about and prayer to St Dorothy (folio 59v),[19] a prose legend of St Agnes (folios 61r–69r),[20] a prose legend of St Agatha (folios 69r–76r), a prose legend of St Barbara (folios 76r–80v),[21] and

---

[12] Kr. Kålund, *Katalog over Den arnamagnæanske Håndskriftsamling*, 2 vols. (Copenhagen, 1888–1894), 2: 480; Jón Þorkelsson, *Om Digtningen på Island i det 15. og 16. Århundrede* (Copenhagen, 1888), 88; Didrik Arup Seip, *Palæografi. B: Norge og Island*, ed. Johs. Brøndum-Nielsen, Nordisk kultur 28:B (Stockholm, Oslo, and Copenhagen, 1954), 137.

[13] C. R. Unger, ed., *Heilagra manna søgur: Fortællinger og legender om hellige mænd og kvinder*, 2 vols. (Christiania [Oslo], 1877), 1: xii.

[14] Konráð Gíslason, ed., *Fire og fyrretyve for en stor deel forhen utrykte prøver af oldnordisk sprog og literatur* (Copenhagen, 1860), xi.

[15] Jón Helgason, ed., *Íslenzk miðaldakvæði: Islandske digte fra senmiddelalderen* (Copenhagen, 1938), 2:341.

[16] Variants from AM 429 12mo (called C) are given in Unger, *Heilagra manna søgur*, 1: 400–21, esp. 400–3, 411–21.

[17] Variants from AM 429 12mo (called C) are given in Unger, *Heilagra manna søgur*, 1: 276–97, esp. 276–94. The poetic legend was edited by Konráð Gíslason, *Fire og fyrretyve for en stor deel forhen utrykte prøver*, 559–60, and stanzas 1 and 31 are printed in Jón Þorkelsson, *Om Digtningen på Island*, 88–89. Jón Helgason, *Íslenzk miðaldakvæði*, 2: 342–46, based his edition of the poem on Copenhagen, Arnamagnaean Institute 721 4to but includes variants from AM 429 12mo (called B).

[18] The prose legend has been edited by Unger, *Heilagra manna søgur*, 1: 322–28, and Kirsten Wolf, ed., *The Icelandic Legend of Saint Dorothy*, Studies and Texts 130 (Toronto, 1998), 88–103. The poetic legend has been edited by Jón Helgason, *Íslenzk miðaldakvæði*, 2: 359–63.

[19] The verse and the prayer have been edited by Wolf, *The Icelandic Legend of Saint Dorothy*, 62.

[20] Variants from AM 429 12mo (called B) are given in Unger, *Heilagra manna søgur*, 1: 15–22.

[21] The legend has been edited by Kirsten Wolf, ed., *The Old Norse-Icelandic Legend of Saint Barbara*, Studies and Texts 134 (Toronto, 2000), 134–43.

a prose legend of Sts Fides, Spes, and Caritas (folios 81r–84v).[22] All the texts are preserved in their entirety with the exception of the legend of St Catherine and the legend of Sts Fides, Spes, and Caritas, which are both defective. In the former, there is a lacuna between folios 18v and 19r. It appears that a gathering consisting of 10 leaves is missing. Of the latter, the conclusion, corresponding to approximately 4 leaves of text, is missing. Considering the fact that folio 84v is quite worn, the 4 leaves would seem to have been lost at an early date, if indeed the codex ever contained the complete text of the legend of Sts Fides, Spes, and Caritas. It seems reasonable to assume that in its original form the codex consisted of 94 or 98 leaves.

Folio 1r is blank; it was no doubt intended as a title page. Folios 14r, 27v, 28r, 48r, and 60r were originally blank. On folios 14r and 27v–28r, the alphabet is written in a seventeenth-century hand, along with the formulaic prayer indicating the sign of the cross (in one instance referring only to the sign [of the cross]): "i nafne faudur | og sonar og anda | heilags amen" (27v), "Signinginn" (28r), and "J nafne fødur og sonar og an[d]|a heilags Amen" (28r). On folio 27v is also written that "þetta er bok Gudrunar | ad leika sier ad þui hun | rifnar ei þo ostillt sie med | fared," which suggest that the manuscript was, at least at one point, in private possession. The scribbles on folio 48r are most likely those of a child practicing letters of the alphabet and are quite similar to those at the bottom of folio 13v. At the bottom of folio 59v, some lines from Hallgrímur Pétursson's (1614–1674) *Passíusálmar* (that is, stanza 1 of hymn 44) are found, also in a seventeenth-century hand: "hropade iesus hatt i stad | hoollds megn og krapt|ur duinar ieg fel minn and|a frelsarinn kuad fad|er i hendur þinar." The first couple of lines of stanza 1 appear again on folio 60r,[23] which includes also all of stanza 2 and the first line of stanza 3: "þu christenn madur þeinck | a þins herra beiskann d[auda] | ad ordum hans og eirni[nng]|a eru þaug læckning n[aud]|a | iesus halldinn i hæst." Stanza 1 and the first line of stanza 2 are also found on the upper half of folio 81r.[24]

The originally blank space on folio 81r was most likely intended for an illumination of Sts Fides, Spes, and Caritas in color or black, for the volume is copiously illuminated. The colors used are red and blue. Full-page, colored illuminations of Sts Margaret, Catherine, Cecilia, and Dorothy are found on

---

[22] Variants from AM 429 12mo (called D) are given in Unger, *Heilagra manna søgur*, 1: 369–76, esp. 369–72.

[23] "hropade iesus hatt hollss matt | og kraptur | hropade iesus hatt i stad holss | og krap."

[24] "hropade iesus hatt i stad | hollds megn og kraptur duin|ar eg fel minn anda frelsar|inn kuad fader i hendur þin|ar. | þu christinn madur þeinck."

folios 1v, 14v, 28v, and 48v, respectively, and on folio 60v there is a full-page illustration of St Agnes in black. All the illuminations are framed, and in appearance the five saints are virtually identical: they all have the same facial features and are depicted with shoulder-length, wavy hair, and are all richly dressed and wearing crowns (with the exception of St Cecilia). What distinguishes the saints are their attributes: Margaret with the staff of a cross,[25] Catherine with the wheel,[26] Cecilia with a book,[27] Dorothy with a basket,[28] and Agatha with a lamb.[29] (Evidently, the illuminator confused St Agatha with St Agnes, whose characteristic iconographic emblem is a lamb; St Agatha's emblem is usually a dish with her breasts.) Smaller illustrations of a similar kind appear also on folios 69r (St Agatha, in black) and 76r (St Barbara, in

---

[25] The frame surrounding St Margaret is red with black borders. Above the frame is written "Sancta Margrieta mey" in a late hand. She is wearing an ankle-length, red-and-white-striped dress with long sleeves and a low, dotted neckline. A red shawl or cape is draped over her shoulders. In her right hand she holds a book, and in her left the staff of a long red cross, upon which a dove is perched.

[26] The frame surrounding the illumination of St Catherine is identical to that surrounding the illumination of St Margaret. St Catherine's blue and red dress, which has an empire waist, a higher neckline, and blue sleeves, is somewhat more elaborate than St Margaret's, and St Catherine's blue shoes are more visible than St Margaret's white shoes, which are almost hidden by her long dress. In her right hand St Catherine holds a sword, and in her left a wheel.

[27] Of the frame surrounding the illumination of St Cecilia only the vertical parts and the bottom part are red. Within the upper horizontal lines of the frame is written "*sancta cecilia ora pro nobis*." Her blue and red dress is quite similar to St Catherine's, but unlike Sts Margaret and Catherine, she is veiled. By St Cecilia's feet lies a naked, bearded man, and St Cecilia is depicted with her bare right foot on his lower back and piercing his right eye with a sword, which she holds in her right hand. In her left hand she holds a book with a forte sign on its cover (presumably to indicate that it is a songbook). In the left margin, a crude copy of the illumination appears in black, though without the man at St Cecilia's feet.

[28] The frame surrounding the illumination of St Dorothy differs from the other three in that the black vertical columns are ornamented. The horizontal lines of the frame contain the following text: "Sancta dorathea ora pro nobis" (in black) and "þetta er darateu [*sic*] saga mey*ar*" (in red). St Dorothy's dress is red and white and quite similar to St Margaret's; however, her shoes are black and pointed. In her left hand she carries a book, and in her right a woven basket with fruits.

[29] It seems reasonable to assume that St Agnes was intended to appear in color as well, for two of the folds in her long dress are colored red. The frame surrounding the illustration of St Agnes consists of two black lines. Within the upper horizontal lines of the frame is written "*sancta* agnes ora p*ro* nob*is*." In her right hand she holds a book, and in her left a long spear.

black). St Agatha is depicted with a torch in her left hand, a book in her right, and a lamb at her feet; and St Barbara with a sword in her left hand, a book in her right, and with what looks like a cactus, but what is probably meant to be a tower, in the background. Moreover, colored illuminations (black and red) are found within the text of the legend of St Margaret on folios 7r, 8r, 10r, and 12v, depicting scenes from her passion.[30] In addition, there are ornamental drawings in black of beasts (or parts of them) at the bottom of folios 35r, 52r, 52v, and 57r,[31] and similar beasts appear in the form of initials on folios 49r (*J*; red) and 76r (*A*; black); the latter is almost idential to the beast on folio 35r. Red chapter titles and initials (blue initials are found on folios 6r and 29r) appear regularly in the first two-thirds of the manuscript. Some of the initials in red and black or black only are quite ornate. The last red initial is found on folio 51r.

On a note accompanying the codex, Árni Magnússon gives the information that he received it from "Páll á Flókastöðum" ("Mitt, feinged af Paale ä Flokastòdum") and lists its contents.[32] This Páll is most likely Páll Ámundason (ca. 1645–1716), son of Ámundi Þormóðsson at Skógar and Solveig Árnadóttir. Páll Ámundason was the administrator of the convent land of Kirkjubær from 1681 to 1708 or 1709 and died at Flókastaðir in Fljótshlíð, where his son-in-law, Björn Thorlacius, served as minister. Páll Ámundason's association with the codex and the nature of its contents make it reasonable to assume that originally

---

[30] The illumination on folio 7r shows St Margaret, with the staff of a long red cross in her left hand and a book in her right, emerging from the belly of a fire-spewing dragon. The illumination on folio 8r shows the saint grabbing the devil's head with her left hand (in her right she holds the long cross) and about to plant her right foot on it. The illumination on folio 10r shows the saint having lifted her foot off the devil's head. And the illumination on folio 12v, which takes up half the page, shows the headsman having just decapitated the kneeling St Margaret, with three angels in the air as spectators.

[31] The beast on folio 35r stands on its two strong hind legs (its front legs are very short and not used for support). It has a long tail, and its head is turned towards its back. Its mouth is wide open, and out of it sticks a long, curled, snake-like tongue. The illustration in the lower left margin by the spine on folio 52r is of only a head, half-human, half-bird. The illustration at the bottom of folio 52v comprises only half a head, one front leg, and a small potion of what is probably a tail. The beast on folio 57r is hardly visible, but appears to be a dragon.

[32] The same information is found in Árni Magnússon's catalogue (*Arne Magnussons i AM. 435A–B, 4to indeholdte håndskriftfortegnelser med to tillæg*, ed. Kr. Kålund [Copenhagen, 1909], 17: "Margretar Saga. de S. Catharinâ. de S. Cæciliâ, og þar i de Tiburtio et Valeriano. Carmen de S. Cæciliâ. de S. Dorotheâ. Carmen de S. Dorotheâ. de S. Agnete. de S. Agathâ. de S. Barbarâ. de S. Sophiâ, desunt nunnulla in calce. Er i 16 blade forme. feinged af Pale á Flokastòdum".

it belonged to the Kirkjubær convent and remained there at least until shortly
after the mid-sixteenth century, when the Icelandic monasteries were dissolved
and all church property was confiscated by order of the Danish King Christian
III (1503–1559; r. 1534–1559). The Kirkjubær convent was leased to the minister Einar Árnason (ca. 1498–1585) in 1554,[33] and what happened to its valuables
remains unknown. It is possible that its treasures ended up in Copenhagen like
those of the cathedral church at Hólar and the monasteries of Munkaþverá
(founded 1155), Möðruvellir (founded 1296), and Þingeyrar (founded 1133).[34]
The convent's collection of books and manuscripts, of which, according to the
inventory of 1397,[35] it had a fair number, not only service books but also twenty
books in Latin and Norse ("xx latinv bækur og norrænv"), was most likely dispersed.[36] Eventually, many volumes were no doubt lost due to improper care;
others, such as prayer-books, saints' lives, and other "popish" literature, were
probably discarded or destroyed.[37] The physical attraction of AM 429 12mo
may explain why the codex was preserved, and its sturdiness (cf. the note on
folio 27v) why it withstood almost intact two centuries of wear and tear before
it found its home in Árni Magnússon's collection in Copenhagen.

III

It is impossible to determine if the legends in AM 429 12mo are copied
from a legendary or from individual lives circulating in Iceland. The latter
seems likely, for although the codex is unified thematically in that the saints

[33] *Diplomatarium Islandicum: Íslenzkt fornbréfasafn*, 16 vols. (Copenhagen and
Reykjavík, 1857–1952), 12: 683–84 (hereafter *DI*).

[34] *DI* 12: 328–30.

[35] *DI* 4: 238–39.

[36] The defective inventory of 1343 lists only service-books (*DI* 2: 781; 8: 5). That
many books were scattered, we have on the authority of Jón Guðmundsson lærði (1574–
1658), who in his *Tijdfordrijf Edur Lijtid Annals Kuer* tells that one book from the Skálholt cathedral had been carried to his distant home district (Strandir), when the cathedral's library was destroyed or dispersed at the introduction of the Reformation, and that
he learned to read from it (Halldór Hermannsson, ed., *Jón Guðmundsson and His Natural
History of Iceland*, Islandica 15 [Ithaca, 1924; repr. New York, 1966], xiv).

[37] Jón Guðmundsson lærði relates that in 1523–24 the Lutheran minister Sigurður
Jónsson made two or three bonfires of the books which had belonged to the Helgafell
church and monastery (established 1184), and which his predecessors had apparently left
undisturbed (Halldór Hermannsson, *Jón Guðmundsson*, xvi). This is, however, the only
known instance of books being committed to the flames in Iceland.

included are all virgin martyr saints, the arrangement of the legends is not *per circulum anni* and seems quite arbitrary.[38] There is nothing to suggest that any of the Icelandic legends contained in AM 429 12mo are original translations. All the legends are extant in manuscripts dating from before 1500 with the exception of the prose legend of St Dorothy, which is preserved only in AM 429 12mo. The Latin source for the legend has been demonstrated to be "a text which was in the main identical with *BHL* 2324, but which differed in regard to certain details, some of which are now found in *BHL* 2325d."[39] A number of errors in the text of the legend, such as "aungu*m*" for "ungu*m*" (50r4), "ei*n*gín*n*" for "eigín" (50v2), "fíoll" for "fíell" (52r15), the repetition of "bren" (53v1), the anticipation of "af sínu*m*" after "h*a*na" in "fr*e*ls þu h*a*na dr*o*ttín*n* mín*n* af sinu*m* krankleika" (54v13–14), and the occasional omission of a word, suggest that the prose text is a copy.

AM 429 12mo is also the oldest manuscript preserving the poetic legend of St Dorothy; the other manuscripts containing the so-called *Dorotheudiktur* or parts thereof date from the nineteenth and twentieth centuries.[40] In Jón Helgason's view, the poem is recorded from oral tradition: "Digtet er uden tvivl nedskrevet efter mundtlig tradition."[41] He bases his assumption on the garbled line "m*e*d gledín*n*e místu uífs" (58r4–5), which, through misrecollection, may have resulted from the confusion of "gud m*e*d gledína ęsta" (58r15) and "s*u*o at bad*a*r místu lífs" (58r3–4). He also notes that the order of the stanzas in the poem as represented by the extant manuscripts is erroneous, and if the description of St Dorothy's *passio* is to follow the prose legend and its Latin source, further rearrangement of the stanzas would be necessary. Jón Helgason comments, however, that it is uncertain if the poem ever followed the prose account accurately. Whether AM 429 12mo is a copy of a now-lost manuscript or presents the original recording of the poem from oral tradition cannot be ascertained.

---

[38] The feast days of the saints are as follows: Margaret (20 July), Catherine (25 November), Cecilia (22 November), Dorothy (6 February), Agnes (21 January), Agatha (5 February), Barbara (4 December), and Fides, Spes, and Caritas (1 August).

[39] Wolf, *The Icelandic Legend of Saint Dorothy*, 76. BHL = *Bibliotheca Hagiographica Latina Antiquae et Mediae Aetatis*, Subsidia Hagiographica 6 (Brussels, 1898–1899; repr. Brussels, 1992); *Supplementum*, Subsidia Hagiographica 12 (Brussels, 1911); *Novum supplementum*, Subsidia Hagiographica 70 (Brussels, 1986).

[40] A copy by Jón Sigurðsson is found in Reykjavík, Landsbókasafn, Jón Sigurðsson 399 4to (only the first stanza); by Steingrímur Thorsteinsson in Copenhagen, Arnamagnaean Institute 920 4to; and by Páll Eggert Ólason in Reykjavík, Landsbókasafn 2166 4to.

[41] Jón Helgason, *Íslenzk miðaldakvæði*, 2: 359.

The legend of St Margaret is extant in numerous manuscripts ranging in date from ca. 1300 to ca. 1550. A thorough examination of all these manuscripts remains to be undertaken. Ole Widding, Hans Bekker-Nielsen, and L.K. Shook distinguish among three main versions of the legend and regard Copenhagen, Arnamagnaean Institute 428a 12mo (ca. 1300–1400) and AM 429 12mo as representatives of the so-called "Margrétar saga II."[42] They identify the source as *BHL* 5303, but note that the introductory section is omitted in the translation. Comparison with the Latin shows that AM 429 12mo is not a copy of AM 428a 12mo, for in several places AM 429 12mo has superior readings or preserves text not included in AM 428a 12mo. These include "theodosíus" (2r2; "theodinus" AM 428a 12mo 1v2), "hofdíngi blot m*ann*a" (2r2; "hofdingi blóta" AM 428a 12mo 1v2–3), "f*yr*ir naf*n* d*r*ottíns j(hesu) c(risti)" (2r12; "f*yr*ir nafn guðs" AM 428a 12mo 2r1), "felldi ha*nn* þeg*ar* hug *til* hen*ar*" (2v7–8; om. AM 428a 12mo), and "eí ma sam*an* koma uelldí þítt *uit* mey þessa þ*ui* at h*un* þíonar eigi godum þínu*m* helldr kallar h*un* a c*r*ist er gydíng*ar* c*r*oss festu" (3r12–15; "Æigi máttu samþykku uerða þessi mey. herra þ*uiat* h*un* er kristín" AM 428a 12mo 2v11–13).

The legend of St Catherine is preserved in its entirety only in Stockholm, Kungliga Biblioteket Perg. 2 fol. (ca. 1425–1445); in Copenhagen, Arnamagnaean Institute 233a fol. (ca. 1350–1375) the beginning is missing, and in AM 429 12mo a middle portion is lost due to a lacuna in the manuscript (see above). Fragments of the legend are found in Copenhagen, Arnamagnaean Institute 238 fol. II (ca. 1300–1350) and 667 4to II (ca. 1400–1500). According to Peter Foote, the beginning and end of the Icelandic legend are derived from a text of the *Passio auct. Pseudo-Athanasio* (*BHL* 1659) with only the first half of the epilogue (*BHL* 1660) included.[43] Foote notes that many passages within the text suggest the same source, but observes that it is also possible to find matter and wording in the Icelandic legend which have parallels only in other versions of the legend, variously *BHL* 1657, 1663, and 1667. Of the five manuscripts, Stock. Perg. 2 fol. and AM 429 12mo appear closest to the Latin. On a number of occasions, AM 429 12mo preserves more accurate and, presumably, more original readings than Stock. Perg. 2 fol., such as "díoclecíano" (15r2–3; "domícíano" Stock. Perg. 2 fol. 74rb9), "latít aungar u*id*barur amot ko*m*a þessu u*o*ro bodi" (15v6–7; "ok setít ǫngur berior j moti þessv vorv bodí" Stock. Perg. 2 fol. 74rb29–30), and "en nu uil ek mẹla líost hiedan j fra suo at alþyda megi skilía mi*n* ord þeir er uid eru stadir" (17r15–17;

[42] Ole Widding, Hans Bekker-Nielsen, and L.K. Shook, "The Lives of the Saints in Old Norse Prose: A Handlist," *Mediaeval Studies* 25 (1963): 294–337, esp. 320.

[43] Peter Foote, ed., *Lives of Saints. Perg. fol. nr. 2 in the Royal Library, Stockholm*, Early Icelandic Manuscripts in Facsimile 4 (Copenhagen, 1962), 26.

En*n* nv vil ek hedan j fra at allír megi skilía mín ord þe*ir* sem vit eru stadd*ir*" Stock. Perg. 2 fol. 74vb1–3). The legend of St Catherine in AM 429 12mo thus cannot be derived from Stock. Perg. 2 fol.; rather the two texts must go back to a common source.

AM 429 12mo is the only manuscript preserving the legend of St Cecilia in its entirety, although it does not include the appended account of the two miracles that took place in Iceland (see n. 65). This account is found only in Stock. Perg. 2 fol., which, like Copenhagen, Arnamagnaean Institute 235 fol. (ca. 1400), contains only a portion of the legend. The source is, according to Foote, a form of the longer recension of the *passio* (*BHL* 1495), though the introductory chapters 1–2 have been omitted in the Icelandic legend.[44] In his edition of the legend, Unger based the text on Stock. Perg. 2 fol. and AM 235 fol. and used AM 429 12mo only to fill in the portion of text not covered by Stock. Perg. 2 fol. and AM 235 fol.[45] Clearly, however, the text in AM 429 12mo is not derived from either of the two manuscripts, for often AM 429 12mo has superior readings or preserves text not included in Stock. Perg. 2 fol. and AM 235 fol., such as, for example, "hafdí h*ann* tuę*r* korun*ur* ski*n*a<n>dí or gullu [*sic*] ok or hínu*m* feguz<t>u*m* grosu*m* (31v5–6; "en*ar* dyrligstv" Stock. Perg. 2 fol. 80vb18, AM 235 fol. 67r38) and "ran*n* up akr auelle u*er*kman*na* m*ed* ol-lu*m* fogru*m* bloma ok dyrlegu*m* grossu*m* (38r17–38v1; "t*oko* akr*ar* m*anna* at f<r>iovazt" AM 235 fol. 68v37).

AM 429 12mo is also the oldest extant manuscript of the poetic legend of St Cecilia. The other manuscript containing the so-called *Ceciliudiktur* is Copenhagen, Arnamagnaean Institute 721 4to (ca. 1500–1550). In addition, there are copies of the text in AM 429 12mo by Jón Sigurðsson in Reykjavík, Landsbókasafn, Jón Sigurðsson 399 4to and by Páll Eggert Ólason in Reykjavík, Landsbókasafn 2166 4to, and there is a copy of Copenhagen, Arnamagnaean Institute 721 4to by Einar Hálfdanarson in Reykjavík, Landsbókasafn, Jón Sigurðsson 112 8vo.[46] AM 429 12mo and AM 721 4to appear to be independently derived from a common exemplar, the date of which remains unknown. The

---

[44] Foote, *Lives of Saints*, 26–27. The longer recension has been edited by Hippolyte Delehaye, *Études sur le légendier romain: Les saints de Novembre et Décembre*, Subsidia Hagiographica 23 (Brussels, 1936), 194–220. Foote notes that "[t]he source for the Icelandic work appears to have been closer to his [Delehaye's] manuscript C than to his manuscript P."

[45] Unger, *Heilagra manna søgur*, 1: 276–97. Stock. Perg. 2 fol. covers 276–279.20 and 289.10–297. AM 235 fol. covers 279.20–287.1. AM 429 12mo covers 287.1–289.10.

[46] A copy of JS 112 8vo by Hálfdan Einarsson is found in Reyjkjavík, Landsbókasafn 848 4to, which, in turn, was copied by Friðrik Eggerz in Reykjavík, Landsbókasafn 936 4to and by Páll Pálsson in Reykjavík, Landsbókasafn 201 8vo (Jón Helgason, *Íslenzk miðaldakvæði*, 2: 341–42).

poem differs from the prose text but appears to be related to the fourteenth-century *Heilagra meyja drápa*,[47] stanzas 18–21 of which concern St Cecilia. Foote draws attention to the fact that both *Heilagra meyja drápa* (st. 19) and *Ceciliudiktur* (st. 17) state that St Cecilia stood six days in the fire before her execution.[48] He also observes that *Ceciliudiktur* (st. 8) mentions the music at St Cecilia's wedding-feast, a detail not included in the prose legend.

Three versions of the legend of St Agnes are extant. The text of AM 429 12mo belongs to what Widding, Bekker-Nielsen, and Shook call "Agnesar saga meyiar I,"[49] and it is the only manuscript which preserves the legend in its entirety. In Stock. Perg. 2 fol., the end is missing, and the fragments AM 235 fol., AM 238 fol. I and II cover only small sections of the text. The source of the legend is, according to Foote, the *passio* of Pseudo-Ambrose (*BHL* 156) in a version closer to that printed in the *Acta Sanctorum* (Jan. II: 351–55) than the one edited by Migne in *Patrologia Latina* (17: 813–821).[50] Foote notes that the Icelandic text is slightly abridged and that the epilogue is omitted. Stock. Perg. 2 fol. has the better text, but on occasion AM 429 12mo preserves readings closer to the Latin or text omitted in Stock. Perg. 2 fol., such as "Ver holldu*m* hatída*r* dag hína*r* helguz<t>o meyia*r* m*ed* salmu*m ok* guds lofí gledesz flokka*r* lyda *ok* fagní *c*ristz olmosor" (61r2–5; "Wær hǫlldum hatidar dag enn*ar* helguztv meyia*r ok* fagni kristz ólmòsu*r*" Stock. Perg. 2 fol. 84ra9–11; "Ver holld*um* hatida*r* dag enn*ar* helguztu meyia*r* agnesa*r*" AM 235 fol. 4vl1–13) and "þa ua*r* kuat þi*ng*s *ok* dreíf þangat mikill fiolldí m*ann*a *ok* ua*r*d þr*e*ta mikill u*m* guds mey" (65r9–10; om. Stock. Perg. 2 fol.). For the portion of the legend not preserved in Stock. Perg. 2 fol., Unger (*Heilagra manna søgur*, 1:15–22, esp. 19–22) based the text on AM 429 12mo, though in some instances the fragments AM 238 fol. I and II have superior readings, such as "*ok* styrkði h*ann* hug henar reisandi manin af d*a*ða" (AM 238 fol. I 2r15–16; "*ok* skryddi hus*it ok* reisti up*p* hin*n* unga m*ann*" AM 429 12mo 65v17–66r1) and "*ok* lifðu marga*r* aðrar meyiar ept*ir* h*e*nar dæmv*m*" (AM 238 fol. II 6r2; "*ok* lífdu marga*r* ept*ir* heNar d*e*mu*m*" AM 429 12mo 68v13).

Altogether five different versions of the legend of St Agatha have been preserved. The source of the various versions is, according to Foote, a form of

[47] Finnur Jónsson, ed., *Den norsk-islandske Skjaldedigtning*, 1A–2A (*tekst efter hånd-skrifterne*) and 1B–2B (*rettet tekst*) (Copenhagen, 1908–1915), 2A:526–39 and 2B:582–97. Jakob Benediktsson, "Helgendigte," *Kulturhistorisk Leksikon for nordisk middelalder* 6 (Copenhagen, 1961), 318–20, esp. 319–20, believes that the poem may be older.
[48] Foote, *Lives of Saints*, 27.
[49] Widding, Bekker-Nielsen, and Shook, "The Lives of the Saints," 298.
[50] Foote, *Lives of Saints*, 27.

the *passio, BHL* 133.[51] Stock. Perg. 2 fol. and AM 429 12mo represent what Unger calls "Agathu saga meyiar I."[52] Stock. Perg. 2 fol. clearly preserves the better text, but in a number of instances AM 429 12mo has more accurate and, presumably, more original readings, such as "Kuíncíanus sigil eyiar iarl heyrdi godann ord rom af einne gaufugri mey er agada het at hon dyrkadi gud" (69r5–12; "Qvíncianus sikileyiar iarll heyrdi godan ordrom vm agatham dyrlíga mey er gudi var helgut" Stock. Perg. 2 fol. 82vb1–3), "þa let Q(uincianus) skera af henne briostit" (72v1–2; "þa let quincianus skera af henne briostín" Stock. Perg. 2 fol. 83rb20–21), and "en er hon lauk bęn sinní þa uoro groenn oll sar henar ok <var> heillt bríost henar" (73v2–3; "ok voru þa heil bríost hennar" Stock. Perg. 2 fol. 83va12). Foote believes that the text of AM 429 12mo "was clearly copied from an archaic exemplar, one that might reasonably be assigned to c. 1200 and ultimately it would seem of Norwegian origin."[53]

The legend of St Barbara is extant also in Stock. Perg. 2 fol. The Latin source is the version of the *passio* listed under *BHL* Suppl. 913a.[54] Stock. Perg. 2 fol. preserves the better text, but in a few instances the text of AM 429 12mo is closer to the Latin than that of Stock. Perg. 2 fol. Accordingly, both manuscripts would seem to be independently derived from the same exemplar, AM 429 12mo probably at several removes.[55]

The legend of Sts Fides, Spes, and Caritas is preserved in full only in AM 235 fol. In Stock. Perg. 2 fol. the first half is missing, and in AM 233a fol. (ca. 1350–1375), the latter half is missing. According to Foote, the Latin source is a form of *BHL* 2971 (cf. *BHL* Suppl., 124–125, no. 3c); he notes, however, that the incipit is like that noted for *BHL* Suppl. 2968b.[56] AM 429 12mo shares some characteristics with AM 233a fol. as opposed to AM 235 fol. (e.g., "Sophía" 81v12–13 and AM 233a fol. 15v14; "Sapientia" AM 235 fol. 36v20), and on occasion the two manuscripts preserve missing or more accurate text than AM 235 fol. Generally, however, the text of the legend in AM 233a fol. appears to have undergone more revision than the texts in AM 235 fol., Stock. Perg. 2 fol., and AM 429 12mo.

The Latin verse about St Dorothy in AM 429 12mo is found also in Copenhagen, Arnamagnaean Institute 418 12mo, a Danish nun's prayer book from ca. 1500, but a connection between the two manuscripts seems unlikely. The Latin prayer to St Dorothy is not known from other Old Norse, Old Danish, or Old

---

[51] Foote, *Lives of Saints*, 27.

[52] Unger, *Heilagra manna søgur*, 1:viii, 1.

[53] Foote, *Lives of Saints*, 27.

[54] Foote, *Lives of Saints*, 26; Wolf, *The Old Norse-Icelandic Legend of Saint Barbara*, 106.

[55] Wolf, *The Old Norse-Icelandic Legend of Saint Barbara*, 103.

Swedish manuscripts, but it resembles the prayer prefacing the legend of Saint Dorothy as represented by *BHL* 2325d.[57] The Latin prayer to Saint Catherine is not preserved in other manuscripts, and its source has not been identified.

IV

Considering the somewhat specialized content of AM 429 12mo, there can be little doubt that the codex was written for use by the nuns in the Kirkjubær convent. Indeed, several of the saints whose legends are included in AM 429 12mo appear to have been especially venerated by the nuns. It is known that the convent owned images of Sts Agnes, Catherine of Alexandria, and Cecilia.[58] Moreover, on becoming abbess of the convent in 1344, Jórunn Hauksdóttir took the name Agnes,[59] and the name of Agatha Helgadóttir, abbess of Kirkjubær from 1293 to 1342, may also be a religious name; it has been pointed out by Magnús Már Lárusson that her family, which produced two bishops (Árni Þorláksson, bishop of Skálholt 1269–1298, and Árni Helgason, bishop of Skálholt 1304–1320) had connections with the area where interest in St Agatha is attested, Borgarfjörður and surrounding regions.[60] Guðný Helgadóttir, abbess of Staður ca. 1332–ca. 1368, appears to have taken the name Kristín on becoming abbess, and Þóra Finnsdóttir, abbess of Staður 1437–1461, seems to

---

[56] Foote, *Lives of Saints*, 28.

[57] Wolf, *The Icelandic Legend of Saint Dorothy*, 62. It also resembles the second prayer appended to the legend of St Dorothy in Lambeth Palace MS. 432, ed. Carl Horstmann, "Prosalegenden," *Anglia* 3 (1880): 293–360, esp. 328.

[58] *DI* 2: 781, 4: 238, 8:5. The convent also owned images of Sts Þorlákr Þórhallsson, Matthew, and Clement. The Virgin Mary was the patron of the convent. Most likely St Þorlákr, bishop of Skálholt (1178–1193), founded the convent at Kirkjubær, where he himself served as priest for six years before he became prior of the monastery of Þykkvibær (founded 1168), though Halldóra, who Anna Sigurðardóttir, *Allt hafði annan róm*, 21–22, believes is the daughter of the priest Eyjólfr Sæmundarson in Oddi, and who was consecrated abbess three years after its establishment, that is, in 1189, and served until 1210 (*DI* 3: 154) most likely assisted him.

[59] Cf. *Skálholtsannáll* s.a. 1344: "Vígð Jorunn abbadis i *Kirkiu* bæ *ok* nefnd Agnes" (Gustav Storm, ed., *Islandske Annaler indtil 1578* [Christiania (Oslo), 1888], 210). Margaret Cormack, *The Saints in Iceland: Their Veneration from the Conversion to 1400* (Brussels, 1994), 75, argues that "[t]he image [of Saint Agnes] owned by the convent appears to have been acquired while she [Jórunn Hauksdóttir] was in office."

[60] Magnús Már Lárusson, "Fornt helgidagaboð (AM. 696, 4to, fragm. XXIX)," *Skírnir* 125 (1951): 199–206.

have taken the name Barbara.[61] In fact, the saints celebrated in AM 429 12mo appear to have been among the most popular female saints in Iceland, with the exception of Sts Dorothy and Fides, Spes, and Caritas.[62] The feasts of Sts Agnes and Cecilia are both listed as Holy Days of Obligation (*löghelgir dagar*) and those of Sts Agatha and Barbara as *leyfisdagar* (days on which it is permitted to work).[63] Observance of the feast of St Catherine was never obligatory, but this is no doubt due to its position in the calendar, a day after the consecutive obligatory feasts of Sts Cecilia and Clement.[64] Similar practicalities may also explain why the feast of St Margaret was not obligatory: her feast on 20 July is also the feast of the Translation of St Þorlákr. Although feast days cannot be used as the sole criterion for measuring the popularity of individual saints, but must be seen in conjunction with other historical evidence such as patronage of churches, the inventories of the various churches corroborate the list of feasts to quite some extent. Thus St Cecilia appears as patron of three churches (Húsafell, Nes [Aðaldalur], and Saurbær [Eyjafjörður]) and co-patron of another three (Otradalur, Refsstaðir [Vopnafjörður], and Arnarbæli [Fellsströnd]), and, in addition to images of her in the three churches of which she was patron as well as at Kirkjubær, there were images at Glaumbær, Valþjófsstaðir, and Vatnsfjörður. Hruni, the monastery of Möðruvellir, Nes, and Saurbær owned copies of her legend.[65] St Agnes is co-patron of Bær

---

[61] Anna Sigurðardóttir, *Allt hafði annan róm*, 99, 129.

[62] St Dorothy figures only rarely in the Icelandic liturgical and historical sources, and evidence of a cult devoted to her is meagre. There is no evidence of a cult devoted to Sts Fides, Spes, and Caritas, and, like St Dorothy, they are not found in the majority of the extant Icelandic calendars (Cormack, *The Saints in Iceland*, 40).

[63] The feasts of Sts Agnes and Cecilia (along with that of Ambrose) were adopted in 1179 under Bishop Þorlákr Þórhallsson, and are said in *Guðmundar saga* to have been prompted by a vision in which St Agnes appeared to one Guðmundr kárhöfði (ed. Jón Sigurðsson and Guðbrandur Vigfússon, *Biskupa sögur*, 1: 420). Of the four female saints (Agnes, Brigida, Cecilia, and Sunnifa), whose feasts are listed as Holy Days of Obligation, only the feast of St Cecilia is included in the 1275 Church Law of Bishop Árni Þorláksson.

[64] Cormack, *The Saints in Iceland*, 88.

[65] St Cecilia's patronage of three churches suggests that the cult of St Cecilia is quite old and predates the thirteenth century, when most of the Icelandic churches were built. St Cecilia is also the only female saint for whom there is a record of miracles in Iceland. Stock. Perg. 2 fol. relates two cures which took place at Húsafell (Unger, *Heilagra manna søgur*, 1: 294–97). The church there had been endowed by Brandr Þórarinsson when Klængr Þorsteinsson was bishop of Skálholt (1152–1176; see Einar Ól. Sveinsson, ed., *Laxdæla saga*, Íslenzk fornrit 5 [Reykjavík, 1934], 227, and and *DI* 1: 217), and although its dedication is first attested in an inventory dated 1504 (*DI* VII: 737), the evidence for interest in St Cecilia in the late twelfth century suggests that her patronage may date from the time stated. The

(Borgarfjörður), and Miðbæli under Eyjafjöll owned a copy of her legend. St Agatha is the primary patron of a half-church (Ingunnarstaðir), co-patron of Laugardælir (Flói) and Melar, and co-patron of an altar at the monastery of Viðey (founded 1226). In addition, masses in honor of St Agatha were sung at Grenjaðarstaður and Langárfoss (half-church), and there were images of her at Steinar, Ufsir, Vellir (Svarfaðardalur), and, as noted above, Kirkjubær. It is also known that there were copies of her legend at Hólar Cathedral and Miðbæli under Eyjafjöll. St Barbara is co-patron of Reykholt and Haukadalur, and there were images of her at Reykholt, Holt (Saurbær), and Möðruvellir;[66] the last-mentioned church also owned a copy of her legend. St Margaret is co-patron of Eyri (Bitra), Laugarnes, and Tröllatunga, and there were images of her in nine churches.[67] Búðardalur, Melur, and the monastery of Viðey owned copies of her legend. St Catherine is the primary patron of Norðurtunga and Eyrar (Einarshöfn) and co-patron of no fewer than eleven churches.[68] More-over, she had, together with St Þorlákr, a chapel dedicated to her at Skálholt, and masses in honor of St Catherine were sung at Eyjólfsstaðir, Gegnishólar,

---

legend of St Cecilia in Stock. Perg. 2 fol. states that "Gudrun Ospaksdottir modir Brandz hafdi mikla virding aa Ceciliu ok let heilagt dagh hennar ok fastadi fyrir" (Unger, *Heilagra manna søgur*, 1: 295), even though it was not a Holy Day of Obligation. As noted above, the feast was adopted as a Holy Day of Obligation in 1179, and while it is possible that the miracles are late compositions designed to justify the adoption of the feast as a Holy Day of Obligation, they give the impression of being genuine records of an early cult.

[66] One such image of St Barbara (Reykjavík, Þjóðminjasafn 14293) has been preserved. In 1950, the upper part of a little figurine of St Barbara was found during excavations of what appears to have been a road-chapel in the late Middle Ages just south of Hafnarfjörður. The figurine, which is made of pipe-clay, now measures 3.3 cm. Vilhjálmur Örn Vilhjálmsson, "Af heilagri Barböru og uppruna hennar," *Árbók Hins íslenzka fornleifafélags 1982* (1983): 171–75, esp. 172–74, draws attention to the fact that the production of such miniature im-ages flourished from the mid-fifteenth century onwards in the Netherlands and Northern Germany and that in Springweg an identical figurine made in Utrecht, the best-known loca-tion of such production, was discovered, which has been dated to the second half of the fif-teenth century. St Barbara is also among the saints depicted on the Hólar bishop Jón Arason's (1484–1550) cope (Reykjavík, Þjóðminjasafn 4401; Kristján Eldjárn, *Hundrað ár í Þjóðmin-jasafni* [Reykjavík, 1973], 35, and Kristján Eldjárn and Hörður Ágústsson, *Skálholt: Skrúði og áhöld* [Reykjavík, 1992], 16–17, fig. 1) and on the large altarpiece donated to the church of Hólar by the same bishop (Kristján Eldjárn and Hörður Ágústsson, *Skálholt*, 39, fig. 45).

[67] These churches are: Goðdalir, Hólmur (Hólmshraun), Hrafnagil, Húsafell, Möðruvellir, Ofanleiti (Westman Islands), Snæfoksstaðir (Grímsnes), Vesturhólshólar, and Þverá (Skagafjörður).

[68] These churches are: Engey (half-church), Eyjólfsstaðir (half-church), Hrísar (half-church), Hruni, Hvalsnes, Hvammur (Vatnsdalur), Kolbeinsstaðir, Kroppur, Nes (Sel-vogur), Staður (Grindavík), and Sæból.

and Oddi. In addition to the images of her at Kirkjubær and at Hvammur, Norðurtunga, Kolbeinsstaðir, and Kroppur, of which she is patron or co-patron, there were images of her in twenty-three churches.[69] Only Hólar Cathedral, Hrafnagil, Höfði (Höfðahverfi), the monstery of Möðruvellir, and Norðurtunga are listed as having copies of her legend.

However, the fact that the codex was probably written for use in the Kirkjubær convent does not necessarily imply that it has its place of origin there. It is not unlikely that the legendary was compiled in the Augustinian monastery of Þykkvibær located only 35 kilometers southwest of Kirkjubær and donated to or purchased by the convent.[70] Certainly, two of the abbots, Brandr Jónsson (1247–1262; d. 1264) and Runólfr Sigmundarson (1264–1307; d. 1307), are known to have engaged in literary activity; the former is believed to have translated *Gyðinga saga* and *Alexanders saga* and the latter the legend of St Augustine. Rúnólfur Sigmundarson is also said to be the one who asked Grímr Hólmsteinsson (d. 1298), priest at Kirkjubær, to compile a legend of John the Baptist. Moreover, the poems *Harmsól*, *Jónsdrápa*, and *Lilja* are all believed to have been composed by clerics at Þykkvibær. *Harmsól* and *Jónsdrápa* have been credited to Gamli, a canon in the monastery in the late twelfth century, and *Lilja* has been attributed to the monk Eysteinn Ásgrímsson (d. 1361). Also, even if the codex originates at Kirkjubær, it does not naturally follow that it was written by females, for a convent's household staff included priests and possibly chaplains or vicars, who could equally have been the ones holding the quill. As noted above, four hands may be distinguished, which may well reflect the number of the convent's male clerical household staff. It is not known how many priests were associated with the Kirkjubær convent around 1500; *Svínfellinga saga* mentions three priests as being at Kirkjubær in 1252 ("Þrír váru prestar á staðnum. Þormóðr hét staðarprestr, annarr Hjalti, þriði Sæmundr") and makes reference also to a deacon named Móðólfr ganimaðr.[71]

---

[69] These churches are: Ás (Holt), Breiðabólstaður, Grunnavík, Hlíðarendi, Hof (Öræfi), Holt (Saurbær), Holtastaðir, Hrafnagil, Hvammur (Laxárdalur), Kaldaðarnes (Flói), Kirkjubær (Hróarstunga), Kross (Landeyjar), Oddi, Ofanleiti (Westman Islands), Reykholt, the convent of Staður, Skúmstaðir, Staður (Grunnavík), Stórólfshvoll, Tjörn (Svarfaðardalur), Þingmúli, the monastery of Þykkvibær, and Viðimýri. St Catherine is also among the saints depicted on Jón Arason's cope (see n. 66).

[70] There are several folk legends that have as their subject the rather "friendly" relationship between the inmates of the two religious houses (Jón Árnason, *Íslenzkar Þjóðsögur og ævintýri*, 6 vols., ed. Árni Böðvarsson and Bjarni Vilhjálmsson [Reykjavík, 1961], 2: 77–78), but these stories are probably fictional and appear to date from after the Reformation.

[71] Jón Jóhannesson, Magnús Finnbogason, and Kristján Eldjárn, ed., *Sturlunga saga*, 2 vols. (Reykjavík, 1946), 2: 99, 93.

Unfortunately, very few details have surfaced about the nuns at Kirkjubær
that can throw light on their activities in general and on their possible involvement in scribal activity specifically. The reasons are self-evident. The Benedictine Rule requested of both its monks and nuns that they remain within
the boundaries of their cloister and avoid all wandering in the world, but for
obvious reasons it was considered to be a more vital necessity for the well-be-
ing of the latter. Moreover, in order to preserve the nuns unspotted from the
world, it was also necessary to keep secular persons outside, for clearly it was
useless to pass regulations forbidding nuns to leave their convents if visitors
from the world had easy access to them and could move freely about within
the precincts. Some interaction with seculars was bound to occur even in the
best-regulated convents, for nuns were often served by layfolk, and it was a
recognized obligation that they should show hospitality to guests, but contact
with the world was no doubt quite limited.[72]
  The Benedictine ideal set study together with prayer and manual labor as
the three bases of monastic life, but this tradition had been largely discarded
by the thirteenth century. As Shulamith Shahar points out, if nuns of a small
convent are found doing manual labor, it is by reason of their poverty.[73] The
two Icelandic convents were not poor,[74] but, given their small size, it is possible that the nuns had to do their own cooking and housework. That the nuns
were not used to outdoor work is evident from a notice concerning the Black
Death in *Lögmannsannáll. s.a.* 1403–1404. It is related that Abbess Halldóra
of Kirkjubær, along with seven nuns and many other people, died from the
disease, with the result that eventually the surviving six nuns had to milk
the cows, and the annalist comments that, having never tried this before, the
nuns were not particularly successful in their efforts.[75]

---

[72] From a letter of 1543 written by Gissur Einarsson, bishop of Skálholt (1542–1548)
and addressed to Abbess Halldóra of Kirkjubær (see below), it is known that the convent
sheltered a woman because of her husband Bergr Ingimundarson's violence against her.
In his letter (*DI* 11: 271), Bishop Gissur requests that the woman be sent back, since her
husband's mistreatment of her did not constitute grounds for divorce.
  [73] Shulamith Shahar, *Die Frau im Mittelalter*, trans. Ruth Achlama (Königstein,
1981), 54.
  [74] See Björn Þorsteinsson and Guðrún Ása Grímsdóttir, "Enska öldin," in Sigurður
Líndal, ed., *Saga Íslands* 5 (Reykjavík, 1990), 5–216, esp. 156.
  [75] "Manndauda aar hid micla a Islandi. . . . Obitus Halldorv abbadisar j Kirkiu bæ.
ok vij systra. enn vi lifdv eptir. Vigd fru Gudrun abbadis Halldors dottir. Eyddi stadinn
þria tima ad mannfolki suo at vm sidir miolkudv systurnar kv fenadinn þær er til uoru.
ok kunnv flest allar lited til sem sen uar. er slikann starfa hofdv alldri fyrri haft" (Storm,
Islandske Annaler, 286).

It is reasonable to assume that needlework and embroidery were the most important occupations that filled the working hours of the nuns.[76] The inventory of the convent's possessions made in 1397 at the request of Vilchin Henriksson, Bishop of Skálholt (ca. 1394–1405), shows that its wealth in embroideries and tapestries was considerable.[77] Evidently, Bishop Vilchin was impressed with the quality of the nuns' work, for in *Lögmannsannáll* it is related *s. a.* 1405 that he arranged for stately wall hangings (*reflar*) to be made in Kirkjubær for all the walls in the large parlor in Skálholt and that he financed the work himself.[78] Anna Sigurðardóttir considers it likely that scenes from saints' lives were depicted on these hangings and points to the example of Ingunn of Hólar, about whom it is said in *Jóns saga helga* that she "vann . . . hannyrðir með heilagra manna sögum" (did needlework with scenes from the legends of saints).[79]

The nuns' unfamiliarity with farm work and their skill in needlework suggest that they were women of gentle birth, and those of the abbesses and nuns that can be identified support this hypothesis. Considering their background, it is reasonable to assume, therefore, that the nuns could read and

---

[76] Elsa E. Guðjónsson, " Með silfurbjarta nál. Um kirkjuleg útsaumsverk íslenskra kvenna í kaþolskum og lútherskum sið," in *Konur og kristmenn: Þættir úr kristnisögu Íslands*, ed. Inga Huld Hákonardóttir (Reykjavík, 1996), 119–62, esp. 133–34.

[77] "Suo mikinn skrvda ä kirkian j kirkjvbæ. iiij oc xx hoklar. xiij kapur. v dalmatikur. sloppar iiij. Altarissklædi til haalltariss ix. til vtalltara v. oc til hvers ferner dvkar til haalltaris med fordvkum. x glitader dvkar. viij manna messvklædi. oc ij messvserker lavser vijgder. vj corporalia" (*DI* 4: 238). For a detailed discussion of these items, see Björn Th. Björnsson, "Myndlist á síðmiðöldum," in Sigurður Líndal, ed., *Saga Íslands* 5 (Reykjavík, 1990), 287–349, esp. 319–20, who argues that the convent in Kirkjubær was a center for embroidery.

[78] "Item liet hann giora j Kirkiu bæ oc lagdi sialfur allann kostnat til (sæmilig)a refla kringum alla storv stofvna. suo onguir uoru fyrr iafnreisvgir. oc . . . þa kirkiunne." It is further noted: "Jtem gaf hann henne sæmelig messo klæde . . . . . reidskap. oc dalmadikv. hver er hofd eru a . . . . . messvr badar jafnan sidan. þvi hann sagdi þa fyrsto messo er hann til landzins jn exulltacione sancte crucis sem fyrr seigir" (Storm, *Islandske Annaler*, 287–88). Elsa E. Guðjónsson, "Með silfurbjarta nál," 135, believes that the comment "lagdi sialfur allann kostnat til" indicates that the nuns received payment for their work.

[79] Anna Sigurðardóttir, *Allt hafði annan róm*, 54, 246; Jón Sigurðsson and Guðbrandur Vigfússon, ed., *Biskupa sögur*, 1: 241. None of these works has been preserved, though an embroidered altar frontal in the church at Skarð in Skarðsströnd (now Þjóðminjasafn 2028; see Kristján Eldjárn, *Hundrað ár*, no. 18) may have its origin in the convent of Staður. In addition to depictions of six saints (Þorlákr, Ólafr, Benedict of Nursia, Magnús, Giles, and Hallvard), it has the embroidered name of Solveig Rafnsdóttir, abbess of Staður 1508–1551 (Elsa Guðjónsson, "Með silfurbjarta nál," 127 n. 14, 134).

write, although admittedly the evidence is slim, for it consists of two comments in *Þorláks saga helga* and *Flateyjarannáll*, respectively. One, which is
found in the so-called C-version of *Þorláks saga helga*, concerns Katrín, abbess of the convent of Staður 1298–1299, who suffered from an illness in her
eyes, which prevented her from reading sacred books ("fieck hun so mikinn
augna kranckleika, ad hun matti sier ecki vid heilagra boka lestur skiemta"),
and was cured through the intercession of St Þorlákr.[80] The other is found in
Flateyjarannáll s. a. 1343 and concerns a nun in Kirkjubær by the name of
Kristín, who had sold herself to the devil by writing a letter ("gefiz hafdi pu-
kanum med brefi") and was, accordingly, burned.[81] Presumably, the letter in
question (a kind of contract with the devil) was impiously irreverent, for, according to *Lögmannsannáll* (which, interestingly, makes no mention of any
letter), she had blasphemed the pope.[82] That there was no formal school in
the Kirkjubær convent is clear from King Christian III's letter of 1542 addressed to Sigvarður Halldórsson (d. 1550), abbot of the monastery of

---

[80] Jón Helgason, ed., *Byskupa sǫgur*, 2 vols., Editiones Arnamagnæanæ A: 13,1–2
(Copenhagen, 1938–1978), 2: 352.

[81] Storm, *Islandske Annaler*, 402. The annalist further notes that she had mistreated
the Body of Christ and slept with many laymen ("hon hafdi ok misfarit med guds likama
ok kastad aftr vm naadahustre laagiz med morgum leikmonnum"). Cf. the account in the
late Icelandic folk legend (Jón Árnason, *Íslenzkar Þjóðsögur*, 2: 77): "Árið sama og Agatha
[i.e. Abbess Agatha Helgadóttir] dó, 1343, kom út Jón Sigurðsson austur í Reyðarfirði
með biskupsvígslu og byrjaði þaðan vísitazíu sína vestur um land sunnan megin og kom
í þeirri ferð sinni að Kirkjubæ. Var þar þá brennd systir ein sem Katrín hét fyrir guðleysi
og fleiri þungar sakir sem á hana voru bornar og sannaþar; fyrst sú að hún hefði bréflega
veðdregið sig djöflinum, annað það að hún hefði misfarið með Krists líkama (vígt brauð)
og snarað aftur um náðhúsdyr, það hið þriðja að hún hefði lagzt með mörgum leikmanni,
og var það því dæmt að hana skyldi brenna kvika" (The same year as Agatha died, 1343,
Jón Sigurðsson, who had been consecrated bishop, came east to Reyðarfjörður and began
his visitation to the east of the country along the southern side, and arrived on this trip
at Kirkjubær. There a nun by the name of Katrín was burned due to her godlessness and
several other severe accusations made and proved against here; the first one was that she
had sold herself herself to the devil by writing a letter, the second that she had mistreated
Christ's body (consecrated bread) and thrown it out through the door to the toilet, and
the third that she had slept with many secular men, and accordingly she was judged to
be burned alive).

[82] "Jtem degraderade hann [Jón Sigurðarson, bishop of Skálholt (1343–1348)] systur
j Kirkiubæ vm paua blasphemiam. ok sidan var hon brend" (274). Anna Sigurðardóttir,
Allt hafði annan róm, 41, attaches much significance to the entry in *Flateyjarannáll* and
argues that Kristín was undoubtedly one of the nuns whose task it was to copy books for
the convent.

Þykkvibær,[83] Brandur Hrafnsson (ca. 1479–ca. 1552), prior of the monastery of Skriða (founded 1493), and Halldóra Sigvaldadóttir, abbess of Kirkjubær,[84] in which he requests that primary schools are to be established in and financed by these religious houses.[85] Nothing came of the king's decree, but it implies that the nuns were capable of serving as teachers, and there can be no doubt that the convent educated young girls who entered in order to take the veil.[86] It is also likely that occasionally the nuns took private pupils, and there are indications that Halldóra Sigvaldadóttir, who, if one accepts Kålund's dating of AM 429 12mo to ca. 1500, was abbess of the convent at the time the legendary was compiled, tutored at least two children. Like other abbesses, Halldóra came from a well-known and distinguished family. Her mother, Þuríðr Einarsdóttir, was the niece of the powerful Björn Þorleifsson (ca. 1408–1467), *hirðstjóri* of Skarð in Skarðsströnd, who was married to Olöf Loptsdóttir. Her father, Sigvaldi Gunnarsson, was a blacksmith, who had worked for Björn Þorleifsson.[87] Þuríðr and Sigvaldi made their home at Síða, where they raised at least six children.[88] One of these children, Einar Sigvaldason, who lived first in Holt at Síða and later at Hraun in Landbrot, passed away

---

[83] Páll Eggert Ólason, *Íslenzkar æviskrár frá landnámstímum til ársloka 1940*, 5 vols. (Reykjavík, 1948–1952), 4: 281, thinks Abbot Sigvarður may be a grandson of Sigvaldi Gunnarsson, Abbess Halldóra's father (see below).

[84] The date of Abbess Halldóra's appointment is unknown, but Anna Sigurðardóttir, *Allt hafði annan róm*, 63, considers it likely that she was consecrated when Stefán Jónsson, bishop of Skálholt (1491–1581) made a visitation to Kirkjubær in 1491. In the inventory which Bishop Stefán had made of the silver owned by the convent, mention is made of the ring which he gave to Sister Halldóra to wear instead of the one he took with him because it was broken (*DI* 7: 232). Her date of birth is nowhere recorded, but she must have been at least twenty-one or thirty, when she was consecrated (Eileen Power, *Medieval English Nunneries c. 1275 to 1535* [Cambridge, 1922], 45; Anna Sigurðardóttir, *Allt hafði annan róm*, 36). Bishop Gissur Einarsson's letter of 1543 (see n. 72) is the last extant document involving Abbess Halldóra and thus serves as a *terminus post quem* for the date of her death, which remains unknown.

[85] *DI* 11: 176–78.

[86] Elsa E. Guðjónsson, "Með silfurbjarta nál," 133–34, draws attention to the priest Björgólfr Illugason's letter of 1413 (*DI* 3: 751–52) to the convent of Staðir, in which he asks that his daughter and niece be educated in the convent in return for payment in the amount of "fim tighi hundrada" (752). The two young women, Steinunn Björgólfsdóttir and Sigríður Sæmundardóttir, took the veil in 1431 along with six other women (*DI* 4: 438).

[87] Einar Bjarnason (cited in Björn Th. Björnsson, "Myndlist," 345) believes that Sigvaldi came from a wealthy family and learned his trade abroad. Evidently he was a man of means; among other things, he built a large church in Vatnsfjörður, and in the so-called *Þáttur um Gissur biskup Einarsson* (Jón Sigurðsson and Guðbrandur Vigfússon, ed., *Biskupa sögur*, 2: 599), it is related that Sigvaldi carved an image of himself on the doorpost of the church.

[88] Páll Eggert Ólason, *Íslenzkar æviskrár*, 4: 280.

before his time, leaving behind his wife, Gunnhildr Jónsdóttir, and six young
children (Anna Sigurðardóttir, *Allt hafði annan róm*, 64). According to Jón
Espólín's (1769–1836) account in *Íslands Árbækur*, Abbess Halldóra supported
her brother's family,[89] and, considering the short distance between Hraun
and Kirkjubær, it is probable that the children were more or less looked after
by her; indeed, one of them, Oddný, later became a nun in the convent. Most
likely, the children were also tutored by Abbess Halldóra. Gissur, who in 1539
was elected bishop of Skálholt, would almost certainly have received some
form of education in the convent before he was sent to the Skálholt cathedral
school and from there to Hamburg for futher studies.

The likelihood that the nuns could read and write and the probability
that they may have taken private pupils do not, of course, constitute proof
that they engaged in literary activities, and the fact remains that there is no
trace of women occupying themselves with the copying of manuscripts. Obviously, it is unsafe to argue from silence that the nuns did not not copy manuscripts; but it is equally unsafe to argue, as Anna Sigurðardóttir and others
have done, that they did, not least considering the fact that their argument —
that nuns abroad concerned themselves with writing — is something of an
overstatement. To be sure, St Bridget of Sweden (ca. 1303–1373) recorded a
number of her revelations,[90] and several literary nuns are found in Germany.[91]

---

[89] Jón Espólín, *Íslands Árbækur í sögu-formi*, 12 vols. (Copenhagen, 1821–1855), 3:
68: "Einar . . . vard eigi gamall, oc lifdi Gunnhildr eptir kona hans, med börninn vid fátæki;
þá var Halldóra abbadys at Kyrkjubæ, frændkona þeirra, dóttir Sigvalda lángalífs hún var
skörúngr mikill, oc qvenna hædst vexti; hún héllt þeim vid" (Einar . . . did not grow old,
and his wife Gunnhildr and their children survived him in poverty. At that time Halldóra
the daughter of Sigvaldr the longlived, their relative, was abbess in Kirkjubær. She was an
outstanding person and very tall. She supported them).

[90] These revelations were subsequently translated into Latin by Matthias Magister
and Prior Peter of Alvastra, her confessors. Interestingly, Lesley Smith, "*Scriba, Femina*:
Medieval Depictions of Women Writing," in *Women and the Book: Assessing the Visual
Evidence*, ed. eadem and Jane H. M. Taylor (London, 1997), 21–44, esp. 26, who observes
that there are very few depictions of women writing in the Middle Ages, comments that
St Bridget is the only female saint who is consistently depicted writing. See also Martha
W. Driver, "Mirrors of a Collective Past: Re-considering Images of Medieval Women," in
Women and the Book, ed. Smith and Taylor, 75–93, esp. 79; and J. Summit, "Women and
Authorship," in *The Cambridge Companion to Medieval Women's Writing*, ed. C. Din-
shaw and D. Wallace (Cambridge, 2003), 91–108.

[91] Judith Oliver, "Worship of the Word: Some Gothic *Nonnenbücher* in their Devotional Context," in *Women and the Book*, ed. Smith and Taylor, 106–22, emphasizes that
"nuns were actively engaged in book production. . . . Dominican nuns in Germany (like
the nuns of Engelberg in Switzerland) made many psalters for their own use, despite
repeated prohibitions against book production by women under Dominican supervision

The convent of Gandersheim in Lower Saxony was renowned for learning in the tenth century through the works of Abbess Roswitha or Hrotsvit (ca. 935–after 1000), who not only wrote religious legends in Latin verse on pagan-Christian conflict, but also composed six dramas or comedies and wrote two epics, one singing the achievements of Emperor Otto the Great and the other celebrating the foundation of the monastery of Gandersheim.[92] In the twelfth century, Abbess Herrad (ca. 1130–1195) compiled and illuminated at Hohenburg in Alsace the *Hortus Deliciarum*, a compendium of all the sciences studied at that time, including theology.[93] The same century also saw also the lives of the two famous nun-mystics and authors, Sts Hildegard of Bingen (1098–1179) and Elizabeth of Schönau (1129–1164), who were both favored with visions.[94] In the next century, the convent of Helfta near Eisleben in Saxony

promulgated in 1249, 1254, and 1263. Beguines (who remained laywomen, but lived like nuns without entering established convents) very likely also engaged in writing and illuminating psalters for their own use in the mid-thirteenth century. . . . In the thirteenth and fourteenth centuries, encloistered nuns also produced numerous antiphonals and graduals. . . . As these psalters and antiphonals indicate, despite the shift of book production to largely urban professional ateliers in the thirteenth century, encloistered women continued to practise this age-old monastic craft in the late Middle Ages. This was especially true in Germany and the Netherlands" (106–7). See also Alison I. Beach, "Collaboration between the Sexes in the Twelfth-Century Scriptorium," in *Monks and Nuns, Saints and Outcasts*, ed. Sharon Farmer and Barbara H. Rosenwein (Ithaca, 2000), 57–75, who offers an interesting study of the collaboration of male and female scribes in two Bavarian double monasteries, Benedictine Admont and Premonstratensian Schäftlarn.

[92] Lerner, *The Creation of Feminist Consciousness*, 48–49, 250–55; Barbara K. Gold,"Hrotswitha Writes Herself," in *Sex and Gender in Medieval and Renaissance Texts*, ed. eadem et al. (Albany, NY, 1977), 41–70. For a useful biography of Roswitha and a discussion of her works, see, for example, Katharina Wilson, *Hrotsvit of Gandersheim: A Florilegium of Her Works* (Woodsbridge, 1998).

[93] For a discussion of Herrad and the *Hortus Deliciarum*, see, for example, Thérèse McGuire, "Two Twelfth-Century Women and Their Books," in *Women and the Book*, ed. Smith and Taylor, 97–105, esp. 97–101.

[94] Joan M. Ferrante, *To the Glory of Her Sex: Women's Roles in the Composition of Medieval Texts* (Bloomington, 1997), 139–74; Lerner, *The Creation of Feminist Consciousness*, 52–64. The visions of St Hildegard were recorded by the monk Vodmar. Other writings by Hildegard include: lives of Sts Disibod and Rupert; two books of medicine and natural history; hymns and canticles of which she wrote both words and music; for diversion, a language of her own composed of 900 words and an alphabet of 23 letters; and also letters to a great number of ecclesiastical and political dignitaries in Germany and abroad. The visions and ecstasies of Elizabeth were written at the instigation of her brother Eckbert, who published them. Her second work, the *Liber viarum Dei*, was written in imitation of the *Scivias* of Hildegard, an account of 26 visions treating the relations between God and man in creation, redemption, and the church.

became under Abbess Gertrud of Hackeborn (1251–1292) the most famous
center of German mysticism and served as the home of several literary nuns
and mystics, who collected books, copied and illuminated them, and learned
and wrote Latin; three of them, Mechtild of Magdeburg (ca. 1209–ca. 1294),
St Mechtild of Hackeborn (ca. 1240–1298), and St Gertrude the Great (1256–
1302), have won fame by their mystic writings.[95] Even in the fifteenth century,
there are examples of German nuns, such as the sisters of St Catherine's in
Nuremberg,[96] who demonstrated interest in book-learning. But when we turn
to England, there is no evidence of any convent that can compare with Gandersheim, Hohenburg, or Helfta, and no record of any nun to compare with
the learned German women. Eileen Power and David N. Bell point out that
the only works ascribed to female monastic authors are a late twelfth-century
Life of St Catherine of Alexandria (an adaptation of an earlier French version
of one of the standard Latin lives of the saint), written in Norman-French by
Clemence, a nun of Barking; a *Life of St Edward the Confessor* (a translation of
the *vita* by Aelred of Rievaulx) written between 1163 and 1169 in Anglo-Norman by a nun of the same abbey; and a translation of Thomas of Ely's Latin
Life of St Etheldreda into pedestrian French as the *Life of St Audrey* by a certain Marie in the early thirteenth century.[97] Nor do nuns in England seem to
have been active in copying manuscripts. Several books can be traced to convents, but there is nothing to suggest that they were written there.[98] Instead,

---

[95] Mechtild of Magdeburg's writings were collected by her friends and were distribut-
ed under the title of *Das fliessende Licht der Gottheit.* The work consists of somewhat dis-
connected compositions: spiritual poems dealing with mystical experiences, love songs
and allegories, visions, moral reflections, and admonitions. Mechtild of Hackeborn was
the spiritual mother of St Gertrude the Great, to whom Mechtild confided the secrets of
her interior life. Gertrude recorded Mechtild's revelations and also edited them under the
title *Liber specialis gratiae.* Gertrude is also known to have worked as a copyist in the monastic scriptorium, and three Latin works are attributed to her: the *Exercitia spiritualia,*
the *Insinuationes,* and the *Preces Gertrudianae,* which, however, is not really authentic.

[96] For a discussion of the convent and the nuns' activities, see Marie-Luise Ehrenschwendtner, "A Library Collected by and for the Use of Nuns: St Catherine's Convent,
Nuremberg," in *Women and the Book,* ed. Smith and Taylor, 123–32.

[97] Power, *Medieval English Nunneries,* 239–40; David N. Bell, *What Nuns Read: Books
and Libraries in Medieval English Nunneries,* Cistercian Publications 158 (Kalamazoo,
1995), 69–70. Power also includes in this list *The Boke of St Albans,* an essay on hawking,
hunting, and coat armor, printed in 1486, by a certain Dame Juliana Berners, who is said
to have been a prioress of Sopwell. See also J. H. McCash, "*La vie seinte Audree,*" *Speculum*
77 (2002): 744–77.

[98] Power, *Medieval English Nunneries,* 240. Bell, *What Nuns Read,* who modifies some
of Power's statements about the education of nuns in medieval England, essentially agrees

the English nuns busied themselves with embroidery, and some of the most famous embroidered vestments now preserved in various places in Italy are believed to be the handiwork of late thirteenth-century English nuns.[99]

Considering the fact that there is no evidence of any Old Norse-Icelandic manuscript having been written by women, and the strikingly similar picture of the activities of medieval English convents, it seems safe to argue that Icelandic nuns did not concern themselves with writing and, by extension, that the hands holding the quill in AM 429 12mo or any other manuscript are not female hands. If the nuns in the Kirkjubær convent were at all involved in the production of the legendary, it would have been in illuminating it, and, given their skills in embroidery and possibly other crafts, this possibility cannot be excluded.[100] The whole trend of medieval thought was against learned women, and even in Benedictine convents, for which a period of study was enjoined by the rule, it seems to have been, at least in Iceland and England, altogether outside the scope of women to concern themselves with writing.

---

with Power on the matter of scribal activities in the convents, arguing that there was no "parallel between the situation in Europe, where female scribes seem to have been common, and England, where they seem to have been exceedingly rare" (66). Regarding the copying of Latin works, he offers the following comments: "An early twelfth-century volume from Nunnaminster — a Latin manuscript containing the *Diadema monachorum* of Smaragdus and a collection of pseudo-Augustinian sermons — was written by an anonymous *scriptrix*, but the evidence for scribal activities on the part of nuns in the centuries following is extremely limited. Sir John Fox suggested that the scribe of William Giffard's Anglo-Norman *Apocalypse* . . . was a member of the Shaftesbury community, but the evidence is tenuous; and the only other cases I can cite are of nuns copying liturgical manuscripts for their own private use. In the fifteenth century, Matilda Hayle of Barking *may* have copied Wycliffite translations of the books of Tobit and Susanna, together with various prayers; at the end of that century or the beginning of the next, Elizabeth Trotter of Ickleton *may* have copied her own collection of Latin *liturgica*; and at about the same time, Margery Birkenhead of Chester *may* have made her own copy of the Chester Processional. None of these cases, however, is incontrovertible. Clearer evidence comes from Syon, where we know that after the suppression of the house in 1539, some of the sisters . . . wrote their own breviaries, but we also know that they wrote them very badly. A large number of nuns could obviously write their own names, but copying an entire manuscript is a very different matter" (66–67).

[99] Power, *Medieval English Nunneries*, 256.

[100] Björn Th. Björnsson, "Myndlist," 330, draws attention to the nickname "hin haga" (the handy) of the nun Guðný of Kirkjubær (d. 1386), but thinks that it may refer to her skills in carving rather than needlework.

Bibliography

Anna Sigurðardóttir. *Allt hafði annan róm áður í páfadóm. Nunnuklaustrin tvö á Íslandi á miðöldum og brot úr krisnisögu.* Úr veröld kvenna 3. Reykjavík, 1988.

Arne Magnussons i AM. *435A–B, 4to indeholdte håndskriftfortegnelser med to tillæg.* Ed. Kr. Kålund. Copenhagen, 1909.

Beach, Alison I. "Claustration and Collaboration between the Sexes in the Twelfth-Century Scriptorium." In *Monks and Nuns, Saints and Outcasts: Essays in Honor of Lester K. Little,* ed. Sharon Farmer and Barbara H. Rosenwein, 57–75. Ithaca, 2000.

Bell, David N. *What Nuns Read: Books and Libraries in Medieval English Nunneries.* Cistercian Publications 158. Kalamazoo, 1995.

BHL = Bibliotheca Hagiographica Latina Antiquae et Mediae Aetatis. Subsidia hagiographica 6. Brussels, 1898–1899; repr. Brussels,1992. *Supplementum.* Subsidia Hagiographica 12. Brussels, 1911. *Novum Supplementum.* Subsidia Hagiographica 70. Brussels, 1986.

Björn Th. Björnsson. "Myndlist á síðmiðöldum." In *Saga Íslands* 5, ed. Sigurður Líndal, 287–349. Reykjavík, 1990.

Björn Þorsteinsson and Guðrún Ása Grímsdóttir. "Enska öldin." In *Saga Íslands* 5, ed. Sigurður Líndal, 5–216.

Cormack, Margaret. *The Saints in Iceland. Their Veneration from the Conversion to 1400.* Brussels, 1994.

Delany, Sheila, trans. *A Legend of Holy Women: Osbern Bokenham,* Legends of Holy Women. Notre Dame and London, 1992.

Delehaye, Hippolyte. *Étude sur le légendier romain. Les saints de Novembre et de Décembre.* Subsidia Hagiographica 23. Brussels, 1936.

DI = Diplomatarium Islandicum. Íslenzkt fornbréfasafn. 16 vols. Copenhagen and Reykjavík, 1857–1952.

Driver, Martha W. "Mirrors of a Collective Past: Re-considering Images of Medieval Women." In *Women and the Book: Assessing the Visual Evidence,* ed. Lesley Smith and Jane H. M. Taylor, 75–93. London, 1997.

Ehrenschwendtner, Marie-Luise. "A Library Collected by and for the Use of Nuns: St. Catherine's Convent, Nuremberg." In *Women and the Book,* ed. Smith and Taylor, 123–32.

Einar Ól. Sveinsson, ed. *Laxdæla saga.* Íslenzk fornrit 5. Reykjavík, 1934.

Elsa E. Guðjónsson. "Með silfurbjarta nál. Um kirkjuleg útsaumsverk ís-lenskra kvenna í kaþolskum og lútherskum sið." In *Konur og kristsmenn:*

Þættir úr kristnisögu Íslands, ed. Inga Huld Hákonardóttir, 119–62. Reykjavík, 1996.

Ferrante, Joan M. *To the Glory of Her Sex: Women's Roles in the Composition of Medieval Texts.* Bloomington, 1997.

Finnur Jónsson, ed. *Den norsk-islandske Skjaldedigtning.* IA–IIA (*tekst efter-håndskrifterne*), IIA–IIB (*rettet tekst*). Copenhagen, 1908–1915.

Foote, Peter, ed. *Lives of Saints. Perg. fol. nr. 2 in the Royal Library, Stockholm.* Early Icelandic Manuscripts in Facsimile 4. Copenhagen, 1962.

Guðbrandur Jónsson. *Dómkirkjan á Hólum í Hjaltadal. Lýsing íslenskra miðalda-kirkna.* Safn til sögu Íslands og íslenzkra bókmenta að fornu og nýju 5, 6. Reykjavík, 1919–1929.

Guðrún P. Helgadóttir. *Skáldkonur fyrri alda.* 2 vols. Akureyri, 1961–1963.

Halldór Hermannsson, ed. *Jón Guðmundsson and His Natural History of Iceland.* Islandica 15. Ithaca, 1924; repr. New York, 1966.

Helga Kress. *Máttugar meyjar. Íslensk fornbókmenntasaga.* Reykjavík, 1993.

Horstmann, Carl. "Prosalegenden." *Anglia* 3 (1880): 293–360.

Hughes, Shaun F. D. "The Reemergence of Women's Voices in Icelandic Literature, 1500–1800." In *Cold Counsel: Women in Old Norse Literature and Mythology,* ed. Sarah M. Anderson and Karen Swenson, 93–128. New York and London, 2002.

Inga Huld Hákonardóttir. "Í nunnuklaustri — Kirkjubær og Reynistaður." In *Kristni á Íslandi,* ed. Hjalti Hugason, 2:225–29. 4 vols. Reykjavík, 2000.

Jakob Benediktsson. "Helgendigte." In *Kulturhistorisk Leksikon for nordisk middelalder* 6: 318–21. Copenhagen, 1961.

Jefferis, Sibylle, and Konrad Kunze. "Passienbüchlein von den vier Hauptjungfrauen." In *Die deutsche Literatur des Mittelalters: Verfasserlexikon,* ed. Kurt Ruh, 325–28. 2nd rev.ed. Berlin and New York, 1989.

Jón Árnason. *Íslenzkar Þjóðsögur og ævintýri,* ed. Árni Böðvarsson and Bjarni Vilhjálmsson. 6 vols. Reykjavík, 1961.

Jón Espólin. *Íslands Árbækur í sögu-formi.* Copenhagen, 1821–1855.

Jón Helgason, ed. *Byskupa sǫgur.* 2 vols. Editiones Arnamagnæana ser. A:13,1–2. Copenhagen, 1938–1978.

———, ed. *Íslenzk miðaldakvæði: Islandske digte fra senmiddelalderen.* Vols 1.2 and 2. Copenhagen, 1936–1938.

Jón Jóhannesson, Magnús Finnbogason, and Kristján Eldjárn, eds. *Sturlunga saga.* Reykjavík, 1946.

Jón Viðar Sigurðsson. "Utenlandske kvinnehelgener på Island i høymid-delalderen." In *Samtíðarsögur: The Contemporary Sagas. The Ninth International Saga Conference, Akureyri 31.7–6.8.1994*, 2:423–34. Reykjavík, 1994.

Jón Sigurðsson and Guðbrandur Vigfússon, eds. *Biskupa sögur.* 2 vols. Copenhagen, 1858–1878.

Jón Þorkelsson. *Om Digtningen på Island i det 15. og 16. Århundrede.* Copenhagen, 1888.

Konráð Gíslason, ed. *Fire og fyrretyve for en stor deel forhen utrykte prøver af oldnordisk sprog og literatur.* Copenhagen, 1860.

Kristján Eldjárn. *Hundrað ár í Þjóðminjasafni.* Reykjavík, 1973.

——— and Hörður Ágústsson. *Skálholt. Skrúði og áhöld.* Reykjavík, 1992.

Kålund, Kr. *Katalog over Den arnamagæanske Håndskriftsamling.* 2 vols. Copenhagen, 1889–1894.

Lerner, Gerda. *The Creation of Feminist Consciousness: From the Middle Ages to Eighteen-seventy.* Oxford, 1993.

Magnús Már Lárusson. "Fornt helgidagaboð (AM. 696, 4to, fragm. XXIX)." *Skírnir* 125 (1951): 199–206.

McCash, J. H. "*La vie seinte Audree,*" *Speculum* 77 (2002): 744–77.

McGuire, Thérese. "Two Twelfth-Century Women and Their Books." In *Women and the Book*, ed. Smith and Taylor, 97–105.

Morgenstern, Gustav. "Notizen." *Arkiv för nordisk filologi* 11 (1895): 95–97.

Mundal, Else. "Kvinner og dikting. Overgangen frå munnleg til skriftleg kul-tur — ei ulukke for kvinnene?" In *Förändringar i kvinnors vilkor under medeltiden. Uppsatser framlagda vid ett kvinnohistoriskt symposium i Skálholt, Island, 22.–25. juni 1981*, ed. Silja Aðalsteinsdóttir and Helgi Þorláksson, 11–25. Ritsafn Sagnfræðistofnunar 9. Reykjavík, 1983.

Oliver, Judith. "Worship of the Word: Some Gothic *Nonnenbücher* in their Devotional Context." In *Women and the Book.* ed. Smith and Taylor, 106–22.

Páll Eggert Ólason. *Íslenzkar æviskrár frá landnámstímum til ársloka 1940.* 5 vols. Reykjavík, 1948–1952.

Power, Eileen. *Medieval English Nunneries c. 1275 to 1535.* Cambridge, 1922.

Seip, Didrik Arup. *Palæografi. B: Norge og Island*, ed. Johs. Brøndum-Nielsen. Nordisk kultur 28:B. Stockholm, Oslo, Copenhagen, 1954.

Shahar, Shulamith. *Die Frau im Mittelalter*, trans. Ruth Achlama. Königstein, 1981.

Smith, Lesley. "*Scriba, Femina:* Medieval Depictions of Women Writing." In *Women and the Book*, ed. eadem and Taylor, 21–44.

Straubhaar, Sandra Ballif. "Ambiguously Gendered: The Skalds Jórunn, Auðr and Steinunn." In *Cold Counsel: Women in Old Norse Literature and Mythology*, ed. Sarah M. Anderson and Karen Swenson, 261–71. New York and London, 2000.

Storm, Gustav, ed. *Islandske Annaler indtil 1578*. Christiania [Oslo], 1888.

Summit, Jennifer. "Women and Authorship." In *The Cambridge Companion to Medieval Women's Writing*, ed. C. Dinshaw and D. Wallace, 91–108. Cambridge, 2003.

Unger, C. R., ed. *Heilagra manna søgur. Fortællinger og legender om hellige mænd og kvinder.* 2 vols. Christiania [Oslo], 1877.

Vilhjálmur Örn Vilhjálmsson. "Af heilagri Barböru og uppruna hennar." *Árbók Hins íslenzka fornleifafélags 1982* (1983): 171–75.

Widding, Ole, Hans Bekker-Nielsen, and L.K. Shook. "The Lives of the Saints in Old Norse Prose: A Handlist." *Mediaeval Studies* 25 (1963): 294–337.

Williams-Krapp, Werner. *Die deutschen und niederländischen Legendare des Mittelalters. Studien zu ihrer Überlieferungs-, Text- und Wirkungsgeschichte.* Tübingen, 1986.

Wilson, Katharina. *Hrotsvit of Gandersheim: A Florilegium of Her Works.* Woodbridge, 1998.

Wolf, Kirsten, ed. *The Icelandic Legend of Saint Dorothy.* Studies and Texts 130. Toronto, 1998.

———, ed. *The Old Norse-Icelandic Legend of Saint Barbara.* Studies and Texts 134. Toronto, 2000.

———, ed. *Heilagra meyja sögur.* Reykjavík, 2003.

THE COMMON TRANSMISSION OF
TRÓJUMANNA SAGA AND *BRETA SÖGUR*

STEFANIE WÜRTH

Within Old Norse-Icelandic literature, *Trójumanna saga* and *Breta sögur* belong to the so-called pseudo-historical translations. These texts are derived from Latin texts dealing with "historical" topics in the broadest sense. *Trójumanna saga* is based on Dares Phrygius's *De excidio belli Trojani*, the history of the Trojan War, a book widely disseminated in the European Middle Ages. As quotations in several other texts prove, it must have been known in Iceland by the end of the twelfth century. Today *Trójumanna saga* is preserved in two versions, both available in very good editions.[1] Version α is closer to the original translation from the beginning of the thirteenth century, but it is preserved only in post-medieval manuscripts. Version β is a younger, revised and interpolated version of *Trójumanna saga*. All extant manuscripts of this version date from the fourteenth century, and in all these manuscripts *Trójumanna saga* is combined with *Breta sögur*, the Icelandic translation of Geoffrey of Monmouth's *Historia regum Britannie*. *Breta sögur*, which has been dated to ca. 1200,[2] constitutes a rather problematic text: since there are only few manuscripts of *Breta sögur*, it is as difficult to compare the translation to its Latin exemplar as it is to compare the different versions of *Breta sögur* to each other. The extant text of *Breta sögur* is a younger revision of an older translation, and in every statement about the style or the characteristics of *Breta sögur* we have to bear this situation in mind. The difficulty of this situation extends to the literature about *Breta sögur*. There is neither a critical

---

[1] Version α has been published in Jonna Louis-Jensen, ed., *Trójumanna saga. The Dares Phrygius version*, Editiones Arnamagnæanæ, Ser. A: 9 (Copenhagen, 1981), and version β in eadem, ed., *Trójumanna saga*, Editiones Arnamagnæanæ, Ser. A: 8 (Copenhagen, 1963). For the history of transmission see the editor's introduction in the earlier of these two volumes.

[2] See Stefanie Würth, *Der "Antikenroman" in der isländischen Literatur des Mittelalters. Eine Untersuchung zur Übersetzung und Rezeption lateinischer Literatur im Norden*, Beiträge zur Nordischen Philologie 26 (Basel and Frankfurt/Main, 1998), 80–82.

edition of the text[3] nor a significant number of scholarly studies. Another problem is the editorial situation of the Latin exemplar, since there is no critical edition of the *Historia Regum Britannie* that takes into consideration all extant manuscripts. But at least there are editions of two versions of the *Historia* which can be used as a basis for the comparison between the Latin exemplar and its Icelandic translation.[4]

The transmission of *Breta sögur*

In all extant manuscripts the text of *Breta sögur* is combined with a text of version β of *Trójumanna saga*. As is the case with version β of *Trójumanna saga*, there is a longer and a shorter redaction of *Breta sögur*. The longer redaction is represented by two manuscripts which are both incomplete: Copenhagen, Arnamagnaean Institute 573 4to and Stockholm, Royal Library, Papp. fol. no. 58.

AM 573 4to: This vellum manuscript from the fourteenth century contains *Trójumanna saga*, *Breta sögur*, and the beginning of *Valvers þáttr*, a text belonging to the genre of courtly romances. The manuscript was written by two different hands: hand 1 is very similar to one of the hands in Copenhagen, Arnamagnaean Institute 764 4to,[5] and hand 2 is identical with the hand of one of the scribes in *Möðruvallabók*, an Icelandic compilation of the fourteenth century.[6] The latter thus provides a date for AM 573 4to of ca. 1330–1370. AM

---

[3] The edition of *Breta sögur* most quoted is Eiríkur Jónsson and Finnur Jónsson, eds., *Hauksbók udgiven efter de Arnamagnæanske håndskrifter no. 371, 544 og 675, 4o same forskellige papirs håndskrifter af Det kongelige nordiske Oldskriftselskab* (Copenhagen, 1892–1896), 231–302. The edition by Jón Sigurðsson, "Trójumanna saga ok Breta sögur," in *Annaler for Nordisk Oldkyndighed og Historie* (Copenhagen, 1848), 102–215, and *Annaler* (Copenhagen, 1849), 3–145, also refers to variants but is not a critical edition in the modern sense. At the Arnamagnaean Institute of the University of Copenhagen, Jonna Louis-Jensen has been working for some time on a new edition of *Breta sögur*. I am grateful to Jonna for permission to use her transcripts of the manuscripts and for providing me with information about the status of her edition. In the following, *Trójumanna saga* will be quoted from Jonna Louis-Jensen's edition (1963); *Breta sögur* will be quoted from Jón Sigurðsson's edition (1848 and 1849).

[4] Neil Wright, ed., *The Historia Regum Britannie. I. Bern, Bürgerbibliothek, MS. 568* (Cambridge, 1985), and idem, ed., *The Historia Regum Britannie. II. The First Variant Version: A Critical Edition* (Cambridge, 1988).

[5] Stefán Karlsson, ed., *Sagas of Icelandic Bishops: Fragments of Eight Manuscripts*, Early Icelandic Manuscripts in Facsimile 7 (Copenhagen, 1967), 26.

[6] Stefán Karlsson, ed., *Sagas*, 28.

573 4to belongs to a larger group of manuscripts which were written in the vicinity of Reynistaður, a Benedictine monastery.[7]

Since the text of *Trójumanna saga* ends on the last page of a complete quire and the text of *Breta sögur* starts on the verso page of the next quire, Jonna Louis-Jensen concluded: "It was obviously the intention to have Br[eta]s[ögur] in a separate codex."[8] But this hypothesis is contradicted by the fact that both *Trójumanna saga* and the first part of *Breta sögur* are written by the same hand. Only in the middle of *Breta sögur* is there a change of scribes. Moreover, there is a clear hint in *Trójumanna saga* that the text will be followed by *Breta sögur*. Whereas in the manuscript of *Hauksbók*, which will be discussed below, the text of *Breta sögur* after King Arthur's death continues to King Aethelstan, foster-father of the Norwegian king Hákon Haraldsson, the text of *Breta sögur* in AM 573 4to concludes with Arthur's death followed by a fragment of *Valvers þáttr*. When Jón Sigurðsson in 1848/1849 edited *Breta sögur*, both parts were still regarded as separate manuscripts. He used the sigla B for variants of hand 1, while in the second part he called them T (=) (Thotts Samling No. 1763).[9]

The second part of AM 573 4to, the part of *Breta sögur* written by hand 2, seems to be based on an exemplar different from that for the beginning of the text. This is indicated by a more verbose and more detailed presentation than in *Hauksbók*. The part of *Breta sögur* written by hand 1 is in the beginning more detailed than is *Hauksbók*, but toward the end it contains several abbreviated passages. In AM 573 4to, in the second part of *Breta sögur*, there are some very interesting additions which occur neither in *Hauksbók* nor in the Latin exemplar.[10] Although some of these additions may be an Icelandic redactor's conclusions from the context, other additions must have been already part of the Latin exemplar, as the comparison with Wace's *Roman de Brut* proves.[11] In general the

---

[7] All these manuscripts can be identified by common orthographical characteristics. See Jonna Louis-Jensen, "Et forlæg til Flateyjarbók? Fragmenterne AM 325 IV β og XI, 3 4to," in *Opuscula* 4, Bibliotheca Arnamagnæana 30 (Copenhagen, 1970), 141–58.

[8] Jonna Louis-Jensen, ed., *Trójumanna saga* (1963), xxxii.

[9] Cf. Kr. Kålund, *Katalog over Den arnamagnæanske Håndskriftsamling*, 2 vols. (Copenhagen, 1888–1894), 1: 735–36.

[10] Cf. for example in AM 573 4to: "En þeir Írar ok Skotar flýðu í ey þá er í voru brunnar Arthi konúngs" (But the Irish and the Scottish fled to an island where the wells of King Arthur were: *Breta sögur* [1849], 93), whereas the *Historia* (§149) does not mention the wells.

[11] Most conspicuous is the passage about the literary and musical entertainment during the crowning ceremony that is found in Wace's text (V. 10544–10556), as well as in AM 573, but which is lacking in the edited versions of the *Historia Regum Britannie* [§157]: "Þá er dryckiu var lokit oc hennar varð í milli, þá voru leikar oc taufl oc saugur. Þar var allzkyns streingleikar: fiðlur oc gígjur, bumbur oc pípur oc simphóníam oc haurpur" (When the drinking was finished and when there was a pause, there were games and

differences between the *Hauksbók*-text of *Breta sögur* and hand 2 in AM 573 4to
are greater than between the *Hauksbók*-text and hand 1 in AM 573 4to. The final
decision about the importance of these differences for the stemma, however, has
to be left open until a critical edition of the text has been prepared.

Stock. Papp. fol. no. 58 is the second manuscript containing the longer redaction. It is a seventeenth-century paper copy of the lost manuscript "Ormsbók" from the fourteenth century. The text of *Breta sögur* in *Ormsbók*, which
covers only the first part of the saga, ends before the main part, the narration about King Arthur. On the basis of their verbal correspondences one
may conclude that the text in *Ormsbók* and the part of AM 573 4to written
by hand 1 were copied from a common exemplar. The original *Ormsbók* was
written in Iceland during the fourteenth century,[12] later came to Norway, and
then to Sweden where it was destroyed, presumably when Stockholm Castle
burnt down in 1697. In the seventeenth century, Olof Verelius wrote an index
for *Ormsbók* indicating that the manuscript contained *Trójumanna saga* and
Breta sögur as a conjoined text together with a number of *riddarasögur*, prose
stories derived from courtly romances. This means that the context of *Breta
sögur* in this manuscript was that of courtly literature.

AM 544 4to, a part of *Hauksbók*, preserves the shorter redaction of *Breta
sögur*. *Hauksbók* is a vellum manuscript consisting of Copenhagen, Arnamagnaean Institute 371, 544, and 675 4to. The manuscript was written between
1301 and 1314 on behalf of Haukr Erlendsson, an Icelander living in Norway.
It consists of a huge compilation starting with *Landnámabók* and *Kristnisaga*
and continues with excerpts from different works of geographical, historical,
or theological interest as well as the Icelandic translation of *Elucidarius*, the
eddic poem *Völuspá*, and calculations concerning the calendar. In addition,
the manuscript contains several sagas, including *Fóstbrœðra saga*, *Hervarar
saga*, *Eiríks saga rauða* as well as *Trójumanna saga* and *Breta sögur*. All three
parts, or booklets, that make up *Hauksbók* are defective.[13] Eiríkur Jónsson and
Finnur Jónsson filled in the lacunae as far as possible using paper copies which

---

chess and stories. There were all kinds of string instruments: fiddles and violins, drums
and pipes and a symphonium and harps: *Breta sögur* [1849], 100–1).

[12] Vilhelm Gödel, *Fornnorsk-isländsk Litteratur i Sverige* (Stockholm, 1897), 20–33,
and idem, "Ormr Snorrasons bok," in *Nordiska Studier tillegnade Adolf Noreen* (Uppsala,
1904), 357–74, here 358, suggests that the manuscript was written in Norway, and therefore he dates *Ormsbók* to the second half of the thirteenth century. But Grén Broberg,
"Ormr Snorrasons bok," *Arkiv för Nordisk Filologi* 24 (1908): 42–66, here 55–56, proves
that this dating cannot be correct.

[13] For a detailed description see Jón Helgason, ed., *Hauksbók: The Arna-Magnæan
Manuscripts 371, 4to, 544, 4to, and 675, 4to*, Manuscripta Islandica 5 (Copenhagen, 1960).

were written during the seventeenth century when *Hauksbók* was more complete than it is today.[14] There are at least fifteen different hands in *Hauksbók*,
some of them writing only very small parts. Hand 1, which wrote the most,
can be identified as the hand of Haukr Erlendsson himself.[15] From a paleo-
graphic point of view the parts of the manuscript written by Haukr can be
divided into four parts, probably written at different times. The current order of the texts probably came into being during the time of Árni Magnússon (1663–1730). The quires containing *Trójumanna saga* (folios 22r–33v) and
Breta sögur (folios 36r–59r) were written between 1302 and 1310. Since Haukr
lived in Iceland from 1306 to 1308 and since all other scribes of the manuscript were Icelandic, these quires may be related to Haukr's stay in Iceland.[16]
Although *Trójumanna saga* and *Breta sögur* are separated by folios 34–35, they
are still a textual unity:[17] *Trójumanna saga* refers to the following *Breta sögur*
as they continue the narration of *Trójumanna saga* with the tale about the
founding of Rome by Aeneas. *Hauksbók* is the only manuscript containing a
complete text of the shorter redaction of *Breta sögur*, including the poem *Mer-
línússpá* and a catalogue of the West-Saxon kings from Caedwalla to Aethelstan. Several later copies or excerpts of *Breta sögur* may have been based on
this redaction of the text.[18]

Finally, there is an extract of *Breta sögur* in Copenhagen, Arnamagnaean
Institute 764 4to. The text is preserved in a short history of the world rendering several passages of *Breta sögur* almost verbatim, briefly summarizing the
passages in between. Similarities of the hands and the orthography also indicate a very close affiliation.[19]

---

[14] Eiríkur Jónsson and Finnur Jónsson, eds., *Hauksbók*.

[15] See the argumentation of Jón Helgason, ed., *The Arna-Magnæan Manuscripts*, x.

[16] Stefán Karlsson, "Aldur Hauksbókar," *Fróðskaparrit. Annales Societatis Scientia-
rium Færoensis* 13 (1964): 114–21, here 119.

[17] Although folios 34 and 35 were written before *Trójumanna saga* and *Breta sögur*,
they must have been inserted later at this place for economical reasons, that is, to complete a quire. See Stefán Karlsson, "Aldur Hauksbókar," 117.

[18] See Jón Helgason, "Til Hauksbóks historie i det 17. århundrede," in *Opuscula* 1,
Bibliotheca Arnamagnæana 20 (Copenhagen, 1960), 1–48, here 15.

[19] See Stefán Karlsson, *Sagas*, 26; Louis-Jensen, "Et forlæg til Flateyjarbók?"; and Peter Foote, ed., *A Saga of St Peter the Apostle. Perg. 4:o nr 19 in The Royal Library, Stockholm*, Early Icelandic Manuscripts in Facsimile 19 (Copenhagen, 1990), xxx. In 1968, in
the binding of an Icelandic manuscript in Trinity College Dublin, a very defective and
hardly readable fragment of *Breta sögur* was found. The foliation of this fragment is very
difficult because it contains a passage which is complete only in *Hauksbók* whereas there
is a lacuna in AM 573 4to at this place.

The common transmission of *Trójumanna saga* and *Breta sögur*

The combination of the Troy story and the history of the Britons was widespread in Europe during the Middle Ages. Although the Latin originals of both texts came independently to Iceland, the translations of *Trójumanna saga* and *Breta sögur* were transmitted together quite early and were obviously considered parts of a coherent story. Within the Icelandic transmission, only late paper manuscripts contain *Trójumanna saga* in a version not interpolated and not combined with *Breta sögur*. The manuscripts containing a combination of the interpolated version β of *Trójumanna saga* and *Breta sögur* can be divided into a longer and a shorter redaction. The longer redactions of both texts are represented by *Ormsbók* and AM 573 4to, while the shorter redactions are preserved only in *Hauksbók*. For a long time, the texts of *Hauksbók* were the basis for all scholarly research on *Trójumanna saga* and *Breta sögur*. Nobody considered the fact that the text of *Hauksbók* represents not the original translation but only a later redaction founded on an individual textual conception. Since the text of *Breta sögur* is only fragmentarily preserved in *Ormsbók* and AM 573 4to, a comparison between the two redactions has to be based mainly on *Trójumanna saga*.

Version β of *Trójumanna saga* differs from version α mainly by using additional Latin sources. But additions and interpolations as well as verbal correspondences and omissions common to both versions prove that they are based on the same translation of the Dares text.[20] In a very early phase of transmission, *Trójumanna saga* was conflated with extracts from the *Ilias Latina* which in the Middle Ages was considered a text of classical antiquity and belonged to the canon of school literature.[21] It may be that the rewriting and interpolation of the Icelandic Dares translation had taken place when *Trójumanna saga* and *Breta sögur* were connected. Since in many manuscripts Geoffrey's text was combined with a version of Dares' text, one which in parts differed quite a lot from Meister's edition,[22] the Latin exemplar of *Breta sögur* might have come to Iceland together with some other interpolated manuscript of Dares' text, which was then used to rework the already existing *Trójumanna saga*.

As noted above, *Hauksbók* contains many different texts. It has repeatedly been maintained that this very diverse material has no systematic order.[23] But

---

[20] Louis-Jensen, ed., *Trójumanna saga. The Dares Phrygius Version*, xii–xv.

[21] Günter Glauche, *Schullektüre im Mittelalter. Entstehungen und Wandlungen des Lektürekanons bis 1200 nach den Quellen dargestellt* (Munich, 1970), 70–71, 110.

[22] Ferdinand Meister, ed., *Über Dares von Phrygien, de excidio Troiae historiae* (Breslau, 1871); see Wright, *Historia Regum Britannie* II, xcvi.

[23] For example, Jón Helgason, ed., *The Arna-Magnæan Manuscripts*, xviii, or *Hauksbók*, lxiii, n. 1.

before accepting such a critical judgment one should recall that the manuscript is defective and therefore the original order of the texts is uncertain.[24] Before *Hauksbók* was damaged, it must have been an impressive and rather thick manuscript, but it was never a manuscript of great splendor: the physical appearance of the manuscript suggests that Haukr was rather economical despite his wealth, for right from the beginning several leaves were defective or irregular and the manuscript's presentation was modest; moreover, it seems to have been heavily used.

Taken together, the texts in *Hauksbók* constitute an encyclopedia focusing on history. All four parts of an encyclopedia are represented: the cosmos, history, science, and ethics.[25] Haukr Erlendsson seems to have been thoroughly interested in history and in his family's genealogy. At the end of the manuscript, *Langfeðgatal* contains persons mentioned in almost all the texts in the manuscript, and in his version of *Landnámabók* Haukr traces seven lines of his own family. The character of an encyclopedia is reflected in the conception of *Hauksbók* as a substitute for a library: it combines the contents of many books containing a large spectrum of knowledge. As a vernacular compilation of learned texts of Latin origin, *Hauksbók* shows that during the thirteenth and fourteenth centuries in Norway and Iceland, as on the European continent, there was an increasing number of non-professional readers interested in learned texts.

The contents of the lost *Ormsbók* can be reconstructed with the help of an index written in the seventeenth century: "Orms Snorrasons Book | Continet Troijomanna Saga. Anundar Jarls Sona Saga; & alia varia, nempe Magus Jarls Saga | Lais Floretz | Berings | Remundars | Eriks Iwenis | Bewis | Myrmans | Parhalops | Enohs & Partiwals Sagor" (The book of Ormr Snorrason contains *Trójumanna saga*, the saga of Önundr jarl's sons, and several others, namely *Magus saga jarls*, the *lais* of Flores, and *Berings saga, Remundar saga, Erex saga, Ivens saga, Bevers saga, Myrmans saga, Partalopa saga, Enoks saga*, and *Parzivals saga*).[26] The interpretation of this index was a matter of discussion between Vilhelm Gödel and Grén Broberg, who both tried to support their differing opinions with the help of later copies and lexicographical excerpts. Although it might still be debated what the exact contents of *Ormsbók* were, especially what "alia varia" (and several others) meant, it can be stated that

---

[24] Stefán Karlsson, "Aldur Hauksbókar," 117–18.

[25] Concerning the categorization and the genre of medieval encyclopedias, see Christel Meier, "Grundzüge der mittelalterlichen Enzyklopädik," in *Literatur und Laienbildung im Spätmittelalter und in der Reformationszeit. Symposium Wolfenbüttel 1981*, ed. Ludger Grenzmann and Karl Stackmann (Stuttgart, 1984), 467–500.

[26] Cf. Grén Broberg, "Ormr Snorrasons bok," 56–57.

"Troijomanna saga" also included *Breta sögur.*[27] The rest of the sagas, the order
of which in the original manuscript is not correctly represented in the index,[28]
consisted of translations of French *lais* and Arthurian romances and of Icelandic courtly romances. That means that in *Ormsbók* the context of *Trójumanna
saga* and *Breta sögur* consisted of courtly literature focusing on entertainment,
delectare, whereas *Hauksbók* was focusing on edification, *prodesse*.

In the fragmentary manuscript AM 573 4to, which is very closely affiliated to *Ormsbók*, *Trójumanna saga* and *Breta sögur* also seem to have been
transmitted amongst courtly literature: after the passage about King Arthur's
death, *Breta sögur* is followed by *Valvers þáttr*, an independent part of *Parcevals saga*. But since the *Ormsbók*-redaction of *Breta sögur* is preserved only in a
copy from the seventeenth century, which does not even continue to the main
part of the saga, we cannot be certain if in Ormsbók *Valvers þáttr* was written
as a continuation of *Breta sögur*.

Although all three manuscripts represent the interpolated version β of
Trójumanna saga, their wording differs so much that this has to be considered in every interpretation.[29] Since all three manuscripts were written in the
fourteenth century and had been copied directly or indirectly from the same
exemplar, we may ask why the redactors altered the texts and what they intended with these alterations. Compared to *Hauksbók*, *Ormsbók* and AM 573
4to differ from each other only in small details, which enable us to conclude
that their characteristics may be traced back to a common exemplar. For this
reason *Ormsbók* and AM 573 4to may be considered as two texts of the same
redaction which can be compared to *Hauksbók*.[30]

At the beginning of *Trójumanna saga*, *Hauksbók* contains an important
addition compared to the redaction in *Ormsbók*/AM 573 4to. The saga proper

---

[27] This can be proven by an entry in Johannes Thomae Bureus's catalogue of 1651:
"Ormer Snorresson, på Pergament, in folio, rätt gammal Suänska, och mächta tätt styl,
om Troiæ förstöring, och Ängelands första bebygning, samt een hoop andra Historier,
angående Frankerike och Tyskland" (Ormr Snorrason, on parchment, in folio, rather old
Swedish and very condensed style, about the destruction of Troy and the first settlement
of England together with a number of other stories concerning France and Germany);
Gödel, "Ormr Snorrasons bok," 357.
[28] Christopher Sanders, "The Order of Knights in Ormsbók," in *Opuscula* 7, Bibliotheca Arnamagnæana 34 (Copenhagen, 1979), 140–56, here 141.
[29] For a detailed comparison of the different redactions of version β of *Trójumanna
saga*, see Stefanie Würth, "Intention oder Inkompetenz," *Skandinavistik* 22 (1992): 1–26.
[30] The interesting question whether the stemma of version β of *Trójumanna saga* can
be extended to *Breta sögur* has to be left open until a critical edition of *Breta sögur* is available. However, there are no arguments against the hypothesis that the interpolated version
of *Trójumanna saga* was, on all levels of transmission, already connected with *Breta sögur*.

is preceded by a mythological prologue in which the antique gods are identified with their Nordic counterparts and connected to world history via a euhemeristic explanation.[31] In addition to this long introduction, *Hauksbók* itself contains two correlated texts. The first passage can be found in chapters 5 and 6 of *Heimslýsing ok helgifræði*[32] under the heading "Huaðan otru hofst". For the most part, this is a translation of an Old English homily written by Ælfric.[33] This text explains that after the building of the Tower of Babel mankind was again seduced by the devil to forget the one and only God. Afterwards, mankind began to worship natural phenomena, like the sun, the moon, and the stars, and even dead people, amongst them Saturn and Jupiter. In accordance with the prologue in *Trójumanna saga*, Jupiter and Thor are also in "Huaðan otru hofst" identified with each other. But both texts refrain from explicitly calling them gods. The theological text as well as *Trójumanna saga* make it clear that the heathen gods are actually men who only by mistake were associated with godlike characteristics. In *Hauksbók* this euhemeristic explanation in *Trójumanna saga* had come about because of the inclusions of material from the *Ilias Latina*. In contrast to the Dares text, in the *Ilias Latina* the gods actively took part in the action. In the *Ættartalan* in *Hauksbók*, Saturn and Jupiter also appear, again without explicitly being called gods; there Haukr traces his ancestors back to Adam and Eve.[34] As in *Trójumanna saga*, Saturn in this genealogy is located on the isle of Crete, but Jupiter is not identified with Thor, who only later is introduced as the grandson of the Trojan king Priam.[35] Priam's grandson Tror is also identified with the Nordic god Thor in the prologue of *Snorra Edda*, which is probably the source of the information in the version of *Langfeðgatal* that is found in *Hauksbók*.[36]

A comparison of these passages makes it clear what Haukr Erlendsson intended when including the prologue in *Trójumanna saga*: a declaration that the human beings worshipped as gods were in fact historical persons and part of Haukr's own genealogy. Thus *Trójumanna saga* in connection with the following *Breta sögur* takes on the value of a historical source. Such a source was important, not only for Norwegian history in general, but also for the history of the family of Haukr, who was a civil servant of the Norwegian king.

---

[31] *Trójumanna saga*, 1.2–5; 18–20, 24–27.

[32] *Hauksbók*, 156–61.

[33] See *Hauksbók*, cxviii–cxix.

[34] *Hauksbók*, 504–6; this genealogy is also preserved in *Diplomatarium Islandicum*, *Íslenzkt fornbréfasafn*, 16 vols. (Copenhagen and Reykjavík, 1857–1952), 3: 5–8.

[35] *Hauksbók*, 504.22–24.

[36] About the different versions of *Langfeðgatal* see Anthony Faulkes, "Descent from the Gods," *Mediaeval Scandinavia* 11 (1978–1979): 92–125; about *Hauksbók* being derived from *Snorra Edda*, 104.

Although the plot of *Trójumanna saga* is the same in *Hauksbók* on the one hand and *Ormsbók* and AM 573 4to on the other, the two redactions differ from each other especially in the arrangement of details. Unlike *Ormsbók* and AM 573 4to, the usually more concise and shorter redaction of the saga in *Hauksbók* contains an addition in the narrative of the Golden Fleece. In the *Ormsbók* redaction (there is a lacuna at this point in the text of the fragmentary manuscript AM 573 4to), when Jason and his companions approach King Laomedon the story mentions only Priam and Hesione as King Laomedon's children.[37] In contrast, *Hauksbók* introduces the family of the Trojan king in much more detail, telling the names of all his children.[38] The genealogy is followed in *Hauksbók* by an account of Hecuba dreaming of her son, who will eventually cause the destruction of Troy, and by the narratives about Paris's youth[39] and the competition among Sif, Freyja, and Frigg. This passage in *Hauksbók* is tied not to Dares' text, but to Ovid's *Heroides* and other, unknown sources. It points to future events which will cause the Trojan War and gives hints about the course of the war and how it will end. Thus *Hauksbók* makes a closer connection between the story of the Golden Fleece and the report of the Trojan War than is the case in the *Ormsbók*-redaction.

While the *Hauksbók* redaction at this early point of the narrative focuses on the key concerns of the saga as a whole (i.e., the description of the war between the Greeks and the Trojans), such future events are, for the time being, left aside in *Ormsbók* and AM 573 4to. Instead, the redaction in *Ormsbók* and AM 573 4to gives many more details than *Hauksbók* about the love-story between Jason and Medea, who express their emotions in verbose dialogues. In *Ormsbók*, Medea's abandonment on the island is described more dramatically and in emotional terms,[40] while in *Hauksbók* Jason obviously leaves Medea because he has finished his political mission and she is no longer of use to him. *Ormsbók* gives the impression that, although Jason leaves Medea of his own free will, he still left her unwillingly; in his fight against Peleus, he depends on the family of his wife. At this stage of *Hauksbók*, Medea is now "out of the saga," but in *Ormsbók* and AM 573 4to, Jason, after his return to Greece, receives a long letter from Medea in which she accuses him, in a very miserable tone, of having abused and betrayed her, and that he has committed a wrong

---

[37] *Trójumanna saga*, 9.7–9.

[38] *Trójumanna saga*, 9.15–19.

[39] In his introduction to *Trójumanna saga*, Haukr also used motifs from indigenous saga literature (Jón Helgason, "Paris i Troja, Þorsteinn på Borg och Brodd-Helgi på Hof," in Lars Svensson et al., eds., *Nordiska Studier i filologi och lingvistik. Festskrift tillägnad Gösta Holm* [Lund, 1976], 192–94).

[40] *Trójumanna saga*, 18.9–17, 19.1–5.

against the gods, who will now decide both their fates.[41] Medea's love for Jason turns to hatred, and the princess asks both Nordic and Greek gods for help. Finally, she threatens Jason with the prophecy that her offspring will become great chieftains and will revenge their relatives.[42] Medea's prophecy has no connection with the main plot of *Trójumanna saga*. This comparison between the two redactions of *Trójumanna saga* indicates that in *Ormsbók* and AM 573 4to it is more important to entertain (*delectare*) than to inform (*prodesse*). While, in the *Hauksbók* redaction, the narrative about Jason and the Golden Fleece is merely intended to explain the reasons for Helen's abduction and thus the onset of the Trojan War, the redaction in *Ormsbók* and AM 573 4to connects this narrative with the detailed love-story of Jason and Medea.

The differences between *Hauksbók*, which concentrates on facts and which strives for an objective style of narration, and *Ormsbók* and AM 573 4to, which are very rhetorical and florid in tone, become particularly clear in the passages which are dealing with Helen and her part in the Trojan War. In both redactions, Helen is mentioned for the first time as a sister of Castor and Pollux in the list of the Argonauts.[43] Here again the redaction in *Ormsbók* and AM 573 4to concentrates on the emotional relationship between Alexander (Paris) and Helen. It then gives a detailed report of the prehistory of Helen's abduction: because of a dream Alexander believes that Helen is the most beautiful of all women, whom Freyja had promised him in the forest of Ida. It is for this reason that Alexander writes a long and very emotional letter to Helen and asks her for her love.[44] In this letter, Alexander repeatedly calls Helen *kurteis* (courtly) and refers to her *kurteisi* (courtliness),[45] and, at the end of the letter, he calls himself "hin*n* kurteisasti madr" (the most courtly man).[46] The words *kurteis, kurteisi,* and *kurteisliga*, cognate with Old-French *cortois* and *cortoisie*, are terms which refer to a person's appearance in the upper class of society,[47] appearing ten times in

---

[41] *Trójumanna saga*, 20.12–14.

[42] *Trójumanna saga*, 21.2–5. The wording in AM 573 4to: "... at synir þessar veslv konv mundv verþa storir hofþingíar ok mundo fæþaz íannars konungs riki ok munv hefna sinna frænda" (That the sons of this poor woman will become great chieftains and that they would be brought up in another king's empire and that they would revenge their relatives: *Trójumanna saga*, 21.10–12).

[43] *Trójumanna saga*, 9.1–3 (= wording in *Ormsbók*) and 9.10; in AM 573 4to this passage is not preserved.

[44] *Trójumanna saga*, 48–50. The text in AM 573 4to has a lacuna before Helen's abduction.

[45] *Trójumanna saga*, 48. 21, 49.4, 6, 22.

[46] *Trójumanna saga*, 50.13–14.

[47] The word *kurteisi* occurs for the first time in a Norse text in the twelfth century, in the *Leiðarvísir* written by Abbot Nikulás. Later, it is also used in the miracles of St Þorlákur,

the *Ormsbók* redaction (it refers on eight occasions to Helen or Alexander).[48] In *Hauksbók*, however, *kurteis* appears in only one instance.[49]

In his letter, Alexander describes his feelings for Helen in detail.[50] Many metaphors are used to illustrate Helen's beauty, which touches Alexander so much that he does not want to rest until he has met her again. Alexander's psyche is that of a lovesick person, a type of character which often appears in medieval courtly literature.[51] Although Alexander in his letter also refers briefly to the virtues of the other Trojans, especially those of his brothers, the rhetoric of the letter as a whole reflects his desire to win Helen's love, even when he speaks about revenge for Hesione's abduction.[52] Just as Telamon's decision about Hesione was founded on love, Alexander wants to take revenge on him for taking Hesione's love, not by taking Helen's person but by taking her love. The argumentation is completely based on Alexander's understanding of the natures of himself and Helen, whereas the political situation is of no importance. Helen answers Alexander with an equally emotional response. However, she also defends the political position of Menelaos.[53] Yet we cannot see any connection with the past events in the letter.

Both redactions of *Trójumanna saga* give a similar description of the preparations for the duel between Alexander and Menelaos. *Hauksbók*, however, gives a concise account of Alexander's acceptance of the challenge, and Menelaos and Alexander function to determine the course of the Trojan War instead of their armies.[54] In the redaction of *Ormsbók* and AM 573 4to, Alexander

---

and since the thirteenth century it has been used quite frequently (Einar Ólafur Sveinsson, *The Age of the Sturlungs* [Ithaca, 1953], 36). About the meaning and the etymology of these words, cf. Jan de Vries, *Altnordisches etymologisches Wörterbuch*, 3rd ed. (Leiden, 1977), 335, and Johan Fritzner, *Ordbog over Det gamle norske Sprog* (Oslo, 1954), 2: 362–63.

[48] *Trójumanna saga*, 48.15, 17, 21, 49.4, 6, 22, 50.13, 56.4. Because of its fragmentary status the version in AM 573 4to can be used only for a comparison of the last passage; the wording in *Ormsbók*: "þar sem hann var allra manna vænstr oc kurteisaztr" (because he was the most beautiful and most courtly of all men: 56.3–4) compared to the wording in AM 573 4to: "er allra manna var uíænstr" (who was the most beautiful of all men: 56.13).

[49] "hann [i.e. Alexander] var allra manna kvrteisastr" (he was the most courtly of all men: *Trójumanna saga*, 10.24).

[50] *Trójumanna saga*, 49.7–14.

[51] The motif of *amor hereos* in Old Norse-Icelandic literature was first dealt with by Anne Heinrichs, "Amor hereos als Gestaltungsprinzip der Rémundar saga keisarasonar," *Skandinavistik* 18 (1988): 125–39.

[52] "oc vel þicki mier þa golldit þeim Girkium firir þat er þeir toko i brott Hesionam. at ek taka à brott þina ast" (and I think the Greeks have been greatly repaid that they robbed Hesione whereas I robbed your love: *Trójumanna saga*, 50.6–7).

[53] *Trójumanna saga*, 50–51.

[54] "þersv iattar Alexandr" (Alexander accepts this: *Trójumanna saga*, 116.23).

answers the challenge with a longer speech, which points out that the fight will be for Helen's love,[55] telling us again during the description of the fight that it is over Helen[56] and the text refers to the anger felt by Menelaos at Helen's abduction. *Hauksbók* just reports the facts of the fight and gives a brief description of the heroes' equipment and some details of their strategy. As we might expect, the redaction in *Ormsbók* and AM 573 4to uses this scene to give a verbose description of the romantic attachment between Alexander and Helen, and Freyja is said to save Alexander from Menelaos' deadly shot. Helen, who in a chapter under the heading "Aanyiandi sinar astir Alexandr ok Helena" (Alexander and Helen renewing their love) has been watching the fight from a tower, grieves in many words for Alexander's fate; his golden locks have been soiled by her former husband. She also describes in detail her bodily reactions caused by her fear for Alexander.[57] Like Alexander, Helen, too, shows the symptoms of *amor hereos* (which strikes men as well as women).[58] Helen ends her lament with the pledge that Alexander shall never again risk his life. Moved by Helen's words, Alexander bursts into tears. In a close embrace, the lovers promise each other their mutual love. By contrast, in *Hauksbók*, Alexander cannot be found, and his mysterious disappearance is not investigated at all.[59] It is not until a later battle that Alexander, without any further comment by the narrator, is listed among the commanders.[60]

Thus in the redaction of the saga in *Ormsbók* and AM 573 4to, Helen plays a more important part than in the *Hauksbók* redaction, which mentions Helen only when she is relevant to the central theme, the Trojan War. Whereas *Hauksbók* always stresses the historical or political situation which is the central aspect of the narrative, *Ormsbók* and AM 573 4to focus on private relationships or emotions. We get a similar impression of the different redactions when we look at the function of the gods in the two redactions of version β of *Trójumanna saga*. All three manuscripts include descriptions of Nordic gods and the

---

[55] *Trójumanna saga*, 116.5–117.3 (= wording in *Ormsbók*), also 116.10–13, 117.8–10 (= wording in AM 573 4to).

[56] "Ok sua sækia þeir grimmliga þetta einvigi er þeir gera firir skylld hinnar fegurstu konu Helenæ" (And they attack so heavily in this duel which they fight because of the most beautiful woman, Helen: *Trójumanna saga*, 119.5–120.1.); wording in AM 573 4to: "þeir sækiaz nu grimlígha oc kosta aflsíns mattvligha firir sok hínnar fogrv konv þeirar er þeir gera þetta eínvighi firir" (Now they attack heavily and struggle with all their power because of the beautiful woman for whom they are fighting: 119.10, 120.8–9).

[57] *Trójumanna saga*, 124.11–12, 125.1–3 (= wording in *Ormsbók*), 124.22, 125.11–13 (= wording in AM 573 4to).

[58] See Heinrichs, "Amor hereos," 133.

[59] *Trójumanna saga*, 124.23, 125.21.

[60] *Trójumanna saga*, 175.

gods of antiquity as existing side by side, but, in *Hauksbók*, the gods are active only in the mythological introduction to the saga. During the main part of the saga, the report of the Trojan War, the gods do not intervene in the actions.[61] In the redaction in *Ormsbók* and AM 573 4to, however, the gods repeatedly take an active part in the action of the saga. Freyja, who is identified with Thor's sister,[62] plays an especially important role, since she has promised Alexander that he will marry Helen. She is actively involved in the events of the war because she gets Alexander away from Menelaos and later also helps her son Aeneas[63] in his duel against Diomedes. Freyja is wounded by Diomedes during this action, and she flies through the air to the highest god in order to lament the boldness of the Greeks. Although *Ormsbók* and AM 573 4to are generally very close and even agree word for word in this passage, *Ormsbók* contains an addition which indicates that its redactor thought that the gods functioned merely as entertainment. Consider the redactor's comments about the gods' actions:

> þa kom þetta ⟨hogg⟩ ecki á Eneam helldr á himneska hond Freyiu ok vard þat mikit sár. Eptir sva gert soker Freya upp um loptin til himnanna. Ok sem hon kemr firi*r* hinn hæsta gud syni*r* hon honum sár sit*t* ok tiar firi*r* honum huersu diarfa Girkier gera sik er þeir hlifa ecki ⟨helldr⟩ godunum enn monnum. þuilika kueinkan bar hon opt firi*r* himna ko-*n*ung. Enn Eneas er nu i valldi gudanna sealfra.

> (Then this blow did not hit Aeneas but rather Freyja's heavenly hand and it was a big wound. After this had happened Freyja gets up through the air. And when she comes to the highest god, she shows him her wound and explains to him how bold the Greeks are when they spare neither gods nor human beings. Such lament she often told the heavenly king. But Aeneas is now under authority of the gods themselves.)[64]

---

[61] Although *Hauksbók*, at the end of the duel between Menelaos and Alexander, mentions that according to "heathen people" Freyja had brought Alexander to a safe place, the redactor distances himself from this utterance by using an ironic formulation: ". . . ok þat er heiðinna manna trva at Freyia tœki Alexandr . . ." (and heathen people believe that Freyja had taken Alexander: *Trójumanna saga*, 123.19–20).

[62] Wording in *Ormsbók*: "þa er Þor hiet þui Freyu systir sinnj" (then when Thor promised this his sister Freyja: *Trójumanna saga*, 230.3–4); wording in AM 573 4to: "þa er Þorr het þvi Freyiu systur sínne" (then when Thor promised this his sister Freyja: *Trójumanna saga*, 230.14–15).

[63] Wording in *Ormsbók*: "Eneas sem var son sealfrar Freyiu" (Eneas who was the son of Freyja herself: *Trójumanna saga*, 112.5–6); wording in AM 573 4to: "Eneas er var son síalfrar Freyu" (Eneas who was the son of Freyja herself: *Trójumanna saga*, 112.17).

[64] *Trójumanna saga*, 140.1–7. Cf. the wording in AM 573 4to: "en þetta hogg kom þo eigi aa Eneam helldr kom þat aa honnd Freyu oc vard þat mikid saar. eftir þetta sækir

Thus in the redaction of *Ormsbók* and AM 573 4to, the outcome of the Trojan War is pre-determined by the gods, whereas in *Hauksbók*, despite Hecuba's dream at the beginning of the saga, the outcome remains open and is decided by the battles.

In the redaction of *Ormsbók* and AM 573 4to the relationship between the gods is unclear for the entire narrative; there is no clear divine hierarchy and their only function is to dramatize the fights and emphasize the tragic fates of the individual heroes. Therefore, much as in the romance-style *riddarasögur*, the fantastic flair in *Trójumanna saga* is strengthened, especially during the emotional scenes with Helen and Medea. In *Hauksbók*, the entertaining aspect of the saga comes second to the historical information, and it is given the encyclopedic characteristics of the manuscript as a whole.[65] Moreover, Haukr Erlendsson draws back from the theme of "Minne" (courtly love), since it does not contribute to the reader's understanding of the War's historical context, just as he does not include detailed descriptions of battle scenes or other descriptive passages lacking elements which contribute directly to the plot. Haukr recites a historical narrative free of irrational and romantic additions, and elucidates the distance between his own time and the time of the reported events. The redaction in *Ormsbók* and AM 573 4to attempts to diminish this distance in order to give the impression that the action takes place in some kind of timeless present.

A comparison of the two redactions of *Breta sögur* lends support to the conclusions we have drawn about the analysis of *Trójumanna saga*. Compared to the redaction in *Ormsbók* and AM 573 4to, the redaction of *Breta sögur* in *Hauksbók* is shortened, concentrating on the historical facts, and it is written in a paratactic, concise style. The cross-references in the text suggest that the redactor had a very good overview of the *Breta sögur* as a whole. He does not use stereotypical characteristics as in the *riddarasögur*, or at least they have been reduced to the minimum required to make sense of the context. This is especially clear in the description of King Arthur's armor, which, in AM 573 4to, takes up twice as much space as in *Hauksbók*:

Freya upp um loftín oc er hon kemr firir godin synir hon saar sitt oc s(egir) huersu diarfir Grikir geraz er þeir hlifa eigi gudunum. en Eneas er nu iualldi gudanna sialfra" (But this stroke did not hit Eneas but it hit Freyja's hand and caused a big wound. Afterwards Freyja flew up into the air and when she came to the gods she showed her wound and told them how bold the Greeks were when they spared not even the gods. But Eneas is now in the hands of the gods themselves: *Trójumanna saga*, 140.15–19).

[65] The tendencies of *Hauksbók*'s reception of the Troy story agree with what can be observed in late medieval German chronicles. See Elisabeth Lienert, "Antikenroman als Geschichtswissen. Zu den kompilierten Trojanerkriegen in der 'Erweiterten Christherre-chronik' Heinrichs von München," in *Die deutsche Trojaliteratur des Mittelalters und der frühen Neuzeit, Materialien und Untersuchungen*, ed. Horst Brunner (Wiesbaden, 1990), 407–56, here 441–46.

AM 573 4to:

Artus konúngr tók þá brynju sína, gerua af hinu harðazta stáli, oc steypir (á) sig; síðan tekr hann hiálm sinn Herepandum, allan gylldan, harðara hueriu stáli oc grafinn í dreki einn af gulli, oc setr á haufuð sèr; þá tekr hann suerð sitt Kaleburnium oc gyrðer sig með, allra suerða bezt, þeirra er þá voru borin í þann tíma; hauggspjót sitt tók hann í haund sèr, þat er Eron hèt, allra spjóta bezt, þeirra er þá voru borin. Hann tekr þá ok skiolld sinn Pridon, hann var þyckr oc þolinn, þar var laugð á með gulli líkneskia Maríe drotníngar, oc á hana hèt hann í raunum aullum til trautz sèr oc fulltíngs. Oc er hann var vapnaðr með sua góðri herneskiu oc ágætri, þá varð allr herrinn glaðr við, er þeir sá sinn haufðíngja oc formann sua vlíkan aullum avðrum, oc treystvz þeir sua vel hans hamíngiu, at þeir gengu aller glaðer til þessar orrosto.

[Then King Arthur took his breastplate made of the hardest steel and puts it on himself. Then he takes his helmet, called Herepandum, which was completely golden and harder than any steel with a golden dragon engraved on it, and puts it on his head. Then he takes his sword, called Kaleburnium, and girds himself; it was the best of all swords being carried in this time. In his hand he took his spear, which was called Eron, the best of all spears which then were carried. He also took his shield called Pridon; it was thick and durable and it bore a golden inlay with Mary the Queen; and actually he used to call on her for help and safety. And he was armed with such good and famous weapons that the whole army was glad when they saw their commander and officer so unlike all others, and they trusted so much in his luck that they all gladly went into this battle: Breta sögur (1849), 92, n. 1]

Hauksbók:

hann var svá herklæddr, at hann hafði fjórfalda brynju; hann hafði hjálm af enu sterkasta stáli, ok grafinn á einn ormr með undarlegum hagleik; hann hafði þat sverð er Kalebúrnum hèt, þat var svá mikit at þat var fám mönnum vâpnhœft; hans skjöldr var gerr af enum sterkustum húðum, ok pentað á jamnan sèr til trausts; hans stóra spjót hèt Ron.

He was armed in this way that he had a fourfold breastplate; he had a helmet from the strongest steel, engraved with a dragon with wonderful skillfulness. He had the sword [called Kaleburnum; this was so big that only few men could use it as a weapon. His shield was made from the strongest skins and the figure of our Holy Lady was painted on it because he always called on her for his own support. His big spear was called Ron: Breta sögur (1849), 90–92]

Hauksbók refrains from using epithets without significance for an under-standing of the plot. Its language is sober and free of rhetorical elements, such as the redoubling of terms and alliteration or references to supernatural in-fluences, whether the help of the Virgin Mary or the king's *hamingja* (i.e., *fortuna*, "luck"). This concentration on the historical facts is in harmony with the tendency of this redactor to explain miraculous or supernatural events in a rational way and to refrain from narrative elements which are unimportant for the plot.

As in the *Hauksbók* redaction of *Trójumanna saga*, the gods in *Breta sögur* do not intervene in the action. If the redactor keeps details of pagan mythology, it is purely out of his antiquarian interests; since the historical characters of the saga believed in heathen gods, the gods form part of the overall historical context:

> Konúngr spurði, hvat Merkúríus veri? Heimgestr svarar: þann kalla sumir Óðinn, ok hafa vârir forellrar mikin*n* trúnað á honum haft, svâ ok á Þór ok Tý, Frigg ok Freyju, höfum vèr því trúað, at þau ráða heimi þessum ok forlögum manna; tóku þeir, konúngr, þat ráð, at eigna þeim daga í hverri viku, at þau þœttist at skyldari til at gæta allssaman, man-na ok missera, ok því kölluðu þeir Óðinsdag ok Týsdag ok Freyjudag.

> (The king asked who Mercurius was. Heimgestr answers: Some call him Odin and our forefathers have believed strongly in him and also in Thor and Tyr, in Frigg and Freyja. We believed that they would determine the world and men's destiny. They decided, O king, to dedicate to each of them one day of the week, because it seemed that they [i.e., the gods] were then even more obliged to take care of everything, men and nature, and therefore they called the days Odinsday, Tyrsday, and Freyjuday.)[66]

The redactor of *Hauksbók* is not very interested in Christian religion either, nor in the history of the Church. As evident from the description of Arthur's weapons, he does not interpret Arthur's veneration of the Virgin Mary as a sign of piety or of his being a good Christian, a view which is also reflected in his account of Arthur's fight with the Saxons. When Arthur realizes that his army will be defeated, "verðr hann ákaflega reiðr, ok bregðr sverði sínu ok höggr á tvær hendr, ok felldi á lítilli stundu lxx manna ok cccc . . ." (he be-comes very angry; he draws his sword and strikes on both sides; and within a short time he killed 470 people . . .).[67] In contrast, in the redaction in AM 573

---

[66] *Breta sögur* (1849), 6.
[67] *Breta sögur* (1849), 92.

4to, the slaying of the 470 enemies is preceded by a long prayer for victory. In *Hauksbók*, important Christian events, such as Christ's birth or the conversion of the British Isles, are merely used as a way of dating historical events. As with *Trójumanna saga*, so with *Breta sögur* Haukr downplays the theme of love. Although he must mention the relationship between Uther Pendragon and Igerna because it explains the animosity between Uther and the Cornish King Gorlois, he gives no details of the attachment or the emotions behind it.[68] Motifs and topics which are characteristic of courtly literature are of no importance in the *Hauksbók* redaction of *Breta sögur*: the text contains no descriptions of courtly feasts and tournaments, and even the famous feast when Arthur is crowned is related in a single sentence: "hann bauð til sín at hvítasunnu öllum konúngum, hertogum ok jörlum, ok öllum höfðíngjum í sínu ríki, ok var hann þá krúnaðr ok svâ drottníng, ok er sú veizla víðfrægjust orðin á norðrlöndum bœði at fornu ok nýju" (At Pentecost he invited all kings, dukes, and earls and all chieftains in his empire; and there he was crowned, as was the queen; and this feast became very famous in all northern countries as well, in the past as well as in the present).[69]

Omissions are particularly noticeable in the *Hauksbók* passages which deal with King Arthur; Finnur Jónsson concludes that "oversætteren var begyndt at blive træt eller utålmodig" (the translator had started to get tired or impatient).[70] In comparison with other British kings, Arthur is dealt with in great detail in Geoffrey's *Historia*, but Haukr could shorten Arthur's biography, because from a Norwegian-Icelandic point of view this king was no more important than any other. The radical omissions in the episodes dealing with Arthur therefore ought not to be explained by the tiredness or impatience of the redactor, but as a result of a desire to give a balanced historical report. Haukr Erlendsson tries to avoid repetitions in his Latin exemplar and to clarify ambiguous or doubtful formulations.[71] As a consequence, his redactions of the texts in *Hauksbók* have a very special and distinctive form.[72] Therefore Jakob Benediktsson's conclusion seems fitting: "Hoveddelen af H[auksbók] er således ikke blot en kompilation, men repræsenterer i flere tilfælde et bevidst redaktionsarbejde"

---

[68] *Breta sögur* (1849), 84–86; cf. the detailed passage in AM 573 4to, which in the edition is cited is among the variants.

[69] *Breta sögur* (1849), 98.

[70] In *Hauksbók*, cvii.

[71] Sven B. F. Jansson, ed., *Sagorna om Vinland. 1. Handskrifterna till Erik den Rödes saga* (Lund, 1944), 114.

[72] "Det visar sig, att man vid en noggrann undersökning av texterna kan få fram en personlig stilvilja, . . ." (Through a detailed investigation of the texts we can find an individual choice of style [. . .]: Jansson, *Sagorna*, 261).

["Thus the main part of Hauksbók is not only a compilation, but in several instances it represents the work of a consciously writing redactor"].[73]
   The ordering of the texts can be explained by two opposing organizing
principles. On the one hand, Haukr tries to collect as much material as possible
about a certain topic. This is especially clear in his version of *Landnámabók,* in
which he collates different sources. On the other hand, Haukr shows a tendency
to condense the texts of his exemplars, which is particularly clear in the case
of *Trójumanna saga.* As Haukr's texts are short and concise, and concentrate
on the central plot, they have very often been thought to represent the arche-
types, but this *brevitas* is, in fact, a characteristic feature of Haukr's style.[74]
Hauksbók emphasizes the historical aspects of the saga by concentrating on
the results of battles, on political decisions or developments, and on the historical consequences of these events. Passages not directly dealing with historical topics are reduced to a minimum necessary for an understanding of
the context of the saga. In *Hauksbók, Trójumanna saga* and *Breta sögur* form a
historical overview, from King Priam in Troy, or even from Saturn and Jupiter/
Thor, down to the English King Aethelstan/Aðalsteinn, foster-father of the
Norwegian King Hákon Haraldsson. As *Hauksbók* also contains a version of
Landnámabók, with genealogies down to Haukr's lifetime, this can be seen as
a historical report, beginning with the earliest ancestors in Troy, continuing
with Haukr's genealogy (in the *Snorra Edda*), and ending with contemporary
Icelandic and Norwegian history.
   In contrast to *Hauksbók,* the redactors of *Trójumanna saga* and *Breta sögur*
in *Ormsbók* and AM 573 4to emphasize the entertaining aspects of the sagas
and concentrate on the narrative highlights. Consistent ordering of events and
logical coherence of the textual elements are of secondary importance. They
give greater weight to situations and to the lives, emotions, and dialogues of the
characters. The narrative units are longer and more coherent than in *Hauksbók.*
Works which belong to the genre of *riddarasögur* "are derivative, one group
translated, the other imitative. They are prose narratives. The aristocratic protagonists are non-Scandinavian; and the settings are outside Scandinavia."[75]

[73] Jakob Benediktsson, "Hauksbók," in *Kulturhistorisk Leksikon for nordisk middelalder* (Copenhagen, 1961), 6: 250–51, here 251.
   [74] Jónas Kristjánsson, *Um Fóstbræðrasögu* (Reykjavík, 1972), 293–94, argued that the
version of *Fóstbræðra saga* contained in *Hauksbók* is the younger redaction of an older
text. This was contradicted by Klaus von See, "Die Überlieferung der Fóstbrœðra saga,"
in idem, *Edda, Saga, Skaldendichtung. Aufsätze zur skandinavischen Literatur des Mittelalters* (Heidelberg, 1981), 443–60.
   [75] Marianne Kalinke, "Norse Romance (*Riddarasögur*)," in Carol J. Clover and John
Lindow, eds., *Old Norse-Icelandic Literature: A Critical Guide,* Islandica 45 (Ithaca, 1985),
316–63, here 317.

They also lack historicity and authenticity, and apologies in the texts allow us to conclude that the *riddarasögur* were criticized for these faults by their contemporary audience.[76] As they are transmitted in *Ormsbók* and AM 573 4to, *Trójumanna saga* and *Breta sögur* fit perfectly into the genre of the *riddarasögur*, as they fulfill many of these criteria: the texts are translated and written in prose; their protagonists are of non-Scandinavian descent and belong to the upper classes of society; and the action takes place outside of Scandinavia. Both sagas are romantic tales that emphasize single episodes and human relationships, integrate supernatural beings into the action, and use a flowery style. In contrast to *Hauksbók*, the redactor of which tries to eliminate precisely those romance elements that would undermine the text's historical credibility, the entertainment value of passages in the redactions in *Ormsbók* and AM 573 4to are more important than the historical meaning of events. In the redactions of *Ormsbók* and AM 573 4to *Trójumanna saga* and *Breta sögur* are the only texts among the other Icelandic pseudo-historical translations which can be compared to the continental "romances of antiquity" which have been adapted to contemporaneous, courtly circumstances. *Trójumanna saga* and *Breta sögur* in the *Hauksbók* redactions cannot be regarded as *riddarasögur*, because Haukr's drastic interventions have revised the conception of the contents, the language, and the style.

These two very different redactions of *Trójumanna saga* and *Breta sögur* were written at about the same time, the late thirteenth or early fourteenth centuries. This suggests that the compilers worked according to some sort of program and chose the texts in keeping with criteria about content. They adapted the language and style of the texts being compiled in conformity with this overall conceptualization. We have to admit that the redactors of the large compilations of the thirteenth and especially the fourteenth centuries worked more independently and in a more self-conscious way than has long been thought. The redactors made use of extensive literary material from which they created independent works with clear themes, which could be adapted to their sagas to suit the tastes and the expectations of different audiences. The younger redactions of *Trójumanna saga* and *Breta sögur* belong to different genres and manifest different worlds of intention.

The old classification of *Trójumanna saga* and *Breta sögur* as "pseudo-historical translations" is based exclusively on the redactions in *Hauksbók*. Although in the twelfth and thirteenth centuries the historical contents of the Latin texts provided the reason for the Icelandic translations, we cannot be sure how long this primarily historical interest in *Trójumanna saga* and

---

[76] Kalinke, "Norse Romance," 318.

Breta sögur continued. Early in the reception of the sagas, as can be seen from the interpolations and the language in the redactions in *Ormsbók* and AM 573 4to and from the stylistic revisions in the young copies of version α of *Trójumanna saga*, to teach, *prodesse*, became less important than to delight, *delectare*.

An excerpt of *Breta sögur* in the manuscript AM 764 4to[77]

AM 764 4to is a vellum manuscript consisting of forty-eight leaves, written ca.1360–1370, either in the Augustinian monastery at Möðruvellir or in the Benedictine convent at Reynistaður.[78] The manuscript was probably written in various stints over a relatively long period of time.[79] For a long time, the codex, which is in places barely readable and contains several lacunae and defective leaves, existed unbound. Two leaves from it have been integrated into another codex (Copenhagen, Arnamagnaean Institute 162M fol.).[80] The manuscript contains a large number of different texts and excerpts, dealing mainly with religious topics.[81] The first part of the manuscript consists of a short history of the world called *Annála bæklingur* (folios 1–23v). While the Icelandic *Veraldar saga* in its order of six ages agrees with Isidore's chronology, AM 764 4to follows Bede's order of eight ages. Excerpts from larger works have been integrated into this historiographic frame, among others a

---

[77] A detailed description of the manuscript can be found in Kålund, *Katalog*, 2: 184–85.

[78] Stefán Karlsson, "Fróðleiksgreinar frá tólftu öld," in Jakob Benediktsson et al., eds., *Afmælisrit Jóns Helgasonar. 30. júní 1969* (Reykjavík, 1969), 328–49, here 117.

[79] Ólafur Halldórsson, "Rímbeglusmiður," in Sigurgeir Steingrímsson et al., eds., *Grettisfærsla. Safn ritgerða eftir Ólaf Halldórsson gefið út á sjötugsafmæli hans 18. apríl 1990* (Reykjavík, 1990), 302–18, here 309.

[80] Mattias Tveitane, *Den lærde stil. Oversetterprosa i den norrøne versjonen av Vitæ Patrum*, Årbok for Universitetet i Bergen, Humanistisk Serie, 1967, no. 2 (Bergen and Oslo, 1968), 17.

[81] The manuscript is mentioned very often because of its varied contents: Ólafur Halldórsson, "Úr sögu skinnbóka," in *Grettisfærsla*, 51–72; idem, "Rímbeglusmiður" (see note 79); idem, "Af uppruna Flateyjarbókar," in *Grettisfærsla*, 427–31; Stefán Karlsson, "Inventio crucis, cap. 1, og Veraldar saga," in *Opuscula* 2, Bibliotheca Arnamagnæana 25 (Copenhagen, 1977), 116–33; Stefán Karlsson, ed., *Sagas*; Peter Springborg, "Weltbild mit Löwe. Die *Imago mundi* von Honorius Augustodunensis in der Altwestnordischen Textüberlieferung," in Pietro Janni et al., eds., *Cultura Classica e Cultura Germanica settentrionale* (Macerata, 1983), 167–219; Matthew J. Driscoll, ed., *Sigurðar saga þǫgla* (Reykjavík, 1992), xxxvi–xxxviii.

geographic introduction,[82] a list of popes to Clement IV,[83] a list of emperors to Frederick II, and smaller legends and miscellanea. The remaining contents of the manuscript consist of more legends,[84] tales from the *Vitae Patrum*,[85] an instruction on interpreting dreams, a historical-geographic overview, treatises dealing with various topics,[86] and annals.

Because the compilation consists of so many small elements, not all parts of the manuscript have yet been identified.[87] At the end of the fifth age, the *Annála bæklingur* contains excerpts, more or less representing its beginning and the end, from *Rómverja saga*.[88] AM 764 4to does not copy the text of its exemplar word for word; instead, it usually quotes small passages, then summarizes a longer passage, and then quotes again word for word.[89] Scholars have only recently noticed that the *Annála bæklingur* (folio 11r8–13 and folios 11v5–12v41) also contains passages from *Breta sögur*. The brief first excerpt from *Breta sögur* is a continuation of the summary of the events of the Trojan

---

[82] See Rudolf Simek, *Altnordische Kosmographie. Studien und Quellen zu Weltbild und Weltbeschreibung in Norwegen und Island vom 12. bis zum 14. Jahrhundert* (Berlin, 1990), 396, 436, 445.

[83] See Springborg, "Weltbild mit Löwe."

[84] The edited texts are: *Remigius saga*, in C. R. Unger, ed., *Heilagra manna søgur: Fortællinger og legender om hellige mænd og kvinder,* 2 vols. (Christiania [Oslo], 1877), 2: 222–27; *Malcus saga*, in Unger, ed., *Heilagra manna søgur*, 1: 437–46; Ole Widding and Hans Bekker-Nielsen, eds., "Elisabeth of Schönau's Visions in an Old Icelandic Manuscript, AM 764, 4o," in *Opuscula* 2, Bibliotheca Arnamagnæana 25 (Copenhagen, 1977), 93–96; "Jóns þáttr biskups Halldórssonar," in Jón Sigurðsson and Guðbrandur Vigfússon, eds., *Biskupa sögur*, 2 vols. (Copenhagen, 1858–1878), 2: 223–30; cf. Hugo Gering, ed., *Islendzk æventyri*, 2 vols. (Halle, 1882–1883), 1: 84–93.

[85] See Tveitane, *Den lærde stil*, 18–22 and passim.

[86] An edition of part of the texts can be found in Ole Widding and Hans Bekker-Nielsen, "A Debate of the Body and the Soul in Old Norse Literature," *Mediaeval Studies* 21 (1959): 272–89.

[87] Ole Widding, Hans Bekker-Nielsen, and L.K. Shook, "The Lives of the Saints in Old Norse Prose: A Handlist," *Mediaeval Studies* 25 (1963): 294–337, list ten legends from AM 764 4to. See Jonna Louis-Jensen in her introduction to *Enoks saga*, in *Opuscula* 5, Bibliotheca Arnamagnæana 31 (Copenhagen, 1975), 225–37, where she among other things deals with the relationships between AM 764 4to and *Ormsbók* and *Disciplina clericalis*. Svanhildur Óskarsdóttir's very thorough study on the manuscripts has not been published yet.

[88] A diplomatic edition of these passages from AM 764 4to can be found in Jakob Benediktsson, ed., *Catilina and Jugurtha by Sallust and Pharsalia by Lucan in Old Norse: Rómverja saga AM 595 a–b 4to*, Early Icelandic Manuscripts in Facsimile 13 (Copenhagen, 1980), 21–22.

[89] Jakob Benediktsson, ed., *Catilina and Jugurtha*, 19–20.

War, and it has verbal correspondences with a passage of *Hauksbók* called "Heimslýsing ok helgifrœði".[90] Finnur Jónsson suspected that this chapter indirectly relates to Isidore, whose text was shortened but also supplemented with additional material (including material from the *Imago mundi* of Honorius Augustodunensis).[91] A passage follows, which summarizes the events from the survivors' flight from Troy until the settlement and naming of Britain by Brutus. Although the text in AM 764 4to is so condensed that there is no verbal correspondence left with *Breta sögur,* there are several clues as to the exemplar the scribe used, in particular the information which is given about the change of names from "Brutus" to "Brito" and the use of the wrong name "Alkrion" instead of "Albion." The change of names, which does not occur in Geoffrey's *Historia,* is found only in the two Icelandic redactions of *Breta sögur.* The incorrect spelling of "Alkrion" indicates that, for this passage, the compiler of AM 764 4to used an exemplar which is very closely affiliated with AM 573 4to, because this manuscript also uses "Alkrion", whereas *Hauksbók* uses "Albíó"[92] and *Ormsbók* uses "Alcion".

The second and longer passage from *Breta sögur* in AM 764 4to begins with the sentence: "Her hefr ad segia af Breta konungum huerir rikt hafa firir higad burdinn" (Here begins the tale about the British kings, those who have reigned before Christ). The reigns of the British rulers from Brutus to Kambelinus are then dealt with in varying detail. A change occurs between passages corresponding verbally with *Breta sögur* and those which summarize heavily and omit large parts of the exemplar. Verbal correspondences in this section indicate an affiliation with AM 573 4to:[93]

---

[90] *Hauksbók*, 155.4–9.

[91] *Hauksbók*, cxvi–cxvii.

[92] *Breta sögur* (1848), 138; the variant from AM 573 4to is not cited in the footnotes of Jón Sigurðsson's edition.

[93] AM 573 4to is quoted from Jonna Louis-Jensen's unpublished transcription of the manuscript, because the passage is not quoted fully in Jón Sigurðsson's edition. The wording in *Ormsbók* (quoted from Louis-Jensen's transcription): "þeir bliesu hátt enn stigu nidur hart ok tok risinn hann sva fast at i sundur geingu tvo rif i hægri siþu Corinei enn eitt i vinstri ok er Corineus var sva fast tekinn þa rann hnum mik i skap ok færdist hann þa i alla avka afls sins ok hefur hann risann uppá axlir sier ok hleypur frammá sæfar hamra med hann ok kastar risanumm þar af framm" (They breathed loudly and stamped hard, and the giant seized him so violently that two ribs broke in Corineus's right side and one in his left; and when Corineus was taken so violently he became very angry and then he added all his power and takes the giant on his shoulders and runs forward to the cliffs and throws the giant down from there). The wording of the passage in *Hauksbók*: "risinn tók hann svâ fast, at iij rifin gengu í sundr í Koríneus, þá varð Koríneus reiðr, ok fœrist í alla

AM 764 4to:

þeir blesu haat ok stigu nidr hart. risin tok Koríneum sua hart at brotnudu rifin íj hægri sidu enn eitt i uinstri Koríneo rann miog iskap en hann uar sua fast tekinn færdiz hann þa i alla auka afls sins hann hof upp risann aa auxl ser ok rann med hann fram siouar hamra nokura ok kastadi honum þar af ofan. [They breathed loudly and stamped hard on the earth. The giant took hold of Korineus so violently that two ribs broke in his right side and one in his left. Korineus became very angry, when he was so violently taken. He used all his power, he put the giant on his shoulders and rushed with him to some cliffs and threw him down from there]

AM 573 4to:

þeir blesu hatt ok stigu hart Risinn tok Koríneum sva fast ad brotnudu ij rif ihans hægri sidu en eitt i [u]instri. Korineo rann miok iskap er hann uar sva fast tekinn færdiz hann þa ialla auka afls sins. hann hof upp risann a auxl ser ok rann med hann fram asiouarhamra [n]ockura ok kastadi honum tar af fram [They breathed loudly and stamped hard. The giant took hold of Korineus so violently that two ribs broke in his right side and one in his left. Korineus became very angry because he was so violently taken. He added all his power; he put the giant on his shoulders and rushed with him to some cliffs and threw him from there]

These two passages are so similar that, taken together with the incorrect spelling of "Alkrion" for "Albion," we might view AM 764 4to as a direct copy of AM 573 4to. This conclusion is supported by the fact that both manuscripts were written in Skagafjörður and thus also show similarities in the scribes' hands.

AM 764 4to is a good example of a compilation which consists of small insertions. Short but coherent passages were separated from their original context and connected to a new text and given new meaning as a result. The compilers used all the sources available to them, the contents of which were relevant in some way to their intention. The only criteria of usefulness was relevance, and even manuscripts like AM 573 4to, which were more entertaining than didactic, could be used as a source.

---

auka afls síns, ok hefir hann síðan risann upp á bringu sèr, ok leypr síðan með honum á sjófargnípur nokkurar" (The giant seized him so violently that Korineus broke two ribs; then Korineus became angry and added all his power and then he takes the giant before his breast and then he runs with him to some cliffs: *Breta sögur* [1848], 140).

Changing function causes alternations

The use of encyclopedic manuscripts characterized both the early and late reception of *Trójumanna saga* and *Breta sögur*. A diachronic overview of the redactions and versions of these sagas proves that the two texts could be adapted as often as was required, either by the compiler or according to the expectations of the compiler's audience. The tendency to *brevitas* in comparison to the Latin exemplars is particularly striking, a tendency which can be seen in the earliest Icelandic versions of both sagas. Omissions and abridgements do not alter the structure of the plot, but they concentrate the *summa facti* of the action. Since contemporary allusions made by early translators were not understood by later redactors and audiences, such allusions also were omitted, although we must recall that the texts are preserved in only a few manuscripts and that, in several manuscripts, the texts were transmitted together.

Medieval Icelandic encyclopedias nearly always focus on historiography, and other genres, such as geography or other learned texts, are subordinated to this historiographic interest.[94] Given that *Trójumanna saga* and *Breta sögur*, too, were integrated into large compilations with such an emphasis on historiography, we may conclude that they were read as informative historical information. They could be read as elements of longer historiographic works, because during the Middle Ages history was considered to be not the history of individuals or of humanity, but the history of limited human communities.[95] Medieval histories of the world are retrospective projections which construct history from histories.

Likewise, the younger redactions of *Trójumanna saga* and *Breta sögur* more or less belong to the genre of historiography, and are transmitted in more, and in better, manuscripts than the older and more detailed versions. Even if we were to begin with an hypothesis that a text is transmitted better the later it comes into being, we can still conclude from the transmission of *Trójumanna saga* and *Breta sögur* that the texts were read mainly as historiographic works, regardless of the intentions which the translators originally connected with these texts. As on the European continent, in Iceland there was a later tendency to integrate the courtly romances, which dealt with topics

---

[94] All examples for Norse encyclopedic manuscripts listed by Simek, *Altnordische Kosmographie*, 25–30, contain one or several historiographic texts, among them mostly a summary of the history of the world.

[95] Arno Borst, "Weltgeschichten im Mittelalter?," in Reinhard Koselleck and Wolf-Dieter Stempel, eds., *Geschichte – Ereignis und Erzählung* (Munich, 1973), 452–56, here 453.

of antiquity, into larger chronicles of world history, and the shorter versions were also preferred in this context.[96] Such shorter redactions were not considered to be a substitute for the longer originals, and both redactions were often transmitted side by side. Later redactions in the style of the *riddarasögur* allow us to conclude that in the fourteenth century *Trójumanna saga* and *Breta sögur* were read as entertaining sagas. Pre-existing Icelandic translations of *Trójumanna saga* and *Breta sögur* were adapted by stylistic revisions and through interpolations from other sources. A common transmission of *Trójumanna saga* and *Breta sögur*, with Arthurian texts in the manuscripts AM 573 4to and *Ormsbók*, proves that these revisions place the sagas in a different genre from that of the original translations. One suspects from the rather poor transmission of *Breta sögur* that their contents were too close to Arthurian literature, so popular in the thirteenth century. With an interest in the historiographic aspect of the sagas declining, *Breta sögur* and *Trójumanna saga* were stylistically reworked to meet the expectations raised by the people's familiarity with *riddarasögur*. As can be seen from the manuscripts AM 573 4to and *Ormsbók*, the struggle for a literary actualization was not successful. The long-winded *Breta sögur*, with more than one glorious hero at the center of its adventures, could not, even in a "modernized" form, compete with *riddarasögur*. Through the Norwegian translations of Chrétien de Troyes' romances, Icelanders were exposed to shorter and more entertaining narratives about King Arthur and his knights, and the transmission of the long and complicated *Breta sögur*, burdened by uninteresting characters, became redundant as entertainment.

Although the transmission of the texts was mostly anonymous, we can see from their many remarks about literary production that the authors and redactors were conscious of their own artistic creativity. There was no literary hierarchy by which to distinguish or grade artistic works of authors, translations, and redactions. Moreover, all who took part in the transmission of literary works could intervene in the process of production. Today, we categorize translations and redactions on the basis of the creative distribution they reflect, on a scale ranging from interlinear translations to free adaptations, and from the verbatim copying of vernacular texts to the independent reworking or re-creation of texts. Each text that is preserved in a medieval manuscript must be seen as the product of individual creative will, even though such will may have been influenced by historical, social, and cultural conditions. A comparison of

---

[96] Rüdiger Schnell, "Prosaauflösung und Geschichtsschreibung im deutschen Spätmittelalter," in Grenzmann and Stackmann, eds., *Literatur und Laienbildung im Spätmittelalter und in der Reformationszeit*, 214–48, here 228–30.

the earliest translations of *Trójumanna saga* and *Breta sögur* and their later redactions proves that the same level of intervention occurred during the transmission. Translations, like redactions, involve a cultural transfer, in which a
literary exemplar is adapted to the expectations of a new audience and to different cultural needs. In the Middle Ages, the alterations which were made to
the text of an exemplar, whether it was in a foreign language or in the same
language, were called "translatio", because "in a manuscript culture to translate means also the turning of a prior text into something more completely itself, or something more than what it literally is."[97]

Large compilations or manuscripts like AM 764 4to show that an author
or redactor could use all the available literature as kind of a construction kit
of references with elements that could be combined freely. The authors and redactors were not concerned whether passages they took were in their sources
in a context intended *prodesse* or *delectare*. Further, depending on the level of
education of each author or redactor, the language of the exemplar was not very
important. Latin and vernacular sources could be combined if their contents
corresponded to each other and if they were relevant to the compilation. Naturally, the intellectual scope of the authors and redactors was limited by the material conditions of their libraries: they could choose only from manuscripts
immediately available to them. There were probably only very few libraries in
Iceland that contained several versions of the same text, and therefore the limit
on materials forced the Icelandic compilers to use their sources creatively, and
to use their own knowledge when they produced new literary works.

Bibliography

Borst, Arno. "Weltgeschichten im Mittelalter?" In *Geschichte – Ereignis und
Erzählung*, ed. Reinhard Koselleck and Wolf-Dieter Stempel, 452–56.
Munich, 1973.

Broberg, Grén. "Ormr Snorrasons bok." *Arkiv för Nordisk Filologi* 24 (1908):
42–66.

Bruns, Gerald L. "The Originality of Texts in a Manuscript Culture."
Comparative Literature 32 (1980): 113–29.

Christoffersen, Marit, and Otto B. Bekken. "Algorismus i Hauksbók i eu-
ropeisk perspektiv." In *The Sixth International Saga Conference 28.7.–
2.8.1985, Workshop Papers,* 1: 131–50. 2 vols. Copenhagen, 1985.

---

[97] Gerald L. Bruns, "The Originality of Texts in a Manuscript Culture," *Comparative
Literature* 32 (1980): 113–29, here 125.

Diplomatorium Islandicum. Íslenzkt fornbréfasafn. 16 vols. Copenhagen and Reykjavík, 1857–1952.

Driscoll, Matthew J., ed. *Sigurðar saga þǫgla.* Reykjavík, 1992.

Einar Ólafur Sveinsson. *The Age of the Sturlungs.* Ithaca, 1953.

Eiríkur Jónsson and Finnur Jónsson, eds. *Hauksbók udgiven efter de Arnamagnæanske håndskrifter no. 371, 544 og 675, 4o same forskellige papirs håndskrifter af Det kongelige nordiske Oldskriftselskab.* Copenhagen, 1892–1896.

Faulkes, Anthony. "Descent from the Gods." *Mediaeval Scandinavia* 11 (1978–1979): 92–125.

Finnur Jónsson, ed. *Alexanders saga. Islandsk oversættelse ved Brandr Jónsson (Biskop til Holar 1263–64).* Copenhagen, 1925.

Foote, Peter, ed. *A Saga of St Peter the Apostle. Perg. 4:o nr 19 in The Royal Library, Stockholm,* Early Icelandic Manuscripts in Facsimile 19. Copenhagen, 1990.

Fritzner, Johan. *Ordbog over Det gamle norske Sprog.* Oslo, 1954.

Gering, Hugo, ed. *Islendzk æventyri.* 2 vols. Halle, 1882–1883.

Glauche, Günter. *Schullektüre im Mittelalter. Entstehungen und Wandlungen des Lektürekanons bis 1200 nach den Quellen dargestellt.* Munich, 1970.

Gödel, Vilhelm. *Fornnorsk-isländsk Litteratur i Sverige.* Stockholm, 1897.

———. "Ormr Snorrasons bok." In *Nordiska Studier tillegnade Adolf Noreen,* 357–74. Uppsala, 1904.

Heinrichs, Anne. "Amor hereos als Gestaltungsprinzip der Rémundar saga Keisarasonar." *Skandinavistik* 18 (1988): 125–39.

Heyse, E. "Ilias latina." In *Lexikon des Mittelalters* 5: 379. Zürich, 1991.

Jakob Benediktsson. "Hauksbók." In *Kulturhistorisk Leksikon for nordisk middelalder* 6: 250–51. Copenhagen, 1961.

———, ed. *Catilina and Jugurtha by Sallust and Pharsalia by Lucan in Old Norse: Rómverja saga AM 595 a–b 4to.* Early Icelandic Manuscripts in Facsimile 13. Copenhagen, 1980.

Jansson, Sven B. F., ed., *Sagorna om Vinland. 1. Handskrifterna till Erik den Rödes saga.* Lund, 1944.

Jón Helgason, ed. *Hauksbók: The Arna-Magnæan Manuscripts 371, 4to, 544, 4to, and 675, 4to.* Manuscripta Islandica 5. Copenhagen, 1960.

———. "Til Hauksbóks historie i det 17. århundrede." In *Opuscula* 1, 1–48. Bibliotheca Arnamagnæana 20. Copenhagen, 1960.

————. "Paris i Troja, Þorsteinn på Borg och Brodd-Helgi på Hof." In *Nordiska Studier i filologi och lingvistik. Festskrift tillägnad Gösta Holm*, ed. Lars Svensson et al., 192–94. Lund, 1976.

Jón Sigurðsson. "Trójumanna saga ok Breta sögur." In *Annaler for Nordisk Oldkyndighed og Historie*, 102–215, 3–145. Copenhagen, 1848–1849.

————, and Guðbrandur Vigfússon, ed. *Biskupa sögur*. 2 vols. Copenhagen, 1858–1878.

Jónas Kristjánsson. *Um Fóstbrœðrasögu*. Reykjavík, 1972.

Kalinke, Marianne. "Norse Romance (*Riddarasögur*)." In *Old Norse-Icelandic Literature: A Critical Guide*, ed. Carol J. Clover and John Lindow, 316–63. Islandica 45. Ithaca, 1985.

Kålund, Kr. *Katalog over Den arnamagnæanske Håndskriftsamling*. 2 vols. Copenhagen, 1888–1894.

Lienert, Elisabeth. "Antikenroman als Geschichtswissen. Zu den kompilierten Trojanerkriegen in der 'Erweiterten Christherrechronik' Heinrichs von München." In *Die deutsche Trojaliteratur des Mittelalters und der frühen Neuzeit, Materialien und Untersuchungen*, ed. Horst Brunner, 407–56. Wiesbaden, 1990.

Louis-Jensen, Jonna, ed. *Trójumanna saga*. Editiones Arnamagnæanæ, Ser. A: 8. Copenhagen, 1963.

————."Et forlæg til Flateyarbók? Fragmenterne AM 325 IV og XI, 3, 4to." In *Opuscula* 4, 141–58. Bibliotheca Arnamagnæana 30. Copenhagen, 1970.

————."Enoks saga." In *Opuscula* 5, 225–37. Bibliotheca Arnamagnæana 31. Copenhagen, 1975.

————, ed. *Trójumanna saga. The Dares Phrygius version*. Editiones Arnamagnæanæ, Ser. A: 9. Copenhagen, 1981.

McTurk, Rory. *Studies in Ragnars saga Loðbrókar and its Major Scandinavian Analogues*. Oxford, 1991.

Meier, Christel. "Grundzüge der mittelalterlichen Enzyklopädik." In *Literatur und Laienbildung im Spätmittelalter und in der Reformationszeit. Symposium Wolfenbüttel 1981*, ed. Ludger Grenzmann and Karl Stackmann, 467–500. Stuttgart, 1984.

Meister, Ferdinand, ed. *Über Dares von Phrygien, de excidio Troiae historiae*. Breslau, 1871.

Ólafur Halldórsson. "Af uppruna Flateyjarbókar." In *Grettisfærsla. Safn ritgerða eftir Ólaf Halldórsson gefið út á sjötugsafmæli hans 18. apríl 1990*, ed. Sigurgeir Steingrímsson et al., 427–31. Reykjavík, 1990.

_____. "Rímbeglusmiður." In *Grettisfœrsla*, ed. Sigurgeir Steingrímsson et al., 302–18.

_____. "Úr sögu skinnbóka." In *Grettisfœrsla*, ed. Sigurgeir Steingrímsson et al., 51–72.

Perkins, Richard. *Flóamanna Saga, Gaulverjabœr and Haukr Erlendsson*. Studia Islandica 36. Reykjavík, 1978.

Sanders, Christopher. "The Order of Knights in Ormsbók." In *Opuscula* 7, 140–56. Bibliotheca Arnamagnæana 34. Copenhagen, 1979.

Schnell, Rüdiger. "Prosaauflösung und Geschichtsschreibung im deutschen Spätmittelalter." In *Literatur und Laienbildung im Spätmittelalter und in der Reformationszeit*, ed. Grenzmann and Stackmann, 214–48.

See, Klaus von. "Die Überlieferung der Fóstbrœðra saga." In idem, *Edda, Saga, Skaldendichtung. Aufsätze zur skandinavischen Literatur des Mittelalters*, 443–60. Heidelberg, 1981.

Simek, Rudolf. *Altnordische Kosmographie. Studien und Quellen zu Weltbild und Weltbeschreibung in Norwegen und Island vom 12. bis zum 14. Jahrhundert*. Berlin, 1990.

Springborg, Peter. "Weltbild mit Löwe. Die *Imago mundi* von Honorius Augustodunensis in der Altwestnordischen Textüberlieferung." In *Cultura Classica e Cultura Germanica settentrionale*, ed. Pietro Janni et al., 167–219. Macerata, 1983.

Stefán Karlsson. "Aldur Hauksbókar." *Fróðskaparrit. Annales Societatis Scientiarum Fœroensis* 13 (1964): 114–21.

_____, ed. *Sagas of Icelandic Bishops: Fragments of Eight Manuscripts*. Early Icelandic Manuscripts in Facsimile 7. Copenhagen, 1967.

_____. "Fróðleiksgreinar frá tólftu öld." In *Afmælisrit Jóns Helgasonar. 30. júní 1969*, ed. Jakob Benediktsson et al., 328–49. Reykjavík, 1969.

_____. "Inventio crucis, cap. 1, og Veraldar saga." In *Opuscula* 2, 116–33. Bibliotheca Arnamagnæana 25. Copenhagen, 1977.

Tveitane, Mattias. *Den lærde stil. Oversetterprosa i den norrøne versjonen av Vitæ Patrum*. Årbok for Universitetet i Bergen, Humanistisk Serie, 1967, no. 2. Bergen and Oslo, 1968.

Unger, C. R., ed. *Heilagra manna søgur: Fortællinger og legender om hellige mænd og kvinder*. 2 vols. Christiania [Oslo], 1877.

Vollmer, F. *Zum Homerus latinus. Kritischer Commentar und Überlieferungsgeschichte*. Munich, 1913.

Vries, Jan de. *Altnordisches etymologisches Wörterbuch*. 3rd ed. Leiden, 1977.

Widding, Ole, and Hans Bekker-Nielsen. "A Debate of the Body and the Soul in Old Norse Literature." *Mediaeval Studies* 21 (1959): 272–89.

——, eds. "Elisabeth of Schönau's Visions in an Old Icelandic Manuscript, AM 764, 4o." In *Opuscula* 2, 93–96. Bibliotheca Arnamagnæana 25. Copenhagen, 1977.

Widding, Ole, Hans Bekker-Nielsen, and L. K. Shook. "The Lives of the Saints in Old Norse Prose: A Handlist." *Mediaeval Studies* 25 (1963): 294–337.

Wright, Neil, ed. *The Historia Regum Britannie. I. Bern, Burgerbibliothek, MS. 568.* Cambridge, 1985.

——, ed. *The Historia Regum Britannie. II. The First Variant Version: A Critical Edition.* Cambridge, 1988.

Würth, Stefanie. "Intention oder Inkompetenz?" *Skandinavistik* 22 (1992): 1–26.

——. *Der "Antikenroman" in der isländischen Literatur des Mittelalters. Eine Untersuchung zur Übersetzung und Rezeption lateinischer Literatur im Norden.* Beiträge zur Nordischen Philologie 26. Basel and Frankfurt/Main, 1998.

Reading from the Margins: The Uses of Old English Homiletic Manuscripts in the Post-Conquest Period[1]

Elaine Treharne

For scholars working in the post-Conquest period, the question of what constitutes Old English and what constitutes early Middle English is a problematic and potentially unsolvable one. In one sense, it does not matter how texts written in English at this time are classified linguistically, since analytical precision is difficult to attain, particularly in the case of a language in transition, as late Old English to early Middle English demonstrates only too clearly. However, the issue is of considerable importance because a failure to classify language realistically — in this case seeing texts written in the twelfth century as neither late Old English nor early Middle English — results in the virtual dismissal of a whole series of manuscripts and their contents from the scholarly canon, purely because they fall outside the chronological boundaries imposed by scholars on language usage and literary production: boundaries that in no way reflect the linguistic or literary facts.

The series of manuscripts to which I refer are those fifty-eight or so literary and legal codices (or fragments of larger volumes that contain English texts) that were produced in the second half of the eleventh century and throughout the twelfth.[2] To these can be added the pre- and post-Conquest manuscripts, numbering over one hundred, that contain annotation, marginalia, and glossing datable to the twelfth century and later that clearly demonstrate the utilization of Old English in the post-Conquest period. There is thus a very considerable number of manuscripts showing a significant use of

---

[1] My focus on manuscripts, and on glosses later in this paper, is especially appropriate in the light of Phill Pulsiano's sustained and exemplary scholarship on glosses, in addition to his work on so many other aspects of Anglo-Saxon manuscript culture.

[2] For which, see N. R. Ker, *Catalogue of Manuscripts Containing Anglo-Saxon* (Oxford, 1957; repr. with supplement, Oxford, 1990), xv–xix.

English, not including the diplomatic material which itself numbers well over
one hundred items datable to the twelfth and early thirteenth centuries.[3]

In terms of the literary culture of this period, the response of many leading scholars to the English texts that survive after the Conquest is one of exclusion or outright dismissal, although in some cases this exclusion might be
attributable to the stated coverage of respective published works:

> The Norman Conquest greatly curbed the influence which Ælfric and
> Wulfstan might have had on the development of English theology and
> prose style . . . The smooth Old English prose [of *Apollonius of Tyre*], so
> suitable for narrative and so different from anything by Alfred, Ælfric,
> or Wulfstan, is a glimpse of a native style that might have developed if
> English had not been replaced by French after the Norman Conquest.[4]

The alternative response of scholars has been generalization about the context of their production. Michael Clanchy, for example, in his influential
From Memory to Written Record, states that:

> Although Anglo-Saxon was not used after the 1070s by the king's gov-
> ernment or by the clergy as a whole, it found defenders in the monastic
> antiquarian reaction which maintained English ways in the face of the
> Norman conquerors. Those monastic houses like Worcester and Roches-
> ter which produced the first cartularies were also among those which
> were most concerned to preserve a knowledge of Anglo-Saxon. Anglo-
> Saxon texts continued to be copied for a century after the Conquest and
> some works survive only in copies made in the twelfth century.[5]

Here, Clanchy attributes the impetus for creating manuscripts containing
Old English to the nostalgic desire for the maintenance of "English ways,"
a form of literary and cultural rebellion in the face of oppression. This, in
itself, would imply that the works produced by the "monastic antiquarians"
possessed no real, serviceable use. In the recent *Cambridge History of Medieval*

---

[3] See, for example, David A. E. Pelteret, *Catalogue of English Post-Conquest Vernacular Documents* (Woodbridge, 1990).

[4] Stanley B. Greenfield and Daniel G. Calder, *A New Critical History of Old English Literature* (London, 1986), 95 and 97 respectively. Note that this volume includes material up
to 1100, while Malcolm Godden and Michael Lapidge, eds., *The Cambridge Companion to
Old English Literature* (Cambridge, 1991), state on the back cover that their volume intends
to introduce "students to English literature of the Anglo-Saxon period from 600 to 1066."

[5] M. T. Clanchy, *From Memory to Written Record*, 2nd ed. (Oxford, 1993), 212.

English Literature, edited by David Wallace, a collection that is set to become a definitive textbook, a chapter on "Old English and its Afterlife" by Seth Lerer[6] seems by its title ready to redress the neglect of Old English manuscripts copied in the post-Conquest period. Lerer brings to the reader's attention three important verses, *The Rime of King William*, *Durham*, and *The First Worcester Fragment* that each demonstrates links to pre-Conquest verse, as well as links to the development of later medieval poetry. Of the numerous substantial prose manuscripts copied in this period, Lerer states:

> Texts that originated in the Anglo-Saxon period were still in use at Rochester a century after the Norman Conquest; mid-twelfth-century manuscripts from Canterbury monasteries (such as British Library, Cotton Caligula A. xv) preserve much of the visual layout of pre-Conquest books, while the glossings, marginalia, and brief transcriptions in many texts . . . illustrate the survival of a trained scribal ability with both the language and the literary forms of Anglo-Saxon England.[7]

He adds:

> Much of what survives of Old English writing in this century-and-a-half, and, in turn, much of what characterizes the literary culture of the period, is the result of certain kinds of antiquarianism or, at the very least, of a certain self-consciousness about writing in a language and in literary forms that are no longer current.[8]

Both Lerer and Clanchy, while variously appreciative of what survives in English from the post-Conquest period, agree that extant texts, whether prose or verse, are the product of an antiquarian energy: a wish to preserve a now defunct literary heritage; a nationalistic "self-consciousness"; the manuscripts effectively petrify linguistic forms and content that have no contemporary usage.

If the English texts of the twelfth century are the result of antiquarianism, there is little point discussing them: they are backward-looking copies of respected older Old English material — antiquities that can reveal little of importance in and of themselves. If, however, as I firmly believe, the opposite is true — that many of the manuscripts were copied for pragmatic purposes,

---

6 *The Cambridge History of Medieval Literature*, ed. David Wallace (Cambridge, 1999), 7–34.

7 Lerer, "Old English," 8–9.

8 Lerer, "Old English," 10.

utilizing a living, contemporary formal written language — then a very different value can be placed on these texts. Moreover, the issue of their linguistic classification becomes crucial. Are these texts copied and sometimes updated, often adapted and re-created, still Old English, thus necessitating a revision of what we mean when we use a term generally employed to indicate texts copied up to *c*. 1050, 1066, or 1100; or are these texts "transitional," linguistically anomalous, and so uncategorizable? My proposal is that while they are often regarded as the latter — hence the scholarly marginalization of the material, until recently — they ought more properly to be seen as belonging to the same Old English literary corpus as the texts in the Exeter Book or as Wulfstan's *Sermo Lupi ad Anglos*.

The purpose of this contribution is to analyze the use of English homiletic texts in the twelfth century and later to illustrate the currency of the vernacular in this period. Peripherally this discussion will also debate the term "Old English": its meaning, its relevance, and its limitations in current scholarship. The argument is that Old English, usually used to refer to the language and texts written in that language from the eighth to the eleventh centuries, might more accurately be used to cover the vernacular language and texts from the twelfth century also, indeed incorporating a number of works composed as late as the early thirteenth century. This will be illustrated by an investigation of the uses of a selection of pre- and post-Conquest English manuscripts by later readers, and by a detailed examination of the contexts of manuscript production and of potential audience for these vernacular texts in this later period.

To demonstrate the limitations of conventional descriptions of post-Conquest English texts as either Old or early Middle English, one could use the example of the English adaptation of Ralph D'Escures's *Sermo in Festis Sancti Marie Uirginis* contained in the mid-twelfth-century London, British Library, Cotton Vespasian D. xiv.[9] It is generally thought of as being among the earliest examples of Middle English texts.[10] The *Peterborough Chronicle Continuations* are similarly referred to as one of, if not *the*, earliest Middle English texts to survive.[11] Yet the *Dicts of Cato* existing in its earliest extant form

---

[9] Ker, *Catalogue*, 277. Ralph D'Escures was Bishop of Rochester, 1108–1114, and Archbishop of Canterbury, 1114–1122. The English adaptation is almost certainly a twelfth-century composition.

[10] See, for example, Margaret Laing, *Catalogue of Sources for a Linguistic Atlas of Early Middle English* (Woodbridge, 1993), 83, where she cites Cecily Clark, *The Peterborough Chronicle 1070–1154* (Oxford, 1970), lii, n. 1, as saying this text is "usually classed as the earliest M[iddle] E[nglish]."

[11] See James Milroy, "Middle English Dialectology," in *The Cambridge History of the English Language*, vol. 2: *1066–1476*, ed. Norman Blake (Cambridge, 1992), 156–206, at 177.

in a manuscript datable to the very end of the eleventh century, and a copy of which is also included in Cotton Vespasian D. xiv, are labeled Old English,[12] as are the *Lives* of Nicholas and Giles in Cambridge, Corpus Christi College 303, both probable post-Conquest translations.[13] The linguistic classification of texts, as should be clear even from this very cursory selection of examples, is at best puzzling, at worst contradictory.

Among the features of late eleventh- or early twelfth-century texts that might have resulted in their classification by linguists as Old or Middle English is the extent of non-West Saxon linguistic forms manifested within the individual text: the higher the number of non-West Saxon elements, the more "early Middle English" the text. Even taking this important element into account, though, the labels commonly applied to post-Conquest texts should be regarded as highly inappropriate within both the dialectology and the chronology of Old English. As Hugh Magennis has pointed out, the earlier of the extant *Lives* of St Margaret, that contained in London, British Library, Cotton Tiberius A. iii, datable to the mid-eleventh century, actually illustrates a "remarkable proportion" of non-West Saxon forms, perhaps attributable to the source, which may have been Anglian. The *Life of Margaret* copied almost a century later in CCCC 303, on the other hand, shows an adherence to late West Saxon forms, despite its mid-twelfth-century date of copying, as do the other anonymous *Lives* within that same manuscript.[14]

This example highlights one of the major problems of our expectations of rigid conformity to late West Saxon within Old English. By Old English, scholars do tend to mean the dominant *Schriftsprache* of West Saxon, coupled with a cut-off date of around 1100. Therefore, texts *originating* from after the Conquest, that is, texts *created* in the late period, that illustrate less adherence to late West Saxon often fall into the category of early Middle English. Chief among these are the *Peterborough Chronicle Continuations*. It appears that when scribes such as those of the *Peterborough Chronicle Continuations* were no longer copying but were writing extemporaneously, they felt no need or,

---

Notably, the chronological division of the *Cambridge History of English Language* series itself indicates that, for the purposes of scholarly neatness, Old English effectively ended in 1066.

[12] By, among others, Greenfield and Calder in *A New Critical History*, 100.

[13] See R. Love, "Hagiography," in *The Blackwell Encyclopaedia of Anglo-Saxon England*, ed. Michael Lapidge, John Blair, Simon Keynes, and Donald Scragg (Oxford, 1999), 226–28, at 227–28, where under the category of "anonymous Old English saints' Lives," Nicholas and Giles are listed as late compositions "mainly intended for private reading."

[14] Mary Clayton and Hugh Magennis, eds., *The Old English Lives of St Margaret*, CSASE 9 (Cambridge, 1994), 97; see also 98–107. For the *Lives* of Nicholas and Giles, see Elaine Treharne, ed., *The Old English Life of St Nicholas with the Old English Life of St Giles*, Leeds Texts and Monographs 15 (Leeds, 1997).

more significantly, were not trained to write late West Saxon. This does indeed suggest the deterioration of a systematic educational program of taught, formal late West Saxon after the Conquest, as the Tremulous Scribe bemoans in the early thirteenth century:

> Þeos lærden ure leodan on Englisc,   næs deorc heore liht, ac hit fæire glod.
> Nu is þeo leore forleten,   and þet folc is forloren.

> [These [teachers] taught our people in English. Theirs was not a dim
>   light, but it shone brightly.
> Now that teaching is forsaken, and the people are lost.][15]

But the evidence of the language of the *Peterborough Chronicle* also shows that for certain monastic cathedral institutions (Rochester, Christ Church, Canterbury, and Worcester, for example), there were those scribes who in their copying still attempted to adhere to "classical" Old English: who saw the communicatory benefits of this most formal English register and employed it. Moreover, some of these manuscript compilers were quite content to assimilate within one codex materials that are entirely "Old English" in their composition with those that are variously "early Middle English" (once again, reference can be made here to Cotton Vespasian D. xiv and Cambridge, Corpus Christi College 303, among other examples). To these manuscript compilers, and the scribes with whom they worked, it seems there was no incongruity in placing texts that appeared phonologically or morphologically very different next to each other; to a greater or lesser extent, these were simply the compilers' required vernacular materials, presumably accepted as equally intelligible to the intended audience.

There appears, *prima facie*, then, to have been a tolerance of linguistic variability within written texts in the earlier post-Conquest period, very much foreshadowing the emergence of remarkably divergent dialectally marked texts in the later twelfth century and thereafter. The scholarly tendency to label variability within late and very late Old English texts as "deviancy" or "corruption" (or even as something else altogether, such as "early Middle English") may be as much a product of our own modern educational insistence on spelling rectitude, as it is a desire to make *medieval* textual orthography fit standard paradigms and declensions. Variability seems not to have prompted too great an anxiety for contemporary manuscript writers or, indeed, for users. English materials copied in the post-Conquest period

---

[15] Quoted in Lerer, "Old English," 23–24. This text, the *First Worcester Fragment*, is contained in Worcester Cathedral Library F. 34.

should therefore not be written off simply as archaic or as a corrupt form of some linguistic *koine* previously more perfect.[16]

A useful example here to illustrate significant linguistic variation within the same textual space is the work of the three scribes in Cambridge Corpus Christi College 303.[17] The two main scribes copy their exemplars with considerable care, replicating the linguistic forms of the Old English with a relative degree of accuracy. The first scribe, A, copied large portions of the manuscript, among which is Ælfric's Homily, *Dominica post Octauis Pentecosten*, at pages 248–252.[18] At page 251/10, the third scribe, C, takes over the copying from Scribe A on this same page. This scribe is responsible for only sporadic and short scribal stints between pages 226 and 254, but he is the most interesting in the context of this debate since his linguistic forms tend to be much more idiosyncratic than those of his colleagues. In the following extract, Scribe A's copying may be compared to the language of the earliest manuscript text of Ælfric's homily, London, British Library, Royal 7 C. xii, dated to the end of the tenth or beginning of the eleventh century:

Royal 7 C. xii:
Becymð þam gecorenum to maran blisse. swa swa on metinge bið forsewen seo blace anlicnys¶ þæt seo white sy beorhtre gesewen; ða gecorenan geseoð symle heora scyppendes beorhtnysse¶ 7 for þi nis nan þing on gesceaftum him bediglod;[19]

CCCC 303:
becumað þam gecorenum to maran blisse¶ swa swa on mætinge bið forsewen seo blace anlicnys þæt seo white si ðe beorhtre gesewen. Þa

---

[16] Milroy, "Middle English Dialectology," 193, states: "Variability in Middle English [equally well applied to the twelfth century] has sometimes been perceived as an obstacle rather than a resource ... In editorial and descriptive commentary, it is very easy to find comments about chaotic or 'lawless' spelling and even editorial judgements to the effect that a given scribe could not have been a native English speaker — so variable is his orthography ... However, judgements of this kind can effectively block further investigation of variable constraints in the texts in question: they can be dismissed as 'corrupt' or 'unreliable' specimens of language."

[17] See Elaine M. Treharne, "The Production and Script of Manuscripts Containing English Religious Texts in the First Half of the Twelfth Century," in *Rewriting Old English in the Twelfth Century*, ed. Mary Swan and eadem, CSASE 30 (Cambridge, 2000), 11–40, esp. 28–31.

[18] Ker, *Catalogue*, 103, item 50. Peter Clemoes, ed., *Ælfric's Catholic Homilies: The First Series*, EETS s.s. 17 (Oxford, 1997), 364–70: "Dominica Secunda post Pentecosten".

[19] Clemoes, *Catholic Homilies* I, 368, lines 110–114.

gecorenan geseoð simle hyre scyppendes beorhtnysse ¶ 7 for ði nis nan
þing on gesceaftum him bediglod.[20]

Within this short excerpt, Scribe A exhibits considerable adherence to the
forms of a late West Saxon exemplar. The dative plural and dative singular
masculine -um inflections are retained, as is the nominative plural ending of
the weak noun (-an). The major significant difference is the monophthongi-
zation of the medial vowel and the unstressing of the final vowel in the genitive plural pronoun, heora, in the earlier manuscript to hyre in CCCC 303.
This proportion of emendation in Scribe A's extensive stints — about fifteen
per cent — of the Standard Old English forms ostensibly illustrated by a manuscript such as Royal 7 C. xii is typical.

This can be contrasted with the work of Scribe C in CCCC 303. At page
251/10, then, Scribe C takes over the copying and his work can also be compared to the same homiletic text in Royal 7 C. xii.

Royal 7 C. xii:
Ic bidde eow mine gebroþra þæt ge beon gemyndige þæs lazares reste.
7 þæs rican wite. 7 doð swa swa crist sylf tæhte¶ tiliað eow freonda on
godes þearfum þæt hi on eowrum geendungum onfon eow into ecum
eardungstowum; Manega lazaras ge habbað nu licgende æt eowerum ga-
tum. biddende eowre oferflowednyssa¶ þeah ðe hi syn waclice geþuhte¶
þeahhwæþere hi beoð eft eowre þingeras wið ðone ælmihtigan.[21]

CCCC 303:
Ic bidde eow mine gebrodra þæt ge beon gemyndige þes lazares reste. 7
þes rican wite. 7 doð swa swa crist tahte. teoliað eow freonda on godes
þearfen¶ þæt hi on eower geendunge onfon eow into ece eardingstowen.
Maniga lazarus ge habbað nu licgenda et eower gaten. biddende eower
godes þeah ðe hi syndde waclice geðuhte¶ þeahhwedere hi beoð eft eower þingeres wið þone ealmihtigan god.

Within this extract, alterations made to the earliest extant manuscript
of the text in Royal 7 C. xii range from the use of <d> for <ð> or <þ> (in gebrodra and þeahhwedere), a feature increasingly common as the twelfth century progresses,[22] to the systematic levelling of dative -um inflections to the

---

[20] CCCC 303, p. 251, lines 1–3.
[21] Clemoes, Catholic Homilies I, 369, lines 123–129.
[22] Roger Lass, "Phonology and Morphology," in Blake, ed., Cambridge History of the
English Language 2, 23–155, at 64, §1.

unstressed *-en* or *-e*. The interchangeability of <e> and <a> or <ea> for late West Saxon <æ> in the orthography of Scribe C may represent a non-West Saxon influence in the scribe's own dialect, but it is also typical of twelfth-century English in general: there is significant variation in the use of <e>, <a> and <æ>, with <æ> eventually dying out in the thirteenth century.[23] The overall preference for <e> exhibited by Scribe C where one might expect <æ> points particularly to the south-east for this scribe's linguistic origins. The intertextual replacement of *oferflowednyssa* ("leftovers", "excess") by *godes* ("gifts")[24] is, again, typical of Scribe C, who often updates specific lemmata[25] with ones he presumably thought to be more appropriate at this late date of compilation. It is not always possible to distinguish scribal innovation from exemplar imitation, but it is unlikely, given the consistency of this scribe's language over a number of distinct texts, that we are seeing anything other than the scribe's own orthographical and lexical preferences.

The question is, is this scribe writing "basically Middle English" as Patrick Stiles has suggested,[26] or is it simply very late West Saxon with some non-West Saxon forms? If it is the latter, then this scribe's stint, as is the case with the whole manuscript, must surely be described as late Old English. Moreover, this is the scribe who is responsible for the checking, rubrication, and some miniation of the manuscript as a whole. It is he who seems to have read through his two, probably less senior, colleagues' writing of the bulk of the English texts comprising the majority of the manuscript. While he is also responsible for the addition of sporadic interlinear glosses updating particular lemmata within the texts,[27] he is also, for the larger part of the text he encounters, seemingly satisfied with his colleagues' efforts in reproducing the usually late West Saxon forms of their exemplars. Put another way, he tolerates considerable variation in the linguistic forms of the manuscript: both the late Standard Old English, and his own transitional idiolect, representing something much less classically paradigmatic, are evidently acceptable and intelligible at this mid-twelfth-century date.

---

[23] Roger Lass, "Phonology and Morphology,"37, §11.

[24] This lexical replacement is seen as a gloss to the text in the earlier manuscript containing this homily, Oxford, Bodleian Library, Bodley 340 + 342, from which this and other homilies in CCCC 303 ultimately derive.

[25] Both by lexical replacement within the texts he himself copied, or through interlinear and marginal glosses written by him in the pages copied by the other two scribes.

[26] In private correspondence cited by Margaret Laing, in the *Catalogue of Sources for a Linguistic Atlas of Early Medieval English*, 23.

[27] As will be discussed below.

It is the case, as mentioned briefly above, that texts such as those of this scribe in CCCC 303 copied from earlier pre-Conquest exemplars have occasionally been labeled by scholars as exemplifying "deviant" forms, with the implication that they will be of little use or interest to the Anglo-Saxonist.[28] The employment of such terms implicitly suggests that there is a literary and linguistic perfection in the pre-Conquest period that is undermined or somehow destroyed by later textual copies. Literary West Saxon is not, however, an invariable form at any point in its history, notwithstanding the paradigmatic rigidity of the university Old English Grammar. As Jeremy Smith suggests, late West Saxon is a "standardized" language, not a Standard:[29] it is one to which scribes aspire, but do not necessarily attain. The point here is that, despite numerous comments by scholars, late West Saxon with its variant forms is a living, utilitarian form of written language throughout the later Anglo-Saxon period, and well into the twelfth century. Its intelligibility is clearly demonstrated by the textual examples cited where by far the majority of the text remains essentially unaltered. The fact that late West Saxon was always a formal register of language, one that would not commonly be a reflection of *parole*, serves to reinforce the argument about the copying of texts in English in the twelfth century: adherence to West Saxon with minor emendations does not imply an antiquarianism or mechanical copying of an archaic language by the scribes responsible; rather, it is an attempt, as it always was, to use the most prestigious register of language for the composition of written texts. Old English in the post-Conquest period, then, is employed as a living language for the writing of formal materials; it was usable, used, and widely comprehended in a non-specialist (that is, not simply antiquarian) context.

The crucial issue in deciding what should be included in the corpus of Old English seems to be neither the evidence of transitional or dialectal forms within texts, nor the issue of date, as both approaches lead to inconsistency and, arguably, a reluctance to engage with this post-Conquest material; but

---

[28] For example, John C. Pope, ed., *Homilies of Ælfric: A Supplementary Collection*, EETS o.s. 259, 260 (London, 1967–1968), 1:178, states: "Deviations [from the Late West Saxon Standard] in certain manuscripts of the twelfth century are of course much more numerous [than in earlier manuscripts] . . .".

[29] Jeremy Smith, *An Historical Study of English: Function, Form and Change* (London, 1996), 66. He adds (67): "Close examination of the written record soon reveals that 'Standard West Saxon' admitted of a good deal more variation than standard Present-Day English. Not only are there certain lexical habits which are restricted to certain monastic scriptoria, but also there seem to be persistent orthographic distinctions between the various scriptorial outputs. Codification of these latter features remains an important task for Anglo-Saxonists." See also Roger Lass, *Old English: A Historical Linguistic Companion* (Cambridge, 1994), especially Chap. 10, "The Dissolution of Old English."

rather the intelligibility and uses of the texts produced in this period. If Ælfric's *Catholic Homilies*, for example, so frequently copied in the twelfth century, can be shown to have been copied by the manuscript compilers with an actual audience in mind, an audience that the manuscript compiler assumed would understand the texts, then one has no option but to regard Old English as an active and useful linguistic medium long after the chronological boundary usually permitted to it.

A significant number of manuscripts contain glosses or marginalia or other work in English of the post-Conquest period focused primarily on homiletic texts, both by Ælfric and by other, anonymous authors. These glosses and annotations can be of various kinds ranging from embedded to interlinear glosses, *signes de renvoi* additions, *notae* marks, and scribbles and notes relating to the texts. It has been remarked, on occasion, that these kinds of activities demonstrate the lack of intelligibility of the original to the post-Conquest reader. In their Introduction to the facsimile of London, British Library, Royal 7 C. xii, for example, Peter Clemoes and Norman Eliason state that:

> The alterations are of significance mainly in revealing how and why, during the course of the eleventh and twelfth centuries, the language and even the handwriting of the text were becoming increasingly difficult to comprehend readily. . . . The later [twelfth-century] annotator who obviously found the text more difficult [than the eleventh-century annotator] (as is indicated by his trouble in separating words, which is evidently why he often puts vertical strokes between them), glosses or changes many words . . .[30]

This interpretation is very plausible, but, I would argue the contrary is actually the case: far from illustrating how little late West Saxon was understood, post-Conquest use of earlier manuscripts shows how extensively comprehensible this material was, the extent to which it was read and used, and therefore how the life and employment of Old English continues long after 1066 or 1100.[31]

---

[30] Peter Clemoes and Norman Eliason, intro., *Ælfric's First Series of Catholic Homilies: British Museum Royal 7 c. xii, fols. 4–218*, Early English Manuscripts in Facsimile 13 (Copenhagen, 1966), 25–26, and n. 1.

[31] Robert McColl Millar and Alex Nicholls, "Ælfric's *De Initio Creaturae* and London, BL Cotton Vespasian A. xxii: Omission, Addition, Retention and Innovation," in *The Preservation and Transmission of Anglo-Saxon Culture*, ed. Paul E. Szarmach and Joel T. Rosenthal, Studies in Medieval Culture 40 (Kalamazoo, 1997), 431–63 discuss the late copying and adaptation of Ælfric, coming to the conclusion (446) that the late copyist "clearly understood his exemplar well enough to edit, augment, and adapt it with some skill."

Glosses found in manuscripts containing English, or glosses in English occurring in Latin texts. are extensive in their number and range, if not in the regularity of their coverage. The most famous glossator and annotator is, of course, the Tremulous Hand of Worcester,[32] though he is not the singular curiosity that he is occasionally stated to be. Certainly the amount of glossing in which he engaged is unsurpassed to date,[33] but the activity itself is more common than I think is generally recognized. And it is not simply extensive glossing that can indicate the widespread nature of the understanding and knowledge of Old English in the post-Conquest period; scribbles can provide additional evidence for the survival of English, and the capability to write in that language. Even in scriptoria such as Salisbury, from which no substantial Old English materials survive in the post-Conquest period, there is evidence that the language was at least known.[34] Dublin, Trinity College 174 (B. 4. 3), a legendary produced at Salisbury, has on its flyleaf a scribe's comment datable to the second half of the eleventh century: "of Searbyrig ic eom."[35] Such seemingly meagre evidence demonstrates that there was at least one scribe capable of writing in the vernacular in that scriptorium in the late Old English period.

Glossing and annotation similarly testify to the existence of twelfth- and thirteenth-century readers of English, who are also trained to write in the vernacular. Far from demonstrating the unintelligibility of a text, these additional textual layers serve rather to illustrate the ways in which the texts were understood. Manuscripts in which glossing and annotation occur often show only occasional attempts to replace one lexeme with another.[36] This can be accounted for by the otherwise wholly understandable nature of the text; that is, only relatively few words require glossing. The manner in which this is performed, too, shows something of the intended purpose of the work on the text: erasing lexemes, as the annotator of Royal 7 C. xii occasionally does, and overwriting them, suggests that the text is meant to be read fluently, perhaps aloud, by someone other than the annotator himself. Otherwise, one

---

[32] For whom see Christine Franzen, *The Tremulous Hand of Worcester: A Study of Old English in the Thirteenth Century* (Oxford, 1991).

[33] It may very well be that careful study of post-Conquest glossing hands in manuscripts of the pre- and post-Conquest period will provide other examples of scribes who were responsible for glossing more than one manuscript.

[34] See Teresa Webber, *Scribes and Scholars at Salisbury Cathedral, c. 1075–c. 1125* (Oxford, 1992), for a detailed study of book production and the interests of the secular canons at this institution.

[35] Ker, *Catalogue*, 143.

[36] As is the case with CCCC 303, for example.

might expect solely interlinear or marginal glossing, which is much less easily simultaneously integrated in a sequential reading process.

Twelfth-century glosses and annotations in Ælfric's First Series of *Catholic Homilies* contained in London, British Library, Royal 7 C. xii can be listed as follows:[37] folio 52r/4 *techt* glosses *belæwed* ("betrayed, incited"); folio 52r/21 *herede* glosses *mærsode* ("praised"); folio 52r/22 *heringe* glosses *onbryrdnesse* ("inspiration"); folio 52v/4 *sage* written over erased *segene* ("said"); folio 52v/23 *welie manne* written above *hwiltidum* ("sometimes"); folio 53v/2, 3 *þet folch* replaces *seo meniu* ("the crowd"); folio 54v/6 *þisum blinde* over erasure; folio 55v/11 *togedere* glosses *on reute* ("in journey together"?); folio 56v/24 *behouede* glosses *gedauenlic* ("fitting, suitable"); folio 58r/8 *brucan* replaces erased *þicgean* ("eat, partake"); folio 58r/12 *staþelwest* overwrites *onbryrd* ("inspired"); folio 58v/17 *weorche* glosses *truwan* ("faith, confidence, pledge"); folio 60r/3 *helle* glosses *nywelnysse* ("abyss"); folio 72v/6 *lare* glosses *biggengum* ("worshipper, learner"); folio 73r/16 *þerfe* replaces *geornfulnyss* ("need, desire"); folio 73r/20 *refe* [*sic*] glosses *gerædum* ("intent, judgement");[38] folio 75r/5 *þogten* glosses *syrewydon* ("plotted, conspired"); folio 76r/6 *helde* glosses *generode* ("rescued, liberated"); folio 81v/19 *twiges* glosses *tua* ("twice"); folio 82r/14 *caseren* glosses *wælræwum* ("cruel, bloodthirsty"); folio 92v/4, 5 *hus* glosses *templ* ("temple"); folio 92v/20, folio 93v/1, *speche* glosses *gereorde* ("speech"); folio 93r/16, 18 *bugað(-an)* glosses *geþeodað(-an)* ("joined, to join"); folio 93v/15, 20, 22, *niminge* glosses *þigene* ("eating, partaking"); folio 95r/14 *costnunge* glosses *syrwungum* ("conspirer"); folio 96v/13 *broþra* glosses *geferena* ("brother" for "companion").

Of these glosses, some have greater significance than others, although all of them are interesting for the light they throw on contemporary twelfth-century conceptions of lexical outdatedness. The glosses *bugað* and the infinitive *bugan* that twice appear at folio 93r in explanation of *geþeodað* and *geþeodan* are paralleled by glosses in the manuscript mentioned initially in this paper, CCCC 303, where a later reader has glossed *geðeodd* with *bugon* at page 220, line 9, and *geðeodað* with *bygd* at page 220, line 15. Similarly, the interlinear glosses at folio 53v, lines 2 and 3 of Royal 7 C. xii, where *þet folch* updates *seo meniu*, is paralleled by the use of *folc* as a gloss for *werod* in CCCC 303, and at least two other manuscripts that were glossed by the Tremulous Hand of Worcester: Oxford, Bodleian Library, Hatton 113, and Cambridge, Corpus

---

[37] Clemoes and Eliason, *Catholic Homilies* I, list virtually all of these glosses and additions to the text in their Introduction, 25–26.

[38] *refe* is probably an error for *rele*. In Oxford, Bodleian Library, Bodley 343, in the homily for Palm Sunday, *gerædum* is glossed by *gerele*. See Clemoes, *Ælfric's Catholic Homilies*, 546, XIV, line 87.

Christi College 178.[39] Such analogous selective glossing demonstrates that not only were there numerous individual readers of these English texts, but that there was a specific group of Old English lemmata that was considered archaic or virtually unintelligible to the user. These sporadic, but consistent, glossing practices across a range of manuscripts of different origins and provenances also indicate that while specific lemmata had lost currency, the overall general intelligibility of late Old English cannot be doubted.[40]

As well as these glosses in Royal 7 C. xii, there are numerous other additions and minor alterations to the text;[41] for example, at folio 56r/12 *to ðam ecan life* is expanded by the addition and clarification of *heofenrices*; at folio 56r/25, *pinungum* is expanded with *hellewite*, again to lend an incontrovertible clarity; at folio 56v/19, *God* is expanded with the addition of *elmicti*; and at folio 57r/5, *þa genealæhte se costnere* is clarified with the marginal addition *þet is se deofel, to þam drictene*. On a number of occasions, such as at folio 56r/18 and folio 59v/17, a proper noun or a determiner plus noun is added to clarify a pronoun: at folio 59v/17, the pronoun *his* is erased and replaced with *þes engles*. In this way, the annotator seeks to clarify his text, in terms both of its lexical intelligibility and its semantic transparency. The consequence of these explanatory interpolations suggests a desire by the glossator to eliminate the potential for misunderstanding in his audience, which might therefore be considered to be less learned than he was, in demanding this interpretative precision, and in need of theological specificity and explanation. Specificity is also the motivation, perhaps, for the appearance of the gloss at folio 96v/13 where *broþra* is written above *geferena*. The context of this particular gloss may indicate the twelfth-century user's intended audience of this homily: "Swa we sceolon eac gif bið an ure 'broðra' [for 'geferena'] on sumere earfoðnysse. ealle we sceolon his yfel besargian. and hogian ymbe þa bote gif we hit gebetan magon."[42] This exhortation to collective charity and concern

---

[39] See Franzen, *Tremulous Hand*. It is significant, though not necessarily surprising, that most of the glosses written into Royal 7 C. xii are paralleled by the exact lexical equivalents in the work of the Tremulous Hand. Franzen's lists (19–23) of English glosses selected by the Worcester scribe illustrate almost all of the glosses cited above in Royal 7 C. xii.

[40] It is obvious, perhaps, but when reading a language that is either archaic or foreign, one glosses only those words that are not understood or for which clarification is required. Since the glosses in these manuscripts do not in any way predominate, it is logical to assert that the vast majority of the Old English text could be understood without interpretation.

[41] For a discussion of which, see Clemoes and Eliason, *Catholic Homilies* I, 26.

[42] Clemoes, *Ælfric's Catholic Homilies*, Homily XIX, *Feria IIIa de dominica oratione*, 334, lines 238–240. "Thus we must (do) if one of our brothers ['companions'] is in some difficulty. We must all pity his trouble, and think about a relief if we can relieve it."

for a "companion" is particularized to one of the "brothers" — surely an interesting alteration pointing to a potentially monastic (or quasi-monastic) audience for these vernacular texts.

There is little in the work of this glossator that is innovative or unusual in the intellectual context of similar activities by other manuscript readers in the twelfth century. Embedded and interlinear lexical glosses and explanatory glosses or notes are frequently found,[43] as has been demonstrated in a small way in the case of the Corpus 303 scribe, and as can be seen in Oxford, Bodleian Library, Bodley 343,[44] together with numerous other manuscripts produced or annotated in the one hundred and fifty years after the Conquest. Embedded glosses occur on numerous occasions within these manuscripts, and illustrate significantly that the scribe is not copying in a *literatim* fashion, but is working editorially.[45] The editorial nature of writing Old English in the twelfth century is irrefutable proof of the currency of late West Saxon and its comprehensibility to those copying and adapting these texts.

In many cases, it seems that the texts being updated — whether by the process of embedded glossing, or subsequent glossing and notational clarification — are being prepared for delivery to a relatively uneducated audience. The glosses from Royal 7 C. xii, for example, occur in clusters within very specific homilies: at folios 51v–56v is Ælfric's *Dominica Quinquagesima*; at folios 56v–62r is *Dominica in Quadragesima*; at folios 71r–76r is *Dominica Palmarum*; at folios 80v–83v is *Dominica I post Pasce*; and at folios 91r–96v is the homily *Feria IIIa de Dominica Oratione*.[46] That the reader of these texts focuses on these homilies in particular is significant for a number of reasons,

---

[43] This is contrary to Andreas Fischer's comment in "The Vocabulary of Very Late Old English," in *Studies in English Language and Literature: "Doubt Wisely": Papers in Honour of E. G. Stanley*, ed. M. J. Toswell and E. M. Tyler (London, 1996), 29–41, where he describes the replacement of obsolete words, or "lexical modernisation," as a "comparatively rare phenomenon" (32). It can be witnessed in many twelfth-century manuscripts, from Cambridge, Corpus Christi College, 302 and 303, to Oxford, Bodleian Library, Bodley 343, and London, British Library, Cotton Vespasian A. xxii — manuscripts that span the period ca. 1100 to the beginning of the thirteenth century.

[44] See Clemoes, *Ælfric's Catholic Homilies*, Appendix C, 543–55.

[45] This is true in the twelfth-century copies of the Gospels in Oxford, Bodleian Library, Hatton 38 also. See Roy Michael Liuzza, "Scribal Habit: The Evidence of the Old English Gospels," in *Rewriting Old English*, ed. Swan and Treharne, 143–65, in which Liuzza describes the types of copying current in manuscripts. See also Fischer, "The Vocabulary of Very Late Old English."

[46] Clemoes, *Ælfric's Catholic Homilies*, Homilies X, XI, XIV, XVI, and XIX respectively.

not the least of which is that in Royal 7 C. xii an earlier glossator than the
one discussed above, of the late eleventh or early twelfth century, had also
selected *Dominica Palmarum* upon which to focus his attention.[47] It is worth
remarking that the glosses and notes appear not to be random, inasmuch as
there are intervening homilies such as those at folios 62r–71r (*Dominica in
media Quadragesima* and *Adnuntiatio Sanctae Mariae*) and folios 76v–80v
(*Dominica Pasce*) that are not glossed or annotated in this manuscript, and
which show no signs of having been read by later readers. The choice of homilies is therefore suggestive of the glossators' particular interests and purposes
in close reading. This in itself is noteworthy enough, but when coupled with
the fact that some of these same homilies also attracted the considerable attention of readers and annotators in other English manuscripts during the
twelfth and thirteenth centuries, it appears that there was significant demand
for English materials for these particular occasions in the church year.[48] One
such text is Ælfric's homily for Palm Sunday, *Dominica Palmarum*. It is contained in numerous manuscript copies, including an incomplete version in
British Library, Cotton Faustina A. ix, and a fragment in the Beinecke Library,
Yale University, Osborn Collection.[49] Of the fourteen manuscript copies and
extracts, at least five contain twelfth- and thirteenth-century annotation and
glossing.[50] For example, Cambridge, Corpus Christi College 302 is an early
twelfth-century homiliary which contains a large number of texts written by
Ælfric and also some anonymous works. Its place of origin and provenance
are unknown though it has textual affiliations with another twelfth-century
homiliary, London, British Library, Cotton Faustina A. ix.[51] CCCC 302 contains a number of glosses and annotations that demonstrate the manuscript
was used by readers in the twelfth and thirteenth centuries. Pages 155–163
of CCCC 302 contain Ælfric's homily from the First Series, *Dominica in die
Ramis Palmarum*. The following lemmata are noted by page and line number:
page 157/20, *hyrsumnysse* glosses *bigengu*; page 159/12, *blissiað* glosses *wul-
driað*; page 159/18, *hrigge* glosses *bæce*. At page 159/26, an interlinear "x" in
the text corresponds to the addition marked by "x" in the margin followed

---

[47] Clemoes and Eliason, *Catholic Homilies* I, 25.

[48] These pre- and post-Conquest English manuscripts, their texts, and the practices of
readers in the centuries following the manuscripts' compilation form one of the focal points
of my forthcoming monograph *Living Through Conquest: The Politics of Early English*.

[49] See Clemoes, *Ælfric's Catholic Homilies*, 290, apparatus for the list of these manuscript versions.

[50] For a late example of this homily, see Mary Swan, "Old English Made New: One
Catholic Homily and its Reuses," *Leeds Studies in English* n.s. 28 (1997): 1–18.

[51] See most recently, Clemoes, *Ælfric's Catholic Homilies*, 30–33.

by *þæt is mid fule synne* which expands on the text; and at page 159/31, *þurh scrift* and *dedbote* is added as an elaboration on the text.[52]

The interests here are clearly in sins and confession, so often the major focus of readers of pre- and post-Conquest manuscripts. Interestingly, Cotton Faustina A. ix, which also contains this text, has thirteenth-century annotations in Latin from folios 103–107 in which the same text, *Dominica in die Ramis Palmarum*, is copied. In this manuscript, the annotations pay particular attention to biblical quotations, such that the Old English "Swa swa se witega cwæð: 'Anra gehwylc manna is gewriðen mid rapum his synna'" is translated marginally into "Utique constringitur funibus peccatorum suorum erat" — a curious admixture of the Bedan homily from which Ælfric might have drawn his Old English phrase[53] and Proverbs 5: 22. A little later, the quotation by Ælfric from Matthew 28: 19–20,[54] "Go forth through all the earth and baptize in my name," has been glossed by its Latin equivalent, "[Euntes ergo docete] gentes omnes, baptizare eos in nomine in patris et Filii et spiritus sancti," but again in a slightly curious form. Perhaps these rather non-direct quotations represent the annotator's memorized Latin biblical text. It is clear that this annotator is most interested in scriptural citations within the Old English. Similar sporadic Latin annotation continues throughout this particular homily, and indeed appears occasionally, though in a less clustered fashion, throughout the manuscript. In addition, pencil crosses and *notae* in the margin draw a reader's attention to particular passages of the text that the annotator clearly felt to be of importance.

While the annotations and glosses in these two latter manuscripts may seem of little intrinsic interest, what they do show is that particular homilies — especially that for Palm Sunday — were of especial significance to different readers using Old English manuscripts as much as a century apart in their practices. By the thirteenth century, there are fewer signs of vernacular glossing; the annotation is Latin, concerns itself with Biblical material in particular, and is fairly full, suggesting the need for rather more drawn-out guidance in the reading process than a simple lemma-gloss would have provided. It is obvious, but requires stating, that the annotators and glossators were perfectly able to read late West Saxon up to two centuries after its literary zenith. Furthermore, one might question the precise purpose of these various marks of readership. It seems entirely likely that this homily, perhaps more

---

[52] At p. 119 of CCCC 302, in the homily *Dominica I in quadragesima* (one of the homilies mentioned in relation to Royal 7 C. xii), the following glosses also occur: page 119/25, *tohogian* glosses *heofian*; page 119/16, *wanswedge* glosses *ælfremedan*.

[53] Godden, *Commentary*, p. 112, note to lines 45–47.

[54] Godden, *Commentary*, p. 113, note to lines 61–68.

than any other, was a key text for later manuscript users, who clearly had few contemporary resources on which they could draw. The use of the text may very well be because of the elaborate Palm Sunday procession that took place in religious foundations throughout the medieval period, and which presumably drew together all the members of the community, whether monastic or secular. Within a specifically monastic context, Ælfric, in his homily, describes the liturgical events,[55] and in his Latin consuetudinary, his "Letter to the Monks of Eynsham," he explains that:

> In Die Palmarum, interim dum matutinalis missa canitur, agatur a sacerdote cum quodam puero, processio in claustro, et finita missa procedant fratres ad maiorem processionem ubi palme benedicendae sunt, albis induti si aura permiserit. Et finita oratione processionis legat diaconus euuangelium 'Turba multa' . . . Transacta processione subsistant ante ecclesiam et decantent pueri deintus 'Gloria laus' cum uersibus . . .[56]

The description here makes no mention of attendance by the laity, but the elaborate nature of the processional ritual, and the importance of the occasion, suggests that all members of the monastery would be in attendance, arguably creating a need for the delivery of didactic material in English. The context in the twelfth and thirteenth centuries may well be similar, thereby explaining the readers' interest in this particular homily. Thus it is that glosses and annotations appearing within this homily demonstrate that what was marginal in terms of its production in the post-Conquest period — manuscripts written in English — became a productive source of educative materials for readers later in the high Middle Ages.

We are not looking here at the personal proclivities of a few individuals that sustained studies of idiosyncratic manuscript readers like the Tremulous

---

[55] Clemoes, *Ælfric's Catholic Homilies*, XIV, 297, lines 195–209.

[56] Christopher A. Jones, ed., *Ælfric's Letter to the Monks of Eynsham*, CSASE 24 (Cambridge, 1998), 124. Jones's translation (125) reads: "On Palm Sunday, while the matutinal mass is being sung, the procession in the cloister shall be carried out by a priest, with a boy [as server]. When the mass is ended, the brothers, dressed in albs if the weather permits, shall conduct the greater procession [to that place] where the palms are to be blessed. And after the processional collect, the deacon shall read the gospel 'A great multitude' . . . At the end of the procession they shall stop before the church where, from within, boys shall sing 'All glory, laud and honour' with its verses . . ." It should be noted that within this elaborate processional rite there is no mention of attendance by the laity. If a monastic context is appropriate for the manuscripts I am discussing here, there seems little reason to assume, *prima facie*, that these codices, their contents, and the subsequent annotation and glosses indicate use by or for the laity.

Scribe might suggest. On the contrary, varying and multiple layers of glossing throughout manuscripts belonging to the pre- and post-Conquest eras demonstrate beyond reasonable doubt that numerous interested religious users found much to plunder for their own use.

In CCCC 303, for example, the contemporary glossing hands, one of which has been analysed above, are not the only signs of use. There is also annotation belonging to a late thirteenth- or early fourteenth-century reader, and one further seventeenth-century notator. The thirteenth- or fourteenth-century glossator and annotator is particularly interesting. The homily principally concerned is the anonymous text for Rogationtide, *Feria III.*[57] He, or she, glosses two Old English lexemes with the French-derived words *senne* and *prude* at page 220/27 for *leahter* and *ofermodignysse* respectively. At page 222/22, *luxuria* glosses *forlyr* in the same hand. These glosses are in the same hand and ink as the marginalia also seen on pages 220, 221, and 222. This activity consists of notes referring to the textual exposition of the three methods of salvation for mankind, and the eight capital sins to be avoided. The first marginal note, at page 220/21 reads "Eleemosina triplex", and it is accompanied by a set of inked dots: one at line 21, two at line 22, and three at line 23, directly referring to the first, second, and third methods of salvation provided in the text. At some level, whether wholly or partly, this very late user of the manuscript is illustrating his or her understanding of the Old English. At page 220/27, "septem capitalis peccata" summarizes the concerns of the Old English text. It, too, is followed by a series of inked dots that correlate to only seven of the sins listed in the Old English. The tag "vana gloria" in the left margin at page 222/5 is the reader's gloss for the eighth capital sin, *idelwuldor*, enumerated in the Old English, but the glossator does not recognize the eight sins catalogued in the Old English (which derive from Irish influence) as against his summary heading of "the seven capital sins" and his sequence of seven dots (the Gregorian tradition, canonically stipulated from the twelfth century). It is obvious from these activities that this annotator had an interest in the fundamental concept of sin and its various manifestations. This would, of course, be of primary concern for someone with pastoral responsibilities, and one might imagine the text being plundered — at this late thirteenth- or early fourteenth-century date — by a writer compiling a confessional manual, along the lines of Robert of Brunne's *Handlyng Synne*. The interest shown in this text parallels that illustrated by other glossators and annotators, placing this glossarial work into a broader vernacular cultural context that includes

---

[57] Ed. J. Bazire and J. Cross, *Eleven Old English Rogationtide Homilies* (Toronto, 1982).

the Tremulous Hand of Worcester;[58] it raises other issues, including the demonstration that this kind of manuscript use in the centuries following the Conquest was not necessarily a regional phenomenon, nor was it an antiquarian and reactive activity as some scholars have claimed. Instead, what seems to be the case from the notes, glosses, and marks in Royal 7 C. xii, CCCC 302, Cotton Faustina A. ix, CCCC 303, and Bodley 343, among many other manuscripts, is the concerted effort by (presumably) native readers to utilize surviving English materials for new purposes. These purposes were undoubtedly bound up with the upsurge of interest in the vernacular in the twelfth and thirteenth centuries resulting from the need to reuse existing texts because of the rarity of new materials produced in English; and, from 1215, the well-known stipulations of the Fourth Lateran Council demanding the provision of religious instruction in the vernacular, with the emergence of subsequent episcopal statutes reaffirming this.[59]

It is notable, though not surprising, to find this continued use of texts that were the bread-and-butter of the establishments that had originally produced them: homilies. It is not the poetry of the Old English period that attracts sustained attention in the later middle ages; neither is it the encyclopedic texts such as the prose *Solomon and Saturn* or *The Dicts of Cato*; neither is it the hagiographic materials so widely collated throughout the eleventh and twelfth centuries. It is perhaps ironic, therefore, that the arguably poor relations of modern scholarly study — the anonymous and, to a lesser extent, the Ælfrician homiletic corpora — were the focus of scholarly research and use for some three hundred years after their composition, emerging again in the sixteenth century as the texts most studied by Matthew Parker and his circle.

The precise environment in which these Old English texts were read and used in the twelfth and thirteenth centuries is difficult to determine.[60] It is generally thought that these religious manuscripts were compiled because homiletic and hagiographic texts were "needed for religious instruction in the vernacular, to lay people as well as to nuns and monks."[61] In the case of

---

[58] See Franzen, *Tremulous Hand*, esp. 191–93.

[59] Dom David Knowles, *The Monastic Order in England From the Times of St Dunstan to the Fourth Lateran Council, 940–1216*, 2nd ed. (Cambridge, 1966), 363–74.

[60] See, for example, Susan Irvine, "The Persistence of Old English in the Twelfth Century," and Elaine M. Treharne, "The Production of Manuscripts Containing English Religious Texts in the First Half of the Twelfth Century," in *Rewriting Old English*, ed. Swan and Treharne, 41–61 and 11–40 respectively. See also Mary P. Richards, *Texts and Their Traditions in the Medieval Library of Rochester Cathedral Priory*, Transactions of the American Philosophical Association 78.3 (Philadelphia, 1988).

[61] Hans Sauer, "Knowledge of Old English in the Middle English Period?" in *Language History and Linguistic Modelling: A Festschrift for Jacek Fisiak on his 60th Birthday*,

Bodley 343, it may have been intended to act as "devotional reading for English speaking monks and nuns" and as "a reading book for secular clergy which could be assimilated and adapted for use in preaching."[62] These conclusions presuppose that preaching was, on occasion, performed in English, and that secular clergy were able to read and assimilate, or copy for themselves, the materials included in these manuscripts. It must also be the case that manuscript compilers in institutions such as Rochester were prepared to give time, effort, and expense to the production of manuscripts in English for the use of English-speaking monks, or for the use of nuns or secular clergy.

These suggestions are interesting theories that could account for the reasons behind the post-Conquest compilation of manuscripts containing English texts. But they are general theories only and, often, they cannot be entirely substantiated by the meagre evidence that the manuscripts themselves provide.[63] In addition, although these homiletic and hagiographic manuscripts can be treated as a group, particularly because of the shared codicological aspects of the volumes, their intended uses may have varied depending on where and when they were produced.[64] In practical terms, the production of manuscripts must have depended on available personnel and materials: the institution had to have at least one compiler or supervisor who recognized the need for English texts; there had to be one or more scribes capable of writing English; at least one Old English exemplar from which texts could be copied was required; and facilities to enable the copying to proceed were necessary.

Contemporary evidence suggests that such a combination of conditions was rare. We know with some degree of certainty of only a few religious institutions that were responsible for copying English, whether religious or secular texts, in the twelfth century: Peterborough (Oxford, Bodleian Library, Laud 636, *The Peterborough Chronicle*; and parts of the *Liber Niger*), Rochester (the *Textus Roffensis*; CCCC 303), Christ Church, Canterbury (the *Eadwine Psalter*; legal documents such as London, British Library, Stowe Charter 43; Oxford, Bodleian Library, Hatton 38; London, British Library, Royal 1.

---

ed. Raymond Hickey and Stanislaw Puppel, Trends in Linguistics, Studies and Monographs 101 (Berlin, 1997), 791–814, at 796.

[62] Susan Irvine, ed., *Old English Homilies from Bodley 343*, EETS 302 (Oxford, 1993), liii.

[63] As Irvine suggests in relation to preaching in *Old English Homilies*, lii–liii, where she states of Bodley 343: "[it] shows no sign of having played any direct role in preaching ... It shows none of the omission marks, changes in punctuation, and marginal additions that appear in eleventh-century manuscripts like D and F, and which would be usual in a manuscript intended or used for preaching. Moreover the material is not uniformly suitable for preaching purposes."

[64] See Treharne, "Production of Manuscripts."

A. xiv), Sherbourne (the Sherbourne Cartulary), St Paul's Cathedral, London (CCCC 383), and Worcester (additions in CCCC 140; possibly Oxford, Bodleian Library, Hatton 116; and Bodley 343).

As so many of the major scriptoria responsible for the production of Latin manuscripts in this period are not represented in this list,[65] one must ask why only a limited number of religious institutions appear to have engaged in the copying of English. Moreover only three of these — Rochester, Christ Church, Canterbury, and Worcester — have more than one significant or extensive vernacular manuscript attributed to them.

It would seem from the evidence of the extant manuscripts that the monastic cathedrals were the establishments most actively pursuing the production of English texts, especially those texts of a religious or didactic nature, and I have spoken of this important factor elsewhere.[66] The audience for these texts must, obviously, be one that understood the vernacular. As indicated above, scholars have most often assumed that it is the secular clergy or the laity or monks or nuns at whom these English manuscripts are aimed. The inclusiveness of this audience, and the implicit homogeneity and stasis of "the laity" over a period of some two hundred years, is doubtful in the light of the historical evidence surrounding the work of the monastic movement in England in the twelfth century. Knowles, for example, in his discussion of monastic education and literary output in the period from ca. 1066 to 1154, states that "Nothing, so far as can be gathered, was written for the benefit of those outside the walls of the monasteries."[67] Other evidence offered by contemporary sources also suggests that far from being occupied with pastoral concerns and with aiding the work of the secular clergy, the Benedictine monks increasingly withdrew from such matters as the twelfth century progressed. In her examination of twelfth-century works of spiritual direction written by monks, for example, Caroline Walker Bynum states:

> One of the symptoms of the twelfth-century religious revival is the frequency with which monks and regular canons undertook the task of providing works of spiritual direction for their brothers. These treatises all share a commitment to the life of the cloister, a desire to flee the world and seek God. But when canons describe relationships in the monastery, they depart from monastic authors in attaching to the ordinary brother an obligation to edify his fellows. In short, canonical

---

[65] Such as Lincoln, Hereford, St Albans, Bury St Edmunds, Durham, and Salisbury.

[66] See Elaine M. Treharne, "The Form and Function of the Twelfth-Century Old English Dicts of Cato," *JEGP* 102 (2003): 465–85.

[67] Knowles, *The Monastic Order*, 501.

authors see regular canons as teachers and learners, whereas monastic authors see monks only as learners.[68]

The twelfth-century *Libellus de diversis ordinibus et professionibus qui sunt in aecclesia* also makes the point that monks, even those who live close to society, should remain isolated from that secular society:

> De ipso autem nomine monachi pauca dicamus. Nomen istud unum uel solum sonat . . . Si autem mouet aliquem quomodo hi qui in ciuitatibus degunt, hoc nomen optinere possint, cum pater Ieronimus dicat, monachum solitudo facit non publicum, respondeo nullum monachum nec affectu nec societate secularibus debere coniungi.[69]

It seems, however, that the concept of monks as insular and inward-looking, as deliberately excluding secular society beyond the monastery walls from their thoughts and deeds, worked only in theory and not in practice. The writer of the *Libellus de diversis ordinibus* finds himself, within a few pages of advocating isolation from secular society for monks, recognizing, perhaps disapprovingly, the reality of the situation in the twelfth-century monastic estate:

> Video enim aecclesias illorum uelint nolint a fidelibus frequentari, assidue eos missas cantare, frequenter euangelium predicare, ad sermonem faciendum in aecclesia cogi, peccata populi de carbone diuini altaris tangere, et annuntiare 'populo scelera' sua.[70]

The writer of this unique work was possibly a canon at Liège,[71] and the orders of canons and monks that he was describing are those found on the Continent and in England in the twelfth century.

---

[68] Caroline Walker Bynum, *Docere Verbo et Exemplo: An Aspect of Twelfth-Century Spirituality* (Missoula, 1979), 35.

[69] G. Constable and B. Smith, eds., *Libellus de diversis ordinibus et professionibus qui sunt in aecclesia* (Oxford, 1972), p. 18. The translation (19) reads: "We shall say little of the name of monk itself. The name means 'one' or 'alone' . . . If it should disturb someone that those who stay in cities should be able to gain this name, and he should say with father Jerome [*Ep.* 42.9, PL 30.291A]: 'Solitude makes the monk, not public life', I shall reply that no monk may be concerned with worldly things either by state of mind or by mixing in society."

[70] Constable and Smith, eds., *Libellus de diversis ordinibus*, 26. This is translated (27): "I see how their churches are frequented by the faithful, whether they desire it or not, how they constantly sing masses, frequently preach the Gospel, must give sermons in church, touch the sins of the people with the coal from the heavenly altar [cf. Is. 6:6–7], and show to the people their wicked doings [Is. 58:1]."

[71] Constable and Smith, *Libellus de diversis ordinibus*, xv.

But his description *De monachis qui iuxta homines habitant, sicut Cluniacenses et eorum similes* cited above would appear to have a particular relevance to English monastic cathedrals, some of which were founded during the tenth-century Benedictine Reform. The Normans increased the number of these foundations during the decades following the Conquest; this suggests that they thought the introduction of monks into cathedral precincts had some potential.[72] Within these foundations, the abbot of the monastery was also the bishop of the diocese, and the monastic church was thus the diocesan seat. It seems that at Rochester, for example, "The people had no parish church of their own and worshipped at the altar of St Nicholas which stood before the rood screen in the nave of the cathedral church."[73] This is reminiscent of the author's words in the *Libellus de diversis ordinibus*: "Video enim aecclesias illorum uelint nolint a fidelibus frequentari." Whether the monks at Rochester appreciated this invasion of their privacy or not, they would have been brought into some contact, albeit distant, with the laity. Indeed, as Oakley illustrates, it is evident that by the fourteenth century the Rochester monks did not wish to have the laity in their church, and a compromise was reached.[74]

This example of the use of Rochester priory by the citizens, reinforced by the information given by the author of the *Libellus de diversis ordinibus*, provides some evidence, however, for the type of situation in which manuscripts containing English religious texts might have been required by monastic institutions: to cater for the laity who used the monks' cathedral on special occasions. This still would not explain why the extant manuscripts contain so little evidence of extensive use — instead one finds mostly targeted use as already shown in this discussion — or who precisely used them. It also presupposes that, despite the general displacement of English as a literary medium following the Norman Conquest, it was used in some establishments instead of Latin for portions of the services in which the laity were involved.

There are examples of twelfth-century monastic preachers using English: as is often cited, Samson, Abbot of Bury St Edmunds in the later twelfth century, preached in English as well as French and Latin, and Senatus was made to preach at Worcester.[75] Contemporary twelfth-century sources, though, are

---

[72] See Knowles, *The Monastic Order*, 619–31. There were nine monastic chapters by the beginning of the twelfth century: Bath, Canterbury, Coventry, Durham, Ely, Norwich, Rochester, Winchester, and Worcester.

[73] Anne M. Oakley, "The Cathedral Priory of St Andrew, Rochester," *Archaeologia Cantiana* 91 (1975): 47–60, at 56.

[74] Oakley, "The Cathedral Priory," 56–57.

[75] See, for example, Clanchy, *From Memory to Written Record*, 205. For Senatus, see Mary G. Cheney, *Roger, Bishop of Worcester 1164–1179* (Oxford, 1980), 58.

usually silent on the matter of preaching specifically, and on religious in-struction in English, especially within monasteries, in general. An interest-ing, but ambiguous, instance of monks being taught in English derives from the Chronicle of Crowland, which is discussed by Clanchy:

> The Crowland chronicle ascribed to Abbot Ingulf, which is itself a com-plex tissue of fact and forgery, records that a fire in 1091 destroyed the abbey's Anglo-Saxon royal charters and other muniments numbering 400 documents. Fortunately, however, Ingulf had removed several du-plicates of these charters from the archive some years earlier *in order to instruct the younger monks in Old English*. These duplicates had there-fore been preserved and upon them Crowland based its claims. This is an ingenious story . . .[76]

No matter whether this is a wholly fictitious cartulary, the indirect comments of Ingulf seem to indicate the need for instructional materials in Old Eng-lish, though here the texts are secular and legal, rather than religious and homiletic.

The evidence of use in the homiletic manuscripts themselves indicates there is little to show that their compilation in the twelfth century or their use in this and later periods was originally intended for a lay audience, or for pastoral work by monks without the monastery's walls. Of course, the texts themselves, and particularly those which are homiletic, are clearly intended to be edifying to the reader; but to reach a conclusion that the manuscripts and their homiletic contents were unambiguously intended to be used pub-licly for a non-specific, homogenous lay audience is premature.

The important issue of use must be particularized with regard to both the immediate context of production, and the period in which the manuscript was compiled and annotated or glossed. This, coupled with a focus on those particular texts that were demonstrably read in this late period, will allow more specific suggestions concerning those who read these manuscripts and why. The context of the manuscripts discussed above was almost certainly monastic; the manuscripts probably remained *in situ* from the time of their creation until the Dissolution of the Monasteries, and this in itself suggests that we should look within the monasteries for the intended readers. The con-tinued applicability of the vernacular texts, certainly in the twelfth century, also points to a specifically monastic audience, but one that featured a need to cater for the *illiterati* within the monastery's lay associates and workers, or monastic *conversi*. For the latter, such use of English religious texts would

---

[76] Clanchy, *From Memory to Written Record*, 148 (emphasis added).

have fulfilled the Benedictine obligation to read a book a year.[77] It seems more likely that in the twelfth century — since novices were often not just young boys, but also older *conversi* — these English texts would have been read to those inexperienced in Latin, and used for the basic explication of Christian doctrine in order to confirm their undertaking of the cenobitic life, or to educate those closely associated with the monasteries' daily functioning. A number of English *conversi* are known to have been accepted at monastic cathedrals such as Christ Church, Canterbury, and there is evidence, as one would expect, for the presence of English monks in monasteries, in the century following the Conquest.[78]

The texts focused upon by post-Conquest readers, as demonstrated above, are those used at moments of high festival in the church year, such as Palm Sunday and Rogationtide, when services, even within a monastic cathedral environment, for example, might have been attended by those who used the Cathedral nave as their parish church — where the monks permitted this — and would certainly have had attendant lay members of the monastic community present. The requirement for English sermons at these crucial liturgical times is clear, and is precisely illustrated by the targeted reading and annotation of these manuscripts' texts for these important occasions. The use of these texts shows clearly the validity of English as a current and contemporary linguistic medium for the edification of *illiterati*, and thus the continuation of the Anglo-Saxon tradition of education in the vernacular. Where such sermons might have been preached and to whom is a matter of less certainty.[79] On high days, the bishop or prior may have preached to the monastic brethren in chapter (though one might assume this would be delivered in Latin); or, he may have preached to the whole monastic community during the main mass. It is to be doubted that these manuscripts themselves were actually used for reading in such a public forum, but they might have been consulted beforehand by the celebrant himself, or, more likely, by one of the monks "researching" the sermon for the celebrant.

The key, therefore, to raising the status of English in the twelfth century and to recognizing the continuation of Old English literary traditions is the acceptance that this material actually had an audience: an audience that would

---

[77] Though one might expect even greater signs of use if this had been the reason why homilies were annotated and glossed.

[78] See, for example, Cecily Clark, "People and Languages in Post-Conquest Canterbury," *Journal of Medieval History* 2 (1976): 1–32.

[79] Milton McC. Gatch, *Preaching and Theology in Anglo-Saxon England: Ælfric and Wulfstan* (Toronto, 1977), 41–57 discusses this issue with clarity for the late tenth and eleventh centuries.

vary depending on the type of material being copied. Most scholars, to date, have not addressed the issue of audience with precision, perhaps because in most cases, to borrow Gatch's phrase, it is an all but unknowable audience.[80] Much, perhaps too much, has been made of Ælfric's declaration of intent in his *Latin Preface* to the First Series of *Catholic Homilies*,[81] such that his words, interpreted as indicating that his series of texts was for preaching to the laity, have become the most obvious answer to scholarly questions about the uses of homiletic texts in English. For post-Conquest English manuscripts, this has been particularly true. The alternative response to the copied texts and created texts in this later period has occasionally been one of dismissal as antiquarianism or a literary or nationalistic curiosity.[82] In this view, homiletic texts are effectively consigned to the monastic library's shelves as material that is non-intelligible from the outset, and becomes increasingly so.

If, however, as I have attempted briefly to do, one can prove that an audience, and therefore a use, existed for these texts, the material must be taken seriously: it can be shown to be linguistically beneficial, useful, and contemporary. Consequently, very late Old English becomes a significant language, one worthy of consideration alongside Latin and French as the smallest, but most widely intelligible, literary language of the Anglo-Norman period.

The issue of audience is therefore crucial in our own attempts to understand these manuscripts. Evidence for the contemporary use of the vernacular — a utilitarian employment of "living" Old English — comes from lexical and accidental modernization, wholesale or partial adaptation, intratextual emendation, and extratextual commentary. All of these activities in no way imply the work of mechanical copyists, or those intent on rescuing for the monastic archive the religious gems of the past. It explicitly reveals the continuity of Old English, its longevity, and its use for particular purposes, as the need arose. The cultural, linguistic, and literary certainty from analyzing the readership of this small selection of manuscripts is that in the post-Conquest period there never was a hiatus in the production and use of English.

---

[80] Milton McC. Gatch, "The Unknowable Audience of the Blickling Homilies," *Anglo-Saxon England* 18 (1989): 99–115.

[81] For a discussion of which, see Gatch, *Preaching and Theology*, 47–50; and, more recently, Jonathan Wilcox, ed., *Ælfric's Prefaces*, Durham Medieval Texts 9 (Durham, 1994), 107–8, 127–28.

[82] Irvine, "The Persistence of Old English," 41–61, shows throughout her study that this scholarly response is not a balanced one.

Bibliography

Bazire, J., and J. Cross, eds. *Eleven Old English Rogationtide Homilies*. Toronto, 1982.

Bynum, Caroline Walker. *Docere Verbo et Exemplo: An Aspect of Twelfth-Century Spirituality*. Missoula, 1979.

Cheney, Mary G. *Roger, Bishop of Worcester 1164–1179*. Oxford, 1980.

Clanchy, M. T. *From Memory to Written Record*. 2nd ed. Oxford, 1993.

Clark, Cecily. "People and Languages in Post-Conquest Canterbury." *Journal of Medieval History* 2 (1976): 1–32.

———, ed. *The Peterborough Chronicle 1070–1154*. Oxford, 1970.

Clayton, Mary, and Hugh Magennis, eds. *The Old English Lives of St. Margaret*. CSASE 9. Cambridge, 1994.

Clemoes, Peter, ed. *Ælfric's Catholic Homilies: the First Series*. EETS s.s. 17. Oxford, 1997.

———, and Norman Eliason, eds. *Ælfric's First Series of Catholic Homilies: British Museum Royal 7 c. xii, fols. 4–218*. EEMF 13. Copenhagen, 1966.

Constable, G. and B. Smith, ed. *Libellus de diversis ordinibus et professionibus qui sunt in aecclesia*. Oxford, 1972.

Fischer, Andreas. "The Vocabulary of Very Late Old English." In *Studies in English Language and Literature: "Doubt Wisely": Papers in Honour of E. G. Stanley*, ed. M. J. Toswell and E. M. Tyler, 29–41. London, 1996.

Franzen, Christine, *The Tremulous Hand of Worcester: A Study of Old English in the Thirteenth Century*. Oxford, 1991.

Gatch, Milton McC. *Preaching and Theology in Anglo-Saxon England: Ælfric and Wulfstan*. Toronto, 1977.

———. "The Unknowable Audience of the Blickling Homilies." *Anglo-Saxon England* 18 (1989): 99–115.

Godden, Malcolm, and Michael Lapidge, eds. *The Cambridge Companion to Old English Literature*. Cambridge, 1991.

Greenfield, Stanley B. and Daniel G. Calder. *A New Critical History of Old English Literature*. London, 1986.

Irvine, Susan. *Old English Homilies from Bodley 343*. EETS o.s. 302. Oxford, 1993.

———. "The Persistence of Old English in the Twelfth Century." In *Rewriting Old English in the Twelfth Century*, ed. Mary Swan and Elaine M. Treharne, 41–61. CSASE 30. Cambridge, 2000.

Jones, Christopher A., ed. *Ælfric's Letter to the Monks of Eynsham.* CSASE 24. Cambridge, 1998.

Ker, N. R. *Catalogue of Manuscripts Containing Anglo-Saxon.* Oxford, 1957; repr. with supplement, Oxford, 1990.

Knowles, Dom David. *The Monastic Order in England from the Times of St. Dunstan to the Fourth Lateran Council, 940–1216.* 2nd ed. Cambridge, 1966.

Laing, Margaret. *Catalogue of Sources for a Linguistic Atlas of Early Middle English.* Woodbridge, 1993.

Lass, Roger. *Old English: A Historical Linguistic Companion.* Cambridge, 1994.

———. "Phonology and Morphology." In *The Cambridge History of the English Language,* Vol. 2: *1066–1476,* ed. Norman Blake, 23–155. Cambridge, 1992.

Lerer, Seth. "Old English and its Afterlife." In *The Cambridge History of Medieval Literature,* ed. David Wallace, 7–34. Cambridge, 1999.

Liuzza, Roy M. "Scribal Habit: The Evidence of the Old English Gospels." In *Rewriting Old English in the Twelfth Century,* ed. Swan and Treharne, 143–65.

Love, R. "Hagiography." In *The Blackwell Encyclopaedia of Anglo-Saxon England,* ed. Michael Lapidge, John Blair, Simon Keynes, and Donald Scragg, 226–28. Oxford, 1999.

Millar, Robert McColl, and Alex Nicholls. "Ælfric's *De Initio Creaturae* and London, BL Cotton Vespasian A. xxii: Omission, Addition, Retention, and Innovation." In *The Preservation and Transmission of Anglo-Saxon Culture,* ed. Paul E. Szarmach and Joel T. Rosenthal, 431–63. Studies in Medieval Culture 40. Kalamazoo, 1997.

Milroy, James. "Middle English Dialectology." In *The Cambridge History of the English Language,* Vol. 2: *1066–1476,* ed. Blake, 156–206.

Oakley, Anne M. "The Cathedral Priory of St. Andrew, Rochester." *Archaeologia Cantiana* 91 (1975): 47–60.

Pelteret, David A. E. *Catalogue of English Post-Conquest Vernacular Documents.* Woodbridge, 1990.

Pope, John C., ed. *Homilies of Ælfric: A Supplementary Colletion.* EETS o.s. 259, 260. London, 1967–1968.

Richards, Mary P. *Texts and Their Traditions in the Medieval Library of Rochester Cathedral Priory.* Transactions of the American Philosophical Association 78.3. Philadelphia, 1988.

Sauer, Hans. "Knowledge of Old English in the Middle English Period?" In *Language History and Linguistic Modelling: A Festschrift for Jacek Fisiak on his 60th Birthday*, ed. Raymond Hickey and Stanislaw Puppel, 791–814. Trends in Linguistics, Studies and Monographs 101. Berlin, 1997.

Smith, Jeremy. *An Historical Study of English: Function, Form, and Change.* London, 1996.

Swan, Mary. "Old English Made New: One *Catholic Homily* and its Reuses." *Leeds Studies in English* n.s. 28 (1997): 1–18.

Treharne, Elaine M. "The Form and Function of the Twelfth-Century Old English Dicts of Cato." *JEGP* 102 (2003): 465–85.

———. *Living through Conquest: The Politics of Early English* (Oxford, 2006) [forthcoming].

———. "The Production and Script of Manuscripts Containing English Religious Texts in the First Half of the Twelfth Century." In *Rewriting Old English in the Twelfth Century*, ed. Swan and Treharne, 11–40.

———, ed. *The Old English Life of St. Nicholas with the Old English Life of St. Giles.* Leeds Texts and Monographs 15. Leeds, 1997.

Webber, Teresa, *Scribes and Scholars at Salisbury Cathedral, c. 1075–c. 1125.* Oxford, 1992.

Wilcox, Jonathan, ed. *Ælfric's Prefaces.* Durham Medieval Texts 9. Durham, 1994.

Elliptical Glossing and Elliptical Compounds in Old English

Joseph P. McGowan

One of the glossarial habits of Anglo-Saxon scribes is "elliptical glossing," a shorthand device by which the second element in common to two compound-formations is mentioned only once. The device gives rise to a class of what might be termed 'manuscript words,' not nonce-formations *per se* but elliptical formations the lexicographer may mark as uncertain, if recorded at all. That a number of the proposed elliptical compounds are attested in full compounded form elsewhere belies the general credence accorded medieval English manuscript readings. The proposed compound formations are of course also proposed manuscript interpretations. As the fullest previous investigation of the phenomenon of elliptical glossing and compounding is Herbert Dean Meritt's 1938 study, an example from Meritt's list may help demonstrate what is meant by such compound-formations:

> in gymnasio: on leornincg ł larhuse (leornincghuse?)
> extales: snædel uel bæcþearm (snædelþearm?)[1]

The notion of elliptical compounding generally involves a schema something like either **a x + bc**, where the elliptical compound envisioned is **ac** (as in the first example from Meritt above, or Modern English *first- and secondhand source*); or, the pattern **a b + c x**, with **ab** representing a known compound and **c** representing a gloss that may only partially explain the lemma but does not make good independent sense, and **cb** the envisioned compound when expanded. The origin of this practice no doubt was a scribal convention for the sake of convenience, writing out one of the compounds, truncating the second (or third), while understood was the transferral of the second element of the complete compound to the incomplete gloss.

---

[1] Herbert Dean Meritt, "Possible Elliptical Compounds in Old English Glosses," *American Journal of Philology* 59 (1938): 209–17, here 211.

By publishing his list of possible elliptical compounds, Meritt was interested in documenting another peculiarity of glossators and, more importantly, bringing to light additional documentation for compounds in the Old English vocabulary or even adding new compounds not before documented. Meritt wrote that "When a new Old English dictionary is published — and the accumulation of Old English scholarship is making this desirable — the handling of possible elliptical compounds will be one, though small, problem to be considered."[2] He suggested that, as a procedure for handling these possible compounds, the entire gloss be cited. That procedure has been followed here; pertinent information regarding additional documentation or related information follows the gloss concerned. Since the dictionary Meritt described as a *desideratum* over half a century ago is currently in progress, the possible compounds have been collated with and checked against Bosworth-Toller and its supplements by Toller and Alistair Campbell, Clark Hall-Meritt, and the *Microfiche Concordance* of the *Dictionary of Old English*, and the DOE itself (fascicles A–F have appeared to date); the compounds have been divided into two groups chosen on the basis of their potential lexicographical significance or as examples from certain types of texts (e.g., in particular, glossaries and glossed psalters) that may yield still more elliptical compounds: the first (A), for which corroborating documentation exists, and the second (B), composed of compounds not recorded elsewhere. In the first section (I), Meritt's possible elliptical compounds have been checked against subsequent dictionaries to test whether accepted; the results show that, except in the case of some Aldhelm glosses (and those from one MS in particular, Brussels, Bibliothèque royale 1650),[3] most of the proposed compounds have not been recorded.[4]

---

[2] Meritt, "Possible Elliptical Compounds," 216–17.

[3] Louis Goossens, *The Old English Glosses of MS. Brussels, Royal Library, 1650 (Aldhelm's* De Laudibus Virginitatis*)* (Brussels, 1974).

[4] DOE practice in dealing with compound formations seems still to be evolving. One example might be given here: the adverb *earsling* (occurring twice in the Paris Psalter, at Ps 6:8 [= 6:11] and 34:5 [= 34:4]) glossing Lat. *retrorsum* is read by the DOE as *on-earsling*, and so will be not be treated until letter O is arrived at some years hence. Where *retrorsum* occurs in other glossed psalters it is rendered as *on bæc, on hinder, underbæcling, on b<a>ecling* (and some other variant readings: see P. Pulsiano, *Old English Glossed Psalters* [Toronto, 2001], 50, 454; see also J. McGowan, "Praefanda Anglo-Saxonica," *Studia Neophilologica* 75 [2003]: 3–10, here 5–7). Undoubtedly, reading *on-earsling* as a morphological unit is supported by the adverbs *onbæcling* and *onhinderling* (as recorded by Clark Hall-Meritt); but, for what it is worth, it is not the form recorded in the manuscripts. Nonetheless, one can argue for it by analogy with other attested adverbs with the form *on*-ROOT-*ling*; so, it is argued here, one may also argue by analogy for the proposed elliptical compounds.

Abbreviations: In the main, citations follow the practice of the *Dictionary of Old English* and the *Dictionary* and its *Microfiche Concordance* have been cited throughout by the project's acronym DOE.

AldV = Aldhelm, *De laudibus virginitatis*

BT = Bosworth, Joseph, and T. Northcote Toller, *An Anglo-Saxon Dictionary* (Oxford, 1898)

BTS = Bosworth, Joseph, and T. Northcote Toller, *An Anglo-Saxon Dictionary, Supplement* (Oxford, 1921)

BTS-Campbell = enlarged addenda and corrigenda to BT by Alistair Campbell (Oxford, 1972)

Clark Hall-Meritt = Clark Hall, J. R., *A Concise Anglo-Saxon Dictionary*, 4ᵗʰ ed. with a supplement by Herbert Dean Meritt (Toronto, 1984)

Cleop Gl = the Cleopatra Glossaries, as edited by John Joseph Quinn and William Garlington Stryker

Corp Gl = the Corpus Glossary (as edited by W. M. Lindsay)

Goossens = Goossens, Louis, *The Old English Glosses of MS. Brussels, Royal Library, 1650* (Brussels, 1974)

Harl Gl = the Harley Glossary (as edited by Robert T. Oliphant)

Kindschi = Kindschi, Lowell, "The Latin-Old English Glossaries in Plantin-Moretus MS 32 and British Museum Additional 32,246" (Ph.D. diss., Stanford University, 1955)

Napier OEG = Napier, A. S. *Old English Glosses, Chiefly Unpublished* (Oxford, 1900)

OLD = *Oxford Latin Dictionary*, ed. P. G. W. Glare (Oxford, 1996)

WW = Wright, Thomas and R. P. Wülcker, *Anglo-Saxon and Old English Vocabularies*, 2 vols. (London, 1884)

I: Elliptical compounds proposed by Meritt 1938

1. ("The uncompounded gloss is fairly obviously complete, either in its meaning or in its ending"⁵).

1.a ("The possible compound is elsewhere documented" [Meritt, "Possible Elliptical Compounds," 210–12])

---

⁵ Meritt, "Possible Elliptical Compounds," 210–13.

(1) *bilustris: twiferum uel hiwum* (for *twihiwum*, at WW 194,30, = *Harley Glossary* B231); not recorded by DOE. Oliphant, in his note to this entry (R. T. Oliphant, *The Harley Latin-Old English Glossary* [The Hague, 1966], 31), expands to *twihiwum*; cf. also *Harley Glossary* B208 *biforma: twihiwe* (= WW 194,20; WW read *biformia* for the lemma) and C1739 *coccum bistinctum: weolocread.* uel *twihiwe godweb* (= WW 212,29).

(2) *cardiacus dicitur qui patitur laborem cordis uel morbus cordis: heortcopa uel ece modseocness uel unmiht* (for *heortece*, at WW 199,33; = *Harley Glossary* C348); not recorded by DOE. See also below I.1.b.4.

(3) *cephalia .i. dolor capitis uel cephalargia: heafodwærc uel ece* (for *heafodece*, at WW 204,8; = *Harley Glossary* [ed. Oliphant; hereafter Harl Gl] C842); not recorded by DOE.

(4) *fasces .i. honores, dignitates, plagas, triumphos: cynedomas uel aldor uel gegerla uel godweb* (for *aldordomas*, at WW 234,18; = Harl Gl F11); not recorded by DOE but accepted by the *Dictionary of Old English*. Compare also the *Lorica* gloss *principatus: aldordomas* (J. H. G. Grattan and C. Singer, *Anglo-Saxon Magic and Medicine* [London, 1952], 134, verse 8), and Cleop Gl (W. G. Stryker, "The Latin-Old English Glossary in MS Cotton Cleopatra A III" [Ph.D. diss., Stanford University, 1951] F128 *fasces: godweb ł ealdordomas* (= WW 402,8). Oliphant expanded to *aldordomas* in his note (p. 172). Cf. Antwerp Gl (Kindschi) B, p. 164, #3 *fasces: ealdordomas.*

(5) *flaminea .i. episcopali gradus: bisceophadas uel sacerd* (for *sacerdhadas*, at WW 239,22; = Harl Gl F406); not recorded by the DOE, but compare AldV 1880 *flaminea: sacerdhadas*, and 4940 *flaminium. sacerdotium: biscophad. sacerdhad* (Goossens). Oliphant expanded the reading to *sacerdhadas* in his note (187).

(6) *gorgoneo: aterlicum oððe biter* (for *biterlicum*, at WW 414,34; = Cleop Gl [Stryker] G117; he advocates expansion to *biterlicum* in his apparatus); not recorded by DOE or DOE (gloss is cited s.v. *attorlic*).

(7) *in gymnasio: on leornincg ł larhuse* (for *leornincghuse*, at coll. gll. ed. K. W. Bouterwek, "Angelsächsische Glossen. 1," *ZfdA* 9 [1853], 401–530, here 405); DOE records only the simplex *leornincg*; compare AldV (Goossens) 3117 *gymnasii: leornunghuses.*

(8) *sollerter: mænigfealdlice ł georn* (for *geornlice*, at Bouterwek, "Glossen," 405); not recorded by DOE.

(9) *pedibus poeticis: mid meterlicum fotum ł scop* (for *scoplicum*, an Aldhelm gl., at Bouterwek, "Glossen," 411); not recorded by DOE though BT reads *scop[licum]* and Goossens, at AldV 299, notes: "*Scop* for *scop[licum]*." Compare Digby AldV (Napier OEG) 199: *pedibus poeticis, .i. metricis: mid scoplicum ł meterlicum fotum*; this clearly seems a case of scribal abbreviation.

(10) *epitaphion, carmen super tumulum* Ɩ *mortuorum: byriensang licleoðsang* 7 *bergelsleoð* Ɩ *sang* (for *forlicsang* or *bergelssang*, at Bouterwek, "Glossen," 427); neither is recorded by the DOE but given in the DOE, s.v. *byrgelssang* ("epitaph, dirge"), deriving from Goossens' note: "Ɩ *sang* for Ɩ *[bergels]sang*".

(11) *atomo: preohthwile beorht* (*beorhthwile*, at Bouterwek, "Glossen," 462); not recorded by DOE, but given tacit acceptance in DOE; cf. also Digby AldV (Napier, OEG) 3247 *in puncto, .i. parte: on beorhthwile*. Meritt cited also Digby AldV (Napier, OEG) 2370 *atomo: beorht* (the preceding lemma *in ictu, .i. in puncto* is glossed *on prince, preowthwile*; Napier suggested reading for the following gl. *beorhthwile*; in his apparatus, p. 64, he cites other occurrences of *beorht(m)hwil*; DOE: "moment, instant," *s.v. beorhthwil*).

(12) *confossa, transfixa: þurhdol þed* (for *þurhþed*, at Bouterwek, "Glossen," 501); not recorded by DOE, but compare Ælfric, *Cath. Hom.* II 35.265.168 *mid sarnysse þurhþyd*, and Ælfric, *LS* (Basil) 272 *and hyne sona þurhþydde....*

(13) *oppidanis: stocweardum burh* (for *burhweardum*, at Bouterwek, "Glossen," 525); not recorded by DOE, though the word does appear at *Exodus* 39a (*abrocene burhweardas*) and *Andreas* 660b (*burhweardas cyme*). Concerning this gloss, Meritt remarked: "From its documented meanings, *burhweardum* does not seem to suit the lemma" (Meritt, "Possible Elliptical Compounds," 211n.). For masc. *burhweard* BT gives "a city-ward or guardian, city-defender," Clark Hall-Meritt "city defender," and DOE "defender of the city, city guardian" (likely a calque of late Lat. *defensor civitatis*). I do not think the lemma should have given Meritt pause; his suggested *burhweardum* to *oppidanis* is not ill-suited; for Lat. *oppidani* Lewis-Short gave "the inhabitants of a town other than Rome, townsmen, townsfolk (esp. when besieged)," with references from Caesar and Livy; perhaps some *Bellum Gallicum* passages gave rise to this gloss, though it may derive from a late Roman context.

(14) *congruant .i. conueniant: gehwærlæcan* Ɩ *riht* (for *rihtlæcan*, at Digby AldV [Napier, OEG]; not recorded by DOE though Napier in his apparatus (p. 3) suggests reading *rihtlæcan*. Such abbreviation is not at all uncommon in the Digby Aldhelm gll.; compare the very next entry, *comparationem: nesse*. For this gloss, clearly incomplete, Napier suggests reading *wiðmetennesse*, citing Digby AldV 587 *in comparatione, .i. assimilatione: unwiðmetenesse* and WW 207,37 (= Harl Gl C1315) *comparatio: wiþmetenes*. Compare also the homily reference (A. S. Napier, *Wulfstan* [Berlin, 1883]) 67: *and heonanforþ ælces yfeles geswican and rihtlæcan....*

(15) *nugaciter .i. utiliter: aworpenlice wac* (for *waclice*, at Digby AldV [Napier, OEG] 2736); not recorded by DOE though for the equivalent entry from the Brussels AldV Goossens notes, "*Wac* for *waclice*" (2651; 321n.).

(16) *machinamentis .i. cogitationibus: orþancum seare* (for *seareþancum*, at Digby AldV [Napier, OEG]); the DOE does not record this expanded gloss, but does record Goossens' *seareþancum* (from AldV 2911 *machinamentis: orþancum l seare*; ironically, Goossens also suggested the possibility of reading *seare[cræftum]*).

(17) *argumentis: mid searecræftum þancan* (for *seareþancan*, at Digby AldV 3016); the DOE did not record expansion of this form but did accept Goossens' expansion of *þancan* to *seareþancan* in the Brussels AldV MS. As Meritt noted, Napier had suggested expansion to *searecræftum* based analogously on Digby AldV 3075 *machinamentis: serewungum, searecræftum* and 3380 *ad argumentum .i. machinamentum: searecræ* (for which Napier suggests *searecræfte*).

(18) *praestaret .i. excelleret: oferþuge stige* (for *oferstige*, at Digby AldV [Napier, OEG] 3133); not accepted by DOE, though Goossens' *[ofer]stige* is recorded.

(19) *lenocinii: hæmedrimes scipes* (for *hæmedscipes*, at Digby AldV [Napier, OEG] 5046); not recorded by the DOE. Compare however Digby AldV (Napier, OEG) 3219 *hymenei: hæmedscipes* and Brussels AldV (Goossens) 3113 *hymenei: hæmedscipes*.

(20) *petulantia: of galscipe wræn* (for *wrænscipe*, at Digby AldV [Napier, OEG] 5290); the entry is printed as *petulantia: of galscipe, wræn*, and Napier suggested reading *wrænscipe*. The word is not recorded by the DOE; cf. Napier's apparatus (134), for occurrence of *wrenscipe* in another MS.

(21) *istoriographus: stærwritere ul gewyrd* (for *gewyrdwritere*, at OEG [Napier] 60.1); as Meritt noted, the form *wyrdwritere* is attested.

(22) *prologus: forerim l tal l saga* (*foresaga*, gl. at Mt 1:1); not recorded by the DOE. Compare two gll. from the Lindisfarne Gospels: *prochemio: in deigilnisi vel in foresaga* (Walter W. Skeat, *The Gospel according to Saint John, In Anglo-Saxon and Northumbrian Versions Synoptically Arranged* [Cambridge, 1878], 187). The DOE records four instances of *foresaga* as an interpretation, glossing Lat. *praefatio, prologus, prooemium, translatio* (s.v. *fore-saga*).

1.b ("The possible compound is elsewhere undocumented")[6]

(1) *matutinum officium: uhtgebed uel þenung* (for *uhtþenung*, at WW 129,32; = Antwerp Gl [Kindschi 1955] A, p. 97, #5); not recorded by the DOE.

(2) *uespertinum officium: aefengebed uel þeowdom* (for *æfenþeowdom*, at WW 129,34; = Antwerp Gl [Kindschi] A, p. 97, #6); not recorded by the DOE but listed in DOE as **æfenþeowdom* ("evening prayer or service, vespers";

---

[6] Meritt, "Possible Elliptical Compounds," 212–13.

fasc. A, p. 96). BT apparently used this gl. for its entry *æfenþeowdom*, m. "an evening service or office"; compare at any rate the fem. noun *æfenþenung*, "an evening service or duty, evening repast, supper" (DOE: "evening meal, supper," "evening service, vespers").

(3) *bibliotheca .i. librorum repositio: bochord uel fodder* (for *bocfodder*, at WW 194,13; = Harl Gl B170); not recorded by the DOE but given as a reconstructed form in DOE ("library, repository for books", s.v. *bōc-fodder*).

(4) *cardiacus dicitur qui patitur laborem cordis uel morbus cordis: heortcoþa uel ece modunseocnes uel unmiht* (for *modunmiht*, at WW 199,33; = Harl Gl C348); not recorded by the DOE. BT cited *modunmeaht* on the basis of the interpreted *[mod]unmiht*. Cf. above, I.1a (2).

(5) *multiformem: þæne mænifealdan l hiwan* (for *mænihiwan*, at Bouterwek, "Glossen," 409); not in the DOE; Meritt notes that evidence for this word can be found among gll. he edited: *multifario: monigheoulice* (cf. H. D. Meritt, "Old English Scratched Glosses in Cotton MS. Tiberius C. ii," *American Journal of Philology* 54 [1933]: 305–22, here 321).

(6) *itinerarium: siðboc foreboc fereld* (for *fereldboc*, at Bouterwek, "Glossen," 454); BTS had documented *færeldboc* on the basis of this gl. Goossens noted: "*Fereld* for *fereld[boc]*?" (277n.). The DOE accepted Goossens' expansion.

(7) *incorruptam .i. inmarcesibilem: unforwurdenlice molsnienlice* (for *unmolsnienlice*, at Digby AldV [Napier, OEG] 60); the whole entry as printed by Napier reads, *incorruptam .i. inmarcesibilem: unforwurdenlice, molsnienlice*, concerning which Napier commented: "The *un-* prefix to *forw-* is intended to do duty also with *molsnienlice*" (3n.). Meritt cites a gloss from Bouterwek (Bouterwek, "Glossen," 407) giving the reading *unformolsniendlic*; Goossens' apparatus notes: "*Mols/(. .c)niendlicne* for *[un]molsniendlicne* or *[unfor]molsniendlicne* (*un-* or *unfor-* to be supplied from *unforwurdendlicne*)" (157n.). The DOE accepted the first of Goossens' suggestions, recording *unmolsniendlicne*.

(8) *prologus: forerim l tal l saga* (for *foretal*, from gll. to Mt 1:1; cf. 1.a.22 above); not recorded by the DOE.

2. ("The incompleteness of the uncompounded gloss is less obvious" [Meritt, "Possible Elliptical Compounds," 213–15]).

2.a ("The possible compound is elsewhere documented" [Meritt, "Possible Elliptical Compounds," 213–14]).

(1) *circumspectio, circuitus: embeþonc uel sceawung* (for *embesceawung*, at WW 204,34; = Harl Gl C964); not recorded by the DOE. Compare however the following glosses to the Durham Ritual: *circumspectione dei:*

ymbsceawung godes (25.5), and *circumspectione dei: ymbsceaunge godes* (116.1).

(2) *constipata .i. consita, repleta, circumdata: embþrungen uel hringed* (for *embhringed*, at WW 209,12; = Harl Gl C1496); not recorded by the DOE.

(3) *collarium: sweorclaþ uel teg uel sal* (for *sweorteg*, at WW 210,36; = Harl Gl C1591); not recorded by the DOE. Meritt also tentatively suggested *sweorsal* (cf. 3.b.1 below). For OE *sweortĕag*, cf. AldV 7 (Napier, OEG; London, British Library, MS. Royal VI. A. vi) 127 *collario: sweorteage* and Antwerp Gl (Kindschi) 859 *millus uel collarium: sweorteh*.

(4) *fantasia .i. imaginatio, admiratio, delusio mentis, reuelatio, multitudo, fantasma: scinlac uel hiw* (for *scinhiw*, at WW 236,6; = Harl Gl F154); not recorded by the DOE. The word occurs a number of times in OE, including an early gl. to Sedulius' *Carmen paschale, portenta: mihtie scinhiu* (= H. D. Meritt, *Old English Glosses* [New York, 1945], 28.429).

(5) *litteraturae: stæfcræftes cyste* (for *stæfcyste*, at Digby AldV [Napier, OEG] 3031); the DOE does not list this expansion (first suggested by Meritt; Napier has no note to the gloss), but lists Goossens' expansion to *stæfcyste* at Brussels AldV 2931 (which he marked with a question mark in his apparatus). The fem. noun *stæfcyst* also occurs at Ælfric, *LS* 23 (Mary of Egypt) 2.593: *Ne ic stæfcyste witodlice ne leornode. . . .*

(6) *archimandrita .i. princeps ouium: hehfæder lareow* (for *hehlareow*, at Digby AldV [Napier, OEG] 3720). The DOE does not list this expansion, but a Cleop Gl entry gives a similar gloss, *archimandrita: heahleareow* (Stryker A106; = WW 342,33). Compare as well these gll.:

  AldV (Digby; Napier, OEG) 3359 didasculis .i. magistris: heahlareowum

  AldV (Brussels; Goossens) 3251 didasculis, magistris, doctorum: heahlareowum

  Cleop Gl (Stryker) G24 gymnosophistis: heahlareowum

A similar cpd. would be neut. *heahleornere*; compare *archimandrita: heah-hyrde . . . heahleornere* (for full gloss, cf. AldV [Goossens] 966), and *archimandrita .i. excelsus magister: hehhyrde, heahleornere* (Digby AldV [Napier, OEG] 910).

2.b ("The possible compound is elsewhere undocumented" [Meritt, "Possible Elliptical Compounds," 214–15]).

(1) *bibiones uel mustiones: muscfleotan uel wurmas mite* (for *muscwurmas*, at WW 121,22; = Antwerp Gl [Kindschi] B, p. 80, #3); not recorded by the DOE. BTS' tentatively suggested *mustwyrm* ("an insect found in wine") based on this glossary entry, but it is not recorded by the DOE either.

(2) *condolomata articula: leoþusar uel geþind* (for *leoþugeþind*, at WW 213,8; = Harl Gl C1786); not recorded by the DOE.

(3) *equester, qui equitat: rædewiga uel cempa* (for *rædecempa*, at WW 228,38; = Harl Gl E305); not recorded by the DOE though Oliphant, in the apparatus to his ed. of the Harl Gl, suggested reading *rædecempa*.

(4) *bolidis: sundgyrd in scipe oððe rap .i. metrap* (for *sundrap*, at WW 358,17; = Cleop Gl [Stryker] B38); not recorded by the DOE, though Stryker accepted the proposed cpd. following BT and Clark Hall-Meritt with the meaning "sounding line."

(5) *nectar: hunig oððe mildeaw* (for *hunigdeaw*, at WW 455,19;= Cleop Gl [Stryker] N143, where Stryker argues for this cpd. based on the context of the lemma [the praef. to *Ænig*. XXVI); not recorded by the DOE. Recorded by the *Oxford English Dictionary* is a first attestation of 1577, in Barnaby Googe's *Heresbach's Foure bookes of husbandry* ("our common people call it Manna, or Hony dewe"; s.v. *honeydew*) and in 1588 in Shakespeare's *Titus Andronicus* ("as doth the honeydew Vpon a gathred Lillie almost withered"; III.i.112), the OED and C. T. Onions' *A Shakespeare Glossary* share for *honey-dew* the gloss: "Sweet sticky substance found on the leaves and stems of plants, held to be excreted by aphides, and formerly imagined to be akin to dew in origin" (s.v.). Long association of nectar (the lemma in question) with honey is amply attested; e.g., νέκταρ μελίσσων from Euripides' *Bacchae* (Liddell-Scott, s.v. νέκταρ). More to the point of the OE form, a proposed **hunig-dēaw* might be analogous to attested *mele-deaw* (found in *The Phoenix* and the glossaries; DOE, s.v. *dēaw*).

(6) *glareas: stancyslas croppas* (for *stancroppas*, at Digby AldV [Napier, OEG] 1812); not recorded by the DOE. OE masc. *stāncrop* is an attested plant-name; cf. *Lacnunga* CXLIII (*stancrop*; Grattan and Singer, *Magic and Medicine*, 178) and CLXXVIII (*stancroppes sæd*; Grattan and Singer, *Magic and Medicine*, 194).

(7) *constellationem: steorwigele mearcunge reonunge* (for *steormearcunge*, at Digby AldV [Napier, OEG] 2631); not recorded by DOE.

(8) *olosericis: of ealseolcenum sidenum* (for *ealsidenum*, at Digby AldV [Napier, OEG] 3161); not recorded by the DOE.

3. ("The gloss may well be taken as it stands, since the uncompounded word occurs elsewhere with the required meaning" [Meritt, "Possible Elliptical Compounds," 215–16]).

3.a ("The possible compound is elsewhere documented" [Meritt, "Possible Elliptical Compounds," 215–16]).

(1) *scopulorum .i. saxorum: stanrocca torra* (for *stantorra*, at Digby AldV [Napier, OEG] 1811); not recorded by the DOE. There is a similar Aldhelm gloss at Digby AldV 2038, *scopulorum .i. saxorum eminentium: stanrocca, torra*, and Meritt mentions WW 147,38 *scopulum: torr* (= Antwerp Gl [Kindschi] B, p. 140, #15). BT lists masc. *stantorr* as "a stone tower" (*Genesis* 1700a, *stiðlic stantorr*; ASPR I), and "a rock, crag, tor" (at Gregory, *Dialogues* 1.12.13; there is also the place-name *Stantorr* [Charter 1819, ed. A. G. C. Turner, "Some Old English Passages Relating to the Episcopal Manor of Taunton," *Proceedings of the Somersetshire Archaeological and Natural History Society* 98 [1953]: 118–26, here 76]).

(2) *marsum: wyrincgalere ł galdre* (for *wyrincgaldre*, at Bouterwek, "Glossen," 519); not recorded by the DOE. As Meritt intimated, this should probably be read as *wyrmgaldre*.

(3) *extales: snaedel uel baecþearm* (for *snædelþearm*, at WW 159,39; = Antwerp Gl [Kindschi] B, p. 180, #11); not recorded as such by the DOE. There is some confusion over masc. *snædelþearm*, most likely due to BT's "*snædel*, (more generally) *snædelþearm*" (s.v. *snædel*); *þearm* generally means "intestine" or "gut" and *snædelþearm* rather more specifically means, and glosses words meaning, "the great gut" (large intestine). This confusion carries over into the DOE; whereas the Harl Gl entries E584 (*extale: rop. snædelþearm. uel smeruþearm. uel bacþearm*; = WW 231,40) and F387 (*fither: snædelþearm*; = WW 239,14) are listed under *snædelþearm*, the Cleop Gl entries 2070 (Stryker 1951; *extale: snædel þearm*) and 2696 (Stryker; *fiber: snædel þearm*) are listed under the simplex *snædel*. This makes no sense considering the relationships of the often semantically grouped glossary batches (one such loosely broken up grouping occurs in the Harl Gl entries F252 ff., especially at F291–F299, F387–F397; see McGowan, "Praefanda Anglosaxonica," 6); Clark Hall-Meritt simply equated *snædel* and *snædelþearm*.[7]

(4) *bilance: twiwæge uel heolore* (for *twiheolore*, at WW 194,28; = Harl Gl B225); not recorded by the DOE. Compare the entry from the Corp Gl (ed. W.M. Lindsay, *The Corpus Glossary* [Cambridge, 1921]) B140 *bilance: tuiheolore* and AldV (Goossens) 1749 *lance: . . . heolore.*

---

[7] And so the *snaedel ðearm* at Occ Gl 83.46 (ed. A. B. Kuypers, *The Prayer Book of Aedeluald the Bishop* [Cambridge, 1902]) should probably be read as a cpd. Compare the Leiden Gl entry (ed. F. Holthausen, "Die Leidener Glossen," *Englische Studien* 50 [1916–1917]), 104, *extale: snedildarm.* OE *snædel* does occur as a simplex; cf. Cleop Gl (J. J. Quinn, "The Minor Latin-Old English Glossaries in MS. Cotton Cleopatra A III" [Ph.D. diss., Stanford University, 1956]), 509 *extale: snædel.*

3.b ("The possible compound is elsewhere undocumented," Meritt, "Possible Elliptical Compounds," 216–17).

(1) *collarium: sweorclaþ uel teg uel sal* (for *sweorsal*, at WW 210,36; = Harl Gl C1591; cf. 2.a.3 above); not recorded by the DOE.

(2) *clauus: steorsceofol oðþe nægl* (for *steornægl*, at WW 312,4; = Cott. Julius A.ii glossary); not recorded by the DOE. Meritt ("Possible Elliptical Compounds," 216–17) mentions the OHG gloss *clauus: stiurnagal* (cf. BT, s.v. *steornægl*).

II: Further possible elliptical compounds

A

1 *Harley Glossary* E603 expedierunt: aræfdon uel ræddon (for *aræddon*)

Not recorded by the DOE; compare WW 20,11 (= Corp Gl [ed. Lindsay] E393) *expedierant: araeddun* and Erfurt Gl (ed. J. D. Pheifer, *Old English Glosses in the Épinal-Erfurt Glossary* [Oxford, 1974]) 366 *expedierunt: aræddun* (the form *aræddon* appears also at the OE Bede 4, 1.254.22). The DOE seems to tentatively accept *aræddon* here as it lists the Harl Gl entry under sense 1.b. of *arædan* ("glossing *expedire*, here 'to arrange, set in order, make ready'"; fasc. A, p. 1490).

2 *Stowe Psalter* 55:7 abscondet: bedihliað ł hidað (for *behidað*)

Not recorded by the DOE. OE *behydan* is recorded glossing Lat. *abscondere, occultare, operire*; cf. also WW 502,29 (= Cleop Gl [Quinn, "Minor Glossaries"] p. 136, #6) *oppilauit: behydde* and Arundel Ps 55:7 *abscondent: behidaþ* (G. Oess, *Die altenglische Arundel-Psalter* [Amsterdam, 1968]).

3 *Lambeth Psalter* 5:7 virum sanguinum: þæne wer þe is blodgita ł geotende ł wer bloda (for *blodgeotende*).

Not recorded by the *Microfiche Concordance* of the DOE, though the DOE accepts the expanded form noting "MS *geotende*" (fasc. B, s.v.). Lindelöf records the expanded form *blodgeotende* in his glossary (U. Lindelöf, *Der Lambeth-Psalter* [Helsinki, 1909]); compare also the dat. pl. at Ps 50:16 in this psalter, *sanguinibus: blodgeotendum*, and the Stowe Ps 54:24, *uiri sanguinum: weras blodgeotende*.

4 *Harley Glossary* C2151 cunabula .i. crepundia. initia. rudimenta. uel panni infantie: cildclaþes uel cradelas. uel primordia (for *cildcradelas*).

> Not recorded by the DOE. The attested cpd. *cildcradol* (DOE: "cradle," and by metonymy, "infancy"), m., appears at Ælfric's *Grammar, cunabula: cildcradulas* (J. Zupitza, *Aelfrics Grammatik und Glossar* [Darmstadt, 1966], 85); cf also WW 419,27 (= Cleop Gl [Stryker] I37) *in cunis: in cildcradelum* and Digby AldV (Napier, OEG) 2156 *in cunis .i. incunabulis: on cildcradelum.*

5 Aldhelm, *De laude virginitatis* [gloss] (Goossens) 328 concretione. coagulatione, creatione: cennunge 7 ren (for *cenren* = *cynren*, n.)

> Not recorded by the DOE. Goossens expands to *cenren* in his note to the gloss; for this sense of *cynren* (normally equivalent to Lat. *genus*, or to Lat. *in generatione* and related phrases as *on cynrene*), cf. Antwerp Gl (Kindschi) 181 *propago: cynren.*

6 *Durham Ritual* glosses 22.22 (ed. A. H. Thompson and U. Lindelöf, *Rituale ecclesiae Dunelmensis* [Durham,1927], 42) reatum: ðeaðsynnignisse ł scyldignis' (for *ðeaðscyldinise* = *deaðscyldignise*)

> Not recorded by the DOE but listed as hypothetical form by DOE (s.v. *deaþsynnignes*: "perh. second element of implied cpd. **deaþscyldignes*", the DOE citing J. McGowan, "Old English Lexicographical Studies" [Ph.D. diss., University of Pennsylvania, 1991]). Lindelöf notes that ðeað- = *deað*-; the form ðeað occurs at Vercelli Hom (ed. P. W. Peterson, "The Unpublished Homilies of the Vercelli Book" [Ph.D. diss., New York University, 1951]), 11.81, the OE version of Augustine's *Soliloquies* 1.31.3, 1.44.8, and 2.63.20, a gloss to Luke (Lindisfarne) 3, and at Arundel Ps 9:15, *de portis mortis: of geatum þeaþes.* The adj. *deaðscyldig* (DOE: "guilty of a capital crime, condemned to death") is attested in OE (e.g., Laws, Edward and Guthrum, cap. 5 *deaðscyldig man scriftspræce gyrne* [F. Liebermann, *Die Gesetze der Angelsachsen*, 3 vols.[Halle, 1903–1916, 1: 128] and Laws II Cnut, cap. 44 *deaðscyldig man* [Liebermann, *Gesetze*, 1: 342]), but not the feminine abstract noun *deaðscyldignes.* The noun is, however, quite an appropriate gloss to the Latin masculine fourth-declension noun *reatus*, which denotes the state of being accused, as of capital crimes; there is also the usage *reatus sanguinis* at Deut 21:8 (on the expiation of the blood-guilt, from murder and other circumstances).

7 *Eadwine Psalter* 1:5 peccatores: firen ł synfullan (for *firenfullan*)

> Similar subst. uses of this adj. appear in this same psalter:
> Ps 10:7 *peccatores: firen ł senfullæn*

Ps 32:10, 70:4, and 74:11 *peccatorum: firenfulre* ł *synfulra*
Ps 108:6 *super eum peccatorem: ofer him ðæ firenfullæn*
Ps 138:19 *peccatores viri: ðæ firenfullæn weræs*

8 *Lambeth Psalter* 45:9 prodigia: foretacna ł beacna (for *forebeacna*)

> Not recorded by the DOE. Lindelöf (*Lambeth-Psalter*) records *forebeac-na* in his glossary; *forebeacen* occurs at Ps 70:7 and with the same lemma at 77:43 *et prodigia sua: 7 his forebeacna* and 134:9 *et prodigia: 7 forebeacna*.

9 *Lambeth Psalter* 1:6 peribit: forwyrð ł losaþ (for *forlosaþ*)

> Not recorded by the DOE.

10 Aldhelm, *De laude virginitatis* [gloss] (Goossens) 917 sollerter: geornful-lice. fræ (for *fræfellice*)

> The DOE records the expanded *fræfellice*, as given by Goossens in his apparatus. See also Meritt's proposed cpd. (1.a.8 above) and Digby AldV (Napier, OEG) 3131 *sollerter: gleawlice, fræfellice*. Here is suggested a broader sense of elliptical glossing, by which the fuller form of the second item is truncated but not to be completed by exactly (i.e., etymologically) the same suffix (rather another adverbial suffix in *-lice*). Something similar may be at work below in II.A.11, but involving an infinitive form.

11 Aldhelm, *De laude virginitatis* [gloss] (Goossens) 4461 industria. astutia: gleawnysse ł georn (for *geornnysse*)

> Not recorded by the DOE. BT records *geornes*, f., in the sense of Lat. *industria, studium*; BTS adds 'diligence, assiduity'; so WW 428,25 *industria: geornesse* (= Cleop Gl [Stryker] 1392); and notice AldV (Goossens) 79 *sollerter curiose: fræflice, mænifealdlice, georn* (= *geornlice*; so Goossens in his apparatus, p. 152; compare also 5167 *elisisse: beswicen, bepæ* [= *bepæcan*]).

12 *Durham Ritual* glosses (Thompson and Lindelöf, *Rituale*, 21) pontifex: hehsceawere ł bisc' (for *hehbisc[e]op*)

> Not recorded by the DOE. Lat. *pontifex* is commonly glossed *heah-bisceop*; plenty of evidence within the Dur. Rit. itself confims the gloss (often abbreviated as *bis', bisc', bisco'*): p. 49, *pontificis: hehbiscopes, pontificis: hehbisco'* (2x); p. 53, *pontificis: hehbisco'*; p. 57, *pontificem: hehbisc'*; p. 72, *pontifice: hehbiscop'*; p. 76, *pontificis: hehbiscob', pontificis: heh-bisco'* (same gloss occurs at p. 77 [3x], p. 78 [1x], p. 88 [1x], p. 91 [2x]); p. 194, *archiepiscopus: hehbisco'*.

13 *Durham Ritual* glosses (Thompson and Lindelöf: 30) laude: herenisse ł lofe
(for *herelofe*)

Not recorded by the DOE. BT and Clark Hall-Meritt record *herelof*, n., as
"praise, fame, glory." Compare the following gll.:

AldV (Goossens) 1751 tropheum. uictoriam ł herelof

AldV (Goossens) 1887 tropheum. signum victorię: herelof

AldV (Goossens) 4400 rumor. fama: herelofa

AldV (Goossens) 4444 rumusculus: herelof ł lysa

Digby AldV (Napier, OEG) 1761 tropeum .i. uictoria: herelof

Digby AldV (Napier, OEG) 1908 tropeum .i. signum victorie: herelof

Digby AldV (Napier, OEG) 4521 rumore: herelofe

Digby AldV (Napier, OEG) 4564 rumusculus: herelof, hlisa

14 Aldhelm, *De laude virginitatis* [gloss] (Goossens) 415 oblectamenta. blan-
dimenta. delectamenta: lustfullunga ł nysse (for *lustfullnysse*)

Not recorded by the DOE; Goossens expands the form in his apparatus. Compare the gloss (ed. Meritt, *Old English Glosses*, #24) 93.1.12
oblectamina: lustfulnessa.

15 *Lambeth Psalter* 12:5 praeualui: is oferswiðrode ł swað (for *oferswað*)

Not recorded by the DOE.

16 *Cleopatra Glossary* (Stryker) A546 astu: gleawnisse 7 sceaf̣ (for *scearpnisse*)

Not recorded by the DOE. Stryker's note reads: "The gloss *sceaf̣* may
be from *scearp* 'sharp, keen, acute of understanding.' BTS gives locu-
tions (under *scearp* VIII) in which *scearp* is used with *gleawnes*" (p. 66).
In the OE versions of Gregory's *Cura pastoralis* is mentioned the *modes
scearpnesse* (Hatton MS; ed. H. Sweet, *King Alfred's West-Saxon Version of Gregory's 'Pastoral Care'* [London, 1871–1872], 99, ll. 9–10), corresponding to the Lat. *aciem mentis*; notice also WW 340,19 (= Cleop
Gl [Stryker] A39) *acies: scearpnes*. Thus OE *scearpnes* would not be an
inappropriate gloss to Lat. masc. fourth decl. *astus.*

17 *Lambeth Psalter* 16:5 uestigia mea: siðstapla ł. wegas ł. fereldu mine (for
siðwegas = *sidwegas*)

Not recorded by the DOE. Cf. *Guthlac* 887b (*of siðwegum*; ASPR III),
Phoenix 337a (*sigað sidwegum*), *Elene* 282b (*of sidwegum*). The glossator
seems to expand upon the *uestigia mea* of Ps 16 in using *(sið)wegas* and
fereldu. Perhaps these latter two gll. are meant to render *uestigium* in the

sense of "the distance of a step" as found in Livy (Lewis-Short, s.v.), or, perhaps figuratively, as "wanderings" or "far tracks." If so, *siðweg* would not be inappropriate.

18 *Eadwine Psalter* 29:12 concidisti: toslite ł curfe (for *tocurfe*)

Not recorded by the DOE. Compare the Lk gloss (W. W. Skeat, *The Holy Gospels in Anglo-Saxon, Northumbrian, and Old Mercian Versions* [Cambridge, 1871–1887], Rushworth Gospels 22:50) *amputauit: toceorf*, and the forms *tocurfon* (3rd pret. pl. act.; Martyrology 5.1893, ed. G. Herzfeld, *An OE Martyrology* [London, 1900]), and infin. *toceorfan* (Ælfric, *LS* [Oswald] 94; *LS* 5.511 and 5.393 [*de inventione crucis*; A. S. Napier, *History of the Holy Rood-Tree* (London, 1894); the form of the latter reference is *toceorfæn*]; Leechdoms I 140.1.11 [T. O. Cockayne, *Leechdoms, Wortcunning, and Starcraft of Early England*, 3 vols. (London, 1864–1866)]).

19 *Harley Glossary* C1803 (= WW 213,17) corimbus .i. uiti racemi. uel botriones. uel circuli: wingeardhringas uel bergan. croppas. bacce (for *winbergan*)

Not recorded by the DOE. OE *winberge*, f., is a well-attested cpd.; compare canticle gloss *winberge geallan ˎ croppas biternesse* (and variants) to *uua fellis et botri amarissimi* and variants (Cant. 7:32) in the *Arundel, Cambridge*, and *Vitellius* Psalters (similar glosses appear in other Psalters: see Pulsiano, *Old English Glossed Psalters*).

20 *Harley Glossary* C1496 (= WW 209,13) constipata .i. consita. replata. circumdata: embþrungen uel hringed (for *embhringed* = *ymbhringed*)

Not recorded by the DOE Cf. WW 48,20 (= Corp Gl [ed. Lindsay] S533) *stipatoribus: ymbhringendum*, 212,38 (= Harl Gl C1760) *conuoluit .i. cingit. circuit: embhrincþ*, and the OE *Cura pastoralis*, Hatton MS (ed. Sweet, *Version*, 111, ll. 8–9) *he bið utane ymbhringed mid ungemetlicre heringe.*

21 *Stowe Psalter* 31:7 circumdedit: ymbtrymdon ł sealdon (for *ymbsealdon*)

Not recorded by the DOE. In the *Stowe Psalter* (ed. A. C. Kimmens, *The Stowe Psalter* [Toronto, 1979]) compare 31:7 *a circumdantibus me: fram ymbsellendum me*; at Ps 87:17–18, the gloss *ymbsealdon* appears three times. OE *ymbsellan* frequently glosses Lat. *circumdare* (frequently in the 3rd pret. pl. forms): cf. *Arundel Psalter* (ed. Oess)16:9, 16:11, 17:5, 17:6, 21:13, 21:17, 39:13, 87:18, 108:3, 114:3, 117:11, 117:12, *Cambridge Psalter* (ed. K. Wildhagen, *Der Cambridger Psalter* [Hamburg, 1910]) 16:9, 17:5, 17:6, 21:3, 21:17, 39:13, 87:18, 108:3, 117:11, 117:12, *Eadwine Psalter* (ed. F. Harsley, *Eadwine's Canterbury Psalter* [London, 1889]) 87:18, etc.

B

1 *Harley Glossary* C2246 (= WW 217,7) cyrographum .i. conscriptio hominis. uel manus. manualis scriptio: gewritræden uel agnung (for *ag(e)nunggewrit*)

> Not recorded by the DOE. The lemma *cyrographum* should read *chirographum* as Oliphant has in his note; Lat. *chirographus* and *chirographon* derive from Grk. χειρόγραφος, -ον, all meaning holograph, autograph, something written in one's own hand, or a type of document meant to reproduce such a form[8] (e.g., Grk. χειρόγραφον, n., "manuscript note; note of hand, bond"; Liddell-Scott, *s.v.*). The OE noun *gewritræden* is not recorded by either BT or BTS, but Clark Hall-Meritt enters "*writræden* f. written agreement." This only roughly approximates the meaning of the lemmata. The proposed *agenunggewrit* would come nearer the sense of "handwritten note" or "document written in one's own hand." Cf. Antwerp Gl (Kindschi) B, p. 66, #11 *cirographum: raedinggewrit uel landgewrit*.

2 *Cleopatra Glossary* (Stryker) A409 (= WW 350,36) auriculum: earwicga ł dros (for *eardrōs*)

> Not recorded by the DOE; DOE, s.v. *ēar-wicga*, discusses the matching of lemma with the second gloss and notes that "other proposed senses include 'earwax'" (fasc. D, p. 690, quoting McGowan, "Lexicographical Studies"). The Latin feminine diminutive noun *auriculum* is elsewhere glossed separately by *earwicga* and *dros*; *drōs* (whence MdE *dross*) generally has to do with "waste" or "filth." Here, since *auriculum* refers to the outer ear, the more specific *eardros*, "ear wax," may be intended (cf. Charm 30 [ed. G. Storms, *Anglo-Saxon Magic* (The Hague, 1948)] *wiþ nædran slite oþþe slege. . . . Do of þinum earan þæt teoru and smyre mid ymb, . . .* , evidencing one use for "ear-dross"). Both glosses seem not so much specific as associative; *earlæppa* would be the more specific gloss to *auriculum*.

3 Aldhelm, *De laude virginitatis* [gloss] (Goossens) 4734 muncipat*us*. princi-pat*us*: burhscipe ł carding (= *earding* for MS *carding*; for *eardingscipe* = *eardungscipe*)

> Not recorded by the DOE; DOE cites only *carding* (= *earding, eardung*) part of gloss and so does not accept the expansion (fasc. B, p. 2454). Latin *principatus* is taken in a secondary sense here (compare the ME gloss

---

[8] Cf. K. A. Lowe, "Lay Literacy in Anglo-Saxon England and the Development of the Chirograph," in *Anglo-Saxon Manuscripts and their Heritage*, ed. P. Pulsiano and E. M. Treharne (Aldershot, 1998), 161–203, here 170–77.

principatus: a prinshode, at WW 683,26). The transferal of *-scipe* fills out the sense to "dominion" or "realm."

4 Plantin-Moretus MS 32 168.14 pinnulae: flaeran uel earlaeppan (for *earflaeran*)

> Not recorded by the DOE (which does, however, suggest a source in Isidore, *Etymologiae* XI.i.48 (ed. W. M. Lindsay [Oxford, 1911]). For such compounding compare *middelflere*, found glossing *interpinnium* (at WW 157,17 [= Antwerp Gl (Kindschi) B, p. 168, #15 *interpinnium uel interfinium: middelflere uel nosegristle*; cf. p. 168, #3 *internasus uel interfinium: nosegristle* and #14 *pinnulae: flaeran uel earlaeppan*], 429,41 [= Cleop Gl (Stryker) I37, where he noted: "read *middelflera*"]).

5 *Harley Glossary* C1874 concentus .i. adunationes multarum uocum: efenhleoþrung uel dream (for *efendream*)

> Not recorded by the DOE. BT, BTS, and Clark Hall-Meritt do not record the fem. abstract noun *efenhleoþrung* (< *hleoþrian*); compare *Phoenix* 621b *efenhleoþre* and Hom S 31.21 (ed. R. Willard, *Two Apocrypha in Old English Homilies* [Leipzig, 1935]) *efenhleoþriende*. For *efendream*, cf. BT s.v. *dream* II "music, rapturous music, harmony, melody, song," and the cpds. *efeneadig, efenbliðe*.

6 *Cleopatra Glossary* (Stryker) F458 fascia: feaxclað ł wræd wriðels (for *feaxwræd*)

> The OE gll. here apparently do not follow Isidore's discussion of *fascia*: '*Fascia est qua tegitur pectus et papillae conprimuntur, atque crispanti cingulo angustius pectus artatur: et dicta fascia quod in modum fasciculi corpus alligat*' (XIX.xxxiii.6, ed. Lindsay). The proposed *feaxwræd*, m., would mean "headband" or "fillet." Compare the Antwerp Gl entries *reticulum: feaxnet* (Kindschi 1955: 116) and *rigula: feaxnet* (124).

7 *Corpus Glossary* 150 (= WW 5,31) amites: fugultreo ł reftras (for *fugulreftras*)

> Not recorded by the DOE. The same lemma and glosses appear at Cleop Gl (Stryker) 357; BT's entry *fugeltras* was corrected to read *fugeltreo* in BTS; for *fugeltreo* Clark Hall-Meritt enters "prop (of a snare for birds)." OE *ræfter* refers generally to "rafter" or "beam"; the Corpus and Cleopatra glosses may be more specific: the elliptically expanded *fugelræfter* would be a prop (most probably a forked stick) for bird-nets. Lat. *ames* denotes a pole or fork "esp. for holding and spreading bird-nets" (Lewis-Short, *s.v.*), "a pole for supporting bird-nets; a rail of a post-and-rail fence, cross-bar" (OLD, s.v.). Compare, for example, Horace, *Epodon* II:

at cum tonantis annus hibernus Iovis
    imbris nivesque comparat,
aut trudit acris hinc et hinc multa cane
    apros in obstantis plagas,
aut amite levi rara tendit retia, . . . (29–33).

Then when the thundring Jove his Snow and showres
    Are gathering by the Wintry houres;
Or hence, or thence, he drives with many a Hound
    Wild Bores into his toyles pitch'd round;
Or straines on his small forke his subtill nets.[9]

OE *reftras* glosses Lat. *amites* at Corp Gl (ed. Lindsay) A533, Ep Gl (Pheifer, *Old English Glosses*) 12, Erf Gl (ed. Pheifer) 30 (*ræfter* also glosses
Lat. *lignum* and *tignum*).

8 *Harley Glossary* D646 (= WW 223,26) discipulatus: lareowdom uel leor-
nung (for *leornungdom*)

Not recorded by the DOE. The gloss *lareowdom* does not exactly fit the
lemma; the proposed cpd. renders better the notion of a state of disciple-
ship or "student-hood." Compare *leornungcræft* at *Elene* 380b.

9 *Harley Glossary* C1232 (= WW 207,1) commentarius: stærtractere. uel
hælsere. tractator. scriptor (for *stærhælsere*)

Not recorded by the DOE. Both *commentarius* and *tractator* have to do
with one who treats academic, particularly literary, matters with annotations or commentaries. OE *hælsere* is itself difficult, but alone the
word makes no sense here. Perhaps as the cpd. *stærhalsere* one could obtain the meaning "one who divines or foretells by means of a text": the
sortes Virgilianae come to mind. Compare the Aldhelm glosses *mathematicorum, i. docentium, l doctorum: tuncgelwitegana . . . tungelwite-
gene l steorgleawe, steorgleawra* (Goossens 2550), and *mathematicorum
.i. doctorum l docentium: tungelwitegana, steorgleawra* (Digby AldV,
Napier OEG: 2630), *stoicorum: stærleornera, leornera* (Goossens 4027),
and *stoicorum: stærleonera* (Digby AldV, Napier OEG 4145).

10 *Harley Glossary* C600 (= WW 202,3) cauterium: mearcisern *uel* tynder (for
tynderisern)

---

[9] The translation of Ben Jonson, published in 1640; *Horace in English*, ed. D. S.
Carne-Ross and Kenneth Haynes (Harmondsworth, 1996), 300.

Not recorded by DOE, OE *tynder* is normally glossed "tinder, fuel"; BT adds the second sense "a burner, an implement which burns," and yet it is found glossing *fomes* (at WW 241,20). Compare *mearcisern* and *stempingisern*. Since a *cauterium* is an instrument for branding, specifically a branding-iron, filling out *tynder* with -*isern* completes the sense.

Many of the peculiarities of late classical and medieval glossators have been only mentioned in passing in notes to editions of the glossaries. Elliptical compounding is just one such practice that may conceal lexicographical data in its practical desire for concision; elliptical glossing is most certainly a device for the convenience of abbreviation:

> *Harley Glossary* F59 (= WW 234,41) fallentis fortune: wægendre gesælignesse uel bepæcendre (for *bepæcendre gesælignesse*);

or

> *Harley Glossary* D613 dissero .i. narro. sepato. interpreto. manifesto. dico. disputo. declaro. expono *uel* profero.ris.e (here Lat. *proferre* is declined in the pres. sing. indic. elliptically).

Other examples of such "grammatical glossing" may be cited from the *Lambeth Psalter*: *et operatur: 7 wyrcð ł 7 byþ wyrcende* (14:2) and *apparebo: beo ætywed ł. æteowie* (16:15). Another peculiar habit of glossators may be called, for convenience's sake, "transverse glossing":

> *Lambeth Psalter* 30:9 in loco spatioso: on feld ł. on stowe bradum ł. on bradre st--- [= stowum]

> *Lambeth Psalter* 32:11 in generatione et generationem: on cnosle ł. on cynne 7 cnosle ł. 7 cynne ł. on mægþe

> *Cleopatra Glossary* (Stryker) N452 nux: hnutbeam ł wælhnutu [= WW 452,34]

These glossarial habits likely point to the sometimes extemporaneous nature of glossing; a great many glossary words are *hapax legomena*, and of these not a few may be nonce-words. The treatment of what, it may be said, the glossators chose not to spell out explicitly but abbreviated in their manuscript entries serves as an indication of how modern lexicographers read the manuscript lexica of their early medieval predecessors. The proposed elliptical compounds enumerated above (as well as those suggested by Meritt in 1938 and reviewed above) serve as an indication of one such peculiar scribal practice and may also serve to recover (or uncover) OE words once plain to the scribes, but now obscured by their methods of abbreviation.

Bibliography

The Anglo-Saxon Poetic Records: A Collective Edition [ASPR], ed. George Phillip Krapp and Elliott Van Kirk Dobbie. 6 vols. New York, 1931–1953.

Birch, Walter de Gray, ed. *Cartularium Saxonicum: A Collection of Charters Relating to Anglo-Saxon History*. London, 1885–1893.

Bosworth, Joseph, and T. Northcote Toller, *An Anglo-Saxon Dictionary* (enlarged by T. Northcote Toller). Oxford, 1898; repr. Oxford, 1989; *An Anglo-Saxon Dictionary, Supplement*, T. Northcote Toller. Oxford, 1921; repr. Oxford, 1980; enlarged addenda and corrigenda by Alistair Campbell. Oxford, 1972.

Bouterwek, Karl Wilhelm, "Angelsächsische Glossen. 1. Die ags. Glossen in dem Brusseler Codex von Aldhelms Schrift *de virginitate*." *Zeitschrift für deutsches Alterthum* 9 (1853): 401–530.

Campbell, A. P., ed. *The Tiberius Psalter, edited from British Museum MS Cotton Tiberius C vi*. Ottawa, 1974.

Campbell, Alistair, *Old English Grammar*. Oxford, 1959.

Clark Hall, J. R. *A Concise Anglo-Saxon Dictionary*. 4th ed. with a supplement by Herbert Dean Meritt. Toronto, 1984.

Cockayne, T. O. *Leechdoms, Wortcunning, and Starcraft of Early England*. 3 vols. London, 1864–1866.

Dictionary of Old English [DOE], ed. Angus Cameron, Ashley Crandall Amos, Antonette diPaolo Healey, et al. Toronto, 1986– . Fascicle *D* (1986), *C* (1988), *B* (1991), *Bēon* (1992), *Æ* (1992), *A* (1994), *E* (1996). *Dictionary of Old English A–F*. Version 1.0. July 2003 (electronic version).

Glare, P. G. W. *Oxford Latin Dictionary*, repr. with corrs. Oxford, 1996.

Goossens, Louis. *The Old English Glosses of MS. Brussels, Royal Library, 1650 (Aldhelm's De Laudibus Virginitatis*. Brussels, 1974.

Gough, J. V. "Some Old English Glosses." *Anglia* 92 (1974): 273–90.

Grattan, J. H. G. and Charles Singer, *Anglo-Saxon Magic and Medicine*. London, 1952.

Harsley, Fred, ed. *Eadwine's Canterbury Psalter*. London, 1889.

Herzfeld, George, ed. *An OE Martyrology: Re-edited from mss in the Libraries of the British Museum and Corpus Christi College, Cambridge*. London, 1900.

Hessels, Jan Hendryk, ed. *A Late Eighth-Century Latin-Anglo-Saxon Glossary preserved in the Library of Leiden Univ*. Cambridge, 1906.

Holthausen, Ferdinand. "Die Leidener Glossen." *Englische Studien* 50 (1916–1917): 327–40.

―――. *Altenglisches Etymologisches Wörterbuch*. 3rd ed. Heidelberg, 1934; repr. Heidelberg, 1974.

Kimmens, Andrew C., ed. *The Stowe Psalter*. Toronto, 1979.

Kindschi, Lowell. "The Latin-Old English Glossaries in Plantin-Moretus MS 32 and British Museum Additional 32,246." Ph.D. diss., Stanford University, 1955.

Klaeber, Friedrich, ed., *Beowulf and the Fight at Finnsburg*. 3rd ed. with 1st and 2nd supplements. Lexington, MA, 1950.

Kuypers, Dom A. B., ed. *The Prayer Book of Aedeluald the Bishop, Commonly Called The Book of Cerne*. Cambridge, 1902.

Lapidge, Michael. "Some Old English Sedulius Glosses from B.N. lat. 8092." *Anglia* 100 (1982): 1–17.

Law, Vivian. "The Latin and Old English Glosses in the *Ars Tatuini*." *Anglo-Saxon England* 6 (1977): 77–89.

Lewis, Charlton T., and Charles Short. *A New Latin Dictionary*. New York, 1907.

Liddell, Henry George, Robert Scott, and Henry Stuart Jones. *Greek-English Lexicon with a Revised Supplement*. Oxford, 1996.

Liebermann, Felix. *Die Gesetze der Angelsachsen*. 3 vols. Halle, 1903–1916.

Lindelöf, Uno. , *Der Lambeth-Psalter: Eine altenglische Interlinearversion des Psalters in der Hs. 427 der erzbischöflichen Lambeth Palace Library*, vol. 1: *Text und Glossar*. Helsinki, 1909.

Lindsay, W. M., ed. *Isidori Hispalensis Episcopi Etymologiarum sive Originum Libri XX*. 2 vols. Oxford, 1911.

―――. *The Corpus Glossary*. Cambridge, 1921.

Logeman, Henri, ed. *The Rule of St. Benet, Latin and Anglo-Saxon, Interlinear Version*. London, 1888.

Lowe, K. A. "Lay Literacy in Anglo-Saxon England and the Development of the Chirograph." In *Anglo-Saxon Manuscripts and their Heritage*, ed. P. Pulsiano and E. M. Treharne, 161–203. Aldershot, 1998.

McGowan, Joseph P. "Old English Lexicographical Studies." Ph.D. diss., University of Pennsylvania, 1991.

―――. "Praefanda Anglosaxonica." *Studia Neophilologica* 75 (2003): 3–10.

Meritt, Herbert Dean. "Old English Scratched Glosses in Cotton MS. Tiberius C, ii." *American Journal of Philology* 54 (1933): 305–22.

———. "Possible Elliptical Compounds in Old English Glosses." *American Journal of Philology* 59 (1938): 209–17.

———. *Old English Glosses (A Collection)*. New York, 1945.

A Microfiche Concordance to Old English. Toronto, 1985.

Mynors, R. A. B., ed. *C. Plinii Caecili Secundi epistularum libri decem*. Oxford, 1963.

Napier, A. S. *Wulfstan*. Berlin, 1883.

———. *History of the Holy Rood-Tree, A Twelfth Century Version of the Cross Legend*. London, 1894.

———. *Old English Glosses, Chiefly Unpublished*. Oxford, 1900; repr. Hildesheim, 1969.

Oess, Guido, ed. *Der altenglische Arundel-Psalter: Eine Interlinearversion in der Handschrift Arundel 60 des Britischen Museum*. Heidelberg, 1910; repr. Amsterdam, 1968.

Oliphant, Robert T., ed. *The Harley Latin-Old English Glossary*. The Hague, 1966.

Page, R. I. "More Old English Scratched Glosses." *Anglia* 97 (1979): 27–45.

Peterson, P. W. "The Unpublished Homilies of the Vercelli Book." Ph.D. diss., New York University, 1950.

Pheifer, J. D. *Old English Glosses in the Épinal-Erfurt Glossary*. Oxford, 1974.

Pulsiano, Phillip. *Old English Glossed Psalters: Psalms 1–50*. Toronto, 2001.

Quinn, John Joseph. "The Minor Latin-Old English Glossaries in MS. Cotton Cleopatra A III." Ph.D. diss., Stanford University, 1956.

Rhodes, E. W., ed. *Defensor's Liber Scintillarum, with an Interlinear Anglo-Saxon Version Made in the Eleventh Century*. London, 1889.

Skeat, W. W. *The Holy Gospels in Anglo-Saxon, Northumbrian, and Old Mercian Versions*. Cambridge, 1871–1887.

Steinmeyer, Elias, and Eduard Sievers. *Die althochdeutschen Glossen*. 5 vols. Berlin, 1879–1922.

Storms, Godfrid. *Anglo-Saxon Magic*. The Hague, 1948.

Stracke, J. Richard. *The Laud Herbal Glossary*. Amsterdam, 1974.

Stryker, William Garlington. "The Latin-Old English Glossary in MS Cotton Cleopatra A III." Ph.D. diss., Stanford University, 1951.

Sweet, Henry, ed. *King Alfred's West-Saxon Version of Gregory's 'Pastoral Care'*. London, 1871–1872.

Thompson, A. H., and Uno Lindelöf, eds. *Rituale ecclesiae Dunelmensis.* Durham, 1927.

Toth, Karl. "Altenglische Interlinearglossen zu Prospers *Epigrammata* und *Versus ad coniugem.*" *Anglia* 102 (1984): 1–36.

Turner, A. G. C. "Some Old English Passages Relating to the Episcopal Manor of Taunton." *Proceedings of the Somersetshire Archaeological and Natural History Society* 98 (1953): 118–26.

Willard, R. *Two Apocrypha in Old English Homilies.* Leipzig, 1935.

Wright, Thomas, and R. P. Wülcker. *Anglo-Saxon and Old English Vocabularies.* 2 vols. London, 1884; repr. Darmstadt, 1968.

Zupitza, Julius, ed. *Aelfrics Grammatik und Glossar.* Berlin, 1880; repr. Darmstadt, 1966.

Abraham Wheelock and the Presentation of Anglo-Saxon: From Manuscript to Print

Peter J. Lucas

Encouraged by James Ussher (1581–1656), archbishop of Armagh, Sir Henry Spelman (1564?–1641), much interested in Anglo-Saxon antiquities and impressed by the richness of their preservation in Cambridge, established an Anglo-Saxon Lectureship in the University, to which Abraham Wheelock was appointed from 1638 until his death. Wheelock (1593–1653) was a Shropshire lad who went up to Cambridge in 1611, where he was resident at Trinity College, graduating BA in 1614, and MA in 1618. He then went to Clare College, as a Fellow from 1619 until his marriage in 1632, being ordained a deacon in 1619 and a priest in 1622, when he became vicar of St Sepulchre's church, and graduated BD in 1624.[1] In 1629 he was appointed University Librarian,

---

ABBREVIATIONS: BL = London, British Library; CUL = Cambridge University Library; CCC = Corpus Christi College, Cambridge; CSJ = St John's College, Cambridge; CSS = Sidney Sussex College, Cambridge; CTH = Trinity Hall, Cambridge; OBL= Oxford, Bodleian Library; STC = Alfred W. Pollard and Gilbert R. Redgrave, *A Short-Title Catalogue of Books printed in England, Scotland & Ireland and of English Books printed abroad 1475–1640*, 2nd ed., 3 vols., rev. William A. Jackson and F. S. Ferguson (London, 1976–1991); TCC = Trinity College, Cambridge; *TSF II* = Hendrik D. L. Vervliet and Harry Carter, *Type Specimen Facsimiles II* (London, 1972); Wing = Donald G. Wing, *Short-Title Catalogue of Books Printed in England, Scotland, Ireland, Wales, British America and of English Books printed in Other Countries 1641–1700*, 1st ed., 3 vols. (New York, 1945–1951); 2nd ed., 4 vols., rev. Timothy J. Crist, John J. Morrison, Carolyn W. Nelson, and Matthew Seccombe (New York, 1982–1998).

[1] There is a good account of Wheelock, to which the present study is indebted, by John C. T. Oates, *Cambridge University Library: A History. From the Beginnings to the Copyright Act of Queen Anne* (Cambridge, 1986), chaps. 7–8. These chapters were based on the Sandars Lectures in Bibliography which Oates delivered at Cambridge University in 1966: *Abraham Whelock (1593–1653): Orientalist, Anglo-Saxonist, & University Librarian*, unpublished typescript deposited in CUL at Cam.b.966.2. For the spelling of Wheelock's name I have preferred that which he and Spelman used in almost all instances in English. Cf. Gerald J. Toomer, *Eastern Wisedome and Learning: The Study of Arabic in Seventeenth-Century England* (Oxford, 1996), 86, n. 151.

a post not sufficiently lucrative at that time to be the sole means of support for someone in Wheelock's position.[2] Spurred on by this stimulus Wheelock took up Spelman's invitation to become his Anglo-Saxon assistant in Cambridge in 1637. As part of the arrangements pertaining to his Anglo-Saxon lectureship he became vicar of Middleton (Norfolk) in 1638, which was in Spelman's patronage.[3] His character was that of a "humble and affable man",[4] a conscientious scholar, willing to please and in need of regular reassurance from his patrons, constantly (over)-anxious about money, modest and somewhat nervous of political instability. He was notably reluctant to travel. In a letter to Sir Symonds D'Ewes of 26 January 1640 (in BL Harley 374, fol. 129r), Wheelock assures D'Ewes that he would come to see him if he were not so busy in Cambridge with his Arabic and his Anglo-Saxon work;[5] and just seventeen days later, in a letter to Sir Henry Spelman of 12 February 1640 (in BL Add. MS. 34600, fol. 209v), Wheelock assures Spelman, who had recently had a fall, that he would have come to see him in the Barbican (London) if his wife had not been ill. Nearly all his extant letters were written from Cambridge.[6] His handwriting, however, is firm and purposeful if not particularly neat (see Fig. 12.1). Many books that he used have an embryonic index of contents of

---

[2] Oates calculates that Wheelock's income from this post would have been about £17 per year (Oates, *Cambridge University Library*, 184). The basic stipend was £3 6s 8d. At the same time the remuneration for the library keeper of Trinity College Dublin was £3: see Lydia Ferguson, "*Custodes librorum*: Service, Staff and Salaries 1601–1855," in *Essays on the History of Trinity College Library, Dublin*, ed. Vincent Kinane and Anne Walsh (Dublin, 2000), 25–38, here 26–27.

[3] On the church and parish, including Wheelock's incumbency, see Francis Blomefield and Charles Parkin, *An Essay towards a Topographical History of the County of Norfolk*, 11 vols. (London, 1805–1810), 9: 30–32.

[4] This quotation is from a brief memorial character-sketch recorded by Thomas Baker in CUL, MS Mm.1.44, p. 476, as being supplied by Wheelock's daughter from an unknown author. William Sclater, *The Crowne of Righteousnes* (London, John Grismond for John Clarke 1, 1654), Wing S916, includes an encomium on the occasion of his funeral: see 27–34.

[5] For Wheelock's work on Arabic see Toomer, *Eastern Wisedome*, 86–93.

[6] MSS containing Wheelock's letters are to be found in BL, MSS Additional 34600, 34601, CUL Dd.3.64, OBL Tanner 67, 70 (to Spelman), BL Harley 374 (to D'Ewes), and CUL Dd.3.12 (Spelman to Wheelock). BL, MS. Harley 7041 contains transcripts by Thomas Baker (s.xviii[1]) of the letters in CUL Dd.3.12; it was from that manuscript (Harley 7041) that the selected letters printed by Sir Henry Ellis (*Original Letters of Eminent Literary Men of the Sixteenth, Seventeenth, and Eighteenth Centuries*, Camden Society I.23 [London, 1843]) were taken. A further (later) series of transcripts survives in CUL Additional MS. 7596. One letter, not present in CUL Dd.3.12, survives in Harley 7041. See Appendix.

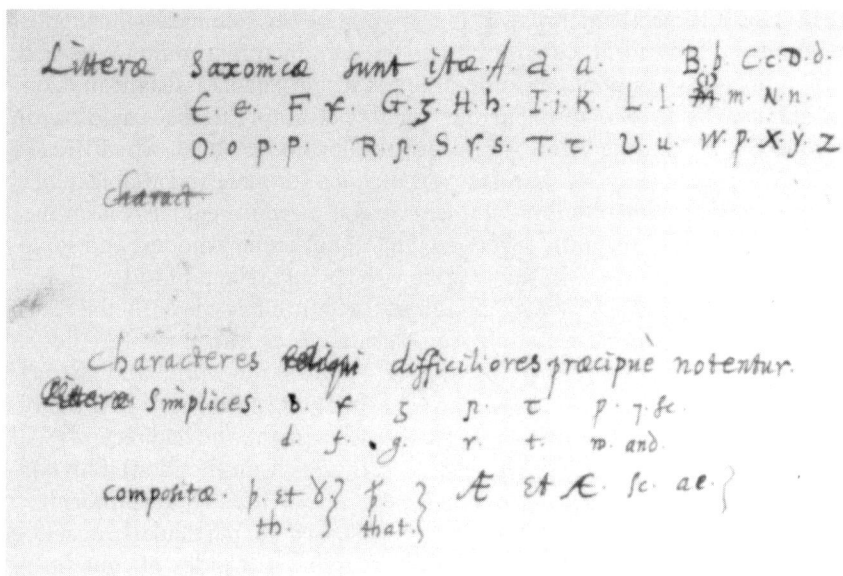

Figure 12.1: BL Add. 34600, fol. 211r: Wheelock's handwritten Anglo-Saxon alphabet (*by permission of the British Library*)

interest to him at the front and/or back. He was a productive scholar. Only six years after his recruitment by Spelman he produced what he is deservedly well known for, his edition of the Anglo-Saxon version of Bede's *Historia Ecclesiastica*, to which Wheelock added an edition of the *Anglo-Saxon Chronicle*, all published in 1643, and for his re-edition of the Anglo-Saxon Laws (the *Archaionomia*, previously edited by William Lambarde in 1568) published in 1644; the two were then combined in a single publication later in 1644.[7]

These books were printed by Roger Daniel (1593?–1667), bookseller and printer in London 1620?–1629?, 1650–1666, and Printer to Cambridge University

---

[7] Abraham Wheelock, ed., William Lambarde's *Archaionomia, sive de Priscis Anglorum Legibus libri* (Cambridge, Roger Daniel for Cornelius Bee [London], 1644), Wing A3605; idem, ed., *Historiæ Ecclesiasticæ Gentis Anglorum Libri V a Venerabili Beda Presbytero scripti; Chronologia Anglo-Saxonica* (Cambridge, Roger Daniel, 1643), Wing B1661; idem, ed., *Historiæ Ecclesiasticæ Gentis Anglorum Libri V a Venerabili Beda Presbytero scripti; Quibus in calce operis Saxonicam Chronologiam, seriem hujus inprimis Historiæ complectentem, nunquam antea in lucem editam, nunc quoque primò Latinè versam contexuimus; Quibus accesserunt Anglo-Saxonicæ Leges, et ultimò, Leges Henrici I nunc primùm editæ* (Cambridge, Roger Daniel for Cornelius Bee [London], 1644), Wing B1662.

1632–1650.[8] To provide the contents with what was considered to be the appropriate style and authenticity of appearance a new Great Primer Anglo-Saxon for the appropriate special sorts was cut to Wheelock's specification (see Fig. 12.2). In the manuscript age the style of script communicated to the contemporary reader part of its meaning (particularly the status of the text

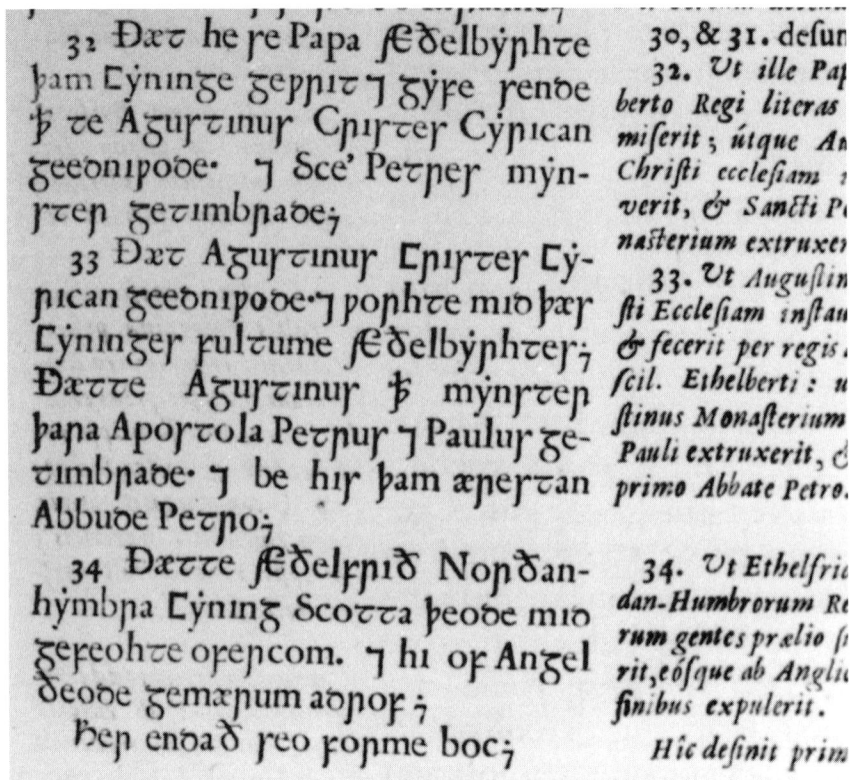

Figure 12.2: Wheelock 1643: D1v (p.10): Text of chapter headings to Bede's *Ecclesiastical History* set in the Wheelockian Great Primer Anglo-Saxon (CUL Pet.A.7.7) (*by permission of the Canon Librarian of Peterborough Cathedral*)

---

[8] David A. McKitterick, *A History of Cambridge University Press, Volume 1: Printing and the Book Trade in Cambridge 1534–1698* (Cambridge, 1992), 168–93, 296–306.

involved).[9] In the age of print it was a tacit assumption (articulated much later) that the type-design used should be in direct accord with the content of what was being printed.[10] To quote John Flood, "Typography is an integral part of the message."[11] Flood's example of a contemporary German graphic poem, "Jetzt", printed entirely in present-day type-designs illustrates the point very neatly. Through his personal touch a designer can also exert a more purposive influence on the typeface.[12] For textual material the age of which is an important aspect of its authoritative appeal, a style mimicking the appearance of letter-forms in authentic manuscripts is very appropriate. Henri-Jean Martin has noted that typography could confer on texts "superstar status: they became codified heralds of an archaeologized knowledge written in dead languages,"[13] an interpretation of typographic power that Martin applied to Latin texts, but is perhaps more appropriate to any attempt to recreate in print the authentic appearance of an archaic form of language such as Anglo-Saxon. As Lotte Hellinga has put it, "typography is the way of expressing . . . cultural allegiance."[14]

Wheelock's Great Primer Anglo-Saxon shows thirty special sorts (including the raised point used for punctuation), with an exceptionally large

---

[9] For discussion see Lucien Febvre and Henri-Jean Martin, *The Coming of the Book: The Impact of Printing 1450–1800*, trans. David Gerard, ed. Geoffrey Nowell-Smith and David Wooton (London, 1976), 78–80. For an overview of the transition from manuscript to printed book see Margaret M. Smith, "The Design Relationship between the Manuscript and the Incunable," in *A Millennium of the Book: Production, Design and Illustration in Manuscript and Print 900–1900*, ed. Robin Myers and Michael Harris (Winchester, 1994), 23–43. For valuable discussion of letter-forms in manuscript and printed book see Stanley Morison, *Selected Essays in the History of Letter-Forms in Manuscript and Print*, ed. David McKitterick, 2 vols. (Cambridge, 1981).

[10] For the concept of the congeniality of the typeface see, e.g., Bror Zachrisson, *Studies in the Legibility of Printed Text*, Stockholm Studies in Educational Psychology 11 (Stockholm, 1965), 76–78. He dates the first articulation of the idea that design should be in accord with content to 1897. Cf. also his discussion of functional considerations (74–76).

[11] John L. Flood, "Nationalistic Currents in Early German Typography," *The Library* 6.15 (1993): 125–41, here 125. For discussion see also Lotte Hellinga, "Printing," in *The Cambridge History of the Book in Britain*, vol. 3, *1400–1557*, ed. eadem and J. B. Trapp (Cambridge, 1999), 65–108, here 71–72.

[12] Cf. Zachrisson, *Studies in the Legibility*, 78.

[13] Henri-Jean Martin, *The History and Power of Writing*, trans. Lydia G. Cochrane (Chicago, 1995), 232.

[14] Lotte Hellinga, "The Bookshop of the World: Books and their Makers as Agents of Cultural Change," in *The Bookshop of the World: The Role of the Low Countries in the Book-Trade 1473–1941*, ed. eadem, Alastair Duke, Jacob Harskamp, and Theo Hermans ('t Goy-Houton, 2001), 11–29, here 12.

A a	N n	
B b	O o	Æ æ
C c	P p	Ð Th ⎰ *Propriè reor pronunciand_a_
Ꝺ ꝺ	Q q	ut Ө in Өıðς, & th in
Ɛ E e	R ꞃ r	ð th ⎱ thing _Anglicé_.
F ꝼ f	S ꞅ ſ	
Ꞡ G ᵹ g	Ꞇ ꞇ t	þ th ⎰ *tanquam* th in **that** vel
Ƕ H h	V Ᵹ u	this, _sed confunduntur_
J ı	Ᵽ p w	hi characteres à scri-
K k	X x	ptoribus.
L l	Y ẏ	
Ꝏ m	Z z	ꝥ that.
		⁊ and
		• comma
		; periodus.

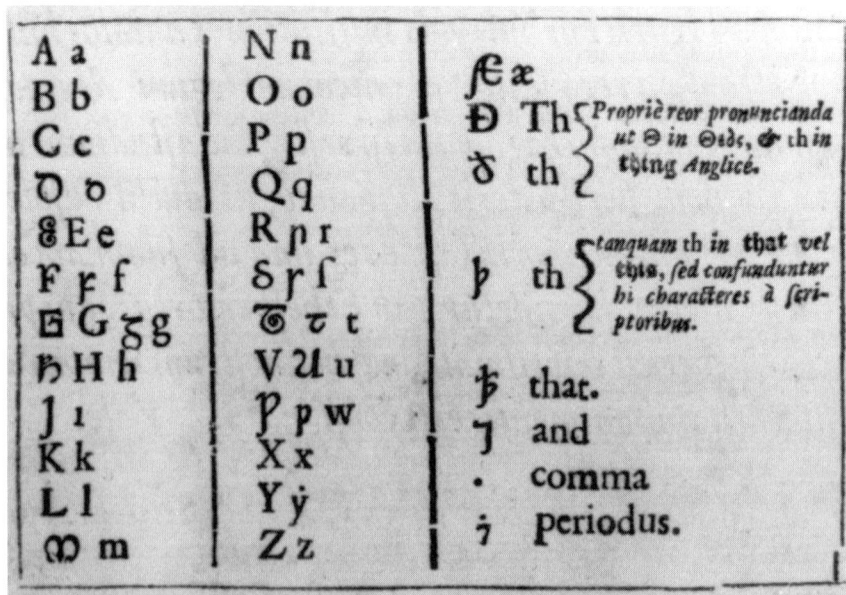

Figure 12.3: Wheelock 1644:¶6v: Reader's Specimen of Anglo-Saxon Sorts, excluding square C (CCC D.3.22²) (*by permission of the Master and Fellows of Corpus Christi College, Cambridge*)

number of capitals (see Fig. 12.3). This set of designs was being cut in London by early 1640, as indicated by a letter from Wheelock to Sir Symonds D'Ewes dated 30 March 1640:

> Typographus noster \ Rogerus Daniel / ... iam nauiter adlaborat monumentis Saxonicis imprimendis. Characteres iam Londini, et politi, ut spero, aut ornantur, aut in ornatu sunt.

> "Our printer, Roger Daniel, is now actively working on printing the Saxon records. The characters are being fitted out now in London, as I hope, and are being got ready or are in preparation." (BL, MS. Harley 374, fol. 143r)[15]

[15] Printed in John Nichols, *Bibliotheca Topographica Britannica*, 8 vols. (London, 1780–1790), 6.2:78.

On 29 April 1641 Wheelock wrote to Spelman:

> Most honored Sir, had not Mr Daniel o^ur printer two seueral times returned to London without my knowlege, on whose courtesie for the deliuerie of my Letters, I wholie depended, I had written a month before. I vnderstand by Mr Daniel, what paines yo^ur w⟨o⟩r⟨shi⟩p hath taken about the Saxon types, in instructing the grauener, for w⟨hi⟩^ch I am much bound to giue you^r w⟨o⟩r⟨shi⟩p thankes. (BL, Additional MS. 34601, fol. 46r)

Evidently Sir Henry Spelman was the source of funds to pay for this new set of type-designs, "instructing" the punchcutter ("grauener").[16] The only known punchcutter in London at that time is Arthur Nicholls, who was active 1632–1653, being one of the four typefounders named in the Star Chamber Decree of 1637.[17] To ascertain the possibility that Nicholls may have cut the Wheelockian Great Primer Anglo-Saxon it is necesssary to go forward in time and work backward. In the Sale-Catalogue of the typefoundry of John James printed in 1782 the Wheelockian Great Primer Anglo-Saxon is one of four Anglo-Saxon fonts shown;[18] the other three are the Spelmanian Great Primer (used for Spelman's *Concilia* of 1639),[19] the Somnerian Pica (used for Somner's *Dictionarium* of 1659),[20] and the Thwaitesian Small Pica (used for Benson's *Vocabularium* of 1701).[21] According to Edward Rowe Mores a Great

---

[16] *OED*, s.v. 'instruct,' v., sense 3: 'To furnish with authoritative directions as to actions . . . ; to direct, command', recorded from 1557. Oates, *Cambridge University Library*, 204 says that Spelman "assisted in their design", but I know of no evidence for this interpretation; the error is taken over by Graham Parry, *The Trophies of Time: English Antiquarians of the Seventeenth Century* (Oxford, 1995), 181, n. 34. The identification of Spelman as the paymaster of the Anglo-Saxon type partly answers the puzzlement of McKitterick, *A History*, 191–92 as to "how the Bede was financed: its Saxon type alone was a considerable investment, for which Daniel was never to find further use."

[17] *A Decree of Starre-Chamber, concerning printing* (London, Robert Barker and assignees of John Bill 1, 1637), G4^v; STC 7757. On Nicholls see John A. Lane, "Arthur Nicholls and his Greek Type for the King's Printing House," *The Library* 6.13 (1991): 297–322.

[18] *A Catalogue and Specimen of the Large and Extensive Printing-Type-Foundery of the late ingenious Mr. John James, Letter-Founder, formerly of Bartholomew-Close, London, deceased*, improved by Edward Rowe Mores, facsimile between pp.104/105 in Edward Mores, *A Dissertation upon English Typographical Founders and Founderies* (1778), ed. Harry Carter amd Christopher Ricks, Oxford Bibliographical Society n.s. 9 (Oxford, 1961), E1^v (= p.[14]), no. 51 (111).

[19] Sir Henry Spelman, *Concilia, Decreta, Leges, Constitvtiones, in re Ecclesiarum Orbis Britannici* (London, Richard Badger 1, 1639), STC 23066.

[20] William Somner, *Dictionarium Saxonico-Latino-Anglicum* (Oxford, William Hall for Daniel White [London], 1659), Wing U163.

[21] Thomas Benson, *Vocabularium Anglo-Saxonicum* (Oxford, Sheldonian Theatre, 1701).

Primer Anglo-Saxon and a Pica Anglo-Saxon came to James from the Grover foundry,[22] Thomas Grover having worked as an apprentice ("servant") for Nicholas Nicholls (son of Arthur); Grover probably succeeded to Nicholls's business.[23] The Pica is the Somnerian Pica, delivered to Oxford University by Nicholas Nicholls in 1656. The identity of the Great Primer that Grover passed on to the James foundry is not clear: it could be either the Spelmanian or the Wheelockian set of designs; Lane assumes it is the Wheelockian,[24] but there is no evidence either way. In fact Arthur Nicholls is the only known candidate as punchcutter for both, unless his son Nicholas was a punchcutter by this time. Although this evidence "is hardly proof that [Arthur] Nicholls himself was responsible for the type used by Daniel in 1643,"[25] it is suggestive.

The Wheelockian Great Primer Anglo-Saxon first occurs in two verse compositions using Anglo-Saxon words offered as contributions to a book of verses published on behalf of Cambridge University to celebrate Charles I's return from Scotland in November 1641.[26] One is by Wheelock, and the other is by William Retchford, a member of Wheelock's college, Clare. Evidently Daniel's efforts to have the completed new designs delivered to Cambridge in 1641 were successful. In the Anglo-Saxon *Bede* and Anglo-Saxon *Chronicle* of 1643 and in the Anglo-Saxon Laws of 1644 they are used in combination with Ameet Tavernier's Great Primer Roman,[27] the same Roman as that used in Spelman's *Concilia* of 1639. Apart from this flurry of activity in Cambridge the Wheelockian set of Anglo-Saxon type-designs occurs only in Marchamont Nedham's English translation of John Selden's *Mare Clausum*, entitled *Of the Dominion, or, Ownership of the Sea*, printed by William Du-Gard in London in 1652 (Wing S2432); presumably Du-Gard acquired these types from Roger Daniel after the latter moved his business to London in 1650. After this publication the Wheelockian set of type-designs disappears from view, apart from a reissue of Du-Gard's printing in 1663 (Wing S2431). The life-span of this type-design was just twelve years (1641–1652). A curiosity occurs in the posthumous 1678 publication of Sir John Spelman's *Ælfredi Magni Anglorum Regis Invicissimi Vita*, ed. Obadiah Walker (aided by Christopher Wase), published

---

[22] Mores, *A Dissertation*, 44–45.

[23] Michael Treadwell, "The Grover Typefoundery," *Journal of the Printing Historical Society* 15 (1980/1981): 36–53, here 37–38.

[24] Lane, "Arthur Nicholls," 305.

[25] David J. McKitterick, *Four Hundred Years of University Printing and Publishing in Cambridge 1584–1984: Catalogue of the Exhibition in the University Library Cambridge* (Cambridge, 1984), 54, item 45; cf. McKitterick, *A History*, 190.

[26] Richard Holdsworth, ed., *Irenodia Cantabrigiensis ob Paciferum Serenissimi Regis Caroli è Scotia Reditum* (Cambridge, Roger Daniel, 1641), Wing C340, A4r, G4r.

[27] Hendrik D. L. Vervliet, *Sixteenth-Century Printing Types of the Low Countries* (Amsterdam, 1968), R20, here occurring with some mixed sorts.

in Oxford at the Sheldonian Theatre (Wing S4934): the Anglo-Saxon type-design used was the Somnerian Pica acquired by the nascent Oxford University Press, but three instances of the Wheelockian Great Primer Anglo-Saxon capital E occur amongst the Somnerian Pica types on 2P2r, 2Q1v, 2Q2.

Tavernier's Great Primer Roman (116 x 2.3: 3.5),[28] with which the Wheelockian Great Primer Anglo-Saxon is combined, first appeared in 1553, and was used widely, reaching London in 1555, Lisbon in 1556, and India (Goa) in 1561. It "is frequent in English books of the 17th century," showing the distinctive letter-forms E, F, L with longer serifs, and the "backward-tilted counters of b, d, p, q".[29] Combined with this Roman (and some other sorts mixed in; see Figure 12.4) the body size of the Wheelockian Great Primer Anglo-Saxon is

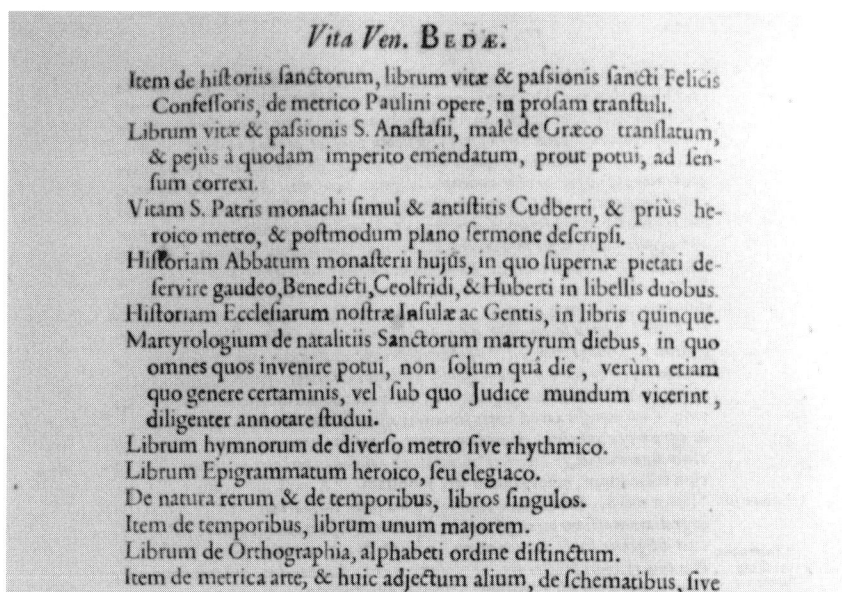

Figure 12.4: Wheelock 1643: B4r (reduced): Part of the list of Bede's works set in Ameet Tavernier's Great Primer Roman (with some mixed sorts) (CUL Cam.a.643) (*by permission of the Syndics of Cambridge University Library*)

---

[28] The convention used follows that explained by Philip Gaskell, *A New Introduction to Bibliography* (Oxford, 1972), 12–16. The first figure is the distance from the top of an ascender to the bottom of a descender multiplied by 20 to obtain the face size corresponding to the body size. The second figure is the x-height of a letter, and the third figure is the height of a capital letter.

[29] Vervliet, *Sixteenth-Century Printing Types*, 254–55.

118 mm for twenty lines: face 116 x 2.3: 3.5 (varies for different capitals). The following special sorts are shown: 12 (lower case) d, e, f, g, i, r, s, t, y; þ, ð, p + 14 (upper case) Æ², C, D, E, F, G, H, I, M, S, T, U, Ð, Ᵹ; + 4 (others) þ,], 7, ˙ (raised point) = 30 sorts. All are shown in the reader's specimen on Fig. 12.3, including the raised point (called a "comma"), except square C, which can be seen in the text of Bede along with many other sorts (including Roman C and G) on Fig. 12.2, where the use of the raised point is also illustrated.

The earlier, sixteenth-century, designs for Anglo-Saxon types exerted a profound influence on later designs, but some seventeenth-century fonts show additional special sorts, and here the influence of continuing contact with manuscripts can potentially be traced. These additional special sorts tend to be capitals. Square C was first used in the Spelmanian set of designs of 1639, where it is the only new sort in that font, created somewhat crudely by taking a Roman E and breaking off the middle arm. Square G first occurs in the Wheelockian set of designs in 1643. Both occur in Anglo-Saxon manuscripts as secondary display capitals in, for example, Cambridge, Corpus Christi College MS. 173, containing the A-version of the *Anglo-Saxon Chronicle* and some Laws (see Fig. 12.5), a manuscript certainly used by Wheelock, and possibly by

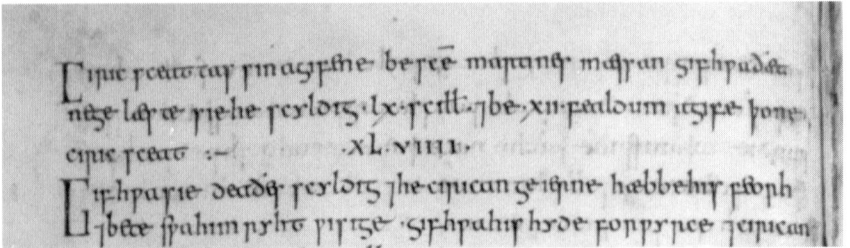

Figure 12.5: CCC, MS. 173, fol. 47v (reduced), Anglo-Saxon Laws of Ine 4–5, ed. Liebermann, *Gesetze*, 1: 90 (*by permission of the Master and Fellows of Corpus Christi College, Cambridge*)

Spelman. Wheelock, Junius, and the Somnerian font use both square C and square G. In the Wheelockian font there are more special sort capitals than in any of these others. The presence of these extra specially-designed letters creates the presumption that Wheelock was sensitive to the graphic form of script letters. In what follows, on the basis that correspondences can be observed between Wheelock's usage and that of the relevant manuscripts, I shall try to characterize the distinctive features of the Wheelockian Great Primer Anglo-Saxon with a view to defining which features show manuscript influence. As will be evident my concern is with what Michael Twyman called the intrinsic (as opposed to the extrinsic) features of verbal graphic language: the range of characters, the font, the style of letter-forms, and the size of letter-forms.[30]

In describing the features of the type-design I follow as far as possible the terminology given for roman type by Philip Gaskell,[31] which is invaluable. According to Gaskell roman letter-forms show stems, diagonals, bowls, counters, strokes, shoulders, arms, tails, spurs, ears, terminals, and serifs. In his "Glossary of Terms," but not in his diagrammatic descriptions of the letters, he also uses the terms ascenders and descenders, which are part of the paleographer's armory, and certainly essential. Gaskell recognized that his nomenclature would require modification for dealing with type-faces other than roman, e.g., italic, and this limitation applies particularly to Anglo-Saxon, since some of the letters are not roman. Gaskell's nomenclature, moreover, was not intended to describe the transition from script to print. Where writing is fluid, produced by the movement of the nib on smooth membrane or paper, type is fixed, the product of sculpting in metal. One of the main differences between humanistic script (of the period just before the development of roman type) and roman type is that, where letters written with the quill show a hooked terminal, either where the nib is led into the stroke, or where the nib is drawn away and lifted from the stroke,[32] letters in roman type show serifs. When a serif was made with a quill it required a separate stroke crossing the main stroke which it introduces or terminates, and the nib had to be held at a different angle.[33] Gaskell's term "hooked terminal" is valuable in that it gives a separate name for the part of the stroke that in type

---

[30] Michael Twyman's distinction between intrinsic and extrinsic features of verbal graphic language ("The Graphic Presentation of Language," *Information Design Journal* 3 [1982]: 2–22, here 11–14) has the merit of being non-judgmental. Scholars interested in the *mise en texte*, the disposition of text in relation to space on the page (i.e., extrinsic features), have referred to "la forme des signes graphiques, ce qui caractérise en réalité la page" as constituting "en quelque sorte le substrat," but this seems to me to be special pleading (cf. Carla Bozzolo, Dominique Coq, Denis Muzerelle, and Enzio Ornato, "Page savante, page vulgaire: Étude comparative de la mise en page des livres en latin et en français écrits ou imprimés en France au XVe siècle," in *La Présentation du Livre*, ed. Emmanuèle Baumgartner and Nicole Boulestreau [Paris, 1987], 122–33, here 131).

[31] Philip Gaskell, "A Nomenclature for the Letter-forms of Roman Type," *The Library* 5.29 (1974): 42–51.

[32] Cf. Harry Carter, *A View of Early Typography up to about 1600* (Oxford, 1969), 48; Juliet Twomey, "Whence Jenson. A Search for the Origins of Roman Type," *Fine Print* 15 (1989): 134–41.

[33] When it was done it was often done sporadically to begin with (cf. Geoffrey D. Hargreaves, "Florentine Script, Paduan Script, and Roman Type," *Gutenberg Jahrbuch* 67 [1992]: 15–34, here 17: re. Florence), although more thoroughly subsequently (26: re. Padua).

is the equivalent of the written approach-stroke or termination-stroke. But it lacks the precision of paleographical usage, which refers, for example, to descenders turned to the left, a description which, besides indicating that the terminal is hooked, states in which direction it is hooked. With these caveats in mind we can proceed.

Given the precedents from previous fonts, the Parkerian Great Primer, the Parkerian Pica, the Lambardian Pica (which also appears in Wheelock's edition of the Anglo-Saxon Laws in the *Glossarium* on 2E1r–4r),[34] and the Spelmanian Great Primer, there is nothing remarkable about the range of sorts selected for representation in the Wheelockian lower case; as in the Lambardian Pica, tongued **e** is included. But the impact made by the font as a whole is distinctive. From the Anglo-Saxon letters there is a general impression of sinuosity (see Fig. 12.2). In addition to the expected curves in the bowls, shoulders, and tails of the relevant letters, there are a number of hooked terminals, as to **d** (ascender), **g** (approach stroke to upper arm), **t** (approach stroke to upper arm), all to the right, and to the left, **f** (descender), **r** (descender), **s** (descender, and upper stroke rolled right over), and **p** (descender). Hooked terminals in such numbers are more characteristic of script than type-design. There is a suggestion of attention to detail in the mimicking of a particular script feature in the way the ascender of **ð** is tagged to the left. Studies of early type-design have shown that "the correct imitation of the best writing was the commonly understood goal,"[35] and there is every reason to suppose that the same approach applies in Wheelock's case.

In the development of roman type-design the upper-case letters were based on classical Latin inscriptional forms with serifs at the terminals.[36] The

---

[34] For the Parkerian Great Primer, see Peter J. Lucas, "'A Testimonye of Verye Ancient Tyme?' Some Manuscript Models for the Parkerian Anglo-Saxon Type-Designs," in *Of the Making of Books: Medieval Manuscripts, their Scribes and Readers: Essays Presented to M. B. Parkes*, ed. Pamela R. Robinson and Rivkah Zim (Aldershot, 1997), 147–88. For the Parkerian and Lambardian Picas see Peter J. Lucas, "Parker, Lambarde, and the Provision of the Special Sorts for Printing Anglo-Saxon in the Sixteenth Century," *Journal of the Printing Historical Society* 28 (1999): 41–69.

[35] Nicolas Barker, *Aldus Manutius and the Development of Greek Script and Type in the Fifteenth Century* (New York, 1992), 69.

[36] See, for example, Felice Feliciano, *Alphabetum Romanum*, ed. Giovanni Mardersteig, trans. R. H. Boothroyd (Verona, 1960). Feliciano recommended that the height of the letter should be ten times the maximum thickness of the stroke: see his comments on the letter A on fol. 1r (trans. 125) and the illustration on 58; he was followed in this respect by Moyllus (Moille), Dürer, and Tory, through whom ideas such as Feliciano's may have filtered through to the sixteenth-century French type-designers: see Matthew Carter, "Theories of Letterform Construction. Part 1," *Printing History* 14 (1992): 3–16.

lower-case letters were then modified to conform to this style so that where
before there were hooked terminals, now wherever possible there were serifs.[37]
The Wheelockian Great Primer Anglo-Saxon shows the opposite process.
Having chosen so many sinuous forms for the lower case, he then proceeded
to choose complementary shapes for as many capitals as possible, so that their
style matched that of the small letters.

The Wheelockian upper case shows a much larger number of sorts (14)
than in the other design sets. The Parkerian Great Primer showed nine (Æ[1],
Æ[2], E, H, M, S; Þ, Ð, Ᵹ), but Wheelock has eliminated the duplication of two
sorts of Æ (keeping the more curvaceous one), and excluded Þ, presumably
on the grounds that Ð will serve in all appropriate instances. He has therefore
added seven more capitals, nearly all consonants: square C, D, F, square G,
I, T, U. Apart from the square letters C and G (on which see further below),
these all add to the overriding impression of sinuosity. The D is a round-
backed form with a short ascender ending in a hooked terminal. F is similar
to the lower-case form, showing a hooked approach stroke at the top of the
stem, and a bowed upper arm with the terminal rolled over. Even I shows a
hooked terminal to its tail. T is the insular form, similar to the lower-case, but
with the stroke terminal scrolled. In the U the left part of the stroke is curved
like a swan's neck, and the right stem has a hooked terminal at the base. Of
the letters also found in earlier fonts Wheelock's E takes the Greek form, as is
to be expected, but both the upper and lower arms show scrolled terminals,
creating a design suggestive of wrought-iron work. H takes the expected uncial form with the right stem curved inwards, but an added feature is the ornamental miniature loop attached to the shoulder-side of the upper stem. M
also takes the expected uncial form and S follows the Parkerian S in showing
the lower part of the stroke closing right back round on to the middle part of
the stroke. Ᵹ shows a hooked terminal to the descender and a rounded bowl.
Of the other special sorts ⁊, the Tironian sign for "and", also shows a hooked
approach stroke and terminal to the descender.

In view of the general preference for sinuous shapes square C and square
G are aberrations (see Figs 12.2, 12.3, and 12.4). However, the square forms are
not often used, and square C is not found at all in Wheelock's second book, his
re-edition of the Anglo-Saxon Laws (1644). On this evidence it is reasonable to
conclude that Wheelock himself was less than wholehearted in his enthusiasm

---

On constructed capital letters cf. Donald M. Anderson, *The Art of Written Forms: The
Theory and Practice of Calligraphy* (New York, 1969), 125–33; for a modern treatment see
David L. Goines, *A Constructed Roman Alphabet: A Geometric Analysis of the Greek and
Roman Capitals and of the Arabic Numerals* (Boston, 1982).

[37] See Carter, *A View*; Twomey, "Whence Jenson"; and Hargreaves, "Florentine Script."

for these square forms,[38] since they do not contribute to the overall impression of sinuosity created by his Anglo-Saxon type-designs when considered as a set.

There are, then, a number of innovations and distinctive features in the Wheelockian Great Primer Anglo-Saxon font:

1. A general preference for sinuous shapes (apart from square C and G), shown particularly by numerous hooked terminals. This feature is correspondingly more important than the following ones, because it applies to a number of letter-forms.

2. Lower-case ð shows the ascender tagged to the left.

3. Upper-case square C.

4. Round-backed D, with a short ascender ending in a terminal gently hooked upwards.

5. E, with both the upper and the lower arms showing scrolled terminals.

6. F, showing a hooked approach stroke at the top of the stem, and a bowed upper arm with the terminal rolled over.

7. Square G.

8. H in uncial form with an ornamental miniature loop attached to the shoulder-side of the upper stem.

9. I, with a hooked terminal at the base of the stem.

10. T, similar to the lower-case, but with the stroke terminal scrolled.

11. U, with the left part of the stroke curved like a swan's neck, and the right stem showing a hooked terminal at the base.

12. ꝑ is rounded, not "square" or sharply angled.

In order to try to ascertain where Wheelock may have found inspiration for his innovations and preferences it is necessary to be sure which manuscripts he used. Only then can we examine the manuscripts to see whether or not they show the features with which those identified as characterizing his font can be matched.

Recent work on the models for early roman type-designs in Italy[39] has argued on the basis of what the Italians call a *coincidenza*. The style of writing exhibited in manuscripts being written at a particular time and place (Padua in the 1460s) provided the model for the type produced at the same time in the

---

[38] Alternatively the paucity of square Cs and Gs is the result of some technical problem with the supply of type.

[39] Twomey, "Whence Jenson" and Hargreaves, "Florentine Script."

same place (Padua 1470). Because of the contiguity of script and type-design there was a transference of letter shapes from one medium to the other: a *coincidenza*. For his Canon Roman (*TSF II*: 1567.16) and English-size Roman type designs (*TSF II*: 1567.22) Claude Garamond followed the design of some letters (a, c, e, m, n, o, u) from the sorts cut by Francesco Griffo for Pietro Bembo in his *De Ætna* (Aldus Manutius 1495), and Giovanni Mardersteig showed that Garamond must have used a copy of the *De Ætna*, which Nicolas Barker suggests was brought back from Italy by Geofroy Tory.[40] An even stronger form of argument is possible. In my analysis of the Parkerian Great Primer Anglo-Saxon, the first Anglo-Saxon type-design,[41] I was able to show that the models for the designs were to be found amongst the manuscripts demonstrably used by Parker and his household, who then instructed the punchcutter. This form of argument is even more compelling than argument by *coincidenza*, and it applies to Wheelock's designs too.

As a reluctant traveler Wheelock apparently never went outside Cambridge to see a manuscript. Consequently nearly all the manuscripts he used were in Cambridge, and still are.[42] This scenario creates a situation analogous to the country-house detective novel: the potential suspects are circumscribed, and, as we shall see, they number about forty. On 27 December 1639 Wheelock wrote from Cambridge to Spelman in London as follows:

---

[40] Giovanni Mardersteig, "Aldo Manuzio e i caratteri di Francesco Griffo da Bologna," in *Studi di Bibliografia e di Storia in onore di Tammaro de Marinis*, 4 vols. (Verona, 1964), 3:105–47, here 133–34, to which attention was drawn by Nicolas Barker, "The Aldine Roman in Paris, 1530–1534," *The Library* 5.29 (1974): 5–20, here 11. Barker says that the relevant letters in three of Garamond's early designs were based on the Aldine model, of which it is sufficient to specify two here: the third he names as "a *gros texte* for display." For discussion of Barker's argument in relation to other work on French Old-Style Romans see Kay Amert, "Origins of the French Old-Style: The Roman and Italic Types of Simon de Colines," *Printing History* 14 (1992): 17–40, here 18–20.

[41] Lucas, "'A Testimonye'."

[42] The manuscripts used by Wheelock are approached from a different point of view by Sue M. Hetherington, *The Beginnings of Old English Lexicography* (Spicewood, TX, 1980), 84–85, 261–64. Her analysis is based on texts cited in an Anglo-Saxon Lexicon compiled by Wheelock (and others) which survives in Harley MS. 761, fols. 2–86. Nearly all the items that she cites occur in my lists below, but exceptions will be dealt with in notes. Difficulty is caused by the fact that entries were put in at different times, and it is by no means certain that Wheelock was responsible for all the entries in the Lexicon, though he was certainly the last to work on it. The present analysis is on firmer ground, although Hetherington's work provides useful corroboration for most of the manuscripts used.

I am at leasure fitting Bede his historie (by the help of six auncient MS.
Three in Lat. & three in Sax.) for the preße; I shall craue all convenient
helps yo⟨ur⟩ worship may afford, w⟨i⟩th the iust acknowlegem⟨en⟩t of
soe great hono⟨ur⟩ to that worke: a work fit to be reviewed since it lays
out the first plantation, & progreße o[f] the Saxon church, & somwhat
of consequence of the Britan⟨n⟩s, & since (by yo⟨ur⟩ worships Leaue,) I
desire to reade this authour, & to compare him w⟨i⟩th Gildas in the most
remarkeable paßages of storie, & Doctrine, Ecclesiastical, & political:
Dr Ward hath borrowed for me Sr Thom: Cottons auncient Latin MS. I
meane Bede his hist. &[c.] & I find both it, & the other two Latin MS.
agree w⟨i⟩th all other new copies concerninge Augustines death before
the death of my oulde neighbors the Monckes of Bangor-Eiscoid. (BL,
Additional MS. 34600, fol. 195)[43]

The only manuscripts from outside Cambridge that Wheelock saw were two
borrowed from Sir Thomas Cotton, who had inherited the great collection
put together by his father, Sir Robert. One was Otho B.xi (since severely damaged in the 1731 fire), containing the Anglo-Saxon version of Bede's *Historia Ecclesiastica* and the *Anglo-Saxon Chronicle* (G), used for collation for
the Bede, and as the main text for the *Chronicle* in Wheelock's 1643 edition
(where the A-version in Cambridge, Corpus Christi College MS. 173, was
used for purposes of collation).[44] The other was a Latin Bede, probably Tiberius C.ii, borrowed through the good offices of Samuel Ward, Master of
Sidney Sussex College. On 31 March 1640 Wheelock wrote to Sir Thomas
asking to be able to keep "these pretious Monuments [in margin:] Bede his
Hist. Lat. et Sax.", i.e., one Latin Bede and one Anglo-Saxon Bede, somewhat
longer than originally projected (BL, MS. Cotton Julius F.vi, fol. 123),[45] and

---

[43] The allusion at the end is predicated on Wheelock's Shropshire origins.

[44] Cf. Angelika Lutz, "The Study of the Anglo-Saxon Chronicle in the Seventeenth
Century and the Establishment of Old English Studies in the Universities," in *The Recov-
ery of Old English: Anglo-Saxon in the Sixteenth and Seventeenth Centuries*, ed. Timothy
Graham (Kalamazoo, 2000), 1–82, here 34–40.

[45] The letter is printed in Sir Henry Ellis, *Original Letters*, 160, no. lviii. In a note Ellis
thinks that both manuscripts were Latin Bedes, but Wheelock claims only to have used
one Latin Bede borrowed from Cotton via Ward, and of the two manuscripts mentioned
in the letter one has to be Otho B.xi. The other manuscript mentioned by Ellis is Tiberius
A.xiv, also an eighth-century Latin Bede (Lowe, *CLA*, Suppl., no. 1703); it is possible that
Wheelock used this manuscript rather than Tiberius C.ii. In the unlikely event that he did
so the tenor of the present argument is not affected. Tiberius C.ii also contains glosses:
see Paolo Vaciago, "Old English Glosses to Latin Texts: A Bibliographical Handlist," *Medioevo e Rinascimento* 4 (1993): 1–67, here 16, no. 64.

he evidently did so.[46] For the text of the Anglo-Saxon translation of Bede's *Historia Ecclesiastica* he followed CUL MS Kk.3.18, collated with Cambridge, Corpus Christi College MS. 41 (borrowed from Corpus by Wheelock)[47] and Cotton Otho B.xi. For the Latin text of Bede he collated Cambridge, Trinity College MS. R.5.22 (s.xiv),[48] Cambridge, Sidney Sussex College MS. 102 (*olim* Δ.5.17; s.xv), and the Cotton manuscript, probably Tiberius C.ii.[49]

The texts used by Wheelock for the West Saxon Genealogical Regnal List require special comment. The work occurs in the 1643 edition of Bede between the preface and the list of chapter headings, as only in Kk.3.18 amongst the manuscripts,[50] which Wheelock followed as his main text. He collated it with two other versions, his B and C. B is Cambridge, Corpus Christi (formerly St Bene't's) College, MS. 173, fol. 1r.[51] C is not Otho B.xi, from which the relevant leaf, now BL Additional MS. 34652, fol. 2, was removed in the early modern period; suggestions for the "culprit" include Sir Robert Cotton himself,[52] and

---

[46] The Latin Bede "bound with my armes" had been borrowed by Ward from Sir Robert Cotton's library earlier (BL, Harley MS. 6018, fol. 159v), and when he lent it to Ussher he wrote (1624) "I will expect the book from you, when you have done with it, for that I would keep it till Sir Robert restore a book of mine": quoted by James P. Carley, "Books Seen by Samuel Ward 'in Bibliotheca Regia', *circa* 1614," *British Library Journal* 16 (1990): 89–98, here 92, from Charles R. Elrington, *The Whole Works of the Most Rev. James Ussher*, 17 vols. (Dublin, 1847–1864), 15:229. Presumably Wheelock restored the manuscript to Sir Thomas after Ward's death in 1642. I am grateful to Professor Carley for drawing his article to my attention.

[47] Timothy Graham, "Abraham Wheelock's Use of CCCC MS 41 (Old English Bede) and the Borrowing of Manuscripts from the Library of Corpus Christi College," *Cambridge Bibliographical Society Newsletter* (Summer, 1997): 10–16, here 13–15.

[48] Bede's *Historia Ecclesiastica* comprises Part I, fols. 1–43. Part III, fols. 72–158, is an eleventh-century copy of the Alfredian translation of Pope Gregory's *Cura Pastoralis*, which must be included amongst the Anglo-Saxon manuscripts possibly studied by Wheelock.

[49] As noted by Oates, *Cambridge University Library*, 204, he also used Cambridge, St John's College MS. 27, a fourteenth-century Latin Bede, but it was not a significant influence.

[50] See David N. Dumville, "The West-Saxon Genealogical Regnal List: Manuscript and Texts," *Anglia* 104 (1986): 1–32. For a diplomatic edition of some of the texts available to Wheelock (CCC 173, CCC 383, Tiberius A.iii, fol. 178, and also extracts copied by Robert Recorde s.xvi in CCC 138) see Bruce Dickins, *The Genealogical Preface to the Anglo-Saxon Chronicle*, Department of Anglo-Saxon Occasional Papers 2 (Cambridge, 1952).

[51] Wheelock also had access to the Genealogical List in Cambridge, Corpus Christi College, MS. 383, fol. 108v/3–26, but there is no evidence that he made any use of it.

[52] As first suggested by Kenneth Sisam, "Anglo-Saxon Royal Genealogies," *Proceedings of the British Academy* 39 (1953): 287–348, here 334, n. 1. Sisam notes that Cotton was working on a genealogy of James I, tracing it back to Alfred.

William L'Isle,[53] but the deed was probably done earlier, in the sixteenth century. C is Tiberius A.iii, fol. 178,[54] which was itself removed from Tiberius A.vi, fols. 1–35,[55] possibly, as Sisam suggested (with different reasoning), by Cotton. These findings are confirmed by the reading at the end of the first paragraph in Dumville's edition: Wheelock reads "winter", a reading that must come from Tiberius A.iii, fol. 178, because all other witnesses have "gear."[56] Presumably Wheelock was supplied by Sir Thomas Cotton with Tiberius A.iii, fol. 178, as well as, or together with, Otho B.xi (which lacked what is now Add. 34652, fol. 2).[57]

---

[53] N. R. Ker, *Catalogue of Manuscripts Containing Anglo-Saxon* (Oxford, 1957, repr. 1991), 234, no. 180.

[54] As noted previously by Dorothy Whitelock, "The Old English Bede," *Proceedings of the British Academy* 48 (1962): 57–90, here 60, and nn. 23–24 on 81. For a zincograph facsimile of fol. 178r see Benjamin Thorpe, *The Anglo-Saxon Chronicle according to the Several Original Authorities*, 2 vols., Rolls Series 23 (London, 1861), 1: pl. vii.

[55] *ASC B*, on which see Simon Taylor, *The Anglo-Saxon Chronicle: A Collaborative Edition*, vol. 4, *MS B* (Cambridge, 1983), xvi–xvii.

[56] Dumville, "The West-Saxon Genealogical Regnal List," 22, textual note 47. The text in Tiberius A.iii, fol. 178, was copied (1) by Laurence Nowell the antiquary (at Sir William Cecil's house in 1562) on fols. 5–6r of BL, Additional MS. 43703, in which there follows a transcript of the Old English version of Bede's *Historia Ecclesiastica* (from Otho B.xi) which lacks the Genealogical Regnal List from what is now Add. 34652, fol. 2 (presumably already removed from Otho B.xi), and (2) by a Parkerian scribe in OBL, MS. Laud misc. 661, fols. 44–45, where it follows a transcript of the *Anglo-Saxon Chronicle* (B) from Tiberius A.vi, to which it originally belonged, and presumably still belonged in Parker's time. Nowell's transcript in Add. 43703 is preceded by the list of popes who sent pallia to Canterbury, a copy evidently taken from Tiberius A.vi, fol. 35v, in which manuscript the list of popes also immediately preceded the Genealogical Regnal List (before that was removed). This evidence suggests that the Genealogical Regnal List (i.e. Add. 34652, fol. 2) was removed from Otho B.xi before Cotton's time, and that the Genealogical Regnal List (i.e. Tiberius A.iii, fol. 178) was removed from Tiberius A.vi at a later time, possibly (by Cotton?) to supply the gap in Otho B.xi (to which there is no objection as regards the relative sizes of the manuscripts, as Otho was originally larger than Tiberius [244 × 177mm as opposed to 228 × 158mm]).

[57] When Francis Junius (1591–1677) made his transcript of the List (OBL MS. Junius 66 [SC 5177], 19–20) from what is now Tiberius A.iii, fol. 178, it was already part of this codex, as he refers to it as coming from the same codex as contained Ælfric's Colloquy, viz. Tiberius A.iii, fol. 60v–64v. On the assumption that Wheelock borrowed what is now Tiberius A.iii, fol. 178 (together with Otho B.xi) and did not go to London to see it, perhaps it joined Tiberius A.iii on return from him; some such explanation is required to account for its incorporation in Tiberius A.iii. I am grateful to David Dumville for reading and commenting on a draft of this paragraph.

Wheelock's appointment to the Lectureship in Anglo-Saxon at Cambridge was encouraged by James Ussher, archbishop of Armagh. Counselled by Ussher, Wheelock inherited the Parkerian view of Anglo-Saxon materials as useful for bolstering the doctrine and practice of the Church of England.[58] This approach, spelt out in the dedication to Cambridge University, is heralded in his letter to Spelman dated 13 June 1638:

> I am now readinge of Beda, with King Alured his translation. which[,] I see, will correct many thinges, . . . but the maine busines which possesseth my thoughtes, is, the discovery (out of Bede, & others, especiallie in manuscripts) of the Apostolical doctrine, by comparinge our present church with the auncient church here in England: which work will most properlie suite with your reader [i.e. Wheelock himself], because he is to be a searcher of truthes out of the fountaines themselues. (BL, Add. MS. 25384, fol. 29v)

Wheelock used his edition of Bede as a vehicle to communicate what he thought of as supporting evidence from other texts, mainly homilies.[59] According to my analysis Wheelock cites passages from eighty-four separate homilies, and he prints in full two of Ælfric's Catholic Homilies, second series: on sig. 3C4v–3E2v "in dedicatione ecclesiae," and on sig.3O3v–3Q2r "in die Pascae."[60] Cambridge manuscripts from which he took this illustrative material include University Library, MSS. Gg.3.28, Ii.1.33, Ii.4.6,[61] Corpus

---

[58] Cf. Michael Murphy, "Abraham Wheloc's Edition of Bede's *History* in Old English," *Studia Neophilologica* 39 (1967): 46–59.

[59] For full details see Peter J. Lucas, *An Analytical Bibliographical Catalogue of Early Printed Books containing Anglo-Saxon printed with Special Sorts* (London, 2008, forthcoming), entry for 1643.1.

[60] Malcolm Godden, *Ælfric's Catholic Homilies: The First Series: Text*, EETS, s.s. 5 (London, 1979), Homily XL, "In Dedicatione," 335–45 and Homily XV, "In Die Pascae," 150–60. For the latter text Wheelock collated the text printed in William L'Isle, *A Saxon Treatise concerning the Old and New Testament. Written about the time of King Edgar (700 yeares agoe) by Ælfricus Abbas, thought to be the same that was afterward Archbishop of Canterburie. Whereby appeares what was the Canon of Holy Scripture here then received, and that the Church of England had it so long agoe in her Mother-tongue* (London, John Haviland for Henry Seile 1, 1623; STC 160), O2v–R3v with that in CUL MS. Gg.3.28, as can be seen in Wheelock's own copy of the 1623 text (CUL Adv.d.48.10).

[61] Annotated by Wheelock, e.g. on fols. 258v–259r.

Christi College MSS. 162,[62] 191,[63] 198, 419,[64] and Trinity College MSS. B.15.34, and R.4.26 (containing Middle English, but the extracts printed by Wheelock utilize his Anglo-Saxon types).[65]

Wheelock also made transcripts of Old English texts for Sir Henry Spelman, which the latter used for his *Concilia* of 1639. For these Wheelock certainly used Corpus Christi College MSS. 201 and 383.[66] Oates suggests that Wheelock also made transcripts of Latin texts for Spelman from Corpus 190 and 279,[67] and from Trinity Hall MS. 1,[68] but while the suggestion is eminently plausible,[69] there are apparently no surviving transcripts to confirm the supposition. Wheelock also transcribed on eight leaves of paper the beginning of Ælfric's homily on the Assumption of the Virgin Mary (*CH*, I.xxx) from Corpus 188, pp. 318/1–326/19, in order to make good the textual lacuna in CUL MS. Gg.3.28, where they are bound in between fols. 94/97.[70]

---

[62] Wheelock also transcribed the end of Ælfric, *CH*, I.xl, from CCC 162, p. 563, in CUL MS. Gg.3.28, fol. 134 top margin, to supply the text missing from this homily (Dominica II in adventu Domini; Peter Clemoes, *Ælfric's Catholic Homilies: The First Series: Text*, EETS s.s. 17 [Oxford, 1997], 530, lines 185–188) as a consequence of fol. 133 being lost.

[63] Wheelock borrowed this manuscript from Corpus: see Graham, "Abraham Wheelock's Use," 14. A transcript of it made for Wheelock survives as BL, MS Harley 440.

[64] Wheelock's embryonic index occurs in Corpus 419 at fols.i–ii[r], pp. 368–70.

[65] Wheelock's embryonic index occurs in TCC R.4.26 at fols.a–d, 164–65.

[66] Wheelock borrowed MS. 201 from Corpus: see Graham, "Abraham Wheelock's Use," 14. His transcript of the Canons of Edgar (dated 25 October 1637) from Corpus 201 survives in BL, Add. MS. 35333, art. 5. In the *Concilia* Spelman claims Corpus 383 (fols. 57v/23–58v/4) as his source for the Law *Be wifmannes beweddunge* (Felix Liebermann, *Die Gesetze der Angelsachsen*, 3 vols. [Halle, 1903–1916]: 1:442–44) on sig. 2M2r.

[67] The "Capitula libri poenitentialis Theodori archiepiscopi" on sig. M5 of the *Concilia*, the "Capitula de Sacerdotali jure Egberti Archiepiscopi" on sig. Y6v–Z1r, and the "Capitula de libro Scintillarum" on sig. Z1v are from Corpus 190, pp. vi–x, as acknowledged for the latter two by Spelman on sig. Y6v and Z1v. The "Synodus S. Patricii" on sig. D1v–2v is from Corpus 279, pp. 1–10, as acknowledged by Spelman on sig. D2v.

[68] The "De fundatione primarum ecclesiarum" on sig. I1v–K1v (pp. 112–124) is from CTH 1 (as ed. Charles Hardwick, *Thomas of Elmham, Historia Abbatiæ S. Augustini*, Rolls Series 8 [London, 1858]: 77/1–90/11, 109/27–110/26, 111/29–113/3, 114/4–116/15, 119/16–124/20), as acknowledged by Spelman on I1v; so also is the "Epitaphium Sancti Gregorii" on E3v (p. 68; as ed. Hardwick, *Thomas of Elmham*, 124–25). The transcript of CTH 1 in BL, MS. Harley 686, is not by Wheelock.

[69] Oates, *Cambridge University Library*, 199. His suggestion that Wheelock made a transcript from CUL MS. Ff.1.27 for Spelman seems improbable since Spelman borrowed the manuscript himself (200, and n. 19).

[70] Wheelock notes on his paper transcript (fol. 2v) that he took the transcript from "Col. Ben. Cantabr. vol.3. p. 318," a reference to Parker's third book of homilies, now CCC

Other manuscripts consulted by Wheelock include Corpus MSS. 138 (from which Wheelock transcribed an unwanted extract for Spelman),[71] 140 (which Spelman asked Wheelock to compare a reading from in his letter of 5 September 1638),[72] and 318, from which the Latin life of Bede, art. 4 (pp. 356–362), was taken to preface the *Historia Ecclesiastica*, University Library MSS. Ff.1.27 (with twelve leaves of index notes by Wheelock),[73] Ff.1.28 (annotated by Wheelock, e.g., fols. 78v, 88v, 138v, 235r), Hh.1.10 (with an embryonic index by Wheelock on fols. iii–vi),[74] Ii.2.4 (in which Wheelock noted on the inside of the front cover that he read it between 3 September 1638 and 17 July 1639),[75] and Ii.2.11 (which Spelman asked Wheelock to compare a reading from in his letter of 5 September 1638).[76] Wheelock must also have seen

---

MS. 188. The transcribed text corresponds to Clemoes, *CH*, 429/4–434/150 ending at the word "eadige". Wheelock's embryonic index occurs in CCC 188 at pp. ii–vii.

[71] Spelman to Wheelock, 22 September 1637 in CUL, MS Dd.3.12, fol. 10. Cf. Oates, *Cambridge University Library*, 198; Spelman thought the extract of little use, and it has apparently not survived.

[72] CUL, MS. Dd.3.12, fol. 31.

[73] The "Synodus apud Acleam" on sig. 2B2r (p. 305) is excerpted from Richard of Hexham in MS. Ff.1.27, p.230a/17–25, as acknowledged by Spelman; for the subject-matter see Arthur W. Haddan and William Stubbs, *Councils and Ecclesiastical Documents relating to Great Britain and Ireland* (Oxford, 1871), 3: 464. In the manuscript there is a mark (and three others on pp. 228, 230) beside this passage in the margin. The mark is somewhat like an H with the two stems consisting of upright spears linked by a double cross-bar tilted down from left to right with a small o between the cross-bars in the centre. It was presumably made by Spelman (not Wheelock). On the manuscript see David N. Dumville, "The Sixteenth-Century History of Two Cambridge Books from Sawley," *Transactions of the Cambridge Bibliographical Society* 7.4 (1980): 427–44, here 433–37.

[74] There is a transcript of CUL MS. Hh.1.10 (Ælfric's Grammar) made for Sir Symonds D'Ewes (who borrowed it from Cambridge) in BL, MS. Harley 8, fols. 5r–72r; the transcript is annotated in the margins by D'Ewes for the purposes of extrapolating words for use in his Dictionary. Hetherington, *The Beginnings*, 263 claims that Wheelock also knew BL MS. Cotton Faustina A.x (Ælfric's Grammar; siglum F), citing as evidence the alleged occurrence in the margin of "corr. F." beside the entry in his Lexicon (Harley 761) for "Lauwerbeam, Laurus"; this entry occurs on fol. 49r, but I could find no sign of the marginal note. I have found no evidence that Wheelock used Faustina A.x.

[75] Wheelock also wrote on fol. 3r "Sum Bibliotheca publicæ Cantabrigiensis", presumably as a reminder to anyone who borrowed it (including himself!) of where it belonged. There are notes by Wheelock on fol. 150r.

[76] Hetherington, *The Beginnings*, 85, 264 claims that Wheelock used BL MS. Royal 1.A.xiv (AS Gospels), but she cites no evidence. In Harley 761, on fol. 88r, there occurs what purports to be a list of sources which read (before it was amended) "Euang: Sax. impressa in Bib: pub. Cant. 2. MS v in Coll. Regal.i.", which I interpret as saying that Foxe's

CUL Ff.1.23[77] and TCC R.17.1 (the Eadwine or Canterbury Psalter),[78] both of which Spelman borrowed through Wheelock's good offices so that his son John could work on them for his edition of the Anglo-Saxon Psalter.[79] Wheelock also presumably saw TCC R.5.16, another manuscript borrowed (on two separate occasions) by Spelman.[80] This information about the manuscripts used by Wheelock is summarized in Tables 1–3, where the first column on the left gives the institution holding the manuscript, the second the class-mark, the third the date when it was written (in which the form s.xi$^{3/4}$ means the third quarter of the eleventh century), the fourth the contents (abbreviated), and the fifth the provenance.[81] Of course, as University Librarian, Wheelock had access to all the manuscripts in the University Library, and, no doubt, to any he wished to see in the Colleges.

Anglo-Saxon Gospels (1571) used as a source occur in CUL Ii.2.11 with variants taken from Royal 1.A.xiv; Hetherington's misreading of MS "in" as "M." and her failure to note what was written first and what was written later (*The Beginnings*, 261, n. 82) has resulted in her misunderstanding. I have found no evidence that Wheelock used Royal 1.A.xiv.

[77] David N. Dumville, "On the Dating of some late Anglo-Saxon Liturgical Manuscripts," *Transactions of the Cambridge Bibliographical Society* 10.1 (1991): 40–57, here 40–41 dates this manuscript earlier in the eleventh century than has traditionally been the case.

[78] For a reduced monochrome facsimile of TCC R.17.1 see M. R. James, *The Canterbury Psalter* (London, 1935). Folios 164r–170v are reproduced in full-size color facsimile in Fred C. Robinson and E. G. Stanley, *Old English Verse Texts from Many Sources: A Comprehensive Collection*, EEMF 23 (Copenhagen, 1991), no. 30. On the manuscript see Margaret Gibson, T. A. Heslop, and Richard W. Pfaff, eds., *The Eadwine Psalter: Text, Image and Monastic Culture in Twelfth-Century Canterbury*, Publications of the Modern Humanities Research Association 14 (London, 1992), with many illustrations, and especially Teresa Webber on "The Script" of the Anglo-Saxon gloss on 13–24, esp. 18–21, with which compare Phillip Pulsiano, "The Scribes and Old English Gloss of the *Eadwine's Canterbury Psalter*," in *Proceedings of the Patristic, Medieval and Renaissance Conference* (Villanova University, Augustinian Historical Institute) 14 (Villanova, PA, 1989), 223–60. See also Vaciago, "Old English Glosses," 9, no. 31.

[79] Sir John Spelman, *Psalterium Davidis Latino-Saxonicum Vetus* (London, Richard Badger 1, 1640), STC 2369. For the borrowing of the Trinity manuscript by Spelman cf. Oates, *Cambridge University Library*, 200–3, and David J. McKitterick in Gibson, Heslop, and Pfaff, eds., *Eadwine Psalter*, 198–99. It was returned together with CUL Ff.1.23 (Spelman to Wheelock, 17 September 1639, in CUL Dd.3.12, fol. 49).

[80] As is evident from Spelman's letter to Wheelock of 8 December 1637 (CUL, MS. Dd.3.12, fol. 15).

[81] Following Ker, *Catalogue*, collated with idem, *Medieval Libraries of Great Britain: A List of Surviving Books* (London, 1964) and idem and Andrew G. Watson, *Supplement* (London, 1987).

Table 1: Manuscripts from which Wheelock took text for printed books or surviving transcripts

Institution	Shelf-mark	Date	Contents	Provenance
CUL	Gg.3.28	s.x/xi	Ælfric, *Homilies*	Durham
	Ii.1.33	s.xii^2	Homilies, Saints' Lives	Exeter
	Ii.4.6	s.xi^{med}	Homilies	Tavistock (Devon)
	Kk.3.18	s.xi$^{3/4}$	AS Bede	Worcester
CCC	41	s.xi^1	AS Bede, Homilies	Exeter
	162	s.xi^{in}	Homilies	South East: Rochester, or Canterbury St Augustine's
	173	s.ix/x-xi^2	AS Chronicle (A)	Canterbury Christ Church
	188	s.xi^1	Homilies	not known
	191	s.xi$^{3/4}$	*Rule of Chrodegang*	Exeter
	198	s.xi^1, xi^2	Homilies	Worcester
	201 (pp.1-178)	s.xi^{in}/xi^{med}	Homilies, Laws, etc.	not known
	201 (pp.179-272)	s.xi^{med}	*Capitula* of Theodulf, etc.	Exeter
	318	s.xiii	Latin Life of Bede, etc.	Rochester
	383	s.xi/xii	Laws	London St Paul's
	419	s.xi^1	Homilies	Canterbury/Exeter
CSJ	27	s.xiv	Latin Bede	Pleshey College (Essex)
CSS	102 (olim Δ.5.17)	s.xv	Latin Bede	Bury St Edmunds
TCC	B.15.34	s.xi^{med}	Homilies	Canterbury?
	R.4.26	s.xiv^2	ME verse Chronicle attrib. "Robert of Gloucester"	not known
	R.5.22 (fols.1-43)	s.xiv	Latin Bede	not known
	(fols.44-71)	s.xii	Latin Saints' Lives	not known
	(fols.72-158)	s.x/xi	OE *Pastoral Care*	Sherborne
BL Cotton	Otho B xi	s.x^{med}/xi^1	AS Bede, ASC (G), Laws	Winchester, Southwick
	Tiberius A.iii, fol.178	s.x^2	WS Genealogical Regnal List	Abingdon, Canterbury St Augustine's
	Tiberius C.ii	s.viii^{ex}	Latin Bede	Lindisfarne

Table 2: Other manuscripts for which there is evidence of use by Wheelock

Institution	Shelf-mark	Date	Contents	Provenance
CUL	Ff.1.27 (pp.1-40, 73-252)	s.xii²/xiii¹	Gildas, Nennius, etc.	Sawley (Yorks)
	Ff.1.27 (pp.253-642, 41-72)	s.xii²/xiv	Gerald of Wales, etc.	Bury St Edmunds
	Ff.1.28	s.xv	Richard of Cirencester	not known
	Hh.1.10	s.xi³/⁴/xii	Ælfric, *Grammar*	Exeter
	Ii.2.4	s.xi³/⁴	OE *Pastoral Care*	Exeter
	Ii.2.11	s.xi³/⁴	Gospels	Exeter
CCC	138	s.xiv	Chronica varia	Norwich
	140	s.xi¹/xii	Gospels, etc.	Bath

Table 3: Other manuscripts for which there is presumed evidence of use by Wheelock

Institution	Shelf-mark	Date	Contents	Provenance
CUL	Ff.1.23	s.xi^med	Glossed Psalter	(?) Canterbury St Augustine's
CCC	173, fols.59-83	s.viii²	Sedulius	Winchester, Canterbury
	190 (A)	s.xi¹	Penitentials	Exeter
	190 (B)	s.xi^med	Ecclesiastical Institutes	Exeter
	279	s.ix/x	Synodus Patricii, Canones	Worcester
TCC	R.5.16	s.xiv	Johannes Glastoniensis	Glastonbury
	R.17.1	s.xii^med	Glossed Psalter	Canterbury Christ Church
CTH	1	s.xv	Thomas of Elmham	Canterbury St Augustine's

Of the twelve features identified above as distinctive or innovatory in Wheelock's Great Primer Anglo-Saxon, lower-case ð with a prominent ascender tagged to the left is characteristic of manuscripts from the second half of the eleventh century.[82] It is probably no coincidence that so many of the manuscripts in the list of those used by Wheelock are from the middle or second half of the eleventh century. However, there are also a number of later medieval manuscripts, and two considerably earlier ones, from the end of the eighth century. So, with the twelve features in mind, I returned to the manuscripts listed in Tables 1–3 to see whether or not they showed similar features. Since hooked terminals are so numerous in Wheelock's type-designs I have limited the search in the manuscripts to descenders turned to the left. The results are set out in Table 4 and include not only Anglo-Saxon manuscripts but also later medieval manuscripts, which cannot be expected to show those features that are exclusively Anglo-Saxon. The material condensed into this Table is generally representative of the usage in each manuscript concerned, but occasionally the usage recorded for individual capitals indicates existence rather than the norm. In CUL Ii.2.11, for example, round-backed D is marked as present, but I found it only on fol. 118v in "Duo". Although occasional variations from the usage recorded here may be found,[83] none are of significance as far as the present argument is concerned.

In Anglo-Saxon manuscripts there was as in other manuscripts a hierarchy of scripts.[84] To state the matter somewhat simplistically with manuscripts from the tenth century onwards in mind: first, at the top of the hierarchy, were illuminated display capitals, secondly there were secondary display capitals,

---

[82] Ker, *Catalogue*, xxxi.

[83] Some manuscripts are written by more than one scribe. For example, CUL Ii.1.33 is written (probably) in two hands, the first of which rarely shows hooked terminals, while the second shows them more frequently. In this case, in the interests of inclusiveness, I have indicated the presence of hooked terminals in the manuscript. Similarly in CCC 198 the main scribes 2 and 4 show hooked terminals, whereas scribes 1 and 3 do not, so I have indicated them as present. In CCC 162 Scribe 2 (p. 565 only) shows ð with the ascender tagged to the left, but, since Scribe 1 does not show the feature, I have marked it as lacking in the manuscript. On the other hand in CCC 190(A) Anglo-Saxon is present only in additions made by various scribes, so the presence of ð with the ascender tagged to the left on p.246 gains an indication of its occurrence in this part of the manuscript. CCC 140 has each gospel written by a separate scribe, of whom only the Matthew scribe sometimes shows hooked terminals, so I have indicated them as absent, since this is the predominant impression given by the manuscript. Fragmentary manuscripts, such as Tiberius A.iii, fol. 178, have insufficient text to show the features of capitals.

[84] The classic statement of this concept is by Berthold L. Ullmann, *Ancient Writing and its Influence* (London, 1932), 113.

Table 4: Summary of Occurrence of Distinctive/Innovatory Features in Relevant AS MSS

MSS	1 Hooked descender terminals	2 ð with ascender tagged to left	3/7 L Li square	4 D round backed	5 Є with scrolled arms	6 F with bowed upper arm	8 Ð with miniature loop	9 I with hooked terminal	10 T with stroke terminal scrolled	11 U with curved left stroke	12 þ with rounded bowl
Cambridge University Library											
Gg.3.28	×	×	✓	✓	×	✓	×	✓	×	✓	✓
Ii.1.33	✓	×	×	×	×	×	×	✓	×	×	✓
Ii.4.6	×	×	✓	✓	×	✓	×	×	×	✓	✓
Kk.3.18	×	×	×	×	×	×	×	×	×	✓	✓
Ff.1.27											
(pp.1–40, 73–252)	–	–	–	✓	×	–	×	–	✓	✓	–
(pp.253–642)	–	–	–	✓	×	–	×	–	×	✓	–
Ff.1.28	–	–	–	–	×	–	×	–	×	×	–
Hh.1.10	✓	✓	×	×	×	×	×	×	×	✓	✓
Ii.2.4	✓	✓	×	×	×	×	×	×	×	✓	✓
Ii.2.11	✓	✓	×	✓	×	×	×	×	×	✓	✓
Ff.1.23	×		✓	✓	×	×	×	×	×	✓	–

Table 4 (cont.)

	1 Hooked descender terminals	2 ð with ascender tagged to left	3 L	7 L square	4 D round backed	5 є with scrolled arms	6 F with bowed upper arm	8 Þ with miniature loop	9 I with hooked terminal	10 T with stroke terminal scrolled	11 U with curved left stroke	12 þ with rounded bowl
Cambridge, Corpus Christi College												
41	×	×	×	✓	×	×	×	×	×	×	×	✓
162	×	×	✓	✓	×	×	–	x?	×	×	–	✓
173	×	×	✓	✓	×	×	×	×	✓	×	×	×
173, fols.59-83	×	–	×	×	✓	×	✓	×	✓	×	✓	–
188	✓	×	×	×	✓	×	✓	×	✓	×	✓	✓
191	✓	✓	×	✓	✓	×	✓	×	✓	×	✓	✓
198	✓	×	×	×	×	×	×	×	×	×	✓	✓
201 (pp.1-178)	×	×	×	✓	✓	×	×	×	✓	×	✓	✓
201 (pp.179-272)	✓	✓	×	×	✓	×	×	×	×	×	✓	✓
318	–	–	–	–	–	×	–	×	–	×	–	–
383	✓	×	×	×	×	×	×	×	×	×	✓	✓
419	✓	✓	×	×	×	×	×	×	✓	×	✓	✓
—												
138	–	–	–	–	–	×	–	×	–	×	–	–
140	×	✓	×	✓	✓	×	×	×	✓	×	✓	✓
—												

Table 4 (cont.)

	1 Hooked descender terminals	2 ð with ascender tagged to left	3 L	7 ʟ square	4 D round backed	5 Є with scrolled arms	6 F with bowed upper arm	8 þ with miniature loop	9 I with hooked terminal	10 T with stroke terminal scrolled	11 U with curved left stroke	12 p with rounded bowl
Cambridge, Corpus Christi College												
190 (A)	x	✓	x	x	✓	x	x	x	✓	✓	✓	x
190 (B)	✓	✓	x	x	x	x	x	x	x	x	✓	✓
279	x	-	✓	x	✓	x	✓	x	x	x	✓	-
Cambridge, St. John's College												
27	-	-	-	-	-	x	-	x	-	x	-	-
Cambridge, Sidney Sussex College												
102	-	-	-	-	-	x	-	x	-	x	-	-
Cambridge, Trinity College												
B.15.34	x	✓	✓	✓	✓	x	x	x	x	x	✓	✓
R.4.26	-	-	-	-	-	x	-	x	-	x	-	-
R.5.22												
(fols.1-43)	-	-	-	-	-	x	-	x	-	x	-	-
(fols.44-71)	x	-	-	-	✓	x	✓	x	x	x	✓	✓
(fols.72-158)	x	x	✓	✓	✓	x	✓	x	x	x	✓	✓

Table 4 (cont.)

	1 Hooked descender terminals	2 ð with ascender tagged to left	L	3/7 L square	4 D round backed	5 ℇ with scrolled arms	6 F with bowed upper arm	8 þ with miniature loop	9 I with hooked terminal	10 T with stroke terminal scrolled	11 U with curved left stroke	12 þ with rounded bowl
Cambridge, Trinity College												
R.5.16	–	–	–	–	–	x	–	x	–	x	x	–
R.17.1	✓	x	✓	x	✓	x	x	x	✓	x	✓	✓
Cambridge, Trinity Hall												
1	–	–	–	–	–	x	–	x	–	✓	–	–
British Library, Cotton MSS												
Otho B.xi[86]	x	x	x	x	x	x	✓	x	x	x	x	✓
Tib. A.iii, fol.178	x	x	x	x	x	x	x	x	x	x	x	x
Tib. C.ii	x	–	✓	x	✓	x	✓	x	✓	x	✓	–

Note: Some manuscripts marked as not showing insular capital T with the stroke terminal scrolled do, nevertheless, show insular-shaped capital T (with a curve but no scroll): viz. CUL Gg.3.28 (fols. 28v, 34v, etc.), Corpus 140 (Scribe 3, fol. 102v), Corpus 188 (p. 447), Corpus 201 (p. 4), Corpus 279 (p. 126), Trinity College R.17.1 (fol. 195v, with illuminated example on fol. 221r), Otho B.xi (fol. 30v), Tiberius C.ii (fol. 60v), and also CUL Ff.1.27 (pp. 253–642, e.g., at p. 286, with round-backed D at p. 303), and Ff.1.28 (fol. 135r; this manuscript also shows capital I with a curved terminal on fol. 79v and U with a curved left stroke (but closed at the top) on fol. 10r).

86 Otho B.xi was seriously damaged by the 1731 fire, so for the purposes of characterizing elements of script I have also examined the leaf detached from it before the fire, BL, Additional MS. 34652, fol. 2, even though there is every indication that Wheelock did not see it.

and thirdly the minuscule of the text. For the capitals that were appropriate to have provided models for the Wheelockian type-designs we should look particularly at the secondary display capitals, since these were made by scribes using the nib to make letter-strokes without ornamentation. These Anglo-Saxon secondary display capitals show a mixture of square, rustic, and uncial forms,[85] such forms often being used by a single scribe, not systematically as in Carolingian manuscripts from Tours,[87] but in conjunction with one another without apparent differentiation. For example, in all relevant manuscripts square C, G, S, and Ᵹ are nearly always accompanied in the same hand by rustic (round) C, G, S, and Ᵹ. Uncial D and M appear side by side with rustic D and M, and uncial E, F, H, and T occur side by side with square E, F, H, and T.

While some features, such as curvaceous U and rounded Ᵹ, are relatively common in the manuscripts, others, such as uncial T with the stroke terminal scrolled, are rare, and some, such as uncial E with scrolled arms, do not occur at all. Some of the post-Anglo-Saxon manuscripts show nothing of relevance to Wheelock's type-designs. Of the Anglo-Saxon ones no one manuscript provides the models for all the design features of Wheelock's Anglo-Saxon sorts. In so far as Wheelock formed his designs on manuscript models he presumably allowed continual reading over a period to stimulate the gradual formulation of a repertoire of suitable designs.

Of the features listed the first is of greater importance than the rest, because it relates to a large number of letter-forms affecting the overall impact made by looking at Wheelock's Anglo-Saxon text on the page.[88] Sinuosity of style is particularly marked in CUL MS. Ii.2.4 (Fig. 12.6), which shows what Ker called "a stately upright script" originating from Exeter in the third quarter of the eleventh century and written by one of the scribes identified with the scriptorium of Leofric, bishop of Exeter (1046–1072).[89] Descenders are regularly turned to the left, and the ascender of ð is tagged to the left. As he records on the inside of the front cover, Wheelock read this manuscript be-

---

[85] For a convenient account of the development of these forms see Sir Edward Maunde Thompson, *An Introduction to Greek and Latin Palaeography* (Oxford, 1912), 272–97.

[87] Ullmann, *Ancient Writing*, 113.

[88] For this reason the manuscript that shows the largest number of features imitated (as enumerated here), viz. CUL Gg.3.28, is not as influential as a primary model as might appear, since it does not present an overall sinuosity of style. For individual letter-forms it was no doubt notably influential.

[89] There is a list of Exeter manuscripts produced before the twelfth century in Patrick W. Conner, *Anglo-Saxon Exeter: A Tenth-Century Cultural History* (Woodbridge, 1993), 3–11. He draws upon the work of Elaine Drage, "Bishop Leofric and the Exeter Cathedral Chapter, 1050–1072: A Reassessment of the Evidence," D.Phil. diss., Oxford University, 1978.

to þam þ ic polðe þenian. Ge hȳpen þa up ahapenan hpæt

falomon cpæð. he cpæð þ ælœr ȳrelȳ rpuma pæpe ofɪp mec-

tu. Ge hȳpen þa eaðmoðan. þ cpufc upe alȳteð hine pȳlpne

ge eaðmeððe emne ðð þone oeað. Ge hȳpen þa upahapenan

hpæt appucen ɪr be heopan heupðe. ꝼ be heopa lapeope þ ɪr

oeopol. bɪc ɪr appucen þ he pȳ cȳnʒ ofɪp ealle þa ofɪp hɪðɪ-

ʒun beapn. ꝼop þam hɪr ofɪp meðu ɪr rpuma. upeꝼ pop lopeꝼ.

ꝼpe oꝼ þanc þe pe mɪð alȳfeðe fȳnðon ɪr ʒoðeꝼ eaðmoðnȳꝼ.

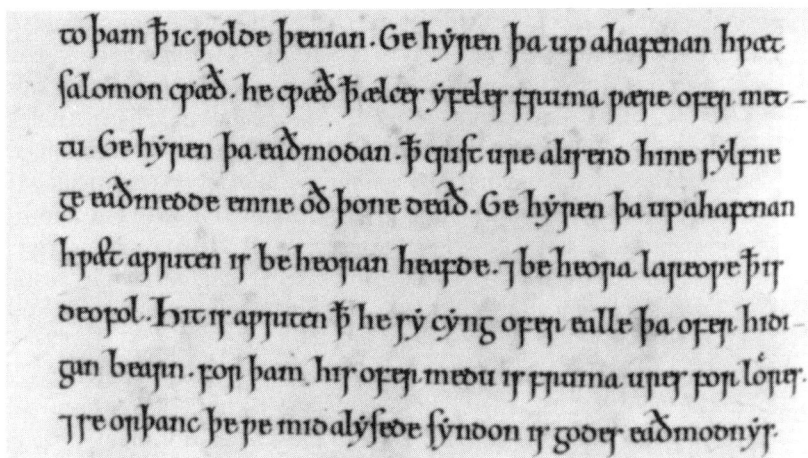

Figure 12.6: CUL, Ii.2.4, fol. 90v (reduced), Anglo-Saxon translation of Pope Gregory's *Cura Pastoralis*, chap. xli, as H. Sweet, ed., *King Alfred's Pastoral Care*, 300/2–9. Exeter script of s.xi[3/4] (*by permission og the Syndics of Cambridge University Library*)

tween 3 September 1638 and 17 July 1639, an extended formative period in his Anglo-Saxon studies.[90] The script is taller than his type-designs, and shows split ascenders (not taken over in the type-designs), but the similarity in sinuosity is strong. Other manuscripts in the group used by Wheelock also show Exeter script of this period, e.g., CCC 190, pp. 351–59 (Ker's items 20–21) and 295–308 (Ker's item 17), where similar features are shown. In fact, nearly a quarter of the manuscripts (or parts of manuscripts) listed (10 out of 41) were in Exeter in the eleventh century, and most of them were produced there, including those produced in Bishop Leofric's scriptorium: CUL Hh.1.10, Ii.2.11, and CCC 190 (B), 191, and 201 (pp. 179–272). This Exeter script of the third quarter of the eleventh century from Bishop Leofric's scriptorium differentiates well between Latin and vernacular forms.[91] It is this script, particularly that in CUL MS Ii.2.4 (Fig. 12.6), that apparently provided the foundation for the overall style of Wheelock's Anglo-Saxon type-designs. To this base he then presumably added the other distinctive letter-forms that he found in various

[90] As noted above, Wheelock was recruited by Spelman in 1637. By the end of that year Spelman regarded him as an equal partner in Anglo-Saxon scholarship (Oates, *Cambridge University Library*, 198).

[91] As noted by T. A. M. Bishop, *English Caroline Minuscule* (Oxford, 1971), 24, commentary to pl. 28 (Corpus 191).

manuscripts as he read them. For some features he apparently took his models from Anglo-Saxon usage in Latin texts; it is unlikely that Wheelock would have made a distinction between Anglo-Saxon and Latin script features, and in any case early Anglo-Saxon manuscripts did not make such a distinction.

The relevant features in the manuscripts with which the corresponding features in his type-designs may be matched are illustrated in the Plates as follows:

1. Hooked terminals. Descenders turned to the left are evident in CUL MS. Ii.2.4 (Fig. 12.6), e.g., "ʃe opþanc" (line 8 = bottom line). They may also be seen in other manuscripts, as CCC 419, p. 308 (Fig. 12.7, line 6), in "ʃppecan" etc.

2. Lower-case ð shows the ascender tagged to the left, as in CUL MS. Ii.2.4 (Fig. 12.6, line 2 in cpæð), CCC 419, p. 308 (Fig. 12.7, line 2 in luриað), TCC B.15.34, p. 79 (Fig. 12.8, line 3 in ða), p. 319 (Fig. 12.9, line 4 in ʃæʒð).

3. Upper-case square C. This feature occurs in CUL Gg.3.28, fol. 44v "CRISTES" (Fig. 12.10, line 3), TCC B.15.34, p. 376 "MARLVS" (Fig. 12.11, line 4), and together with square G (feature 7) in CCC 173, fol.47v "Liрic" (Fig. 12.5, line 1).

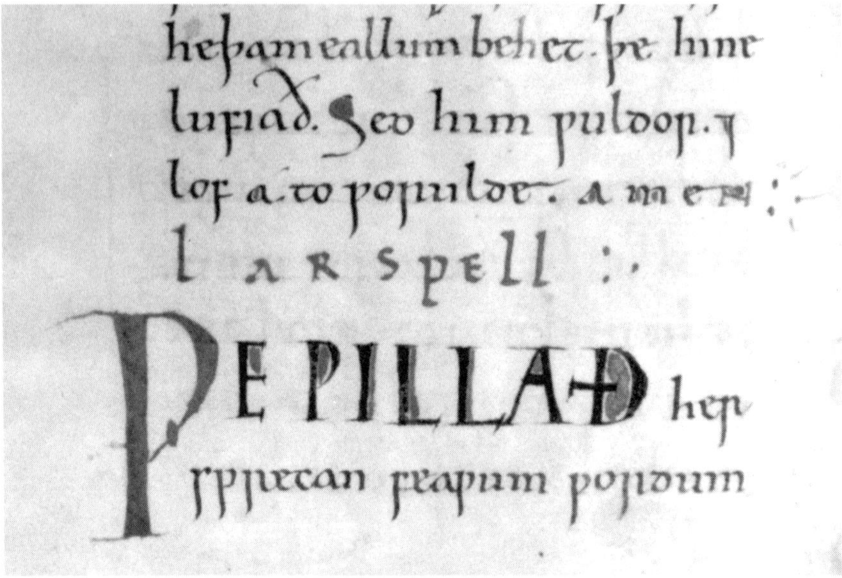

Figure 12.7: CCC, MS. 419, p. 308 (reduced), Anglo-Saxon homily "Larspell" for the 4th Sunday in Lent, as Belfour, *Twelfth-Century Homilies*, 50, beginning (*by permission of the Master and Fellows of Corpus Christi College, Cambridge*)

Figure 12.8: TCC, MS. B.15.34, p. 79 (reduced), Ælfric, Homily "Dominica III post Pascha," ed. B. Assmann, *Angelsächsische Homilien und Heiligenleben* (Kassel, 1889), 73, beginning (*by permission of the Master and Fellows of Trinity College, Cambridge*)

Figure 12.9: TCC, MS. B.15.34, p. 319 (reduced), Ælfric, *CH* I.xxiv, "Dominica IIII Post Pentecosten," ed. P. Clemoes, *Ælfric's Catholic Homilies: The First Series*, EETS s.s. 17 (London, 1997), 371, beginning (*by permission of the Master and Fellows of Trinity College, Cambridge*)

Figure 12.10: CUL, Gg.3.28, fol. 44v (reduced), Ælfric, *CH* I.xiv, "Dominica Palmarum," coll. Clemoes, *Catholic Homilies*, 290, beginning (*by permission of the Syndics of Cambridge University Library*)

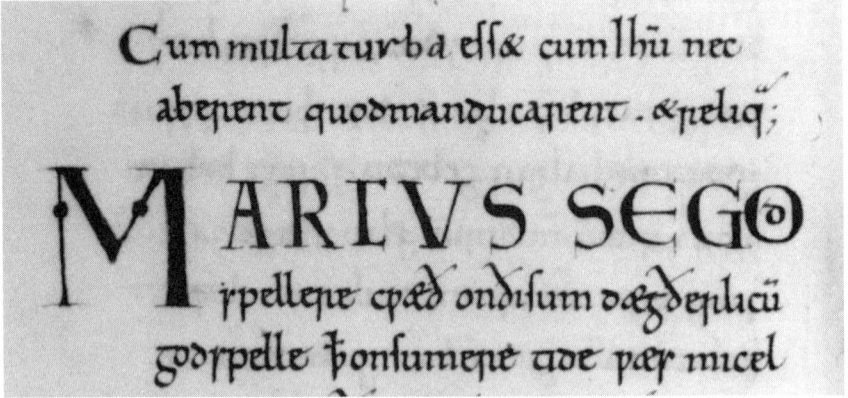

Figure 12.11: TCC, MS. B.15.34, p. 376 (reduced), Ælfric, *CH* II.xxv, "Dominica VIII post Pentecosten," ed. M. Godden, *Second Series*, 230, beginning (*by permission of the Master and Fellows of Trinity College, Cambridge*)

4. Round-backed **D**, with a short ascender ending in a terminal gently hooked upwards, as in TCC B.15.34, p. 319 "GOD" (Fig. 12.9, line 3). Cf. CUL Gg.3.28, fol. 131v "Driht⟨en⟩" (Fig. 12.12, line 7), CCC 201, p. 190 "Dolum" (Fig.12.13, line 2), also Tiberius C.ii (s.viii), fol. 75r, "Deniq:" (Fig. 12.14, line 1).

5. E, with both the upper and the lower arms showing scrolled terminals. Unless transferred from scrolled T this feature does not occur in manuscripts,

Figure 12.12: CUL, Gg.3.28, fol. 131v (reduced), Ælfric, *CH* I.xl, "Dominica II in adventum Domini," coll. Clemoes, *First Series*, 527–8 (*by permission of the Syndics of Cambridge University Library*)

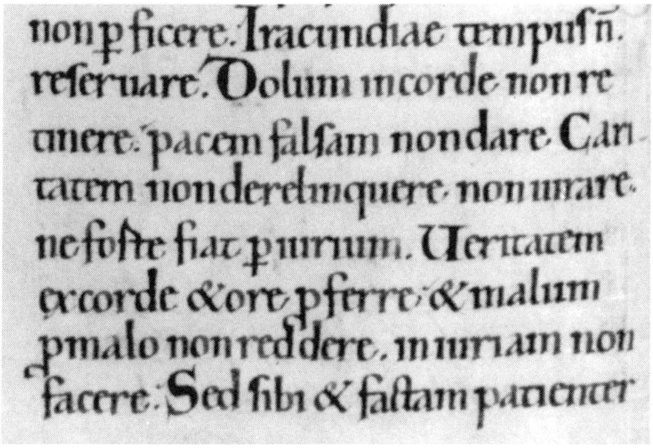
non p ficere. Iracundiae tempus n.
reseruare. Dolum in corde non re
tinere. pacem falsam non dare. Cari
tatem non derelinquere. non iurare.
ne forte fiat p iurium. Veritatem
ex corde & ore p ferre. & malum
p malo non reddere. iniuriam non
facere. Sed sibi & factam patienter

Figure 12.13: CCC, MS. 201, p. 190 (reduced), *Capitula of Theodulf*, ed. Hans Sauer, *Theodulfi Capitula in England: Die altenglische Übersetzung, zusammen mit dem lateinischen Text*, Münchener Universitäts-Schriften 8 (Munich, 1978), 326/23–29, chap. xxi, §§ 22–30 (*by permission of the Master and Fellows of Corpus Christi College, Cambridge*)

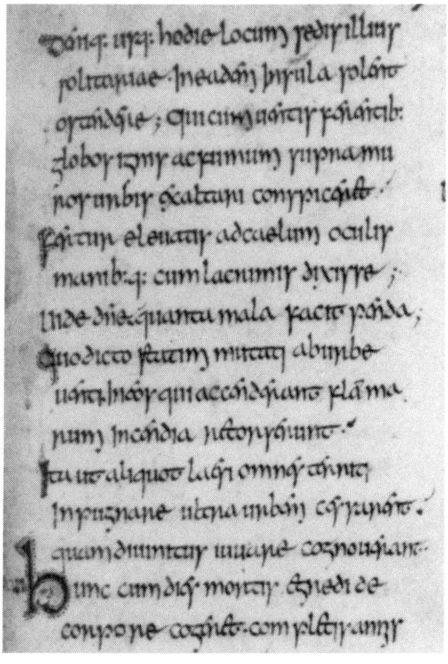

Figure 12.14: BL Cotton Tiberius C.ii, fol. 75r (reduced), Bede, *Historia Ecclesiastica*, III.xvi–xvii, ed. Bertram Colgrave and R. A. B. Mynors, *Bede's Ecclesiastical History of the English People* (Oxford, 1969), 262 (*by permission of the British Library*)

although it is certainly authentically Anglo-Saxon, for example, in its resemblance to the design of wrist-bands known as Class A.[92] The wrist-band illustrated by John Hines is from Holywell Row (nr Mildenhall, Suffolk).[93] Since this particular wrist-band was excavated by the archaeologist T. C. Lethbridge at some time between 1929 and 1948 it was not available to Wheelock, but he may have seen something similar, which served to inspire his design for Anglo-Saxon capital ϵ. Another possible source of inspiration is uncial E with the spaces between the arms shaded to indicate prominence; the shading with metallic ink was applied with a circular motion to provide a ball of colour, as in CCC 188, p. 241 "Erant" (Fig. 12.15, line 5).

6. F, showing a hooked approach stroke at the top of the stem, and a bowed upper arm with the terminal rolled over, as in CUL Gg.3.28, fol. 157v "Foþ" (Fig.

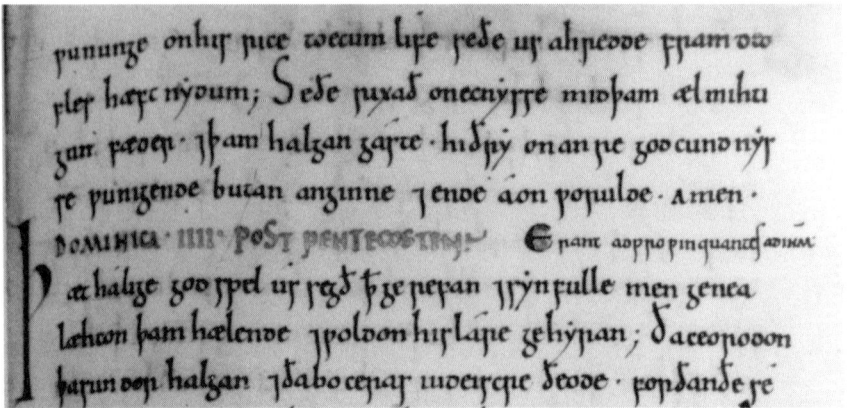

Figure 12.15: CCC, MS. 188, p. 241 (reduced), Ælfric, *CH* I.xxiv, "Dominica IIII post Pentecosten," coll. Clemoes, *First Series*, 371, beginning (*by permission of the Master and Fellows of Corpus Christi College, Cambridge*)

---

[92] I am grateful to Dr Carole Biggam (Glasgow) for drawing my attention to this resemblance.

[93] John Hines, *The Scandinavian Character of Anglian England in the Pre-Viking Period*, British Archaeological Reports, British series 124 (London, 1984), p. 382, fig. 2.5. I am most grateful to Jean Somerville, Project Director for the Cambridge Museum of Archaeology and Anthropology, for her helpfulness in locating this item (no. Z7112B) so that I could examine the original.

Figure 12.16: CUL MS. Gg.3.28, fol. 157v (reduced), Ælfric, *CH* II.ix, "Sancti Gregorii Pape," ed. Godden, *Second Series*, 72, beginning. Note the cross-reference in Wheelock's hand to 'Serm.51', i.e., CUL MS. Ii.1.33 (*by permission of the Syndics of Cambridge University Library*)

12.16, line 2), also Tiberius C.ii (s.viii), fol. 75r "Fenꞇuꞃ" (Fig. 12.14, line 6).

7. Upper-case square G, as in CUL Gg.3.28, fol. 157v "Ᵹregorius" (Fig. 12.16, line 8), TCC B.15.34, p. 319 "\HA/LIGE" (Fig. 12.9, line 3), and together with square C (feature 3) in CCC 173, fol. 47v "Ᵹriꝼ" (Fig. 12.5, line 4).

8. H in uncial form with an ornamental miniature loop attached to the shoulder-side of the upper stem. This feature does not occur in manuscripts. It may have been inspired by h with a bar across the ascender in "DRIЪTLIᴄAN" in CCC 162, p.44 (Fig. 12.17, line 2). Although this h is undoubtedly an error — "drih" with a bar across the ascender of h is an abbreviation for OE *drihten* "lord", as in the same manuscript, p. 252/10 — it may still have provided the idea for the ornamentation in the printed sort. Another possible influence is uncial capital Ъ with an ornamental motif on the ascender, as in CCC 419, p. 73 "ЪER" (Fig. 12.18, line 4); cf. also Tiberius C.ii (s.viii), fol. 75r, "Ъunc" (Fig. 12.14, line 15).

9. I, with a hooked terminal at the base of the stem, as in CUL Gg.3.28, fol. 255r "Ic" (Fig. 12.19, line 2), also Tiberius C.ii (s.viii), fol. 75r, line 19, "In" (not illustrated).

10. T, similar to the lower-case,[94] but with the stroke terminal scrolled. This feature occurs rarely in the manuscripts. An outstanding example is that in

---

[94] Some manuscripts show small t with the stroke curled to distinguish it from Latin, e.g., Oxford, Corpus Christi College, MS. 197, illustrated in Ker, *Catalogue*, pl. II.

Figure 12.17: CCC, MS. 162, p. 44 (reduced), Anglo-Saxon homily "Be þam drihtli-
can sunnandæg folces lar," ed. A. S. Napier in *An English Miscellany Presented to Dr.
Furnivall*, ed. W. P. Ker and idem (Oxford, 1901), 357, beginning (*by permission of the
Master and Fellows of Corpus Christi College, Cambridge*)

Figure 12.18: CCC, MS. 419, p. 73 (reduced), Anglo-Saxon homily "Angelorum nomina,"
ed. A. S. Napier, *Wulfstan* (Berlin, 1883), 226 (no.xlv), beginning (*by permission of the
Master and Fellows of Corpus Christi College, Cambridge*)

Figure 12.19: CUL Gg.3.28, fol. 255r (reduced), Ælfric, Anglo-Saxon version of *De
temporibus anni* (excerpt), ed. H. Henel, EETS o.s. 213 (London, 1942), 2, Preamble
and §§ I.1–4 (*by permission of the Syndics of Cambridge University Library*)

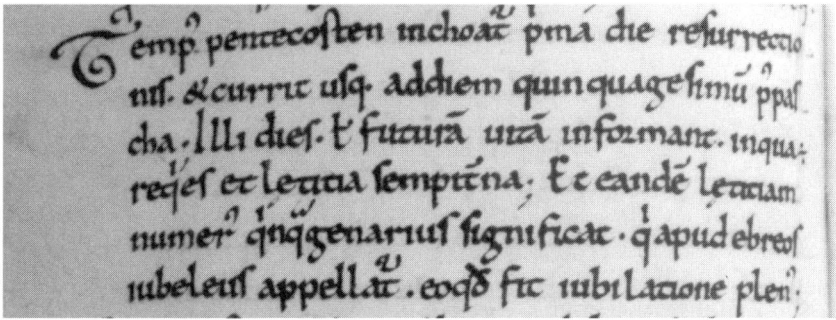

Figure 12.20: CCC, MS. 190, p. 236 (reduced), from *De Septem Ecclesiasticis Gradibus*, 'De Sacerdotibus, Lectiones de Pentecosten,' ed. (excerpted) Bernhard Fehr, *Die Hirtenbriefe Ælfrics*, BaP 9 (Hamburg, 1914), repr. with suppl. Peter Clemoes (Darmstadt, 1966), 243/7–9 (*by permission of the Master and Fellows of Corpus Christi College, Cambridge*)

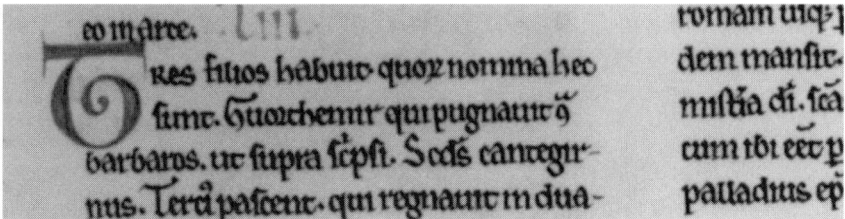

Figure 12.21: CUL Ff.1.27, p. 35 (reduced), from the *Historia Brittonum* (here attrib. Nennius), coll. Theodor Mommsen, *Chronica Minora saec. IV. V. VI. VII*, MGH AA 13 (Berlin, 1898), 192a/8–12 (*by permission of the Syndics of Cambridge University Library*)

Corpus 190, p. 236 "Temp⟨us⟩" (Fig. 12.20, line 2), and Wheelock would have seen others in later manuscripts, such as CUL Ff.1.27, p. 35 (Fig. 12.21, line 2), and CTH 1. For such a T with a curl but not a scroll see CUL Gg.3.28, fol. 44v "To hwi" (Fig. 12.10, line 11), fol. 131v "To ðam", "To ðy" (Fig. 12.12, lines 10, 11).

11. U, with the left part of the stroke curved like a swan's neck, and the right stem showing a hooked terminal at the base, as in CCC 201, p. 190 "Ueritatem" (Fig. 12.13, line 5), TCC B.15.34, p. 79 "URE" (Fig. 12.8, line 2). Cf. also CUL Gg.3.28, fol. 44v "Unꞇyȝað" (Fig. 12.10, line 8), fol. 131v "Undeꝼꞃꞇandað" (Fig. 12.12, line 5), "Uꞃ" (Fig. 12.12, line 2).

12. Þ is rounded, not "square" or sharply angled. This feature is common in the manuscripts, e.g., CUL Gg.3.28, fol. 131v "Þeꝥodlice" (Fig. 12.12, line 1), fol. 255r "Þiꞇodlice" (Fig. 12.19, line 4), CCC 419, p. 308 "ÞE ÞILLAÐ" (Fig. 12.7, line 5).

Roman typefaces triumphed "over the various national letter styles in much of Europe after 1530," e.g., "Black Letter" (Textura) in England, because of "the prestige of their origins and the prestige of the Latin texts for which they seemed a natural means of expression."[95] It was the essence of this triumph that Archbishop Parker aimed to recreate when he had his own Anglo-Saxon types made, probably through the auspices of his Latin secretary, John Joscelyn. Through the choice of authentic letter-forms and the prestige of the ancient English texts printed with them, Parker's Great Primer Anglo-Saxon too was a prestige typeface.[96] The predominant influence on Parker's type-designs was Worcester manuscripts, and MS. Junius 121 in particular. Despite Wheelock's familiarity with this kind of script in CUL MS. Kk.3.18, which he used as his base text for the Anglo-Saxon Bede, he has apparently rethought the process through, using as his model Exeter script from Leofric's scriptorium of the third quarter of the eleventh century. Wheelock's Great Primer Anglo-Saxon is combined with Tavernier's Great Primer Roman (with some mixed sorts). One of the great advantages of Roman type is that the presence of serifs increases readability, the gelling of words on the page.[97] Wheelock's Anglo-Saxon type in practice retained serifs in letters that were not provided with Anglo-Saxon special sorts, but in other letters where special sorts were provided, serifs were generally dispensed with in favor of sinuosity of shape. Whereas Exeter script from Leofric's scriptorium (Fig. 12.6) shows an evenness of sinuous approach, this consistency is not evident in Wheelock's text (Fig. 12.2) because it is an amalgam of standard roman and special Anglo-Saxon sorts. Wheelock's rethinking of the process went so far as to re-model the same lower-case letters as were used in previous Anglo-Saxon fonts, and to extend the number of upper-case special sorts. His decision not to repeat Parker's second Æ, or Þ, suggests that expense may have been a consideration. Certainly it would have been much more expensive to design special sorts for every letter of the alphabet.[98]

The combination of Wheelock's Great Primer Anglo-Saxon, which is modeled on script, and Tavernier's Great Primer Roman, which is, of course,

---

[95] Martin, *The History*, 304.

[96] Lucas, "'A Testimonye'."

[97] As opposed to legibility, which is the distinguishability of individual letters, a distinction made by Walter Tracy, "Legibility and Readability: The Vocabulary of Type, 1986," in *Typographers on Type: An Illustrated Anthology from William Morris to the Present Day*, ed. Ruari McLean (London, 1995), 170–72, here 170–71.

[98] For some remarks on the costs of creating a (partial) Anglo-Saxon font see Lucas, "Parker," 44–45. Compare Sir Henry Spelman's remark (about a different matter) in his letter of 5 October 1638: "my mynde & purse be not of like dimension."

modeled on earlier designs of roman type, was not a marriage made in heaven. But it was a good working partnership that clothed Wheelock's scholarship in graceful attire, sufficiently attractive and interesting still to be talked about today. In a different context Matthew Carter used the phrase "nostalgic pastiche" to describe a type-design that looks back to various earlier models without thinking through the new design's contemporary purpose.[99] Wheelock's Anglo-Saxon type-designs are not a pastiche, because they look to a consistent model to inform them: Exeter script from Leofric's scriptorium. They are nostalgic in the sense that they were a deliberate attempt to re-create typographically the style and impact of handwriting in authentic manuscripts. This style has even been extended to some letters that do not show such features in the manuscripts: the most notable instance is the E with its "wrought-iron curlyhues" possibly taken over from T. However, the adopted mode of presentation was not just a matter of taste, still less of acceding to the preferences of readers, but rather an attempt to enshrine authority in elegance, the elegance of authenticity. Wheelock has securely established himself in the tradition begun by Parker of presenting Anglo-Saxon with as much authenticity as possible.[100]

Bibliography

Amert, Kay. "Origins of the French Old-Style: The Roman and Italic Types of Simon de Colines." *Printing History* 14 (1992): 17-40.

Anderson, Donald M. *The Art of Written Forms: The Theory and Practice of Calligraphy.* New York, 1969.

Barker, Nicolas. "The Aldine Roman in Paris, 1530-1534." *The Library* 5.29 (1974): 5-20.

---

[99] Matthew Carter, "Now We Have Mutable Type, 1990," in *Typographers*, ed. McLean, 182–86, here 184.

[100] A version of this paper was presented to the Cambridge Bibliographical Society in October 2001. It is a pleasure to thank both the Bibliographical Society (London) for granting a subvention in support of the research associated with the present article and the Neil Ker fund of the British Academy for making a grant towards the cost of acquiring photographs of the manuscripts. For advice on aspects arising in the writing of it I should like to thank Carole Biggam, Elisabeth Leedham-Green, and Peggy Smith, and for commenting on a draft version as well Lotte Hellinga and Hendrik Vervliet. I am solely responsible for the views expressed and for any errors.

———. *Aldus Manutius and the Development of Greek Script and Type in the Fifteenth Century.* New York, 1992.

Benson, Thomas. *Vocabularium Anglo-Saxonicum.* Oxford, 1701.

Bishop, T. A. M. *English Caroline Minuscule.* Oxford, 1971.

Blomefield, Francis, and Charles Parkin. *An Essay Towards a Topographical History of the County of Norfolk.* 11 vols. London, 1805-1810.

Bozzolo, Carla, Dominique Coq, Denis Muzerelle, and Enzio Ornato. "Page savante, page vulgaire: étude comparative de la mise en page des livres en latin et en français écrits ou imprimés en France au XVe siècle." In *La Présentation du Livre,* ed. Emmanuèle Baumgartner and Nicole Boulestreau, 122-33. Paris, 1987.

Bremmer, Rolf. "The Correspondence of Johannes de Laet (1581-1649) as a Mirror of his Life." *LIAS: Sources and Documents Relating to the Early Modern History of Ideas* 25 (1998): 139-64.

Carley, James P. "Books Seen by Samuel Ward 'in Bibliotheca Regia', *circa* 1614." *British Library Journal* 16 (1990): 89-98.

Carter, Harry. *A View of Early Typography up to about 1600.* Oxford, 1969.

Carter, Matthew. "Now We Have Mutable Type, 1990." In *Typographers on Type: An Illustrated Anthology from William Morris to the Present Day,* ed. Ruari McLean, 182-86. London, 1995.

———. "Theories of Letterform Construction. Part 1." *Printing History* 14 (1992): 3-16.

Clemoes, Peter. *Ælfric's Catholic Homilies: The First Series: Text.* EETS s.s. 17. Oxford, 1997.

Conner, Patrick W. *Anglo-Saxon Exeter: A Tenth-Century Cultural History.* Woodbridge, 1993.

Dickins, Bruce. *The Genealogical Preface to the Anglo-Saxon Chronicle.* Department of Anglo-Saxon Occasional Papers 2. Cambridge, 1952.

Drage, Elaine. "Bishop Leofric and the Exeter Cathedral Chapter, 1050-1072: A Reassessment of the Evidence." D. Phil. diss., Oxford University, 1978.

Dumville, David N. "On the Dating of Some Late Anglo-Saxon Liturgical Manuscripts." *Transactions of the Cambridge Bibliographical Society* 10 (1991): 40-57.

———. "The Sixteenth-Century History of Two Cambridge Books from Sawley." *Transactions of the Cambridge Bibliographical Society* 7 (1980): 427–44.

————. "The West-Saxon Genealogical Regnal List: Manuscript and Texts." *Anglia* 104 (1986): 1-32.

Ellis, Henry. *Original Letters of Eminent Literary Men of the Sixteenth, Seventeenth, and Eighteenth Centuries.* Camden Society 1.23. London, 1843.

Febvre, Lucien, and Henri-Jean Martin. *The Coming of the Book: The Impact of Printing 1450-1800*, trans. David Gerard, ed. Geoffrey Nowell-Smith and David Wooton. London, 1976.

Feliciano, Felice. *Alphabetum Romanum*, ed. Giovanni Mardersteig, trans. R. H. Boothroyd. Verona, 1960.

Flood, John L. "Nationalistic Currents in Early German Typography." *The Library* 6.15 (1993): 125-41.

Ferguson, Lydia. "*Custodes librorum*: Service, Staff, and Salaries 1601-1855." In *Essays on the History of Trinity College Library, Dublin*, ed. Vincent Kinane and Anne Walsh, 25-38. Dublin, 2000.

Gaskell, Philip. *A New Introduction to Bibliography*. Oxford, 1972.

————. "A Nomenclature for the Letter-forms of Roman Type." *The Library* 5.29 (1974): 42-51.

Gibson, Margaret, T. A. Heslop, and Richard W. Pfaff, eds. *The Eadwine Psalter: Text, Image, and Monastic Culture in Twelfth-Century Canterbury.* Publications of the Modern Humanities Research Association 14. London, 1992.

Gneuss, Helmut. *Handlist of Anglo-Saxon Manuscripts: A List of Manuscripts and Manuscript Fragments Written or Owned in England up to 1100.* Tempe, AZ, 2001.

Godden, Malcolm. *Ælfric's Catholic Homilies: The Second Series: Text.* EETS s.s. 5. London, 1979.

Goines, David L. *A Constructed Roman Alphabet: A Geometric Analysis of the Greek and Roman Capitals and of the Arabic Numerals.* Boston, 1982.

Graham, Timothy. "Abraham Wheelock's Use of CCCC MS 41 (Old English Bede) and the Borrowing of Manuscripts from the Library of Corpus Christi College." *Cambridge Bibliographical Society Newsletter* (Summer 1997): 10-16.

Haddan, Arthur W., and William Stubbs. *Councils and Ecclesiastical Documents relaing to Great Britain and Ireland.* Oxford, 1871.

Hardwick, Charles, ed. *Thomas of Elmham, Historia Abbatiæ S. Augustini.* Rolls Series 8. London, 1858.

Hargreaves, Geoffrey D. "Florentine Script, Paduan Script, and Roman Type." *Gutenberg Jahrbuch* 67 (1992): 15-34

Hetherington, Sue M. *The Beginnings of Old English Lexicography*. Spicewood, TX, 1980.

Hellinga, Lotte. "The Bookshop of the World: Books and their Makers as Agents of Cultural Change." In *The Bookshop of the World: The Role of the Low Countries in the Book-Trade, 1473-1941*, ed. eadem, Alastair Duke, Jacob Harskamp, and Theo Hermans, 11-29. 't Goy-Houton, 2001.

———. "Printing." In *The Cambridge History of the Book in Britain*, Vol. 3, *1400-1557*, ed. eadem and J. B. Trapp, 65-108. Cambridge, 1999.

Hines, John. *The Scandinavian Character of Anglian England in the Pre-Viking Period*. British Archaeological Reports, British Series 124. London, 1984.

Holdsworth, Richard, ed. *Irenodia Cantabrigiensis ob Paciferum Serenissimi Regis Caroli è Scotia Reditum*. Cambridge, 1641.

Holt, Peter M. *Studies in the History of the Near East*. London, 1973.

James, Montague Rhodes. *The Canterbury Psalter*. London, 1935.

Kaufmann, Claus M. *Romanesque Manuscripts 1066-1190*. Survey of Manuscripts Illuminated in the British Isles 3. London, 1975.

Ker, N. R. *Catalogue of Manuscripts Containing Anglo-Saxon*. Oxford, 1957; repr. with a supplement, Oxford, 1990.

——— . *Medieval Libraries of Great Britain: A List of Surviving Books*. London, 1964.

——— and Andrew G. Watson. *Medieval Libraries of Great Britain: A List of Surviving Books. Supplement to 2nd Edition*. London, 1987.

Lane, John A. "Arthur Nicholls and his Greek Type for the King's Printing House." *The Library* 6.13 (1991): 297-322.

Liebermann, Felix. *Die Gesetze der Angelsachsen*. 3 vols. Halle, 1903-1916.

L'Isle, William. *A Saxon Treatise Concerning the Old And New Testament*. . . . London, 1623.

Lowe, E. A. *Codices Latini Antiquiores*. Part 2, *Great Britain and Ireland*. Oxford, 1935; 2nd rev. ed. Oxford, 1972.

Lucas, Peter J. *An Analytical Bibliographical Catalogue of Early Printed Books Containing Anglo-Saxon Printed with Special Sorts*. London, forthcoming.

——— . "Parker, Lambarde, and the Provision of the Special Sorts for Printing Anglo-Saxon in the Sixteenth Century." *Journal of the Printing Historical Society* 28 (1999): 41-69.

———. "'A Testimonye of Verye Ancient Tyme?' Some Manuscript Models for the Parkerian Anglo-Saxon Type-Designs." In *Of the Making of Books: Medieval Manuscripts, their Scribes and Readers: Essays Presented to M.B. Parkes*, ed. Pamela R. Robinson and Rivkah Zim, 147-88. Aldershot, 1997.

Lutz, Angelika. "The Study of the Anglo-Saxon Chronicle in the Seventeenth Century and the Establishment of Old English Studies in the Universities." In *The Recovery of Old English: Anglo-Saxon in the Sixteenth and Seventeenth Centuries*, ed. Timothy Graham, 1-82. Kalamazoo, 2000.

McKitterick, David A. *Four Hundred Years of University Printing and Publishing in Cambridge 1584-1984. Catalogue of the Exhibition in the University Library Cambridge.* Cambridge, 1984.

———. *A History of Cambridge University Press*, Vol. 1: *Printing and the Book Trade in Cambridge 1534-1698.* Cambridge, 1992.

Mardersteig, Giovanni. "Aldo Manuzio e i caratteri di Francesco Griffo da Bologna." In *Studi di Bibliografia e di Storia in onore di Tammaro de Marinis*, 3: 105-47. Verona, 1964.

Martin, Henri-Jean. *The History and Power of Writing*, trans. Lydia G. Cochrane. Chicago, 1995.

Mores, Edward. *A Dissertation upon English Typographical Founders and Founderies* (1778), ed. Harry Carter and Christopher Ricks. Oxford Bibliographical Society n.s. 9. Oxford, 1961.

Morison, Stanley. *Selected Essays in the History of Letter-Forms in Manuscript and Print*, ed. David McKitterick. 2 vols. Cambridge, 1981.

Murphy, Michael. "Abraham Wheloc's Edition of Bede's *History* in Old English." *Studia Neophilologica* 39 (1967): 45-59.

Nichols, John. *Bibliotheca Topographica Britannica.* 8 vols. London, 1780-1790.

Oates, John C. T. *Abraham Whelock (1593-1653): Orientalist, Anglo-Saxonist, and University Librarian.* Sandars Lectures in Bibliography 1966. Unpubl. typescript, C.U.L. Cam.b.966.2.

———. *Cambridge University Library: A History. From the Beginnings to the Copyright Act of Queen Anne.* Cambridge, 1986.

Parr, Richard D. D. *A Collection of Three Hundred Letters Written between the most Reverend Father in God James Usher, Late Arch-bishop of Armagh and Primate of All Ireland, and others.* London, 1686.

Parry, Graham. *The Trophies of Time: English Antiquarians of the Seventeenth Century.* Oxford, 1995.

Pollard, Alfred W., and Gilbert R. Redgrave. *A Short-Title Catalogue of Books Printed in England, Scotland, and Ireland and of English Books Printed Abroad 1475-1640*. 3 vols. 2nd ed. rev. William A. Jackson and F. S. Ferguson. London, 1976, repr. 1991.

Pulsiano, Phillip. "The Scribes and Old English Gloss of the *Eadwine's Canterbury Psalter*." In *Proceedings of the Patristic, Medieval, and Renaissance Conference* (Villanova University, Augustinian Historical Institute) 14, 223-60. Villanova, PA, 1989.

———, and A. N. Doane, eds. *Anglo-Saxon Manuscripts in Microfiche Facsimile*. 12 vols. Binghamton, NY and Tempe, AZ, 1994- .

Ravius, Christianus. *Sesqui-Decuria Epistolarum Adoptivarum ex variis orbis partibus commissarum*. London, 1648.

Robinson, Fred C., and E. G. Stanley. *Old English Verse Texts from Many Sources: A Comprehensive Collection*. EEMF 23. Copenhagen, 1991.

Sclater, William. *The Crowne of Righteousness*. London, 1654.

Sisam, Kenneth. "Anglo-Saxon Royal Genealogies." *Proceedings of the British Academy* 39 (1953): 287-348.

Smith, Margaret M. "The Design Relationship between the Manuscript and the Incunable." In *A Millennium of the Book: Production, Design, and Illustration in Manuscript and Print 900-1900*, ed. Robin Myers and Michael Harris, 23-43. Winchester, 1994.

Somner, William. *Dictionarium Saxonico-Latino-Anglicum*. Oxford, 1659.

Spelman, Henry. *Concilia, Decreta, Leges, Constitutiones, in re Ecclesiarum Orbis Britannici*. London, 1639.

———. *Psalterium Davidis Latino-Saxonicum Vetus*. London, 1640.

[Star Chamber]. *A Decree of Starre-Chamber, concerning Printing*. London, 1637.

Taylor, Simon. *The Anglo-Saxon Chronicle: A Collaborative Edition*. Vol. 4. MS B. Cambridge, 1983.

Temple, Elżbieta. *Anglo-Saxon Manuscripts 900-1066*. Survey of Manuscripts Illuminated in the British Isles 2. London, 1976.

Thorpe, Benjamin. *The Anglo-Saxon Chronicle according to the Several Original Authorities*. 2 vols. Rolls Series 23. London, 1861.

Toomer, Gerald J. *Eastern Wisedome and Learning: The Study of Arabic in Seventeenth-Century England*. Oxford, 1996.

Thompson, Edward Maude. *An Introduction to Greek and Latin Palaeography*. Oxford, 1912.

Tracy, Walter. "Legibility and Readability: The Vocabulary of Type, 1986." In *Typographers on Type*, ed. McLean, 170-72.

Treadwell, Michael. "The Grover Typefoundery." *Journal of the Printing Historical Society* 15 (1980/1981): 36-53.

Twomey, Juliet. "Whence Jenson. A Search for the Origins of Roman Type." *Fine Print* 15 (1989): 134-41.

Twyman, Michael. "The Graphic Presentation of Language." *Information Design Journal* 3 (1982): 2-22.

Ullmann, Berthold L. *Ancient Writing and Its Influence*. London, 1932.

Vaciago, Paolo. "Old English Glosses to Latin Texts: A Bibliographical Handlist." *Medioevo e Rinascimento* 4 (1993): 1-67.

Vervliet, Hendrik D. L. *Sixteenth-Century Printing Types of the Low Countries*. Amsterdam, 1968.

——, and Harry Carter. *Type Specimen Facsimiles II*. London, 1972.

Wheelock, Abraham, ed. William Lambarde's *Archaionomia, sive de Priscis Anglorum Legibus libri*. Cambridge, 1644.

——, ed. *Historiæ Ecclesiasticæ Gentis Anglorum Libri V a Venerabili Beda Presbytero scripti; Chronologia Anglo-Saxonica*. Cambridge, 1643.

——, ed. *Historiæ Ecclesiasticæ . . . ; Quibus in calce operis Saxonicam Chronologiam, seriem hujus inprimis Historiæ complectentem, nunquam antea in lucem editam, nunc quoque primò Latinè versam contexuimus; Quibus accesserunt Anglo-Saxonicæ Leges, et ultimó Leges Henrici I nunc primùm editæ*. Cambridge, 1644.

Whitelock, Dorothy. "The Old English Bede." *Proceedings of the British Academy* 48 (1962): 57-90.

Wing, Donald G. *Short-Title Catalogue of Books Printed in England, Scotland, Ireland, Wales, British America and of English Books Printed in Other Countries 1641-1700*. 3 vols. New York, 1945-1951; 2nd ed., rev. Timothy J. Crist, John J. Morrison, Carolyn W. Nelson, and Matthew Seccombe. 4 vols. New York, 1982-1998.

Zachrisson, Bror. *Studies in the Legibility of Printed Text*. Stockholm Studies in Educational Psychology 11. Stockholm, 1965.

Table 5: Manuscripts in Tables 1-4 with references to Helmut Gneuss, *Handlist of Anglo-Saxon Manuscripts: A List of Manuscripts and Manuscript Fragments Written or Owned in England up to 1100* (Tempe, AZ, 2001); Ker, *Catalogue*; A. N. Doane, gen. ed., *Anglo-Saxon Manuscripts in Microfiche Facsimile*, 13 vols. (Tempe, AZ, 1994-); Elżbieta Temple, *Anglo-Saxon Manuscripts 900-1066*, Survey of Manuscripts Illuminated in the British Isles 2 (London, 1976); Claus M. Kauffmann, *Romanesque Manuscripts 1066-1190*, Survey of Manuscripts Illuminated in the British Isles 3 (London, 1975); also E. A. Lowe, *Codices Latini Antiquiores*, part 2, *Great Britain and Ireland* (Oxford, 1935).

	Gneuss	Ker	ASMMF	Temple	Kauffman
Ff.1.23	4	13	93	80	
Ff.1.27 (pp.1-40, 73-252)	14	No	94		102
(pp.253-642)	No	No	94		102
Ff.1.28	No	No	No		
Gg.3.28	11	15	95		
Hh.1.10	13	17	97		
Ii.1.33	No	18	98		
Ii.2.4	14	19	99		
Ii.2.11	15	20	100		
Ii.4.6	18	21	101		
Kk.3.18	22	23	103		
CCC 41	39	32	25	81	
CCC 138	No	No	No		
CCC 140	44	35	30		
CCC 162	50	38/41	33		
CCC 173	52	39	34		
173, fols. 59-83	53	40	34	Lowe II.no.123	
CCC 188	58	43	37		
CCC 190	59	45	38		
CCC 191	60	46	39		
CCC 198	64	48	41	88	
CCC 201, fols.1-178	65	49	42		
fols.179-272	66	50	42		
CCC 279	81	No	No		
CCC 318 (art.4)	No	No	No		
CCC 383	102	65	55		

	Gneuss	Ker	ASMMF	Temple	Kauffman
CCC 419	108	68	58		
CSJ 27	No	No	No		
CSS 102 (olim Δ.5.17)	No	No	No		
TCC B.15.34	177	86	80	74	
TCC R.4.26 (ME)	No	No	No		
TCC R.5.16	No	No	No		
TCC R.5.22, fols.1-43	No	No	81		
fols.44-71	No	No	81		
fols.72-158	180	87	81		
TCC R.17.1	No	91	85		68
CTH 1	No	No	No		
Cotton Otho B.xi	357	180	217		
Tiberius A.iii, fol.178	364	188	223		
Tiberius C.ii	377	198	232	Lowe II.no.191	

Appendix

An Inventory of Wheelock's correspondence with Sir Henry Spelman, Sir John Spelman, and Sir Symonds D'Ewes.[101]

Language: English unless otherwise stated.

---

[101] This list aims at completeness, but further letters may well turn up. For Wheelock's letter to [Johannes de Laet] see Rolf H. Bremmer, "The Correspondence of Johannes de Laet (1581–1649) as a Mirror of his Life," *LIAS: Sources and Documents Relating to the Early Modern History of Ideas* 25 (1998): 139–64, here 156. For his correspondence with Ussher see Richard D. D. Parr, *A Collection of Three Hundred Letters Written between the most Reverend Father in God James Usher, Late Arch-bishop of Armagh and Primate of all Ireland, and others* (London, 1686), Wing S4663. For Wheelock's correspondence with Sir Thomas Adams about his Arabic professorship at Cambridge see the extracts from Adams's letters printed by Peter M. Holt, *Studies in the History of the Near East* (London, 1973), 37–42. For his letters to Christianus Ravius of 12 Nov. 1647 and 11 Feb. 1648 see Christianus Ravius, *Sesqui-Decuria Epistolarum Adoptivarum ex variis orbis partibus commissarum* (London, 1648), Wing R.315, 28–32. For his other correspondence relating to Arabic matters see Toomer, *Eastern Wisedome*, 87–91, where he makes use of the Samuel Hartlib papers at Sheffield University, also available on CD-Rom; copy-extracts from letters by Wheelock to Hartlib (the first dated 12 Nov. 1647) are at fols. 33/4/1A–4A.

Status: o = original
a = original written by an amanuensis
d = draft
c = copy
s = summary
p = printed (by)

Document: [Institution,] class-mark, fol. nos (art. no.)

Dates: Those between 1 January and 25 March have been adjusted to conform to the modern calendar year beginning on 1 January.

Abbreviations: F   French
L   Latin
HenryS   Sir Henry Spelman
JohnS   John Spelman (son)
RogerS   Roger Spelman (grandson)
W   Abraham Wheelock

Manuscripts:

Add.7596	=	CUL, MS Additional 7596
Add.34600	=	BL, MS Additional 34600
Add.34601	=	BL, MS. Additional 34601
Dd.3.12	=	CUL, MS. Dd.3.12
Dd.3.63	=	CUL, MS. Dd.3.63
Dd.3.64	=	CUL, MS. Dd.3.64
Harley 374	=	BL, MS. Harley 374
Harley 7041	=	BL, MS. Harley 7041
Tanner 67	=	OBL, MS. Tanner 67
Tanner 70	=	OBL, MS. Tanner 70

1637

HenryS to W   30/06/37   Barbican/Cambridge   Dd.3.12, fols. 6–7   o
c by Baker in Harley 7041, fol. 40rv; c in CUL Add. 7596, item 1;
Begins: Good Mr Wheelock I accoumpe my selfe very happy in your acquaintance.

HenryS to W   04/08/37   Barbican/Cambridge   Dd.3.12, fols. 8–9   o
c by Baker in Harley 7041, fol. 40r; c in CUL Add. 7596, item 2; p
Ellis, *Original Letters*, 153, no. 64;
Begins: Good Mr Wheelock I thanke you for yo⟨ur⟩ love and curtuosie towardes me.

HenryS to W   22/09/37   London/Cambridge   Dd.3.12, fols. 10–11   o
c by Baker in Harley 7041, fol. 40v; c in CUL Add. 7596, item 3;
Begins: S⟨er⟩ I am mutch in yo⟨ur⟩ debt. . . .

W to HenryS   04/10/37   Cambridge/Barbican   Tanner 70, fols. 174–75   o
Begins: Right worshipful, this weeke we had the com⟨m⟩encem⟨en⟩t in publick . . .

HenryS to W   12/10/37   Barbican/Cambridge   Dd.3.12, fols. 12–13   o
                c by Baker in Harley 7041, fols. 40v–41r; c in CUL Add. 7596,
                item 4;
Begins: Good Mr Wheelock Yo⟨ur⟩ curtuosie and greate paynes. . . .

HenryS to W   04/11/37   Barbican/[Cambridge]   Dd.3.12, fol. 14   o
                c by Baker in Harley 7041, fol. 41r; c in CUL Add. 7596, item 5;
Begins: Good Mr Wheelock I was troubled. . . .

HenryS to W   08/12/37   Barbican/Cambridge   Dd.3.12, fols. 15–16   o
                c by Baker in Harley 7041, fol. 41r; c in CUL Add. 7596, item 6;
Begins: S.P. I receiued yo⟨ur⟩ laste weekes l⟨ett⟩re. . . .

HenryS to W   24/01/38   Barbican/[Cambridge]   Dd.3.12, fol. 19   o
                c in CUL Add. 7596, item 7;
Begins: S.P. I haue yet no nere matter to write. . . .

HenryS to W   02/02/38   Barbican/Cambridge   Dd.3.12, fols. 20–21   o
                c in CUL Add. 7596, item 8;
Begins: Mr Wheelock I thanke you for yo⟨ur⟩ transcript⟨es⟩ | yesterday receiued,

HenryS to W   06/04/38   Barbican/Cambridge   Dd.3.12, fols. 22–3   o
                c by Baker in Harley 7041, fol. 41v; c in CUL Add. 7596, item 9;
Begins: Mr Wheelock I haue not yet answered | yo⟨ur⟩ l⟨ett⟩re of a fortnight since. . . .

JohnS to W   06/04/38   Barbican/Cambridge   Dd.3.12, fols. 73–4   o
                c by Baker in Harley 7041, fol. 46v; c in CUL Add. 7596, item [38];
Begins: S⟨er⟩ I giue you many thanks for yo⟨ur⟩ paines y⟨ou⟩ pleased | to take in my
behalfe, ...

HenryS to W   04/05/38   Barbican/Cambridge   Dd.3.12, fols. 24–25   o
                c by Baker in Harley 7041, fols. 41v–42r; c in CUL Add. 7596,
                item 10;
Begins: SP. You know I haue a very faire & antient | interliniarie Latino Saxonicu⟨m⟩
Psaltar. . . .

HenryS to W   08/06/38   Barbican/Cambridge   Dd.3.12, fols. 26–27   o
                c by Baker in Harley 7041, fol. 42r; c in CUL Add. 7596, item 11;
Begins: I thanke you for yo⟨ur⟩ l⟨ett⟩re and paynes. . . .

HenryS to W   15/06/38   Barbican/Cambridge   Dd.3.12, fols. 40–41   o
                c in CUL Add. 7596, item 12;
Begins: Mr Wheelock many intervenient occasions | put it out of my mynde to write
unto you | in tyme.

HenryS to W   31/08/38   Barbican/[Cambridge]   Dd.3.12, fol. 28   o
              c by Baker in Harley 7041, fol. 42r; c in CUL Add. 7596, item 13;
Begins: Mr Wheelock. I was gladde to rec[eiue] yo⟨ur⟩ l⟨ett⟩re | but sory. . . .

HenryS to W   05/09/38   Barbican/Cambridge   Dd.3.12, fols. 29–30   o
              c by Baker in Harley 7041, fol. 42rv; c in CUL Add. 7596, item 14;
Begins: Mr Wheelock. As of the Saxon Psalter there | is mutch variety in the Mss.

HenryS to W   28/09/38   Barbican/Cambridge   Dd.3.12, fols. 31–32   o
              c by Baker in Harley 7041, fol. 42v; c in CUL Add. 7596, item 15;
              p Ellis, *Original Letters*, 154–55, no. 55;
Begins: Mr Wheelock I gave my lo. of Ely thank⟨es⟩ in yo⟨ur⟩ | behalfe. . . .

HenryS to W   05/10/38   Barbican/Cambridge   Dd.3.12, fols. 33–34   o
              c by Baker in Harley 7041, fol. 42v; c in CUL Add. 7596, item 16;
Begins: Good Mr Whelock though my mynde & purse | be not of like dimension

HenryS to W   02/11/38   Barbican/Cambridge   Dd.3.12, fols.35–6   o
              c by Baker in Harley 7041, fol. 43r; c in CUL Add. 7596, item 17;
              p Ellis, *Original Letters*, 156–57, no.56;
Begins: Mr Wheelock (to lett all other matter⟨es⟩ reste in | sylence for this tyme)

HenryS to W   08/11/38   Barbican/Cambridge   Dd.3.12, fols. 38–9   o
              c by Baker in Harley 7041, fols. 43rv; c in CUL Add. 7596, item 18;
Begins: Mr Wheelock I am very ill vsed by yo⟨ur⟩ | Cambridge Carrier. . . .

W to HenryS   13/11/38   Norwich/Barbican   Tanner 67, fols. 43–44   o
Begins: Right w⟨orshipfu⟩ll. I haue cause to pray for yo⟨ur⟩ worship. . . .

HenryS to W   30/11/38   Barbican/[Cambridge]   Dd.3.12, fol. 37   o
              c by Baker in Harley 7041, fol. 43r; c in CUL Add. 7596, item 19;
Begins: Mr Wheelock yf you haue or may finde Middleton better then I reported it . . .

W to HenryS   05/12/38   Cambridge/-   Dd.3.64, fols. 5–6   o
Begins: Right worshipful, my most bounden dutie remembred: Mr Rylie . . .

HenryS to W   22/12/[38]   Barbican/Cambridge   Dd.3.12, fols. 17–18   o
              c by Baker in Harley 7041, fols. 41rv; c in CUL Add. 7596, item 20;
Begins: S.P. yf all thing⟨es⟩ falle out to yo⟨ur⟩ mynde | at Middleton. . . . The sequence
in Add. 7596 suggests 1638 rather than 1637

W to HenryS   [1638?]   Cambridge/Barbican   Add. 34600, fols.197–198 o
Begins: Right worshipfull, After my humble dutie p⟨ro⟩mised | I am bound to giue . . .

HenryS to W   14/01/39   Barbican/Cambridge   Dd.3.12, fols. 42–43   o
              c by Baker in Harley 7041, fol. 43v; c in CUL Add.7596, item 21;

Begins: I haue nothing at this tyme, but my | Comendacons to you, supposing by yo⟨ur⟩ former | l⟨ett⟩res that it may be I shall see you ere long | at Londen, . . .

HenryS to W   31/05/39   Barbican/[Cambridge]   Dd.3.12, fol. 44   o
c by Baker in Harley 7041, fol. 43v; c in CUL Add. 7596, item 22;
Begins: Mr Wheelock I haue nothinge to write but si vales | bene est ego quidem valeo.

HenryS to W   28/06/39   Barbican/Cambridge   Dd.3.12, fols. 45–6   o
c by Baker in Harley 7041, fols. 43v–44r; c in CUL Add. 7596, item 23;
Begins: Mr Wheelock. After many commendacons | I sende you herew⟨ith⟩ a translation. . . .

W to HenryS   15/07/39   Cambridge/Barbican   Add. 34600, fols. 174–75 o
Begins: Right w⟨orshipfu⟩ll. After my most humble service remembred; | soe soone as . . .

W to HenryS   20/07/39   Cambridge/Barbican   Add. 34600, fols.176–77 o
Begins: Right w⟨orshipfu⟩ll. After the remembrance of my dutie, | I haue made what . . .

HenryS to W   13/09/39   Barbican/Cambridge   Dd.3.12, fols. 47–48   o
c by Baker in Harley 7041, fol. 44r; c in CUL Add. 7596, item 24;
Begins: In mutch businesse at this tyme I can|not write mutch vnto you. . . .

HenryS to W   17/09/39   Barbican/Cambridge   Dd.3.12, fols. 49–50   o
c by Baker in Harley 7041, fol. 44r; c in CUL Add. 7596, item 25;
Begins: S.P. | I sent you by the laste week⟨es⟩ Carrier both | Trinitie Colledg Psalter. . . .

HenryS to W   20/09/39   Barbican/Cambridge   Dd.3.12, fols.51–52   o
c by Baker in Harley 7041, fol. 44rv; c in CUL Add. 7596, item 26;
Begins: S.P. I wroth vnto you the laste weeke & sent | you by the Carriers. . . .

HenryS to W   28/09/39   Barbican/Cambridge   Dd.3.12, fols. 53–4   o
c by Baker in Harley 7041, fol. 44v; c in CUL Add. 7596, item 27
(date wrongly copied as 8 September);
Begins: Mr Wheelock I am mutch troubled w⟨ith⟩ the | scandall layde vppon me. . . .

W to HenryS   20/11/39   Cambridge/Barbican   Add. 34600, fols. 188–9 o
Begins: Most trulie honored, & learned; I acquainted o⟨ur⟩ Vice-chancelo⟨ur⟩. . . .

HenryS to W   29/11/39   Barbican/Cambridge   Dd.3.12, fols. 55–6   o
c by Baker in Harley 7041, fols. 44v–45r; c in CUL Add. 7596, item 28;
Begins: SP. | I continew my firste intent about o⟨ur⟩ Lecture of Church and Saxon Antiqq. . . .

TCC to HenryS 02/12/39   Add. 34600, fols. 193–94 a
Begins: Clarissime Vir, Honoratissime D⟨omi⟩ne, | Etsi noster animus ad gratulandum. . . .

W to HenryS   04/12/39   Cambridge/Barbican   Add.34600, fols.191–92 o
Begins: Most honored Sir, with my humble service: I am euer bound | to giue. . . .

W to HenryS   27/12/39   Cambridge/Barbican   Add. 34600, fols. 195–96 o
Begins: Right w⟨orshipfu⟩ll. my humble dutie bindeth me to giue some testimonie. . . .

D'Ewes to W   26/00/39   Bury/Cambridge   Harley 7041, fol. 60   c
Begins: Kind Mr Whylocke/ Your printing of Bede alone, without some other . . .

HenryS to W ˙   10/01/40   Barbican/Cambridge   Dd.3.12, fols. 57–8   o
              c by Baker in Harley 7041, fol. 45r; c in CUL Add. 7596, item 29;
Begins: I received yo⟨ur⟩ l⟨ett⟩res, and those other very cur|tuouse from the M⟨aster⟩. . . .

W to HenryS   15/01/40   [Cambridge]/BarbicanAdd. 34600, fols. 205–6   o
Begins: Right wor⟨shipfu⟩ll: w⟨ith⟩ my most humble service euer | remembred; I am. . . .

W to D'Ewes   26/01/40   Cambridge/Stow Hall   Harley 374, fols.129–30 o
              p Ellis, *Original Letters*, 157–59, no. 57;
Begins: Most Learned, & trulie noble Sir; how much I am bound to serve you, . . .

W to D'Ewes   02/02/40   -/Stow Hall   Harley 374, fols. 131–132 o
Begins: Noble Sir, I am not soe much cheered w⟨ith⟩ yo⟨ur⟩ | most quick lines, . . .

W to HenryS   05/02/40   Cambridge/Barbican   Add. 34600, fols.207–208 o
Begins: Right w⟨orshipfu⟩ll. & most honoured, I confes I am to | blame that before. . . .

W to D'Ewes   09/02/40   Cambridge/Stow Hall   Harley 374, fols.133–134 o
Begins: Noble Sir, I giue yo⟨ur⟩ worship thankes for yo⟨ur⟩ many letters. . . .

W to HenryS   12/02/40   Cambridge/Barbican   Add. 34600, fols. 209–210 o
Begins: Right w⟨o⟩r⟨shipfu⟩ll: my humble service remembred, I am very sorrie to heare . . .

W to HenryS   [11/03/40]   [Cambridge]/Barbican   Add. 34600, fols. 221–222 o
Begins: Most honored Sir \After my humble service, &/ I cannot in few wordes expreße . . .

HenryS to W   12/03/40   Barbican/Cambridge   Dd.3.12, fols. 59–60   o
              c by Baker in Harley 7041, fol. 45r; c in CUL Add. 7596, item 30;
Begins: Mr Wheelock w⟨ith⟩ my commendacons. After | 7. weekes languishinge. . . .

HenryS to W   20/03/40   Barbican/Cambridge   Dd.3.12, fols. 61–62   o
              c by Baker in Harley 7041, fol. 45rv; c in CUL Add. 7596, item 31;
Begins: SP. | I rec[eived] yesternight yo⟨ur⟩ l⟨ett⟩res by ye Poste who | tolde me. . . .

W to HenryS   31/03/40   Cambridge/Barbican   Add. 34601, fols.4–5   o
Begins: Most noble Sir, with my most humble service promised; | I was not a little . . .

HenryS to W   24/04/40   Barbican/Cambridge   Dd.3.12, fols. 63–64   o
        c by Baker in Harley 7041, fol. 45v; c in CUL Add. 7596, item 32;
Begins: SP. I forgot the 2 laste weekes to | write vnto you about the rent. . . .

W to HenryS   28/04/40   Cambridge/-   Add. 34601, fols. 8–9   o
Begins: Most honored sir, my humble service euer remembred; I giue | you heartie
thankes

D'Ewes to W   18/05/40   'Hawh' [?Hawkedon]/   Harley 7041, fol. 60v   c
        Cambridge
Begins: Mr Wheelocke/ Excuse my shorte scribble, amidst the multitude of busines.

W to HenryS   27/05/40   Cambridge/Barbican   Add. 34601, fols. 10–11   o
Begins: Most honored Sir, I am trewlie sensible how fauourablie | yo⟨ur⟩ worship hath

HenryS to W   05/06/40   -/Cambridge   Dd.3.12, fols. 65–66   o
        c by Baker in Harley 7041, fols. 45v–46r; c in CUL Add. 7596,
        item 33;
Begins: Mr Wheelock I pray trouble not yo⟨ur⟩ | thought⟨es⟩ or your lovinge wife. . . .

W to HenryS   13/06/40   Cambridge/Barbican   Add. 34601, fols. 12–13   o
Begins: Right w⟨o⟩r⟨shipfu⟩ll. Euer honoured Sir, I am much comforted, & incouraged

HenryS to W   26/06/40   Barbican/Cambridge   Harley 7041, fol. 48v   c
        p Ellis, *Original Letters*, 161, no. 59;
Begins: Mr Wheelock / I have acquainted my Lˢ Grace of Armagh, & my L:~ | Bishop
of Elye with the intended Lecture. . . .
        Baker says at the end: 'This is an original under seal, w in Sʳ Hen: Spelman's
        own hand. | It is lodged inter Archiva with the Draught affixed'.
Proposal for Saxon Lectureship   Dd.3.12, fols. 80–81   o
        c in CUL Add. 7596, item [37].

W to HenryS   30/06/40   [Cambridge]/Barbican   Add. 34601, fols. 16–18   o
Begins: Most honored Sir, I most humblie thanke you for takeinge | such paines about

W to HenryS   14/07/40   [Cambridge]/Barbican   Add. 34601, fols. 19–20   o
Begins: Right w⟨o⟩r⟨shi⟩p⟨fu⟩ll. I am bound to giue yo⟨ur⟩ worship | all thanks for this

W to HenryS   19/07/40   Cambridge/Barbican   Add. 34601, fols. 21–22   o
Begins: Most noble S⟨ir⟩. before my setting forward for Middleton I thought

W to HenryS   09/08/40   Middleton/Barbican   Add. 34601, fols. 23–24   o
Begins: Right noble S⟨ir⟩, I am now by the blessinge of god, & yo⟨ur⟩ | w⟨orshi⟩ps
fauo⟨ur⟩

W to HenryS   27/10/40   [Cambridge]/Barbican   Add. 34601, fols. 25–26   o
Begins: Right w⟨o⟩r⟨shi⟩p⟨fu⟩ll. I am bound to thanke god for yo⟨ur⟩ safe returne;

HenryS to W   30/10/40   Barbican/Cambridge   Dd.3.12, fols. 67–68   o
                c by Baker in Harley 7041, fol. 46r; c in CUL Add. 7596, item 34;
Begins: Mr Wheelock yo⟨ur⟩ longe silence as not having | heard of you. . . .

W to HenryS   [00/11/40]   [Cambridge]/Barbican   Add. 34601, fols. 28–29   o
Begins: Right w⟨o⟩r⟨shi⟩p⟨fu⟩ll. with my humble service euer remembred; I | haue
presented yo⟨ur⟩

W to HenryS   [00/00/40]   [Cambridge]/Barbican   Add. 34601, fols. 39–40   o
Begins: Most honoured S⟨ir⟩; my humble dutie euer remembred; | I could defer noe
longer

HenryS to W   09/11/40   Barbican/Cambridge   Dd.3.12, fols. 69–70   o
                c by Baker in Harley 7041, fol. 46r; c in CUL Add. 7596, item 35;
                c in Add. 34601, fol. 27; p *Original Letters*, 163–164, no. 61;
Begins: Mr Wheelock / it is a great comfort | to me in the latter ende of my dayes. . . .

HenryS to W   27/11/40   Barbican/Cambridge   Dd.3.12, fols. 71–72   o
                c by Baker in Harley 7041, fol. 46r; c in CUL Add. 7596, item 36;
Begins: Mr Wheelock I thanke you for yo⟨ur⟩ farther | paynes in my behalfe. . . .

W to D'Ewes (L) ante02/11/40 Cambridge/Stow Hall   Harley 374, fols. 172–173 o
Begins: Quas (nobilißime Domine) Latiu⟨m⟩ | antiquu⟨m⟩, aut Græcia, aut Judea, . . .

W to D'Ewes (L) 01/12/40   Cambridge/Westminster Harley 374, fols. 162–163   o
Begins: Nobilißime domine, licetne inter tot curaru⟨m⟩ publicaru⟨m⟩ turbas, . . .

W to D'Ewes (L) 28/12/40   Cambridge/Westminster Harley 374, fols. 166–167   o
Begins: Nobilißime Domine; excusatione opus mihi erit, quod | post deceßu⟨m⟩. . . .

W to D'Ewes (L) 30/03/41   -/Westminster   Harley 374, fols. 143–144   o
                p Nichols, *Bibliotheca*, 6: 78–9;
Begins: Nobilißime Domine, vnde mihi excusatio pro tam | diuturno silentio. . . .

W to D'Ewes   00/00/[41]   -/Stow Hall   Harley 374, fol. 145   o
                p Nichols, *Bibliotheca*, 6: 79–80;
Begins: Right w⟨orshipfu⟩ll. with my humble service; I was glad to hear | from you; . . .

W to D'Ewes (L) 13/04/41   Cambridge/-   Harley 374, fols.146–147   o
Begins: Gratulantur mihi per quam læte. . . .

Jo Walden to W 08/10/41   Barbican/Cambridge   Dd.3.12, fols. 78–79   o
                c by Baker in Harley 7041, fol.46v; c in CUL Add.7596, item [39];
                p *Original Letters*, 170–171, no. 65;
(HenryS's death) begins: Worthy S⟨er⟩ | I haue now a sorrowfull occasion of writinge. . . .

W to D'Ewes (L) 04/11/41   Cambridge/-   Harley 374, fols. 164–165   o
Begins: Nobilißimo Academico, iuxtà et politico, et | pro Suffolcensibus . . .

W to D'Ewes (L) 23/09/42   Cambridge/Westminster Harley 374, fols. 209–210   o
Begins: Nobilissime Domine; quod prima hæc qua⟨m⟩ | in luce⟨m⟩ dedimus, . . .

W to RogerS   10/03/45   Cambridge/-   Add. 34601, fol. 55–55bis   o
Begins: Be pleased (worthie Sr.) to accept this | present token, as a testimonie . . .
On the occasion of presenting Sir Henry Spelman's grandson with a copy of Bede + Laws

W to RogerS   12/10/49   Middleton/-   Add. 34601, fol. 56   ?o
Begins: Right worthie Sr. I am to craue yo⟨ur⟩ fauour | in dispencinge with me till . . .

Three Studies on the Manuscript Text of Beowulf: Lines 47b, 747b, and 2232a[1]

J. R. Hall

For more than a decade I have been studying the *Beowulf* manuscript and its supplementary evidence, most notably transcripts A and B. I here present my findings for three places, each concerned with a lost or damaged reading and each illustrating a different kind of difficulty. In the first study, on line 47b, I consider a crux in which the evidence of transcripts A and B on how to spell the word to be restored clashes with the spelling of the word elsewhere in *Beowulf*. Solving the puzzle entails scrutinizing anew readings in the two transcripts and taking into account Thorkelin's 1815 edition. In the second study, on line 747b, I adjudicate between rival restorations by determining which better matches the few ink traces left in a virtually illegible manuscript reading. The question is complicated by the fact that I reached somewhat different conclusions the two times I directly investigated the reading in the manuscript. In the third study, on line 2232a, I support a reading proposed a century ago and recently reintroduced. I show that the history of handling the crux long obscured what is otherwise a fairly evident restoration. A reason it eluded scholars so long is the common assumption that all lost readings in the manuscript result from the Cotton fire of 1731.

---

[1] I welcome the opportunity to dedicate this essay to the memory of Phill Pulsiano. Some of the research was done at various times when he and I were working in the Students Room in the old British Library building. Phill was an ideal scholar-friend. During library hours, he was always willing to take time from his own work to advise one on a troublesome manuscript reading. After hours, he was a boon companion in restaurant and pub. We had, I once told him, a trying friendship — I was forever trying to keep up with his letters (he could compose a page on the computer at breathtaking speed), with his scholarship (from year to year his list of publications grew exponentially), and with his literal pace (he could outstride an Old Norse giant). I look forward in the next life to resuming our pinball competition, in which, at the moment, Phill holds an exiguous lead.

Line 47b: *g[el]denne, g[yl]denne,* and the Standard of Evidence

Line 47b occurs when the poet describes the ship funeral of Scyld Scef-ing. After saying that his followers placed many treasures in the ship near the king's corpse, the poet continues:

Þa gyt hie him asetton   segen ge[l]denne
heah ofer heafod,   leton holm bera*n*,
geafon on garsecg;   (47–49a)[2]

Then also they set up for him a standard *ge[l]denne*
high over head, let the sea take (him),
gave (him) to the ocean.

The form *ge[l]denne*, as given in Dobbie's edition, is misleading. In the manu-script *g* — obscure but intact except for its cross-bar — comes at the end of line 1 on fol. 130r.[3] The letters that once followed *g* are gone with the loss of the upper right corner of the folio. Line 2 begins with *denne*, entirely intact. In presenting the damaged text as *ge[l]denne*, Dobbie gives the impression that the manuscript for certain once had *e* after *g*. In reality *e* is the reading of transcripts A and B but not necessarily of the *Beowulf* manuscript. In my discussion I cite the form as *g . . . denne*, the ellipsis indicating that the resto-ration of the lost letters is speculative.

The first scholar to confront the problem in print was Sharon Turner, who in his *History of the Anglo-Saxons* (1805) translates *segen* and its defec-tive fellow form as "golden banner."[4] Turner is almost certainly correct that *g . . . denne* is the remains of the OE word for "golden." The very phrase "segen gyldenne," meaning "golden standard," occurs at *Beowulf* 1021a, when the poet (cunningly linking Beowulf to Scyld Scefing) enumerates the rewards

---

[2] Quotation of *Beowulf* is from Elliott Van Kirk Dobbie, ed., *Beowulf and Judith*, ASPR 4 (New York, 1953). In the present passage Dobbie italicizes *n* in "bera*n*" to indicate that the letter is lost from the manuscript but is supported by one of the two transcripts.

[3] In giving folio numbers, I follow the system used by Julius Zupitza, ed., *Beowulf. Auto-types of the Unique Cotton MS. Vitellius A xv in the British Museum*, EETS o.s. 77 (London, 1882); 2nd ed., *Beowulf Reproduced in Facsimile from the Unique Manuscript British Museum MS. Cotton Vitellius A. xv*, ed. Norman Davis, EETS 245 (London, 1959).

[4] *The History of the Anglo-Saxons*, 4 vols. (London, 1799–1805), 4: 400. In the 2nd ed., 2 vols. (London, 1807), 2: 295, Turner similarly translates as "gilt banner." In the 3rd ed., 3 vols. (London, 1820), 3: 329, he translates as "flowing banner," likely misled by Thorkelin's 1815 edition (later discussed) from his earlier, correct belief that the damaged OE form is the word for "golden."

Hrothgar bestowed on Beowulf for slaying Grendel. But it is unlikely that Turner knew line 1021a in the poem; in the first edition of his *History* he gives no evidence of having studied *Beowulf* beyond line 742a.

If Turner did not know line 1021a, where did he get the notion of translating *g . . . denne* as "golden"? Perhaps he simply struck gold, guessing that a form beginning with *g* and ending with *denne* and describing a standard in the context of treasure would be the OE word for "golden." Or perhaps, knowing that *-ne* in *denne* is an adjectival declension suffix that would not be included in a headword, he checked the Lye-Manning dictionary (1772) for a word beginning with *g* and ending with *den* and found two appropriate headwords: *Gelden*, glossed "Aureus," and *Gylden*, which redirects readers to the headword *Gildan*. Under the headword *Gildan*, Turner would have seen the citation *gilden*, together with the alternate spelling *gylden*, glossed "Aureus, inauratus."[5] *Gelden / gilden / gylden*: spelling variants of the same golden word. The stressed vowel did not matter to Turner — he was translating and did not need to reconstruct the OE form — but it matters to us, who want to restore the original manuscript reading as precisely as possible.

John M. Kemble in his edition of *Beowulf* is the first scholar to restore the word as *g[yl]denne* — or, to be more exact, as *(gyl) denne* (first edition, 1833) or *[gyl]denne* (second edition, 1835), overlooking the fact that *g* should not be in parentheses or brackets since enough of it remains to identify the letter with certainty.[6] In neither edition does Kemble explain why he chooses *y* as the stressed vowel rather than *i* or *e*. Among the unpublished notes he made in 1834–1835 in preparing his second edition, however, is this comment on the restored form *(gyl) denne* in his first edition: "The first syllable is quite gone in the MS. I made the suggestion from l. 2035 [= 1021a]. Similarly in l. 5531 [= 2767b], we have segn eall gylden, where by the way the omission of the masculine inflection is not very intelligible."[7] In citing "segen gyldenne" and "segn eall gylden," Kemble is much less concerned with the vowel in the stressed syllable of *gylden* than with adducing evidence that twice elsewhere in *Beowulf* a form of *gylden* modifies *segen*. It is nonetheless significant that

---

[5] Edward Lye, *Dictionarium Saxonico et Gothico-Latinum*, ed. Owen Manning, 2 vols. (London, 1772), 1: s.vv. *Gelden, Gylden, Gildan*.

[6] *The Anglo-Saxon Poems of Beowulf, The Travellers Song and the Battle of Finnes-burh* (London, 1833); 2nd ed., 2 vols., with translation (1835–1837). See (half-)line 94 (= line 47b in editions numbering by full lines). In the 1833 edition *(gyl)* is separated from *denne* by space.

[7] London, British Library, Add. MS. 36531, opposite printed page 4. In the manuscript the pages of Kemble's first edition are interleaved with blank pages on which he added a wide range of textual and explanatory notes.

in both cases cited by Kemble the adjective is spelled *gylden* rather than *gilden* or *gelden*. In fact in the four other occurrences of the adjective in *Beowulf*, the stressed vowel is always *y*: "swyn ealgylden" 1111b, "gyldnum beage" 1163a, "gylden hilt" 1677a, and "hring gyldenne" 2809b. If we limit the evidence to the manuscript text of *Beowulf* as it stands, we will restore *g . . . denne* at line 47b as *g[yl]denne*.

It would be hasty, however, to limit the evidence to the manuscript text of *Beowulf* as it stands. Here, as elsewhere for letters lost from *Beowulf*, we should take into account transcripts A and B, which enable us to supply, overall, more than two thousand now lost letters.[8] In the present case both transcripts record the first two letters of the defective form as *ge*.[9] If, like Dobbie, we accept their evidence here as definitive, we will restore the defective reading as *g[el]denne*.

What practical difference does it make if we restore as *g[el]denne* or *g[yl]denne*? This difference: *g[el]denne* would be a Kentish spelling and would give striking — and unexpected — support to the claim that *Beowulf* at some point passed through Kentish hands.[10]

Most editors simply ignore the *e*-spelling of the transcripts.[11] However, the first scholar to publish a comprehensive study of the transcripts, Kemp Malone,

---

[8] In *The Thorkelin Transcripts of 'Beowulf'*, Anglistica 25 (Copenhagen, 1986), Kevin S. Kiernan at first says that the transcripts allow us to restore about two thousand letters lost from the text of *Beowulf* (ix) but later gives the number as fewer than 1,970 (144). I put the number at beyond two thousand.

[9] Here and elsewhere for readings of the transcripts, see Kemp Malone, ed., *The Thorkelin Transcripts of Beowulf in Facsimile*, EEMF 1 (Copenhagen, 1951). For A's reading see p. 2, line 8; for B's, p. 3a, line 1. A digitized facsimile of the transcripts is also available in Kevin Kiernan, with Andrew Prescott et al., *Electronic Beowulf*, 2 CDs (London and Ann Arbor, 1999).

[10] For the argument that *Beowulf* went through a Kentish recension, see Eduard Sievers, "Zu Cynewulf," in *Neusprachliche Studien: Festgabe Karl Luick zu seinem sechzigsten Geburtstage dargebracht von Freunden und Schülern* (Marburg, 1925), 60–81, here 81; and Fr. Klaeber, *Beowulf and the Fight at Finnsburg*, 3rd ed. with 1st and 2nd supplements (Boston, 1950), lxxxix–xc. On *e* for *y* (where *y* results from *i*-mutation) as Kentish, see Alistair Campbell, *Old English Grammar* (Oxford, 1959; corr. ed. Oxford, 1977), § 288. Although restoring as *ge[l]denne*, Dobbie, 117, notes: "Nowhere else in Beowulf, however, do we find a form with *e* for etymological ȳ, unless *trem*, l. 2525, is one (cf. *trym*, Maldon 247, which may be a late form of *trem*)."

[11] According to Birte Kelly, "The Formative Stages of *Beowulf* Textual Scholarship: Part I," *Anglo-Saxon England* 11 (1983 [1982]): 247–74, at 257, and "Part II," 12 (1983): 239–75, at 241, three editors since 1950 — Dobbie, Gerhard Nickel, and Howell D. Chickering, Jr. — restore as *ge[l]denne*.

forcefully supported the *e*-spelling. In his pioneering essay (1949), Malone declares, "The reading *gyldenne* of the editions is not justified; the proper reading is *ge(l)denne*."[12] Malone sent a copy of the essay to Fr. Klaeber in Germany. In his edition, first published in 1922 and repeatedly revised since then, Klaeber had adopted the *y*-spelling, *g(yl)denne*, without discussion, but in his thank-you note to Malone, dated 30 May 1950, Klaeber says, "Your meticulous scrutiny of the Thorkelin transcripts furnishes all possible details about A and B and gives us some valuable new readings, such as *for his unsnyttrum* and *ge(l)denne*."[13] In the second supplement to his third edition of the poem (1950), Klaeber again cites "for his unsnyttrum" 1734a and *ge(l)denne* 47b among the valuable readings highlighted by Malone's essay (463). Of the two readings, however, Klaeber includes only "for his unsnyttrum" in his "list of textual changes" introduced by the second supplement (470).[14]

Similar ambivalence is reflected in Kevin S. Kiernan's shift of position over the years. In his study of the Thorkelin transcripts (1986), he accepts A as preserving the reading of the *Beowulf* manuscript and restores as "g(e)[l]denne" (47), in which parentheses signal a letter supplied from transcript A and square brackets a speculative restoration. In his edition in the *Electronic Beowulf* (1999), however, Kiernan reads "g(y)[l]denne" in the edited text and **g[yl]denne** in the glossary. The parentheses around *y* in the edited text indicate that the letter is supplied from transcript A alone or from

---

[12] "Readings from the Thorkelin Transcripts of *Beowulf*," *PMLA* 64 (1949): 1190–1218, at 1192. Similarly Malone remarks in *The Nowell Codex: British Museum Cotton Vitellius A. xv Second MS*, EEMF 12 (Copenhagen, 1963), 50.2: ". . . the MS reading before the fire was doubtless *gel*; the editorial reading *gyl* must be reckoned an emendation of the inherited text."

[13] Kemp Malone papers, box 11 (folder), Special Collections, Robert W. Woodruff Library, Emory University, quoted by permission. The word "furnishes" is written above the word "contains," crossed out. (The letter came to my attention from Helen Damico's citing it in "'My Professor of Anglo-Saxon was Frederick Klaeber': Minnesota and Beyond," in *The Preservation and Transmission of Anglo-Saxon Culture*, ed. Paul E. Szarmach and Joel T. Rosenthal [Kalamazoo, 1997], 73–98, at 90.) In the phrase "for his unsnyttrum" 1734a, the new reading is *for*, lost from the *Beowulf* manuscript but recorded in transcript A. The reading as reported by Malone was quite new to Klaeber. In Zupitza's facsimile edition of *Beowulf*, on which Klaeber depended decisively for knowledge of both the *Beowulf* manuscript and transcripts A and B, Zupitza had neglected to note A's *for*.

[14] Perhaps Klaeber stayed with *g(yl)denne* because he did not wish to part company with his former teacher at the University of Berlin, Zupitza, who, in his facsimile edition (*Reproduced*, 4), is aware that transcripts A and B read *ge* as the first two letters of the defective form but still restored the syllable as *g[yl]*. Zupitza was suspicious of *e* in each transcript (discussed below).

transcripts A and B together. The fact that *y* is in italics indicates that Kiernan has emended A's or A and B's reading.[15] Kiernan gives further details in the glossary, s.v. **g[yl]denne**: "(**ge** A, **ge** B, for **gyl**; usu. em., usu. rest)." This is shorthand for saying that A and B both read *e* after *g*, that their *e* is usually emended by editors to *y*, and that the next letter missing from the manuscript and not recorded by AB is usually restored as *l*.

As Klaeber's wavering and Kiernan's change of position suggest, there is something to be said for either side of the question: favoring *g[yl]denne* is the fact that the stressed syllable is spelled with *y* six of six times elsewhere in the poem; favoring *g[el]denne* is the fact that *e* is recorded after *g* in both transcripts. I hope to resolve the conflict in the standard of evidence by reconsidering the readings of transcripts A and B.

Transcript A. In his facsimile edition of *Beowulf* (1882), Julius Zupitza notes that in the transcript *e* of *ge* is written with "another ink and hand" than *g* (4). In his *PMLA* article on the two transcripts, Malone observes, "A first wrote *segen g*, left after it a four-letter blank space, and followed this with *denne*; later, in A's later hand and with another ink, an *e* was added to the *g*; still later the *d* of *denne* was crossed (and thereby made an *ð*); the cross-mark was done in a way characteristic of B's hand but unlike A's; A did not fill out with dots the space left blank between *ge* and *denne*; this space signalizes something illegible" ("Readings," 1192). In his book on the transcripts, Kiernan notes that A added *ge* some time after he had copied *segen* and that Thorkelin later crossed A's *d* in *denne* to make it into *ð* (*Transcripts*, 47). In the *Electronic Beowulf*, Kiernan, borrowing a phrase from Zupitza, says that *e* of *ge* is written with "another ink and hand" than *g* (note on facsimile of fol. 130r).

I agree with Kiernan (first account) that *g* as well as *e* — not *e* alone — is a later reading in the transcript: in the sequence "segen ge," the *g* in *segen* and the *g* in *ge* differ, the *g* in *segen* being A's earlier form of the letter, the *g* in *ge* being A's later form. Clearly, some time after he finished copying the page as a whole, A went back and inserted *g* at the beginning of the blank space he had left after *segen*. I also agree with Zupitza, Malone, and Kiernan (second account) that the *e* in *ge* is not written in the same ink and hand as the preceding *g*. The question is more complex, however, than a change of ink and hand suggests.

What has not been noted till now is that obscurely underlying the imitation Insular minuscule *e* in *ge* is an earlier *e*, that this earlier *e* appears to

[15] For the meaning of italics and other conventions in Kiernan's edited text, see the *Electronic Beowulf* under Help Index | Guide, Electronic Texts, Edition, 2–4. In a note to the facsimile of fol. 130r in the *EB*, Kiernan suggests that "perhaps bottom tip of y-descender [survives] below loop of g" and queries if AB mistook "top of dotted y . . . for e?"

have been a looped *e*, and that the ink in which it was written is lighter than that used for the preceding *g*. Further, the ink used to draw the Insular minuscule *e* on top of the looped *e* seems to match the ink used to convert *d* of A's original *denne* to *ð*. Since, as Kiernan rightly claims, it is certain that it was Thorkelin who crossed A's original *d* to make it into *ð*, it is almost certain that it was Thorkelin who wrote the Insular minuscule *e* over the looped *e*. Equally important, it seems it was Thorkelin who wrote the original looped *e*: A does not write looped *e*'s, and what can be seen of the looped *e* is like the looped *e*'s Thorkelin makes in his own transcript. In short, it seems that the A copyist at no time wrote *e* after *g* in transcript A. Thorkelin appears responsible for the letter in both stages, the looped *e* and the imitation Insular minuscule *e* later superimposed on the looped *e*.

　　Transcript B. Zupitza says that *ge* at the end of line 1 is written "with another ink" (4); he does not comment on B's *ðenne*. Malone in his essay remarks that "B wrote *segen ge- denne*; later, with another ink, he crossed the *d*; his dash serves the purpose elsewhere served by a dot in his text" ("Readings," 1192). Kiernan first describes *ge-* as written "later, on dots" and *ð* in *ðenne* as revised from *d* (*Transcripts*, 47). In the *Electronic Beowulf* Kiernan, echoing Zupitza, says that *ge* is written "with another ink" (note to facsimile of fol. 130r). I agree with Zupitza and Kiernan against Malone that Thorkelin added *ge* later. He first wrote *segen* plus two (possibly three) dots at the end of line 1 and *denne* at the beginning of line 2. Later, in lighter ink, he wrote *ge* (*g* covering the second dot), added a hyphen after *ge*, and crossed the ascender of *d* in his original *denne* to make the letter into *ð*. The fact that Thorkelin added a hyphen after *ge* and altered *d* to *ð* in apparently the same ink in which he wrote *ge* is revealing. He could hardly have copied the hyphen from the *Beowulf* manuscript (which does not use hyphens), and he certainly altered *d* to *ð* without manuscript authority. Like the hyphen, the cross-stroke inserted to convert *d* into *ð*, and other readings in transcript B in lighter ink,[16] Thorkelin's *e* almost certainly was not copied from the *Beowulf* manuscript. Further, he probably got *g* of *ge* — the two letters written in the same ink and as a unit — from transcript A rather than from the manuscript itself.

　　In adding *e* to transcript A and *ge-* to transcript B, what did Thorkelin have in mind? What he had in mind is that a common morpheme might be the solution to a common problem in the burned *Beowulf*, the loss of letters at the end of a manuscript line. He alighted on this solution because none other seemed likely.

---

　　[16] On the unreliability of B's readings on dots and in lighter ink, see Kiernan, *Transcripts*, 138–40. In my view transcript B is much more reliable than Kiernan believes; I agree with him, however, that B's readings on dots and in lighter ink are not trustworthy.

Restoring "segen g . . . denne" as "segen g[yl]denne" with the meaning "golden standard" was not a live option for Thorkelin. When he comes to the very phrase "segen gyldenne" 1021a (*Poëma*, 78, line 16) he mistranslates it as "Signum solvendæ," taking *gyldenne* not as a form of the adjective *gilden / gylden* but as a form of the verb *gildan / gyldan,* glossed in Lye-Manning as "Reddere, restituere, solvere."[17] Since he did not understand *gyldenne* at line 1021a although it is well preserved in the text, he was not likely to think of restoring *g . . . denne* as *g[yl]denne* at line 47b: Thorkelin was on his own. Ingenuity may be no real substitute for sound learning, but in his day modern OE scholarship was in its cradle, and he was often obliged — and perhaps inclined from his confident knowledge of Old Icelandic — to rely on inventive speculation. He knew that *ge-* is a frequent prefix in OE, one that in Lye-Manning's dictionary is even printed with a hyphen when it occurs in headwords. Working with transcript A (probably before he began his own transcript), he speculated that *g . . . denne* might be restored as **gedenne* and added a provisional looped *e* in light ink after A's *g.* But a problem arose when Thorkelin later checked Lye-Manning and found no such OE word. He did, however, find a somewhat similar form in the verb *Ge-þenian,* glossed "Extendere."[18] The challenge now was to figure out how to make his **gedenne* look more like a form of *geþenian.* He knew that thorn and eth are interchangeable in *Beowulf* and that *geðenian* would mean the same as *geþenian.* With a quick stroke of the quill he converted A's *d* in *denne* to *ð* and then drew a small imitation Insular minuscule *e* over his own speculative looped *e* in transcript A. Later, to bring transcript B into harmony with transcript A, Thorkelin inserted *ge* in transcript B in the space after *segen* that he had earlier left blank

---

[17] Thorkelin's treatment of lines 1020–1021 is best evaluated when his OE text and translation are printed in parallel as in his edition (*Poëma*, 78, lines 14–17):

Forgeaf þa Beowulfe	Dedit tunc (Rex) Beowulfo
Brand Healfdanes	Lanceam Halfdani
Segen gyldenne	Signum solvendæ
Sigores to leane	Victoriæ mercedi

Thorkelin's tricky Latin may be translated: "Then he (the king) gave Beowulf Healfdene's spear, a sign in payment for the victory that deserved to be rewarded." (My thanks to D. R. Howlett for clarifying the Latin; I am alone responsible for the actual translation.) However one construe the passage, it is important to note that in Latin Thorkelin does not take *solvendæ* as modifying *signum,* which presumably means that in OE he does not take *gyldenne* as modifying *segen.*

[18] I am grateful to E. G. Stanley, who owns a copy of Lye-Manning that once belonged to Thorkelin and that, presumably, he used in working on his edition, for checking s.v. *Ge-þenian* for annotations. Unfortunately for my purposes, Professor Stanley reports there are no marks in the dictionary associated with the word.

except for dots, added a hyphen after *ge* to remind himself that *ge* at the end of line 1 is the prefix *ge-*, and crossed the *d* of his original (and accurate) *denne* to make *ð* and *ðenne*.[19]

Thorkelin had now arrived at the phrase "segen geðenne" or — to cite the form used in his edition, in which he replaced all the eths of the transcripts with thorns — "segen geþenne." Since Lye-Manning defines *segen* as "Signum, indicium. *Item*, Insigne, vexillum, labarum," and *geþenian* as "Extendere," one might expect Thorkelin to have translated "segen geþenne" as "signum extensum," i.e., "standard stretched out, unfurled banner."[20] Instead, Thorkelin translated "segen geþenne" as "aplustre expansum." We cannot ascertain precisely what Thorkelin meant by *aplustre* since Latin dictionaries define the term somewhat differently and we do not know which dictionary he used. However, an authoritative dictionary of the time, Facciolati and Forcellini's *Lexicon*, defines *aplustre* in a way well suited to the context in Thorkelin's edition: as an elaborate ship ornament placed at the top point of the stern.[21]

And that brings me to the context in Thorkelin's edition. He had no idea that the lines describe Scyld Scefing's sea-funeral. He thought they describe a fleet of ships setting out on an expedition.[22] Presumably the ship with the expanded ornament was the ship of command. Thorkelin well knew that *segen*

---

[19] Earlier I quoted Malone's view in his essay ("Readings," 1192) that Thorkelin's "dash serves the purpose elsewhere served by a dot in his text." What Malone here calls a "dash" he more accurately calls a "hyphen" in the *Nowell Codex*: "B's hyphen marks a missing or illegible letter here" (50.2). B's hyphen does not mark a missing or illegible letter here. It is an end-line hyphen that serves the same purpose as an end-line hyphen today: to signal the continuation of a word on the next line, as is shown in the very first line of transcript B, when Thorkelin puts a hyphen after *De* to show that the letters should be taken with the first two letters on line 2, *na*, to make *Dena*.

[20] This is pretty much what Turner did. Faced with Thorkelin's "Segen geþenne" (*Poëma*, 6, line 18), Turner in his third edition abandoned his earlier translations, "golden banner" and "gilt banner," in favor of "flowing banner" (n. 3 above). This is an intelligent response to Thorkelin's "geþenne," which Turner likely believed was the real manuscript reading.

[21] Jacobus Facciolati and Ægidius Forcellini, *Lexicon Totius Latinitatis* (Padua, 1805), 1: s.v. *aplustre*: "navis ornamentum ex tabulis confectum, & in summitate puppis positum, & plerumque in modum pinnarum, aut cristæ efformatum, & versus proram recurvum." A similar definition is given in another authoritative dictionary of the time, Charles du Fresne Du Cange, *Glossarium ad Scriptores Mediæ et Infimæ Latinitatis* (Frankfurt, 1762), 1: s.v. *aplaustrum* ("pro *Aplustrum*, vel *Aplustre*"): "tabulatum ad decorandum superficiem navis adpositum."

[22] See Chauncey B. Tinker, *The Translations of Beowulf: A Critical Bibliography*, Yale Studies in English 16 (New York, 1903), 17; and Franklin Cooley, "Early Danish Criticism of *Beowulf*," *English Literary History* 7 (1940): 45–67, at 48.

means "standard,"[23] but a simple standard even unfurled was not sufficient to set the most important ship apart from the others. (A "golden banner," had the restoration g[yl]denne occurred to Thorkelin, may have sufficed.) Thorkelin's "aplustre expansum" seems a far sight from the Beowulf poet's "segen gyldenne," but perhaps they share a perspective. The poet ornaments a ship by giving it a distinguished standard; the scholar distinguishes a ship by giving it a special ornament.

I have attempted to understand how Thorkelin arrived at restoring g... denne as geþenne. I do not insist that my reconstruction is accurate in fine detail. I do say, however, that e in ge of transcripts A and B is not based on the Beowulf manuscript and that Thorkelin, an editor faced with the task of furnishing an intelligible text, speculatively added e after g. We should not follow him. We should follow the spelling of the word's first syllable always elsewhere in Beowulf. We should restore line 47b as g[yl]denne.

Line 747b: "[him] ræhte ongean," "[him swa] ræhte ongean," and the Reach for Restoration

In describing Grendel's attack on Beowulf, the poet employs the phrase "ræhte ongean":

> Forð near ætstop,
> nam þa mid handa   higeþihtigne
> rinc on ræste,   ræhte ongean
> feond mid folma;   (745b–48a)

> Forward, nearer, he stepped,
> then with a hand grabbed the strong-hearted
> warrior at rest, "ræhte ongean"
> the foe with a palm.

In his Sir Israel Gollancz Memorial Lecture, Fred C. Robinson finds "ræhte ongean" suspect for two reasons: first, ongean, taken as a preposition meaning "toward," has no object; second, "lacking an unaccented syllable before

---

[23] See Thorkelin's edition, (Poëma), e.g., 78.16 (= 1021a) segen "signum"; 92.12 (= 1204a) segne "signis"; 206.5 (= 2767b) segn "vexilla"; 206.23 (= 2776b) segn "signa." I do not know why Thorkelin construes seg(e)n as a plural in the last three instances, but at least he shows he knows what the word means.

ræhte, it [the half-verse] is metrically short."[24] A reasonable answer to Robinson's first objection is to take *ongean* not as a preposition meaning "toward" but as an adverb meaning "opposite" or, perhaps more idiomatically in modern English, "out":

Forward, nearer, he stepped,
then with a hand grabbed the strong-hearted
warrior at rest, reached out,
the foe with a palm.[25]

Robinson's second objection, that "ræhte ongean" as it stands is metrically deficient, is more difficult to counter. One would expect the half-line to have an unstressed syllable before *ræhte* to make a B-verse or an unstressed syllable after *ongean* to make an A-verse.[26] A common solution to the problem, emending *ongean* to *togeanes*, revises the half-line into a neat A-verse but requires a major rewriting of the manuscript form. Robinson contends that the scribe did not mangle a word but simply omitted one. Citing the half-verse "him gangað ongean" from *Paris Psalter* 84, 9:1a and the half-verse "þe him foran ongean" from *Beowulf* 2364b, Robinson suggests that "ræhte ongean" be restored as "[him] ræhte ongean": Grendel "reached toward him," i.e., toward Beowulf. In a single move Robinson would both provide an object

---

[24] "*Beowulf* in the Twentieth Century," *Proceedings of the British Academy* 94 (1997): 45–62, at 56.

[25] In *Beowulf: An Edition with Relevant Shorter Texts* (Oxford, 1998), 72–73, Bruce Mitchell and Fred C. Robinson note with regard to lines 745b–749, "The stated actions are clear, but it is not always clear which of the two combatants is the actor. The confusion in the dark hall is mirrored in the language of the narrative." In the present case it is certain that the subject of *ætstop* is Grendel. But later in the passage *feond*, the subject of *ræhte* (or a variation on understood *he*, subject of *ræhte*), might be taken in reference to Beowulf, in which case "opposite" would be an effective translation of *ongean*: "Forward, nearer, he [Grendel] stepped, then with a hand grabbed the strong-hearted warrior [Beowulf] at rest; the foe [Beowulf] reached opposite with a palm." In the first translation of the passage into English, in 1837 (n. 6 above), Kemble renders *ongean* as meaning "out" and understands the one reaching as Beowulf: "He (*Beowulf*) reached out his hand . . ." (31, Kemble's parenthetical insert).

[26] Although "ræhte ongean" is unmetrical in the Sievers system, which Robinson follows, it is metrical in the system propounded by A. J. Bliss, *The Metre of Beowulf* (Oxford, 1958), 140, where the phrase is classified as 2E1a. (My thanks to A. N. Doane for bringing the point to my attention.) For cogent criticism of Bliss's treatment of E-verses (which allows such syllabic patterns as ´x x ´), see Thomas Cable, *The Meter and Melody of 'Beowulf'* (Urbana, 1974), 45–64.

for *ongean,* taken as a preposition, and repair the meter of the line. He notes that the reading is not new: Moritz Trautmann in 1904 proposed it as an emendation, and Michael Swanton in 1978 proposed it as a restoration (Robinson, *"Beowulf* in the Twentieth Century," 57, n. 34).[27]

Robinson turns now to the manuscript context of "ræhte ongean." The words occur at the beginning of line 7 on fol. 131r (or, in the alternate system of numbering, fol. 149r). Near the end of line 6 in the manuscript is an apparent *h,* partly obliterated, followed by several obscure letter fragments. Robinson notes that John C. Pope long ago suggested that the letter fragments once composed the words "him swa" but asserts that Pope's *swa* is not well grounded:

> What makes Pope's reading problematic is the awkward *swā* in *him swā ræhte ongēan.* Apparently Pope thought it was necessary to have *him swā* because in the manuscript the erasure has room for five or six letters, not just three, and Pope assumed that any reconstruction must fill up the amount of space in the manuscript. But this assumption is fallacious. Whatever the scribe was removing when he erased the letters was presumably wrong. Otherwise, why would he have erased it? Therefore a reconstruction of the intended word need not fill the space left by the erased incorrect letters.[28]

Robinson's reasoning makes good sense if we suppose that the letters in question were in fact deliberately erased by the scribe.

Pope, however, does not believe that the scribe deliberately erased the letters. "I strongly doubt," he says, "that they were erased intentionally, because corresponding places on the two sides of the preceding leaf are likewise obscured, as if something had been spilled there. It should be legitimate, therefore, to fill in the gap" (*Rhythm,* 372). Pope's reasoning makes as good sense as Robinson's. If the letters were obliterated by accident, as suggested by the fact that the preceding leaf has suffered corresponding damage, then we should expect the obliterated letters to be intelligible in the context. Supposing "him swa" to be the reading obliterated at the end of fol. 131r6, Pope gives this translation of lines 745b–748a: "He stepped forth nearer, took then

---

[27] Moritz Trautmann, ed., *Das Beowulflied* (Bonn, 1904), 42–43; Michael Swanton, ed., *Beowulf* (Manchester, 1978; rev. ed. Manchester and New York, 1997), 68–69. Trautmann is actually restoring rather than emending. He cites the manuscript reading as "ræste : : :"; the colons indicate the loss of text from the manuscript. See also n. 33 below.

[28] Robinson, *"Beowulf* in the Twentieth Century," 56–57. For Pope's discussion see *The Rhythm of Beowulf,* rev. ed. (New Haven, 1966), xxxi, 237, 372.

with his hand the stout-hearted warrior in his bed — he reached toward him so, the fiend, with his grip" (xxxi). Apart from the inclusion of "so," this is comparable to Robinson's translation: "forward [and] nearer he (Grendel) approached; he grasped then with his hand at the strong-hearted warrior in his resting place; the foe (Grendel) reached toward him (Beowulf) with his palm" (Robinson's brackets and parentheses).[29]

As noted, Robinson rejects "him swa" as the obliterated reading. He speculates that the reading was *handa*, a reading deliberately deleted by the scribe:

> Conjecturally, we may reconstruct the process of error. The erasure consists of a partially erased *h* followed by a letter which Zupitza thought had probably been an *a* before it was erased. Now above and to the right of the erasure in the preceding line of the manuscript are the letters *han*, the first syllable of *handa*, which is completed in the next line. Apparently, when the scribe went to write *him*, his eye was caught by the neighbouring word *handa* in his exemplar, and he copied that. Then noticing his mistake, he erased *handa*, all except for the initial *h*, which he intended to complete as *him*. But he neglected to complete the correction. We can with considerable confidence complete his correction for him, being guided by syntax, sense, metre, and by the vestigial evidence in the manuscript.[30]

On 9 March 1998 I examined this place in the *Beowulf* manuscript, beginning with the damaged *e* of the preceding form *onræste*, to determine if the "vestigial evidence" supports Robinson's argument. In reporting my findings, I quote from my original notes both because first impressions claim greater immediacy and more objectivity than edited accounts and because the notes show explicit awareness that my having *handa* in mind may have conditioned what I saw.

> *e* of onræst*e* definite. remains of so-called *h* consistent with *h* but ascender truncated and offstroke of *h* curved right: [sketch]. After "h" is a blotted curved stroke on line consistent with beginning of *a* or *æ* or

---

[29] *Beowulf: An Edition with Relevant Shorter Texts*, 72.

[30] "*Beowulf* in the Twentieth Century," 57. (It is not literally true that "above and to the right of the erasure in the preceding line of the manuscript [line 5] are the letters *han*." Only *h* now survives; *an* must be supplied by transcripts A and B. See Zupitza, *Reproduced*, 36.) Years before Robinson suggested that the erroneous reading obliterated after *ræste* on line 6 was *handa*, Kemble (line 1488) suggested that the correct reading to be restored after *ræste* is *hand*. Did the traces in the manuscript suggest *hand* to Kemble?

e[.] the *d* seems most in evidence. The erasure seems original to me. The traces remaining seem consistent with *handa* — but I was looking for the word. Faded shine-thru may impede reading.[31]

Included in my notes is a sketch of the obliterated reading as a whole. The sketch depicts from left to right: 1) an *h*-like figure with a very short ascender, 2) a curve on the baseline like the left side of a bowl, 3) some minim-like marks as though for *m* or *n*, 4) a *d*-like shape with an obscure bowl, and 5) a minim-like mark slightly curved like the left side of a bowl.

I also studied the place on 12 July 1999 with an edited version of my earlier report before me. In response to my edited version's statement that "*e* of *onræste* is definite," I inserted "very faint but" before "definite." Concerning the obliterated letters after the *h*-like figure, I noted, "Am more impressed with possible *an* now than earlier, less impressed with possible *d* & final 'letter'." In fact, in response to my edited version's statement that "Following other small marks is a *d*-like shape, after which is a slightly curved minim," I double underlined "*d*-like shape" and noted, "Cannot see this now. Possible ascender; cannot really see a '*d*-like shape'." I also underlined "slightly curved minim" in my edited statement and noted, "Cannot see this now." Further, I drew a sketch of the obliterated reading as a whole. The sketch shows from left to right: 1) an *h*-like shape missing the upper half of its ascender, 2) an *a* with a definite beginning of the onstroke and a definite end of the offstroke but with the upper part filled in by a hazy outline, 3) an *n*-like shape missing the lower half of its first minim, and 4) a short vertical line to the upper right of the *n*-like shape and labeled "beginning of ascender?" After the sketch I remarked, "cannot really see a final 'letter'; looks like emptiness."

I have quoted my two firsthand reports, made sixteen months apart, on an obscure reading in the *Beowulf* manuscript. The reports do not agree in vital ways. In the report of 9 March 1998 I claim to see a *d*-like shape — indeed, I say "the *d* seems most in evidence" — followed by a curved minim, whereas in the report on 12 July 1999 I cannot confirm a *d*-like shape but only the possible beginning of an ascender, after which I see no fragment at all.

I believe that two factors largely explain the differences in the reports. The first is that I was able to spend more time studying the reading in March 1998, when I devoted more than three-quarters of an hour to the task, than in July 1999, when I was able to spend no more than fifteen minutes. My experience is that verifying really difficult manuscript readings takes nearly as long as

---

[31] In quoting from my notes here and hereafter I silently expand abbreviations (e.g., "def" to "definite," "beg" to "beginning," "sms" to "seems").

making the reading in the first place. The second factor is that the conditions under which I examined the *Beowulf* manuscript changed. In March 1998, I studied it in the Students Room at the British Library building on Great Russell Street, Bloomsbury; in July 1999, I studied it in the Manuscripts Reading Room at the new building on Euston Road, St. Pancras. When indistinct traces of ink and faint patterns in parchment are in question, the lighting need not be dramatically different to yield different results.[32]

I trust my report of 9 March 1998, when I studied at length fol. 131r6, end. My assertion that "the *d* seems most in evidence" is a strong statement for someone of my skeptical bent, especially when what I characterized as "so-called *h*" is more pronounced in facsimiles. However, I also trust my report of 12 July 1999, in which I could not confirm the earlier reported "*d*-like shape" followed by a curved minim-like fragment but found *an* a more plausible reading than earlier. Given the altered circumstances, this report is probably as accurate as the first. Combining the two reports, I conclude that the vestigial evidence is wholly consistent with and moderately supports Robinson's assertion that *handa* was once written at the end of line 6. Certainly the evidence better supports Robinson's *handa* than Pope's "him swa": Pope's *i* does not fit the fragment coming immediately after apparent *h*, and I saw no evidence of a descender for wynn (or for any other letter).[33]

What perplexes me more than the lack of complete accord between my two reports is Pope's strong argument that the letters at the end of line 6 were not deliberately erased "because corresponding places on the two sides of the preceding leaf are likewise obscured, as if something had been spilled there." I agree that whatever damaged fol. 131 recto, line 6, end, at the same time damaged the corresponding places on the preceding folio, 146: on 146 recto, line 6, end, *horn* (704a) is still legible but blurred; on 146 verso, line 5, beginning,

---

[32] I learn from Carl T. Berkhout, who worked alongside Phill at the British Library more often than anyone else, that Phill thought that different lighting conditions could so influence legibility that scholars should specify the dates they study controversial manuscript readings. Zupitza evidently held the same conviction a dozen decades ago. Of a speculative reading, *metodes?*, on 198v4 he says, "I thought I saw all those letters pretty distinctly (except the two first strokes of *m*) on the tenth of September 1880, but on no other day. On the 12th of Sept., 1882, I thought I was able to read [*w*]*igendes* || *egesan*] *an* torn . . ." (*Reproduced*, 144).

[33] However, Trautmann, "Berichtigungen, Vermutungen und Erklärungen zum Beowulf," *Bonner Beiträge zur Anglistik* 2 (1899): 121–92, here 167, thought he could discern *him* in Zupitza's facsimile, and Pope himself thought the traces in the facsimile might be read as "*him sw* (the *s* high, only the lower half of its stem visible, the *w* [wynn] showing quite plainly below the line)" (*Rhythm*, 372).

letters are lost before *an* (722b); and on 146 verso, line 6, beginning, letters are lost before *bolgen* (723b). Further, on fol. 131 itself, verso, line 6, beginning — which corresponds to the letters obliterated after *onræste* on the recto — *n* is blurred beyond recognition, and *ede* is blurred but legible (767a).[34]

We can but speculate on what caused the damage. Pope suggests that liquid had been spilled on fol. 131. This may be close to the truth but not the whole truth. Suppose all but *h* of the original reading after *onræste* was intentionally erased. Perhaps the roughness of the erased surface caused this part of the folio to retain more water than elsewhere during and after the Cotton Library fire in October 1731.[35] Or, better, suppose that an early antiquary applied a liquid agent to try to recover the erased reading — as apparently occurred in the case of readings on fol. 179 — and the agent contaminated contiguous readings.[36] Be that as it may, the empirical evidence favors Robinson's suggestion for the obliterated letters over Pope's.

In the *Electronic Beowulf*, Kiernan proposes another reading for the end of fol. 131r6. In connection with an ultra-violet (UV) digitized image of the place, he remarks, "6. after **ræste** an erasure of about five letters, of which the first two appear with UV as **he**, perhaps followed by **on** (if so, an eye-skip to the following line)." Kiernan's possible "eye-skip to the following line" makes sense only if he, like Robinson, envisions an eye-skip made by the scribe in reading the exemplar: it is quite unlikely that the scribe of the Cotton *Beowulf* had copied "he on" at the end of line 7 before writing whatever letters (now largely obliterated) he copied at the end of line 6.

Kiernan is more confident of seeing *he* than *on*. Although when I first studied the place in March 1998 I reported, "After 'h' is a blotted curved stroke

---

[34] We know from transcripts A and B that the original reading was *dynede*. Now *dy* is simply gone.

[35] On the question of erasure or accidental effacement, it may be noted that in his diplomatic edition of *Beowulf*, published in 1881 (n. 49 below), Wülcker, independent of Zupitza, also refers to the loss of text after *ræste* as the result of "rasur" (*Bibliothek*, 1.1: 46). On the Cotton fire and its aftermath, see Andrew Prescott, "'Their Present Miserable State of Cremation': The Restoration of the Cotton Library," in *Sir Robert Cotton as Collector: Essays on an Early Stuart Courtier and his Legacy*, ed. C. J. Wright (London, 1997), 391–454. See esp. 394: "... the water used to extinguish the blaze had caused as much damage as the flames."

[36] In *Beowulf with the Finnesburg Fragment*, 3rd ed., rev. by W. F. Bolton (New York, 1973), 12, C. L. Wrenn suggests that someone applied a "disastrous chemical reagent" to fols. 179r and 198v in an "attempt to improve their legibility." In the *Electronic Beowulf*, under Help Index | Guide, Electronic Texts, Edition, 2–3, and in his comments on the digitized images of fol. 179r, Kiernan adduces visual evidence to support Wrenn's point. See also n. 56 below.

on line consistent with beginning of *a* or *æ* or *e*," my sketch of the fragments in July 1999 leads me to think that *æ* and *e* are much less likely than *a* as the original letter after apparent *h*.[37] Certainly if the original letter after apparent *h* was *æ* or *e*, the *e*-head is now wholly gone. Kiernan does not specify whether his speculative *on* is written solid after his speculative *he* — as *heon* — or whether *he* and *on* are separated by a small space to mark them as separate words. I would argue that the remaining letter fragments are too close together to admit of a word space and that the fragments in third position are not consistent with *o*: it may be possible to reconstruct the original reading as *heno* (or even *hemo*), but *he on* and *heon* are inconsistent with the evidence.

Thanks to Kiernan and the *Electronic Beowulf,* scholars need not study the manuscript firsthand to get a firsthand sense of the manuscript. In the *Electronic Beowulf* the ultra-violet image in black and white and the regular image in color seem to suggest that the first three letters of the obliterated form were *h*, *a*, and *n*. I see, however, virtually no evidence in the two images for *d* and only the most arbitrary evidence for the curved minim that I report after *d* in my examination of March 1998. It is important to remember, however, that the regular color images of the *Electronic Beowulf* can be altered in size but not otherwise modified.[38] In using the *Electronic Beowulf*, one cannot alter lighting conditions or the angle of vision as when working directly with the manuscript. Studying the manuscript directly — with all the expense and inconvenience that entails — remains the best way to study it.

Studying the manuscript directly, Zupitza, twelve decades ago and without looking for any letters in particular, observed, "after *ræste* an erasure of some five letters, of which the first seems to have been *h*, the second possibly was *a*" (*Reproduced*, 36). I believe that Zupitza is correct and that Robinson's speculative restoration of the entire obliterated form as *handa* best agrees with the evidence that time and chance have left us.

---

[37] An advantage of relying directly on one's original notes instead of on an edited version is that in my edited version I had deleted reference to the possibility that the fragments after apparent *h* might be the remains of *e*. Had not Kiernan later suggested *e* as the possible second letter, I might have left *e* entirely out of account. Although I do not believe that the second letter was *e*, the record shows that on first studying the place I thought *e* quite possible.

[38] Unlike the regular folio images in color, the ultra-violet images accessed by double clicking on the hotspots cannot be altered in magnification.

Line 2232a: *eorð[hu]se, eorðse[le]*, and the Construction of Error

Referring to a costly cup in the dragon's treasure-laden lair, the poet says, according to Dobbie's edition:

þær wæs swylcra fela
in ðam eorð[hu]*se*   ærgestreona,   (2231b–2232)

there were many such
ancient treasures in that *eorð[hu]se*.

Dobbie italicizes *se* in "eorð[hu]*se*" to indicate that the two letters are not found in the *Beowulf* manuscript and that only one of the transcripts has the reading. In his textual note on the crux Dobbie comments: "**2232** eorðhuse] Restored by Zupitza and most later edd. The reading *eorðsele*, adopted by Holder (2 ed.) and Trautmann, following a suggestion by Kluge, ignores the evidence of transcript B that the next to the last letter of this word was *-s-*" (233). Dobbie's assertion that transcript B records the word's penultimate letter as "*-s-*" is not accurate. Transcript B reads "eorðse . ." — not "eorð . . se." I would like to clinch the case for Friedrich Kluge's reading and trace the tradition of misconstruing the evidence in transcript B.

Transcript B is best understood against the backdrop of the *Beowulf* manuscript. Lines 2231b–2232, earlier quoted from Dobbie's edition, occur in the manuscript on fol. 179v3–4:

. . . þær wæs swylcra fela inðā eorð
. . . ær ge streona

I insert ellipsis at the beginning of each line to signal lost letters. The letters lost before *þær*, line 3, do not bear on the present problem. Those lost before *ær*, line 4, are the heart of the matter.

When Thorkelin executed his transcript of *Beowulf*, he copied line 3 and the first part of line 4 in the manuscript as follows:

. . . . . þær væs svylcra fela inðan eorð
se . . er ge streona (102a.3–4)

Twice, in *væs* and *svylcra*, Thorkelin transcribes wynn as *v*. This is not a simple copying error since at the time he believed that wynn should be so transcribed. Later, coming to understand that wynn should be transcribed as *w*, Thorkelin altered *v* to *w* in both words (as in many others) in transcript B. He also later altered his original *n* in *inðan* to *m*. Again, Thorkelin's original *n* is not a simple transcriptional error since he recognized the macron over *a* in manuscript *inðā* as a sign of abbreviation; he merely resolved it incorrectly at first. That leaves but a single direct error in transcript B here: Thorkelin's transcription of *ær*, line 4, as *er*.[39] This is a difficult manuscript reading, *æ* being barely legible; the letter has been half erased, and the *e*-part has no tongue. So much for Thorkelin's shortcomings in this particular place.

What he has given us in the passage — something for which we otherwise have no evidence — is brief but valuable. In the *Beowulf* manuscript no letters now survive before *ær*, line 4, and transcript A records no letters (including *ær*) for the beginning of the line before *ge streona* (65.15). For the beginning of line 4, however, Thorkelin records *se* plus two dots. That means he gives us evidence for a noun beginning *eorðse-* in reference to the dragon's lair, *eorð* coming at the tail of line 3 in the manuscript and *se* once coming at the head of line 4. Are there any words in *Beowulf* referring to the lair beginning *eorðse-*? As Kiernan has recently noted, there is *eorðsele* "earth-hall," occurring at lines 2410a and 2515a.[40]

Eorðse[le] rests on more secure foundations than does Zupitza's *eorð[hu]se*. First, *eorðhus*, unlike *eorðsele*, does not occur in *Beowulf* in reference to the dragon's lair; in fact, *eorðhus* does not occur anywhere in *Beowulf* or elsewhere in OE verse. Second, *eorðse[le]* agrees with Thorkelin's firsthand transcription of the *Beowulf* manuscript as "eorð | se . .," whereas *eorð[hu]se* supposes that Thorkelin's reading is really an error for "eorð | . . se."

Eorðse[le] is so clearly superior to *eorð[hu]se* that one wonders how *eorð[hu]se* has been left standing generation after generation. Thorkelin's edition of *Beowulf* is partly to blame. Earlier I noted that in transcript B Thorkelin first transcribed fol. 179v3–4 in the manuscript as follows:

> . . . . . þær væs svylcra fela inðan eorð
> se . . er ge streona

I also noted that Thorkelin later revised *væs* to *wæs*, *svylcra* to *swylcra*, and *inðan* to *inðam* in transcript B. In his 1815 edition (*Poëma*, 167, lines 7–10), he incorporated these revisions and introduced other changes as well.

---

[39] Kiernan, *Transcripts*, 81, believes there were two other errors in the passage as originally copied: he holds that Thorkelin first wrote *indan* and *eord* for manuscript *inðā* and *eorð* and only later corrected *d* in each reading to *ð*. I have studied firsthand only *ð* in *eorð*. My finding is that *ð* was *ð* from the start and that Thorkelin did not add the cross-stroke at a later stage. To judge by the versions of transcript B in Malone's facsimile and in the *Electronic Beowulf*, the *ð* in *inðan* was also *ð* from the start, but this is no more than an impression.

[40] See the *Electronic Beowulf*, glossary, s.v. *eorðsele*; and the note to the facsimile text of *Beowulf* on the manuscript reading at the head of fol. 179v4.

. . . .
Þæ wæs swylcra fela   *Ibi erant tales multi*
In þam eorþ . . . .   *In ista terra . . . .*
Se . . er gestreona   *Ille . . . . . opum*

These lines differ much from the lines in transcript B. On line 7 Thorkelin gives an entire half-line of dots as against five dots in transcript B for what in the *Beowulf* manuscript was likely the loss of a single word before *þær*. On line 8 he misprints *þær* of transcript B as *þæ*. And on line 9 he inserts four dots after *eorþ*. This seemingly innocuous departure from transcript B leads to a nocuous error: the interpretation of the letters *se* at the head of line 4 of Thorkelin's transcription of fol. 179v as a new word — the definite masculine article *se* (translated "Ille") — instead of as the immediate continuation of a word beginning *eorþ* ("eorð | se . ." = "eorðse . .").[41]

Thorkelin's departure in his edition from the evidence of his transcript exerted direct influence on N. F. S. Grundtvig, who in 1829 took a handwritten text of *Beowulf*, based on transcripts A and B and Thorkelin's edition, to London from Copenhagen to collate against the *Beowulf* manuscript.[42] In writing his handwritten text, Grundtvig — who perhaps supposed that Thorkelin knew best how to interpret his own transcript — followed Thorkelin's edition instead of Thorkelin's transcript and gave the lines as

in þam eorð . . . . .
se . . er ge-streonum.[43]

In collating the lines with the *Beowulf* manuscript in summer 1829, Grundtvig crossed out "se . . er ge-" and corrected his speculative *streonum* to *streona*.[44]

When Grundtvig finally published his edition some three decades later, in 1861, he presented the text as follows:

[41] Note that in giving *eorþ* in his edition, Thorkelin also departs from his transcript in substituting *þ* for *ð*. Throughout his edition he uses *þ* when *ð* occurs in his transcript.
[42] On the collation see Birte Kelly, "The Formative Stages of Modern *Beowulf* Scholarship, Textual, Historical and Literary, Seen in the Work of Scholars of the Earlier Nineteenth Century" (Ph.D. diss., Queen Mary College, University of London, 1979), 90–110.
[43] Copenhagen, Royal Library, Grundtvig-Arkiv Facs. 307, fol. 101v, lines 4451–4452. (Fol. 101v, displaced toward the end of Facs. 307, is Grundtvig's original version of lines 4432–4466; fol. 67v, which also contains the lines, is a fair copy of his original text and collation and is once removed his original study of the lines in the *Beowulf* manuscript.)
[44] He should not have crossed out "er ge-" but have replaced "er" with "ær" (although *æ* is difficult) and have let stand "ge" (distinctly legible in the manuscript).

in þám eorð . . . *fe,*   4455
ǽr-gestreóna,

Italics in Grundtvig's edition indicate letters borrowed from A or B or other early witnesses like Kemble (= K). Grundtvig has a textual note on each (half-) line: "4455 . . . se. B. scræfe. K." and "4456 er. B. ǽr. K."[45] In his note to 4455, Grundtvig misrepresents transcript B as reading ". . . se" (instead of "se . ."), and he compounds the problem by giving ". . . *fe*" in his text, implying that B's *s* is a transcriptional error for what in the manuscript was once *f*. Why *f*? Grundtvig wants to allow for Kemble's restoration, *scræfe* "cave." In his edition, however, Kemble had put *scræfe* in parentheses to signal that it is a speculative restoration, "in ðam eorð(-scræfe)," while giving *ǽr* on the next line without parentheses to show that it is the actual manuscript reading, "ǽr-gestreóna" (lines 4459–4460). Grundtvig, however, ignores Kemble's parentheses and presents *fe* as attested by Kemble as once present in the manuscript.

Little wonder that other scholars followed suit. The first edition published after Grundtvig's was Moritz Heyne's, in 1863, in which the half-line is printed as "in þam eorð[scrä]fe," which clearly implies that "fe" (as distinct from Grundtvig's *fe*, in italics) exists in the manuscript, an implication given greater currency by the fact that the reading is repeated in Heyne's second edition (1868) and third edition (1873).[46] The second German scholar to publish an edition after Grundtvig's was Christian W. M. Grein, who, like Heyne, printed the half-line as "in þam eorð[scrä]fe" in 1867.[47] If we can pardon Grundtvig, who had directly studied the manuscript and transcripts A and B, for printing *fe* as though he had real evidence that the letters were once in the manuscript, we shall have to pardon Heyne and Grein for misinterpreting Grundtvig and printing "fe" as though the letters were simply the manuscript reading. Neither had set eyes on the manuscript.

Nor had any German scholar to date reported firsthand on the manuscript text of *Beowulf* — despite the fact that Germans were leaders in the field of *Beowulf* studies and that nearly six decades had passed since Thorkelin's edition made *Beowulf* known to the world of Germanic learning. That soon changed. In the mid-1870s three German scholars journeyed to London

---

[45] *Beowulfes Beorh eller Bjovulfs-Drapen, det Old-Angelske Heltedigt, paa Grund-Spoget* (Copenhagen, 1861), 76. Grundtvig should have put "ge" of "*ǽr*-gestreóna" in italics, citing A, B, and Kemble in support, since he had deleted "ge" in 1829. See n. 44 above.

[46] *Beovulf. Mit ausführlichem Glossar herausgegeben* (Paderborn, 1863).

[47] *Beovulf nebst den Fragmenten Finnsburg und Valdere* (Kassel, 1867).

to ponder the manuscript in person: Eugen Kölbing in summer 1875, Richard Paul Wülcker later the same year (and again in 1878), and Alfred Holder in fall 1876.[48]

Kölbing, a twenty-nine-year-old scholar from Breslau, was the first to publish a report. In "Zur Beóvulf-handschrift" (1876), he comments on the crux: "v. 2233. eorð ms. eord H[eyne] 1. 2. 3. Das[selbe] eorð . . . . fe ær" (110). The first part of Kölbing's note means that the manuscript reading is *eorð* but that Heyne in his three editions prints *eord* instead. In the second part of the note Kölbing says that the manuscript reads "eorð . . . . fe ær." Both parts of the note are inaccurate. Heyne reads *eorð*, not *eord*, and Kölbing (who elsewhere uses a bar to indicate the end of scribal lines) should have recorded the manuscript reading as "eorð | . . . . ær." In reporting "fe" as present in the manuscript, Kölbing is even more misleading than Grundtvig, Heyne, and Grein: Grundtvig in reading "eorð . . . *fe*" at least used italics to signal that he had no firsthand evidence for *f* and *e*, and Heyne and Grein in reading "eorð[scrä]fe" at least did not claim to base their texts on a personal examination of the manuscript.

In his diplomatic edition of 1881, Wülcker, the second German scholar to report on the manuscript text of *Beowulf*, transcribes line 3 and the first part of line 4 of fol. 179v as follows:

. . . . . . þær[4]) wæs swylcra fela in ðā eorð[5])
. . . . . e[6]) ær gestreona

---

[48] Wülcker (n. 49 below) does not specify when he began transcribing the manuscript in 1875, but it seems to have been after Kölbing collated it in the summer. At the end of his report, "Zur Beóvulf-handschrift," *Archiv für das Studium der neueren Sprachen und Literaturen* 56 (1876): 91–118, here 117–18, Kölbing, writing in December 1875, complains that because of him others have since gone to London to collate the manuscript. He mentions Sievers, Wülcker, and Zupitza. This may be true of Wülcker but not of Sievers and Zupitza, each of whom had got to London years before Kölbing. Sievers, at the age of 21, saw the *Beowulf* manuscript in 1871, when he collated *Judith*, the poem following *Beowulf*. See Eduard Sievers, "Collationen angelsächsischer Gedichte," *ZfdA* 15 (1872): 456–67. Zupitza spent six months in England in 1872. If Zupitza was back in England in late 1875, it was likely not to collate *Beowulf* but to further his edition, *The Romance of Guy of Warwick: The Second or 15th-century Version*, EETS, e.s. 25–26 (London, 1875–1876). See Arthur Napier, "Julius Zupitza," *Archiv für das Studium der neueren Sprachen und Literaturen* 95 (1895): 241–58, here 242–43. Evidently, the first time Zupitza worked with the *Beowulf* manuscript was in August 1880 (Zupitza, *Autotypes*, v). It appears that F. J. Furnivall asked Zupitza to edit the facsimile not because he was a well-known *Beowulf* scholar (he was not) but because Furnivall knew him from his work on *The Romance of Guy of Warwick*, published by Furnivall's EETS. See also n. 53 below.

Wülcker's notes 5 and 6 concern the present argument. In n. 5 he says, "*So hat die hs.*," by which he would correct Kölbing and anyone else who might think that the letters missing from the word beginning *eorð* on line 3 once came at the end of line 3 rather than the beginning of line 4. In n. 6 Wülcker gives earlier readings from, respectively, Thorkelin's edition, transcript B, Kemble, Grundtvig, and Kölbing: "*Thork.* eorþ . . . . Se . . er gestreona; *B.* eorð . . . se. *K.* eorð (scræfe) ærgestreona; *Gru.* eorð . . . *fe ær*gestreona; *Kö.* eorð . . . . fe ær."[49] One might quibble with Wülcker for omitting the accents and hyphens in citing Kemble's reading and Grundtvig's, but the real inaccuracy in n. 6 — the report of the reading in transcript B as "eorð . . . se" instead of "eorðse . ." — is not of Wülcker's making: Grundtvig was the only scholar to have published a firsthand account of readings in transcripts A and B, and other scholars were wholly dependent on it. Wülcker could not have known that Grundtvig got the reading wrong.

Wülcker cannot be absolved, however, for printing the first part of line 4 in the manuscript as ". . . . . e⁶) ær gestreona," as though an "e" survives in the manuscript immediately before "ær."[50] It does not, nor, if transcript B is to be believed, did such an "e" survive when Thorkelin saw the manuscript more than eight decades before Wülcker. If Wülcker thought he saw an identifiable fragment of "e" immediately before "ær," he should have put the letter in italics (as is his practice elsewhere) to indicate its provisional nature. Wülcker repeats the reading, however, both in the 1883 reprint of his diplomatic edition and in the companion critical edition.[51] In the critical edition he gives "*Hs.* eorð . . . . . e" (along with readings of other editors) in a textual note and in the text itself reads "in þam eorð*scræfe*" — exactly equivalent to what Grein had read a decade and a half earlier ("eorð[scrä]fe") without benefit of having seen the manuscript. In his diplomatic edition Wülcker (wrongly) recorded "e" as surviving before "ær" on line 4 in the manuscript, but in his diplomatic edition he certainly did not record "f" as surviving before "e." Whence the letter in Wülcker's critical edition? From Grundtvig's edition, whose reading Wülcker cites

---

[49] *Bibliothek der angelsächsischen Poesie begründet von Christian W. M. Grein. Neu bearbeitet, vermehrt und nach eignen Lesungen der Handschriften herausgegeben von Richard Paul Wülcker* (Kassel, 1881), 1.1:106.

[50] Wülcker could have avoided the error had he consulted — and trusted — the work of an Englishman who had studied the manuscript firsthand shortly before he had. In *Beowulf, A Heroic Poem of the Eighth Century* (London, 1876), 144, Thomas Arnold (brother of the more famous Matthew) reads "eorð-[scræfe]," clearly implying that no letter of the second part of the compound survived.

[51] *Das Beowulfslied nebst den kleineren epischen, lyrischen, didaktischen und geschichtlichen Stücken* (Kassel, 1883).

in his textual note as "eorð . . . fe." Like Heyne and Grein, Wülcker ignores the fact that Grundtvig put "fe" in italics to signal that he had not actually seen the letters but based the reading on "se" in transcript B.

Holder did better. In his 1881 diplomatic edition he prints line 3 and the first part of line 4 of fol. 179v as follows:

> • • • þær wæs swylcra fela in ðā eorð
>
> • • • • e ær ge streona[52]

In Holder's diplomatic edition italics signal a reading no longer in the manuscript but supported by early evidence. The edition is without textual notes, however, and he does not specify his source of *e* before "ær." The second edition, published in 1882 and also without textual notes, is practically a reprint of the first. One of the few changes concerns the crux in question. Holder adds a fifth point before *e* at the head of line 4: • • • • • *e*. Did he add the point to accommodate the five letters of *scræf*? Yes. It was the final attempt to prop up Kemble's "eorð(-scræfe)," dilapidated after five decades, a reading Holder himself would soon happily leave behind.

The year 1882 saw the publication of a book far more influential than the second edition of Holder's diplomatic edition: Zupitza's facsimile edition of *Beowulf*, in which a transliteration of the text in modern type faces photographs of the folios. Zupitza had a huge edge over other scholars. F. J. Furnivall, director of the Early English Text Society, secured him the loan of transcripts A and B to use in parallel with the *Beowulf* manuscript,[53] and for the first time Thorkelin B's reading of the head of fol. 179v4 was accurately cited: "*se . . er ge streona*" (104). As it happens, however, Zupitza could not withstand the textual tradition beckoning him back six and a half decades to 1815, when Thorkelin transmuted "eorð | se . ." of transcript B into "eorþ . . . . | Se . ." of his edition. Implying that the transcript reading "eorð | se . ." is an error for "eorð | . . se," Zupitza in his transliterated text reads "eorð- | [hu]se."

Zupitza's new restoration had early impact. In his critical edition (1884), Holder reads "eorð-*hûse*" and gives this textual note: "2232 –hûse *Zupitza* • •

---

[52] *Beowulf*. I. *Abdruck der Handschrift im British Museum, Cotton. Vitellius A. xv* (Freiburg i. B., [1881]). I make no attempt to reflect Holder's use of Insular minuscule for certain letters. The first edition is rare (the only copy I have seen is in the Universitätsbibliothek Freiburg); 2nd. ed. 1882; 3rd ed. 1895.

[53] J. R. Hall, "F. J. Furnivall's Letter to the Royal Library, Copenhagen, Asking that the Thorkelin Transcripts of *Beowulf* Be Sent to London for the Use of Julius Zupitza," *Notes and Queries* 45.3 (1998): 267–72.

se α."⁵⁴ In Holder's critical edition the siglum "α" stands for an original manuscript reading based on early evidence. Here α evidently indicates that "⁚ se" is taken from transcript B. Despite the fact that Zupitza clearly reports B's reading as "*se . . er ge streona*," Holder reverses the points and letters, filtering Thorkelin's transcript through Zupitza's text. In his first appendix, a list of early evidence for damaged manuscript readings, Holder repeats the error, this time, however, explicitly ascribing the reading to transcript B (101).

Eleven years later, in the third avatar of his diplomatic edition (1895), Holder sprang a surprise. He abandoned "⁚ se" as the former manuscript reading, based on his understanding of Zupitza's report on transcript B, and presented the former manuscript reading as "⁚⁚⁚ e." We have beheld Holder at work like this before. In his 1881 diplomatic edition, he had given the former manuscript reading as "⁚⁚⁚⁚ e"; in the 1882 diplomatic edition he had given it as "⁚⁚⁚⁚⁚ e." Why did he now decide that the number of letters lost before *e* was three and not five? The reason becomes clear in the 1899 version of Holder's critical edition, in which he discards Zupitza's "eorð-*hûse*" in favor of "eorð-*sele*," his only comment being this textual note: "2232 sele *Kluge* ✶✶✶e α." Besides accrediting the new reading to Kluge, Holder gives "✶✶✶e" as the manuscript reading, which of course reflects the reading in his diplomatic edition of 1895 and affords a neat three-letter niche for *sel* to fill. In his first appendix, a list of early evidence for damaged manuscript readings, Holder duly reports (as in his 1884 critical edition) the reading of transcript B as "✶✶se." To accommodate Kluge's restoration, Holder must accept "e" in B's putative "✶✶se" but silently reject B's "s." The crowning irony is that Holder need not have resorted to editorial legerdemain. B's real reading, "se . .," accurately reported by Zupitza, cogently supports Kluge's hunch that the original manuscript reading was not *eorðhuse* but *eorðsele*.

Kluge's restoration was accepted by Trautmann in his edition (1904) but did not fare well thereafter, perhaps because editors continued to understand B's reading through Zupitza's text rather than textual note. When Malone published his facsimile edition of the transcripts in 1951, however, scholars no longer had to rely on Zupitza's report for B's reading but could see it for themselves. Even so, Zupitza's influence lived a long afterlife.

In the preface to his 1953 edition Dobbie (vi) thanks Malone for facilitating his use of photographs of the transcripts even before the publication of Malone's facsimile edition in 1951, but for line 2232a Dobbie seems to have relied on Zupitza's text rather than his own eyes. Otherwise it is difficult to

---

⁵⁴ *Beowulf. II. Berichtigter Text mit knappem Apparat und Wörterbuch* (Freiburg i. B., 1884; 2nd. ed. 1899).

understand Dobbie's assertion, quoted earlier, that Kluge's proposed *eorðsele* "ignores the evidence of transcript B that the next to the last letter of this word was -*s*-." In the *Nowell Codex*, Malone himself remarks of fol. 179v4, "at the head of the line A has only a blank space before *ge* but B has *se . . er ge*; the MS has only *ær ge*; B's dots should have been put before, not after *se*, of course; the usual restoration is *huse* (Z)."[55] In *'Beowulf' and the 'Beowulf' Manuscript* (New Brunswick, 1981), Kiernan presents fol. 179v4 as reading "::se) ær ge streona swa hy on gearda" and says, "The reading at the beginning of the line, before the parentheses, is based on Thorkelin B" (240). The reading may be based on Thorkelin B, but it is not Thorkelin B's reading. It would be more accurate to say that the reading is Zupitza's textual embodiment of B's reading. In *The Thorkelin Transcripts of 'Beowulf'* (1986), Kiernan does not list any letters lost on fol. 179v that can be restored through transcript B (80). When he comes to consider B's work on line 4, Kiernan comments, "se . . er (for . . seær? e/æ — MS gone?)" (81), which I take to mean, first, that B's "se . . er" may be an error for ". . seær"; second, that the letter B transcribed before *r* as *e* is an error for *æ*; and, third, that the manuscript reading may have been gone when B recorded "se . ." (i.e., "se" may be only editorial speculation by B). However, a decade later in the revised edition of *'Beowulf' and the 'Beowulf' Manuscript* (Ann Arbor, 1996), Kiernan, in giving his reading of fol. 179v4, replaced the inaccurate "::se)" of his first edition with the accurate "se::)" (240). And three years later Kiernan, now editing the poem for the *Electronic Beowulf*, combined B's "eorð | se . ." with the poet's use of *eorðsele* at lines 2410a and 2515a and concluded that the best restoration at line 2232a is *eorðse[le]*.

More than two centuries after Thorkelin executed transcript B we finally got the restoration right. What took us so long? One reason is that no scholar outside Denmark knew of B's reading until the appearance of Grundtvig's edition in 1861, and then Grundtvig wrongly reported the reading as ". . . se." But even after Zupitza rightly reported B's reading in 1882, it took us a dozen decades to arrive at a fairly straightforward restoration. And that suggests a second reason it took us so long: editorial inertia, by which I do not mean editorial languor (OE editors being gluttons for labor) but the understandable tendency of editors to move in the same direction decade after decade unless deflected from the well-traveled course. Kemble's *eorð[scræfe]* ruled the dragon's roost for half a century to the extent that Grundtvig emended B's "se" to "fe" to accommodate the restoration and Holder and others simply cast aside B's "s." And then Zupitza's proposed restoration, *eorð[hu]se*, took such blind-

---

[55] Malone, *The Nowell Codex*, 85.2–86.1. (What I refer to as fol. 179v is fol. 183v in the numbering system Malone follows.)

ing command that for more than a century scholars read B's reading through the prism of Zupitza's text.

A third reason it took so long to arrive at *eorðse[le]* is that scholars tend to make a certain assumption concerning the loss of text in the manuscript, an assumption Malone seems to reflect when he says that "B's dots should have been put before, not after *se*, of course." Why "of course"? Because Malone apparently supposes that *Beowulf* always suffered loss from the outer margins inward. True for textual loss resulting only from the Cotton fire of 1731, but fol. 179 suffered textual loss from both deliberate erasure and the fire. The leaf also attests an attempt by someone to restore erased text.[56] The restorer could not restore all erased readings. Fol. 179r shows nine instances in which he restored letters at the beginning of a line, then had to leave a gap before restoring later letters. On line 12, for example, he restored *ð* at the beginning but could not restore other letters until he reached mid-line.

Something similar occurred, I believe, at 179v4. In the late eighteenth century Thorkelin found himself looking at a line in which the restorer had restored (or, less likely, in which Thorkelin himself had restored) the first two letters on the erased line but not the next two. Thorkelin recorded the two letters, *se*, to which he added two dots. In time the beginning of the line (along with the beginning of other lines on the leaf) crumbled away, a delayed result of the fire more than fifty years before Thorkelin. Thorkelin did not know what to make of the reading. Today we do, after generations of misinterpreting the evidence.

The history of scholarship on the crux makes it easy to believe that we are now perpetrating and perpetuating other misreadings that future generations will regard as risible errata.

Bibliography

Arnold, Thomas, ed. *Beowulf, A Heroic Poem of the Eighth Century*. London, 1876.

Berkhout, Carl T. "*Beowulf* 2200–08: Mind the Gap." *American Notes and Queries* 15.2 (2000): 51–58.

Bliss, A. J. *The Metre of Beowulf*. Oxford, 1958.

---

[56] For a persuasive account of the erasure and partial restoration, see Carl T. Berkhout, "*Beowulf* 2200–08: Mind the Gap," *American Notes and Queries* 15.2 (2002): 51–58. Perhaps the same person who restored some of the text also applied chemical reagent to the folio (n. 36 above).

Cable, Thomas. *The Meter and Melody of Beowulf.* Urbana, 1974.

Campbell, A. *Old English Grammar.* Oxford, 1959; corr. ed. Oxford, 1977.

Cooley, Franklin. "Early Danish Criticism of *Beowulf.*" *English Literary History* 7 (1940): 45–67.

Damico, Helen. "'My Professor of Anglo-Saxon was Frederick Klaeber': Minnesota and Beyond." In *The Preservation and Transmission of Anglo-Saxon Culture,* ed. Paul E. Szarmach and Joel T. Rosenthal, 73–98. Kalamazoo, 1997.

Dobbie, Elliot Van Kirk, ed. *Beowulf and Judith.* ASPR 4. New York, 1953.

Du Cange, Charles du Fresne. *Glossarium ad Scriptores Mediæ et Infimæ Latinitatis.* Frankfurt, 1762.

Facciolati, Jacobus, and Ægidius Forcellini. *Lexicon Totius Latinitatis.* Padua, 1805.

Grein, C. M. W., ed. *Beovulf nebst den Fragmenten Finnsburg und Valdere.* Kassel, 1867.

Grundtvig, N. F. S., ed. *Beowulfes Beorh eller Bjovulfs-Drapen, det Old-Angelske Heltedigt, paa Grund-Spoget.* Copenhagen, 1861.

Hall, J. R. "F. J. Furnivall's Letter to the Royal Library, Copenhagen, Asking that the Thorkelin Transcripts of *Beowulf* Be Sent to London for the Use of Julius Zupitza." *Notes and Queries* 45.3 (1998): 267–72.

Heyne, M., ed. *Beowulf. Mit ausführlichem Glossar herausgegeben.* Paderborn, 1863.

Holder, Alfred. *Beowulf I. Abdruck der Handschrift im British Museum, Cotton. Vitellius A. xv.* Freiburg i. B., 1881; 2nd ed. 1882; 3rd ed. 1895.

———. *Beowulf II. Berichtigter Text mit knappem Apparat und Wörterbuch.* Freiburg i. B., 1884; 2nd ed., 1899.

Kelly, Birte. "The Formative Stages of Modern *Beowulf* Scholarship, Textual, Historical, and Literary, Seen in the Work of Scholars of the Earlier Nineteenth Century." Ph.D diss., Queen Mary College, University of London, 1979.

———. "The Formative Stage of *Beowulf* Textual Scholarship: Part I." *Anglo-Saxon England* 11 (1983 [1982]): 247–74. "Part II." *Anglo-Saxon England* 12 (1983): 239–75.

Kiernan, Kevin. *The Thorkelin Transcripts of 'Beowulf'.* Anglistica 25. Copenhagen, 1986.

———, Andrew Prescott, et al., eds. *Electronic Beowulf.* 2 CDs. London and Ann Arbor, 1999.

Kemble, John M., ed. *The Anglo-Saxon Poems of Beowulf, The Travellers Song, and the Battle of Finnes-burh.* London, 1833; 2d ed., 2 vols., with trans. London, 1835–1837.

Klaeber, Fr., ed. *Beowulf and the Fight at Finnsburg.* 3rd ed. with 1st and 2nd supplements. Boston, 1950.

Kölbing, Eugen. "Zur Beóvulf-handschrift." *Archiv für das Studium des neueren Sprachen und Literaturen* 56 (1876): 91–118.

Lye, Edward. *Dictionarium Saxonico et Gothico-Latinum*, ed. Owen Manning. 2 vols. London, 1772.

Malone, Kemp. *The Nowell Codex: British Museum Cotton Vitellius A. xv Second MS.* EEMF 12. Copenhagen, 1963.

———. "Readings from the Thorkelin Transcripts of *Beowulf.*" *PMLA* 64 (1949): 1190–1218.

———, ed. *The Thorkelin Transcripts of Beowulf in Facsimile.* EEMF 1. Copenhagen, 1951.

Mitchell, Bruce, and Fred C. Robinson, eds. *Beowulf: An Edition with Relevant Shorter Texts.* Oxford, 1998.

Napier, Arthur. "Julius Zupitza." *Archiv für das Studium des neueren Sprachen und Literaturen* 95 (1895): 241–58.

Pope, John C. *The Rhythm of Beowulf.* Rev. ed. New Haven, 1966.

Prescott, Andrew. "'Their Present Miserable State of Cremation': The Restoration of the Cotton Library." In *Sir Robert Cotton as Collector: Essays on an Early Stuart Courtier and his Legacy*, ed. C. J. Wright, 391–454. London, 1997.

Robinson, Fred C. "*Beowulf* in the Twentieth Century." *Proceedings of the British Academy* 94 (1997): 45–62.

Sievers, Eduard. "Collationen angelsächsischer Gedichte." *ZfdA* 15 (1872): 456–67.

———. "Zu Cynewulf." In *Neusprachliche Studien: Festgabe Karl Luick zu seinem sechzigsten Geburtstage dargebracht von Freunden und Schülern*, 60–81. Marburg, 1925.

Swanton, Michael, ed. *Beowulf.* Manchester, 1978; rev. ed. Manchester and New York, 1997.

Tinker, Chauncey B. *The Translations of Beowulf: A Critical Bibliography.* Yale Studies in English 16. New York, 1903.

Thorkelin, Grímur Jónsson. *De Danorum Rebus Gestis Secul. III et IV. Poëma Danicum Dialecto AngloSaxonica.* Copenhagen, 1815.

Trautmann, Moritz. "Berichtigungen, Vermutungen, und Erklärungen zum Beowulf." *Bonner Beiträge zur Anglistik* 2 (1899): 121–92.

——, ed. *Das Beowulflied.* Bonn, 1904.

Turner, Sharon. *The History of the Anglo-Saxons.* 4 vols. London, 1799–1805; 2nd ed., 2 vols., 1807; 3rd ed., 3 vols., 1820.

Wrenn, C. L., ed. *Beowulf with the Finnesburg Fragment.* 3rd ed., rev. by W. F. Bolton. New York, 1973.

Wülcker, Richard, ed. *Das Beowulfslied nebst den kleineren epischen, lyrischen, didaktischen, und geschichtlichen Stücken.* Kassel, 1883.

——, ed. *Bibliothek der angelsächsischen Poesie begründet von Christian W. M. Grein. Neu bearbeitet, vermehrt und nach eignen Lesungen der Handschriften herausgegeben von Richard Paul Wülcker.* 1. Band. 1. Hälfte. Kassel, 1881.

Zupitza, Julius, ed. *Beowulf. Autotypes of the Unique Cotton MS. Vitellius A. xv in the British Museum.* EETS, o.s. 77. London, 1882; 2nd ed., *Beowulf Reproduced in Facsimile from the Unique Manuscript British Museum MS. Cotton Vitellius A. xv,* ed. Norman Davis. EETS 245. London, 1959.

——, ed. *The Romance of Guy of Warwick: The Second or 15th-century Version.* EETS, e.s. 25–26. London, 1875–1876.

What's In A Number? The Physical Organization of the Manuscript Collections of the British Library

Andrew Prescott

"Knock boldly at the gate; the porter will open it . . . A flight of steps leads to the principal entrance. Go on. Do not fear any surly looks or impertinent glance from any person in attendance. You are upon safe ground here. You are come to see your own property. You have as much right to see it, and you are as welcome therefore to see it, as the highest in the land. There is no favour in showing it you."

Advice on visiting the British Museum, from an article in The *Penny Magazine*, 7 April 1832, in a scrap book on the history of the Museum compiled by Sir Frederic Madden, vol. 1, f. 44, British Library, C.55.i.1[1]

I

Every manuscript is a palimpsest. Apart from the original text and contents (frequently, of course, in themselves complex constructions), there are invariably additions to the manuscript which mark its passage through time, right up to the present day. London, British Library, Harley MS. 863 is an Exeter manuscript, dated by Neil Ker to the third quarter of the eleventh century. It

---

[1] All manuscripts cited are in the British Library. I am grateful to the former Manuscripts Librarian, Dr. Christopher Wright OBE, as well as to Michelle Brown, Pamela Porter, John Rhatigan, Ruth Greenwood, and Christopher Fletcher for their assistance in the compilation of this paper. Where references are not provided for particular statements, they are from personal knowledge gained as a curator in the Department of Manuscripts from 1979 to 2000, or are from documents in the archives of the Department of Manuscripts which do not have a convenient means of citation.

would have been familiar to Phillip Pulsiano because of the short interlinear Old English gloss of the *Quicumque vult* on folio 107. The Exeter origins of the manuscript are evident at every turn: the *Quicumque vult* and other canticles follow an Exeter calendar and psalter, while the manuscript concludes with a litany of Exeter usage. At the beginning is a sight familiar in many medieval manuscripts, a flyleaf covered with post-conquest scribbles: copies of Latin couplets, notes of ownership, pen trials, and so on, in a great variety of different hands. A modern user of the manuscript, anxious to pursue a particular line of research, might be tempted to rush past the flyleaf and its scribbles, but those with more time will perhaps pause, and reflect how the doodles on this flyleaf can convey for twenty-first-century readers a feeling of affinity and contact with their long-dead predecessors. Moving on to the calendar in Harley MS. 863, the reader will note that it also has many additions and annotations. These are working notes which correct and supplement the contents of the calendar, but they nevertheless add to the sense that the manuscript remained for many centuries after its first creation an open, live object, being actively improved and developed, a shared and used inheritance.

At a certain point in time, the manuscript changes, and is viewed differently by its users. The medieval readers who scribbled in the manuscript took its character for granted, and did not comment explicitly on its contents. Then, in the seventeenth century, it became necessary for somebody to make a note on the flyleaf saying that this is a very old psalter and suggesting a date when it was written. The manuscript had became an object of curiosity to be interpreted, analyzed, and cared for, to be carefully looked after by curators, those gatekeepers standing between the manuscript and its readers.

Accordingly, the later layers of the palimpsest of Harley MS. 863 change. The scribblings on the manuscript have a new significance. They tell the curators how to look after the manuscript and how to keep it safe. On the flyleaf of Harley MS. 863 are two obscure sets of numbers, one added in ink in the eighteenth century:

$$\frac{62.B.4}{863}$$

and another added beside it in pencil:

$$\frac{14 \ D}{1}$$

A large ungainly hand has numbered the folios in pencil. A gnomic note at the end apparently relates to the foliation, but appears to be added sometime after the folio numbers were inserted:

1*

27*

123

125ff.

FM Ex^d Feb 1877

These more recent additions to the palimpsest do not only consist of writing. The ownership of the manuscript by the British nation is proclaimed by the insertion of bright red stamps throughout, the bibliographical equivalent of planting a flag in a new colony. At the beginning and end of the manuscript (fols. 1v, 122v) are large and obtrusive square red stamps, reading "MUSEUM BRITANNICUM," while a smaller, more discreet stamp with the words "BRITISH MUSEUM" around a small crown, more sensitively placed in the margins, occurs at frequent intervals throughout the manuscript (e.g. fols. 5v, 9v, 12v, 20v, 25v, 29v, 35v).

To ensure that the manuscript looks worthy of ownership by a national institution, it has been rebound. This rebinding evidently took place sometime after 1877, as the note on foliation has been specially inset into the end papers. The special status of the manuscript as part of the first collections to enter the British Museum after its foundation in 1753 is proclaimed on the front cover of the manuscript, with its gold tooling showing the Harley arms. On the other hand, the strong, utilitarian nature of the binding, in a dark and dingy institutional blue, indicates that the manuscript was expected to suffer the stress and strain of delivery to a reading room and use by scholars, and a strong binding was used which would provide the best form of protection for the delicate contents of the volume. The information on the spine of the binding is limited: PSALTERIUM, BRIT MUS., HARLEY 863, the three pieces of information that the custodians of the manuscript felt were most important to identify it. But the spine also has two small printed labels on it: at the top 693, at the bottom D.2.

Even in manuscripts which do not contain medieval scribbles of the sort found in Harley MS. 863, these later layers of the palimpsest — curatorial notes of accession number, placing, foliation, together with ownership stamps — are present. The apparently baffling curatorial codes in Harley MS. 863 are in fact easy to interpret. The ink number beginning 62.B.4 is an early British Museum pressmark, dating from the late eighteenth century, when the Harley manuscripts were arranged on the museum shelves in a subject order. The pencil numeration 14.D./1 is the pressmark assigned to the manuscript when it was moved from the original home of the British Museum, Montagu House, to Sir Robert Smirke's new building in 1827, and the subject classification scheme for the Harley manuscripts was abandoned. The number 693 on the spine means that, while the British Library was still in the British Museum building at Bloomsbury, the manuscript was placed in the press numbered 693, which was located in the "Select Lobby," a specially secure area where the most precious manuscripts were stored, adjacent to the "Students' Room"[2] of the Department of Manuscripts. The bottom label on the spine of Harley MS. 863, "D.2," means that the manuscript was placed on the fourth shelf down in press 693, and was at one time the second item on the shelf. In fact, the use of a number on the spine to indicate the position of a volume on the shelf was abandoned by the 1930s, so this pressmark label helps date the rebinding of the manuscript, which can thus be placed between 1877 (the date of the foliation note) and 1939. The 693D shelfmark recorded in these two labels on the spine of Harley MS. 863 still defines the location of the manuscript in the British Library's new premises at St. Pancras, but it no longer relates to a particular place or shelf.

The square "MUSEUM BRITANNICUM" stamps date from the eighteenth century. These large stamps were prominently placed in the middle of folios to prevent initials or letters being cut out. By 1845, it was considered that there was a greater risk that individual text pages might be extracted from a manuscript, and the practice of stamping a much larger number of folios, but with a smaller stamp, was introduced. Foliation is also related to security. Folio numbers were not simply inserted so that scholars could give accurate references, but, more importantly, to enable curators quickly to establish whether all the folios that were supposed to be in a particular volume were in fact there. The foliation note at the end of Harley MS. 863 simply indicates that there are 123 folios in the manuscript, together with two which, for unexplained reasons (most likely misnumbering), had been given starred numbers.[3] FM was Frederick Mackney, who was one of the attendants who

---

[2] All Departments of the British Museum are obliged to allow researchers access to collections not on display. The rooms provided in these Departments for public consultation of the collections are known as the "Students' Room," presumably because the term "Reading Room" was inappropriate for the consultation of artefacts. The use of the term "Students' Room" by the Department of Manuscripts when it was at Bloomsbury reflected this convention.

[3] Starred foliations are currently used in the British Library whenever an omission in the foliation has been discovered after the number of folios for a particular manuscript is

undertook simple clerical tasks in the Department of Manuscripts in the late nineteenth century. Mackney's foliation note indicates that he did not insert the folio numbers himself, but had simply examined ("Ex^d") the foliation, that is, he had checked that every folio was numbered, and that the numeration was in a correct sequence, and had recorded the number of folios in the foliation note at the end. The foliation therefore dates from before Mackney's examination in 1877. By the 1870s, folio numbers had begun to be entered generally as small, discreetly placed pencil numbers on the top right-hand corner of the recto. The ungainly character of the folio numbers in Harley MS. 863 suggests they were added much earlier, perhaps in the early nineteenth century (maybe in connection with the preparation of the published catalogue of the Harley manuscripts), as before that time folio numbers were generally entered in ink.

Mackney's work as a foliator appears in a number of the British Library's most famous manuscripts. He undertook, for example, the refoliation of Cotton MS. Vitellius A.xv, which contains *Beowulf*, in 1884.[4] On this occasion, the foliation note tells us that Mackney himself inserted the folio numbers, while they were checked by his colleague, George Gatfield. It would be fascinating to know more about these shadowy clerks, whose numbering of the leaves of so many manuscripts scholars still follow, and sometimes deplore, but the British Museum's records only enable us to trace their slow ascent through the lower ranks of the public service, and otherwise leave them in Pooter-like obscurity. The Keeper of Manuscripts, Sir Frederic Madden,[5] showed his appreciation of the work of the attendants by his annual donation to the life assurance society which the attendants formed in 1856, and to which both Mackney and Gatfield belonged, but even the records of this society show us little more than a group of prudent, steady clerks. On her death in 1908, Mackney's widow, Sarah, left the life assurance society more than £800. The Mackneys must have been models of Victorian prudence to have accumulated such a substantial nest-egg.[6]

---

entered in the foliation register. Here they were perhaps used by Mackney in the course of his examination to avoid having completely to refoliate the manuscript.

[4] Andrew Prescott, "'Their Present Miserable State of Cremation': The Restoration of the Cotton Library," in *Sir Robert Cotton As Collector*, ed. C. J. Wright (London, 1997), 391–454, at 452 n. 302.

[5] Sir Frederic Madden (1801–1873), Assistant Keeper of Manuscripts, 1828–1837; Keeper of Manuscripts, 1837–1866.

[6] Reports of the British Museum Attendants Mutual Life Assurance Society, shelved at British Library pressmark PP. 1423.tt.

II

The importance of later medieval and early modern inscriptions in understanding the history of a manuscript is now widely understood. How important is it also to investigate these later, curatorial, levels of the palimpsest? Does a better understanding of details such as those outlined for Harley MS. 863 assist in analyzing and contextualizing the contents of the manuscript, or are they mere antiquarian details? In order to answer these questions, it is necessary briefly to review the major categories into which these later interventions fall. Each type of intervention has a different significance and a different bearing on our understanding of the manuscript. In attempting briefly to survey the nature of these curatorial interventions, an immediate difficulty is that practice varies widely from library to library and even from collection to collection. Although certain practices, such as foliation, can be regarded as standard, there is no consistency in how they are implemented. In some libraries, flyleaves, preliminary material, and blank leaves are regarded as integral parts of the manuscript and assigned folio numbers; in other libraries, these items may be left unfoliated or assigned roman or starred folio numbers. Policies on stamping or the recording of shelfmarks can be even more diverse. Some manuscript libraries have procedures which are not to be found anywhere else, such as the British Library's practice (dating apparently from the early twentieth century) of inserting printed slips at the beginning of the manuscript on which details of the publication of texts in the manuscript were recorded.[7] This in itself provides an immediate justification for attempting to record and describe these practices. However, it means that it is impossible to give an overview of curatorial activity which covers all libraries. Consequently, the following general comments apply only to the British Library, and they may not hold true in, for example, the Bodleian Library or the Parker Library (and archives like the Public Record Office are completely different again).

The major categories of curatorial intervention in a medieval manuscript are generally stamping, foliation, binding, and, largest and most complex of all, the various processes involved in registering and physically storing the manuscript, including notes on acquisition, allocation of registration numbers, and records relating to the placing of the manuscript on the shelf. It is also worth noting that, with collections of papers, the curator actually determines the detailed order and structure of the documents within the volume

---

[7] These "bibliographical slips" were usually completed by the most junior members of the curatorial staff, as a chore regarded as good training, during their spell as Deputy Superintendents of the Students' Room.

in which they are bound. When collections of papers such as the Paston Letters are acquired, they generally appear in the British Library as a loose and unsorted collection of documents, frequently in cardboard boxes and other containers. These loose documents are put in order by a curator, who assigns dates to undated material and seeks to identify relationships between the documents, which help determine their place in the volume. This process of "arrangement," as it is known, follows a series of arcane British Museum house rules, which have been continued by the British Library. After the collection has been bound into volumes, the range and extent of this curatorial arrangement will not be apparent to the reader, and the process is not recorded in any way. On the whole, "arrangement" is a process which concerns only modern papers, but is worth noting here as part of the mediation a curator undertakes between the original document and its user.

One of the first actions of the Trustees of the newly-created British Museum was to order on 5 November 1756 that all the Museum's books and manuscripts be stamped with an ownership mark. Dr. John Ward, one of the Trustees, was asked to procure a suitable stamp, and he provided a sample on 3 December, which was the large square stamp which occurs at the beginning and end of Harley MS. 863. In February 1757, the Principal Librarian instructed the Museum's bookbinders to apply the stamp to each book and manuscript. As far as possible, the stamp was to be placed in the same place in each volume. In July 1757, it was ordered that the manuscripts should be stamped in red. Identifying the manuscripts was by no means as simple a task as one might think. A Major Edwards had made a bequest to help maintain the Cotton Library. This included a small collection of printed books, which had been stored with the Cotton manuscripts. Consequently, for stamping purposes, these printed items were treated as manuscripts, and stamped in red.[8]

For printed books, where collections were frequently dispersed among the general sequence, stamps can provide important evidence of provenance, and can be vital in helping to reconstitute the myriad of smaller libraries which are hidden away in the vast British Library printed collections. From an early date, color-coding was used to indicate how printed books were acquired, with red for purchases, yellow for donations, and blue for books deposited in accordance with copyright legislation. Stamps in printed books are also dated, which can again assist in establishing provenance and even, sometimes, approximate date of publication. Nevertheless, as Phil Harris has emphasised, stamps can be deceptive; they were often applied sometimes after the acquisition of the book, when information about how the book was acquired had been

---

[8] P. R. Harris, *A History of the British Museum Library 1753–1973* (London, 1998), 5–6.

forgotten, and there was even one case where books donated to the Museum were deliberately stamped as purchases, in case it was afterwards necessary to sell them as duplicates.[9]

By contrast with printed books, stamps are much less useful as evidence for the curatorial history of manuscripts. No color-coding system was adopted for the stamping of manuscripts. The old square stamps at the beginning and end of volumes were both ugly and poor deterrents against the removal of particular pages. One of the anxieties of Sir Frederic Madden when he became Keeper of Manuscripts at the British Museum in 1837 was that large parts of the collections had not been stamped. Madden immediately instructed that the Additional Charters, a sequence begun by his predecessor Josiah Forshall,[10] should be stamped and also checked that the stamping of the Additional Manuscripts was up to date.[11] Madden also introduced for new acquisitions the practice of stamping each individual document. In 1845, the scholar James Orchard Halliwell had attempted to sell to the Museum some manuscripts which had been stolen from Trinity College Cambridge, and this prompted Madden to reconsider the security of the Museum's own collections. He pointed out to the Trustees that volumes in the Cotton, Harley, Lansdowne and other collections were stamped only at the beginning and the end, and that it would be easy to remove a single document from the manuscript. He drew attention to a case where a horoscope of Queen Elizabeth I had apparently been stolen from Cotton MS. Titus B. ii. He proposed that "such MSS. of the Cotton, Harleian, Lansdowne and other collections as consist of original letters or distinct documents or treatises, should be separately stamped, as the practice is at present, and has been in regard to the Additions made to the Department since the year 1837." [12]

Madden's proposal was accepted. The work began with the stamping of the Cotton manuscripts. Stamping at this time was not carried out within the curatorial departments, such as Printed Books or Manuscripts, but rather in the office of the Museum Secretary, as part of a process of registration the bureaucratic circumlocution of which was such that it was rather pointless. This procedure was abandoned in 1849, and the curatorial departments took direct responsibility for stamping.[13] The smaller red stamps in the Cotton and

---

[9] Harris, *History*, 24–25, 44–45, 152–53.

[10] Josiah Forshall (1795–1863), Assistant Librarian of Manuscripts, 1824–1828; Under-Librarian of Manuscripts, 1828–1837; Secretary of the British Museum, 1828–1850. The sequence of Additional Charters was begun in 1829: T. C. Skeat, *The Catalogues of the Manuscript Collections in the British Museum* (London, 1951), 14–15.

[11] Additional MS. 62001, fol. 54v.

[12] Additional MSS. 62004, fol. 71v; 62025, fol. 45.

[13] Harris, *History*, 205, 225.

Harley collections are all part of this onerous work of stamping individual documents or articles in these collections, the progress of which can be traced in the *Annual Reports* of the British Museum and which was not complete until 1865, shortly before Madden retired. Between 1845 and 1865, over twenty thousand manuscript volumes were stamped in this way.[14]

The developments in stamping procedures for the British Library's manuscripts since the time of Madden have largely concentrated on the need to ensure that the stamping process provides a high level of security, while minimising the damage done to the manuscript. Specially designed dies and inks are used; stamps are applied, for example, to the reverse of documents bearing handwriting; some categories of manuscript, such as highly illuminated manuscripts or papyri, are not stamped because the process would cause an unacceptable level of damage. Since the 1840s, separate registers have been kept recording the number of stamps in each manuscript. The aim of these registers is to assist in identifying whether documents have been removed from a manuscript, since they record the number of stamps that should be found in the volume. However, this information can generally be more rapidly established by checking the volume's foliation, so the stamping registers are of limited value. Although the stamping of manuscripts is a fundamental part of the curator's armory against the book thief, the stamps in manuscripts, unlike the stamps in printed books, generally add little to an understanding of the provenance or history of the manuscript.

Stamps generally excite little interest among scholars, except sometimes to lament obtrusively placed stamps. By contrast, the foliation of manuscripts has incited passionate debates. A substantial part of Kevin S. Kiernan's groundbreaking book, *Beowulf and the Beowulf Manuscript*, is a plea for reconsideration of the "official" foliation of Cotton MS. Vitellius A. xv.[15] Likewise, Peter Meredith and Richard Beadle criticised the 1882 foliation of the official register containing the text of the York Play, Additional MS. 35290, because of its failure to include blank leaves which were part of the original manuscript, and their facsimile therefore uses a third foliation, specially devised by them (but one which, of course, does not appear in the original manuscript).[16] In some cases, these concerns reflect the fact that, for various reasons, an older foliation has been used by scholars, and use of the current

---

[14] Harris, *History*, 225–26, 277.

[15] Kevin Kiernan, *Beowulf and the Beowulf Manuscript*, 2nd ed. (Ann Arbor, 1996), xxi–xxiv, 65–169.

[16] Richard Beadle and Peter Meredith, *The York Play: A Facsimile of British Library MS Additional 35290*, Leeds Texts and Monographs, Medieval Drama Facsimiles 7 (Leeds, 1983), x–xi. The foliation in this case was again the work of Frederick Mackney.

Library foliation can cause confusion among scholars. These discussions also perhaps express an anxiety that the foliation represents an "official" view of the actual structure of the manuscript, and that, by using this foliation, a scholar is implicitly accepting one particular view of the manuscript. However, like stamping, foliation was, as has been seen, the work of relatively low-grade staff who were not manuscript scholars. Its primary functions are, first, to provide an easy means of checking that all the leaves that were supposed to be in the manuscript were there; second, to assist in the rebinding of manuscripts; and, finally, to facilitate easy reference to a particular page both for internal housekeeping purposes (cataloguing, photography, and so on) and by scholars writing about the manuscript. For both these purposes, the original physical structure of the manuscript is to a large degree an irrelevance; the important thing is to have a clear and consistent sequence.

Foliation is still carried out by administrative staff within the Department of Manuscripts, and treated as a clerical process. The modern rules are based on those promulgated in the 1960s by the then-Keeper of Manuscripts, Theodore Cressy Skeat.[17] Foliation numbers are entered as far as possible on the top right-hand corner of the recto of the leaf (ideally about three-quarters of an inch from the top and side of the folio) in a small, clear hand, using pencil. All leaves bearing writing are foliated; blank leaves (whether or not part of the original manuscript) are left unfoliated.[18] Arabic numerals are generally used, but extraneous material is indicated by the use of small roman numerals (with stubs treated as part of the main foliation sequence). Previous foliations and numerations are not erased, but instead lightly struck through by the foliator in pencil. Details of the foliation are entered in a small slip inserted at the end of the manuscript, which records the number of folios, the initials of the clerk who entered the folio numbers, the initials of the clerk who examined the foliation (that is to say, checked that the folio numbers were in the right sequence and conformed to the house style), and, finally, the initials of the curator who sent the manuscript to receive its folio numbers, and who may perhaps have given special instructions as to how the numbers were to be inserted. Dates of all these stages in the foliation process are also given. The use of pre-printed slips for foliation supplanted the entry of these details

---

[17] Theodore Cressy Skeat (1907–2003), Assistant Keeper, Department of Manuscripts, 1931–1948; Deputy Keeper, 1948–1961; Keeper of Manuscripts, 1961–1972.

[18] At least, this was the rule stipulated by Skeat. In the case of medieval manuscripts, the omission of blank folios from the foliation sequence can be inconvenient (for example, it may be necessary to refer to blank folios in describing scribal practice), and, in recent years, blank folios in medieval manuscripts have increasingly been assigned folio numbers.

directly on the end-papers of the manuscript sometime in the 1960s, perhaps at the same time as Skeat's rules were compiled. From at least the 1840s, registers have been kept which record the information in the foliation note, so as to provide a safeguard against its erasure or alteration. Identification of those involved in the foliation process is straightforward: it is simply a matter of checking the initials against the lists of attendants or, from 1949, clerical officers, which are given in the British Museum establishment lists.

The foliation rules currently in use are the result of a long process of development reaching back to the earliest days of the British Museum. The driving force in the elaboration of these rules has been, again, security and protection against theft. It seems that initially foliation practice was fairly haphazard. Planta records that, on starting his catalogue of the Cotton manuscripts, he found that use by readers had caused a number of volumes, particularly those damaged by the fire of 1731, to fall into a state of "great, and in many instances, irretrievable confusion." Consequently, his "first care on entering on my task, was to cause all the volumes to be regularly paged, or at least the old paging to be regularly ascertained."[19] At this time, folio numbers were entered in ink, and the folio statement, beginning with the Latin word "Constat," simply states the number of folios in the manuscript. It seems that the task was already at this stage a clerical one, as the foliation notes are generally in the same hand, not Planta's. Another enduring feature of foliation practice already established by Planta's time was the placing of the folio number on the top right-hand corner of the recto. The practice of entering folio numbers in pencil, rather than ink, was introduced in the 1820s. Madden improved the record-keeping associated with foliation. The earliest recorded folio registers date from the 1840s,[20] and in 1847 Madden "gave instructions that hereafter the number of folios in each MS shd be entered in the Day-Book of MSS. folio'd."[21] However, Madden did not pay much attention to the actual procedure of foliation, and indeed his work on the restoration of the Cotton manuscripts in some cases introduced deep confusion into the foliation of particular manuscripts. After Madden inserted recovered material in Vitellius C. viii, for example, there were *two* sets of leaves which bore the folio numbers 148–153, a situation which was not rectified until 1875.[22]

[19] Prescott, "'Their Present Miserable State'," 401.

[20] Lists of hand and shelf catalogues, etc., in the Department of Manuscripts, compiled by Richard Sims, in a volume of miscellaneous papers dating from the period of Madden's Keepership in the archives of the Department of Manuscripts.

[21] Additional MS. 62005, fol. 20.

[22] Prescott, "'Their Present Miserable State'," 428.

A separate Manuscripts Students' Room was not provided in the British
Museum until 1885, and manuscripts were read in the main Reading Room,
a situation which continued for some time even after a special Manuscripts
room was opened, so that as late as 1913 more than seventy manuscript volumes were delivered to readers in the main Reading Room.[23] Madden's con-
tempt for the famous Round Reading Room of the British Museum was not
simply due to his hatred of the Keeper of Printed Books, Antonio Panizzi,[24]
who was largely responsible for the design of the reading room; he was concerned about how the security of the manuscripts could be ensured in such a
large room. In the years immediately after the opening of the Round Reading
Room, the difficulty of preventing entry by unauthorised persons was a constant source of concern. Pages were found missing from reference books; the
Keeper of Printed Books suspected that readers had taken them to the lava-
tories and ripped pages out there.[25] It was not until 1873 that a regulation was
introduced requiring all readers to show their tickets on entry to the Reading
Room (afterwards substantially modified because of protests by readers) and
a police officer was employed to patrol the Reading Room to guard against
thefts.[26] The use of manuscripts in the main Reading Room exposed them
to great risk; in 1879, a thirteenth-century French manuscript, Royal MS. 16
E.VIII, disappeared altogether after it had been returned by a reader, possibly
mixed up with some printed books, where perhaps it lingers still.[27]

An even greater threat than the loss of whole manuscripts in the Reading
Room was the abstraction of individual leaves. As early as 1836, an Assistant
in the Department of Manuscripts, John Holmes,[28] proposed that one of the
curators in the Department of Manuscripts should check each volume on its
return to the Department of Manuscripts to ensure that no folios had been
removed.[29] This idea was firmly resisted by Madden during the period of his

[23] Andrew Prescott, "The Panizzi Touch: Panizzi's Successors as Principal Librarian," *British Library Journal* 23 (1997): 194–236, at 205–6.

[24] Sir Anthony Panizzi (1797–1879), Keeper of Printed Books 1837–1856; Principal
Librarian 1856–1866. Panizzi was the effective creator of the British Museum Library in
its modern form, remains the presiding genius of the British Library, and was arguably
the greatest librarian who ever lived. Madden despised Panizzi, and the antagonism between the two had a profound influence on the history of the British Museum Library: see
further Michael Borrie, "Panizzi and Madden," *British Library Journal* 5 (1979): 18–36.

[25] Harris, *History*, 283.

[26] Harris, *History*, 287–88, 359–60.

[27] Harris, *History*, 360; Prescott, "The Panizzi Touch," 225.

[28] John Holmes (1800–1854), Assistant in the Department of Manuscripts, 1830–
1850; Assistant Keeper of Manuscripts, 1850–1854.

[29] Prescott, "The Panizzi Touch," 228.

Keepership, on the grounds that his staff had no time to carry out such checks. One of the first actions of Madden's successor, Edward Augustus Bond,[30] was to introduce such a check, which is still carried out to this day. The new system almost immediately proved its effectiveness, when in June 1867 it was found that folios 151 and 198 had been removed from Lansdowne MS. 5. The introduction of this system of checking the manuscripts made it important to ensure that manuscripts were foliated on a consistent basis, and over the next twenty years many manuscripts were refoliated in order to ensure that all leaves bearing writing had folio numbers, so that a curator, hurriedly checking at the end of the day through the manuscripts used by readers, could easily spot whether there was a gap in the volume. These refoliations have irritated and confused scholars ever since, but they have played a vital part in ensuring the safety of the manuscript.[31]

This process of refoliation was thus driven by security needs, and on the whole says little about the structure of the manuscript. The main case in the British Library's collections where modern foliations can provide useful codicological information is the case of the Cotton manuscripts restored by Sir Frederic Madden. Here, the various notes made by Madden can assist in tracing the process by which he sorted the individual leaves after they had been flattened, cleaned, and mounted.[32] This is unusual, however. The importance of the foliation is nevertheless not limited to its role in ensuring the security of the manuscript. As a means of referencing a particular leaf, it provides a key link in the whole network of housekeeping records used to maintain a manuscript library; not only the catalogue, but also indexes of photographic work, conservation records, the stamping registers, and so on. For this reason, since the "great refoliation" undertaken in the 1870s and 1880s, further substantial refoliations have not taken place. Since the folio number provides a kind of "unique identifier" for each leaf, it is best not to change it. An exception to this rule (and there are always some in any manuscript library) is the Vitellius Psalter, Cotton MS. Vitellius E. xviii, which was refoliated in 1959 in order to place the surviving fragments in a better order.

Rebinding is the most obvious and dramatic example of curatorial intervention. Again, the security of the manuscript has been a major consideration, but attitudes have shifted as different views of the nature of the manuscript

---

[30] Sir Edward Augustus Bond (1815–1898), worked on the records of the Augmentations Office of the Exchequer 1833–1838; Assistant in Manuscripts 1838–1854; Assistant Keeper of Manuscripts 1854–1866; Keeper of Manuscripts 1866–1878; Principal Librarian of the British Museum 1878–1888.

[31] Prescott, "The Panizzi Touch," 200, 228–29 n. 46.

[32] Prescott, "'Their Present Miserable State,'" 427–28.

have prevailed. In the eighteenth century, the text of the manuscript was seen as the primary concern, so that for example the *mise en page* of a medieval manuscript was thought to be of little interest, and the cropping of a volume by the binder was considered an acceptable practice. By the mid-nineteenth century, cropping had been abandoned, but the status of the binding as an integral part of the manuscript as an artefact was given little thought. The prime concern was to make sure that the leaves of the manuscript were protected against the buffeting involved in delivering a volume to the reader, and many antiquarian bindings were replaced with robust new bindings. Since the Second World War, the significance of the binding in understanding the manuscript has received greater attention, and boxing has been more extensively used to extend the life of older bindings, though, in the end, all bindings give out and have to be replaced. The primary function of the binding in providing security and protection to inner leaves is reflected in the development of binding practice in the British Museum and Library. In the late eighteenth and early nineteenth centuries, bindings were often elaborately tooled, and delicate materials such as Russia leather were used. By the middle of the nineteenth century, patterns which were both more robust and cheaper were used, with full leather binding being gradually abandoned.

The pattern of binding established by the end of the nineteenth century continues to be used in the Library. Examples such as Arundel MS. 60, a psalter with an Old English gloss, which was rebound in 1966, and where the binder sought to recreate a medieval binding by using wooden boards, are extremely rare. This is partly because cost has always been a major consideration in binding; in order to reduce the cost of the extensive rebindings undertaken in the 1780s, smaller manuscripts in both the Royal and Harley collections were frequently bound together, although separate numerations for the constituent manuscripts were retained.[33] However, security and cost have not been the only factors affecting the curatorial approach to manuscript binding in the British Library. In the old British Museum building, space was always short, and this constantly militated against both extensive boxing (which causes manuscripts to take up more shelf space) and flattening of roll manuscripts (desirable from a conservation point of view, but requiring extensive large flat storage shelves). In the British Museum building, large parts of the older collections, such as the Cotton, Harley, and Royal collections, were on public display in glazed presses in the great Manuscripts Saloon at the south end of the King's Library, which from 1857 was one of the major public thoroughfares in the Museum. Up until the move from the British Museum,

---

[33] Harris, *History*, 18–19.

curators were conscious that these manuscripts were in public view, and this militated against boxing, which made the presses containing the manuscripts look less imposing, and encouraged rebinding, so that the manuscripts would look at their best on the shelves. This awareness that the manuscripts, when placed on their shelves, were on show to the public also encouraged the continuation of a system of color-coding for the bindings, whereby different subject categories were given different colored boards, a system probably originating in the late nineteenth century.

A reader confronted with a medieval volume which has been rebound in the last two hundred years naturally wishes to know when it was rebound and if anything is known about its previous binding. If the rebinding was undertaken in the past sixty years, the date of the rebinding can be easily established by looking on the back endpaper, where the date of the rebinding is noted, usually with a note that it was checked on return from the bindery by the Executive Officer at that time in charge of supervising bindery work. The history of any binding work prior to 1950 has to be established by checking the binding index, an administrative record which lists work undertaken on particular manuscripts and cross-references the requisition to the binder. Unfortunately, systematic records of this kind were introduced only in the 1880s.[34] Prior to that, the only records are informal memoranda of binding work that were kept by individual keepers or the general statistics included in the British Museum annual report. From the nineteenth century, old covers, if they were deemed of bibliographical interest, were sometimes pasted in the new binding. This had the unfortunate effect, however, of warping the new binding, so more recently the practice has been established of retaining the old covers of a manuscript separately if they were thought to be of interest. Unfortunately, the user of the manuscript has no way of knowing whether or not old covers have been retained in this way, since the information is generally not recorded in the catalogue. The only way of finding out if there are any old covers from a particular manuscript is to ask one of the curators.

The binding indexes and the retention of old covers are examples of information which is available only to curators, and which the reader has no means of otherwise knowing. These examples are, however, unusual. Otherwise, where stamping, foliation, and binding are concerned, the manuscript itself contains all the information that is recorded about these processes, and is readily ascertainable by the reader without curatorial assistance. This forms

---

[34] Although earlier records may have been destroyed; see p. 505, below. Madden's personal papers as Keeper also include some material relating to binding: see e.g. Additional MSS. 62577, 62068–62069.

a contrast with the documentation relating to the physical placing of the manuscript on the shelf. The information in a manuscript stating where it should be kept and noting any restrictions governing access to it are, generally, completely incomprehensible to the outsider, and, even once one understands the housekeeping system, the notes in the manuscript itself may require reference to secondary documentation of various types to be fully understood.

III

In order to understand the records and processes associated with the physical storage of the manuscript, or the "placing" of the manuscript as it is known, it is essential first to describe the different buildings in which the manuscript collections of the British Library have been housed since the establishment of the Museum in 1753. This is also vital to understanding housekeeping information entered in the manuscripts themselves. For example, on the inside front cover of Arundel MS. 60, there is an erased pencil annotation, "GR4." GR stands for Grenville Library, the gallery immediately to the east of the main entrance of the British Museum, which was originally intended to provide storage for manuscripts, but which, much to the fury of Sir Frederic Madden, was allocated to the Department of Printed Books to accommodate the library of Sir Thomas Grenville, the Library's most important single acquisition of rare printed books.[35] Despite the fact that the room fell in the territory of the Department of Printed Books, it was used for nearly a century from 1890 for the display of illuminated manuscripts,[36] and "GR4" indicates that Arundel MS. 60 was once displayed in one of the exhibition cases in the Grenville Library. Similarly, the pencil annotations "SAL" found in other manuscripts refer to the Manuscripts Saloon, the great room to the east of the Grenville Library and at the southern end of the King's Library, where the

---

[35] On this infamous episode, see for example Borrie, "Panizzi and Madden," 27–30. Madden apparently remained unaware of Panizzi's plans also to annex the Manuscripts Saloon: Harris, *History*, 178.

[36] Harris, *History*, 319. The way in which long-term exposure to light causes illuminations to fade was not particularly appreciated at this time. The sunlight streaming through the windows of the Grenville Library, at that time unprotected by blinds, was found in 1929 to have caused some openings in illuminated manuscripts to have faded: Harris, *History*, 484. This led to the use of curtains on the showcases to protect the manuscripts. Later, blinds were installed on the windows, and the use of curtains discontinued. The way in which exhibition under these conditions caused particular openings to fade is still readily noticed in many of the Library's most well-known illuminated manuscripts.

bulk of the Library's great foundation collections and other early manuscript collections were kept. Users of the Anglo-Saxon manuscripts in the British Library will certainly at some time have been given a manuscript described as a "Safe Z" manuscript, which has to be handled with particular care. It is natural for the reader to wonder what Safe Z is. Why are Safes A-Y never mentioned, and do they exist? How did Safe Z get from Bloomsbury to St. Pancras? Is it still the same safe? Such questions reflect the reader's natural curiosity to know what the curatorial gatekeeper is doing with the manuscripts and, above all, about what he or she might have hidden away elsewhere.

Since the establishment of the British Museum, the manuscript collections have been housed in three different buildings: Montagu House, on the site of the present British Museum building, a seventeenth-century mansion in the French style built for the first Duke of Montagu and purchased by the Trustees in 1754 as a home for the newly founded Museum; the present British Museum building, built by Sir Robert Smirke between 1826 and 1852, but with important additions and remodellings, such as the White Wing, built in the early 1880s; and of course their present home, the British Library building by Sir Colin St. John Wilson, to which the manuscript collections were moved between July and December 1998. At both Montagu House and the British Museum, large parts of the collections were in bookcases which were, in different ways and at different times, on display to visiting members of the public. This had an effect on the way the manuscripts were stored and treated. At St. Pancras, the manuscripts are, by contrast, in a store hidden away from public view. Nevertheless, the arrangement of the manuscripts on the shelves at St. Pancras is still fundamentally determined by the procedures developed for the previous buildings, and in particular the British Museum building.

Montagu House contained two floors, connected by an imposing staircase. The fundamental arrangement of the Museum library consisted of printed books downstairs and manuscripts upstairs, with the various manuscript collections stored in separate rooms. A snapshot of the arrangement of the manuscripts at Montagu House is provided by the earliest official guide to the Museum, the 1808 *Synopsis of the Contents of the British Museum*.[37] Climbing the great staircase, the visitor arrived in a large state room, containing a miscellaneous collection of modern works of art from all the countries of the world, ranging from Europe to the Sandwich Islands. The visitor then

---

[37] *Synopsis of the Contents of the British Museum* (London, 1808), 4–14. For a plan of the rooms at Montagu House, see Harris, *History*, Plan B. The various plans reproduced by Harris are essential in tracing the development of the manuscript storage in both buildings at Bloomsbury.

passed into a series of three rooms facing south towards Great Russell Street. The first had been emptied, ready to receive a collection of antiquities. The second was occupied by the recently acquired Lansdowne manuscripts. In the next room was to be found, in three presses between the windows, Thomas Birch's collections of manuscripts (Additional MSS. 4101–4478) and in presses III–XXX the Sloane Manuscripts. Other recesses in this room had been used to house some other small collections, such as Hastead's collections on the history of Kent (Additional MSS. 5478–5539).

From this room, the visitor passed into another series of three rooms, this time looking northward, over the beautiful gardens of Montagu House. The first room contained the bulk of the Harley manuscripts. In the next room were the remainder of the Harley manuscripts, an odd mixture of biblical, patristic, and parliamentary material, together with manuscripts acquired since the establishment of the Museum, which were still largely kept in their component collections. Finally, the visitor passed into the seventh room, containing "The Royal Library of Manuscripts. Deposited in XXXIII Presses" and "The Cottonian Library of Manuscripts. Deposited in XXI Presses." Leaving this room, the visitor returned to the saloon at the top of the staircase.

Montagu House was dark, decaying, and damp. Sir Frederic Madden, who had joined the Manuscripts Department in the last days of Montagu House, when the manuscripts had already been moved out, stated that the only way to see the contents of one of the rooms containing the Harley manuscripts had been by the reflected light of freshly fallen snow.[38] His predecessor as Keeper of Manuscripts, Josiah Forshall, vividly described how the manuscripts in Montagu House "were scattered over three or four rooms in the old building, some of which were used as reading rooms. These rooms were generally inconvenient; one of them was so dark that in the brightest day a tin reflector was used to find the manuscripts."[39] Sir Robert Smirke later described how props for the floors were concealed in bookcases and the heating flues created a serious fire risk.[40] As the Museum grew, and bulky acquisitions such as the Towneley Marbles, the Elgin Marbles, and, above all, the King's Library arrived, the inadequacies of Montagu House became more evident and the need for new premises more pressing, so Montagu House was progressively demolished and replaced by Smirke's celebrated building.

The first stage in the construction of Smirke's building was the east wing, which was initially slotted in behind the north-east corner of Montagu

---

[38] Additional MS. 38791, fols. 29–32v: it is unclear whether this is Madden's own recollection or that of Richard Kay, whose notes he was here copying.

[39] *Report from the Select Committee on the British Museum* (1836), no. 4373.

[40] Harris, *History*, 56.

House and ran almost the length of the large gardens of Montagu House to the north. This wing was intended for the reception of the King's Library, the library of George III acquired by the Museum in 1823. The first rooms of this wing to be completed, and thus the oldest part of the Museum, were three rooms at the southern end of the King's Library, which were to become the heart of the Department of Manuscripts' accommodation at Bloomsbury: the Manuscripts Saloon, the Middle Room, and the South Room. The Manuscripts Saloon was an imposing room at the southern end of the King's Library, lined from floor to ceiling with book presses for the storage of manuscripts. At the ground floor level were presses with space for up to ten shelves of manuscripts. Above was a gallery with a further series of presses reaching up to the ceiling. The gallery walkway was protected by a flimsy metal rail which provided little feeling of security for those walking along the narrow gangway in order to reach the manuscripts stored in the gallery presses. The condition of this rail gave anxiety from the earliest days of the Department of Manuscripts' occupation of this room, especially as the use of hoists attached to the rail to raise manuscript volumes to the gallery seriously weakened the rail.[41] At the corners of the room, the gallery rail also supported large leather-covered book rests, added at the request of Sir Frederic Madden in 1848, and intended for the consultation of manuscripts stored in the gallery presses.[42]

At the time of the opening of the room in 1827, the book presses in the Manuscripts Saloon contained as much shelving space as all the various rooms on the upper floor of Montagu House put together: 1,750 linear feet on the ground floor and 800 in the gallery, a total of 2,550 linear feet, compared with 2,547 linear feet available for the storage of manuscripts in Montagu House.[43] The room was completed by the end of January 1827, and all the manuscripts were in their new home by the end of Easter week 1827.[44] The collections moved into the Manuscripts Saloon were therefore generally those which had been acquired before 1827 and which had been at Montagu House, such as the Sloane, Cotton, Harley, Royal, and Lansdowne manuscripts, and the bulk of the volumes in these collections continued to be kept in the Manuscripts Saloon for the rest of their time at Bloomsbury. Indeed, a report of 1859 describes the

---

[41] Harris, *History*, 110.

[42] Additional MS. 62006, fol. 57v.

[43] Harris, *History*, 57.

[44] Although some individual manuscripts and collections were left on display in rooms in Montagu House after the move. For example, the 1834 Synopsis notes that the Magna Carta, the Doubleday collection of seals, a papyrus, and various specimens of miniature writing were still on display in rooms in Montagu House: *Synopsis of the Contents of the British Museum* (London, 1834), 1–2, 12.

Cotton Manuscripts occupying broadly the same presses in the Saloon, numbers 17–27, in the north-east corner of the room, where they were by the time
they left the Museum building in 1998.[45] However, individual volumes did not
remain in the same place. As additional accommodation became available elsewhere, some manuscripts were moved out of the Saloon. For example, there was
a major rearrangement of the Saloon Gallery when new shelving became available in the Middle Room in the 1840s.[46] Moreover, particular volumes in the
Saloon were progressively designated as "Select" and removed to more secure
accommodation elsewhere in the Department, particularly during the period
before the Second World War. The effect of rebinding, which might increase
the size of volumes, also meant that individual volumes were moved about,
and space became available which was used to accommodate a few more recent
acquisitions. Nevertheless, the broad shape of the collections on the shelves of
the Manuscripts Saloon just before they left Bloomsbury for St. Pancras in 1998
would have been familiar and understandable to the two curators who super-
vised the transfer of the manuscripts from Montagu House to the Manuscripts
Saloon, Sir Henry Ellis, then Keeper of Manuscripts,[47] and Josiah Forshall.

Smirke built the King's Library with a view to conveying the splendour
and importance of the great collection built up by George III. Consequently
he did not use aisle presses, perhaps the most familiar form of arrangement
of bookshelves, since, although these allow the most effective use of space in
accommodating the maximum number of books per square foot, they fail to
convey the scale of the collection readily to the viewer. By contrast, the arrangement adopted by Smirke for the King's Library, with presses flush to the
wall, and every wall covered from floor to ceiling with shelving, gave an exag-
gerated impression of the size of the collection, suggesting it was much larger
than it really is. Smirke adopted a similar procedure for the arrangement of
the manuscripts in the Manuscripts Saloon. Both the King's Library and the
Manuscripts Saloon were designed to create a strong visual impact on the
visitor. This was emphasised by the way in which some doors leading off the
King's Library and the Saloon were concealed by false bookshelves, complete
with fake leather spines, elaborately tooled with title and manuscript number

[45] Lists of hand and shelf catalogues, etc., in the Department of Manuscripts, compiled by Richard Sims, in a volume of miscellaneous papers dating from the period of
Madden's Keepership in the archives of the Department of Manuscripts.

[46] See e.g. Additional MS. 62002, fols. 41, 42v, 44v.

[47] Sir Henry Ellis K. H. (1777–1869), Assistant Librarian in the Department of Printed
Books of the British Museum 1805–1806; Keeper (or more correctly Under Librarian) of
Printed Books, 1806–1812; Keeper (or Under Librarian) of Manuscripts 1812–1828; Prin-
cipal Librarian 1828–1856. Author of the *General Introduction to Domesday Book* (1833).

information, carefully composed by Madden so as to be convincing.[48] Concern about damp meant that the presses in the Saloon originally had open wire doors. In order to protect the manuscripts from dust, a small leather flap, on which the shelf letter designation was elaborately printed, was hung from each shelf. These flaps survived even when they were no longer necessary, as the doors of the presses were progressively glazed after the room came to be used for exhibitions and members of the public regularly admitted.

The Manuscripts Saloon later became one of the major galleries of the British Museum through which thousands of visitors would pass each day; but until 1885, it was instead the main office area of the Department of Manuscripts, where the various curators and attendants had their desks, and even wash-stands in which to wash their hands. In some ways, use of the Saloon as an office must have been a very convenient arrangement, since all the manuscripts would have been readily to hand, but in other ways it was very unsatisfactory. The room was very dark, and extra windows had to be added to the room, creating gaps in the numeration of the presses.[49] There were constant problems about damp, lack of ventilation, and poor heating.[50] A conduit lined with slate had be installed around the edge of the room to reduce the risk of damp in the book presses.[51] Readers were required to read particularly valuable manuscripts in the Saloon itself, and room had to be found for them.[52] Above all, in the early days of the Saloon, there was a constant flow of attendants conducting visitors through the Manuscripts Saloon to view the King's Library.[53] When this ceased to be a problem, the movement of books between the Grenville Library and the King's Library was found to be an equal nuisance.[54] Indeed, Madden's annoyance about the use of the room adjacent to the Manuscripts Saloon for the Grenville Library was not only due to the loss of presses intended for manuscripts, but also because of the fact that his Department's main office became something of a passageway between two areas of the Department of Printed Books.[55]

---

[48] Additional MS. 62003, fol. 53v.

[49] Additional MS. 62025, fols. 5v–6.

[50] Harris, *History*, 109–10, 177.

[51] *Report from the Select Committee on the British Museum* (1836), no. 2287.

[52] Harris, *History*, 155, 158, 285–86.

[53] Harris, *History*, 68.

[54] Additional MS. 62028, fol. 13.

[55] Panizzi's 1857 catalogue of exhibited printed books refers to "an apartment containing manuscripts," meaning the Manuscripts Saloon. In the copy of this catalogue in the Department of Manuscripts archives, Madden has deleted "an apartment containing" and inserted "The Department of."

In 1851, as a response to the large number of visitors in London for the Great Exhibition, the King's Library and Manuscripts Saloon were opened to the public and exhibitions of printed books and manuscripts arranged there. This meant moving desks out of the way in the Manuscripts Saloon to accommodate the exhibition cases, with staff trying to work while large numbers of the public were passing through the room.[56] Not surprisingly, this was a great inconvenience, and Madden was furious when it was proposed in 1856 that the King's Library and Saloon should be permanently opened to the public.[57] Smirke produced designs for exhibition cases and also for screens which would shield the curators from the curious gaze of the public. The exhibition cases took up about two-thirds of the floor space in the centre of the Saloon, with the officers of the Department crammed into the remaining third.[58] This accommodation problem was not finally resolved until 1885, with the opening of new offices in the White Wing. The exhibition cases in the Manuscripts Saloon were at first crammed full of exhibits, containing in 1859 some 232 items. The tendency over the next fifty years was to put more and more material on display. This was partly achieved by using the bottom of the show cases for (very inaccessible) displays, a practice which continued until the 1930s. This must have been not only unsatisfactory for the visitors, but damaged the manuscripts, because of the oblique angles at which volumes were displayed.[59] Eventually, the bottom part of the show cases were converted into cupboards, which provided valuable storage space for particularly large volumes and boxes. It was in these "Saloon Cupboards," for example, that the huge volumes containing the charters in Cotton MS. Augustus ii were kept. Another series of Saloon Cupboards were the large cupboards to the right and left of the corner of the room immediately adjacent to the King's Library, which were specially fitted out (probably in the late nineteenth century) for the storage of glazed papyri, some of which are more than eight feet in length.[60]

---

[56] Harris, *History*, 195–96.

[57] Harris, *History*, 250; Additional MS. 62011, fols. 60–65; 62027, fols. 78v, 80.

[58] Harris, *History*, 250.

[59] This is shown by photographs of exhibition cases in the 1930s in the archives of the Department of Manuscripts.

[60] For a view of the Manuscripts Saloon in 1986, showing the exhibition cases and cupboards below them, see Harris, *History*, fig. 19. The Magna Carta case is the case running right to left on the right hand side of the picture. The case just in front of the entrance to the King's Library contained the Lindisfarne Gospels and the Moutier-Grandval Bible. One set of the large wall cupboards which contained glazed papyri can be seen just beyond it.

To the south of the Manuscripts Saloon were the other two parts of the original Manuscripts accommodation at Bloomsbury, the rooms which became known as the Middle Room (immediately to the south of the Manuscripts Saloon) and (to the south of the Middle Room) the South Room. Both these rooms were initially used as reading rooms, the rooms first being occupied by readers in the spring of 1827. In his book on the history of the British Library Reading Rooms, Phil Harris describes this opening phase in the career of these two rooms as follows: "They were fitted out to accommodate about 120 readers, but were soon under heavy pressure. The ventilation was far from adequate and in 1859, John Winter Jones[61] (then Keeper of Printed Books) wrote with considerable feeling about the smell of these particular rooms, when they were full of readers. The normal entrance to the Middle and South Rooms [at this time] was not from the Manuscripts Saloon at the south end of the King's Library but by a door which was reached through a small archway from the front courtyard and up a steep and narrow flight of exterior stone steps. These led to a lobby where readers left their sticks and umbrellas. This was so small, cold and uncomfortable that the attendant stationed there often complained that a dog would not remain in such a situation unless he was chained up."[62] This dingy lobby afterwards formed part of the storage in the South Room.

The Middle and South Rooms quickly proved unable to accommodate the number of readers, and it became necessary to use the Manuscripts Saloon to provide overflow reading room accommodation.[63] In 1833, it was agreed to construct new larger reading rooms to the north of the King's Library. These were finally opened in 1838.[64] During this early part of the Museum's history, there was no separate reading room for Manuscripts, and printed books and manuscripts were read in the same room. When the new Reading Rooms were opened in 1838, a special cart was ordered to transport manuscripts securely through the King's Library.[65] When these reading rooms were in turn replaced by the famous Round Reading Room in 1857, part of the reason for Madden's furious condemnation of the room as totally unsuited to its purpose was the difficulty of supervising the use of manuscripts in such a large room.[66]

---

[61] John Winter Jones (1805–1881), Keeper of Printed Books 1856–1866; Principal Librarian, 1866–1878.

[62] P. R. Harris, *The Reading Room* (London, 1979), 6–7.

[63] Harris, *Reading Room*, 7; Harris, *History*, 86–87.

[64] Harris, *History*, 88–89.

[65] Additional MS. 62001, fols. 46v–47.

[66] He described it as "a splendid room, but perfectly unsuited, I think, to its purpose": Borrie, "Panizzi and Madden," 32.

Certain particularly valuable manuscripts were consulted in the offices of the Department of Manuscripts itself. This was the origin of the category of "Select" manuscripts, and Madden's designation of an increasingly large number of manuscripts as "Select" led to complaints from the Trustees that Madden was allowing too many readers to work in the Manuscripts offices, and that he was running an unofficial Reading Room there.[67] Even after a separate reading room for Manuscripts was opened in 1885, manuscripts were still available to readers, and as late as 1913 some manuscripts were still being consulted there.[68] The strict division between the Manuscripts and Printed Books reading rooms seems to have come into force only after the First World War. While it was obviously desirable that there should be a separate reading room for manuscripts, it was difficult to arrange to consult printed books with the manuscripts. It was only with the move to St. Pancras that it once again became a straightforward matter to read printed books together with manuscripts.

When the manuscripts had been moved from Montagu House, it was found that there was not quite enough room to accommodate them all conveniently in the Saloon, so a small overflow was shelved in the Middle Room, probably in the gallery, with charters apparently in drawers at ground level.[69] Presumably the Middle Room was also used for the storage of new acquisitions of manuscripts in the 1830s, such as the Arundel and Burney manuscripts.[70] Following the opening of the new Reading Rooms in 1838, the Middle and South Rooms became available for the storage of manuscripts. Sir Frederic Madden, who had just taken over as Keeper of Manuscripts, enthusiastically set about having the rooms refurbished.[71] Like the Manuscripts Saloon, the Middle Room was covered on all four sides with book shelves, again from floor to ceiling, with a gallery which connected to the Saloon gallery. The arrangement of the manuscripts in the Middle Room occupied much of Sir Frederic Madden's time in 1840,[72] and, as in the Manuscripts Saloon, features of the broad physical arrangement of the collections established by Madden, such as the positioning

---

[67] Andrew Prescott, Michelle Brown, and Richard Masters, "The Survey of Illuminated Manuscripts," in *Towards the Digital Library: The British Library's Initiatives for Access Programme* (London, 1998), 130–47, at 131–32.

[68] Prescott, "The Panizzi Touch," 205–6.

[69] Harris, *History*, 57. On the charter drawers, see e.g. Additional MS. 62022, fols. 13, 52.

[70] But note that Madden stated in 1836 that the Saloon was adequate for storage of all manuscripts acquired up to that date: *Report from the Select Committee on the British Museum* (1836), nos. 2168–2169.

[71] Additional MS. 62022, fol. 52.

[72] See e.g. Additional MS. 62023, fols. 64, 68, 79, 88v–89.

of the Arundel and Burney manuscripts in the ground-floor presses of the Middle Room, were retained right up until the departure of the Manuscript Collections from Bloomsbury. The 1912 *Guide to Exhibited Manuscripts* in the British Museum explains that only a photograph of the Articles of the Barons and Magna Carta was on display, apparently for reasons of security and conservation. The originals could, however, be inspected on application "within the barrier of the Department." This apparently refers to the Middle Room, and as a result the Middle Room became known as the Magna Carta Room.

Magna Carta left the Middle Room, to be displayed in a hardwood display case positioned in the centre of the Saloon in 1960, when it was agreed that the Map and Egerton rooms could be remodelled so as to provide additional storage.[73] Temporary shelving was erected in the Middle Room to house material from these rooms while the refurbishment was carried out. These huge steel racks were separated from public areas by a wooden partition which formed a small temporary entrance lobby to the Department. The work in the Map and Egerton Rooms took nearly ten years to complete. Shortly afterwards, it was proposed to remodel the South Room, and so the temporary shelving was used to house the contents of the South Room. This work again proved extremely protracted, and by the time that the storage in the South Room was again available, a massive acquisition had been made in the form of a huge archive of plays deposited by the Lord Chamberlain's Office. The great steel racks in the Middle Room were used to store a large part of the huge sequence of green boxes containing these plays, so that the temporary measure of 1960 was still in use in the late 1980s.[74]

Eventually, in 1988 demand for a separate British Library bookshop meant that the plays were moved to storage at Woolwich, the temporary shelving was demolished, and the Middle Room was reclaimed as an exhibition space. The exhibition cases (with their associated cupboards) which had contained the illuminated manuscript displays in the Grenville Library were moved into the Middle Room, and a new display of illuminated manuscripts prepared.[75] The

---

[73] For a listing of the six items displayed in this case, see G. R. C. Davis, *Magna Carta* (London, 1982), 34–38.

[74] Harris, *History*, 628–29. The sorry saga of the refurbishment of these rooms and the temporary shelving in the Middle Room is told in documents preserved in a large box file of accommodation documents in the archives of the Department of Manuscripts.

[75] The register of the location of exhibited manuscripts in the archives of the Department of Manuscripts states that the displays of illuminated manuscripts in the Grenville Library were withdrawn in November 1988, and the new displays in the refurbished Middle Room installed on 27 February 1989. The refurbished Middle Room was reopened to the public shortly afterwards.

chequered history of the Middle Room vividly illustrates the inflexibility of the manuscripts storage at Bloomsbury and the consequent use of elaborate temporary measures which in themselves became equally inflexible. At the time of the move to St. Pancras in 1998, the Middle Room provided the main area for marshalling and control of crates containing manuscripts. Appropriately, at the end of the move, it was the scene of a farewell party where the curators said adieu to Bloomsbury with a lively ceilidh.

One of Madden's great interests was the collection of charters and seals, which seem to have been accommodated after the move from Montagu House mostly in drawers in the Middle Room, with some of the seals remaining in one of the upper rooms in Montagu House. Madden was anxious that some of the space made available when the Middle and South Rooms ceased to be reading rooms should be used to provide improved accommodation for charters and seals. In 1838, Madden noted that Smirke had recommended that the South Room should be fitted up for charter and roll storage "below the gallery, with wainscot doors, either on all four sides, or on the north, east and west sides."[76] The South Room had been fitted in this way, with drawers and special deep cases for roll storage, by the end of 1840. The need for large roll storage was made more pressing by the deposit in the British Museum in 1833–1834 of the Chancellors' Rolls, the series of duplicate pipe rolls, the unwieldy character of which caused great problems in the Reading Room, and which were eventually to be transferred to the Public Record Office in 1862.[77] The South Room remained fitted out in this way until the 1970s, when it was completely renovated, with the insertion of new floors, a strongroom area, and modern shelving, and air conditioning, so that no hint was left of its original character and it seemed as if it could have been a modern purpose-built storage area.

The development of the accommodation of the Department of Manuscripts at Bloomsbury was a process of ad hoc addition of new areas around these three core rooms of the Manuscripts Saloon, Middle Room, and South Room. The first additions formed part of the process by which Smirke's building was gradually pieced together and Montagu House demolished during the 1840s and 1850s. The most important addition was intended to be the large room to the west of the Manuscripts Saloon. The connecting doors to this room apparently replaced windows in the west of the Saloon, making the problem of light in the Saloon worse. However, as has been seen, the new

---

[76] Additional MS. 62022, fols. 12v–13. At the same time, Madden also recommended the purchase of tin cases for the storage of rolls. A number of rolls in the Manuscript Collections are still stored in these cases.

[77] John D. Cantwell, *The Public Record Office 1838–1958* (London, 1991), 222; Harris, *History*, 279.

manuscripts room was allocated to the Grenville Library, despite the fact that Madden had already moved some of the most valuable manuscripts to special cases there.[78] Consequently, he had to wait until 1848 until there was the first substantial increase in the manuscripts storage area, when a room was built on land in the south-west angle between the Manuscripts Saloon and the Middle Room, which was reached through a door from the Middle Room. Madden was by this time desperately short of storage for large manuscripts, and used the new accommodation to assemble there various maps, drawings, and other large volumes. The room consequently became known as the Map Room.[79] Smirke's plans for the new entrance hall to the Museum included a waiting room, to the right of the entrance doors, abutting the Map Room. The need for office and storage space was too pressing to allow this room ever to be used for its original purpose. At first it was used by the Department of Printed Books, but eventually in 1858 it was allocated to the Department of Manuscripts, and Madden used it to assemble together the Egerton manuscripts, so called because they are purchased from the proceeds of a fund bequeathed by Francis Henry Egerton, eighth Earl of Bridgewater.[80] The room consequently became known as the Egerton Room.

The Map and Egerton Rooms were originally similar in shape and appearance to the Middle Room, but, like the South Room, all trace of the original layout of the storage areas there was obliterated when the shelving in the rooms was remodelled between 1966 and 1968, with an additional floor of shelving being inserted. At this time, the possibility of the British Museum library being removed into a separate building was under active consideration, and it was stipulated that the new shelving should be free-standing, so that it could be removed if the manuscripts were transferred to a new building and the rooms reinstated. The then-Keeper, Theodore Skeat, even suggested that the shelving should be designed so that it could be transferred wholesale to any new accommodation. Consequently, the shelving was made of pressed steel painted in a dingy institutional green, and problems with the steel caused repeated delays with the remodelling of the rooms. Once completed, the upper floor was used chiefly for the storage of charters removed

---

[78] Borrie, "Panizzi and Madden," 27–28; Harris, *History*, 178–79. As late as 1879, Thompson argued that the only solution for the accommodation problems of the Department of Manuscripts was the return of the room used to house the Grenville Library: Harris, *History*, 317.

[79] Harris, *History*, 178; Additional MS. 62027, fol. 37v.

[80] Harris, *History*, 178–79. The Bridgewater Fund was supplemented by a further bequest in 1838 by Egerton's cousin, Charles Long, Baron Farnborough, a Trustee of the Museum.

from the South Room, and more economically shelved in large green boxes. The original name of the room was reflected in the large numbers of Egerton manuscripts still to be found in the presses around the wall of the first floor, and in the storage of large boxes containing rolled maps, brass rubbings, and other material needing deep storage in a press at the entrance to the ground floor level. In their remodelled state, the rooms contained nearly a quarter of the Department's storage space in its last days at Bloomsbury.[81]

The Departmental territory was also extended to the east. At the southeast corner of the Manuscripts Saloon was the entrance to a room which became Sir Frederic Madden's own study. The room had a glass roof, so that Madden complained constantly about the temperature of the room, which was excessively cold in winter and unbearably hot in summer.[82] A new office for the Keeper of Manuscripts was provided with the opening of the White Wing in 1885, and in 1936 Madden's old study was in use as a workshop. At the suggestion of a Museum Trustee, Lord Crawford, a special exhibition room for Bibles was constructed in this small room, which opened in 1936, and the room became known as the Bible Room. The specially-built exhibition cases again incorporated cupboards providing storage for boxes and large manuscripts. The room also served as an entrance to the Manuscripts Students' Room. With the remodelling of the Library's exhibitions in the 1970s, the room became a temporary exhibitions room, known in honour of the man who initiated the conversion of the room into a gallery as the Crawford Room.[83]

Madden's study was enlarged as part of the small extension to the east of the Middle Room built in 1847.[84] This included a long room to the south of Madden's study, connected by a door, which was intended to provide space for the sorting of manuscripts. The provision of space for the sorting of manuscripts was always a constant problem, and indeed still has not been satisfactorily resolved even at St. Pancras. As part of the remodelling of this area at the time of the construction of the White Wing, it was substantially reduced in size, and became after 1885 the office occupied by the attendants such as

---

[81] Harris, *History*, 628; box file marked "Accommodation" in Department of Manuscripts archives.

[82] The room can be clearly identified from Plan E in Harris, *History* (it is marked "Officer"). The other room marked "Officer" was occupied by the Assistant Keeper of Manuscripts, who was cast into darkness when one of the windows of his room was blocked by the building of the new Long Room: Harris, *History*, 177. Prescott, "'Their Present Miserable State'," 449 n. 203, wrongly identifies Madden's study as the Interview Room.

[83] Harris, *History*, 484–85.

[84] Harris, *History*, 177; Additional MSS. 62006, fol. 19; 62025, fols. 25v–26.

Gatfield, where routine tasks such as foliation were undertaken. When the Attendants became clerical officers in 1949, the room became known as the Clerks' Room. Another office situated off the Manuscripts Saloon had an entrance in the north-east corner, diametrically opposite that of Madden, and was occupied by the Assistant Keeper of Manuscripts.[85]

The most substantial extension of the accommodation of the Department of Manuscripts was the building of the White Wing, built to the east of the Saloon and the Middle Room between 1882 and 1885 with money bequeathed by William White, who during his lifetime had lived near the Museum.[86] The land on which the White Wing was built was formerly the Principal Librarian's garden. Part of it had been used for a bindery, and it was here that the disastrous bindery fire of 1865, which destroyed and damaged some Cotton manuscripts, occurred.[87] With the building of the White Wing, a new bindery was built to the north of the Museum (which still houses part of the British Library's conservation service). The White Wing included accommodation for the Departments of Printed Books, Prints and Drawings, and Medieval and Later Antiquities, as well as Manuscripts, and included on its opening a Newspaper Reading Room and a Students' Room for Prints and Drawings. It is not feasible here to trace the complete history of the use of this building, which latterly housed much of the Department of Oriental Manuscripts and Printed Books. The main areas used by the Department of Manuscripts will simply be noted.

From the Middle Room, a corridor led through to the Manuscripts Students' Room. The Manuscripts Students' Room originally comprised the ground floor of the southern part of the White Wing, but by the 1940s it was proving too small, and in 1956–1957 an extension of the room was built at the bottom of the gloomy central well in the middle of the wing. This had the peculiar effect of creating what were virtually two inter-connected reading rooms, which raised potential problems of supervision, so the remodelling of the room included the building of a central desk which looked out over both rooms, where the curators responsible for supervising the room sat.[88] Part of the remodelling of this room included improved storage for the most valuable

---

[85] Harris, 177. The room was afterwards connected with the Long Room, and used for oriental materials, and became known as the Sanskrit Library. From the 1980s, it was occupied by the Exhibitions Section of the British Library.

[86] Harris, *History*, 312–13.

[87] Prescott, "'Their Present Miserable State'," 419–20.

[88] A picture of the original Manuscripts Students' Room before its enlargement is Harris, *History*, fig. 62; a photograph of the enlarged room, showing the newly added room, is Harris, *History*, fig. 98.

manuscripts. The "Select Lobby," which offered state-of-the-art storage conditions for these manuscripts, was immediately to the north of the Students'
Room extension, and there was a direct entrance to the lobby from the Issue
Desk at the western end of the extension. Following the enlargement of the
room in 1957, readers fed their requests for manuscripts through a hole in the
wall beside the issue desk, where they dropped into a tray in a room where
the Library Assistants, who were responsible for fetching the manuscripts,
collected and sorted orders. The LAs room, as it was known, also contained
wooden cupboards for the storage of photographic negatives. From the corridor connecting the Middle Room and the Students' Room ran the imposing West Staircase which led up to office accommodation. This comprised a
room allocated to the Assistant Keeper (or AKR), the Keeper's Room (KR),
and finally the magnificent Dickensian space of the Working Room, where
the curators worked. All these rooms contained substantial book space, and
allowed the development of a substantial working library of reference books.
A staircase at the eastern end of the Working Room led to the three East
Rooms, which provided further office space, but which also contained presses used for manuscript storage. The East Rooms were also accessible by means
of a door at the east end of the original Students' Room.

The story of the extension of the Students' Room illustrates how, like other
areas of the Museum, the White Wing was subject to remodelling and impro-
vised improvements during the century in which the Department of Manuscripts was there. Temporary wooden partitions were used for demarcation
between the East Rooms and the offices of the Department of Medieval and
Later Antiquities. When the newspaper storage was moved to Colindale in
1906, this area (on the ground floor corridor leading from the Manuscripts
Saloon to what was originally the Newspaper Reading Room) was fitted out
with presses for material from the oriental collections. This in turn was used
for manuscript storage when the oriental collections themselves moved to Store
Street in the 1980s. This area was known as the North Lobby. The corridor
from the Manuscripts Saloon, which provided access to the select lobby before
the extension of the Students' Room, and was consequently known as the Select Lobby Corridor, was also lined with glazed presses, and used to store collections of modern historical papers, including the bulk of the papers of William Gladstone. Above all, underneath the west stairs leading to the Keeper's
and Assistant Keeper's Rooms, there was a small strongroom, with an imposing door built by Chubbs, the famous safe-makers. This became known as Safe
Z, although at the time it was the only safe in the Department. The designation
probably reflects the evolution of the grading system of manuscripts, and was
meant clearly to distinguish the outstandingly valuable manuscripts from the
next category, the "A*" grade manuscripts. The small, airless Safe Z could

accommodate only a few very precious manuscripts. The exact date when Safe Z was inserted under the west stairs is uncertain. It gave every appearance of having been part of the original furnishings of the White Wing, but the chronology of the development of the grading system of the manuscripts suggests that Safe Z may not have been installed until towards the end of the First World War, or even later. More work needs to be done on this point. When moved to St. Pancras, the Safe Z manuscripts were placed in a special penned area. The St. Pancras pen could accommodate a larger number of manuscripts, which permitted an extension of the "Safe Z" category, which is still retained at St. Pancras, despite the fact that it no longer refers to a single safe.[89]

The most important expansion of the storage area of the Department of Manuscripts in the twentieth century was the expansion into the Residence. During the eighteenth and nineteenth centuries, the senior officers of the Museum were required to live on the premises.[90] The blocks jutting out to the south on the extreme east and west of the forecourt of the famous entrance of Smirke's south front of the Museum were designed to provide houses for the Museum's Keepers, and thus became known as the Residences, each Residence being given a number. The house of the Principal Librarian, the Director of the Museum, was in the east wing in the nineteenth century. A corridor connected it with the main Museum building, the entrance to the corridor being immediately to the east of the South Room.[91] There was a small waiting room at the entrance to this corridor. Like its bigger brother off the entrance hall, this waiting room was of little use, and Panizzi relinquished the room to provide extra office space for the Department of Manuscripts.[92] This little room had a chequered history, mostly being used as a rather inconvenient office, but on one occasion even being converted into a temporary toilet for use during a royal visit, and finally ending up as an "Interview Room." This room led to Residence no. 1. This Residence was allocated to the Department of Manuscripts as office space in 1948. It was used to house curators working on modern historical papers, and the constant need for storage space meant that the walls of both the Residence corridor and most of the rooms in the Residence itself quickly became covered with presses containing manuscripts (although, for security and conservation reasons, the Residence was generally only ever used for the storage of modern papers).

---

[89] Prescott, Brown, and Masters, "The Survey," 131–33.

[90] Harris, *History*, 4, 62, 107, 113, 302, 442–43, 565, 570, fig. 54.

[91] The building of the Residence corridor was part of the extension works which included the building of the Clerks' Room as a sorting room: Harris, *History*, 177.

[92] Harris, *History*, 177.

It was through the Residence Corridor and Residence that the manuscripts left Bloomsbury. Building work on the Great Court scheme meant that the forecourt of the British Museum building could not be used for the vans which transported the crates containing manuscripts from Bloomsbury to St. Pancras. A special entrance for the vans was created in the Museum railings along Montague Street. One of the rooms on the ground floor of the Residence was specially converted so that the crates could be brought along the Residence corridor, up a ramp, through an exit specially constructed in a large window, onto a special hoist, and thus into the vans.

When the manuscripts were moved from Montagu House into the Saloon and Middle Room, the complex arrangement in the different upper rooms at Montagu House was replaced by a single integrated arrangement. Likewise, in moving the manuscripts from Bloomsbury to St. Pancras, the complex sprawl of manuscripts through all the various rooms occupied by the Department at Bloomsbury, running from the Saloon through the Middle Room to the Residence corridor and beyond, was replaced by a single integrated sequence at St. Pancras, occupying one very large room. The architect of St. Pancras, Colin St John Wilson, pointed out at an early stage of planning of the new building that Smirke's method of arranging book presses around the wall, while looking spectacular, was wasteful of space. The validity of Wilson's comment is spectacularly demonstrated by the way in which the whole contents of the ground floor presses in the old Manuscripts Saloon fit into twenty or so "ranges" at St. Pancras. Unlike the printed book storage, the manuscripts storage is above ground and uses fixed shelving. The main sequence of manuscripts runs in a continuous series of presses arranged along an aisle running almost the entire width of the building. The Lord Chamberlain's Plays, returned from Woolwich, are in a separate aisle, and an area of deep shelving, adjacent to the entrances to the Manuscripts offices, contains the contents of all the various cupboards which were underneath the exhibition cases and elsewhere at Bloomsbury. Just like the Saloon in 1830, everything is clear and logical. One must wait and see whether the pressure of the inexorable growth of the collections means that ad hoc measures of the sort repeatedly adopted at Bloomsbury since 1840 will be necessary. Perhaps by 2150 the physical geography of the Manuscript collections at St. Pancras will be as complex as it was at Bloomsbury.

IV

Manuscripts Saloon, Middle Room, East Rooms, Residence Corridor, Grenville Cupboards, Safe Z, Select Lobby. How did anyone ever find anything at Bloomsbury? This is a matter of more vital interest to the scholar than it might at first seem, since it fundamentally determines how the scholar can find out what manuscripts are in the British Library, and whether or not the researcher can be sure that a long-lost text or an unimagined masterpiece is not, in fact, lurking somewhere in that huge sequence of manuscripts. In 1844, Madden noted in his work diary that "The indexes of the contents of the Cotton volumes in MS. Birch 4628 are copied from the MS. Harl. 4622 pts i and ii and, strange to say, in the last edition of the Harleian catalogue this no. 4622 is omitted altogether!"[93] If that is the case, how did Madden know where Harley MS. 4622 was, and how could he establish its contents? In 1847, Madden again noted that "I saw by the index to the minutes that on 9 May 1835 the Sloane MS 2640 was reported as missing, and on 12 December 1835 Harl. 6037. Both the MSS are now on the shelves."[94] How had Madden established this? Had he simply happened to notice the volumes on the shelves and remembered that they were said to have been lost? Such questions tap into a fundamental anxiety of humanities scholars, namely how far the curatorial gatekeeper has material that the scholar cannot know about and cannot hope to discover, but which might help answer the questions the scholar is researching.

The scholar's lifeline is the catalogue. However, the catalogue is often demonstrably incomplete. The most spectacular example of this is the Cotton catalogue compiled by Joseph Planta. Since Planta's time, dozens of manuscripts described by him as having been destroyed in the fire of 1731 have been recovered and restored by Forshall, Madden, and others. Yet the catalogue in the Manuscripts Reading Room at St. Pancras (and indeed the version now available on-line) gives few clues as to their survival. In order to establish their present condition, it is necessary to refer to specialist catalogues, such Ker's *Catalogue of Manuscripts containing Anglo-Saxon*. Ker also refers to manuscripts for which, at the time he was writing, there was no catalogue available, such as the collections of Cotton fragments. How did Ker know they were there? Assuming he asked a curator, how did the curator know what was there and, above all, how can we be sure that the curator accurately traced all the material which might have been lurking in that labyrinth of manuscript storage areas at Bloomsbury?

The answers to these questions lie in two key housekeeping documents, the hand lists and the shelf lists. These record the pressmarks assigned to individual manuscripts. The manuscript number (such as Additional MS. 14360) is sometimes inaccurately described by manuscript scholars as the pressmark. In fact, this number is simply a convenient means of succinctly

---

[93] Additional MS. 62004, fol. 28v.
[94] Additional MS. 62006, fols. 26v–27.

identifying a particular manuscript volume. The numbers have developed in a variety of ways, but are most commonly (as in the case of the Additional and Egerton sequences in the British Library, the two sequences which are still "live" and to which manuscripts are still added) accession numbers. They do not indicate where a manuscript is shelved. The manuscripts are arranged on the shelf in a size sequence (so as to place volumes of approximately the same size together, the best arrangement from a conservation point of view).

In order to locate the manuscript, a concordance is required. This is the hand list. The hand list is a list of the manuscripts in each collection, arranged in manuscript number order, with information on the location and grade of each manuscript, and occasional notes of transfers, invalid numbers, surrogates, and so on. When a manuscript is requested by a reader, the hand list is used by the staff retrieving it to find out where it is placed. When checks are made to ensure that no manuscripts are missing, a list of the manuscripts in order on the shelf is also needed. This is the shelf list. The shelf list is a list of the manuscripts in the order in which they are found on the shelf. It also notes which manuscripts are bound together or boxed. It was used at Bloomsbury during verification, a stock check of the shelves which took place during the annual closed week. The function of the hand and shelf lists is most succinctly described in a memorandum dating from about 1879 by the then Keeper of Manuscripts, Edward Maunde Thompson:[95] "Each MS. (in addition to its own individual number) has two small printed labels attached to the back, one placed at the top and the other at the bottom of the volume. The first bears the number of the press, the second the letter-mark of the shelf and the number of the volume in its order on the shelf: e.g. the Additional MS. 28816 bears the labels marked 176 and G.5, indicating that it is the fifth book on the G shelf in Press 176. The hand lists contain lists of the MSS with their pressmarks. The shelf lists contain lists of the presses and shelves with the volumes which they contain."[96]

The hand and shelf lists thus essentially consist of huge sequences of numbers, but nevertheless, as the central housekeeping records, they provide the most authoritative statement of exactly what is in the British Library's manuscript collections. How did the hand and shelf lists evolve, and how accurate are they as statements of the contents of the manuscript collections? The early history of these lists and the system of placing is difficult to reconstruct because of the destruction during the earlier part of the twentieth century of all the oldest hand and shelf lists. Two lists survive, compiled in

---

[95] Sir Edward Maunde Thompson (1840–1929), Assistant in the Department of Manuscripts 1862–1871; Assistant Keeper of Manuscripts, 1871–1878; Keeper of Manuscripts, 1878–1888; Principal Librarian, 1888–1909.

[96] Prescott, "The Panizzi Touch," 224.

1852 and 1858, of the 'inventories, registers, hand and shelf catalogues & c. in the Department of Manuscripts.'[97] These were drawn up by Richard Sims, an interesting figure who, apparently under a misapprehension as to the exact nature of his duties, accepted a position as an Attendant in the Manuscripts Department. His abilities far exceeded the duties required of him, and he was used by Madden not only to maintain many of the working records of the Department and organise binding work but also for simple indexing and cataloguing work. On his own initiative, he produced an index to the heraldic visitations, still a valuable reference work, and the first detailed guide to the British Museum Library for readers. Sims was evidently Madden's sergeant-major, and his periodic threats to resign unless he was promoted filled Madden with great apprehension. Eventually, with Panizzi's assistance, Madden was able to have him appointed as a transcriber.[98]

Sims' list gives details of a large number of hand catalogues for each manuscript collection, dating back in some cases to the eighteenth century, together with a similarly wide range of shelf catalogues. There were also parallel series of inventories and drawer lists for the charter and seal collections, together with early binding, folio, and stamping registers. The archives listed by Sims also included detailed records of all manuscripts issued in the reading room since 1758, with the register from 1816 to 1857 alone running to sixty-four volumes in folio; a register of visitors to the Department; a register of artists authorised to make drawings from the manuscripts; and a register of presses cleaned. Hardly any of these records survive today, which can only be regarded as a bibliographical disaster of the first order. In particular, all the various hand and shelf-catalogues, inventories, and drawer lists have disappeared. The earliest surviving hand and shelf lists all date from the 1920s, although one hand list of the charters and rolls compiled in the 1850s has been preserved and a fragment of an early nineteenth-century shelf list may also have been preserved. The circumstances of this loss are not documented, but easily enough guessed at. Sims' lists state that all the records not in current use were stored in a "closet in the Middle Room." It is mainly these records which have disappeared. The closet was presumably the cupboard immediately by the door from the Middle Room to Residence Corridor. This cupboard appears to have been cleared out at some point in the 1930s in order to store photographic negatives. Presumably the archives listed by Sims were disposed of at the same time.

---

[97] In a volume of miscellaneous papers in the archives of the Department of Manuscripts.

[98] Details of Sims' life are scattered through Madden's diaries, but see also Harris, *History*, 223, 235, 236&n, 258n, 307. After Madden's retirement, Sims became an Assistant in the Department of Manuscripts.

In addition to the lack of early placing records, the reconstruction of the early system of placing in the Manuscripts Department is further hampered by variations in terminology. The early use of the term "hand catalogue" or "hand list" does not necessarily correspond to the modern use. When the system of annual visitations of Museum Departments by the Trustees was introduced in 1805, it was recommended by a sub-committee of the Trustees that "the under-librarians and their assistants should proceed immediately to make hand catalogues of the contents of each case and shelf of books, noting the distinctive mark of each compartment; the number of each book upon each shelf, and the short title of each book; and they recommend this with the more confidence, as they are informed that by the aid of such hand catalogues an annual visitation is made of the Bodleian Library in Oxford."[99]

The preparation of such hand catalogues was recommended for both the manuscripts and printed books. The compilation of such hand catalogues for the printed book collection was an immense task, and in 1827 the Keeper of Printed Books, Baber, was finally able to report that they were nearing completion.[100] The best description of the printed-book hand catalogues was given by Panizzi before the 1836 Parliamentary Committee: ". . . these are catalogues in which the headings only are entered with a topical arrangement, if I may so express myself: the titles are arranged as the books stand on the shelves; for instance, in those days we went by rooms, and if there was 7. A.c, on a book, it meant that the book stood in the seventh room, in press A., and on shelf c; and it had a number, moreover, which meant that it occupied a particular place on a particular shelf. The advantage of the hand catalogue is immense for the security of the collection, because if we had not the hand catalogue, upon seeing that a book was missing from its place, I should not know what was the missing book, but if I know that the tenth book on shelf c, in Press A, of the seventh room is wanting, by the hand catalogue I see that it is 'Virgil,' for instance; and then I go to the general catalogue, and I find that the 'Virgil' which stands in the seventh room, Press A., shelf c, number 10, is such a 'Virgil' and then I can trace it."[101]

Panizzi stressed that the hand catalogue of printed books was not the slightest use for readers and was merely "to know what particular book is on a particular shelf." After the twenty years spent in their compilation, the hand catalogues had become "good for nothing, and mere waste-paper" as soon as

---

[99] *Report from the Select Committee on the British Museum* (1836), 519–21.

[100] F. J. Hill, "The Shelving and Classification of Printed Books," in *The Library of the British Museum: Retrospective Essays on the Department of Printed Books*, ed. P. R. Harris (London, 1991), 1–74, at 54.

[101] *Report from the Select Committee on the British Museum* (1836), no. 9597.

the books had been moved from Montagu House into the new building.[102] Although Panizzi had submitted to the Trustees specimen sheets for hand catalogues recording the new arrangement of the printed books, these were never completed. The reason, Panizzi conceded to the parliamentary committee, was that the new hand catalogue could not be compiled until the general catalogue was finished, since the hand catalogue contained only the headings. The function of the hand catalogues was eventually taken over by the fourth copy of the general catalogue.[103]

The preparation of such hand catalogues for the manuscript collections was not as laborious an undertaking as for the printed books. Moreover, there was not the same cross-checking to the general catalogue required as with the printed book collections. It is unclear whether these early hand catalogues, also sometimes described as inventories, included details of the contents of each manuscript. There is in a volume of early papers of the Manuscripts Department a page which looks as if it may have come from an early hand catalogue. This lists the "contents of this case" in shelf order, with a short title for each. Establishing the titles of each manuscript, particularly in the case of such foundation collections as the Sloane Manuscripts, must have been a complex task. The value of the title reference must also have been limited.

Despite their name, the early nineteenth-century hand catalogues performed the same function as the modern shelf lists and do not correspond to the present hand lists at all. It is consequently impossible to establish accurately to which form of document the nineteenth-century lists of old inventories in the Department of Manuscripts referred to. Sims' 1858 list gives two different categories of inventory for the manuscript collections: hand catalogues and shelf catalogues. The hand catalogues are older, and include a number for the Harley, Sloane, and early Additional and Royal Manuscripts which date from 1787 or 1791 and thus predate the Trustees' instruction for the preparation of detailed shelf inventories. This suggests that the terminology had already by this date begun to shift and that the hand catalogues are aids for locating a manuscript, not shelf inventories. On the other hand, the earliest shelf catalogues date from 1810 and some of the Sloane and Additional shelf catalogues were arranged by groups of presses. This confirms that Sims' shelf catalogues were indeed shelf inventories of the sort stipulated by the Trustees in 1805.

To add further to this confusion, some of the main bibliographical catalogues were in the nineteenth century regularly referred to as hand catalogues or hand lists. In 1836, no information about recent additions to the manuscript collections was available in the Reading Room. Madden introduced

---

[102] *Report* (1836), nos. 9598–9600.
[103] Hill, "The Shelving," 54–55.

a written register which contained brief details of the latest additions to the collections together with details of how the manuscripts had been acquired and their pressmarks.[104] This register of additions was in Madden's time referred to most commonly as the "hand list" of additions, but also sometimes as the "hand catalogue," the "brief catalogue of the Additional Manuscripts," and the "Register of Additions." It was only under Bond that this confusing variety of nomenclature was abandoned, and the term "register" consistently used for this series. As more detailed descriptions for the final Catalogue of Additions were prepared, these were copied into a fuller catalogue kept in the Departmental offices. When sufficient copy had been accumulated, this catalogue was then published, and the relevant volume of the register withdrawn from the reading room.[105] This register is still preserved in the Departmental archives, and can be useful in tracing provenance information for acquisitions made in the nineteenth century, when such information was not always included in the printed catalogue.

Manuscripts were entered in the register in the Reading Room only when they had been arranged and bound and were in a fit condition for issue. In order to keep a check on the allocation of Additional Manuscript numbers, Madden had a private pocketbook in which he made rough notes of acquisitions and their numbers.[106] Subsequent Keepers also kept a similar aide-memoire, and this was the origin of the rough register. These early rough registers were also known as hand lists or hand catalogues. The "hand catalogues" incorporated into the collections with other records of Madden's Keepership are in fact early volumes of the rough register. The formal register maintained under Madden and Bond became unnecessary as the issue of the catalogue of additions became more prompt, but, as the published catalogue began to fall into arrears after the Second World War, a copy of the "rough register" was once again made available to readers to give details of recent accessions.

Up until the 1870s, then, the term hand list or hand catalogue was applied indiscriminately to a wide variety of records in the Department of Manuscripts.

---

[104] The creation of such a register in 1854 is noted in the annual report of Madden for that year, in the archives of the Department of Manuscripts.

[105] At least this was the practice in the late nineteenth century: Prescott, "The Panizzi Touch," 224. By the 1970s, the procedure was that manuscript copy for the catalogue was placed in a series of wooden boxes kept on the White Wing landing opposite the Assistant Keeper's Room. Copies of the descriptions were also placed in a folder in the Students' Room. The process of cumulation prior to publication could be a very lengthy one: in 1998, one of these wooden boxes still contained a few descriptions for the new Cotton catalogue begun sixty years previously. As projects were abandoned, the contents of the boxes could in themselves become archival items.

[106] Additional MSS. 62042–62066.

The more precise terminology used today was only introduced under Bond's Keepership from 1866 to 1878. As a result, it is very difficult to interpret references to hand lists or hand catalogues in early records of the Department. Thus, in a report to the Trustees on 8 July 1840, Madden states that "The remaining portion of the Additional MSS. have been arranged in the New Room [the Middle Room]. References in the hand catalogues have been made to the greater part of those in the gallery of the Saloon, and the binder is now placing press-marks on them . . ."[107] It is impossible here to know exactly what Madden was referring to. It could be any one of a number of possibilities: hand catalogues giving the order of the manuscripts on the shelf, something like the modern shelf lists, hand catalogues in manuscript number order giving the location of each manuscript, something like the modern hand lists, or the register in the Reading Room.

Despite these difficulties, enough information can be gleaned to give a broad picture of the development of the placing system in the Department of Manuscripts and the evolution of the present hand and shelf lists. The placing method preferred by the first Keepers of Manuscripts at Montagu House was the arrangement of the manuscripts in each collection by subject. This principle was adopted for the arrangement of both the Harley and Sloane collections. In 1764, Charles Morton, the then-Keeper of Manuscripts, made the following report to the Trustees: "It is an order of the Trustees that the Sloanian Manuscripts be classed according to the subjects: & there seems to be a propriety in following the heads or subjects which were approved for the Harleian Manuscripts. These were six principally; viz. Divinity, Law, Physick, Philosophy, History & Philology. The preparations for this arrangement, by fixing numbers to/upon each manuscript, suiting those numbers to the catalogue and index, and completing the distinction of subjects upon the back of each MSS are now finished, through the Committee's indulgence of Mr Nelson: & little more remains, than to report them actually upon the shelves, which can be performed by the messenger, with a very small supervising: after which then titles will be affixed to the presses, & the shelf of each manuscript noted in the catalogues."[108]

The difficulties of any subject arrangement of manuscripts are now widely recognised. Manuscripts frequently contain a number of different works on completely unrelated subjects. Establishing the main subject content of a particular manuscript is inevitably a matter of subjective judgement. At best, any subject classification produces a large and unwieldy class of miscellanea.

---

[107] Additional MS. 62023, fol. 68.
[108] Additional MS. 45751, fol. 49

At worst, important material can be placed in inappropriate categories and become effectively unfindable. The difficulties of using even a catalogue arranged on subject principles, such as Ayscough's catalogue of the Sloane collection, are formidable.[109] The problems posed by trying to make such an arrangement actually on the shelf are even greater. The unwieldiness of a subject based arrangement of manuscripts is evident from Morton's return of the number of Sloane Manuscripts in each class. Physic was, of course, the largest group, with 1490 volumes, but the next largest category was "miscellanies" with 674. Philosophy contained 452 volumes, history 317, philology 206, divinity 187, law 104, and oriental, including rolls, 127. This gave a total of 3175 Sloane manuscripts, which is considerably short of the present total of 4100 manuscripts. The reasons for such a large discrepancy are not clear: Morton noted "that there is a deficiency upon the face of the catalogue of above 300 vols.," but does not offer any further explanation.[110]

The subject arrangement of the Harley manuscripts is explained in detail in the 1808 *Synopsis* of the contents of the Museum.[111] The categories used were as follows:

> Bibles, biblical books, commentaries, Korans, rituals, etc.; Fathers of the church; Polemics, homilies; Ascetics; Journals of the Houses of Lords and Commons, parliamentary rolls and miscellanies; Jurisprudence; Medicine; Philosophy; Ecclesiastical history; Epitaphs, funeral ceremonies, etc.; Collections on the history of typography; Genealogical and heraldical miscellanies; Visitations of heralds, arranged by counties; Scots, Irish and Welsh pedigrees, and Heraldics; Foreign pedigrees and heraldics; History of France and Italy; Seguier's collection respecting the history of France; Collections respecting the history of Scotland; Collections respecting the history of England; Collections respecting the University of Cambridge, by Mr T. Baker, etc.; Collections respecting Domesday Book, etc.; Historical, biographical, numismatical, and other collections, chiefly respecting Great Britain and Ireland; Miscellanies; Greek classics; Latin classics; Modern poetry, music, etc.; and grammars, lexicons, catalogues and miscellanies.

The different subject categories were not placed in any logical order. Moreover, while some of the classifications such as "Jurisprudence," "Medicine,"

---

[109] Samuel Ayscough, *A Catalogue of the Manuscripts in the British Museum Hitherto Undescribed* (London, 1782). On this catalogue, see further the preface to *Catalogue of Additions to the Manuscripts 1756–1782.*

[110] Additional MS. 45751, fol. 54v.

[111] *Synopsis*, 8–10.

and "Philosophy" are reasonable, it is difficult to see the distinction between "collections respecting the history of England" and "historical, biographical, numismatical, and other collections, chiefly respecting Great Britain and Ireland." The reason why there should be, for example, a separate section of "collections respecting Domesday Book" is not clear. Generally, at Montagu House the presses in each room were numbered separately in roman numerals, but the presses containing the Harley manuscripts were subdivided into sections numbered in arabic numerals so that the pressmark was expressed in the form 3/IV, C, with the letter referring to the shelf on which the manuscript was placed. These Montagu House pressmarks can still be seen written in ink on the flyleaf of many Harley manuscripts.

The effort of arranging the Sloane and Harley manuscripts in this fashion seems to have exhausted the curators responsible for arranging the manuscripts on their arrival at Montagu House, and the Cotton and Royal manuscripts were placed in their original order on arrival in the Museum. The use of separate rooms to house the different collections at Montagu House facilitated such a mixed system of storage. In the 1808 synopsis, there is an apologetic note, regretting that the Cotton and Royal collections "are not classed in strict scientific order."[112] Thus, in their first years in the Museum, the Cotton manuscripts, for example, remained placed in their original Emperor order. The 1808 synopsis reports that the Cotton manuscripts occupied twenty-one presses which is more than those allowed for by the original Emperor system. This suggests that the Emperor system had by 1808 been disrupted in some way, perhaps because extra space was required to accommodate the appendices and the manuscripts stored in cases, and perhaps also because individual Emperor groups ran into more than one press. It was therefore necessary to insert into the manuscripts Montagu House press-marks, with the press written in Roman numerals and a letter designating the shelf. These press-marks, written in pencil on inside fly leaves, can still be found in a number of Cotton manuscripts.

Since the Harley and Sloane manuscripts had been rearranged according to subject groupings, the manuscript number itself was insufficient to locate a manuscript. Details of the shelfmark had to be entered into the catalogues so that a particular manuscript could be located when it was requested in the Reading Room. Moreover, it was difficult under such an arrangement to establish whether all the manuscripts were present. This prompted the compilation of inventories of the Harley and Sloane collections to assist in locating particular manuscripts and to facilitate checking. Sims' 1858 list records two such inventories, apparently arranged in manuscript number order, dating

---

[112] *Synopsis*, 14.

from 1787. These have been lost, but it seems reasonable to assume that they are the distant ancestors of the modern hand lists. Since the Cotton and Royal manuscripts were in the same order on the shelf as in the catalogue, there was no such pressing need for an inventory of these collections. However, the main catalogues for these collections did not record the losses by fire. Moreover, in both cases, although the manuscripts were in the same sequence as the catalogue, these divisions covered more than one press, and there was some need to check the position of the manuscripts on the shelf. These considerations prompted, according to Sims' list of the manuscript archives, the compilation in 1791 of inventories of both the Royal and Cotton collections.

In the earliest days of the Museum, it seems that checking of the manuscripts stock was mainly limited to ensuring that all manuscripts were returned from the Reading Room. On Christmas Eve 1762, Charles Morton pointed out to the standing committee of the Trustees that "Since the opening of the Museum it has been the practice at Christmas, and twice or thrice at Whitsuntide, to balance the account of the manuscripts with the reading room, by bringing back all such as were there, back to the department, and cancelling the receipts, and opening a new account after the holidays. This usage, which was calculated for the safety of the manuscripts, and to prevent other inconveniences of long accounts, was neglected last Christmas."[113] Morton suggested to the committee that this balance should be made that Christmas, and that there should be a standing order for such a check. Sims' list reveals that, following the order of the Trustees for the compilation of catalogues listing the manuscripts in shelf order, such inventories were compiled for the Royal and Cotton manuscripts in 1810. Although these made checking of the manuscripts on the shelf much easier, it seems that such checks took place relatively infrequently. John Holmes, then an Assistant in the Department of Manuscripts, in evidence to the Parliamentary Committee in 1836, stated that every year the inventories of the department were inspected in order "to ascertain whether every manuscript is in its place, or, if not in its place, by whom it is in use." He was forced to return to the committee and admit that he was mistaken: such an examination had in fact taken place only "twice during the time that I have been in the Museum, between six and seven years; namely in 1831 by Sir Frederic Madden, the Assistant Keeper; and in 1835, by the Reverend Henry Coxe and Mr Upton Richards, two of the assistants." The decision as to when such a check should be made and how often rested entirely with Forshall as Keeper.[114]

[113] Additional MS. 45751, fols. 12v–13.
[114] *Report from the Select Committee on the British Museum* (1836), nos. 4031–4033, 4260–4269.

In 1824, a new set of shelf lists was drawn up, presumably to facilitate the move from Montagu House to the Manuscripts Saloon.[115] Josiah For-shall, who seems to have undertaken most of the work in planning this move, was firmly opposed to any form of subject arrangement in the placing of the manuscripts. He declared to the parliamentary committee in 1836 that "It is scarcely possible, without unbinding and even cutting up manuscripts to make anything like a regular classification of them upon the shelves of a library, seeing that 10 or 12 manuscripts upon very different subjects are not infrequently bound in a single volume, and sometimes several written upon the same fasciculus of paper or vellum." In his enthusiasm, however, Forshall slightly distorted the case by claiming that the manuscripts "have always been arranged as they are now; that is, according to the numbers by which they are designated, and this is the best arrangement for manuscripts."[116] As has been seen, a simple arrangement by number had not prevailed at Montagu House, and the arrangement adopted in the Manuscripts Saloon marked a more radical departure with previous practice than his statement to the Select Committee suggests. When the manuscripts were moved into the Manuscripts Saloon, they were for the first time placed according to a consistent principle, broadly by accession number, but qualified by the need to group manuscripts of similar size together on the same shelf, with the smallest manuscripts at the top and the largest at the bottom. The number of the press was painted above it, using roman numerals, as at Montagu House, but in a continuous sequence around the room. On the spine of each manuscript, the binder fixed a panel giving the number of the press and the letter of the shelf where it was placed in the form Plut[eus, Shelf] XXXIV. C. In other words, when moving the manuscripts from Montagu House into the Manuscripts Saloon, Sir Henry Ellis and Forshall, as the curators responsible for the move, invented and implemented the system of placing which was to prevail throughout the time that the Manuscript collections were at Bloomsbury.

The subject arrangements of the Harley and Sloane collections vanished with the move from Montagu House, and the old shelfmarks of the Cotton and Royal collections ceased to be "live" pressmarks. The mixed system of placing at Montagu House was replaced by an integrated system apparently devised by Forshall. Forshall's system had many advantages. It was more conservation-friendly, in that it avoided mixing volumes of different sizes on the shelf. Above all, it was readily extensible. New manuscripts could simply be allocated to presses at the end of the sequence, and as new presses became available, they could be added to the sequence. As it turned out, the system

---

[115] According to the list of manuscript archives drawn up by Richard Sims.
[116] *Report from the Select Committee on the British Museum* (1836), nos. 4374–4375.

could even readily accommodate the addition of different categories of storage, such as cupboards and safes. Forshall's system was to serve the Department of Manuscripts very well throughout its time at Bloomsbury, and is still the basis for the organisation of the manuscripts on the shelves at St. Pancras. Appendix One shows the numerical distribution of presses in the different rooms at Bloomsbury at the time of the move to St. Pancras in 1998, and illustrates how Forshall's system was extended as the accommodation at Bloomsbury was gradually extended and remodelled. Inevitably the move of the manuscripts from Montagu House required the compilation of a complete new set of inventories in both manuscript number and shelf order, which are duly noted in Sims' list as extant in 1852. The inventories in manuscript order still seem to have been primarily used at this time for checking rather than locating the manuscript when required in the Reading Room. The pressmarks were entered in a "reference catalogue" for this purpose — some catalogues with the pressmarks entered in this form can still be found.

The flexibility of Forshall's placing system is further illustrated by the way in which it readily coped with transfers of material into other Departments and institutions. As the Museum grew, its various departments were progressively split up and reorganised to form new, increasingly more specialised Departments. As these new Departments were created, material was transferred to their custody and reorganised in storage areas controlled by the new Department. The most substantial rearrangement of the collections of the Department of Manuscripts during its time in Bloomsbury was the creation of the Department of Oriental Manuscripts and Printed Books. Shortly after the retirement of Madden in 1866, the incoming Principal Librarian, John Winter Jones, pointed out the increase in the number of oriental manuscripts and recommended the establishment of a Keeper of Oriental Manuscripts. At this stage, the Keeper of Oriental Manuscripts ran a sub-department of the Department of Manuscripts. Decisions about acquisitions of oriental manuscripts continued to be made by the Keeper of Manuscripts, and this sometimes produced conflict. When Edward Maunde Thompson became Principal Librarian, he recommended the establishment of a separate Department of Oriental Printed Books and Manuscripts, which was duly carved out from the collections, staff and acquisitions funds of both the Department of Printed Books and the Department of Manuscripts.[117]

---

[117] Harris, *History*, 409. From 1974, this Department was known as the Department of Oriental Manuscripts and Printed Books (757). The Department of Manuscripts was never renamed "Western Manuscripts" due to the fact that Oriental Manuscripts had initially remained formally a sub-department of Manuscripts.

These processes involved the transfers of large numbers of manuscripts, including material from the Sloane, Cotton, and Harley collections, to the new Department, which organised its collections in a different way. These transfers were recorded by deleting the Manuscripts shelf mark entry in the hand list and noting that the item had been transferred to Oriental. The hand list is the only record of these transfers, since the Oriental manuscripts acquired before 1866 remain in their appropriate place in the catalogues, giving the impression to the unwary reader that they are still in the custody of the Department of Manuscripts.[118] The hand lists are therefore essential in, for example, tracing which oriental Cotton or Harley manuscripts were moved into the Oriental Collections. The Oriental manuscripts were not the only categories transferred as the Museum grew and the number of Departments were multiplied. Artefacts which had formed part of the Manuscript collections, such as a tonsure ring which had been one of the Cotton charters[119] or the clog almanacs which had been part of the Harley collection, were transferred to the Department of Medieval and Later Antiquities. Objects which required curatorial expertise not available in the Department of Manuscripts were moved to a more appropriate department, such as the manuscripts containing Mexican picture writing, which were transferred in the 1920s to the Department of Ethnography. Some categories moved in and out of Manuscripts custody: there was, for example, briefly a separate Department of Maps between 1866 and 1880. Transfers between different departments of the Museum and Library continue right up to the present day; as recently as 1998 all music manuscripts and correspondence between musicians were transferred to the Music Library and arranged in the music storage area at St. Pancras according to a new system. The hand lists provide the only record of all these transfers, and are the essential documents in attempting to trace the original structure of particular manuscript collections.

---

[118] Inevitably the process of identifying and transferring the oriental manuscripts was not 100% successful, and the hand list provides the key for identifying the handful of oriental items which escaped the net, and are still in the western manuscript collections, such as a volume of Chinese botanical drawings in the Lansdowne collection which was never transferred: Lansdowne MS. 1244. Two other volumes of Chinese drawings in the Lansdowne collection were, nevertheless, transferred to Oriental Departments, Lansdowne MS. 1242 to Oriental Antiquities, still part of the British Museum, and Lansdowne MS. 1243 to Oriental Collections in the British Library. To add further to the confusion, the prints in Lansdowne MS. 1242 were, according to Madden, pasted into a blank volume from the Sloane collection. Madden notes that these three volumes were all previously in the Prints and Drawings collection: Additional MS. 62004, fols. 31v–32.

[119] Cotton Charter xvi.73.

While the vast majority of the manuscript volumes of the Department of Manuscripts were thus encompassed by Forshall's new pressmarking system, there were some major categories of material which fell outside the main sequence. The most important of these were the charter and seal collections, the development of which deserves a separate study, but which can be briefly outlined here. The distinction between charters and manuscripts has, since the earliest development of the manuscript collections of the British Library, been an extremely rough and ready one. As is well known, the most precious of Cotton's charters were placed within the Emperor pressmark system, as part of the huge volumes which formed Augustus ii, but other charters, such as the sealed copy of Magna Carta which is now Cotton Charter xiii.31a, were kept in a separately shelved series of loose charters. Fundamentally, the distinction was between documents which could be easily bound up, which became part of composite manuscripts, and those which could not be readily incorporated in volumes, which were retained as separate charters.[120] This is still broadly the basis on which the distinction between manuscripts and charters is made today. The naming of the charter collections can often be deceptive. The Cotton Charters, for example, include material which was designated prior to 1866 as miscellaneous charters, so include charters purchased by the Museum in the eighteenth century as well as material acquired by Sir Robert Cotton.[121] The point at which the Sloane Charters were first so designated is mysterious,[122] and most of the Lansdowne Charters were rescued by Madden from a box of refuse.[123] The sequence of Additional Charters was first begun by Forshall in 1829. Confusingly, the Additional Rolls form part of the Additional Charter sequence; charters in roll form are given accession numbers within the Additional Charter range but are then generally referred to as Additional Rolls rather than Additional Charters. (The same principle applies to the Egerton Charters and Rolls.)[124]

---

[120] Skeat, *The Catalogues*, 13–14, observes that "Many [charters], especially those which formed part of the older collections were bound up in volumes of MSS. Conversely, that masterpiece of English twelfth-century drawing, the Guthlac Roll, is numbered, not as a MS., but as Harley Roll Y.6 . . . there is no hard-and-fast line delimiting MSS. and charters, and the division, especially in the case of later documents on paper, is very largely a matter of convenience, often depending on whether the documents can best be kept separately in boxes as charters, or bound up in book form." In a footnote, Skeat goes on to point out that the Shakespeare Mortgage Deed is categorised as a manuscript, Egerton MS. 1787, and that of 449 original papal bulls in the British Library's collections, at least 156 are bound up in manuscript volumes.

[121] Prescott, "'Their Present Miserable State'," 430.

[122] Skeat, *The Catalogues*, 16–17.

[123] Prescott, "'Their Present Miserable State'," 447–48, n. 154.

[124] Skeat, *The Catalogues*, 14–15.

Unlike the manuscripts, the numbers originally used for some of the charter collections were also pressmarks. Thus, Cotton Ch. xiii.1 was the first item in the thirteenth charter drawer. Even when the series of Additional Charters was instituted, it appears that the numeration also indicated its placing. Likewise, the numbers adopted for the sequence of Detached Seals reflected their placing. Detached Seal xlvi.5 would be the fifth item in the forty-sixth seal drawer. However, gradually during the later nineteenth century this relationship between number and placing became disrupted, and the numbers used for the charters and seals became, like the manuscript numbers, simply a handy way of referring to the individual item. By 1964, the basis on which the roman numerals in the Detached Seal numbers was allocated had been forgotten, and it was proposed by the Keeper of Manuscripts that the roman figure should be changed at the end of 1965, and thereafter every ten years. In fact, the roman numerals were changed at the end of 1965 and 1970, and since then the roman number has been changed every five years. Since the charter and seal collections were in these ways treated differently within the housekeeping systems of the Department of Manuscripts, the documentation recording them was also different. No shelf list was ever compiled for the charter and seal collections until this information was computerised in the 1990s.[125]

A drawback of Forshall's new placing system for the manuscripts was that the placing of the individual volumes on the shelf was a very formal and cumbersome process. This can be seen from Madden's work in arranging the manuscripts in the Middle Room in 1840. Madden pointed out to the Trustees that each manuscript moved had to be "cleaned, classed in size, placed, pressmarked [by the binder] and entered [in the inventories and catalogues]."[126] The whole process took place under Madden's personal supervision. Manuscripts not yet bound or finally placed were given a temporary placing. When the time came to place the manuscripts, they were carefully graded according to size and placed on the shelf. When they were finally "fixed" they were given to the bookbinder for labelling with their pressmark. Because of the formal labelling on the spine, it was difficult to change the position of a manuscript once it was finally placed on the shelf, so that backlogs easily built up. One reason why the "temporary" appropriation of the new West Room to the Grenville Library was so annoying to Madden was that it was impossible to finally place manuscripts while he was still not sure whether or not this room would eventually be available to him. Moreover, since the pressmark

---

[125] *The British Library Catalogue of Additions to the Manuscripts 1956–1965* (London, 2000), 1, 626.

[126] Additional MS. 62023, fol. 32.

was noted in the reference catalogue, it made it difficult to complete the catalogue while the pressmark was still not fixed. In 1847, Madden pointed out to the Trustees that "Part of the Addl MSS for the years 1842 and 1843 and all acquired since are at present without pressmarks, and consequently without a permanent reference catalogue. The inconvenience felt on this account is very great, and Sir FM for some time past has anxiously looked forward to the new room, as a means of enabling him to locate the whole, and have permanent press-marks affixed to them by which alone they can easily be found, when wanted, and if one is missing or misplaced, can readily be traced."[127] Similar delays were created by the glazing of the presses in the Saloon and Middle Room, and by other building works there.[128] Wherever a rearrangement took place the compilation of a new inventory was necessary, and Sims' lists shows that it was necessary to revise all the inventories of most of the different collections more than once during the 1840s and 1850s. In August 1840, Madden recorded in his work diary that "In consequence of the MSS. in the Gallery and Outer Room having been out so often before any Inventory made, I was apprehensive great mistakes might occur. I therefore resolved to have an inventory of each Press taken, as also verify the numbers in regular order. This I began with Bromley."[129]

Madden experimented with methods of labelling the manuscripts. Shortly after he became Keeper, he proposed to the Trustees that "with respect to the verification of the MSS. when returned [from the Reading Room]" a procedure used in the Bodleian Library "which appears extremely satisfactory" should be adopted: "each row of volumes, as they stand in order on the shelves, should be marked with a large number in white, black or red paint, from no. 1 to the highest number on the shelf, as by this means, if a volume were missing or out of place, it could immediately be detected and with the aid of a hand catalogue, the whole collection might easily be verified by one of the assistants once in every twelve months. In the library of Printed Books small printed numbers are attached, but these are liable to come off, and do not sufficiently strike the eye. Manuscripts also are not so likely to shift their places as Printed Books, but even were this required, it would be very easy to wash off the painted number and substitute another."[130]

---

[127] Additional MS. 62027, fol. 77v.

[128] Madden's report for 1850, in the archives of the Department of Manuscripts, states that the completion of glazing in the Middle Room and the Saloon Gallery had allowed more than two thousand volumes finally to be pressmarked. This work continued in 1851.

[129] Additional MS. 62002, fol. 54.

[130] Additional MS. 62002, fol. 15v.

The Trustees instructed Madden to prepare one shelf of manuscripts in this fashion as a specimen of this method, which was found satisfactory and duly adopted. Its implementation, however, proved difficult. In 1840, Madden reminded the Trustees of this plan. He reported that following their approval of the scheme "The old Royal collection was completed, and this plan proves of the most essential service in verifying this collection. In Feb. 1839 the painter Ingham, who was employed on this service, was unable to give any more of his time to it, being employed elsewhere, and thus to the detriment of the department of MSS. it has continued ever since. Sir FM would therefore suggest that Ingham should resume the work thus commenced on those days of the week in which he acts only as attendant in the public rooms, or that the Trustees would employ someone else in his place." At the same time, Madden proposed that "numbers to the presses may be painted on tin, and affixed in a similar manner to those on the presses in the Department of Printed Books, the utility of which in both Departments is obvious."[131] Madden's request for the renewal of Ingham's service was accepted and by the end of 1840 he had numbered the Lansdowne, Hargrave, Harley, and Burney manuscripts.[132] However, Madden's bold scheme in the end proved impracticable. The painting was too time-consuming and the difficulty of then changing the placing of a manuscript was too great. By 1859, the painted numbers on the manuscripts had been washed off.[133] Instead, Madden reverted to having the placing of the volume tooled by the binder on the spine of the manuscript.

Another drawback of Forshall's system of manuscript placing was that volumes could easily be misplaced and would be difficult to find once misplaced. The only way of ensuring that volumes were not misplaced was by regular verification, that is, by checking the shelves against the shelf inventories to ensure that all the volumes were present and correct. The process of "numerical verification" was described by John Holmes in his evidence to the 1836 parliamentary select committee. It comprised "an examination which involved ascertaining whether the manuscripts are still in the Museum and forthcoming; it does not apply to the internal state of the manuscripts, I think not even to the binding; it is an examination of the several inventories of the collections." The volumes were not removed from the shelves "but as all the volumes have a number on the back, it is easy to see if a manuscript is missing." Holmes was forced to admit that this procedure amounted to "little

---

[131] Additional MS. 62023, fol. 53.

[132] Additional MS. 62002, fols. 45, 54; 62023, fols. 53, 68, 79.

[133] Note by Richard Sims in a volume of miscellaneous papers in the archives of the Department of Manuscripts.

more than counting them [the manuscripts] over."[134] Nevertheless, Madden afterwards declared that numerical verification was "the only certain mode of verification."[135]

Under Madden, wholesale verification of the collections was only undertaken every ten years. In his work diary for 2 May 1847, Madden records that he "Began with the other officers of my Department to verify the whole of the MSS. I took myself the old Royal, and verified great part of it, marking in the Hand Catalogue the alterations necessary. Mr Holmes took the Harleian, Mr Richards the Additional, Mr Bond the Lansdowne and Mr Cureton the Oriental ..."[136] This procedure took some time. Madden himself completed the verification of the Royal manuscripts on 4 May, but "could not proceed with the Cotton until a new inventory was made, which I ordered forthwith. Mr Cureton completed the Oriental MSS."[137] It was not until 9 June that Madden received from Bond, his Assistant Keeper, a return of the verification of the Additional, Sloane, Hargrave, Arundel, Burney, and Egerton manuscripts.[138] A new inventory of the Harley manuscripts had proved necessary, and Madden records that on 25 November Holmes, the senior assistant, brought him the "new numerical inventory" of the Harley manuscripts which had been verified by him. Madden notes that the only numbers missing were those which were missing in 1825 and several much earlier.[139]

The next complete verification did not take place until 1857. Madden's report on this exercise stated that "the whole of the various collections of manuscripts have been verified by the Shelf and Hand Lists, and new Lists made and copied fair."[140] In fact, Madden's work diary indicates that the check of the hand lists was not complete: "The verification of the collections by the shelf lists has been completed, and partly also by the hand lists."[141] The growth of the collections and their more frequent use in the Reading Room made more frequent verification desirable, and in the September closed week in 1865, the attendants verified all the collections apart from the charters and the rolls with the shelf lists.[142]

---

[134] *Report from the Select Committee on the British Museum* (1836), nos. 4031–4033, 4260–4269.

[135] Additional MS. 62028, fol. 80v.

[136] Additional MS. 62005, fols. 81–81v.

[137] Additional MS. 62005, fol. 81v.

[138] Additional MS. 62005, fol. 88v.

[139] Additional MS. 62006, fol. 25.

[140] Report for 1857, in the archives of the Department of Manuscripts.

[141] Additional MS. 62001, fol. 71v.

[142] Annual Report of the Keeper of Manuscripts for 1865, in the archives of the Department of Manuscripts.

It was the vigorous Bond who placed this stocktaking activity on a more regular basis and thus provided the catalyst by which the modern form of hand and shelf list emerged. One of Bond's first actions after becoming Keeper was to have the collection verified by the shelf lists and the hand lists during the closed weeks in 1867. Thereafter, annual checks were made during a closed week.[143] The check was made against the shelf list, and the regular annual verification was the major means by which the accuracy of the hand and shelf lists was ensured. The autumn closed week and the process of verification, in which all staff took part, was perhaps the major landmark in the year at Bloomsbury. It was this regular process of numerical verification against the shelf which ensured that the hand and shelf lists provided definitive listings of all the valid manuscript numbers at Bloomsbury. A manuscript might, as Madden found, be missing from the catalogue. However, if a manuscript was missing from the hand or shelf lists it could not be located and, logically, could have no existence. It is the hand list which enables the gatekeeper to know what is in his care.

The value of the hand list can be seen from looking at just one example, the hand list of the Cotton manuscripts. This lists all valid Cotton manuscript numbers, and is the only way, for example, of establishing where old covers have been separately preserved. It also indicates where Cotton manuscripts have been transferred to other collections. It provides a definitive listing of which manuscripts omitted from Planta still survive, identifying a number of manuscripts (such as Galba A. xx, Galba A. xxi, and Galba E. xiv) which are not noted in Thomas Smith's pre-fire catalogue and are also omitted by Planta, and the existence of which can otherwise be traced only from the appendix to Casley's catalogue of the Royal manuscripts. In short, the Cotton hand list illustrates vividly how a mere list of numbers can conceal the rich curatorial history of a manuscript collection. It is not practicable to reproduce the hand list here, and the use of the hand lists in day-to-day retrieval of manuscripts means that it is impossible to make them available for scholarly perusal. However, eventually this information will probably be recorded in an automated requesting system, and be disseminated in this way.

The main adjustment made in the placing system after the time of Bond was the dropping of the third element of the pressmark, which described the position of the manuscript on the shelf. Instead, manuscripts were placed in manuscript number order on each shelf, so that its position could be deduced without the extra element in the pressmark. As part of the preparation for the move of the manuscripts to St. Pancras, the information in the hand and shelf lists was mounted on a computer data base. However, the nature of Forshall's

---

[143] Prescott, "The Panizzi Touch," 200.

system of placing, as refined and modernised by Madden and Bond, meant that it could be adapted to St. Pancras. The manuscripts were simply retained in their shelf mark sequence, and the manuscripts placed in that sequence on the new presses at St. Pancras. This means that the pressmark became in a sense a "virtual" pressmark. At Bloomsbury, the pressmark 39A meant that the manuscript was found on shelf A of a press numbered 39. At St. Pancras, it means that it follows 38G and precedes 39B. However, a decision was taken not to abandon the practice of closed weeks with the move to St. Pancras. The annual verification does not now take place, but a system of rolling checks has been instituted. It is to be hoped that this will still ensure that the hand and shelf lists retain that great accuracy as statements of the contents of the British Library's Manuscript Collections which was their hallmark from the time of Bond onwards.

V

Much of Phillip Pulsiano's scholarly research took place in the Manuscripts Students' Room of the British Library at Bloomsbury. He was fascinated by how the place worked, and in particular by how the scholar could be sure that there were not new and unexpected things hidden away in unexpected nooks and crannies of those rooms which he loved so much. This essay has been an attempt finally to answer the question Phill so frequently asked me: Do you think there could be an Anglo-Saxon manuscript hidden away in that room? The existence of the hand and shelf lists, mere lists of numbers but checked and refined by a constant process of verification over more than a hundred years, mean that there are no unexpected hidden caches of "refuse" in the British Library's Manuscript collections of the sort that Ellis, Forshall, and Madden found.[144] The accuracy of the shelf lists is reflected in the fact that no hidden or lost items from the Manuscript collections came to light in the move to St. Pancras.

---

[144] The Manuscripts Reading Room copy of the catalogue of the Harley manuscripts includes at the end a series of additional handwritten entries comprising Harley manuscripts rescued by Ellis and Forshall from refuse. On 11 December 1837, Madden "Looked over some bundles taken out of the S.E. closet of reading room [i.e. the Middle Room], containing refuse of Lansdowne, Hargrave, Burney, Sloane, Spindler, Cole, [illegible] and Mangly papers. Such as I think worth preserving I shall have bound": Additional MS. 62001, fol. 20v. The notebook by William Harvey recording his discovery of the circulation of blood was, as late as 1875, found among duplicates in the Department of Printed Books: Prescott, "The Panizzi Touch," 221.

The nature of the British Library's housekeeping systems is such that "discoveries" are made in three ways. First, detailed collation between the catalogue and hand list may reveal the existence of items which, for one reason or another, have not been recorded in the catalogue. This is unlikely in the case of recent acquisitions, but may well happen with earlier collections. However, the number of volumes which can be identified as having slipped through the scholarly and curatorial net in this way is likely to be very small. Second, there are items described fully in the catalogue which scholars simply have never looked at. A letter of manumission given to the Kentish rebels in 1381 was listed in the index of charters in the nineteenth century, but nevertheless escaped scholarly attention until 1984.[145] There are doubtless many more treasures which have been fully described by the curators, but ignored by scholars. Finally, and most important, new discoveries can be made by the re-examination of the contents of manuscripts which have been described in only a cursory fashion in the relevant catalogue. The reliance of the housekeeping system on numerical verification means that the contents of the volumes are rarely systematically examined as part of the housekeeping activities of the Department of Manuscripts. The way in which a systematic survey of the contents of volumes could reap great dividends, particularly for manuscripts described in the early catalogues (the Harley, Sloane, and Cotton collections and Additional and Egerton manuscripts acquired before 1875) was spectacularly demonstrated by the Survey of Illuminated Manuscripts, in which a team of curators led by Michelle Brown and Scot McKendrick, breaking with the tradition of numerical verification, checked all volumes in the Department of Manuscripts to identify illuminated and early manuscripts, and made some remarkable discoveries.[146]

The move to St. Pancras took place at the time of Phill's last illness. One of the reasons he was determined to visit London during the last summer of his life was that he wanted to see the Manuscript collections in their new home at St. Pancras and to try the system there. By this stage, I had already left the Library to work at the University of Sheffield, but we had a last snatched conversation in the new Manuscripts Reading Room at St. Pancras. I afterwards regretted not speaking to him during the few weeks before he died, but we both knew that, in that last conversation in the Manuscripts Reading Room, we had chosen the most appropriate place to say goodbye.

---

[145] Cotton Charter iv.51: Andrew Prescott, "Writing About Rebellion: Using the Records of the Peasants' Revolt of 1381," *History Workshop Journal* 45 (1998), 1–27, at 26 n. 118.

[146] On this project, see e.g. Prescott, Brown, and Masters, "The Survey," 130–47.

Appendix

Distribution of Manuscript Press Numbers at Bloomsbury at the Time of the Move to St. Pancras, 1998

Press numbers	Location
1–79	Manuscripts Saloon, ground floor
83–112	MSS Saloon gallery
113–155	MSS Saloon gallery
156–205A	Middle Room
206–243	Middle Room gallery
244–263	Select Lobby Corridor
274–320	North Lobby
325–434	Map and Egerton Room, ground floor
435–541	Map and Egerton Room, 1st floor
542–569	North Lobby
574–577	West Stair presses
584–640	East Rooms 1–3
643–696	Select Lobby (Select MSS.)
697–716	Select Lobby Corridor
717–769	Select Lobby (Select MSS.)
770–818	Residence I
865–958	South Room, ground floor
959–1046	South Room, first floor
1047–1093	South Room, second floor

Bibliography

Ayscough, Samuel. *A Catalogue of the Manuscripts in the British Museum Hitherto Undescribed*. London, 1782.

Beadle, Peter, and Peter Meredith. *The York Play: A Facsimile of British Library MS Additional 35290*. Leeds Texts and Monographs, Medieval Drama Facsimiles 7. Leeds, 1983.

Borrie, Michael. "Panizzi and Madden." *British Library Journal* 5 (1979): 18–36.

[British Museum]. *Report from the Select Committee on the British Museum*. London, 1836.

[British Museum]. *Synopsis of the Contents of the British Museum*. London, 1808, 1834, etc.

Cantwell, John D. *The Public Record Office 1838–1958.* London, 1991.

Harris, P. R. *A History of the British Museum Library 1753–1973.* London, 1998.

————. *The Reading Room.* London, 1979.

Hill, F. J. "The Shelving and Classification of Printed Books." In *The Library of the British Museum: Retrospective Essays on the Department of Printed Books*, ed. P. R. Harris, 1–74. London, 1991.

Kiernan, Kevin. *Beowulf and the Beowulf Manuscript.* 2nd ed. Ann Arbor, 1996.

Prescott, Andrew. "The Panizzi Touch: Panizzi's Successors as Principal Librarian." *British Library Journal* 23 (1997): 194–236.

————. "'Their Present Miserable State of Cremation': The Restoration of the Cotton Library." In *Sir Robert Cotton as Collector*, ed. C. J. Wright, 391–454. London, 1997.

————. "Writing About Rebellion: Using the Records of the Peasants' Revolt of 1381." *History Workshop Journal* 45 (1998): 1–27.

————, Michelle Brown, and Richard Masters. "The Survey of Illuminated Manuscripts." In *Towards the Digital Library: The British Library's Initiatives for Access Programme*, 130–47. London, 1998.

Skeat, T. C. *The Catalogues of the Manuscript Collections in the British Museum.* London, 1951.

CONTRIBUTORS

A. N. Doane is professor emeritus of English at the University of Wisconsin-Madison. With Phill Pulsiano he founded "Anglo-Saxon Manuscripts in Microfiche Facsimile."

Peter Foote is professor emeritus of Scandinavian Studies at University College London. He has written numerous books and articles. A number of the latter were re-published on the occasion of his sixtieth birthday and his retirement from the chair of Scandinavian Studies in *Aurvandilstá: Norse Studies* (1984). His most recent publication is his edition of *Jóns saga Hólabyskups ens helga* in the Editiones Arnamagnæanæ series (Copenhagen, 2003).

J. R. Hall, Professor of English at the University of Mississippi, has published widely on Old English literature.

Ólafur Halldórsson was a research fellow at the Stofnun Árna Magnússonar in Reykjavík, Iceland, 1963–1990. He has prepared and published numerous philological editions of medieval Icelandic texts, his main work being the Great Saga of Óláfr Tryggvason (*Óláfs saga Tryggvasonar en mesta*), which was published in three volumes, 1961–2000. His most recent book, *Text by Snorri Sturluson in Óláfs saga Tryggvasonar en mesta*, was published in 2001.

Joyce Hill is Visiting Professor at the University of Leeds, where she formerly held the Chair in Old and Middle Language and Literature. She is currently Director of a national policy unit for higher education throughout the U. K.

Marianne Kalinke is a Center for Advanced Study Professor of Germanic Languages and Comparative Literature at the University of Illinois at Urbana-Champaign. Her publications include *King Arthur North-by-Northwest* (1981), *Bridal-Quest Romance in Medieval Iceland* (1990), and *The Book of Reykjahólar: The Last of the Great Medieval Legendaries* (1996). Since 1981, she has been managing editor for German and Scandinavian of the *Journal of English and Germanic Philology*.

Kevin Kiernan is T. Marshall Hahn Sr. professor emeritus of Arts and Sciences at the University of Kentucky. He is editor of the *Electronic Beowulf* and is currently preparing an electronic edition of Alfred the Great's Old English translation of Boethius's *Consolation of Philosophy*. With computer scientists at the University of Kentucky, he has developed an Edition Production Technology (EPT) for humanities projects.

Peter J. Lucas, now Emeritus Professor, taught Old And Middle English in Dublin for nearly forty years and has recently been teaching Anglo-Saxon in the University of Cambridge, where he is affiliated to Wolfson College. He has published extensively in Old and Middle English and the history of the English Language and is presently researching the early printing of Anglo-Saxon.

Joseph McGowan is currently associate professor of English at the University of San Diego. He has edited the sermons of Augustine of Ancona (c. 1243–1328) and is at work on volume 2 of *Old English Glossed Psalters: A Collective Edition* (Toronto).

Andrew Prescott was from 1979–2000 a curator in the Department of Manuscripts, The British Library. He was one of the principal collaborators in Professor Kevin Kiernan's Electronic Beowulf project, and has written a number of studies of the history of the Department of Manuscripts. He is now Director of the Centre for Research into Freemasonry, University of Sheffield, the first Centre of its kind to be established in Britain.

Elaine Treharne is professor of Medieval Literature at the University of Leicester, and President of the English Association. She works on English manuscripts from 1000–1200 and is author of the forthcoming book, *Living Through Conquest: The Politics of Early English*.

Gernot Wieland teaches Old English in the English Department at the University of British Columbia. He is author of *The Latin Glosses on Arator and Prudentius in Cambridge, University Library Manuscript Gg.5.35*, and editor of *Waltharius* and *The Canterbury Hymnal: Ms BL 37517*. He has most recently co-edited two Festschriften, with Christa Canitz, *From Arabye to Engelond: Medieval Studies in Honour of Mahmoud Manzalaoui on his 75th Birthday*, and with Sian Echard, *Anglo-Latin and its Heritage: Essays in Honour of A.G. Rigg on his 64th Birthday*. His main interests lie in manuscript studies, Anglo-Latin, and the influence of early Christian Latin literature on the Anglo-Saxons.

Jonathan Wilcox, Professor of English at the University of Iowa, writes extensively on Old English homilies and manuscripts (including editing several fascicles of Anglo-Saxon Manuscripts in Microfiche Facsimile) and is past editor of the *Old English Newsletter*.

Kirsten Wolf is the Torger Thompson Chair and professor of Old Norse and Scandinavian linguistics at the University of Wisconsin-Madison. Her primary areas of research are Old Norse-Icelandic philology and hagiography. She has prepared and published several editions of medieval Icelandic texts, including *Saga heilagrar Önnu* (2001) and *Gyðinga saga* (1995). Her most recent books are *Heilagra meyja sögur* (2003) and *Daily Life of the Vikings* (2004).

Stefanie Würth is professor in the Scandinavian section of the German Department at the University of Tübingen, Germany. Her publications include *Elemente des Erzählens: Die þœttir der Flateyjarbók* (1991) and *Der "Antikenroman" in der isländischen Literatur des Mittelalters* (1998).

General Index

Abel, Danish King (r. 1250–1252): 120–121, 166, 169

Abingdon: 234

Absalom and Ahitophel: story of in 2 Samuel 15–16 *See* Samuel

Accede ad musas vatum Thamesina iuuentus (sixteenth-century poem): 8

Adam of Bremen: 109, 138, 140–143, 145–145, 169–170

Adams, Sir Thomas: Wheelock's correspondence with 431

Ælfric: "Supplement" to glossary 68; scriptorium of 30; alliterative style of 89; metrical prose of 255; "Admonitio ad filium spiritualem" 253–54; *Catholic Homilies* 29–30, 238–43, 339–355, 363, 401–02, 415–16, 418–19, glosses on 341; *Colloquy* 400; *De Auguriis* 34; *De Duodecim Abusivis* 28–29; *De Falsis Deis*: 28–29; *De temporibus anni* (OE) 420; *Grammar* 370, 403; *Interrogationes Sigewulfi* 28–29; Letters, to Brother Edward 249, to the Monks of Eynsham 243, 248, 345, to Sigeweard 247, 249–50, to Wulfgeat of Ylmandun 249–50, to Wulfsige 242, 245, to Wulfstan 242, of Christ to Abgarus 34; *Lives of Saints* xvi–xvii, 27–40, 85–106, 229–59, 363, of Martin 230, of Thomas 230, of Mildred 230, prefaces to 242–43, 246, 249–50; Translations, of Genesis 247, of Joshua 247, of Kings 251, of Maccabees 248; "Wyrdwriteras Us Secgað" 251

Aelred of Rievaulx: *Life of St. Catherine of Alexandria*: 290

Æthelmær, patron of Ælfric: 246–50, 254, 258

Æthelred, King: 248

Æthelstan, West Saxon King (d. 939): 299, 301, 315

Æthelweard, patron of Ælfric (fl. 975–998): 27–28, 241, 246–50, 254, 258

Aggesøn, Sven: 109, 152, 155–156

Agatha Helgadóttir, abbess of Kirkjubær (1293–1342): 280, 286

Agathu saga: 279

Agnesar saga: 278

Ágrip: 139, 149–150, 164

Alcuin (735–804): 44, 67, 77, 244; *carmina* 2, 5

Albeck, Gustav (1906–1995): 152, 156

Aldhelm: 73; glosses of 360; *De laudibus virginitatis* 267, 361–62, 366, 370–72, 374

Alfred, King (871–899): 246, 401

Alexanders saga: 283

Alfífa, mother of King Sveinn Knútsson of Norway: 116–117, 146

Alfræði íslenzk: 140–142

Ambrosius saga: 178

Ámundi Þormóðsson: 273

Andreas: 363

Anglo-Saxon Chronicle: 148–149, 151, 248, 385, 390, 392, 398, 400

Anna Sigurðardóttir: 266, 280, 285–288

Annals: *Annála bæklingur* 317–318; *Annales Essenbecenses* 157; *Annales Fuldenses* 138; *Annales Lundenses* 146, 149–150, 160–61; *Annales Nestvedienses* 164; *Annales regni Francorum* 138; *Annales Ryenses* 146, 149, 157–161, 164, 166; *Annales Slesuicenses* 157; *Annales Sorani* 164; *Annales vetustissimi* 139, 168; *Flateyjarannáll* 138–139, 141, 155, 159, 168, 286; *Gottskálks annáll*: 138, 141, 155, 168; *Høyers annáll* 159, 165; *Konungs annáll*: 138, 141–142, 152–153, 155, 165, 168; *Lögmannsannáll* 138, 168, 284–286; *Oddaverja annáll*: 138, 155; *Resens annáll* 138, 159, 168; *Skálholts annálar*: 138–139, 141

Arator: 3, 5, 8, 12–13, 15, 23 *Historia apostolica* xvi, 2–3, 5–6, 8, 12, 15, 19, 22; letter to Vigilius 13

Ríkiza, queen of King Eiríkr of Sweden: 120–121, 162–163
Rime of King William: 331
Richard of Hexham: 403
Robert of Brunne: *Handlyng Synne* 347
Roger of Howden: 149
Rómverja saga: 318
Roskilde: 120–121, 130, 141
Roswitha (Hrotsvit), abbess of Gandersheim (ca. 935–after 1000): 289
Rufinus: translation of Eusebius's "Historia Ecclesiastica" 61–62, 64, 68
Runólfr Sigmundarson, abbot of Þykkvibær (1364–1307): 283

Sæmundr, priest at Kirkjubær (1252): 283
St. Alban's, church: 153, 350
St. Augustine's, Canterbury: *See* Canterbury, St. Augustine's
St. Catherine's, convent in Nuremberg: 290
St. Hallvard's, church: 156
St. Liudger of Essen-Werden, Parish of: 45
St. Pancras, *See* British Library
St. Peter's, church in Hedeby: 164
St Sepulchre's Church: 383
Saints (*see also* Saints' Lives): Alban: 257; Ambrose: 281, 179; Andrew: 268; Anne: 178; Anthony, desert father: 179, 200, 214; Audrey: 290; Barbara: 270, 272–273, 275, 279, 281–282; Basil: 268; Basilissa: 85; Benedict: 253, 285; Bridget of Sweden: 281, 288; Caritas: 268, 271, 275, 279, 281; Catherine of Alexandria: 268–272, 275–277, 280–283, 290; Cecilia: 268, 270–272, 275, 277–278, 280–283; Christina: 268; Christopher: 178; Clement: 280–281; Constance: 34; Disibod: 289; Dorothy: 269–272, 275, 279, 280–281; Etheldreda: 290; Fides: 268, 271, 275, 279, 281; George, martyr: 178; Gertrude the Great: 290; Giles: 285, 333; Gregorius: 179, 187; Hallvard: 285; Henry II, emperor: 179, 200; Hildegard of Bingen: 266, 289; Holy Helpers: 178; Judith: Ælfric's homily on 251–52; Julian: 85; Knútr, Danish Duke:

112–113, 118–119, 154–155, 163; Knútr, Danish King (r. 1080–1086): 109, 112–113, 116–121, 151–153, 157, 167; Laurence: 120–121, 161; Lawrence, martyr: 178; Macarius: 34; Magnús: 285; Margaret of Antioch: 270–273, 275–276, 281–282; Marina: 268; Matthew: 280; Matthias: 251; Médard: 76; Mildred: prose life of 252, 258; Nicholas: 333, 352; Nicholas of Tolentino: 179; Oswald: 257: 178–179; Paul: 34; Roch, hermit: 179; Rupert: 289; Sebastian, martyr: 178; Servatius: 179; Seven Sleepers: 179; Silvester, pope: 179; Sophia: 268, 279; Spes: 268, 271, 275, 279, 281; Stephen, martyr: 178; Sunnifa: 281; Terrentianus: 34; Þorlákr: 280–282, 285–286, 308; Veronica, prose life of: 252
Saints' Lives: vernacular and based on Ælfric's *Lives of Saints* 238, scarcity of surviving female lives in Old English 252; anonymous Old English (Nicholas and Giles) 333; of St. Margaret 333; on Rogationtide (*Feria III*) 347; *See also* Ælfric, *Lives of Saints*
Samson, Abbot of Bury St. Edmunds (fl. 12 c.): 352
Saxo Grammaticus: 157
Scripts: Carolingian, with Insular symptoms 47, minuscule of the Corbie type 47; "Maurdramnus" minuscule 48; Anglo-Caroline minuscule Style IV: 4
Sedulius: *Carmen Paschale* 5, 232, 366
Seip, Didrik Arup (1884–1963): 270
Selden, John (1584–1654): 390
Senatus, prior of Worcester: 352
Series ac brevior historia regum Danie: 136, 151, 155
Series et genalogiæ regum Danorum: 161
Series regum Danie ex necrologio Lundensis: 136
Servius: "Commentary on Vergil's *Georgics*" 63
Shahar, Shulamith: 284
Shakespeare Mortgage Deed: *see Manuscript Index*: BL Egerton MS. 1787
Sherbourne Cartulary: 350

Þingeyrar, monastery: 274
Þóra Finnsdóttir (Barbara), abbess of Staður (1437–1461): 280
Þorláks saga helga: 286
Þormóðr, priest at Kirkjubær (1252): 283
Þykkvibær, monastery: 280, 283, 287

Unger, C. R. (1817–1897): 270, 277–279, 282
Ussher, James (1581–1656), archbp. of Armagh: 383, 398, 400, 431
Utrecht: 42–44, 282

Valvers þáttr: 298–299, 304
Veraldar saga: 317
Versibus egregiis decursum clarus arator: 2
Vigilius (fl. 537–555): 13
Vilchin Henriksson, bishop of Skálholt (ca. 1394–1405): 285
Vilhjálmur Örn Vilhjálmsson: 282
Virgil: 57–58, 68
Visio Pauli: 268
Vitae Patrum: 318
Völuspá: 300

Wace: Roman de Brut: 299–300
Wanderer (Old English poem): 234
Wanley, Humphrey (1672–1726) : 31
Werden: 42, 46–47, 50, 77; abbey of 43–45, 49, dissolution of 45; Werden Probstei (formerly Werden Pfarrhof) 41–43
Werden Glossary: See Glossaries
Werden Heptateuch: See Manuscript Index: Düsseldorf, Universitäts-bibl. A. 19 + Tokyo, T. Takamiya

Werden Pfarrhof: See Werden Probstei
Wessner, Paul (1870–1933): 43
West Saxon, Late: nature of 333–355
Westman Islands: 282–283
Wheelock, Abraham (1593–1653): xviii–xix, 383–439, passim; edition of Bede's Historia Ecclesiastica 385; re-edition of Archaionomia 385
Widding, Ole: 179, 276, 278
Wilson, Sir Colin St. John: 487, 502
Wolf, Kirsten: 184, 186, 190, 194, 196, 198, 202, 212, 214, 220
Women: audience for Ælfric's work 252–59; in medieval Iceland, and oral transmissionof poetry 266, as copyists 266–267, 290, as illuminators 289, 291, as instructors 286–288, as poets 265, as scribes 265–291, as translators 267, daily occupations of 284–285, 290–291
Worcester: 232, 256, 330, 334, 350, 352, 422
Worcester Fragment: 331, 334
Wulfgeat of Ylmandun: 249
Wulfsige, Bishop of Sherbourne (993–1001): 242, 249
Wulfstan, Archbishop and homilist (d. 1023): 242, 245; Commonplace Book of (Cambridge, Corpus Christi College 265, part I) 232, 249; Sermo Lupi ad Anglos 332
Wülcker, Richard Paul (1845–1910): 462

Zainer, Günther (d. 1478): 176
Zupitza, Julius (1844–1895): 445–47, 455, 457–59, 462, 464–67

Manuscript Index